A Writer's Workshop

Crafting Paragraphs, Building Essays

Third Edition

Bob Brannan

Johnson County Community College
Overland Park, Kansas

 Higher Education

Boston   Burr Ridge, IL   Dubuque, IA   New York   San Francisco   St. Louis
Bangkok   Bogotá   Caracas   Kuala Lumpur   Lisbon   London   Madrid   Mexico City
Milan   Montreal   New Delhi   Santiago   Seoul   Singapore   Sydney   Taipei   Toronto

Higher Education

Published by McGraw-Hill, an imprint of The McGraw-Hill Companies, Inc., 1221 Avenue of the Americas, New York, NY 10020. Copyright © 2010, 2006, 2003. All rights reserved. No part of this publication may be reproduced or distributed in any form or by any means, or stored in a database or retrieval system, without the prior written consent of The McGraw-Hill Companies, Inc., including, but not limited to, in any network or other electronic storage or transmission, or broadcast for distance learning.

✪ This book is printed on recycled, acid-free paper containing a minimum of 50% total recycled fiber with 10% postconsumer de-inked fiber.

5 6 7 8 9 0 DOW/DOW 2

ISBN: 978-0-07-338568-6 (Student Edition)
MHID: 0-07-338568-9
ISBN: 978-0-07-727564-8 (Annotated Instructor's Edition)
MHID: 0-07-727564-0

Editor in Chief: *Michael Ryan*
Publisher: *David S. Patterson*
Director of Development: *Dawn Groundwater*
Sponsoring Editor: *John Kindler*
Developmental Editor: *Anne Stameshkin*
Editorial Coordinator: *Jesse Hassenger*
Marketing Manager: *Allison Jones*
Production Editor: *Alison Meier*
Media Project Manager: *Thomas Brierly*
Design Coordinator: *Laurie Entringer*
Cover and Interior Design: *Maureen McCutcheon*
Photo Research: *Brian J. Pecko*
Production Supervisor: *Tandra Jorgensen*
Composition: *10/12 Palatino by Aptara®, Inc.*
Printing: *45# New Era Matte Recycled, R. R. Donnelley*

Cover images: tree sapling © Don Nichols; recycle symbol © Carol Stone

Credits: The credits section for this book begins on page C-1 and is considered an extension of the copyright page.

Library of Congress Cataloging-in-Publication Data

Brannan, Bob.
    A writer's workshop: crafting paragraphs, building essays / Bob Brannan. —3rd ed.
      p. cm.
    Includes bibliographical references and index.
    ISBN-13: 978-0-07-338568-6 (acid-free paper)
    ISBN-10: 0-07-338568-9 (acid-free paper)
    1. English language—Paragraphs—Problems, exercises, etc. 2. English language—Rhetoric—Problems, exercises, etc. 3. English language—Grammar—Problems, exercises, etc. 4. Report writing–Problems, exercises, etc. I. Title.
    PE1439.B69 2009
    808'.042—dc22
                                                             2008034959

The Internet addresses listed in the text were accurate at the time of publication. The inclusion of a website does not indicate an endorsement by the authors or McGraw-Hill, and McGraw-Hill does not guarantee the accuracy of the information presented at these sites.

About This Book

Overview

The third edition of **A Writer's Workshop: Crafting Paragraphs, Building Essays** engages developing writers with a **hands-on, process-oriented, collaborative,** and **conscientious** approach to writing. Throughout, it **links lessons to previous experience and future application,** treating students as writers and writing as a dynamic process.

Hands On …

A *Writer's Workshop* advocates that the best way to learn to write well is by writing. This book offers a wealth of opportunities for students to write paragraphs and essays about topics that interest them, encouraging writers to draw on their own experiences. Along the way, it provides both instruction on and practice using essential sentence-level skills that will help writers clearly express their ideas.

Process Oriented …

The text's central focus and user-friendly design ensure that "process" is more than a buzzword in writing *and* reading. The assignment chapters offer thorough process break-downs, revision strategies, and **Journal/Blog prompts** in the context of actual assignments. Each assignment chapter features multiple walk-throughs (one per chapter is annotated) of student work in multiple drafts and stages of revision, as well as a variety of suggested and illustrated prewriting approaches.

Collaborative …

Every chapter offers **Working Together** activities, opportunities for collaborative learning and practice. **Feedback** prompts in assignment chapters encourage workshopping at all stages of the writing process.

A *Writer's Workshop* is also offered as a paperless e-book.

Conscientious …

A *Writer's Workshop* is McGraw-Hill Higher Education's first "green" textbook. This approach is reflected in production materials, partnership, and content.

- **Green production materials:** Each book is produced using 10% recycled paper stock certified by the Sustainable Forestry Initiative (SFI). The books are printed with soy inks.

- **Green partnership:** McGraw-Hill is pleased to announce that in the spirit of A *Writer's Workshop*'s commitment to conservation, we are partnering with the Arbor Day Foundation, the million-member nonprofit conservation and education organization, to plant 50,000 trees in our nation's forests (destroyed by insects, disease, and devastating wildfires) during the next three years. The book's website will be updated to list any local activities McGraw-Hill and the

Conservation in Context

Arbor Day Foundation will be sponsoring to promote environmental awareness. Visit www.mhhe.com/brannan to see how many trees have been planted and learn how you can get involved.

- **Green content:** *A Writer's Workshop* features a recurring theme of conservation, incorporating **Conservation in Context** activities, tips, writing assignments, and readings (such as Al Gore's Nobel Prize acceptance speech) reflecting a range of environmental topics. Conservation is a fitting focus for *A Writer's Workshop,* which motivates students to build on what they know with readily available tools—and to use their writing, reading, and studying energies wisely. Students are encouraged to try prewriting, drafting, and revising on the computer, saving not only paper but also money and time. Throughout this text, all prewriting samples are displayed as if they were on-screen, rather than in a handwriting font, showing that tech-savvy can also mean earth-friendly. Journal/Blog prompts are designed so that journals can be kept, shared, and graded online.

At The McGraw-Hill Companies, environmental responsibility is an integral part of overall corporate citizenship. As such, we strive to minimize our environmental footprint by closely monitoring and developing strategies to reduce the environmental impact of our operations and our office facilities. This partnership with the Arbor Day Foundation and the content of *A Writer's Workshop* represent one step toward that goal; we hope that you will support this effort and encourage us with your feedback.

Linking to Previous and Future Experience ...

In select chapters, **Linking to Previous Experience** sections help developing writers connect what they already know about processes and concepts to lessons in the book. **Linking to Future Experience** sections wrap up main points and tie writing skills and patterns to future applications, giving further purpose to what students are practicing.

Shortly after they leave this course, our students may find themselves wrestling with a researched argument in Comp I, a term paper in history, or perhaps a process description in a health sciences course. I hope that this text helps you to help your students reach and even exceed these goals.

Organization

 Unit 1

Getting Our Feet Wet engages students with the writing and reading process.

- **Chapter 1** gives students many opportunities to practice essential writing strategies like discovering ideas, organizing, drafting, revising, and editing. The chapter closes with diagnostic assignments that instructors can use to help assess students' writing skills.

- **Chapter 2** focuses on reading strategies useful in any college course: identifying topic and thesis sentences, analyzing a text for key examples, and rewording material (through summary or paraphrase) to make it a writer's own. The activities are linked to Chapter 3 so instructors can quickly move students into the assignment chapters of *A Writer's Workshop.*

 Unit 2

Crafting Paragraphs introduces students to the paragraph as the building block of composition.

- **Chapter 3** provides a comprehensive treatment of paragraph structure and development.

- **Chapter 4** offers detailed suggestions for revising paragraphs from rough through final drafts.

ASSIGNMENT CHAPTERS

- **Chapters 5–11** cover seven patterns of development (definition and argument are covered in Unit 3), taking students through all phases of the writing process.

 Unit 3

Building Essays moves students from writing paragraphs into writing essays.

- **Chapter 12** focuses on essay form and development, devoting special attention to introductions and conclusions.

- **Chapter 13** helps students either expand a paragraph from Unit 2 or begin an essay focusing on one of the patterns of development.

- **Chapter 14** offers illustrated advice for revising rough, second, and final essay drafts.

ASSIGNMENT CHAPTERS

- **Chapters 15–18** cover definition and persuasion, essay exams, and research essays; each emphasizes combining the patterns of development from Unit 2.

 Unit 4

Polishing Style suggests strategies students can use to improve their writing style through sentence variety **(Chapter 19)** and word choice **(Chapter 20).**

SPECIAL FEATURES *of the Assignment Chapters*

- **Journal/Blog Entries and Feedback prompts encourage students to work reflectively and collaboratively to plan, develop, and improve writing assignments.**

- **Developing Skills and Exploring Ideas sections walk students through concepts, offering practice in skills needed to write effectively in each pattern of development.**

- **Three Student Models. Two student models illustrate key points for building a paragraph or essay in that pattern (with prereading questions and analytical marginal annotations). A third student model is included under "Writing Assignment" as an annotated walk-through, showing multiple drafts and stages of revision.**

- **Writing Assignment—located within a rhetorical context that asks students to think about their audience and purpose. Each assignment offers the following features:**

  1. **Discovering Ideas: provides prewriting suggestions and topic lists**

  2. **Organizing Ideas: focuses students with key organizational points like thesis and topic sentences**

  3. **Drafting: offers important reminders to ease students into their first draft**

  4. **Revising Drafts: includes in-context special points notes and a specially tailored checklist for writers and peer reviewers. Each stage of the revision process is illustrated in the annotated student model.**

- **Alternate Assignments give students additional focused topics and specific suggestions for developing them.**

Unit 5

Practicing Sentence Sense reviews common problems developmental writers have with grammar, spelling, and punctuation. In **Chapters 21–28,** the operating principle is that less is more—that students can learn to punctuate effectively, express themselves clearly, and achieve a degree of syntactic fluency without an overemphasis on grammar and punctuation rules. Grammar study is applied directly to students' own writing, with examples drawn from their daily lives. As elsewhere in the book, special concerns of ESL students are highlighted with English Review Notes.

Additional exercises and quizzes are available on the book's Online Learning Center at www.mhhe.com/brannan, which also links to more than 3,000 practice opportunities on Gateway.

Unit 6

Learning from Professional Readings includes eighteen professional readings from print and online sources, as well as one work of art, *Cans Seurat*. The collection includes a humorous illustration piece on the value of short words, a definition essay on hoarders and a persuasive call to address global climate change.

Key Features of *A Writer's Workshop*

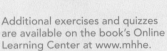

- **Linking to Previous Experience, Linking to Future Experience.** Each chapter in Units 1, 2, and 3 calls upon familiar ground as a point of entry through the **Linking to Previous Experience** feature, then closes with **Linking to Future Experience,** which explores this concept's usefulness beyond the course or classroom. In other chapters, the relevance of acquiring various skills is explored under the heading **What Are We Trying to Achieve and Why?**

- **Activities.** Each chapter offers an array of practice opportunities, including collaborative and online exercises:

  - **Working Together Activities** suggest collaborative work within exercises. **Feedback** prompts encourage workshopping in pairs or small groups.

  - **Working Online Activities** engage students with the book's website (www.mhhe.com/brannan) and other Internet sites for specific exercises and writing assignments. The online **Review Quiz** at the end of each chapter gives students a convenient way to test their understanding before moving on.

- **Conservation in Context.** Boxes, activities, or assignments suggest specific ways to discuss or practice conservation during the writing process. Readings, visuals, and examples explore environmentally themed topics such as alternative energy, global climate change, and overfishing.

Conservation in Context

- **More than 200 possible writing topics** for **illustrated assignments,** with additional **alternate assignments.** One alternate assignment per chapter is linked to an image or images, encouraging visual literacy and providing a helpful way in for visual learners.

- **Journal/Blog Entries.** These exercises help students make the connection between the chapter assignment and their lives, calling for specific, detailed examples and reinforcing the integration of a writer's aims. In many entries, **Feedback** prompts encourage workshopping drafts in groups and commenting on classmates' posts.

- **Hints.** Useful marginal suggestions and cross-references connect new concepts with previous ones and help students solve specific rhetorical problems.

- **English Review Notes.** In the book's margins, these tips provide helpful guidance for nonnative speakers while avoiding marginalizing labels. Additional student resources include in-depth explanations of grammar concepts throughout the text and online practice opportunities on Gateway (see www.mhhe.com/brannan).

SPECIAL FEATURES *for Instructors*

1. **Flexibility in teaching approaches. This text offers a great deal of explicit instruction on fundamental sentence grammar and mechanics, allowing instructors to shape a course that focuses primarily on these issues. However, as a fully developed composition textbook,** *A Writer's Workshop* **encourages instructors to integrate grammar and mechanics into meaningful writing assignments so that students have a real context in which to develop their skills in standard edited English.**

2. **Instruction linked to a rhetorical context. Writing assignments are grounded in the rhetorical triangle: text, writer, and reader, paying particular attention to audience.**

Supplements Package

Supplements for Instructors

- **Annotated Instructor's Edition (ISBN 0-07-727564-0).** The teaching edition of *A Writer's Workshop* consists of the student text with embedded answers to activities. Marginal **Teaching Ideas** on almost every page provide suggestions for using the text in class.

- **Online Learning Center** (www.mhhe.com/brannan). This companion website offers password-protected instructional aids and resources. Among other features, this includes the **Instructor's Manual** written by Bob Brannan. This guide provides comprehensive commentary on every chapter, sample syllabi, alternative writing assignments, peer response worksheets, and more.

Supplements for Students

- ✔ **FREE Online Learning Center** (www.mhhe.com/brannan). *A Writer's Workshop*'s companion website, powered by Catalyst 2.0, offers a host of instructional aids and additional resources for students, including grammar exercises with feedback, writing activities for additional practice, guides to doing research on the Internet and avoiding plagiarism, useful web links, and additional content for Chapter 18: Writing a Research Essay, including a helpful assignment walk-through.

- ✔ **FREE access to Gateway,** the self-paced tutorial carefully crafted to strengthen and expand students' writing and editing. It is the ultimate resource for grammar and usage instruction. Offering **over 3,000 exercises and quiz questions** for additional practice in basic grammar, usage, punctuation, spelling, and techniques for effective writing, this new program allows the user to practice at his or her pace. **Gateway** makes writing and editing meaningful!

- ✔ **Additional Supplements.** See www.mhhe.com/brannan for more on: Passport for College Writing / Catalyst 3.0 /*The New McGraw-Hill Exercise Book* by Santi Buscemi / *The McGraw-Hill Exercise Book for Multilingual Writers* by Maggie Sokolik / *A Writer's Journal* by Lynee Gaillet / *The McGraw-Hill Student Planner*.

- ✔ **Dictionary and Vocabulary Resources.** We also carry a full line of Merriam-Webster reference books. To find the right one for your students, visit www.mhhe.com/brannan.

E-Book Alternative

Paperless eTextbook
CourseSmart is a new way find and buy eTextbooks—including *A Writer's Workshop*. At CourseSmart you can save up to 50% off the cost of a print textbook, reduce your impact on the environment, and gain access to powerful web tools for learning. CourseSmart has the largest selection of eTextbooks available anywhere, offering thousands of the most commonly adopted textbooks from a wide variety of higher education publishers. CourseSmart eTextbooks are available in one standard online reader with full text search, notes and highlighting, and email tools for sharing notes between classmates. For further details contact your publishing representative or go to www.coursesmart.com.

Acknowledgments

Many people have contributed to the success of this and previous editions of this text. First, I would like to thank Senior Sponsoring Editor John Kindler for working hard to bring this project together. His vision from the beginning was of a current and topically engaging developmental writing textbook for the *adult* writer and a book that would model the "green" theme that McGraw-Hill has committed itself to. John's vision is of a major multinational corporation that is beginning the paradigm shift necessary if people are to thrive in the twenty-first century. Sustainability, people living in balance with the earth, is a goal that we cannot afford to put off any longer.

I would also like to thank the Developmental Editor in charge of this book, Anne Stameshkin, who through her organizational skills, expertise with language, good humor, and gentle but insistent encouragement has kept me on task even when I have felt overwhelmed. Thanks, too, to the rest of the editorial and marketing team: Editorial Coordinator Jesse Hassenger, Director of Development Dawn Groundwater, Market Development Editor Nanette Giles, Marketing Manager Allison Jones, and Publisher David Patterson for various and important contributions in helping shape, shepherd, and promote this text. Thanks to ESL Specialist Joyce Stern for providing the English Review Notes. Alison Meier, our production editor, has kept the manuscript flow going smoothly and helped the Brannan series become a reality. Beverley DeWitt has done a terrific job of copyediting. Thanks to Laurie Entringer and Maureen McCutcheon for creating an exciting yet clean design. And Brian Pecko, our photo researcher, has helped me find images that make the text a more effective teaching and learning tool. I would like to offer a special thank you to the colleagues of mine at Johnson County Community College who have reviewed and offered many valuable suggestions for improving this text:

Maggie Ackelson	Shaun Harris
Danny Alexander	Sandy Hastings
Andrea Broomfield	Monica Hogan
Diane Canow	Mary Pat McQueeney
Dave Davis	Jim McWard
Maureen Fitzpatrick	Holly Milkowart
Mary Grace Foret	Tom Reynolds
Keith Geekie	Ted Rollins
Beth Gulley	Matthew Schmeer
Greg Harrell	Marilyn Senter

The two most important people in my life I have saved for last: my wife, Beth, and my daughter, Lauren. They have had to endure my many absences from their lives as I have closeted myself, growling at their invitations to pretend, for an hour or so, to be a real human. Beth has carried more than her share of the parenting load and missed more than a few dates with me during this process, but she hasn't kicked me out yet, so I still have hope. Lauren has grown into a beautiful 12-year-old who can't well remember a time when her dad hasn't been busier with his books than perhaps he should have been. Beth and Lauren, I love both of you deeply. Thank you for being part of my life.

Bob Brannan

Contents

CHAPTER 7

Illustrating through Examples *136*

CHAPTER 8

Creating and Explaining Groups (Classification) *165*

CHAPTER 9

Recognizing Causes, Explaining Effects *186*

CHAPTER 10

Explaining Activities: Doing or Understanding Them (Process Analysis) *211*

CHAPTER 11

Exploring Similarities and Differences (Comparison or Contrast) *234*

UNIT 3 Building Essays *260*

CHAPTER 12

Introducing the Essay *261*

CHAPTER 13

Expanding Paragraphs into Essays **297**

What Are We Trying to Achieve and Why? **298**

> LINKING TO PREVIOUS EXPERIENCE **298**

CHAPTER 14

Revising Essays **328**

> LINKING TO PREVIOUS AND FUTURE
> EXPERIENCE **329**

Revising Essays

CHAPTER 15

Defining Terms, Clarifying Ideas **340**

What Are We Trying to Achieve and Why? **341**

> LINKING TO PREVIOUS EXPERIENCE **341**

CHAPTER 16

CHAPTER 17

CHAPTER 18

*The Online Learning Center at www.mhhe.com/brannan features
a full walk-through of the research paper assignment in stages.

CHAPTER 22

Coordination, Subordination,
and Parallelism *530*

CHAPTER 23

Run-ons, Comma Splices, and Sentence
Fragments *540*

CHAPTER 24

Verbs: Form and Agreement *552*

CHAPTER 25

Pronouns: Reference, Agreement,
and Form *567*

CHAPTER 26

Adjectives and Adverbs: Words
That Describe *578*

CHAPTER 27

Commas, Other Punctuation Marks, and Mechanics 586

CHAPTER 28

Spelling and Sound-alike Words 605

UNIT 6 Learning from Professional Readings 617

(* indicates a reading new to this edition)

Getting Our Feet Wet

1

Practicing the Writing Process

[*These climbers prepare for their journey by consulting a map. What other steps have they taken to ready themselves? In what ways can you prepare yourself to begin the writing process?*]

KEY TOPICS

- How do we begin to write?
- After breaking ground—into the writing process
- Steps in the writing process
  - Discovering ideas
  - Organizing ideas

- Drafting
- Revising
- Editing
- Proofreading
- Diagnostic writing assignments

How Do We Begin to Write?

The first step in beginning to write is to think of yourselves as writers—not necessarily easy to do. Many view the act of writing as mysterious and think successful writers have lucked into their talent. But, just like you, accomplished writers have to work hard at their craft. They can be confused at first, uncertain about where their ideas will come from. Often they produce some genuinely bad writing in their early drafts and agonize over the final shape of their words—and what others will think of the work.

Whatever your past experiences with writing, you share in the common experience of everyone who seeks to commit words to paper. When you write, be it a brief paragraph or long essay, you *are* a writer, with all the hard work, the aggravation, and the satisfaction that come with it.

How do writers get started? To focus your efforts, ask yourself several questions.

Questions to Ask at the Start of a Writing Project

1. **What is my purpose?** People write for many reasons, often having several for the same project, although one purpose usually predominates. Primary reasons for writing are to entertain, explain ideas and information, and persuade. There are, of course, other reasons for writing, such as to express emotions or explore ideas.

2. **Who is my audience?** Most student writing is done for teachers. However, in "real-world" writing, you need to be able to communicate effectively with different readers, ranging from fairly general audiences to very specific ones. Knowing who your audience is will help you decide what and how much to say.

3. **What, exactly, is the project?** Writing out your goals will help you to focus your thoughts. In class your instructor will give you an assignment guide, or you will follow the assignment instructions in the text. Determine what the project calls for: purpose, audience, overall organization, length, and draft due dates.

4. **How can I develop a real interest in the project?** Avoid taking a passive attitude, an "I don't care, whatever" approach; instead, seek a connection with the assignment and topic. Sometimes you will have to write to specific requirements, sometimes not. When a topic is assigned, you can still find some part of it that is appealing. When you can choose a topic, take time to find an interesting one, rather than going for the seemingly easiest one. If you can commit to the project, you are more likely to enjoy the writing process—and to end up with a better grade.

Good writing is not easily accomplished; it takes time. To achieve the best results, first gain a clear overview of the project, and then apply effective study skills.

KEY STUDY SKILLS

1. Listen carefully in class, ask questions, and take notes, especially when your instructor writes on the chalkboard, uses the overhead projector, or posts information online.

These key study skills will help you understand every writing assignment.

2. Take handouts home to study or complete.

3. Participate fully in class activities and discussion.

4. Pay attention to any instructions your instructor gives you to clarify writing projects in this text.

5. Study the textbook's student models for further guidance.

After Breaking Ground—into the Writing Process

We all have gone through steps to produce written paragraphs and essays, so we all have *a* writing process. For some of us, that process has worked well; for others . . . not so well. The rest of this chapter explains the writing approach many of us already unconsciously use. However, the writing process varies with individuals, and you should freely adapt it to what works best for you.

Steps in the Writing Process

Gathering and shaping ideas and putting words on paper are a natural sequence for most of us, but writers seldom move through this process like a train moving on a track, beginning at one point and progressing to the final destination. In fact, you will often find yourself brainstorming for ideas in the middle of a paper, editing as you notice an error, and sometimes substantially reorganizing when the work seemed nearly complete.

THE WRITING PROCESS

1. Discover ideas
2. Organize ideas
3. Draft
4. Revise
5. Edit
6. Proofread

Discovering Ideas

How many times have you been faced with a writing project and found that you have nothing to say? It is a common, frustrating occurrence. Instead of smacking your keyboard or simply giving up, why not try one or several of the following methods for discovering ideas?

Freewriting

Freewriting is rapid, uncensored writing. Fast drafting or freewriting lets you get ideas on paper—some of which may be usable. To practice this method, set aside time—say, 5 to 10 minutes—and write nonstop, without censoring ideas or worrying about grammar, spelling, and punctuation. Even if you run out of thoughts, keep writing or typing.

If you have no idea of what to write, freewriting can help you uncover ideas. Freewriting for this purpose may begin with or include sentences like the following:

English Review Note

While freewriting, don't worry about grammatical errors. Leave a blank if you can't think of a word in English.

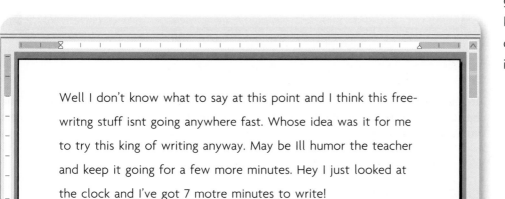

Well I don't know what to say at this point and I think this free-writng stuff isnt going anywhere fast. Whose idea was it for me to try this king of writing anyway. May be Ill humor the teacher and keep it going for a few more minutes. Hey I just looked at the clock and I've got 7 motre minutes to write!

Keep producing words even when you do not seem to be getting anywhere. Although no one has been able to explain why, the mere act of writing triggers more words and, often, usable ideas. Then, with a topic in hand, you can try **focused freewriting**—uncensored writing on a general topic:

HINT

Focused freewrites can give your writing direction.

I get to chose from a list of places or come up with my own place. I don't k ow what the best way is. Maybe I'll try some of the outside places on the list I like the outdoors fishing, hnting, hiking in themountains. I like being aroung the trees and plants. I seem to have always liked being outside ever since I was a little kid. How about that trrehouse my brother and I built when we were how old? About 11 and 13. Eric was pretty good at figuring out how to get the main platform built and braced into the trees. He was always better at building stuff than I was but we worked preety ell on that job. Let's see I'm sup-posed to be comeing up with a descriptionof something. May be the treehouse could work. I wonder if it's still there? I could

BRIEF FOCUSED FREEWRITE

drive back into the oldneighborhood and look I guess. How
many trees, 3. We had to nail on to those big old catalpa trees
in our backyard in South Bend. Dad would only let us put it up
about 10–12 feet from the ground. No way to get up high into
those huge branches. . . .

In this freewrite, the author discovers several ideas for a descriptive paper. The backyard, the tree house, or the author's former house might make interesting subjects to explore.

ACTIVITY 1.1 *Focused Freewriting*

Select a topic from the list below and write nonstop on it for 5 minutes. Remember, don't worry about grammar, spelling, or punctuation or whether ideas get tangled.

airport	gym	subway
attic	interstate	swimming pool
beach	kitchen	wharf
cafeteria	library	woods
football field	restaurant	zoo

Clustering

Clustering is another good prewriting technique. With this method you write a single word in the center of a page and then jot down around it any words it brings to mind. After linking several words to the original word, you connect more words to the second set. Keep extending your network of linked words until you find a grouping that seems interesting.

SAMPLE
CLUSTER

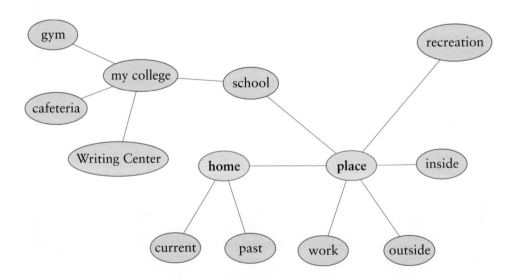

If the author wanted to select the "home" cluster to begin a more **focused cluster,** the next step might look like this:

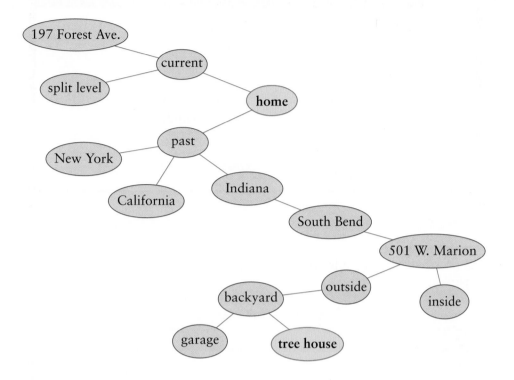

SAMPLE
FOCUSED
CLUSTER

Now the author has arrived at the tree house as a possible topic for his description paragraph. He might choose to cluster again for specific details, or he might try another method for generating ideas, like brainstorming or listing.

ACTIVITY 1.2 *Focused Clustering*

Select a topic from the list in Activity 1.1 (or continue with the one you have already chosen), and create a focused cluster like the one preceding. Work for 5 minutes, trying to fill a page with word associations.

ACTIVITY 1.3 WORKING ONLINE: *Making Online Clusters*

As an alternative to Activity 1.2, visit http://bubbl.us/edit.php to create your own cluster (or idea map) online. You can color-code your cluster and choose from a variety of "bubble" shapes and structures. When you're done, save and post or print your cluster. Return to this site when you're brainstorming your next paragraph or essay assignment.

Brainstorming (Listing)

In **brainstorming,** either by yourself or with others, you list in a word or phrase every idea that occurs to you when you think about a general topic. If we extended the tree house topic from the clustering activity, we might end up with a list like this:

SAMPLE LIST

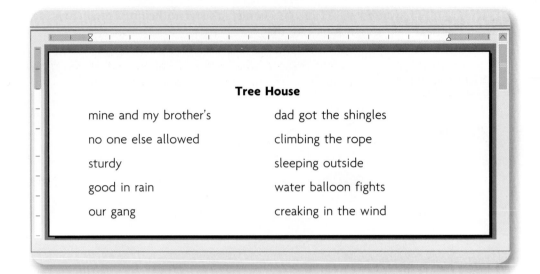

Tree House

mine and my brother's	dad got the shingles
no one else allowed	climbing the rope
sturdy	sleeping outside
good in rain	water balloon fights
our gang	creaking in the wind

If we **focus** the list, we can concentrate primarily on generating the specific words and sensory details that make up a good description. (For more on description, see Chapter 5.)

SAMPLE
FOCUSED LIST

Try a focused brainstorming list to generate details about your topic.

Tree House

Specific Words	Sensory Details
10–12 feet off ground	Sight: colors—red shingles, gray
three catalpa trees	boards, green leaves
backyard	Sound: boards creaking, wind
by redbrick patio	in branches, cars passing in
rope to climb—no stairs or	alley, mower running, boys
ladder	laughing and shouting
rope to swing from	Touch: rough feel of bark,
red shingles	splinters, rope in my hands,
white pine walls	heat and humidity
painted slate gray	Smell: fumes from cars passing,
	cut grass, clean air after rain
	Taste: baloney sandwiches on
	white bread with mustard,
	potato chips

After you have created a list that is somewhat focused, you will likely have a rough outline that you can use to develop or rearrange ideas.

ACTIVITY 1.4 *Brainstorming (Listing)*

Choose a new topic from the list in Activity 1.1 (or use the topic you have already chosen), and create a list of descriptive phrases that apply to it. Include words that help you visualize the place or that suggest sound, touch, taste, or smell.

Journalist's Questions

After you have a fairly clear idea of your writing topic, you can ask yourself the classic journalist's questions *who, what, when, where,* and *why.* You should also add *how* and *what was the result.* To continue with our tree house example:

Journalist's questions provide the framework for news articles, especially the lead paragraphs.

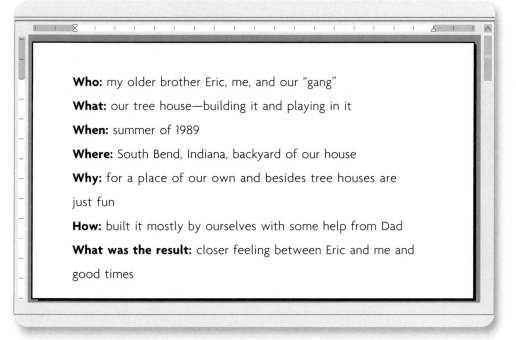

Who: my older brother Eric, me, and our "gang"

What: our tree house—building it and playing in it

When: summer of 1989

Where: South Bend, Indiana, backyard of our house

Why: for a place of our own and besides tree houses are just fun

How: built it mostly by ourselves with some help from Dad

What was the result: closer feeling between Eric and me and good times

SAMPLE QUESTIONS

ACTIVITY 1.5 *Journalist's Questions*

Select a topic from the list in Activity 1.1 (or continue with the one you have been working with), and create a list of answers to the preceding questions.

Patterns of Development

Another way to generate material for your paper is to turn the **patterns of development** into questions and then apply them to your topic.

- **Narration:** telling a brief story to make a point

    What kind of story could I tell to show my reader the tree house?

- **Description:** using vivid details to paint a picture

  What details do I remember that could help my reader visualize the tree house?

- **Illustration:** giving examples to illustrate some point

  What examples could I give to explain the importance of the tree house?

- **Comparison/contrast:** showing how your subject is like and unlike similar subjects

  What could I compare or contrast the tree house to that my reader would know?

- **Classification/division:** putting your subject into a group, breaking it into parts

  What group does the tree house fit into? What are the parts of the tree house?

- **Cause/effect:** telling what actions can affect your subject and what effects can flow from it

  How did the tree house come about? What were its effects on me?

- **Process analysis:** telling how your subject works

  How did the tree house work? What regular activities did I do there?

- **Definition:** telling the essential characteristics of your subject

  What makes the tree house unique?

- **Persuasion:** trying to convince someone to agree with you or to perform some action

  How could I persuade my reader of the value a tree house can have for a child?

ACTIVITY 1.6 *Patterns of Development*

Select a topic from the list in Activity 1.1 (or continue with the one you have been working with), and create a list of questions like the ones preceding. Next, answer each question in a sentence or two.

Browsing for Ideas

If you've chosen a topic but aren't sure how to focus it, try a quick online search for relevant images, articles, quotations, and sites that will get you thinking. As you go, note URLs you might want to return to later. This pre-writing method can provide quick inspiration, but limit your browsing time to 5–10 minutes; otherwise, it may prove more distracting than helpful. As shown in the following pages, a Wikipedia search on tree houses might remind the student writer of his experience building the tree house with his brother. Looking at the images and following links to other, more focused sites could serve to trigger memories and give the writer ideas to focus on. Note: Wikipedia is a great place to start your browsing search, but because the site's content can be updated by any user, be sure to double-check the information presented here.

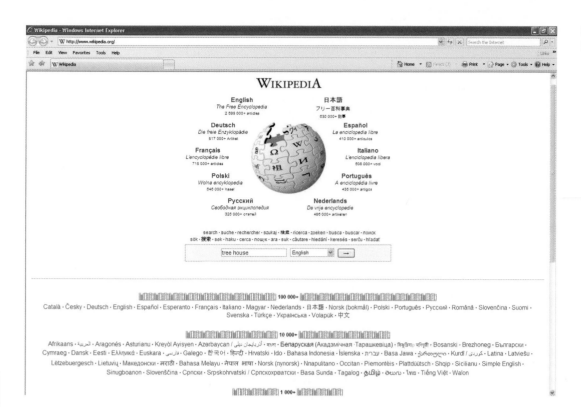

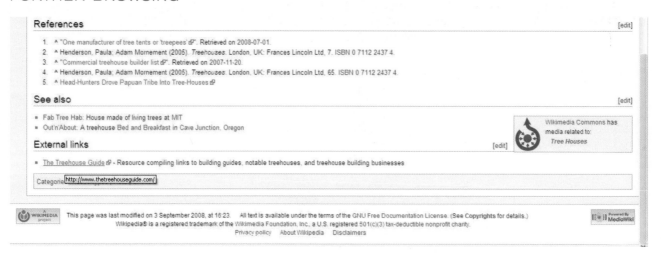

References   [edit]

1. ^ "One manufacturer of tree tents or 'treepees' &". Retrieved on 2008-07-01.
2. ^ Henderson, Paula; Adam Mornement (2005). *Treehouses*. London, UK: Frances Lincoln Ltd, 7. ISBN 0 7112 2437 4.
3. ^ "Commercial treehouse builder list &". Retrieved on 2007-11-20.
4. ^ Henderson, Paula; Adam Mornement (2005). *Treehouses*. London, UK: Frances Lincoln Ltd, 65. ISBN 0 7112 2437 4.
5. ^ Head-Hunters Drove Papuan Tribe Into Tree-Houses &

See also   [edit]

- Fab Tree Hab: House made of living trees at MIT
- Out'n'About: A treehouse Bed and Breakfast in Cave Junction, Oregon

Wikimedia Commons has media related to: *Tree Houses*

External links   [edit]

- The Treehouse Guide & - Resource compiling links to building guides, notable treehouses, and treehouse building businesses

Categorie[http://www.thetreehouseguide.com/]

WIKIMEDIA project This page was last modified on 3 September 2008, at 16:23.   All text is available under the terms of the GNU Free Documentation License. (See Copyrights for details.) Wikipedia® is a registered trademark of the Wikimedia Foundation, Inc., a U.S. registered 501(c)(3) tax-deductible nonprofit charity.   Powered By MediaWiki
Privacy policy   About Wikipedia   Disclaimers

ACTIVITY 1.7 WORKING ONLINE: *Browsing for Ideas*

Using Wikipedia or a search engine, such as Google, choose a key word or words from your focused freewrite (in Activity 1.1) or cluster (in Activity 1.2). What sites do you find, and are they interesting and relevant to your topic? If so, how might they help you focus or further explore it? Limit your browsing to under 10 minutes.

Journal/Blog Entries

A **journal** or blog in which you write for a few minutes every day can be a good general source of ideas. If you decide to keep a personal journal (paper or online), or your instructor assigns one, this additional daily writing can give you valuable practice in organizing and expressing your thoughts. You can also gain some insights into yourself and the world around you.

The suggestions for **Journal/Blog entries** that appear throughout Units Two and Three can help you complete major writing assignments. If you respond to them thoughtfully, the entries you write will help you discover, focus, organize, and develop your ideas. Remember, your ideas are what count most. While it is never a bad idea to edit your work (even in your journals), grammar, spelling, and punctuation should be a low priority. The **Feedback** component provides opportunities for collaborative thinking and input at all stages of the writing process.

Considering Your Audience

While we sometimes write only for ourselves, more often we write for others. These "others" may be a relatively general audience, or they may be quite specific. And we may direct our work toward several kinds of readers, often a more specific group within a larger secondary audience. When you consider a writing topic, you will usually find that knowing who you are writing to will help you generate and select interesting ideas.

If you were describing an action/adventure film like *Armageddon* to two friends—one a sci-fi fan and one who prefers more serious, "literary" films—which of the following two paragraphs would you be likely to use with each friend?

A. This movie makes you think an asteroid is really going to slam into earth. The opening special effects are great! Blazing chunks of rock rain down on New York City, exploding cars, tearing craters in the streets, punching holes through skyscrapers, and throwing people all over the place. The action is nonstop. From the meteorite bombardment, to Bruce Willis finding his daughter in bed with one of his oil drillers and then chasing after him with a shotgun, through the astronaut training and mission to blow up the asteroid—you can't even get up to hit the restroom, or you'll miss too much.

B. There's plenty of action in the film, but not all of it is explosions. The relationships really make the movie interesting. Bruce Willis plays a loving father who is having difficulty communicating with his daughter and accepting that she has become a woman. To complicate matters, she is in love with one of Willis's employees, who returns her love, and their relationship adds tension to the film. The audience is not sure how Willis will ultimately react to the young man. As the film progresses, several characters must make difficult personal decisions, ultimately testing their loyalty, courage, and sense of self-sacrifice.

Let what you know about your audience help focus your material.

While much of your writing will appeal to a fairly large "general" audience, within it you will usually be able to appeal to a smaller group.

Clearly, the details in version A should capture the attention of the sci-fi fan while the details in version B should interest the friend who favors more serious films. Writers must constantly generate details and then select the ones that will interest their particular readers.

age	education	particular knowledge of a subject
sex	political affiliation	level of intelligence
race/ethnicity	religion	wants
country	social groups	needs
region	hobbies	goals
city	sports	prejudices
neighborhood	special interests	personality
occupation	general knowledge	expectations

If you develop a sense of your audience, you are more likely to write in an engaging way—and come closer to enjoying the process of the writing.

ACTIVITY 1.8 *Considering Your Audience*

Assume that you have rented the film *The Wizard of Oz* for the evening and are trying to persuade two friends to watch it with you. One friend doesn't mind children's stories but thinks a 60-year-old movie will be boring. The other friend doesn't like children's stories but does like horror and supernatural films. List three points you could make or examples you might choose to convince each of your friends to watch the movie with you. (If you have not seen *The Wizard of Oz*, choose any film you have enjoyed, list two friends who might not like it for different reasons, and then list three examples/points that would help persuade each person.)

Organizing Ideas

If you have tried prewriting, you should have some ideas for your paper. Before moving ahead, though, you must decide on a central point—a **rough topic sentence** for a paragraph or a **working thesis sentence** for an essay. Your topic or thesis sentence should consist of your topic plus a statement that expresses an opinion, attitude, or feeling about it. For instance, in the tree house description, the author might want to focus on enjoyment:

feeling about topic   topic

My brother and I had a world of good times in our backyard tree house.

Once you have a central point, you could just plunge into the draft, writing furiously and hoping for the best. Sometimes this approach works well, especially if the material falls into a natural order or if you happen to have a "feel" for the best organizing method. Often, though, you will not be sure what to do with all the words in front of you. In that situation, you need to reconsider your purpose (to entertain, explain, or persuade), review the assignment instructions for suggestions, and try some informal or formal **outlining.**

Rough Outlines

A **rough outline** usually consists of a simple list of ideas. For example, if you chose to describe a place, you might try a spatial method for organizing (moving from one side to another, inside to outside, top to bottom, or front to back) and

Help focus your paper with a central point.

then create a rough or "scratch" outline. After reviewing the brainstorming lists for the tree house example (see pp. 7–8), the author might choose to arrange the descriptive details about the tree house from bottom to top, creating the following rough outline:

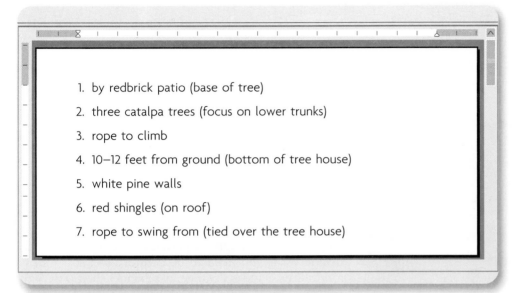

1. by redbrick patio (base of tree)

2. three catalpa trees (focus on lower trunks)

3. rope to climb

4. 10–12 feet from ground (bottom of tree house)

5. white pine walls

6. red shingles (on roof)

7. rope to swing from (tied over the tree house)

To see a detailed informal outline for an essay, turn to Chapter 12.

Once this structure is set, the writer can add more details from the brainstorming list or from additional brainstorming, such as the chalky smell of the brick, the rough feel of the bark, and the deep yellow of the rope.

ACTIVITY 1.9 *Creating Rough Outlines*

Look back at your list from Activity 1.4 and rearrange the examples/details, moving from one side of your place to another, inside to outside, top to bottom, or front to back.

Formal Outlines

Formal outlines have numbered and lettered categories and subcategories. They are particularly useful for longer writing projects, such as essays. Here is the pattern of a formal outline:

Review carefully the organization of formal outlines in English.

Thesis Statement (Controlling Idea of Essay)

   I. First topic sentence (first main supporting idea)

     A. First supporting example

       1. First specific supporting detail

       2. Second specific supporting detail   } paragraph one

         a. Additional supporting detail

         b. Additional supporting detail

     B. Second supporting example

  II. Second topic sentence (second main supporting idea) } paragraph two

(This pattern continues for the length of the essay.)

Use a formal outline to help plan an essay.

Create a formal outline based on your list in Activity 1.9. For help, download the Outlining Tutor at www.mhhe.com/brannan. Or use the site's Outline Template to create an outline in Microsoft Word.

Remember that more drafts will come.

Drafting

With the ideas and details you have discovered in hand and the overall shape of your paper determined, you can confidently begin the first draft.

[In a paragraph, describe your ideal work space.]

Preparing a Work Space

Before jumping into the writing, consider your surroundings. If you feel comfortable working in a noisy environment, any environment will probably work for you. If you need quiet to concentrate, though, find a place where you will not be disturbed. Set aside ample time to complete your writing goal; perhaps 30 minutes is enough, or perhaps several hours. Then decide what you need to be comfortable: soft music, a window, a glass of juice, a relaxing chair. Are you more productive curled up in bed, or do you get more done in the computer lab? Create an environment that will help you work efficiently.

Moving Ahead

As you begin to write, focus on your main idea (topic or thesis sentence), purpose, and audience. The goal of the first draft is to create material for the coming revisions, so grammar, spelling, and punctuation should not be major concerns (though writers occasionally backtrack to correct minor errors as they go). Focus on getting ideas on paper. If you continually stop writing and then start again, you can lose your train of thought and end up with unity problems. However, rereading your work in progress, especially for content, can also keep you connected to each unfolding idea.

Try to keep at your work for the scheduled time, but feel free to go beyond the time limit if the words are coming easily. Resist the impulse to be negative about the draft. There will be ample time to look more critically at your writing later. Finally, if you have difficulty resuming a draft in a new writing session, try leaving an idea or even a sentence unfinished and then beginning at that point.

SOLUTIONS FOR BREAKING OUT OF WRITER'S BLOCK

1. Return to your central point. Be sure you have written out a rough topic or working thesis sentence at the top of the page, and reread it frequently as you compose.

2. Try any of the discovery methods discussed in this chapter.

3. Talk to yourself on paper. Begin a written "conversation" about your writing problem.

4. Talk to yourself out loud, or speak with another person. Often, simply verbalizing things can help you clarify a fuzzy idea or give you a new direction.

5. Read what others have written. *A Writer's Workshop* offers many models for your assignments. See how other writers have solved the problems you face.

6. To get around the "perfection syndrome" that sometimes freezes writers, let yourself produce clunky, awkward sentences. You might be surprised at how many usable ideas and even sentences result.

7. If you are writing an essay and the introduction is a problem, start writing the body paragraphs. If your first body paragraph is not working, move on to the next.

8. Take a break. Sometimes a 10-minute trip to the kitchen is just what you need. Other times you may need a break of a day or so, thinking about the paper occasionally to let the ideas sort themselves out.

In drafting, keep self-criticism to a minimum.

If you are a fast writer but find that your draft is becoming scattered, slow down and reflect. If you typically write slowly, try freewriting to speed the process up.

ACTIVITY 1.11 *Drafting*

Following the "Breaking Out of Writer's Block Solutions," select one of the topics you have developed so far, write a topic sentence to focus it, and then write a rough draft of 200 to 300 words.

EARTH-FRIENDLY DRAFTING

There are many advantages to drafting on the computer instead of on paper; you can avoid unnecessary waste and work. Typing your draft means that you won't have to transfer your thoughts from one medium to the other later. It's also easier to revise on the screen than on paper, where scratched out words make a passage difficult to read. ●

Revising

Unlike drafting, revising requires a more critical (but not negative) frame of mind and a willingness to look closely at your work, knowing that it can be improved. As you rework your draft, by yourself and with others, you will be looking to add, shift, and delete material.

Very little about revision is easy; in fact, it may be the hardest part of the writing process. To revise effectively, you need to learn what problem areas to look for, gain insight into what you want to say, and let go of words and sentences that aren't working. Sometimes you will even need to throw out that first rough draft and start over. If you want to see your writing improve, you must join the many professional writers who may moan and groan as they revise, but who do so until they shape a product they can be proud of.

Remember not to be overly concerned with grammar, spelling, or punctuation at this point; save that for editing.

HINT

Revision = adding, cutting, and rearranging material.

After giving the draft some time to "cool off" (try for at least a day), remind yourself again of your purpose and audience, and look closely at your topic or thesis sentence. Taken as a whole, does your paper seem to grow from your main point? Jot down any reactions you have, positive or negative, and then reread the draft, following this list of priorities:

REVISION PRIORITY CHECKLIST

1. **Content:** The content of your work is the most important feature.
   - ☐ Check your ideas for clarity: Can you and other readers understand your point?
   - ☐ Be sure you have enough examples and details to convey your meaning and satisfy readers' curiosity.
   - ☐ Check for unnecessary points, examples, or details—anything that is repetitive or will distract readers from the central idea.

2. **Organization:** Make sure readers can follow your ideas.
   - ☐ Check your topic or thesis sentence to see if it still clearly guides readers.
   - ☐ Review the overall organizational pattern. If you chose a spatial arrangement, for instance, make sure you have been consistent in ordering details.
   - ☐ Look closely at how your sentences and paragraphs flow together. If transitions or other connectors are needed, use them.
   - ☐ Check your ending: Does it link to the main point of your paper and leave readers with something to reflect on?

3. **Style:** Word choice and arrangement can make writing easy or difficult to follow.
   - ☐ What words are not working well?
   - ☐ Is your meaning fuzzy?
   - ☐ Do you repeat words unnecessarily?
   - ☐ Do you have enough variety in the length, type, and beginnings of your sentences?
   - ☐ Where can you tighten sentences, eliminating words that serve no purpose?

4. **Mechanics:** The last element to check in your paper is mechanics—grammar, spelling, and punctuation. When you move into more polished drafts, you will edit out mechanical errors that keep you from communicating clearly.

As you practice revising, you will get better at it. Moving slowly through your drafts and focusing on one category to revise at a time will make this process more manageable.

Group Revising: Working Together

What if you have tried to revise by yourself in the past without much luck? Fortunately, in your writing class, you will have the help of fellow students and your instructor. In each chapter of this book, Working Together activities provide specific opportunities for collaborative learning, writing, and revising.

To profit most from collaborative work, you should be open to constructive criticism. Although none of the students in your group is an English teacher, you don't have to be an expert to respond to another's draft. Simply letting a student author know that an idea is unclear or that a paragraph seems to be drifting can be invaluable.

Each assignment chapter in this book gives advice on discovering ideas, organizing, drafting, and beginning to revise. Also, the revision chapters, 4 and 14, offer step-by-step suggestions for improving your drafts. However, for some general suggestions to make group revising productive, read through the following lists:

How the Writer Can Help the Reader

1. In a sentence or two at the top of your draft, specify your audience and purpose.

2. Tell your reader your main point.

3. Direct the reader to any part of the paper you have specific concerns about—for example, "I'm not sure about my topic sentence. Does it tell you what I think is the main point?" or "Do you think I might have too many details about sound in the first half of the paragraph?"

4. After your paper has been read, listen carefully to the reader's responses, and then ask for clarification of any comments you didn't understand.

5. Do not let a reader overwhelm you. Be selective in the advice you follow. Have several other readers comment on suggestions for revision, especially if a suggestion feels wrong for your paper.

How the Reader Can Help the Writer

1. Ask about the audience, purpose, and main point.

2. Read the draft quickly and tell what you liked or thought the author did well.

3. Answer any questions the author has about the draft.

4. Reread the draft again slowly, using the revision checklists in each revision chapter. Jot notes in the margins of the paper. A helpful shorthand is to draw a straight line under words, phrases, and sentences that you particularly like and a wavy line under any part that seems questionable.

5. Share your honest reactions with the author. But remember, neither of you should expect the other to be the "teacher." Your job is simply to give the best response you can as you understand the assignment requirements.

6. Remember to role-play the designated audience as you read, and respond as you think that person or group would.

ACTIVITY 1.12 WORKING TOGETHER: *Revising*

Get together with one or more group members and trade drafts. Using the preceding lists, offer each other comments and suggestions that will help you produce better-developed and more clearly written drafts.

Editing

After revising your paper several times for material, organization, and style, it's time to focus on mechanics—grammar, spelling, and punctuation. Hopefully, hearing the word *grammar* doesn't make your eyes glaze over or the sweat start

Concentrate on your most serious errors first.

to trickle. The object of editing is simply to make your writing more readable, to help readers better understand and enjoy your ideas.

One goal of this text is to help you solve *most* of your problems with grammar, punctuation, and spelling. So don't despair. Even if you think that you'll never figure out where all the commas and other "stuff" go, you will learn most of what you need to know to write clearly and correctly by the end of the term.

The following are some pointers for effective editing:

HOW TO EDIT

1. Go *slowly*, stopping often. When you edit, you will tend to see whole word groups as you are used to seeing them, rather than how they actually appear on the page. Your mind will fill in the blanks for missing words, register a *there* as *their*, or create or eliminate pauses for commas in an unpredictable fashion.

   To help you concentrate, try putting your finger below each word of your printed draft. Go line by line, stopping frequently at the end of completed thoughts. If you are not sure about a possible mistake, write a question mark and continue. But don't simply ignore it, hoping the problem will go away. It won't.

2. Read through your paper many times, each time focusing on just a few kinds of errors.

3. Begin an Improvement Chart after your instructor hands back your diagnostic writing sample. List your most common errors in the Improvement Chart at the back of this book. This list will help you track and then correct them. Does it make more sense to memorize all the rules in a 500-page handbook or to figure out the handful of mistakes that cause *you* the most problems?

4. Use the handbook section in this text (Unit Five) and a supplemental handbook if your instructor requires one. As you write papers, your instructor will mark many errors, some of which will be pattern errors. The handbooks give examples of such errors and show how to correct them.

5. Allow enough time for others to review your work with you: classmates, friends, family members, writing center tutors, and your composition instructor.

6. Word process your draft. Errors are generally more noticeable on a cleanly word processed page than on a handwritten one, and you have the advantage of using spell and grammar checkers.

Try covering the line that follows the one you are editing, to keep your eyes from jumping ahead as you work.

Learn your pattern errors. See Activity 1.13.

Unit Five examines problems with grammar, spelling, and punctuation in detail, but the following list will give you an overview of common errors:

MAJOR CATEGORIES OF MECHANICAL ERRORS

English Review Note

Your peers—particularly those who work in the writing center—can be a great editing resource. If English isn't your first language, ask a native speaker to help you edit your work.

1. Grammar
   A. Subject/verb agreement (pp. 560–565)
   B. Verb tense shift (pp. 559–560)
   C. Correct verb form (pp. 553–560)
   D. Pronoun agreement (pp. 570–572)
   E. Pronoun shift (pp. 575–577)
   F. Pronoun case (pp. 573–575)

G. Pronoun reference (pp. 568–570)

H. Parallelism (pp. 537–539)

 I. Misplaced and dangling modifiers (pp. 582–584)

2. Punctuation

A. Run-on sentences/comma splices (pp. 541–546)

B. Sentence fragments (pp. 546–551)

C. Unnecessary commas (pp. 596–597)

D. Commas to introduce main clauses (pp. 588–590)

E. Commas to enclose nonessential words or set them off at the end of main clauses (pp. 590–592)

F. Commas to divide main clauses (pp. 592–594)

3. Words

A. Spelling (pp. 606–616)

B. Sound-alike and look-alike words (pp. 610–616)

C. Wrong words (pp. 478–481, 491–497)

D. Missing words (p. 68)

E. Capitalization (pp. 600–601)

| **ACTIVITY 1.13** | WORKING ONLINE: *Diagnostic Editing Tests*

For practice revising and editing on the sentence level, take the four Diagnostic Editing Tests at www.mhhe.com/brannan. These can help you identify specific editing concerns to watch for in your own writing.

Proofreading

Proofreading is your final step. After you have closely edited your most recent draft and caught all the mechanical errors possible, print out a copy of the final version, the one you plan to turn in for a grade. You might think that this version is as polished as you can make it. But chances are this draft still contains problems that you can catch and correct—before your instructor does.

HOW TO PROOFREAD AND PREPARE YOUR FINAL MANUSCRIPT

1. Check for typographical errors such as misspelled, run-together, and omitted words. Often, when fixing errors in the editing stage, writers slip up in small ways on the keyboard. *Be sure to spell check once again.*

2. Check the following items carefully: font size (12 point), line spacing (double space), margins (1 inch), and title. Remember to capitalize all words in the title, even small ones like *is* and *do*, except articles (*a, an, the*), prepositions (*of, in, to,* etc.), and coordinating conjunctions (*and, but, so,* etc.). If articles, prepositions, or conjunctions begin or end a title or follow a colon, however, capitalize them.

3. Spell check any additional required material, such as outlines. Staple or paperclip your pages. Avoid putting the paper in a plastic sleeve, which most instructors consider a nuisance.

ACTIVITY 1.14 | *Proofreading*

Proofread your paper and hand it in to your instructor. Be sure to read your teacher's comments and corrections carefully when he or she returns the paper, and then list all errors on your Improvement Chart.

Linking to Future Experience

You will use some variation of the writing process for every paper assignment in college, including those in this class. Use this chapter as a reference when working on future paragraphs and essays. Remember that even experienced writers benefit from idea clusters, outlines, collaborative revision, and careful proofreading.

Because your instructor may ask for them, save your prewriting and organizing notes so you can turn them in along with your draft.

Diagnostic Writing Assignments

Before you begin any of the assignments below, review this chapter's advice on discovering ideas, organizing, and drafting. Try at least one prewriting method, and aim to write a single paragraph of 200 to 300 words. After you have a revised draft in hand, be sure to edit and proofread it carefully.

Option 1: Description

Describe a room that you are familiar with and comfortable in. If you can visit the room (e.g., a room in your home), you might try listing details of the surroundings and then arranging the details spatially (one side to the other, front to back, bottom to top—see p. 84). Consider taking a photograph that you can use as a reference. Remember to state some central point or main idea about the room in your first sentence. As an alternative assignment, describe the rooms in the photograph on the facing page.

Option 2: Narration

Tell a story about some event in your life that you remember well and that has affected your view of yourself, another person, or the larger world. You could use several of the discovery methods discussed in this chapter to find ideas, but you might begin with general clustering and then try a focused cluster. Arrange your details chronologically (as if you were reliving the event from beginning to end—see p. 122). State some main point or reason for telling the story in your first sentence.

Option 3: Exposition

Explain why you are in college and what you hope to gain from this experience. You could use several of the discovery methods discussed in this chapter to find ideas, but you might begin with general freewriting and then try a focused freewrite. Arrange your reasons, starting your paragraph with the least important one and ending with the most important (see p. 139). State some overall point or reason for being in school in your first sentence.

 ACTIVITY 1.15 WORKING ONLINE: *Writing Process Review*

Take the Chapter 1 Review Quiz at www.mhhe.com/brannan.

Chapter Summary

1. Clarify the writing project.

2. Commit yourself to the work.

3. Practice the writing process:
   A. Discover.
   B. Organize.
   C. Draft.
   D. Revise.
   E. Edit.
   F. Proofread.

4. Be flexible in approaching the writing task. Try alternatives when necessary.

5. Don't despair. Help for your writing abounds, but you must become an active learner, seeking out the help that you need to succeed.

Making the Most of Reading

2

[*How do you feel about reading? What specifically do you like most or least about it? What advantages do you see to becoming a more effective reader?*]

KEY TOPICS

- Is there a method to effective reading?
- Prereading: Preparing to understand
- Reading: Processing ideas
- Reading: Focusing and recording main ideas
- Postreading: Retaining ideas

Is There a Method to Effective Reading?

When you were a child learning the alphabet and beginning to puzzle out words —*c-a-t, d-o-g, p-i-g*—reading was a mysterious and difficult process. As you advanced in school, this process became more comprehensible, but your reading tasks have also become more difficult. As a college student and an adult you are expected to read, understand, and evaluate complex texts. When you confront large, abstract reading assignments, you might sometimes feel as if you are back in elementary school, trying to untangle the mysteries of language. To make college-level reading more rewarding, this chapter will help you again become conscious of the reading process and learn some of the *techniques* that help effective readers remember, comprehend, and evaluate ideas.

We can divide the reading process into three stages:

1. **Prereading:** preparing to understand
2. **Reading:** processing ideas
3. **Postreading:** refining and retaining ideas

Prereading: Preparing to Understand

Reading, like writing, is best understood as a process. Just as you discover and organize ideas before writing a first draft, so too should you size up a text before you begin reading it. Here are three useful approaches:

1. **Skim** all signposts.
2. **Skim** beginnings and endings.
3. **Link** new information to previous knowledge.

Signposts

All textbooks use signposts (visual aids) to help readers focus on the main points in each chapter, much like road signs guide travelers. The title itself will usually contain the main idea of the chapter. Next you will often find chapter previews, sometimes in the form of lists or brief summaries. Within the chapter, the major headings and subheadings form a chapter outline. Brief summaries or lists of essential points often appear at the ends of main sections, and many chapters conclude with a summary of (or questions on) the chapter's primary ideas. Text boxes and marginal notes highlight significant points and ask questions to help readers reflect on the material. Finally, key words and passages are boldfaced, italicized, or shaded to emphasize a point. Skimming through a chapter and noting these reading aids may take a few minutes, but it is time well spent.

Beginnings and Endings

Chapters in textbooks are organized in much the same way as paragraphs and essays. Each chapter has a central focus (thesis), which divides into several topics. These, in turn, are divided into subtopics, all of which are then developed through examples, details, and explanations. Before you read the body of the chapter, it helps to read the chapter introduction and concluding paragraphs or chapter summary. For more in-depth knowledge, skim the body paragraphs, focusing on the first and last sentences of each. All paragraphs should contain a unifying idea, and that idea will frequently be stated as a clear topic sentence.

Connections: Linking New to Previous Knowledge

After you have previewed a chapter, pause for a moment of reflection. What have you just read? What does it mean to you at this point? How do the terms and ideas fit into your previous experience? We all have a large store of knowledge to draw from. When you link new information to what you already know, you remember more efficiently. Within almost all new material, you can usually find something familiar to help fix the new information in your mind. If you have little actual experience with a topic, you will still have associations with it and can make useful comparisons that will help you understand and remember it.

Signposts create a chapter outline.

While previewing, remember not to read the body of the text; simply sample what the chapter will present in more depth.

ACTIVITY 2.1 *Previewing a Chapter*

Turn to Chapter 3 and skim the signposts, the beginning, and the ending. After 5 minutes of skimming, answer the following questions.

1. What is the chapter focus? _____

2. What are three essential parts of a body paragraph? _____ _____

3. What are three ways of organizing ideas within a paragraph? _____ _____

4. What is a topic sentence? _____

5. What are the three ways of developing a paragraph? _____ _____

6. What does it mean when we say that a paragraph is coherent? _____ _____

7. What are five ways to achieve coherence in a paragraph? _____ _____

8. Based on your prior knowledge, how would you describe the concept of *coherence* in a paragraph? What does the word *coherence* mean to you? What image or association comes to mind when you think of it? For example, the text uses the image of glue or tape. _____ _____ _____ _____

Reading: Processing Ideas

After previewing a chapter, the next step involves active reading, in which you read the body of the text. During active reading you may often pause to think about the author's message, sometimes backing up to reread. Complicated material like a college textbook requires careful reading. As active readers move through a text, they interact with it, asking questions, anticipating the author's next point, agreeing or disagreeing with ideas, and linking new information to their previous knowledge.

Here are three useful habits to develop as you read through any text:

1. **Anticipate** and **react** to the author's points.
2. **Visualize** what the author is explaining or detailing.
3. **Link** new ideas to previous ones.

Anticipating and Reacting

When you preview a chapter, you guess at what the body of the text will assert. Then, as you read, you react to the more detailed information. For example, if an author makes an arguable statement like "The Second Amendment provides for militias, not individual gun ownership," you can tentatively agree or disagree, depending on the examples and explanations that follow. In a passage in which the author develops an extended comparison of, for example, a school to a prison, a reader might respond in several ways:

- **Uncertainty:** "What in the world does the writer mean by this comparison?"
- **Guesses:** "I wonder if he means school before college, when education is still mandatory?"
- **Disagreement/agreement:** "I don't/do see many similarities here."
- **Comprehension:** "Oh, I see. He means the teachers are like prison guards."

Experienced readers carry on a running *internal* conversation with the text, but they also sometimes express themselves *aloud*.

Remember that all writing—from a comic strip to a calculus textbook—comes from people who are trying to communicate. When writers don't communicate clearly, readers must puzzle out meaning for themselves. Interacting with a text is the most important way to become a more effective reader.

Visualizing

Another active-reading technique is to visualize the author's words. We all form images in our minds. What kinds of pictures do you see in the following description?

> The redwood table was covered with summer picnic food: bowls of potato salad, baked beans, deviled eggs, and sweet pickles. Hot dogs sizzled on the grill alongside hamburgers, soaking up flavor from smoking mesquite chips. Mom and Dad rested on the bench for a moment, sipping iced tea and gazing fondly at their three children, who laughed as they pushed their swings higher and higher still into the clear blue sky.

This brief paragraph includes only a few of the details we would see if we were actually there. But if we work with the writer, we can fill in others, making the scene come alive. For example, does the picnic table have a tablecloth? If so, what kind and color—possibly plastic with a red-and-white-check pattern? Maybe there are trees nearby, other families lounging on blankets, and other children climbing monkey bars. Writers select details to stimulate readers' imaginations. Active readers then do most of the work themselves.

Even writers who are not purposely writing a description will include many details to illustrate their points, using key words to trigger images in readers' imaginations. In the following passage, some words may be unfamiliar, but others—like *island* and *volcanic*—probably create pictures in your mind.

> In mid-September of 1835, the *Beagle* arrived at the Galápagos Islands, a volcanic archipelago straddling the equator 600 miles west of the coast of Ecuador.

Perhaps you visualize sandy beaches and palm trees or a volcano spewing molten lava. We all form images differently, but creating vivid pictures helps us remember material—and makes reading more interesting.

Linking New to Previous Knowledge

As you read, it is crucial to connect new ideas to previous knowledge. For example, linking the *Beagle*'s arrival at the Galápagos Islands to some other event of the mid-1800s you are familiar with—say, the beginning of Queen Victoria's reign—will help you put Charles Darwin's voyage in context, an important step toward understanding. Whenever you link previous knowledge to new ideas through associations and comparisons, you help yourself understand and remember.

ACTIVITY 2.2 *Developing Active-Reading Habits*

This activity returns you to Chapter 3, this time to read in more depth. Turn to the pages listed for each of the three topics below. Read the material carefully, and then practice the three active-reading habits (listed here).

EXAMPLE: Turn to pages 40–41 and read the information on revising topic sentences.

A. Anticipate and react: *Oh no, more about topic sentences. Now I'm supposed to make the topic sentence more interesting? What if I'm not even all that interested in this topic?*

B. Visualize: *When I think of a tool, I see hammers, saws, rakes, pliers, wrenches, drills—I just need to create a picture in my mind of my garage.*

C. Link to previous knowledge: *Specific words fall into a "more limited category" than ones like them. This makes sense to me if I think of cars in general or my own Toyota Corolla, which is more specific than hundreds of other kinds of cars.*

1. Read about examples and details versus explanations (pp. 42–44).

   A. Anticipate and react: _____

   _____

   B. Visualize: _____

   _____

   C. Link to previous knowledge: _____

   _____

2. Read about layering examples (p. 44).

   A. Anticipate and react: _____

   _____

B. Visualize: _____

_____

C. Link to previous knowledge: _____

_____

3. Read about unity (pp. 46–47).

A. Anticipate and react: _____

_____

_____

B. Visualize: _____

_____

_____

C. Link to previous knowledge: _____

_____

ACTIVITY 2.3 WORKING ONLINE: *Reading Websites*

Apply the three active-reading habits to reading this web page. Then answer this question: How is reading online different from reading in print?

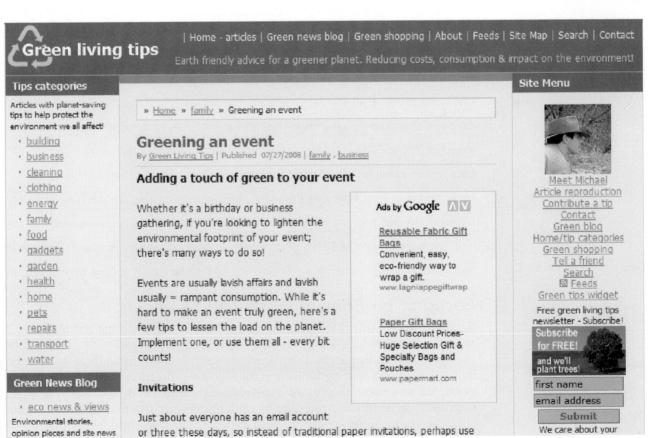

Reading: Focusing and Recording Main Ideas

Knowing a few common patterns for organizing and developing ideas will make your reading easier and more efficient the first time through. Also, using a pencil and highlighter will make the material easier to review.

Here are several strategies to help focus your reading and record information:

1. **Look** for thesis, topic, and summary sentences.
2. **Focus** on primary (essential) examples.
3. **Look** for repeated material.
4. **Notice** the patterns of development.
5. **Learn** to annotate, outline, summarize, and paraphrase.

Looking for Thesis, Topic, and Summary Sentences

For more on thesis, topic, and summary sentences, see Chapter 12.

Thesis sentences contain the main idea of an essay; **topic sentences** contain the main idea of a paragraph. Both sentences state, "This is my topic, and this is what I'm going to say about it." Essays and textbook chapters usually have a thesis statement in the opening paragraphs. Within body paragraphs, the first or second sentence is often a topic sentence, and at the end of the paragraph, there may be a summary sentence that reiterates the main idea. Look for these sentences when you preview a text, and then concentrate on them while reading. In the following paragraph, the topic sentence is shaded.

Developing Body Paragraphs

After a writer has established a workable topic sentence, he or she must next move into the heart of the paragraph, the support sentences. Depending on the writer's purpose, the audience's expectations, and the topic itself, these supporting sentences might range from several to several dozen. "Twenty-four sentences!" you might think to yourself when faced with a lengthier paragraph or essay assignment. "How in the world am I ever going to fill up all that white space?" The answer is, the same way that writers have been filling up paragraphs, essays, books, and other kinds of writing since words were first pressed into wet clay. After you have declared your main point, you will illustrate it with **examples, details,** and **explanations.** These are the simple tools of the trade. And no matter how long the writing project runs, writers use the same kinds of material over and over to "fill up the space," sometimes artfully, sometimes not. In the next few pages, we will take a look at exactly what solid support is: what it consists of, how much is enough, when it is relevant, and how to be sure it is clear to your readers.

Focusing on Primary (Essential) Examples

Paragraphs are built from detailed examples and explanations not all of which are critical to a reader's understanding of the paragraph's main idea. Writers often use secondary examples and explanations simply to reinforce their most important points. When reading for information, you should concentrate on the primary examples and most important explanations. Don't be distracted by the less-important ones. In the preceding sample paragraph, the main points that support the topic sentence are in bold type. The other supporting points—the possible text length, a writer's reaction to a long project, and the reference to clay tablets—are secondary and useful primarily to develop the main idea.

Looking for Repeated Material

Textbooks in particular will repeat and elaborate important ideas, providing many examples and explanations. When you notice repeated material within a paragraph or chapter section (often in lists, charts, summaries, headings, and boxes), pay special attention; it is probably important. In the sample paragraph below, notice that the idea of support is repeated several times.

Noticing the Patterns of Development

In Chapter 1, we looked briefly at the patterns of development, which writers use to expand and clarify their ideas and examples in predictable ways. For instance, in the paragraph below, we find imagined dialogue, which is a narrative element. Then the paragraph begins to tell how writers develop their ideas—the process-analysis or how-to pattern. Illustrating through examples, using vivid descriptive details, making comparisons, speculating about causes and effects, defining terms—when we begin to recognize these patterns, the ideas and information contained within them become easier to understand and to recall.

Learning to Annotate, Outline, Summarize, and Paraphrase

Annotating and Outlining

Active readers often find it helpful to **annotate** a text, underlining or highlighting important points while writing marginal notes to record reactions to the material. It is common to write questions, agree/disagree with a point, express surprise, link an idea with one found elsewhere in the text, and so on. You might number examples, star passages, circle prominent facts, and connect information with arrows.

There is no one best way to annotate, but, in general, highlight selectively. It will not help you focus on critical parts of the text if you highlight three-fourths of it. Note the following sample annotation:

Try different methods for recording your interaction with a text to find one that works for you.

Sample Annotation

After a writer has established a workable topic sentence, he or she must next move into the heart of the paragraph, the support sentences. Depending on the writer's purpose, the audience's expectations, and the topic itself, these supporting sentences might range from several to several dozen. "Twenty-four sentences!" you might think to yourself when faced with a lengthier paragraph or essay assignment. "How in the world am I ever going to fill up all that white space?" The answer is, the same way that writers have been filling up paragraphs, essays, books, and other kinds of writing since words were first pressed into wet clay. After you have declared your main point, you will illustrate it with **examples**, **details**, and **explanations**. These are the simple tools of the trade. And no matter how long the writing project runs, writers use the same kinds of material over and over to "fill up the space," sometimes artfully, sometimes not.

Here's the main point.

No set length for a paragraph!

What does this "wet clay" reference mean?

How can this be? Over and over? It's got to be more complicated than that.

ANNOTATING

Taking reading notes in the margins of your text saves paper, and it's also helpful when rereading or reviewing material for a test. Annotations are signposts that you can design especially for yourself. ●

Conservation in Context

Informal "scratch" outlines can also be useful for retaining information. Here is how we might outline the paragraph on support sentences:

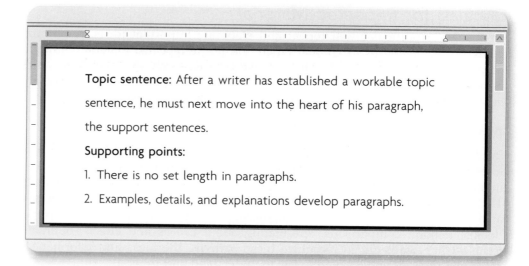

Topic sentence: After a writer has established a workable topic sentence, he must next move into the heart of his paragraph, the support sentences.

Supporting points:

1. There is no set length in paragraphs.

2. Examples, details, and explanations develop paragraphs.

Paraphrasing and Summarizing

Paraphrasing and summarizing the material you read helps you remember it because doing so requires you to put a text's ideas into your own words. In a **paraphrase,** you retain both primary and secondary examples. Therefore, a paraphrase is longer than a **summary,** which consists only of the main idea and significant examples. Here is how the support sentences paragraph might be paraphrased or summarized:

SAMPLE
PARAPHRASE

The main point of this paragraph is how to develop paragraphs. The author says that paragraphs have no set length but that their size depends on what the writer wants to accomplish, what readers expect to hear, and maybe how complicated the subject is. Support sentences consist of examples, details, and explanations.

SAMPLE
SUMMARY

This paragraph states that writers need to use examples, details, and explanations when developing paragraphs.

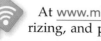

ACTIVITY 2.4 WORKING ONLINE: *Writing to Learn*

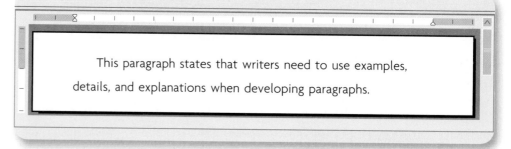

At www.mhhe.com/brannan, practice annotating, outlining, summarizing, and paraphrasing with the Writing to Learn exercises.

ACTIVITY 2.5 | *Focusing and Recording Main Ideas*

Read through the following paragraph excerpt, underlining the topic sentence and any primary examples. Next, annotate in the margins to show your reactions. Finally, write a brief scratch outline and a one-sentence summary of the paragraph.

Organizing Body Paragraphs

So far we have looked closely at the parts of a body paragraph and discussed a number of important ways to focus and develop them. But paragraphs and essays also benefit from an overall organizational plan, and there are several methods that are useful, depending on what you want to accomplish. If your primary goal is to describe, you might choose a spatial method of arrangement, organizing the parts of your description from side to side, front to back, near to far, inside to out, or bottom to top. If your primary goal is to tell a story—to entertain, explain, or persuade—you would choose a chronological pattern, relating events as they unfold in time. If you are most interested in communicating information—telling how something works, defining an idea, giving some history—or persuading, you might select order of importance, that is, beginning with your least important or interesting idea and ending with the most significant. Whatever overall method you choose, keep in mind that, especially in writing longer papers, you will often combine methods. For instance, a persuasive essay with reasons primarily arranged from least to most convincing might include a story that is arranged chronologically, or the essay might need to arrange some scene spatially.

Scratch Outline

Topic sentence (main point): _____

_____

Supporting points:

1. _____

2. _____

3. _____

4. _____

Summary (one sentence): _____

ACTIVITY 2.6 | WORKING ONLINE: *Find the Focus*

Practice summarizing with this online activity; limit each summary to ten words: http://www.mhhe.com/socscience/english/allwrite3/seyler/se03/finding.mhtml.

Postreading: Retaining Ideas

When you finish a reading assignment, you can simply move on to the next item on your to-do list, or you can take a few minutes to review, making your future recall of the material easier. When you stop reading, keep interacting with the text by asking questions like "What do I think of the material just covered? How does it fit with my experience? Are there any special points that I agree or disagree with, any ideas or suggestions that I will use from now on or that I think are useless?" Forming opinions will help you remember important ideas.

There are many ways to review effectively: silently skimming main points, stating them aloud, or organizing your thoughts on paper. These specific suggestions will help you review any reading assignment:

1. **Repeat the prereading step,** focusing especially on signposts.

2. **Summarize or outline the main points.** This may only require pulling together the paragraph summaries you have already written or listing the main points that you underlined when you annotated.

3. **Quiz yourself** on the material as if your instructor were asking the questions. If you can't answer your own questions, reread.

4. **Try to define any important term or idea** in a sentence of 20 words or less. Can you remember (or come up with) an example that helps to define the term or support the idea?

5. **List** what you feel are the three most important points from your reading.

| **ACTIVITY 2.7** | WORKING TOGETHER: *Practicing Postreading Strategies* |

Using any of the five preceding suggestions, review Chapter 2; then, in small groups, list the *essential* points about reading that you need to remember. Limit your list to ten points and use them to write the Chapter Summary below.

Chapter Summary

1. _____

2. _____

3. _____

4. _____
   _____

5. _____
   _____

6. _____
   _____

7. _____
   _____

8. _____
   _____

9. _____

10. _____
   _____

Remember that topic sentences are usually the first or second sentence but can be located elsewhere in a paragraph.

Crafting Paragraphs

2

BRANNAN

Writing Paragraphs

3

[*In this photo, the three women are solving a puzzle, putting the many pieces together to make a complete picture. Explore in a paragraph how writing is like working on a puzzle.*]

KEY TOPICS

- What is a paragraph?
- Writing a topic sentence
- Developing body paragraphs
- Writing a concluding sentence
- Organizing body paragraphs
- Connecting sentences—achieving coherence
- Selecting a title

What Is a Paragraph?

So far we have discussed the writing and reading processes, reviewing in general how compositions grow. Now we will look more specifically at one writing unit—the paragraph—to see how its pieces fit together and how it works in relation to larger units of writing. You've been writing paragraphs for years; in this chapter you will simply learn more about how they work and how you can write even more effective ones.

A **paragraph** is a collection of related sentences that are clearly connected to one another and that make some point. Paragraphs come in several varieties:

- Introductory
- Body
- Concluding
- Transitional

HINT

Paragraphs usually work together.

Our focus throughout Unit Two will be on the body paragraph. We will be developing paragraphs as single units of thought while remembering that paragraphs generally work together in essays. We will practice focusing a paragraph with a topic sentence; developing that main idea with specific, relevant support; and concluding the paragraph forcefully.

There is no set length for a paragraph; the kind of writing and the audience for it usually determine the number of sentences. For example, newspapers favor shorter paragraphs, whereas articles in academic journals often include paragraphs that fill a page. The paragraphs you write in Unit Two will usually run 250 to 300 words, or around fifteen sentences.

Body Paragraph

Topic sentence = topic + statement

Body of paragraph (contains sentences to support the topic sentence):

1. Connector
2. First example, reason, or detail
3. Support for first example

1. Connector
2. Second example, reason, or detail
3. Support for second example

(Additional examples, reasons, or details as needed to develop paragraph)

Concluding sentence:
1. Connector
2. Link to topic sentence
3. Expanded thought

Essay

Introductory paragraph

Body paragraph 1

Body paragraph 2

Body paragraph 3

Concluding paragraph

To contrast the paragraph with the essay and to get a sense of the parts of a paragraph, take a look at the diagrams on this page.

The **body paragraph** has three basic parts: topic sentence, support sentences, and concluding sentence. As you can see, the essay also has an introduction and a conclusion, but they are entire paragraphs. We will study introductory and concluding paragraphs in Unit Three.

To see a student
model paragraph with
the parts labeled, turn
to pages 43–44.

A body paragraph is
not an essay.

Although in some
languages it is
considered impolite to
begin with a strong,
direct point, English
readers expect such
an approach. In fact,
you should state
your point as directly
as possible to show
that you value your
readers' time.

Writing a Topic Sentence

All effective paragraphs have a **main point,** that is, some reason for their author to put that group of sentences together. Writers frequently state explicitly what a body paragraph will be about in a topic sentence. Usually the paragraph's first sentence, a **topic sentence,** indicates the direction of the author's and the readers' mental journey. Like a compass guiding a backpacker through unfamiliar terrain, the topic sentence can help readers find their way from one end of a paragraph to the other, without taking needless detours along the way.

Which of the following sentences both limits the topic and expresses a statement or opinion that you think the author could develop in a single paragraph?

A. I have a brother named Jason.

B. Many families have more than one boy.

C. My brother Jason is a great guitarist.

Sentences A and B are simply factual observations that give the reader no sense of what else the writer might want to say about them. Sentence C, on the other hand, limits the topic ("Jason") and makes a clear statement or assertion about it ("is a great guitarist") that we would expect the author to discuss further. A clearly expressed opinion or statement combined with a well-focused topic gives you and your readers the direction you need to move through the rest of the paragraph.

HOW TO WRITE A TOPIC SENTENCE

1. Limit the topic.

Since we are working with paragraphs, your scope must be fairly narrow. For example, instead of trying to take on the topic of global environmental problems, you might discuss a personal commitment to recycling.

Sometimes writers list several parts of their topic in a **forecasting statement** like this: "If people want to begin to recycle, all they need to do is call Deffenbaugh Waste Disposal, make a bit of extra room in their garage, and be prepared to separate the 'hard' from the 'soft' trash."

2. Make a clear statement about it.

Your topic sentence should state an opinion or controlling point. For instance, don't say, "Many people recycle in the United States"—a general factual statement that could lead in many directions. Instead, express a point, like this: "I learned the hard way how important it is to recycle."

3. Use specific word choices.

Strive to make your topic sentence interesting, since it is your introduction to the rest of your paragraph. You might begin with a rough topic sentence like "My brother is a great guitarist." But by adding more specific details, you could write a far more interesting sentence, such as this one: "My brother Jason toured all last summer with Architecture in Helsinki, playing some terrific solo riffs."

ACTIVITY 3.1 *Recognizing the Parts of Topic Sentences*

In the following group of topic sentences, underline the topic once and the statement being made about it twice.

EXAMPLE: My dad, Charlie Martin, <u>had a way of making us smile in</u> the middle of difficult situations.

1. Global warming is accelerating faster than most scientists predicted.
2. Hot air balloon rides are fun but more dangerous than most people think.
3. "Road rage" affects people from all walks of life.
4. All day care facilities should require a state license.
5. I think cemeteries are very restful places.

Focusing Topic Sentences

Good topic sentences are broad enough to let the writer develop a subject with specific examples, explanations, and details but narrow enough to allow the subject to be covered in a paragraph. Notice how the following broad topic sentences can be narrowed:

UNFOCUSED   Most people look forward to holidays.

WORKABLE   I always look forward to spending Thanksgiving with my relatives in Dallas.

UNFOCUSED   In the fall nature slows down and prepares for winter.

WORKABLE   While much of nature slows down in the fall, squirrels seem to be in perpetual motion as they prepare for the long winter months ahead.

ACTIVITY 3.2 *Focusing Topic Sentences*

Revise the following topic sentences to narrow their focus. Consider drawing on your own experiences or general knowledge to make a specific point about each topic.

EXAMPLE: Having to stay in the hospital can be a miserable experience.

Revised and limited: *One of the most miserable experiences of my life was being hospitalized for knee surgery last June.*

As you decide how to limit each statement, imagine that you will have to write a paragraph based on your revised topic sentence.

1. There are ways to preserve the environment.

   _____

2. Education costs a great deal in this country.

   _____

   _____

3. Computers are often used by students.

   _____

4. There are many SUVs on the road today.

   _____

   _____

5. Most people take precautions when they learn of a tornado warning.

   _____

   _____

Often, when you reread drafts of your paragraphs, you will see that the supporting sentences take you in a slightly different direction than what you stated in the topic sentence. Sometimes this requires deleting or modifying the supporting sentences, and sometimes it means reshaping the topic sentence.

ACTIVITY 3.3 *Deducing Topic Sentences*

Read each of the following groups of sentences from the body of a paragraph, state a topic that matches them, and then write a suitable topic sentence.

EXAMPLE: Jinyi opened her first present and clapped her hands in delight. Her parents, brothers and sisters, and the rest of the family wished her well. Jinyi's mother brought the cake, with 10 candles blazing, into the room. Her father hugged her and whispered, "You are the best daughter a father could ever hope for."

Possible topic: *Jinyi's tenth birthday party*

Possible topic sentence: *Jinyi had a wonderful time on her tenth birthday.*

1. One major mistake new college students make is too much partying. Another problem many students have is zoning out in class. Whereas cramming used to cut it in high school, daily study is now required. It is difficult to balance schoolwork with jobs.

Possible topic: _____

Possible topic sentence: _____

_____

2. I never realized that marriage would have so many bumps in the road. Being a good partner requires more than giving 50-50. A couple must communicate daily. Another important practice is regularly showing affection.

Possible topic: _____

Possible topic sentence: _____

3. Dad told us to burn the leaves, and my older brother Jim thought gasoline would help. After we had the leaves raked in a big pile, Jim poured on a mayonnaise jar full of gas. "Go ahead and light them," he ordered me. When the leaves exploded, I was knocked flat on my back.

Possible topic: _____

Possible topic sentence: _____

_____

Revising Topic Sentences

A **rough topic sentence** is enough to begin a draft of your paragraph with, but when you polish a topic sentence, you can make it more informative and interesting. One way to improve a topic sentence is to use *specific* words wherever possible. Selecting a specific word simply means choosing a word that fits into a more limited category than another, similar word.

Compare the following word lists:

A	B
tool	hammer
plant	rose bush
person	Thomas Jefferson
energy source	coal
animal	horse

Notice that the words in column B are more specific; that is, they are part of a larger group that the words in column A represent. For instance, the first word in column A, *tool,* includes the first word in column B, *hammer,* as well as such items as a screwdriver, paintbrush, or shovel. The more specific the word you choose, the sharper the image it creates—and the more interesting the sentence becomes.

Look at the following topic sentences. The first in each pair is the rough topic sentence, and the second has been polished by adding <u>specific words</u>.

ROUGH TOPIC SENTENCE   My vacation didn't turn out too well.

REVISED TOPIC SENTENCE   My vacation to <u>Ft. Lauderdale</u> was a <u>disaster</u>.

ROUGH TOPIC SENTENCE   Our day care center has had a problem recently.

REVISED TOPIC SENTENCE   <u>Peppermint Patty's</u> day care has sent <u>six children</u> home this week with <u>pinkeye</u>.

ROUGH TOPIC SENTENCE   My family's table manners need some work.

REVISED TOPIC SENTENCE   <u>Elbows on the table, arms stretched across plates as hands reach for the salt shaker, brothers and sisters outshouting one another</u>—my family's table manners need some work.

ACTIVITY 3.4 *Polishing Topic Sentences*

Rewrite the following sentences, making them more interesting by adding specific words where appropriate.

1. Rough topic sentence: I like working on my car.

   Revised topic sentence: _____

2. Rough topic sentence: Many voters are excited about the election.

   Revised topic sentence: _____

   _____

3. Rough topic sentence: I know now why I am finally back in school.

   Revised topic sentence: _____

   _____

4. Rough topic sentence: My husband has to work too much.

   Revised topic sentence: _____

   _____

5. Rough topic sentence: Living in a new country is difficult.

   Revised topic sentence: _____

   _____

HINT

For more on specific language, see pp. 75–78.

Developing Body Paragraphs

After writers establish a workable topic sentence, they must next write sentences that support it. These sentences are developed with examples, details, and explanations—the basic tools of the trade. No matter how long the writing project, we use these tools over and over to "fill up the space" and show why and how our topics matter.

The next few sections explore support: what it is, how much is enough, when it is relevant, and when it is clear.

Kinds of Support

Writers support their topic sentences with specific examples, details, and explanations.

Examples

An **example** illustrates some part of a statement by showing a specific instance of it. Whenever you are asked for more information to help someone understand an idea, chances are that you will give an example. For instance, you might say to a friend, "Baseball is boring." Your friend, a baseball fanatic, immediately replies, "What do you mean by that?" When you tell her that the pitcher and the catcher have most of the fun, that half the time the infielders and outfielders are so stationary they might as well be asleep, and that you would like to see a little more body contact, like in football, you have provided a list of examples.

For more on using examples in writing, see Chapter 7.

Your body paragraph should explain your main point, not just repeat it. Paragraph development in English may differ from that in your native language.

TYPES OF EXAMPLES

1. **Personal examples:** based on your own experiences. To illustrate how frustrating preschoolers can be, you could tell a story about the time your 4-year-old sister locked herself in the bathroom for 2 hours.

2. **Facts:** commonly accepted truths—for example, "Some trees lose their leaves in the fall."

3. **Statistics:** numerical facts—for example, "The earth is 93,000,000 miles from the sun."

4. **Information** gathered from print sources (books, newspapers, magazines, etc.), electronic sources (including the Internet), interviews, TV, and radio.

5. **Second-hand anecdotes:** things that happened to someone else.

6. **Comparisons,** including metaphors/similes—for example, "The flute is basically a pipe with holes drilled in it."

7. **"What-if" situations:** speculation about what could happen, such as what would happen if you decided to stop working on Fridays.

8. **Dialogue** created or reported to express a point.

Details

Just as we need examples to illustrate general statements, we need **details** to make examples more interesting. Details help sharpen an image or clarify an idea. To make the example of your little sister's locking herself in the bathroom more vivid, you could name some parts of the scene, then add **modifiers** and **sensory details:**

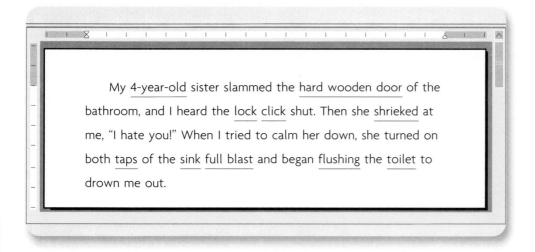

My 4-year-old sister slammed the hard wooden door of the bathroom, and I heard the lock click shut. Then she shrieked at me, "I hate you!" When I tried to calm her down, she turned on both taps of the sink full blast and began flushing the toilet to drown me out.

Explanations

You can use examples to develop much of your writing, but sometimes you need more. What if the reader does not understand the example or how it relates to your point? You can offer **explanations**—reasons that justify behavior, tell how things work, or anticipate possible outcomes. Explanations are vital when you develop a main point because they connect examples and guide readers through your ideas.

Suppose a reader's reaction to the example of the preschooler's behavior is "That doesn't seem so frustrating to me. Why didn't you just walk away and forget it?" The writer would need to explain that the child was his responsibility and that it would have been too dangerous to leave her locked in a bathroom by herself, especially while she was having a tantrum.

Explanations work with details and examples to "fill up the white space." In the following paragraph, you will find three major examples to support the topic sentence, an explanation following each major example, and details throughout to make the examples and explanations more vivid for the reader.

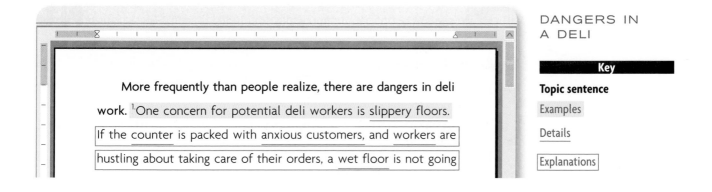

DANGERS IN A DELI

Key
Topic sentence
Examples
Details
Explanations

More frequently than people realize, there are dangers in deli work. [1]One concern for potential deli workers is slippery floors. If the counter is packed with anxious customers, and workers are hustling about taking care of their orders, a wet floor is not going to take top priority. During the rush what's going to stop an employee from running too fast, which could result in a serious wipeout? [2]In addition to slippery floors, working around chemicals should not be taken lightly. When cleaning the glass, you might end up with ammonia sprayed in your eyes. Both pan degreaser and sanitizer are used at dish time, and it only takes one splash in the sink to send someone on her way to the emergency room. [3]But the part of the job that is most dangerous is using the meat and cheese slicer. Whether operating the slicer or simply cleaning it, you risk cutting yourself. With just one careless slip near the sharp blade, you could end up with one less finger. A new person on the job might be a little nervous because of the possible injury that deli work entails, but luckily safety training is a requirement.

Concluding sentence

Sufficient Support

Detailed examples and clear explanations are important; you must have enough of them to fully illustrate your ideas. However, all too often inexperienced writers think a topic has been fully presented when the development is thin or repetitive.

To avoid underdevelopment, fill your paragraphs with layers of specific examples: The further readers move into a paragraph, the more specific it should become. Each major point should be clarified with detailed examples and explanations that increasingly limit and focus the paragraph's main idea:

Layer examples from general to specific.

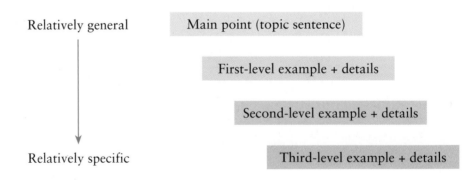

Relatively general → Main point (topic sentence)

First-level example + details

Second-level example + details

Relatively specific → Third-level example + details

Practically speaking, in one-paragraph papers, you will regularly be descending only one or two levels.

Read the following to see what the deli paragraph sounds like once we strip away the second-level examples, details, and explanations:

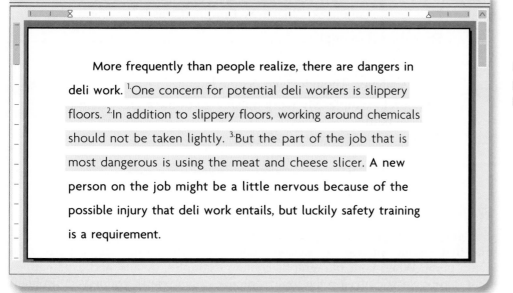

More frequently than people realize, there are dangers in deli work. [1]One concern for potential deli workers is slippery floors. [2]In addition to slippery floors, working around chemicals should not be taken lightly. [3]But the part of the job that is most dangerous is using the meat and cheese slicer. A new person on the job might be a little nervous because of the possible injury that deli work entails, but luckily safety training is a requirement.

Does this version of the deli paragraph read more like a paragraph or an outline?

This version reads more like an *outline*. The main ideas are there, but nothing more.

ACTIVITY 3.6 | *Creating Sufficient Support*

Each sentence group below begins with a topic sentence followed by a first-level example. To further develop each topic, create a second-level example that adds more specific information (details and explanation).

EXAMPLE: Topic sentence: People should avoid jogging because it hurts more than helps them.

First-level example: For instance, jogging can be bad for a person's joints.

Second-level example: *I have had problems with my knees, and my ankles swell if I run for more than half an hour.*

1. Topic sentence: Making it to class on time is difficult for several good reasons.

   First-level example: First, students have difficulty finding a parking space.

   Second-level example: _____

   _____

2. Topic sentence: I learned how to budget my money the hard way.

   First-level example: One lesson was to stop eating out so often.

   Second-level example: _____

   _____

3. Topic sentence: My family's annual trip to Silver Dollar City was fun this year.

   First-level example: I most enjoyed my time on the lake.

   Second-level example: _____

   _____

4. Topic sentence: Painting my house this spring was a valuable experience.

First-level example: Another way I profited was by saving money.

Second-level example: _____

_____

5. Topic sentence: Though some people hate it, I love doing yard work.

First-level example: My work outside gives me a great chance to observe nature.

Second-level example: _____

Unity = all examples and explanations clearly relating to a paragraph's main point.

The writer should show that all ideas in a paragraph are relevant.

Relevant Support—Achieving Unity

Sometimes even fully developed secondary support and examples include material that—while interesting, accurate, and worthwhile—may distract from the main point. When your paragraphs contain examples, details, and explanations that do not clearly develop the topic sentence (main point), you have a problem with **unity.**

Always consider your audience and try to gauge whether they would view any of your material as distracting or unnecessary. If you write out a controlling topic sentence and then look at it often as you work, you will have less trouble with unity.

In the following descriptive paragraph, do you think the underlined sentences reinforce or distract readers from the main point?

The paragraph's main point

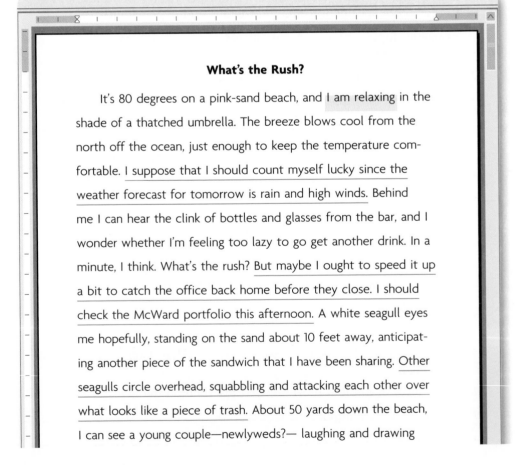

What's the Rush?

It's 80 degrees on a pink-sand beach, and I am relaxing in the shade of a thatched umbrella. The breeze blows cool from the north off the ocean, just enough to keep the temperature comfortable. I suppose that I should count myself lucky since the weather forecast for tomorrow is rain and high winds. Behind me I can hear the clink of bottles and glasses from the bar, and I wonder whether I'm feeling too lazy to go get another drink. In a minute, I think. What's the rush? But maybe I ought to speed it up a bit to catch the office back home before they close. I should check the McWard portfolio this afternoon. A white seagull eyes me hopefully, standing on the sand about 10 feet away, anticipating another piece of the sandwich that I have been sharing. Other seagulls circle overhead, squabbling and attacking each other over what looks like a piece of trash. About 50 yards down the beach, I can see a young couple—newlyweds?— laughing and drawing shapes in the wet sand. Beyond them the surf is gentle, breaking softly on the flat shelf of the beach. In the distance, rocking gently in the swells, a boat heads out to sea, its red flag with white diagonal stripe flapping. I glance down at the snorkeling gear I brought and think maybe it's time for a little action, but then the bartender is standing by my chair, another glass of soda and lime in hand. "Michael," he says smiling, "how about a little refresher?" There goes my resolve. "Thanks, I think," I tell him. As I flop back onto the lounge chair, I remind myself that this is my vacation. There is a time for work and a time for rest, and a wise person knows when each is appropriate.

English Review Note

In some languages, it is not uncommon to digress or go off the topic. Although indirectly related details may seem interesting, they can confuse the reader.

CONSERVING WORDS

Think of words as valuable resources and your paragraph as how you can use them. Part of keeping paragraphs unified and relevant is paying attention to these concerns on the sentence level. Consider when you've used "padding"—words that merely make a sentence bulkier, not more meaningful. ●

Conservation in Context

ACTIVITY 3.7 *Determining Relevant Support*

Look closely at the following paragraph and then underline the three sentences that seem to stray too far from the topic sentence. In the space after the paragraph, explain why each sentence you marked does not belong.

Primary audience: American college students ages 18–22.

When I was 10 years old, I used to live for baseball. Summer signaled the time school was finally over, and my friends and I could hit the park. We never wasted any time. Eight boys ranging in age from 7 to 15 met at our house for breakfast, filled up their water bottles, and headed down to the park. We almost always had it to ourselves. Of course, there was one time when the city held their Fourth of July celebration there. Down went the Frisbees to mark the bases, out came the gloves, bats, and balls, and then began the all-day games. You might think that a group of kids couldn't stay focused on anything all day, but we did. This was like our little World Series. Part of it was just love of the game; part of it was the competitive spirit. We all wanted to win. My brother was the most competitive of all of us and would fight over the strikes and the foul or fair balls. After countless innings,

HINT

See Chapter 20 for more on writing concisely.

balls chased into the street, and blisters from swinging the bat too many times, we would call it a day. I knew that later in the evening I might sneak a quick game of basketball in with my brother in our driveway. The sun would finally set on the eight of us, sweating, dehydrated, and covered in dirt from sliding into bases and diving for grounders. Whoever had the most wins, it didn't really matter. We went home happy, knowing that the next day we could play baseball again.

1. _____

2. _____

3. _____

Clear Support

After revising your paragraph for sufficient and relevant support, you might think that you are home free. But there is still one more vital point to check for—clarity. Achieving **clarity**—explaining examples, reasons, and word choices completely—is essential if readers are to fully understand your paragraph. One of the surest ways to check for clarity is to imagine a specific audience reading your work so that you can anticipate and answer their questions.

For example, in the baseball paragraph from Activity 3.7, there are several words, phrases, and ideas that might puzzle some readers. The idiomatic expression "my friends and I could hit the park" could be misinterpreted by readers unfamiliar with it. (Why would young people want to beat the ground at the park?) In the next sentence, readers might wonder about 7-year-olds playing baseball with 15-year-olds. Are the ages accurate? More explanation might be needed. The stated audience (American college students ages 18–22) would not have any difficulty with words and phrases like *Fourth of July, World Series, strikes,* and *diving for grounders,* but other readers might.

As you reread your work, checking for clarity, try to role-play your audience. And as other readers give you input, ask these questions frequently: "Do you understand all of my ideas? Are my examples and explanations clear? Do any of the words puzzle you or seem to need further explaining?"

HINT

Clarity = clear explanations and precise word choices.

HINT

Role-playing your audience can help with clarity.

English Review Note

Avoid using translations; they can be confusing to readers.

ACTIVITY 3.8 *Achieving Clarity in Word Choices*

As you read the following paragraphs, think about the audience and what they might know; then underline any word or phrase that might need additional explanation.

EXAMPLE: Audience: 12-year-olds learning about fly-fishing

First you must select the proper fly for the weather and water conditions. I would suggest a <u>dry fly</u> <u>number 12</u>, perhaps a <u>Royal Wulff</u>. Your <u>leader</u> should be <u>tapered</u>, with no more than a <u>3X tippet</u>, and you must be particularly careful using the <u>improved clinch knot</u> with which you will attach the fly to the tippet.

1. Audience: person training to be a waiter

   Be careful on Friday and Saturday evenings during the rush. Orders are coming fast off the wheel, and the servers will blow past you pretty quickly coming off the line. Always check with the manager to see if any

menu items have been 86ed, and be sure to check the special.

2. Audience: a young uncle who has volunteered to baby-sit (but who has no experience with toddlers) getting instructions on changing a diaper

Be careful not to use the Kleenexes; they're too rough. Use the wipes.

And don't wipe her from back to front. Go the other way. If it's before

bedtime, use a day diaper. If she's ready for bed, don't use the old night

diapers because we want her to start using the pull-ups now. You will

find the cloth diapers and all the other diapers in the drawers under the

changing table, but don't try to use the cloth diapers for anything but

padding the table. And, oh yes, don't use the Diaper Genie; it's a hold-

over from Alexis's baby days.

ACTIVITY 3.9 | *Achieving Clarity in Explanations*

As you read the following paragraph, think about the audience; then underline any phrase or sentence that fails to explain its point clearly. In the space below the paragraph, explain what more readers would need to know.

Audience: first-year community college students beginning the registration process

All new students must attend a preadvising session, so set some time

aside and find the right room for the session. Next, go get an application, fill

it out, and turn it in. Be sure to create a PIN and record it for future use—

this is important! If you want to enroll in credit classes, you must take the

assessment tests. Of course, not everyone has to take all the tests, and not

doing well on the tests will not keep you from attending the college, but

not taking the tests at all will.

_____

_____

_____

Writing a Concluding Sentence

As important as it is to begin a paragraph well and to develop the body fully, writers need to end their paragraphs with equal care. Although many short and medium-length body paragraphs in essays do not use summary or "clincher" sentences, longer body paragraphs commonly do, and one-paragraph papers should as well. The paragraphs you write for assignments in Unit Two should end decisively with a single sentence (sometimes two) that brings the paper to a satisfying finish.

For more on sentence
connectors, see
pp. 54–57.

Don't be afraid
to express strong
emotional conclusions.

HOW TO WRITE A CONCLUDING SENTENCE

1. **Use a connector:** Remember to use a transitional word (e.g., *finally, aside from, on the other hand, consequently*) or other sentence connector in the first part of the concluding sentence.

2. **Link to the topic sentence:** Always remind your readers of the topic and the statement you made about it in your topic sentence. You may simply repeat a word or, better still, find a synonym. Some paragraphs benefit from briefly mentioning (in a word or two) some important example, reason, or image from the body.

3. **Expand the thought:** Leave your readers with something to think about besides the statement in your topic sentence. This added thought should extend the discussion in the supporting sentences of your paragraph. Use any of the following methods:

   A. Express an emotion.

   B. Give a judgment or opinion.

   C. Ask a related question.

   D. Make a reflective statement.

   E. Say how your topic has affected your behavior or outlook on life.

   F. Make an ironic observation.

WHAT TO AVOID IN CONCLUDING SENTENCES

1. Do not simply repeat the topic sentence or a slightly altered version of it. Show your readers that you have some good reason for writing the paragraph and for them to read it.

2. In searching for an interesting ending, don't drift off into the twilight zone. Your final thought should grow logically from the paragraph.

3. Do not end with a cliché or worn phrase such as this one: *So, as you can see, I was caught between a rock and a hard place.*

4. Do not announce that you are ending the paper: *Well, it's time to end this paragraph, so . . . .* A brief summary of important examples or points, your expanded thought, and the white space at the bottom of the page will let readers know you have finished.

For more on clichés
and worn phrases, see
Chapter 20.

Expanded Thought

There is no one "right" way to conclude a paragraph or essay. Actually, conclusions, like introductions, are often detachable parts of the larger writing project. As you change one, you will frequently need to change the other. Take a moment to examine the six possible concluding sentences that could end the following paragraph. Which do you prefer?

An Oak Deeply Rooted—or a Tumbleweed?

Many people would define the ideal life as one in which they can live where they want to, when they want to. The Midwest appeals to people from all over the country who want housing that is still affordable, a small city with lots of green spaces, and an environment that is relatively low in crime. But when summer comes, people head for the mountains in droves. In an ideal situation a couple would have a small, well-furnished cabin in a rugged mountain chain like the Rockies and spend time there from July through September. They could spend time backpacking, fishing the lakes and streams, rafting the rivers, horseback riding, and mountain biking. However, mountain winters are rugged, so there comes a time when many people feel the most desirable destination is the beach. In January, when the temperatures in the middle and northern part of the country are dipping well below zero, in a mass exodus, winter-shy crowds head for the southern rim of our country and beyond. And why not? Who wants to bundle up in four layers of clothes and a down coat just to waddle outside to check the mail? Beach residents can look forward to sailing, motorboating, jet skiing, windsurfing, fishing, snorkeling, diving, and strolling along the beach. Aside from the gentler weather and fun activities, it seems easier to find large groups of like-minded people of various ages to socialize with. _____

HINT Any of the possible concluding sentences could be inserted here.

POSSIBLE CONCLUDING SENTENCES

A. It would be fun to have the freedom and money to live wherever a person wanted to, and it is a shame that more people in this affluent country of ours can't do it.

B. But if people want this kind of lifestyle, they need to work hard and save so they can earn it.

C. With so many places to visit and new experiences awaiting us, who wouldn't want to travel the country as the seasons turn?

D. In the long run, although it would be wonderful to have the freedom and the money to move from place to place, attitude and health probably count more than wherever people live.

E. But even with the opportunities for fun that multiple homes could bring, I think I would miss my friends and family too much to stay away from my *real* home too long.

F. So, if you like this vision of a future, be sure to take it easy while you're young, don't work too hard, don't worry about an education that will lift you upward, and by all means max out those credit cards today—you'll be living the ideal life before you know it.

Any of these possible conclusions could be the "right" way to end this paragraph. Try several possible endings as you revise your drafts, searching for one that best fits your topic, purpose, audience, and tone (humorous, serious, sad, and so on).

HINT Try several concluding sentences to end your draft.

ACTIVITY 3.10 *Selecting Concluding Sentences*

In each of the following three sets of sentences, you will find a topic sentence and three concluding sentences. Circle the letter of the strongest closing sentence; in the space provided, explain why you think it works best.

1. Topic sentence: Whenever I close my eyes trying to remember the "good old days," the first thing that comes to mind is my friends calling me a wuss.

Possible concluding sentences:

A. I have a career goal today, which I am close to achieving, of becoming a travel agent.

B. Several of my childhood friends are currently in jail.

C. Although I wouldn't want to relive these childhood experiences, they have helped me become more sensitive to other people's fears and insecurities.

_____

_____

2. Topic sentence: I was 15 years old and had never before lost a tae kwon do tournament, but this St. Louis match was a big one, and I was a little worried.

Possible concluding sentences:

A. With only 5 seconds left, my opponent's parents began to cheer with tears in their eyes.

B. But losing this tournament helped me to see that there will always be someone better, so I should never stop learning and practicing what is important to me.

C. Martial arts are a good way to stay in shape if you are willing to spend the time at them.

_____

_____

3. Topic sentence: So, as my life in America began, I was surprised at the great difference between Korean high school and American high school.

Possible concluding sentences:

A. Though I miss my home and friends, I'm glad that I was able to experience the freedom I found in my American high school.

B. In Korea, I had no choice; there was a required academic program that couldn't be disputed by the students.

C. The way that the high schools dealt with sexuality between males and females was very different because of the different cultures.

_____

_____

ACTIVITY 3.11 *Creating Concluding Sentences*

Read through the following paragraph, and create two closing sentences that are different from the one provided. Use any two of the six methods (A–F) listed on page 50.

Death Strikes

There were many people in the water waiting to put their boats on their trailers at Hillside Lake on that tragic July afternoon. I felt hot and sticky waiting on the lake, frantically maneuvering my small aluminum boat closer to the ramp, but I knew my turn was still a long way away. Slowly, ominous black clouds that had been building on the horizon rolled closer and closer. Thunder shook the huge lake as if it were a glass of water, vibrating, nearly ready to fall off some gigantic rock and shatter on the ground. Suddenly the sky began to pour, as if someone had opened a faucet. I remember looking at the old man in the boat next to me and how his head turned so quickly. I can remember hearing a high-pitched hum, like a camera flash charging up. Quickly, instinctively, I jerked my head around to my left toward the shore and saw the massive bolt of lightning fly down from the sky into a man's chest. He arched his back and was thrown into the water. The lightning hit him as though a refrigerator had been dropped on him. He was only 33 years old, and he died right in front of me, a sight that will stay in my memory, like a stain, forever. Death can strike anyone at any time, and I know now that eighteen does not mean immortal.

Concluding sentence

Other possible concluding sentences:

1. _____
   _____
2. _____
   _____
   _____

Organizing Body Paragraphs

In addition to a topic sentence that provides focus, paragraphs benefit from an overall organizational plan, which depends on the writer's purpose.

If your primary goal is to describe, you might choose **spatial** arrangement, organizing the parts of your description from side to side, front to back, near to far, inside to out, or bottom to top. If your primary goal is to tell a story—to entertain, inform, or persuade—or explain a process, you might choose **chronological** order, relating events as they unfold in time. If you are most interested in communicating information—telling how something works, defining an idea, or giving some history—you might select **order of importance,** that is, beginning with your least important or interesting idea and ending with the most significant.

Whatever method you choose, especially in writing longer papers, you will often combine methods. For instance, a persuasive essay with supporting points primarily arranged from least to most convincing might include a story that is arranged chronologically or a description arranged spatially.

For more complete explanations of these organizational methods, as well as paragraph examples, turn to the following pages:

- Spatial: pages 84–86, 87–89
- Chronological: pages 115–117, 122–123
- Order of importance: pages 139–140, 144–147

Essays often combine organizational patterns.

Connecting Sentences—Achieving Coherence

After establishing an overall pattern for your paper, formulating a working topic sentence, and writing a first draft, read your paper for **coherence.** An effective paragraph or essay is *unified;* that is, all the examples and explanations clearly

Coherence = linking
sentences with
connecting words.

relate to the main idea expressed in the topic or thesis sentence. If unity relates to **ideas,** then coherence relates to the paper's **structure,** what holds the sentences together. It might help to think of the related word *adhesive,* a useful sticky substance (like tape or glue) that can keep your sentences from falling apart.

Writers can link sentences and paragraphs in several ways, and you probably use these methods quite naturally even as you churn out rough drafts. But when you omit necessary connectors, you can confuse readers. Consider the following passages, and decide which seems clearer to you:

A. _____ I prepared for surgery _____ the vet clinic _____ I work, I was administering anesthesia to a miniature black poodle _____ respiration stopped _____ the heart _____ beating. I quickly scrambled _____ the side of the small _____ to start _____.

B. As I prepared for surgery at the vet clinic where I work, I was administering anesthesia to a miniature black poodle when respiration stopped and the heart stopped beating. I quickly scrambled to the side of the small poodle to start respiration.

The omission of several transitional words and three repeated words in version A makes it difficult for us even to follow the information, much less enjoy what the writer has written.

HINT

In your own work, you
should become aware
of these devices, which
will help your writing
"stick together."

METHODS FOR ACHIEVING COHERENCE

1. Transitions
2. Repetition
3. Synonyms
4. Pronouns
5. Reference to a main idea

Transitions

Transitions (also called "connectors") are the most common method writers use to create coherence. Transitional words and phrases guide a reader through your writing like street signs help you to find your way in a city.

TABLE 3.1 COMMON TRANSITIONS

FOR LOCATING OR MOVING IN SPACE (PARTICULARLY USEFUL IN DESCRIPTIVE WRITING)			
above	east (west, etc.)	inside	over
against	elsewhere	in the distance	surrounded by
alongside	far off (away)	into	there
around	farther on	near	through
at the side (end)	forward	next to	to
backward	from	off	to the right (left)
behind	here (close to here)	on	under
below	in	on the other side	up
beyond	in back	onto	upstairs
by	in between	opposite	
down	in front of	out of	

FOR MOVING IN TIME
(PARTICULARLY USEFUL IN NARRATIVE WRITING)

after	first (second, etc.)	next	suddenly
afterward	immediately	now	then
at last	in the meantime	often	time passed
awhile	in the past	once	until
before	later	previously	when
earlier	long ago	recently	while
finally	meanwhile	soon	

All References to Calendar Time and Calendar Events
ago (days, weeks, months, years)
one day (days of the week, months of the year, seasons, holidays)
that morning (afternoon, evening)
today (tonight, yesterday, tomorrow)

All References to Clock Time
any clock numbers used with a.m./p.m. (12:00 a.m., 1:00 p.m., etc.)
a few minutes (seconds, hours)

All References to Regular Meals
during breakfast (brunch, lunch, dinner)

FOR ADDING MATERIAL
(PARTICULARLY USEFUL IN WRITING THAT EXPLAINS HOW SOMETHING WORKS)

again	as well as	furthermore	likewise
also	besides	in addition	moreover
and	further	last	next

FOR GIVING EXAMPLES AND EMPHASIS
(PARTICULARLY USEFUL IN EXPLANATORY AND PERSUASIVE WRITING)

above all	especially	in particular	one reason
after all	for example	in truth	specifically
another	for instance	it is true	surely
as an example	indeed	most important	that is
certainly	in fact	of course	to illustrate

FOR COMPARING
(PARTICULARLY USEFUL IN WRITING THAT FOCUSES ON SIMILARITIES AND DIFFERENCES)

alike	both	like	resembling
also	in the same way	likewise	similarly

FOR CONTRASTING
(PARTICULARLY USEFUL IN WRITING THAT FOCUSES ON SIMILARITIES AND DIFFERENCES)

after all	dissimilar	nevertheless	though
although	even though	on the contrary	unlike
but	however	on the other hand	whereas
difference	in contrast	otherwise	yet
differs from	in spite of	still	

FOR SHOWING CAUSE AND EFFECT (PARTICULARLY USEFUL IN EXPLANATORY AND PERSUASIVE WRITING)			
accordingly	because	hence	then
and so	consequently	since	therefore
as a result	for this reason	so	thus

FOR SUMMARIZING AND CONCLUDING (PARTICULARLY USEFUL AT THE END OF BODY PARAGRAPHS AND AT THE BEGINNING OF CONCLUDING PARAGRAPHS)			
finally	in conclusion	in short	that is
in brief	in other words	largely	to summarize

ACTIVITY 3.12   *Achieving Coherence through Transitions*

Using Table 3.1, locate and underline all the transitional words in the following paragraph excerpt. The first sentence has been marked as an example.

English Review Note

Review these transitions and their meanings. Note the prepositions and articles that may be part of the phrase.

Paddling down Kansas and Missouri rivers is one of my favorite pastimes, but I have had some awful experiences on them. One aggravation I have learned to deal with is bad weather. Our first night on the river, everybody is excited and raising hell—till the rain comes. For some reason the rain clouds seem to follow us down into the river valleys and then open up. Fellow campers and I usually wake up in a huge mud puddle, and we are lucky if we don't have to swim to the trucks to get clean, dry clothes. While uncertain weather might seem bad enough, having a friend get hurt is worse. Once my friend Matt flipped his canoe in front of mine, and I couldn't stop in time. Matt caught the bow of my canoe in his right eye. The cold, clear spring water of the Current River did not stop the huge purple lump above his eye from swelling.

ACTIVITY 3.13   WORKING ONLINE: *Using Transitions*

Practice using transitions in paragraphs at http://cla.univ-fcomte.fr/ english/paragraph/tutorial_4/trans_hotpot/trans1.htm. If you run into trouble, take the Transitions Tutorial on the same site.

Repetition

Repeating a word or phrase is the second most common method for creating coherence in writing. However, if you repeat words needlessly, you risk boring your reader. Which of these sentence groups uses repetition more effectively?

HINT

Repeating a word or phrase is a common and useful way to connect sentences.

A. Every summer, after school was over in Venezuela, two of my cousins used to come to my parents' house to spend their vacation time with us. My cousins and I didn't realize at that young age that my grandfather, who lived with us, was having a hard time trying to sleep. Kept awake every night by my cousins' loud voices and laughter, my grandfather decided to play a joke on my cousins and me that didn't turn out to be as funny as my grandfather thought it would be.

B. Every summer, after school was over in Venezuela, two of my cousins used to come to my parents' house to spend their vacation time with us. We didn't realize at that young age that my grandfather, who lived with us, was having a hard time trying to sleep. Kept awake every night by our loud voices and laughter, he decided to play a joke on us that didn't turn out to be as funny as he thought it would be.

If version A seems a bit awkward, it is because the writer has overused repetition, instead of offering some variety by substituting pronouns such as *we* (for *my cousins and I*), as in version B.

Synonyms

Using **synonyms**—words with identical or nearly identical meaning—or short phrases in place of another word or phrase is a good alternative to repetition. For example, in version A above, the author could have created variety by naming her two cousins and using the word *children* to refer to herself and her cousins.

Repeating words can make your writing less interesting and also indicates a limited vocabulary. Use a dictionary to find appropriate synonyms and make use of pronouns.

ACTIVITY 3.14 WORKING TOGETHER: *Achieving Coherence through Repetition and Synonyms*

Working with a partner, cross out unneeded repetition in this paragraph; then write in necessary replacement words in the space above the line. Do not cross out every repeated word, though—artful repetition is desirable. Compare your revision to those of other groups.

Everyone has experienced the thrill of victory, but I have yet to see a comeback as sweet as the 1997 Chapman versus Abilene football game. Chapman and Abilene are two class 4A high schools located in north-central Kansas, and Chapman and Abilene have one of the fiercest football rivalries in the state of Kansas. At first, the game seemed like any other football rivalry game. Chapman would get a touchdown, and then Abilene would answer with another touchdown. Both Chapman and Abilene had a strong passing game, but Chapman could run the football better than Abilene could run it.

Pronouns

You use **pronouns**—words that can replace nouns (*she, it, who, them*)—so unconsciously that you might overlook them as a way to improve coherence. Read the following two sets of sentences and decide which is more coherent and clear:

A. Bill's boss told him that his office would be relocated while major renovations were completed on their building. The rest of his staff were worried that his office relocation would put him too far away to stay in touch with day-to-day problems. But Jim assured everyone that his office project would be handled quickly and that he would be back on the front line with his co-workers before they knew it.

Be careful not to overuse pronouns. Also, be sure that each pronoun clearly refers back to a specific noun.

CHAPTER 3 Writing Paragraphs   **57**

Copyright © 2010 The McGraw-Hill Companies, Inc. All rights reserved.

For more on pronouns and pronoun reference, see Chapter 25.

B. Bill's boss told him that Bill's office would be relocated while major renovations were completed on their building. The rest of Jim's staff were worried that Bill's office relocation would put him too far away to stay in touch with day-to-day problems. But Jim assured everyone that Bill's office project would be handled quickly and that Bill would be back on the front line with his co-workers before they knew it.

If version A seems difficult to understand, you might notice the overuse of *his*. Pronoun reference becomes especially tricky when a pronoun could be referring to several different nouns, as is the case with Bill and Jim. A good general rule when revising for both coherence and clarity is to check pronouns several times to be sure the noun they refer to will be clear to your readers.

ACTIVITY 3.15 *Achieving Coherence through Pronouns*

In the following paragraph excerpt, cross out unneeded or confusing pronouns, and write in the replacement words in the line above.

Smokey lived with me for $8\frac{1}{2}$ years and was my good friend. But then she contracted a feline virus comparable to HIV in humans. During the time she was sick, she also got cancer, which caused a lump on her neck just behind her head. We had it removed once in hopes that it would save her life, but instead it came back. When it returned, it was twice as big as it had been, and it only took half the time to form. My mother and I decided that it would be best to put her down. It was the hardest decision of my life, but I loved her too much to see her in such pain.

Take care to distinguish between *he/she* and *him/her*.

Reference to Main Ideas

You can also achieve coherence within and between paragraphs by linking main ideas or examples. For instance, notice how the following paragraph excerpt begins to develop the idea of *merciless teachers* in the topic sentence, continues with the synonym *cruel,* and reinforces the idea of cruelty with the word *punish.*

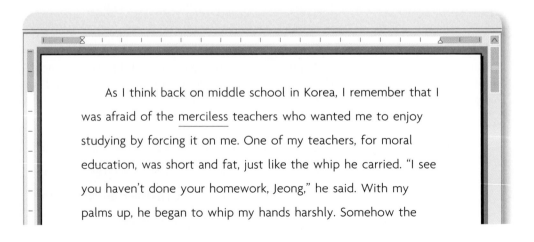

As I think back on middle school in Korea, I remember that I was afraid of the merciless teachers who wanted me to enjoy studying by forcing it on me. One of my teachers, for moral education, was short and fat, just like the whip he carried. "I see you haven't done your homework, Jeong," he said. With my palms up, he began to whip my hands harshly. Somehow the pain ended with me crying and begging, "I will do it next time, teacher!" Another cruel man, my history teacher, liked to use his green baby bamboo stick to punish me when I didn't score more than 80 percent on his exams.

Effective writers rely on all five methods we have discussed—transitions, repetition, synonyms, pronouns, and references to the main idea—to achieve coherence, often using several in the same sentence.

Selecting a Title

With your paper almost finished, it is time to expend one last bit of creative energy—choosing a title. But why do you need one in the first place?

A title's primary purpose is to attract readers. In "real-world" writing, authors are competing for readers' attention, time, and money, so any device that increases the authors' chances of success is welcome. You, too, are competing for your audience's attention. Whether you are working on a personal project, a business proposal, or a paper for a professor, including a title captures your readers' interest and sets up a positive expectation.

As you draft, be alert to any image or phrase that might make a good title. If nothing seems promising, brainstorm alone or with others when the paper is complete. Whenever you create your title, remember that it should accomplish two goals: interest readers and indicate your slant on the topic.

If you had to choose one of the following papers from each pair to read on the basis of the title, which would most interest you?

You may find a good title in a phrase or sentence in your draft.

1. A profile of a hard-working mother:
    A. "My Mom the Worker"
    B. "She Kept the Ship Afloat"
2. A story about a child sneaking one too many cookies:
    A. "Children Should Mind Their Parents"
    B. "Slamming the Lid on Andrew"
3. A personal narrative about a serious accident:
    A. "A Bad Wreck"
    B. "Crawling through the Wreckage"

In each case, version B is more vivid and inviting.

HOW TO WRITE EFFECTIVE TITLES

1. Keep titles short (roughly one to eight words). People can read and process a shorter title more efficiently. Readers confronted with a long title may think that the paper to follow will also be hard work.
2. Link the title to your main idea or dominant impression.

For more on metaphors,
see pp. 498, 500.

For more on audience
profiling, see pp. 46–49.

For more on tone,
see Chapter 20.

3. Create an image:

   A. Use a metaphor or other comparison. Notice the first title example above. What do you suppose "the ship" refers to?

   B. Use specific words, sensory details, active verbs, and words with *-ing* endings. Notice that the second and third title examples use *-ing* words to convey action.

4. Use a question. Look back at the paragraph "What's the Rush?" (p. 46).

5. Make a play on words. Notice in the second title example that "slamming the lid" brings to mind the slang expression "put a lid on it," meaning to stop some behavior. A play on words can add a humorous touch to a paper when the topic and tone warrant it.

6. Refer to something that your audience might know about and find engaging: sports; world, national, or local news; literature; religion; social groups; life roles (employer, employee, parent, brother, sister); jokes or song lyric references; and so on.

WHAT TO AVOID IN TITLES

1. Clichés and worn phrases. Recycled comparisons bore readers. Don't title a paper "The Wait That Seemed an Eternity" or "The Night That Sent Shivers down My Spine." These kinds of clichés will *send shivers down your instructors'* spines, may make them *break into a cold sweat,* and will certainly make them feel as if they will be reading your paper *for an eternity.*

2. Inappropriate tone. The tone of your work is the feeling you have about your topic and the emotions you want your readers to experience (happy, playful, sad, bitter, angry, formal). If, for instance, your topic and your treatment of it are serious, sad, or angry, don't use a light-hearted title.

3. Waiting until 5 minutes before class to write it. If the title contributes to the overall impact of your paper, why gamble on inspiration at the last possible moment?

FORMATTING

1. Capitalize all words in your title—even small ones like *do, is,* and *can*—except articles (*a, an, the*), prepositions (*in, on, to,* etc.), and coordinating conjunctions (*and, but, or, nor, for, so, yet*). However, the first and last words of the title and any word following a colon should be capitalized.

2. Do not enclose in quotation marks or underline a title placed on a title page or above the first line of text.

3. Be sure to center the title on the page.

ACTIVITY 3.16 WORKING ONLINE: *Paragraph Review*

To test yourself on the main topics discussed in this chapter, complete the crossword puzzle under Chapter 3 at www.mhhe.com/brannan.

Body paragraphs make up the bulk of most writing assignments, and the information in this chapter will come in handy as you develop papers of any length. The skills of unity, clarity, and support extend far beyond coursework. If, for example, you were writing a cover letter, you would want to present a *unified* reason for pursuing the position and a *clear* description of your previous experience, complete with specific *supporting* examples.

Chapter Summary

1. A paragraph is a unified and coherent collection of sentences that is most often grouped with other paragraphs.

2. Body paragraphs must have a central point, which is often expressed in a topic sentence located as the first sentence in the paragraph.

3. A topic sentence consists of the topic plus a statement of opinion or attitude. It should be focused and as interesting as you can make it.

4. Paragraphs are developed with examples, details, and explanations.

5. Paragraph support should be sufficient, relevant, and clear.

6. Paragraphs benefit from specific word choices and specific examples.

7. Concluding sentences should end a paper decisively. One way to end effectively is with an expanded thought.

8. Three types of organizational patterns for paragraphs are spatial (description), chronological (narrative), and order of importance (explanatory and persuasive). These methods often overlap.

9. A paragraph is unified when all examples, details, and explanations relate to a central point, which is expressed in the topic sentence.

10. In coherent paragraphs, sentences are clearly linked using transitions, repetition, synonyms, pronouns, and references to the main idea.

11. A title's primary purpose is to attract readers, and good titles are brief, linked to the main idea, and engaging.

Revising Paragraphs

4

[*Artists are only one group of people who constantly rework or revise to improve their final product. In what ways do you see revision working in your own life? In what activities (such as specific sports, hobbies, or job skills) do you try to improve? Pick one activity and tell how practice has helped you get better at it.*]

KEY TOPICS

- Revising paragraphs: An introduction
- Revising first-stage drafts
- Revising second-stage drafts
- Editing
- Proofreading

Linking to Previous Experience

Revision is part of your everyday life, as you find yourself trying to improve your parallel parking skills, your recipes, your dance moves, or the organization of your living space. Or perhaps you often try to find faster ways to get from one location to another. If you lift weights or try yoga, you are revising your body. And each time you take a class, you revise your mind and critical thinking skills. Whether you are improving upon a pie crust recipe or a paragraph, revision takes time and effort; most people do not have a natural talent for it. However, if you are willing to invest the energy, it is a rewarding process, and you can gradually become your own best editor.

Revising Paragraphs: An Introduction

Working with key concepts introduced in Chapters 1 and 3, this chapter will help you revise writing by providing questions to help you think critically about your draft. As you work through specific assignments in Chapters 5–11, you can return to this chapter for help with revising paragraphs or to Chapter 1, pages 17–19, for reminders about general revision strategies.

HINT

Effective revising begins with a can-do attitude.

Revising First-Stage Drafts

As you revise a first-stage draft, concentrate primarily on the main points you want to make. Consider your focus: Are you following the assignment as your instructor has explained it? Have you narrowed your topic so that you can express it briefly in a topic sentence? Have you arranged your examples logically and thoroughly explained them? Does your last sentence link to your topic sentence and make a final point?

The following questions will help you as you begin revising your first draft.

1. **Have you discussed several examples (steps, groups, causes or effects, or the like)?** To fully develop your paragraph, you will need several points to expand the main idea stated in your topic sentence.

2. **How effective is your topic sentence?** Your topic sentence has two functions: to identify and limit the topic. Let the reader know what your paragraph will explore, sometimes by including a **forecasting statement**. Also, use specific language wherever possible.

   | VAGUE TOPIC SENTENCE | Restaurants don't always make a lot of money. |
   | FOCUSED TOPIC SENTENCE | The Olive Garden where I work is losing business for three reasons. |

3. **Have you arranged your main examples, steps, groups, or causes or effects by space, time, or importance?** If you are explaining a process or telling a story, you will order the steps by time; otherwise, arranging by order of importance is usually the best method.

4. **Have you written a subtopic sentence to introduce each main example, step, group, cause or effect, or point of comparison or contrast?** While not all paragraphs use subtopic sentences, many do, and they can strengthen your paragraph in several ways. Subtopic statements guide your readers, they guide you, and they create emphasis.

English Review Note

Visit your college's writing center for assistance in revising your drafts.

HINT

For more on subtopic sentences, see pp. 138–139 and the student models in Unit Two.

For more on layering examples, see Chapters 3 and 7.

For questions on revising a first-stage draft of a descriptive paragraph, see p. 95. For revising a narrative paragraph, see pp. 124–125. For revising an illustration paragraph, see pp. 154–155.

5. **Are your main examples well developed?** Each major point that you introduce for your readers should be thoroughly detailed and explained. Specific words, sensory details, active verbs, *-ing* words, dialogue, descriptions of setting and people, and comparisons can all help. Practice the principle of layering examples, becoming increasingly specific.

6. **Are your examples relevant (pp. 46–48)?** Avoid examples that might be interesting but nevertheless distract from the main point.

7. **How well connected are sentences within the paragraph (pp. 53–59)?** First drafts usually need more transitions for adding material (*also, in addition*), giving examples (*for instance, for example*), and emphasizing points (*in particular, especially*). For overall coherence, remember to use the other connectors as well: repeat words, synonyms, pronouns, and references to main ideas.

8. **How effective is your concluding sentence (pp. 49–53)?** Your final sentence should use a connector, refer back to the topic sentence, and expand the main idea of the paragraph. While drafting, if you decided that an idea seemed out of place in the body, the idea might make a good expanded thought in the conclusion.

FOCUSED TOPIC SENTENCE The Olive Garden where I work is losing business for three reasons.

FOCUSED CONCLUDING SENTENCE If the Olive Garden management would eliminate or even reduce these causes, business would quickly increase.

JOURNAL / BLOG ENTRY 4.1

To help you focus on the revision process and to alert your instructor to your progress, list three *specific* changes you have made or feel you ought to make from your first to second rough draft. Refer to the preceding first-stage draft questions, and answer as specifically as possible.

FEEDBACK *In a sentence or two, say what you like best about a classmate's draft. What do you like best about your own?*

Revising Second-Stage Drafts

Depending on your writing habits, you may have a draft that is fairly close to final now, or you may still need to address major content and organizational concerns. If at this point you are comfortable with most of the content of your draft, you can focus on word- and sentence-level revision. The following questions will help you find problems in your second-stage drafts for all paragraph assignments in Unit Two.

1. **Have you used specific language (pp. 75–76)?** Your paragraph will include both general and specific words, but remember that specific words sharpen an image. You could sharpen the focus on "old clothes" by saying "old blue jeans and a baggy KU Jayhawks sweatshirt."

2. **Have you developed sensory details thoroughly?** Description and narration thrive on sensory details (sight, sound, touch, smell, taste), but all writing can benefit from them. Revise your sentences using the five senses,

without relying too much on sight. Which of the following sentences creates a sharper image?

A. A dessert eaten by a campfire tastes better than one eaten at home.

B. The hot, white, melting marshmallows fresh from the fire stick to my fingers and almost burn me as I pop them too quickly into my mouth.

Revise your own sentences to add sensory details wherever they will help.

3. **Are you choosing "active" verbs to describe action?** Verbs that show action are usually a better choice than more "static" verbs (*be, do, have,* and *make* are common culprits). Which of the following sentences creates the sharper image?

A. The children <u>are having</u> a good time bowling.

B. The small children <u>are jumping, clapping,</u> and <u>screaming</u> as their balls <u>hit</u> the pins.

Revise your own sentences to add active verbs wherever they are needed.

4. **Are you using any *-ing* words? (See Chapter 24.)** Present participles (verb forms with an *-ing* ending) can also convey action. Which of the following sentences creates the sharper image?

A. I can hear the trees move.

B. I can hear the leaves <u>rustling</u> and branches <u>brushing</u> against each other.

Revise your own sentences, adding *-ing* words wherever they are needed.

5. **Are the sentences in your paragraph varied in length? (See Chapter 19.)** Your writing can be more interesting when you vary the length of your sentences. After polishing word choices, count the words in each sentence. If you find that more than three or four sentences in a row are roughly the same length, either combine two of them or divide a longer one.

6. **Are the beginnings of your sentences varied?** If even two sentences in a row in your draft begin with the same word, such as *the,* you might need to change an opening or combine sentences to break up the pattern. Also look for too many similar openings, even if the sentences are not together.

7. **Have you repeated a word or phrase so often that it becomes noticeable?** While some repetition is fine, too much becomes boring. Compare the following sentences. Which sounds repetitive?

A. I like to spend time at the <u>pond</u> because the <u>pond</u> is a relaxing place. Of all the <u>ponds</u> I have visited in <u>the</u> last 20 years, <u>this pond</u> is the one that will forever live in my memory.

B. I like to spend time outdoors in relaxing surroundings, and there is one <u>place</u> in particular that I enjoy. Of all the <u>ponds</u> I have visited in the last 20 years, this is the <u>one</u> that will forever live in my memory.

Revise your own sentences to cut or replace words that are repeated too often.

8. **Have you included words that serve no purpose?** Cluttered writing can bore and confuse, whereas concise writing involves readers and clarifies ideas. Which of the following sentences is concise, and which is cluttered?

A. The meat hotdogs, long and thin, sizzle <u>with a sizzling sound</u> as they cook, <u>roasting,</u> and drip <u>meaty hotdog juices</u> off the end of the <u>wooden stick.</u>

B. The hotdogs sizzle as they cook and drip juices off the end of the stick.

Revise your own sentences to cut nonessential words.

Avoid stacking modifiers in front of words—for example, "a sleek, shiny, turbocharged, gas-guzzling black Mustang."

For more on active verbs, see Chapter 24.

For more on unnecessary repetition and unneeded words, see Chapter 20.

To help you focus on revision and alert your instructor to your progress, list three *specific* changes you have made or feel you ought to make to your second draft. Refer to the second-stage draft questions, answering them specifically. Next, in several sentences state what you like best about your draft so far.

FEEDBACK *Exchange work with a classmate and use the second-stage draft questionnaire to make constructive suggestions. What is the strongest feature of this person's draft? What does he or she say is the strongest part of yours?*

Editing

Like many students you might be tempted to hurry through the editing stage. This impulse is understandable—it is often a long journey from brainstorming to final draft.

Aside from being overanxious to complete the writing excursion, you might not always know what to look for in your final draft. For instance, if you don't know the rule that tells you where to put the comma, how are you supposed to recognize the spot where the comma is missing?

Well . . . it would be great if there were a quick fix for grammar, spelling, and punctuation errors, but the simple truth is that all writers grapple with them for a long time. Yet even if you are not a "comma whiz," you can still catch many mistakes if you are willing to read your work *slooowly* and carefully.

The following paragraphs have a number of the common mechanical errors listed here:

English Review Note

Edit for these common errors: **(1)** missing articles ("an," "a," "the") **(2)** missing parts of verb forms and tenses (ex: I have ~~study~~ studied English for two years.).

COMMON ERRORS

- Misspelled words
- Sound-alike words
- Missing words
- Wrong words
- Sentence fragments
- Comma splices
- Run-on sentences
- Faulty capitalizations
- Incorrect apostrophes
- Missing commas
- Unneeded commas
- Faulty pronoun reference
- Faulty pronoun agreement
- Verb tense shifts

HINT

Editing these practice paragraphs will help you with your own revision. To edit your work effectively, slow your reading to a crawl.

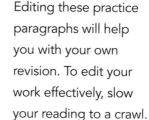

ACTIVITY 4.1 WORKING ONLINE: *Editing Review*

Test your editing skills by reading through each paragraph on the following page slowly, putting a finger on every word if necessary, to see how many mistakes you catch. Use the correction symbols feature at www.mhhe.com/brannan or consult the list in the back of this book.

Editing Review

1. As I glance down at the windowsill I often, think, about the many dead insects, lying their one can only assume that the bugs want there last moments alive too be my porch. Its small body makes quite a feast, for the two Barn Spiders that share my porch with me. The webs' are always filled with one delicacy, or anothr, one spider, in particular has, woven quite a spectacular web, against the old, paint-chipped corner. While I am inhaling, my first cup of morning fuel. A magnificent gust of wind blows thru. The sweet smell my neighbors freshly cut grass fills the air so flagrantly, that I can barely notice the thick humidity building for the day ahead.

To see the corrected version of excerpt 1, turn to p. 88 and look at the first half of "Waking Up the Right Way."

2. When I went to Middle School in korea. I was afraid of sevral merciles teachers, who seemed too want me to enjoy studying forcing it on me. My Moral Education Teacher was one of these crule educators, he was short, and fat like the whip he carried to enforce there every whim. "I see you have'nt done your homework Jeong", he would say. He orders me to hold my palms up and, then he begins to whip my hands harshly.

To see the corrected version of excerpt 2, turn to p. 144 and look at the beginning of "Teaching with Whips."

3. Panick and fustration our a sure fire recipe, for tears but I fought them of and strugled too remain calm, for my girls. Suddenly I hear a voice, say "Listen I have a cell phone, do you want to call someone to come pick you up". As I turned toward the voice I saw an older gentleman, who looked a lot like my dad. Begining to cry I explained how helples I felt.

To see the corrected version of excerpt 3, turn to p. 130 and look at the middle of "Do Unto Others . . ."

4. In order too help customers shop more efficiently, in Toys "R" Us, the store is divided into three overrall categories: areas for older children, toddlers, and babies. The older chidren have four major areas. Blue, Pink, R-Zone, and Silver piles of toys for everyone. Boys mostly head for the blue section, and items like the GI Joe's Hotwheel's and Lego's. In no time, at all, the boys can have Lego race tracks assembled, on he floor, and be racing miniature batmobiles after the "bad guys."

To see the corrected version of excerpt 4, turn to p. 172 and look at the beginning of "Shopping the Easy Way."

ACTIVITY 4.2 WORKING ONLINE: *More Editing Review*

Go to www.mhhe.com/brannan to practice editing three more paragraphs, the corrected versions of which are in this text.

If you caught all but two or three errors in any paragraph, congratulations; you are a careful editor! If you missed more than five or six, try to slow down.

REVISING ON-SCREEN

Conserve paper and time by revising and editing your paragraphs on the computer. Microsoft Word and other word-processing programs offer helpful editing features like "Track Changes" that help you keep track of as many drafts as you want—and comment on classmates' papers. ●

Problems to Watch for When Editing

1. **Spelling errors:** Use your computer's spell checker first, and then try to find at least one other reader who is a fairly good speller. Remember, too, to consult a good dictionary.

Look for these errors as you edit your own draft.

For help with spelling and sound-alike words, see Chapter 28.

For more on clarity, see Chapter 20.

2. **Sound-alike words:** A common example is using *there* for *their* or *they're.* Keep adding sound-alike words that cause you problems to your Improvement Chart (in the back of this book), and try to memorize these repeat errors. Writers usually keep making the same handful of mistakes—unless they identify and correct them—till doomsday.

3. **Missing words:** Read slowly to detect these errors. Sometimes reading each sentence backwards can help, and covering the sentence ahead of the one you are editing can keep you from jumping ahead too quickly.

4. **Wrong words:** Be suspicious of words that sound too fancy. If you often thumb through a thesaurus looking for words, you might be using them incorrectly. You probably already know words that express your meaning well, and, in most contexts, more common words are usually the best choices. Your readers can help by alerting you to words you may be using incorrectly, and then you can use a dictionary to decide.

5. **Sentence fragments:** Remember two common types of incomplete sentences:

PHRASE FRAGMENT	Running to the store for bread and a six-pack of Coke. (The word group lacks a subject and a verb and is not a complete thought.)
SUBORDINATE CLAUSE FRAGMENT	Because he is the kind of man we want for mayor. (The word group has a subject and verb, but the subordinating word *because* makes it an incomplete thought.)

You can correct most fragments (Chapter 23) by joining them to another sentence or adding words to make them complete sentences.

6. **Comma splices/run-ons:** These errors happen when two sentences are joined incorrectly with only a comma or with no punctuation at all:

COMMA SPLICE	The cement is freezing, it instantly numbs my feet.
RUN-ON	The cement is freezing it instantly numbs my feet.

There are at least five easy ways to fix these errors (Chapter 23).

Note: In dialogue, be careful to avoid this kind of comma splice:

> Roxanne shouted, "Get out of here, nobody gives a damn about you anyway!"

Instead write:

> Roxanne shouted, "Get out of here! Nobody gives a damn about you anyway!"

People often speak in short sentences and fragments. Don't be afraid to use this kind of sentence in your dialogue.

In English, remember to capitalize days and months.

See Chapter 27 for more on using apostrophes, commas, and other punctuation.

7. **Capitalization:** Capitalize each **proper noun** (a specific/unique person, place, or thing; see Chapter 27). In your titles capitalize most words, even little ones like *is* and *one.* But do not capitalize articles (*a, an, the*), prepositions (*to, on, of, in,* etc.), and coordinating conjunctions (*and, but, so,* etc.) unless these words begin or end a title or follow a colon.

8. **Apostrophes:** Use to show ownership or to mark the omission of a letter in a contraction: "Maria's calculator isn't working."

9. **The Big Three comma categories:** These categories govern perhaps half the common uses of the comma:

   A. Use commas to introduce single words, phrases, and subordinate adverb clauses before a main clause (cue words: *because, as, if, when,* etc.).

   EXAMPLE: If I finish my paper early, I will watch *The Matrix Reloaded* again.

B. Use commas to enclose nonessential words, phrases, or clauses within a main clause or to set them off at the end of a main clause (cue words: *who/which*, etc.).

> EXAMPLE: *The Matrix Reloaded,* which continues *The Matrix,* uses more computer animation and special camera effects than the first film.

C. Use commas to divide main clauses joined by *and, but, or, so, yet, for,* or *nor.*

> EXAMPLE: Neo gains more powers in this sequel, and he uses them outside of the Matrix against the machines.

10. **Unnecessary commas:** As you learn the handful of rules that help with comma placement, you will move away from the old standby: "I put commas where I hear pauses." Using your ear helps with punctuation—but only about half the time: a 50 percent average. Try to avoid unneeded commas such as those in the following examples:

> INCORRECT   I went to Burger King for lunch, and then to McDonald's for dinner. (Your ear might tell you to pause, but a comma is not needed unless the two word groups you are joining with *and* are complete sentences.)

> CORRECT   I went to Burger King for lunch and then to McDonald's for dinner.

> INCORRECT   I eat three 13-ounce bags of potato chips every day, because I want to have a heart attack. (You might naturally pause before *because,* but it begins an essential clause that explains *why* this person eats so foolishly and so should not be set off with a comma.)

> CORRECT   I eat three 13-ounce bags of potato chips every day because I want to have a heart attack.

11. **Faulty pronoun reference and agreement:** Pronouns must refer to a specific noun, and they must agree with that noun in number:

> REFERENCE ERROR   Florence was talking to Abby when *she* saw the accident. (Clarify *she* reference: *she* = Abby.)

> AGREEMENT ERROR   *Each* of the players want a raise. (*All* . . . want . . .)

For more on pronoun problems, see Chapter 25.

After editing as carefully as you can on your own, it is time to get help. Every writer—professional and beginner—benefits from having others look at his or her work. You will undoubtedly spend class time in collaborative editing, but don't stop there. Work with your instructor. If your school has a writing center, you will find wonderful support there to help you through every stage of the process, including editing.

JOURNAL / BLOG ENTRY 4.3

When your draft is in good shape—with the important details in place, words carefully chosen, and sentences flowing well—review your Improvement Chart to focus on pattern errors. *Slooowly* edit your paper, word by word, line by line. In your journal or on your blog, list three errors from your draft, and then show the corrections. What steps are you taking to avoid repeating these errors?

Proofreading

Proofreading is the last step in preparing your paper. Assuming that you have closely edited your draft and caught most of the mechanical errors, you can now print out a final copy, the one you will turn in for a grade. You might think you are finished because, after all, you have just spent several hours editing. But there are still common problems to check for, ones you can correct before your instructor does.

HOW TO PROOFREAD AND PREPARE YOUR FINAL MANUSCRIPT

1. Check for typographical errors such as misspelled, run-together, and omitted words. Often, when fixing errors in the editing stage, writers slip up in small ways on the keyboard. Be sure to spell check once again.

2. Check the following items carefully: font size (use 12-point type), line spacing (double space, including the heading), margins (1 inch), and title capitalization.

3. Spell check any required material, such as outlines and audience profiles.

4. Staple or paper clip your pages. Avoid putting the paper in a plastic sleeve. (Most instructors find these more troublesome than impressive.)

On the following page, you will find both a title page and a one-paragraph paper without a title page. Check with your instructor to see which format he or she prefers. Notice that the title in both cases is neither underlined nor enclosed in quotation marks, and all information is double-spaced.

JOURNAL / BLOG ENTRY 4.4

Reflecting for a moment on the work you did in and out of class to produce your final draft, take 5 minutes to write a paragraph telling your instructor about what challenges you had to overcome, how you dealt with them, and what strategies you think might be most important to apply to your upcoming writing assignments this semester.

FEEDBACK *Comment on other students' findings and experiences, sharing strategies for successful revising.*

SAMPLE TITLE PAGE

Title centered

12-point font

No underline

No quotation marks

All information double-spaced

All information at least 1 inch from the top of the page

Death Strikes

by

Terry Gwin

Composition 100, Section 37

Professor Brannan

September 26, 2008

SAMPLE PAPER (NO TITLE PAGE)

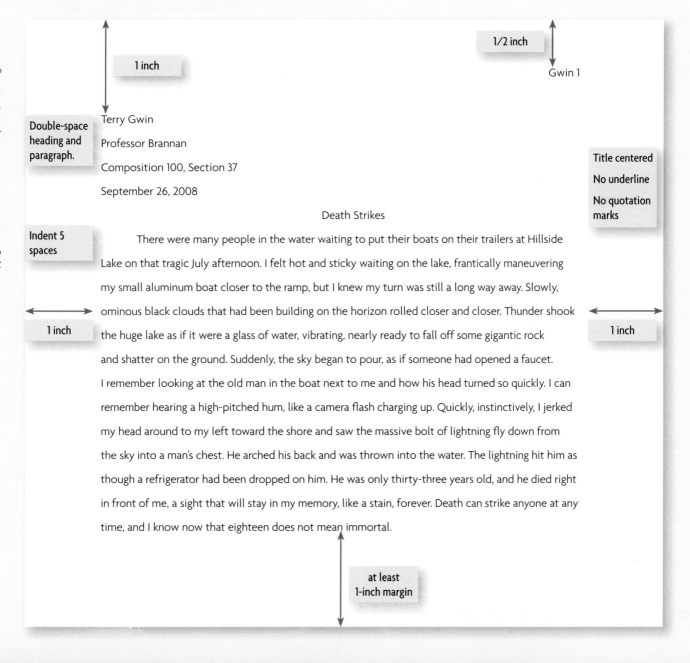

1/2 inch

1 inch

Gwin 1

Double-space heading and paragraph.

Terry Gwin

Professor Brannan

Composition 100, Section 37

September 26, 2008

Title centered

No underline

No quotation marks

Death Strikes

Indent 5 spaces

     There were many people in the water waiting to put their boats on their trailers at Hillside Lake on that tragic July afternoon. I felt hot and sticky waiting on the lake, frantically maneuvering my small aluminum boat closer to the ramp, but I knew my turn was still a long way away. Slowly, ominous black clouds that had been building on the horizon rolled closer and closer. Thunder shook the huge lake as if it were a glass of water, vibrating, nearly ready to fall off some gigantic rock and shatter on the ground. Suddenly, the sky began to pour, as if someone had opened a faucet. I remember looking at the old man in the boat next to me and how his head turned so quickly. I can remember hearing a high-pitched hum, like a camera flash charging up. Quickly, instinctively, I jerked my head around to my left toward the shore and saw the massive bolt of lightning fly down from the sky into a man's chest. He arched his back and was thrown into the water. The lightning hit him as though a refrigerator had been dropped on him. He was only thirty-three years old, and he died right in front of me, a sight that will stay in my memory, like a stain, forever. Death can strike anyone at any time, and I know now that eighteen does not mean immortal.

1 inch

1 inch

at least 1-inch margin

Linking to Future Experience

You will have the opportunity to practice more specific revision techniques in each assignment chapter of this text; for information on revising essay-length work, see Chapter 14. Revising is a valuable skill you will practice in all of your classes and, as discussed on page 63, in every part of your life. Revision means improvement in your writing, and that's the goal of this class.

Chapter Summary

1. Revising is a common process that people go through in any activity at which they want to improve.

2. Revision can be done alone, but writers profit from the input of others.

3. Revising is an ongoing act that writers follow throughout the process of producing their final work.

4. It is more effective to revise for larger concerns in rougher drafts, working on overall organization and content rather than style and editing issues.

5. As drafts progress, writers should pay more attention to style concerns.

6. When drafts are largely complete, writers focus on serious editing for mechanical errors. An Improvement Chart (see the back of this book) can be especially useful during editing.

7. After a draft has been edited closely and printed out as a "final" copy, writers should proofread one last time.

Picturing a Place (Description)

[*Many scenes convey a feeling or overall impression when we look at or experience them. How would you describe in a few words the overall (dominant) impression or feeling you have when viewing this picture of a college dorm room?*]

KEY TOPICS

- Developing skills and exploring ideas in descriptive paragraphs
  - Using specific, concrete language
  - Using the five senses
  - Establishing and strengthening the dominant impression
  - Organizing descriptions by using spatial arrangement
  - Locating the reader in space and time
- Analyzing student models: Descriptive paragraphs
- Writing a descriptive paragraph

What Are We Trying to Achieve and Why?

Setting the Stage

Describing is the process of relating details to help another person see what we have seen or experienced. It is the act of painting a picture with words. But good descriptions do more than just give readers a picture of a scene; they use the other senses (hearing, touch, taste, smell) to involve the audience more completely. When we provide (and listen to) descriptions that offer unique points of view on a subject—subjective descriptions—we enrich our lives, communicating personal experiences and extending the boundaries of what we can know through our senses alone.

In this chapter, we will learn about describing in general and about describing a place in particular. Within descriptions, we will practice identifying and conveying a **dominant impression.**

Linking to Previous Experience

What describing have you done in the past? Perhaps you have described a vacation, for example, a ski trip with friends or a visit to your sister in a nearby city. On that ski trip, what did the mountains look like? How much snow fell, what were the temperatures, and how crowded were the lift lines? When you visited your sister, did you drive or take the bus? What did her apartment look like? How would you describe the city's sounds, smells, and energy? If you ate at a restaurant, what was the food like? If you have not been on a vacation for a while, when was the last time you described a scene or an individual closer to home? Perhaps you have detailed another person's clothing to a friend or described your child for an acquaintance who also has a youngster in your child's preschool. We describe daily, and being able to do it well is a useful skill.

JOURNAL / BLOG ENTRY 5.1

Name three things, people, or places you have described recently (e.g., a new car, a friend, or a workplace). Using specific details, briefly develop one of those descriptions for your instructor and/or classmates. What value do you see in being able to describe well?

| FEEDBACK | *Compliment a classmate on a specific description. Now ask for more details in another classmate's description.*

Developing Skills and Exploring Ideas in Descriptive Paragraphs

To describe effectively, we will build on the following composition techniques:

1. Using specific, concrete language
2. Using the five senses

3. Establishing and strengthening the dominant impression
4. Organizing the description by using a spatial arrangement
5. Locating the reader in space and time

Using Specific, Concrete Language

Using Specific Language

To create effective descriptions, writers should understand the concept of **general versus specific language.** If you make a relatively general statement (e.g., in a topic sentence), you should support it by using the most specific words you know. Specific language will help you create vivid images. The larger the group— or category—that contains a word, the more general the word is. And, conversely, the smaller the group, the more specific the word is—as shown by the nested circles below:

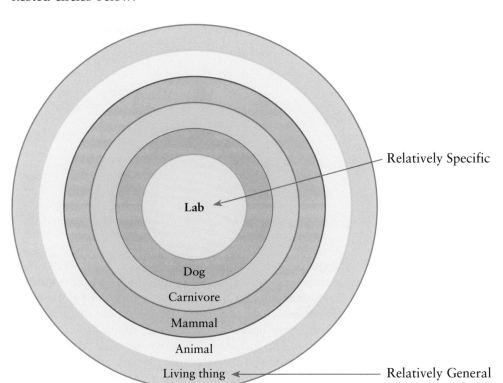

The same concept is illustrated by the Language Line below:

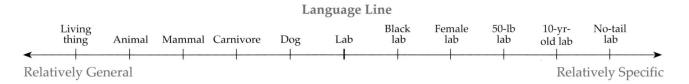

As we move along the Language Line, choosing more specific nouns, the group the word belongs to shrinks, in the process creating an image. To make the image even sharper, you can add details (modifiers such as *small* and *old*). Using concrete, specific words results in a fairly clear picture of a small old black lab missing her tail. We could probably pick her out of a group of dogs in a park, and she is a far cry from the opposite end of the spectrum (merely a "living thing"). You can easily apply this process of narrowing the category to your own descriptions.

ACTIVITY 5.1 *Narrowing the Category*

For each of the five words in column I below, select a more specific word for column II and an even more specific word for column III, and then add two modifiers to the words in column IV.

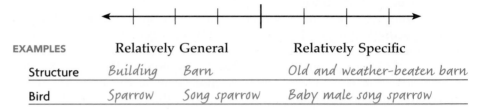

EXAMPLES	Relatively General		Relatively Specific	
Structure	*Building*	*Barn*	*Old and weather-beaten barn*	
Bird	*Sparrow*	*Song sparrow*	*Baby male song sparrow*	

I (Noun)	II (Noun)	III (Noun)	IV (Modifiers + Noun)
1. Machine			
2. Human being			
3. Reptile			
4. Scenery			
5. Business			

Using Concrete Language

Abstract words refer to qualities, processes, or ideas (goodness, photosynthesis, freedom) and emotions (love, fear, pity). **Concrete** words represent things that we can experience with our senses (chair, car, hamburger—cement or concrete is also "concrete"!). Abstract words are necessary in writing; they allow us to talk about ideas and states of being. For instance, when we discuss "democracy," most of us understand that it means self-rule through elected officials within a society that guarantees certain freedoms. However, when people become unclear about a term or disagree with basic assumptions about it, the abstraction needs to be clarified with specific examples, which are often illustrated with concrete terms. In your descriptive paper you will write about specific, concrete places, but you will also make clear your abstract feelings about the place—your dominant impression—by using specific, concrete words.

For more on exploring definitions, see Chapter 15.

ACTIVITY 5.2 *Using Abstract versus Concrete Language*

Write in column II a word or phrase that is more concrete than the abstract words in column I. Remember that concrete words are often specific examples used to show what a person means by the more abstract term.

I **Abstract** (idea, quality, emotion)	II **Concrete** (knowable through senses: has weight, color, smell, texture)

EXAMPLE
Happiness *a smile* _____

EXAMPLE
Love *a kiss* _____

EXAMPLE
Football defense *a sacked quarterback* _____

1. Comfort _____
2. Activity _____
3. Tranquility _____
4. Death penalty _____
5. Transportation _____

Using the Five Senses

Because people come to know their world through their five senses—sight, hearing, touch, smell, and taste—suggesting these senses in writing helps to involve readers in your description. Consider the following two paragraph excerpts, and decide which one makes you feel more a part of the scene:

A. I am back at the pond again tonight, relaxing and noticing the stars. As I listen, I can hear the sounds of the woods around me. Animal noises tell me that I have truly made it back to my favorite spot. I can see that the fire is about ready, so I get out the food I brought and settle down for some late night snacks.

B. As the brilliant, yellow moon shines down, reflecting off the pond, little waves ripple across the surface. While gazing at the sky, I can see millions of sparkling stars and, from time to time, even view one falling. The blazing embers leave a smoke trail rising upward from the fire. Through the darkness of the night, I can see the shadows of the trees, silhouettes of the horses, and swooping bats. The sounds of the night surround me: the murmur of voices in the distance, leaves rustling, and branches brushing against each other. From the nearby pond and surrounding trees, I can hear the unique chorus of the tree and bullfrogs. As the train whistles by, the cries of howling coyotes drift on the wind. From time to time I can even hear the lonesome hooting of an owl. As the popping and crackling of the fire dies down, the embers are ready for cooking.

The language in the second paragraph suggests two senses, sight and sound, as you can see by the shaded sight and boxed sound details. Although the author has not suggested taste, smell, and touch, she has still created a memorable scene.

ACTIVITY 5.3 WORKING TOGETHER: *Using the Five Senses*

Working in a group, locate all the sensory details in the following paragraph, and then list them under the appropriate columns on the sensory chart. Most of the specific words are *sight* details, colors included (see Activity 5.1). The excerpt also includes sound and touch

but few smell or taste details. If you removed all the sensory details, would this description be less interesting to you?

Jumping feet first off the gently rolling boat, the salty taste of seawater in my mouth, I feel the warm Caribbean waters close over my head. Sinking slowly in a swirl of frothy silver bubbles, I look back up to the surface to see the dark hull of the dive boat steadily receding. Beneath me broken shafts of sunlight filter past the tips of my black fins as I kick back and forth, keeping the descent under control. At 30 feet I begin to kick harder and inflate my BC, the sudden sound of compressed air rushing past my ear. Another 10, 20, 30 feet, and there I hover, weightless, over the plateau. Spread out to 100 feet in all directions, green and purple sea fans bend gently in the mild surge as rainbow-colored parrotfish graze on the reef, the sound of their teeth grinding chunks of coral audible even under 60 feet of water.

Sensory Chart				
Sight	Sound	Touch	Smell	Taste

Too many sensory details can be too much of a good thing. The point is not to cram as many into a paper as possible, or even to represent all five senses, but rather to use these details selectively wherever they can enhance an image.

ACTIVITY 5.4 *Using the Five Senses*

On separate paper, brainstorm sensory details for one of the following places. Be alert to any details that might help show a central focus or dominant impression/feeling. Don't be surprised if you come up with more details under sight and sound than any other sense.

1. Cafeteria at lunch hour (dominant impression: activity/fast pace, maybe even confusion or chaos!)

2. Church wedding (dominant impression: excitement/happiness, maybe even communal spirit of love)

3. Zoo (dominant impression: *either* depression/confinement, maybe even animals in misery, *or* relaxation, maybe even contentment, animals happy to have a life so easy—try for one of these, remembering that, as always in focused description, you *choose* the details that you want your readers to see)

4. Summer camp (dominant impression: happy confusion/expectation/fun)

Establishing and Strengthening the Dominant Impression

The elements of description that we have discussed—general/specific words, abstract/concrete words, and sensory details—can work together to establish the dominant impression—the overall feeling about the person, object, animal, or place that is being described.

For instance, if you wanted to describe a zoo as a depressing place (see Activity 5.4), you might focus on images of overcrowded, understimulated animals, like the coyote pacing endlessly behind the bars of his small cage. But you could find sensory details to support other, more positive dominant impressions—such as a child gazing with wonder at a giraffe or the sight of sea lions playing.

Your task, then, is to *focus* on details that suggest a feeling for or impression of a place. Telling readers your feelings or thoughts about the place can also help them understand your dominant impression.

The writer must control the dominant impression, choosing details to make a point. Thoughts and feelings can make the dominant impression stronger.

ACTIVITY 5.5 *Establishing the Dominant Impression*

Read each of the paragraphs below, determine the dominant impression, underline the words that show it, and then write it out in a word or two.

> EXAMPLE: In the huddle I heard the quarterback calling the play, but I couldn't connect the words to a meaning. My ears were ringing, and my head throbbed from the last tackle. I looked down at the chewed-up turf beneath my cleats and saw a blur of legs and shoes and dirt and torn grass. I leaned harder than I should have needed to on John and Scott and felt my knees giving out. "Oh, no," I thought, "I'm losing it in the middle of the game!"

Dominant impression: *losing consciousness*

1.   People show up to the ball game excited, with no age in their eyes, just pure enjoyment for a game they love. I notice the parents most, teaching and telling their children about the "greats" of the game and their fond memories of when they were young. The cheer from the crowd explodes with sheer excitement when the baseball cracks off the bat for the first time. During the seventh inning stretch I can sense the excitement in the air as the colorful lights dance off of the high water fountains, and the fans and players move about in an almost rhythmic motion. For nine innings fans of all ages act like they did when they were kids, wearing gloves and trying to catch foul balls and home runs.

Dominant impression: _____

2.   I had never met the man who worked in this garage, but I could see that he was a neat freak. First off, how many people carpet their garage floor—cement at that! And the carpet was clean, like it had just been vacuumed that morning. All the bigger equipment—extension and stepladders, wheelbarrow, snowblower, lawn mower, weed eater, leaf blower—was neatly stacked around the whitewashed walls. There were no spider webs in the windows or corners, not in this place. The shelves on the west wall, where most of the garage junk was kept, put

me in mind of a hardware store, a neat one, like the True Value down the way. This guy must have been saving Gerber baby food jars from half a dozen kids to collect enough for all the little loose nuts, bolts, screws, washers, nails, tacks, brads, staples, and what not that he had lined up in precise, evenly spaced and *labeled* rows. It was enough to make a slob like me a little sick to my stomach.

Dominant impression: _____

Not all descriptions are well focused from the beginning. In fact, rough drafts often include examples, details, or commentary that, while perhaps interesting, are nevertheless distracting. When you develop a single idea or feeling within a paragraph, most words should be directly connected to the dominant impression.

Avoid details that distract from the dominant impression.

ACTIVITY 5.6 | *Strengthening the Dominant Impression*

Read the example paragraph below and notice the underlined words that distract the reader from the stated dominant impression. Next, read "The Late Night Place to Be," state what the author wants the dominant impression to be, and then underline any words that you think detract from that dominant impression.

EXAMPLE: Dominant impression for "Ground Zero": *messiness*

Ground Zero

My bedroom is a mess. I have never been much of a neat freak, so it's hard for me to do all the routine "house chores." In fact, if you look around, you will see what I mean. I can't seem to hang a picture straight on the walls, and my poster of The Arcade Fire has come untaped at the upper right corner so that it sags a little. The wallpaper behind the poster is a weird flower pattern, roses, I think. Along the wall opposite the doorway, I have my stereo and new CD player (the old one died last week). The queen-sized bed is a disaster; it looks more like an animal's nest than a place for humans. There are three pillows propped up against the oak headboard and two lying on the carpet. The elastic has worn out around the pale-blue bottom sheet, so it has curled up at the corners, leaving the ancient mattress bare. I like to snack in bed, so I've left the remains of old meals spread out on and under it: an old pizza crust with red sauce . . . well, kind of dark red sauce now, a Big Mac box, an old French fry or two (they may still be good; I'll try them in a minute), and some kind of crumbs—no, I think it's sand. A red and green quilt is lying in a pile by the end chest, where it slipped off a month ago, in May, when the weather got too warm for me to need it anymore, and I'm afraid to look under the bed for what I might find there. My desk is littered with papers and old Kleenexes (some used, some not, but, hey, at least I'm ready for the next blow), and there is usually an open can of Coke on it, sticky at the bottom (someday I'll learn how to drink without spilling). The wastebasket overflows. My parents can't believe I'm comfortable living like this, and I wouldn't mind having it cleaner, but, hey, messy is so much easier.

1. Write out the dominant impression for "The Late Night Place to Be":

_____

2. Underline details that distract from the dominant impression.

The Late Night Place to Be

I like being part of all the action in the gym, especially late at night. The bright lights of the place shine through plate glass windows, illuminating the parking lot as I arrive at 1:00 a.m. After checking in, I head to the mezzanine, on the left side of the gym, next to the cardiovascular area. As I walk upstairs, I can identify the sounds of the room. I hear the heavy breathing of the sweaty runners as their feet pound strongly against the treadmills, which are lined up against the back wall. The room is carpeted in dark pink and is full of cardiovascular equipment such as NordicTracks, stair steppers, and stationary bicycles, and most of the machines are, surprisingly, in use. The carpet feels good on my feet after a hard night working in the restaurant, and I wonder if the other people here appreciate it too. Management has kept the gym neat: the walls are freshly painted, the mirrors clean, and all the resistance machines look practically new. The fresh look improves my attitude and makes it somehow easier for me to work out harder. Although there are plenty of people, the place doesn't look crowded, but it is noisy. The beeping sound from various machines marks people getting on and off and setting different resistance levels. Looking down to the main area of the gym, across from the reception desk, I can see two girls talking and hear part of their conversation as they work out. Near the back wall, about 60 feet away from the reception desk, three men are working with free weights. I can hear the clink and clank of the metal weights as they lay them down. Although it might seem strange to some that all this activity is going on so late at night, to me, and maybe the rest of the people in the gym, this is the best way to relax at the end of a long day.

Writing the Topic Sentence

In Chapter 3 we learned that most body paragraphs in essays and single-paragraph papers should begin with a topic sentence. The topic sentence of a descriptive paragraph should include the place and the dominant impression.

To make the topic sentence more interesting, you can add a sensory detail, an action, and specific words. Notice the following basic topic sentence:

place + dominant impression

ROUGH TOPIC
SENTENCE
The bar and grill is noisy.

This is a perfectly acceptable *working* topic sentence, but as you begin to polish your draft, you might want to make your sentence more interesting:

action/sound specific words   specific words

REVISED TOPIC
SENTENCE
If I fired a .44 magnum in the Longbranch Saloon on

specific words   dominant impression

a Friday night, there is so much noise that no one would notice.

ACTIVITY 5.7 | *Topic Sentences*

Read the following sentences, and circle the number of each that you think would make a good *rough* topic sentence for a place description:

1. My kitchen has a linoleum floor.
2. My house has a relaxing place to spend time in.
3. My studio apartment measures 12 by 18 feet.
4. For a memorable place to vacation, skiing is the best.
5. Farm ponds are pretty busy places.

Now make one of the topic sentences that you chose more interesting by adding a sensory detail (color, sound, touch), an action, or a specific word.

Your choice of rough topic sentence: _____

_____

Your revised topic sentence: _____

_____

_____

Writing the Concluding Sentence

Your concluding sentence should wrap up the main point that you have stated in your topic sentence. In an essay, of course, you will have room to expand a concluding thought into a full paragraph, but with single-paragraph papers you should limit yourself to one final sentence (or two) with these parts: a connector, place, and link to the dominant impression.

To make the final sentence more effective, you can add details, specific words, and an expanded thought linked to the dominant impression. Here is a rough concluding sentence followed by a more polished version:

connector   dominant impression

ROUGH CONCLUDING
SENTENCE
After last call the volume begins to drop as

place

everyone leaves the Longbranch for home.

connector   sound detail   dominant impression

REVISED CONCLUDING
SENTENCE
After last call the shouted conversations and the

sound detail   action

banging together of beer mugs begin to die down,

HINT

Strong concluding sentences expand your dominant impression.

action   place

and everyone heads out from the bar into the night,

expanded thought

alone again till the next time they come back to their

home away from home.

ACTIVITY 5.8 *Concluding Sentences*

Items 1–4 contain rough topic sentences that could work to begin a paragraph that describes a place and rough concluding sentences that might work to end the paragraph well. Circle the number of any sentence that would make an acceptable *rough* conclusion.

1. My kitchen is an easy place to work in. (rough topic sentence)
    With all this equipment to work with, my kitchen is efficient. (rough final sentence)

2. My house has a relaxing place to spend time in. (rough topic sentence)
    If I plastered and repainted, all the rooms would look better. (rough final sentence)

3. My studio apartment is well organized. (rough topic sentence)
    I really don't spend much time in my studio apartment. (rough final sentence)

4. For a memorable place to vacation, skiing is the best. (rough topic sentence)
    Snow skiing in the mountains is great fun. (rough final sentence)

Now, for a more interesting ending, revise one of the rough concluding sentences you circled, remembering to include a connector, the place, and the dominant impression. The following example will help you revise:

To make a concluding sentence stronger, use an expanded thought, specific words, sensory details, or an action.

EXAMPLE

ROUGH TOPIC SENTENCE	Farm ponds are pretty busy places.
ROUGH CONCLUDING SENTENCE	With so much going on in them, farm ponds are fun to visit.
REVISED CONCLUDING SENTENCE	

With all the frantic animal action at my uncle's pond, some people might think no one could rest there, but for me, it's one of the most relaxing places I can spend time at on a late spring afternoon.

Your choice of rough concluding sentence from the list of four: _____

_____

Your revised concluding sentence: _____

_____

Organizing Descriptions by Using Spatial Arrangement

All writing that is easy to read follows an organizational strategy. In writing description, an author will often choose **spatial arrangement**—organizing details from one point in space to another so readers can visualize the scene. In describing a person or an animal, you might progress from the head to the feet; for a place like a room, you might begin at the ceiling and work down to the floor or perhaps begin at the entrance and then move inward. Spatial arrangement is usually flexible, giving writers freedom to choose an approach, which they should then follow consistently.

ACTIVITY 5.9 *Organizing Descriptions*

The following lists of place details are jumbled. Read through them, and then number the details using the spatial arrangement given in parentheses, with 1 as the first detail in a paragraph and 6 as the last.

> EXAMPLE: Topic sentence: My attic is the dirtiest place in the house. (Arrange details from bottom to top.)
>
> __2__ The floorboards are covered with dust.
>
> __4__ Two small windows are streaked and smeared.
>
> __6__ The rafters have cobwebs hanging from them.
>
> __1__ I can feel grit beneath my feet on the stairs going up.
>
> __3__ Old furniture has the dust of ages accumulating on it.
>
> __5__ Boxes of ancient books are piled to the ceiling.

1. Topic sentence: First Watch on a busy Sunday morning is a study in efficiency. (Arrange details from front to back.)

   _____ Outside the restaurant a host is taking names for seating.

   _____ At the far end of the line, I can see the cooks efficiently cranking out the food.

   _____ In the lobby, coffee and tea are set for waiting customers.

   _____ At the front desk a manager greets people while checks are being processed in an orderly way.

   _____ Bussers clear, wipe, and reset tables quickly.

   _____ Behind the food line I can hear the dishwashers hard at work.

2. Topic sentence: The poolroom grew quiet, and time seemed to slow as everyone around the table concentrated on the last shot of the game. (Arrange details from bottom to top.)

   _____ The TVs on the walls seemed to blur out, and the sound became just so much white noise.

   _____ Overhead, the blades of the ceiling fans were frozen in place.

   _____ People stopped shuffling their feet.

   _____ Lucky Ed was draped over his cue—the stick, cue ball, and eight ball his whole universe.

   _____ As Ed's right hand drew the cue back, the crowd leaned forward in anticipation.

   _____ Bottles of Budweiser were dangling at their sides—no one dared to move before the shot.

3. Topic sentence: Monastery Beach on a hot July afternoon is full of activity. (Arrange details from distant to closer as you stand in the parking lot at the edge of the beach.)

_____ Scuba divers are putting their fins on at the edge of the surf.

_____ In the middle of the beach, a handful of giggling kids tries to get a kite up into the air.

_____ In the distance a fishing boat loaded with tourists chugs along.

_____ Forty yards out from shore a sea otter floats on his back in the kelp, banging away at an abalone he has wrenched from the ocean floor.

_____ Waves pick up height 10 yards from the beach as they curl and break over the few brave swimmers.

_____ Where the beach meets the parking lot, seagulls cluster around trash cans, squabbling among themselves for scraps.

Review these English transitions carefully, especially the prepositional phrases.

Locating the Reader in Space and Time

Linking sentences with connectors is essential for readers to follow the flow of your ideas. Aside from repeated words, synonyms, pronouns, and references to the main idea, description especially benefits from time and space transitions like the following:

FOR LOCATING OR MOVING IN SPACE

above	by	in the back	over
against	east (west, etc.)	into	there
alongside	far off (away)	near	to the right/left
around	in	next to	under
at	in between	on	upper

FOR MOVING IN TIME

after	first (second, etc.)	next	suddenly
afterward	immediately	now	then
at last	in the meantime	often	time passed
awhile	in the past	once	until
All references to calendar time and calendar events: last week, a few months ago			
All references to clock time			

ACTIVITY 5.10 *Locating the Reader in Space and Time*

In "Ground Zero" underline all the space connectors once and time connectors twice.

Ground Zero

My bedroom is a mess. I can't seem to hang a picture straight on the walls,

and my poster of The Arcade Fire has come untaped at the upper right corner

There are only a few time connectors. Use the preceding lists and the complete lists on pages 54–56 to locate the transitions.

so that it sags a little. The queen-sized bed is a disaster; it looks more like an animal's nest than a place for humans. There are three pillows propped up against the oak headboard and two lying on the carpet. The elastic has worn out around the pale-blue bottom sheet, so it has curled up at the corners. I like to snack in bed, so I have left the remains of old meals spread out on and under it: an old pizza crust with the red sauce . . . well, kind of dark red sauce now, a Big Mac box, an old French fry or two, and some kind of crumbs—no, I think it's sand. A red-and-green quilt is lying in a pile by the end chest, where it slipped off a month ago, and I'm afraid to look under the bed for what I might find there. My desk is littered with papers and old Kleenexes, and there is usually an open can of Coke on it, sticky at the bottom. The wastebasket overflows. My parents can't believe I'm comfortable living like this, and I wouldn't mind having it cleaner, but, hey, messy is so much easier.

ACTIVITY 5.11 | *Locating the Reader in Space*

Fill in the blanks with the space transitions from page 85.

1. After walking into the movie theater, you have to go _____ or _____ to get to the film you came to see.

2. Driving _____ the garage, I could see my work cut out for me.

3. The weight room is located _____ of the club.

4. In most houses you can find a mirror _____ the vanity.

5. The boathouse is _____ the dock.

Analyzing Student Models: Descriptive Paragraphs

The following models show ways to describe inside and outside locations: how to develop and arrange details, and how to polish sentences for readability. As you focus on each model, take a few minutes to read the prereading commentaries and annotations and then to carefully answer the questions for postreading analysis. This commentary and analysis will help you better understand why the writing is successful, so you can write stronger descriptive paragraphs yourself.

➤ Prereading Exploration for "By the Pond"

In the following paragraph, the author's purpose is to write a description that communicates to her classmates a special feeling she has about a place. Before you jump into the reading, think about the elements of effective descriptive writing that we have discussed and answer the following questions:

1. How should the author try to focus the paragraph?

2. What kinds of details do you suppose the author will use to develop the paragraph?

3. What is the difference between a relatively general and a relatively specific word, and which tends to create the most vivid image?

Before continuing with the paragraph, read the first and last sentences, and then, as you read, look for descriptive details and explanations that reinforce the dominant impression.

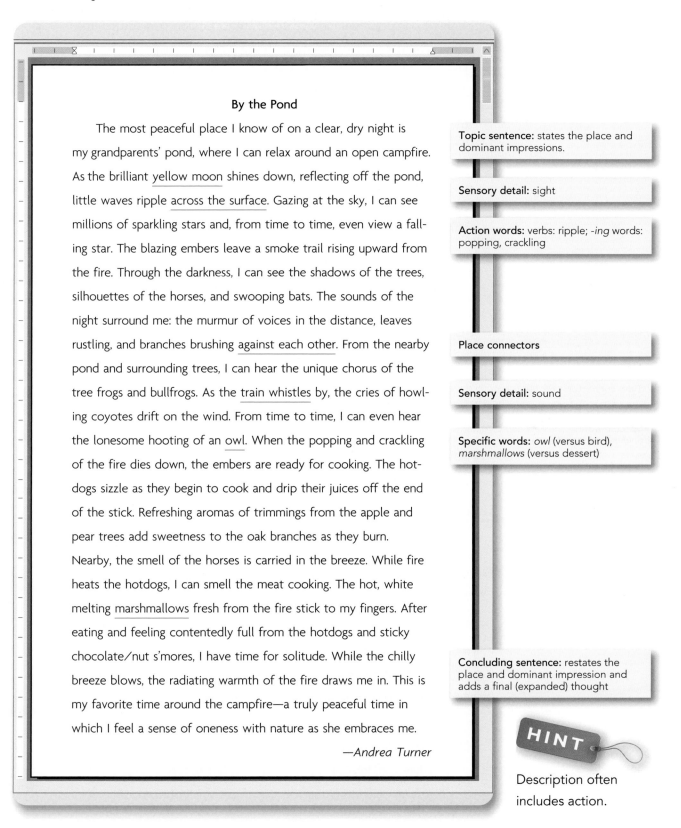

By the Pond

The most peaceful place I know of on a clear, dry night is my grandparents' pond, where I can relax around an open campfire. As the brilliant <u>yellow moon</u> shines down, reflecting off the pond, little waves ripple <u>across the surface</u>. Gazing at the sky, I can see millions of sparkling stars and, from time to time, even view a falling star. The blazing embers leave a smoke trail rising upward from the fire. Through the darkness, I can see the shadows of the trees, silhouettes of the horses, and swooping bats. The sounds of the night surround me: the murmur of voices in the distance, leaves rustling, and branches brushing <u>against each other</u>. From the nearby pond and surrounding trees, I can hear the unique chorus of the tree frogs and bullfrogs. As the <u>train whistles</u> by, the cries of howling coyotes drift on the wind. From time to time, I can even hear the lonesome hooting of an <u>owl</u>. When the popping and crackling of the fire dies down, the embers are ready for cooking. The hotdogs sizzle as they begin to cook and drip their juices off the end of the stick. Refreshing aromas of trimmings from the apple and pear trees add sweetness to the oak branches as they burn. Nearby, the smell of the horses is carried in the breeze. While fire heats the hotdogs, I can smell the meat cooking. The hot, white melting <u>marshmallows</u> fresh from the fire stick to my fingers. After eating and feeling contentedly full from the hotdogs and sticky chocolate/nut s'mores, I have time for solitude. While the chilly breeze blows, the radiating warmth of the fire draws me in. This is my favorite time around the campfire—a truly peaceful time in which I feel a sense of oneness with nature as she embraces me.

—Andrea Turner

Topic sentence: states the place and dominant impressions.

Sensory detail: sight

Action words: verbs: ripple; *-ing* words: popping, crackling

Place connectors

Sensory detail: sound

Specific words: *owl* (versus bird), *marshmallows* (versus dessert)

Concluding sentence: restates the place and dominant impression and adds a final (expanded) thought

HINT

Description often includes action.

➡ Prereading Exploration for "Waking Up the Right Way"

So far, we have discussed important elements of description like specific word choices, sensory detail, and clear focus (dominant impression). But we have not said much about how you can add to the overall impression of the place by revealing your thoughts and feelings about it. Take 30 seconds to skim the next paragraph, noting the topic and concluding sentences; then look closely at the highlighted passages, which reveal the author's thoughts and feelings.

1. How would you describe these thoughts/emotions?

2. How do they link to the stated dominant impression of tranquility?

3. After reading the model more carefully, respond to these questions: How accurate was your judgment of the paragraph, based only on the quick skim? What value do you see in skimming as a prereading technique?

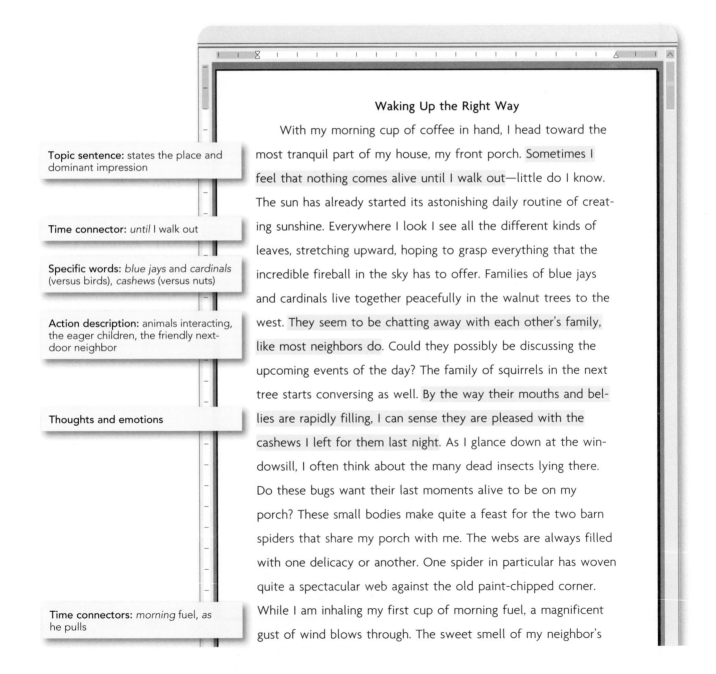

Topic sentence: states the place and dominant impression

Time connector: *until* I walk out

Specific words: *blue jays* and *cardinals* (versus birds), *cashews* (versus nuts)

Action description: animals interacting, the eager children, the friendly next-door neighbor

Thoughts and emotions

Time connectors: *morning* fuel, *as he pulls*

Waking Up the Right Way

With my morning cup of coffee in hand, I head toward the most tranquil part of my house, my front porch. Sometimes I feel that nothing comes alive until I walk out—little do I know. The sun has already started its astonishing daily routine of creating sunshine. Everywhere I look I see all the different kinds of leaves, stretching upward, hoping to grasp everything that the incredible fireball in the sky has to offer. Families of blue jays and cardinals live together peacefully in the walnut trees to the west. They seem to be chatting away with each other's family, like most neighbors do. Could they possibly be discussing the upcoming events of the day? The family of squirrels in the next tree starts conversing as well. By the way their mouths and bellies are rapidly filling, I can sense they are pleased with the cashews I left for them last night. As I glance down at the windowsill, I often think about the many dead insects lying there. Do these bugs want their last moments alive to be on my porch? These small bodies make quite a feast for the two barn spiders that share my porch with me. The webs are always filled with one delicacy or another. One spider in particular has woven quite a spectacular web against the old paint-chipped corner. While I am inhaling my first cup of morning fuel, a magnificent gust of wind blows through. The sweet smell of my neighbor's freshly cut grass fills the air so fragrantly that I barely notice the thick humidity building for the day ahead. As I am taking in the fresh aroma of the morning dew, my attention is drawn to a group of young children who are eagerly on their way to the first day of school. My next-door neighbor waves to me and hollers "Morning to ya!" and then starts his trek to work. As he pulls his pickup from our shared driveway, the gray dust from the gravel leaves a chalky taste in the morning air. Like clock-work (at 7:20 a.m.), Rex, the German shepherd who lives in the backyard behind me, starts his morning barking routine. So, along with most experiences in life, my morning relaxing time has come to a temporary halt. Heading back inside to get dressed, I know that I'm ready for the challenges awaiting me in my day. I'm ready to face each one, relaxed and confident, because I started in my favorite place—my porch.

—Stacey Becker

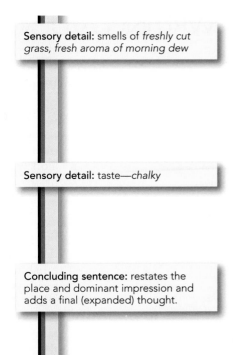

Sensory detail: smells of *freshly cut grass, fresh aroma of morning dew*

Sensory detail: taste—*chalky*

Concluding sentence: restates the place and dominant impression and adds a final (expanded) thought.

POSTREADING QUESTIONS FOR PARAGRAPH ANALYSIS: DESCRIPTION

Note: Questions 1–10 apply to either student model.

1. What is the dominant impression of the paragraph?
2. What two important points does the topic sentence include?
3. What words in the concluding sentence link to the topic sentence?
4. Name one or more action descriptions that support the dominant impression, and then explain how the action does this.
5. Name three specific words, and list a more general word for each (pp. 75–76).
6. List sensory details, trying to find several for each sense.
7. List at least three time and three space connectors (p. 85).
8. Name three active verbs and three *-ing* words that the author uses to show action.
9. What is your favorite image in this paragraph? Why do you like it?
10. To improve the paragraph, what three sensory details or specific words could be added to support the dominant impression?
11. In the seventh sentence of "Waking Up the Right Way," the author asks a question. Is there any value in asking readers an occasional question? Why do you think Becker does it?
12. Can you think of a more interesting title for "By the Pond"? Can you link a title to the paragraph's dominant impression? See pages 88–89.

Active verbs show specific action: The horse *gallops* versus moves; see pp. 508–509.

WRITING A DESCRIPTIVE PARAGRAPH
Summarizing the Assignment

Write a single paragraph of roughly 250 to 300 words that paints a verbal portrait of a place. The place can be indoors and more or less surrounded by four walls (a room in a house, a store in a mall, a library), or outside (a park, a favorite fishing hole, a basketball court). Your goal is to focus on a general feeling or overall impression you want to convey about the place. This dominant impression will help shape and develop the paragraph.

Establishing Audience and Purpose

Select any person or group you think might be interested in the location you will describe, and write your paragraph for that audience. For instance, if you chose a fishing pond on a friend's farm in southern Miami County, Kansas, you could write your description specifically for your friend, knowing that you would both share memories of the place. Or you could choose a larger yet specific audience—say, the readership of a magazine like *Kansas Wildlife & Parks*—who would know something about the land near the pond but would not actually have been there. Your composition instructor is always at least a secondary audience, so write to show him or her that you are learning descriptive strategies.

Your overall purpose is to convey information and a feeling about a place, to help readers see it through your eyes.

Working through the Writing Assignment

Discovering Ideas

Your instructor may assign one place for the whole class to write about. If the choice is left to you, however, there are many possible topics. The good news is that you can select a place that you know well and care about. Just don't allow yourself to feel overwhelmed by too much freedom. You might be tempted to put off choosing a place and fall behind on the assignment, or you might settle on a first, quick choice, whether you care about it or not. Avoid these pitfalls and choose a topic that really interests you. Involving yourself in a writing project will help you have more fun with writing and will usually produce better work.

The following topics lists may help get you off to a good start.

Choose several possible places before you fix on one.

For additional description topics, see Chapter 5 at www. mhhe.com/brannan.

POSSIBLE TOPICS: **DESCRIPTION**

Inside places to describe

- Any room in your house
- Restaurant
- Auto repair shop
- Department store
- Museum
- Gym
- Bowling alley
- Library

- Nature center
- Dance studio
- Pet store
- Music store
- Hospital
- Movie theater
- Fishing boat
- Airport
- Subway station

- Boxing arena
- Stable
- Recycling center
- Funeral home
- Hardware store
- Greenhouse
- Tattoo/piercing shop

Outside places to describe

- Beach
- Park
- Mountains
- Pond, lake, or river
- Stadium
- Zoo
- Interstate (at rush hour)
- Parking lot
- Fountain

- Municipal landfill
- Pig or cattle pen (corral)
- Woods
- Summer camp
- Construction site
- Race track (car, horse, dog)
- Basketball court

- Swimming pool
- Wildlife sanctuary
- Garden (any type)
- Historic site
- Cemetery
- Outdoor concert
- Amusement park
- Field (corn, wheat)

Conservation in Context

DESCRIBING A PLACE

Choose one of the outdoor spaces above as a topic and focus your description either on the balance of nature in the scene—how all the plants and animals depend on one another—or describe how people have had a negative impact on the place (e.g., pond/park: oil slick, food wrappers, cans, and other waste or pollutants). ●

ACTIVITY 5.12 WORKING ONLINE: *Use the Description Writing Tutor*

For additional topics in description, look under Chapter 5 at www.mhhe.com/brannan. And for more descriptive writing strategies, download the Description Writing Tutor.

If you haven't found a possible topic from these lists, think of the places where you regularly go: home, work, and school. Also consider the places where you pursue your interests. What hobbies do you enjoy? Do you target shoot, play in a band, or prepare gourmet meals? How about sports, team and individual? We all lead varied lives that offer many possible place topics.

Whatever place you select, limit how much of it you describe. For instance, a college campus is too large a topic for this paragraph assignment, but the school cafeteria could be just right. The Lake of the Ozarks is, again, too large, so settle for a particular part of it that you know well.

After you have decided on a place, go there if you can and take a few notes. While you can draw many details from memory, you will probably miss important ones. Even professional storytellers, who are paid to create scenes from their imagination, often visit a place to record details. Several suggestions to help with your own note taking follow.

HINT

Visit your place and take notes.

Prewriting

Sit quietly at your place for a few minutes. If you can't go there, try to remember as vividly as possible what it was like. Look around, listen carefully, and open your senses—all five of them. Search for a dominant impression to focus on. Use the following guidelines as you take notes:

- Describe how the place makes you feel. Is it busy and loud, or slow and quiet? Are you outside in one of nature's spectacles—sunset, snowstorm, or fog?

Listing is one of several useful prewriting methods for description.

For more on metaphors and similes, see pp. 498, 500.

- Create a list of sensory impressions: sight, sound, touch, smell, and taste. Sight and sound are often the most noticeable. Name objects as specifically as possible, and try to include colors.

- Observe how the people in your place interact. Are they friendly, cooperative, competitive, angry, isolated, quiet, busy, rowdy, or what? Write down some of their dialogue.

- Record the dimensions of the area and where important objects are in relation to each other.

- As you observe the place, try to create a comparison, perhaps as a metaphor or simile—for example, "The waiter was as busy as a squirrel burying acorns in autumn."

If a dominant impression is not yet clear, don't despair; but don't write an unfocused description either. Your instructor, writing group members, writing center staff, friends, and family can all give useful input.

PREWRITING—SUMMING UP

1. Make a list of several places to describe (using the topic lists as a guide). Carefully consider and choose a place that interests you.

2. Limit the size of the place you intend to describe.

3. If possible, go to the place and take detailed notes of the things and people there.

4. In your list include sensory details, specific details, and actions.

5. Decide on a dominant impression.

JOURNAL / BLOG ENTRY 5.2

Describe the overall feeling of your place in a few words. Review your prewriting notes, and then state the dominant impression in one sentence. (Remember, a place can feel different to different people, and there are often several ways to express a dominant impression.)

FEEDBACK   *Discuss different interpretations (and examples) of the term domi-nant impression with other students online or in class.*

Delete distracting details—keep only those details that show the dominant impression.

Organizing Ideas

Now it is time to choose and arrange the sensory details, specific descriptions, and actions from your prewriting to create an overall impression. In your notes, you will probably find unneeded details, even some that contradict the dominant impression. These details should be cut. As you begin to draft, other useful details will come to mind, so be receptive to them. Good ideas come to writers *throughout* the process of drafting and revising.

Following is a prewriting list for Jo Lucas's place paragraph, "Our Family Outing" (pp. 96–101); several details are crossed out because they distract from the overall impression of activity and family fun.

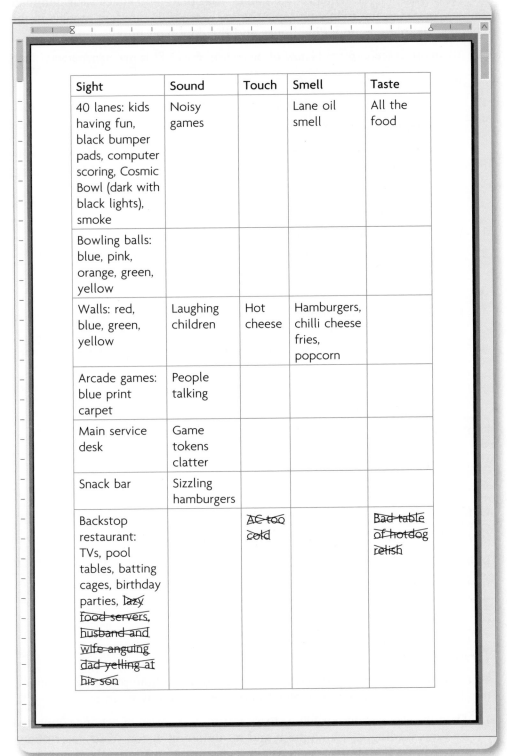

Sight	Sound	Touch	Smell	Taste
40 lanes: kids having fun, black bumper pads, computer scoring, Cosmic Bowl (dark with black lights), smoke	Noisy games		Lane oil smell	All the food
Bowling balls: blue, pink, orange, green, yellow				
Walls: red, blue, green, yellow	Laughing children	Hot cheese	Hamburgers, chilli cheese fries, popcorn	
Arcade games: blue print carpet	People talking			
Main service desk	Game tokens clatter			
Snack bar	Sizzling hamburgers			
Backstop restaurant: TVs, pool tables, batting cages, birthday parties, ~~lazy food servers, husband and wife arguing dad yelling at his son~~		~~AC too cold~~		~~Bad table of hotdog relish~~

Arrange the specific words and details that you decide to keep in a roughly spatial order. Jo Lucas organized her description as she progressed into and through the family fun center. However you arrange your details—top to bottom, front to back, and so forth—be consistent.

Next write a topic sentence that names your place and states your dominant impression, as in the following topic sentences from the student models in this chapter. The place is underlined once and the dominant impression twice:

A. The most peaceful place I know of on a clear, dry night is my grandparents' pond, where I can relax around an open campfire.

B. With my morning cup of coffee in hand, I head toward the most tranquil part of my house, my front porch.

Follow the topic sentence with description, and locate readers within the scene by using space and time transitions (words like *above, near, after,* and *finally*).

Move from the topic sentence directly into the description.

ORGANIZING—SUMMING UP

1. Write out your dominant impression in a word or two.
2. Cut any details from your prewriting list that conflict with the dominant impression.
3. Arrange your details spatially.
4. Review the list of transitions—especially space transitions—and other connectors on pages 54–56.
5. Write a rough topic sentence that names the place and states the dominant impression.

JOURNAL / BLOG ENTRY 5.3

Your description will benefit from spatial organization—that is, details listed from top to bottom, outside to inside, one side to another, or far to near. Can you picture yourself in a fixed spot inside a room, or do you see yourself walking through the place? After reviewing your notes, write a brief paragraph explaining how you will organize your description and why this method makes sense to you.

Drafting

You are now almost ready to write the first draft. But before plunging in, review the drafting suggestions in Chapter 1 and keep the following in mind:

1. Describe a place; do not tell a story. A story is a series of actions connected by time, leading to a high point and resolution of action. Your description may have action, but the actions are there only to reinforce the dominant impression.
2. Feel free to include action description along with dialogue.
3. Occasionally, tell readers what to think about your details and how you feel about them (see the student models in this chapter).
4. Add plenty of details. Specific words and sensory details are essential. Even if you overdescribe in the first draft, you can cut unneeded material later.

After completing the first rough draft, write two short, reflective paragraphs. In the first, tell what you like most about your draft and why; in the second, tell what you like least and why. Be specific. This self-assessment can help you decide where to begin revising.

FEEDBACK *In one paragraph, tell a classmate what you like best about his/her draft, and then address one aspect you have questions or concerns about.*

Revising Drafts

First-Stage Drafts

At this stage, you should focus on content (scene description: specific words, sensory details, thoughts, and feelings) and organization (arranging and connecting ideas). Rereading your draft, ask yourself the following questions:

1. **Are you really describing a place and not slipping into a narrative (story)?** While a well-told story will have lots of action leading to a high point or climax, a descriptive paragraph usually contains little or no action.

2. **Is your topic sentence effective (Chapter 3)?** Have you included the place being described and a limiting statement about it? Try adding a word or two of sensory detail (a detail about color, sound, or touch perhaps) and using specific words, such as the name of the place.

3. **Does your description have an overall point (dominant impression)?** Many rough drafts include random details of sight, sound, and other senses. However, you are not merely a camera recording any picture that comes in front of your lens. You are a person with a point to make about your place, so your details should reinforce that point.

4. **Are you occasionally telling your readers what to think about the details?** Readers often need some brief explanation within a sentence to reinforce a dominant impression.

5. **Are you occasionally letting your readers know how you feel about the place?** Because this is a subjective description, you should let your reader know your thoughts and feelings about the place—as long as they help reinforce the dominant impression. (See "Waking Up the Right Way," pp. 88–89.)

6. **Are you using enough specific language?** Your second draft will be stronger when you make some images more specific.

7. **Are you using sensory details?** Remember to use other senses—not just sight—in building images. But avoid overdescribing, cramming too many details into a sentence.

8. **Is your concluding sentence effective?** Does it include each of the following: a connector, a word that echoes the dominant impression, and a comment about your place (expanded thought)? Stick with one or, at most, two sentences, and you will end your one-paragraph paper effectively.

9. **Are all the sentences in the paragraph well connected?** First drafts often need more time and space connectors. Reread each sentence, imagining that you are directing a photographer who is filming your place. You will tell the photographer what to shoot, using phrases like "to the left of the mirror," "in front of the picture window," and "next to the refrigerator."

For more on the dominant impression, see pp. 79–82.

For more on specific words, see pp. 75–76.

For more on connectors, see pp. 54–56.

To help you focus on the revision process and alert your instructor to your progress, list three *specific* changes you have made or feel you ought to make in going from your first to second draft, responding to the specific first-stage draft questions in the preceding list. Next, in several sentences, state what you like best about your draft.

Second and Final Drafts

For advice on revising and then editing further drafts of your work, turn to Chapter 4.

Annotated Student Model: "Our Family Outing"

Let's look closely at how another student successfully worked through the writing process: gathering ideas, drafting, revising, and editing to create a well-focused, vivid description of a family fun center. The prewriting list for this paragraph is on page 93.

As you read, keep in mind that revision seldom occurs in tidy stages. Sometimes, for example, you will edit early in the process of writing a draft and change content later. However, the following draft stages will help focus your revision efforts.

First-Stage Draft

As you work through your first draft, watch for these problem areas:

- Unfocused dominant impression
- Too many sentences leading into the description
- Weak concluding sentence
- Too few specific words and sensory details

How many of these problems can you identify in Jo's first draft?

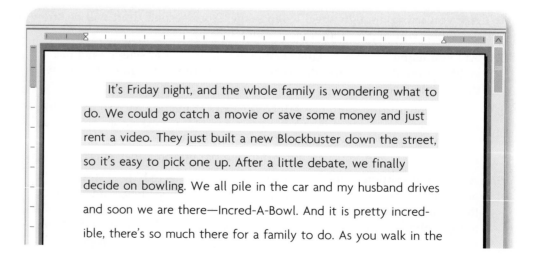

It's Friday night, and the whole family is wondering what to do. We could go catch a movie or save some money and just rent a video. They just built a new Blockbuster down the street, so it's easy to pick one up. After a little debate, we finally decide on bowling. We all pile in the car and my husband drives and soon we are there—Incred-A-Bowl. And it is pretty incredible, there's so much there for a family to do. As you walk in the place you can see all kinds of activity. People are laughing and talking, employees are busy checking out bowling shoes, and you can see the balls rolling down the alleys into the pins. There is a huge arcade with brightly lit and noisy arcade games. You can also see people helping customers. Further along is the snack bar. You can smell the aroma of freshly popped popcorn and hamburgers on the grill. If you keep looking, you will see the Backstop restaurant with televisions mounted around the room, near the ceiling. Each television is on a different sports channel, so you dont miss a play of any sport. They have put the bumper pads in the gutters for the small kids so they can knock over a few pins. Tonight is the Cosmic Bowl. This means turning the regular lights off and turning the black lights on. They turn the smoke machines on and this gives the effect of outer space. The bowling balls glow as they roll down the lanes. Everyone is laughing and enjoying themselves.

Second-Stage Draft

In Jo's second-stage draft, she adds sensory details, specific words, and locator phrases.

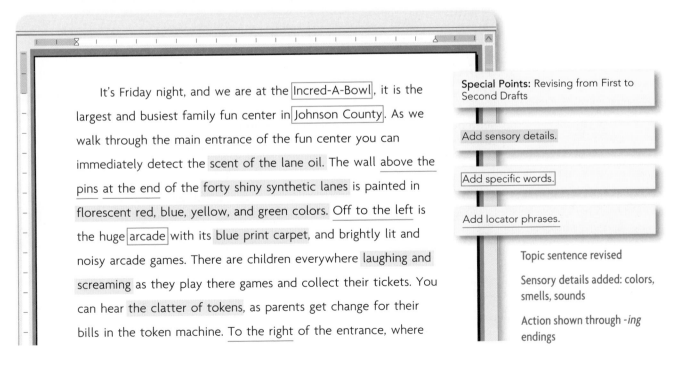

It's Friday night, and we are at the Incred-A-Bowl, it is the largest and busiest family fun center in Johnson County. As we walk through the main entrance of the fun center you can immediately detect the scent of the lane oil. The wall above the pins at the end of the forty shiny synthetic lanes is painted in florescent red, blue, yellow, and green colors. Off to the left is the huge arcade with its blue print carpet, and brightly lit and noisy arcade games. There are children everywhere laughing and screaming as they play there games and collect their tickets. You can hear the clatter of tokens, as parents get change for their bills in the token machine. To the right of the entrance, where

Special Points: Revising from First to Second Drafts

Add sensory details.

Add specific words.

Add locator phrases.

Topic sentence revised

Sensory details added: colors, smells, sounds

Action shown through -ing endings

we came in, is the control desk. Here people are talking, laughing, and helping customers. Further down the crowded concourse is the snack bar. You can smell the aroma of freshly popped popcorn, and hamburgers sizzling on the charbroil grill. To the left of the snack bar is the Backstop restaurant. It is decorated with all kinds of sports memorabilia. There are thirteen-inch televisions mounted around the room, near the white ceiling. Each television is on a different sports channel, so you dont miss a play of any sport. Upstairs in the restaurant are pool tables and batting cages. Back downstairs there are some birthday parties going on. They have put the bumper pads in the gutters for the small kids. They are now jumping, clapping, and screaming as their pink, blue, yellow, green, and orange balls hit the pins. The computerized scoring is a nice feature. Because it allows the parents to participate in the fun instead of having to keep score. Tonight Incred-A-Bowl is having a Cosmic Bowl. This means turning the regular lights off and turning the black lights on above the lanes. They also turn the smoke machines on and this gives the effect of outer space. The blue, pink, orange, green, and yellow bowling balls glow as they roll down the lanes. Everyone is laughing and enjoying themselves. This is a great place to keep family ties close.

Specific words added

Another location added

Locator phrases added

Action shown through -*ing* endings

Expanded thought in conclusion

Closing sentence added

Third-Stage Draft

Moving into a third-stage draft, Jo polished her work for word choices and sentence variety. Note how she adds sensory details and specific words, combines sentences for variety, substitutes synonyms for repeated words, and deletes unnecessary material.

Title added

Special Points: Revising from Second to Third Drafts

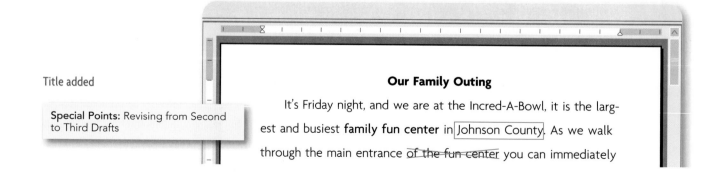

Our Family Outing

It's Friday night, and we are at the Incred-A-Bowl, it is the largest and busiest **family fun center** in Johnson County. As we walk through the main entrance ~~of the fun center~~ you can immediately detect the scent of the lane oil. The wall above the pins at the end of the forty shiny synthetic lanes is painted in florescent red, blue, yellow, and green colors. Off to the left is the huge arcade with its blue print carpet, and brightly lit, ~~and~~ noisy arcade games. There are children everywhere laughing and screaming as they play there games and collect their tickets. You can hear the clatter of tokens, as parents get change for their bills in the token machine. To the right of the entrance, where we came in, is the control desk. Here seven people are talking, laughing, and helping customers. Further down the crowded concourse is the snack bar where you can smell the aroma of freshly popped popcorn, and hamburgers sizzling on the char-broil grill. Someone has just purchased an order of chili cheese fries. It looks so sinful, with its homemade chili and hot nacho cheese. To the left of the snack bar is the Backstop restaurant, which is decorated with all kinds of sports memorabilia. There are thirteen-inch televisions mounted around the room near the white ceiling. Each **tv** is on a different ~~sports~~ channel, so you don't miss a play of any sport. Upstairs in the **restaurant** are pool tables and batting cages. This is where many parents take their **sons and daughters** to practice batting the upcoming baseball season. Back downstairs there are some birthday parties going on. They have put the black bumper pads in the gutters for the small **kids** who are now jumping, clapping, and screaming as their pink, blue, yellow, green, and orange balls hit the pins. The computerized scoring is a nice feature. Because it allows the parents to participate in the fun instead of having to keep score. Tonight Incred-A-Bowl is having a Cosmic Bowl which means turning the regular lights off and turning the black lights on above the lanes. They also turn the smoke machines on and this gives the effect of outer space. The ~~blue, pink, orange, green, and yellow~~ multicolored bowling balls glow as they roll down the lanes. Everyone is laughing and enjoying themselves here at Incred-A-Bowl, a great place to keep family ties close.

Add sensory details.

Add specific words.

~~Delete unneeded words.~~

Combine sentences for variety.

Substitute synonyms for repeated words.

Material added

Material added

Final-Editing Draft

Here is the last draft of "Our Family Outing," the one that Jo has carefully edited. Now is the time to slow down, focusing on each word and applying the grammar and punctuation rules you have learned so far, especially for the use of commas.

Special Points: Editing Final Drafts

1. **Misspelling**
2. **Sound-alike word**
3. **Missing word(s)**
4. **Wrong word**
5. **Sentence fragment**
6. **Comma splice/run-on**
7. **Faulty capitalization**
8. **Incorrect apostrophe**
9a. **Comma(s) needed: Introductory word(s)/ phrase/clause**
9b. **Comma(s) needed: Nonessential word group(s)**
9c. **Comma(s) needed: Main clauses with coordinating conjunction**
10. **Unneeded comma**

Our Family Outing

It's Friday night, and we are at the Incred-A-Bowl, it [6] which is the largest and busiest family fun center in Johnson County. As we walk through the main entrance [9a] you [4] I (or we) can immediately detect the scent of the lane oil. The wall above the pins at the end of the forty shiny synthetic lanes is painted in florescent [1] fluorescent red, blue, yellow, and green colors. Off to the left is the huge arcade with its blue print carpet, [10] and brightly lit, noisy arcade games. There are children everywhere laughing and screaming as they play there [2] their games and collect their tickets. You [4] I (or we) can hear the clatter of tokens, [10] as parents get change for their bills in the token machine. To the right of the entrance, where we came in, is the control desk. Here seven people are talking, laughing, and helping customers. Further down the crowded concourse is the snack bar, [9b] where you [4] I (or we) can smell the aroma of freshly popped popcorn and hamburgers sizzling on the charbroil grill. Someone has just purchased an order of chili cheese fries. It looks so sinful, [10] with its homemade chili and hot nacho cheese. To the left of the snack bar is the Backstop restaurant, which is decorated with all kinds of sports memorabilia. There are thirteen-inch televisions mounted around the room near the white ceiling. Each tv [7] TV is on a different sports channel, so you [4] customers dont [8] don't miss a play of any sport. Upstairs in the restaurant are pool tables and batting cages. This is where many parents take their sons and daughters to practice batting for the upcoming baseball season. Back downstairs there are some birthday parties going on. They have put the black bumper pads in the gutters for the small kids [9b] who are now jumping, clapping, and screaming as their pink, blue, yellow, green, and orange balls hit the

pins. The computerized scoring is a nice feature.[5] Because it
allows the parents to participate in the fun instead of having to
keep score. Tonight Incred-A-Bowl is having a Cosmic Bowl[9b],
which means turning the regular lights off and turning the black
lights on above the lanes. They also turn the smoke machines
on[9c], and this gives the effect of outer space. The multicolored
bowling balls glow as they roll down the lanes. ~~Everyone is~~[4] All
the people are laughing and enjoying themselves here at Incred-
A-Bowl, a great place to keep family ties close.

—Jo Lucas

FINAL-DRAFT CHECKLIST: DESCRIPTION

Before turning in your final draft for a grade, review this checklist. You may find that, as careful as you think you have been, you've still missed a point or two.

☐ 1. Are you describing a place and not slipping into a narrative (story)?

☐ 2. Does your description have an overall point (dominant impression)?

☐ 3. Are you occasionally telling readers what to think about the details?

☐ 4. Are you letting readers know how you feel about the place?

☐ 5. Are you using enough specific language?

☐ 6. Are you using enough sensory details?

☐ 7. Is your topic sentence effective?

☐ 8. Is your concluding sentence effective?

☐ 9. Are all the sentences within the paragraph well connected?

☐ 10. Are you using active verbs and -ing words to describe action?

☐ 11. Have you varied the length and beginnings of your sentences?

☐ 12. Have you used synonyms for words that are repeated too often?

☐ 13. Have you cut unneeded words?

☐ 14. Have you written an interesting title? Have you checked its capitalization?

☐ 15. Have you prepared your paper according to the format expected by your instructor?

HINT

For more on any of these points, see Chapter 4.

HINT

Check to see if you need to include a title page, double space, leave at least 1-inch margins, and use a 12-point font.

16. Have you edited closely (including having at least one other person proofread)? Have you checked your Improvement Chart for pattern errors?

17. Have you looked specifically for the following errors: misspellings, sound-alike words, missing words, wrong words, sentence fragments, comma splices/run-ons, faulty capitalizations, incorrect apostrophes, missing commas, and unnecessary commas?

Alternate Writing Assignments

While the focus of this chapter has been on evoking a place, there are many other uses for description. For any of the assignments, be sure to do the following:

- Decide on a dominant impression.
- State the dominant impression in your topic sentence.
- Use specific words and sensory details to develop the dominant impression.
- Conclude with a sentence that restates the dominant impression and makes a final point.
- Connect your sentences with time and place transitions.

1. **Describe an event.** Rather than create a story with organized action leading to a high point, capture the feeling of the event. Perhaps, as in the accompanying photo, you have witnessed a dramatic moment at a sporting event and can communicate that feeling. This picture shows the soccer players' joy in scoring—the dominant impression. You could help readers understand the excitement at the game by describing how people reacted,

what they said and did. The players are jumping in the air, clapping hands, smiling, and shouting to one another. Undoubtedly, the coaches and spectators are also showing their happiness. Think about an event that you remember well or, better yet, go to one with the purpose of capturing a dominant impression through close observation and detailed note taking.

2. **Describe a person.** Find someone you know well or someone you are around enough to observe his or her appearance (physical look and clothing) and actions (the way he or she walks, stands, and sits; his or her body language and mannerisms). Listen to the person and record some characteristic dialogue. Your goal is to create a verbal portrait so that someone who has not met this person would recognize him or her from your description. Focus your description with a dominant impression, such as sloppy, well groomed, athletic, lazy, talkative, shy, funny, or angry.

3. **Describe an object.** Select an object and detail its appearance. This object could range from the small and ordinary (salt shaker, toaster oven, wrench) to the large and more unusual (construction crane, new Corvette, office building). Your goal is to capture the dominant impression of the object through description. For instance, your salt shaker might be exceptionally functional. You could describe what it looks like and how well it does its job of dispensing salt. The construction crane might suggest power. You could describe the large metal parts and then show the machine in action.

4. **Describe an animal.** Select a household pet (dog, cat, hamster, iguana), farm animal (cow, horse, pig, chicken), or wild animal in your neighborhood (squirrel, rabbit, bird, garter snake). Again the trick is to focus the description through a dominant impression, a defining trait of the animal. It might be easy and obvious to choose a trait like sloppiness for a pig. But it could be more challenging to show the intelligence or lovable qualities of the pig.

5. **Describe a product.** There are a zillion possible products you could describe. Limit the field by sticking to one you use regularly. For instance, you might describe your favorite breakfast cereal. Why do you find it appealing? You could focus your description on characteristics like taste, texture, and length of time it stays crunchy.

6. **Describe a work of art.** Bring this painting to life for someone who has never seen it. What is its dominant impression? Describe its details, colors, style, and textures. While your description will likely focus largely on what you *see*, try using your other senses a little, too. What would this image "sound," "smell," or "feel" like? What mood does it convey, and how does it make you feel? Are the colors loud or warm or sinister?

For more variety in approaching Alternate Assignment 6, choose to describe any work of art displayed in the Collections Database of the Metropolitan Museum of Art: http://www.metmuseum.org/works_of_art/index.asp. In your paragraph, be sure to note both the artist and title of the work.

Linking to Future Experience

Determining the Value of Description

Descriptive skills will make you a better reader and improve your writing at work, home, and school. You will use description in almost any writing assignment, regardless of its purpose or pattern. Description is also an important part of all conversations and social interactions—in person, over the phone, and online. But the most valuable benefit of learning to describe well is developing the ability to observe your surroundings closely. Now that you have worked through the activities in this chapter, analyzed the model paragraphs, taken notes for your own descriptions, and workshopped drafts, you will find yourself noticing more of the world around you—and seeing it more clearly.

Chapter Summary

1. Describing is the process of using details to build vivid images.

2. Descriptive writing relies on specific words and sensory details.

3. Words can be relatively general or relatively specific—the more specific a word, the clearer the image.

4. Description is often found in narrative, expository, and persuasive writing.

5. Writers often focus description with a dominant impression.

6. A topic sentence in a paragraph describing a place should name the place and state the dominant impression.

7. Descriptions are often organized spatially.

8. Time and space transitions are needed in descriptive writing.

9. Subjective descriptions are strengthened by the inclusion of thoughts and emotions.

10. Action—including people moving and speaking—is often part of description.

11. Writing is not complete until it has been revised and carefully edited.

Telling Your Own Story (Narration)

6

[*Professional storytellers entertain us in writing, orally, and visually, as in TV and film. In a paragraph, tell what kinds of stories you like best (such as action, romance, comedy, fantasy), and tell why.*]

KEY TOPICS

- Developing skills and exploring ideas in narrative paragraphs

  - Creating conflict, suspense, and a climax

  - Finding the significance of a story

  - Building a story that shows as well as tells

- Using effective dialogue

- Including metaphors and similes to add clarity and interest

- Analyzing student models: Narrative paragraphs

- Writing a narrative paragraph

What Are We Trying to Achieve and Why?

Setting the Stage

People have been in the storytelling business for a long time, perhaps for as long as humanity has existed. A universal impulse, spanning all cultures, moves people to share their experiences with one another. We are drawn together by the stories of our own culture and by learning those of others. Whenever we tell someone what we have done during the day—the bargain we got while shopping, the math exam we aced, the ticket we got speeding to school—we are telling a story, or **narrating.**

Linking to Previous Experience

Narration comes naturally to us. Since we first learned to speak, we have been telling those around us about our lives, stories that have helped us release emotions, reveal some part of ourselves, influence others, and entertain. In this chapter, you will work more consciously with the elements of personal narrative, learning how to fashion them into a focused and interesting story. As you gather material, you will look for the significance of your story and test this definition of personal narrative: *Someone doing something somewhere for some reason.*

You already have significant experience responding to written narratives. Movies begin as screenplays, and most TV programming is scripted. Much of what we read for entertainment is fiction, beginning with the picture books read to children and progressing to short stories and novels.

You also create your own narratives. Though few of us have the skills of an accomplished fiction writer, we all talk about ourselves, work associates, friends, and family members (perhaps too much sometimes!). Whenever you begin a conversation with a line like "You'll never guess who I saw Ted Wilson's wife with last night," you are launching into a narrative.

And if you have ever kept a diary, e-mailed a friend with news or gossip, or completed a school assignment about an incident in your life, you were writing narrative. If you worked through Chapter 5 in this book, you have written a description of a place, an assignment that contains many elements of narration: specific language, sensory details, active verbs, clearly linked sentences, and a unified dominant impression.

JOURNAL / BLOG ENTRY 6.1

Recall and list three instances during the past week when you told someone about something that happened to you. Summarize each incident in several sentences, describing what happened in each. Next, list whom you told each story to and what your purpose was: to release frustration, communicate information, express your feelings, persuade, or simply make her or him laugh. How well did you succeed in each instance?

FEEDBACK *Read a classmate's three stories and tell him or her which seems most interesting to you—and why.*

Developing Skills and Exploring Ideas in Narrative Paragraphs

To learn how to write effective personal narrative, we will practice the following:

1. Creating a narrative that has conflict, suspense, and a climax
2. Finding the significance or meaning of a story
3. Building a story that shows as well as tells
4. Using effective dialogue
5. Including metaphors and similes to add clarity and interest

Creating Conflict, Suspense, and a Climax

Perhaps it is human nature to be more interested in narratives that involve conflict than those that do not. As a species surviving many centuries of struggle with other species and with natural forces, we may well have no choice in the matter. Our instincts might simply tell us, "Look out: possible negative outcome. Pay attention!" Whatever the case, you will find **conflict**—the potential for events to go wrong—critical to your story, and you should arrange the action so as to keep your reader in **suspense** (wondering) about the outcome or **climax.**

The central conflict in your story might be one of these:

- A person dealing with another person or group—for example, your boss treats you poorly.
- A person dealing with her- or himself—for example, you are learning to control your temper.
- A person coping with the environment—for example, your air conditioner is broken, and it is 100 degrees outside.

In the first example, we might have two very different stories to tell:

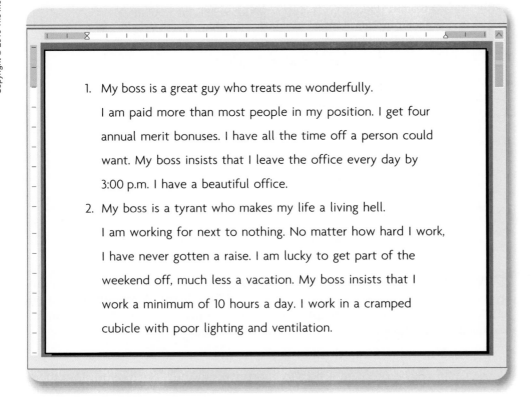

1. My boss is a great guy who treats me wonderfully.

   I am paid more than most people in my position. I get four annual merit bonuses. I have all the time off a person could want. My boss insists that I leave the office every day by 3:00 p.m. I have a beautiful office.

2. My boss is a tyrant who makes my life a living hell.

   I am working for next to nothing. No matter how hard I work, I have never gotten a raise. I am lucky to get part of the weekend off, much less a vacation. My boss insists that I work a minimum of 10 hours a day. I work in a cramped cubicle with poor lighting and ventilation.

Most of us might envy the fortunate soul in version 1, but we would probably be more interested in knowing how the poor stiff in version 2 is going to improve his or her life.

If we were to create a brief narrative based on version 2, we might choose a few hours in the day of our person—let's call him Oscar Jamieson—when it looked like his life was going to take a turn from bad to worse. Oscar will be arriving at 7:30 a.m. at the Sprint, building where he works.

Action Outline

Conflict	Oscar has a confrontation with his boss today.
Lead-in	He is worrying about the billing statement he mishandled yesterday.
Developing the conflict—actions to build suspense	• Hearing through a co-worker on the way to his office that he is in big trouble
	• Finding a brief "come-see-me" note in his in-box from his boss
	• Wondering, worrying, and avoiding the confrontation all morning
	• Getting a phone call from the boss, who orders him to "Get in here now!"
	• Seeing the assistant look up, shake his head, and look down at his desk
	• Entering the boss's office and seeing her scowl from behind her desk
	• Standing helplessly while the boss rages about the billing statement mess
	• Listening to the dreaded words "You're fired!"
Climax	Seeing his boss suddenly fall back in her chair, clutching her chest; calling the secretary. The boss sends word from the hospital that on doctor's orders, she's taking early retirement—immediately.
Resolution	Finding out that Oscar's best friend has been promoted to the boss's position and that Oscar, too, is up for a promotion

What looked at first like a horrible day for Oscar (the good guy) turned out instead to be the end of a career for his boss (the villian). Although this action outline is a bit simplistic—people are seldom simply good or bad—it demonstrates several important elements of story structure:

- **Lead-in:** a brief introduction to arouse interest and set the stage
- **Conflict:** the problem a person encounters in the story

- **Suspense:** the reader's uncertainty about the outcome of the conflict
- **Climax:** the high point of the action
- **Resolution:** the result of the climax—the point of the story (significance)

ACTIVITY 6.1 | WORKING TOGETHER: *Creating Conflict, Suspense, and a Climax*

With group members, choose a topic from one of the three categories listed below (or from the topics listed on p. 119), and decide what the conflict is. If you choose an event that actually happened to a group member, ask questions about the event. Next, describe the conflict in a single sentence, and then write an action outline as illustrated above.

1. An embarrassing moment: speaking in public, asking for a date, having forgotten your wallet or purse in a restaurant when the bill is presented, being caught in a lie

2. An unpleasant moment as a consumer: returning defective merchandise, being overcharged, suspecting a mechanic of cheating

3. A public confrontation: handling a traffic accident, being pulled over by a police officer, arguing in a restaurant, dealing with a neighbor, protecting your property

Action Outline

Topic:

Conflict:

Lead-in:

Actions to develop conflict and build suspense:

A. _____

B. _____

C. _____

D. _____

E. _____

F. _____

Climax:

Resolution:

Finding the Significance of a Story

A story should have a point. Without one, the story is likely to be confusing, boring, or both. In Oscar Jamieson's narrative, we can see that he has been freed from a tyrant who has been making his life miserable. There is a clear progression from the anxious beginning of his day to the triumphant end. But even in a story with a clearly resolved conflict, the writer can directly state the action's significance. For example, here are several points that could emerge from Oscar's story:

- After people have suffered enough, if they have faith and can hang on, they may eventually be rewarded.

- There is justice after all.

HINT

Writers choose the meaning of their stories. The significance of a story won't always be clear to you at first.

- Bullies and tyrants tend to come to a bad end.
- It's pointless to feel too worried or depressed about a bad situation before you know the outcome.
- Having experienced cruelty, people often resolve to become kinder.

Any of these ideas or a combination of them could be the main point of the story. It is the author's privilege to choose. The main point, however, should come naturally from the event and not feel tacked on at the end. For example, it would seem forced to use Oscar's story as a warning to people to eat better and exercise to avoid a heart attack or to show how a friend can help you get promoted. In your own narratives, the significance will not always be clear at first, but as you tell the tale, a point should emerge.

ACTIVITY 6.2 | WORKING TOGETHER: *Finding the Significance of a Story*

Skillful writers of serious fiction often imply many shades of meaning. Less-experienced writers, though, need to focus on one meaning and make it clear. The following story, "On the Brink," has several possible points, but none that are explicitly stated. If the writer were part of your group, what suggestions could you give to clarify a meaning? Read and discuss the model, and then write out three possible points the story could make.

On the Brink

As I prepared for surgery at the vet clinic where I now work, I was administering anesthesia to a miniature black poodle when respiration stopped, and the heart stopped beating. I scrambled to the side of the small poodle to start respiration, also giving epinephrine (adrenaline) and dopram, trying to get the heart beating again. Not sure what else to do, I yelled frantically for Dr. Erickson, and he came into the room saying, "What the hell is going on in here?" After assessing the situation, he began to assist me in trying to revive the limp, almost lifeless poodle lying on the surgical table. It seemed there was no hope for the small black poodle when a single breath came from its lungs, then another, and another. However, the battle had just begun, for the dog had no heartbeat, but it was breathing. The doctor and I had never seen anything like it before. Often there will be a heartbeat and no breath, but never the other way around. After a few more minutes, we got the dog's heart beating, but the big question then was whether we should go ahead with the exploratory surgery as planned or let the animal come out of anesthesia, in which case it would risk dying from the abdominal swelling. We decided to go ahead with the surgery, trying to save the poor poodle from certain death. As we cut open the body cavity to find out what was causing the swelling, the uterus expanded and swelled out of the animal's body cavity. We immediately removed the infected uterus, sutured the body cavity, and quickly brought the dog out of anesthesia to observe it for other difficulties.

List of Possible Meanings

EXAMPLE: *It amazes me to see how creatures can hold on to life.*

1. _____

2. _____

3. _____

Building a Story That Shows as Well as Tells

Creating a story requires the ability both to show and to tell. When you **show** readers something, they are able to interpret the scene or idea for themselves. When you **tell** readers about something, you interpret for them. Which of the two following passages tells and which shows?

A. We were growing more frightened by the moment.

B. As late as it was, one of my cousins, my brother Tama, and I were still up, talking over some gruesome scenes from *The Exorcist*, in our minds once again hearing Linda Blair roar out "MERRIN!" in her demon voice and seeing her head turn completely around. Suddenly, we all heard a scratching sound at the outside of the door and an awful noise that sounded like someone groaning in pain: "Ooohhh-aaaghh!"

If you chose passage A for telling and passage B for showing, you are correct. Telling is more economical; it gets the point across fast. However, telling often involves only the mind, leaving out the heart. And while showing requires more words, if done well it can involve readers on several levels as they react to the characters' speech and actions, and experience the sensory details. Good writers interweave showing and telling, using one to clarify and reinforce the other, as in the following passage:

Showing and telling work together in an effective narrative.

> As late as it was, one of my cousins, my brother Tama, and I were still up, talking over some gruesome scenes from *The Exorcist*, in our minds once again hearing Linda Blair roar out "MERRIN!" in her demon voice and seeing her head turn completely around. We were growing more frightened by the moment when suddenly we all heard a scratching sound at the outside of the door and an awful noise that sounded like someone groaning in pain: "Ooohhh-aaaghh!"

Rough drafts often suffer from too much telling and too little showing. But if you realize the power of showing and are willing to work at it, you can create narratives that truly move an audience.

First drafts often tell too much and show too little.

ACTIVITY 6.3 | *Building a Story That Shows and Tells*

The following sentences tell a reader how to interpret a situation. Write a sentence that shows the same statement.

EXAMPLE

Telling: My brother was concerned about my grandfather lying on the floor.

Showing: *My brother screamed, "Mom, help, grandpa is dying!"*

1. Telling: Josh felt sick again today.

    Showing: _____

You can show with sensory details, a person's actions, and a person's statements.

2.   Telling: The whole family felt sad as they gathered around the casket.

Showing: _____

_____

_____

3.   Telling: The customer service representative did not appear interested in my story.

Showing: _____

_____

_____

4.   Telling: Now I finally understood that Adrian was a bigot.

Showing: _____

_____

_____

5.   Telling: Batur was overjoyed when his semester grades arrived.

Showing: _____

_____

Using Effective Dialogue

Dialogue—the words people speak—is an important way to show. Whereas narratives can be written without dialogue, stories usually benefit from it. Having the characters in your story speak can reveal their qualities, add important information, and make the mood or feeling of the story stronger. When you tell the story by speaking as its **narrator,** you also add variety and reveal more of yourself.

There are three kinds of "speech" in narrative: direct and indirect dialogue and revealed thought. **Direct dialogue** reproduces the words spoken by a character and is the most powerful:

DIRECT DIALOGUE   I couldn't keep my mouth shut any longer: "I'm not going to sit here and listen to you bad-mouth my brother one more second!"

Notice that within the quotation marks the verb tense shifts from the narrator's past tense to the present tense.

Indirect dialogue reports what someone else said, but not in his or her exact words:

INDIRECT DIALOGUE   My brother Tama told me he didn't believe in any of this supernatural nonsense.

Compare this to "Tama said, 'I don't believe in ghosts and all that other creepy stuff.'" Notice how the words change as the brother speaks for himself.

We use indirect dialogue when what is said has less importance to the story than direct dialogue would give it. We also use it to make the story go faster, to move readers more quickly to important events.

Revealed thought is the narrator thinking aloud:

REVEALED THOUGHT   I was thinking, "Oh my God, I am not dreaming. It is real!"

Notice that when the narrator reveals thought, instead of just telling the story, the verb tense shifts from past to present. This tense shift helps readers feel more involved with the story, as if they are really in the scene.

English Review Note

Narrators must follow the conventions of standard edited English, so their writing "voice" will differ somewhat from their speaking voice.

HINT

In dialogue, put periods, question marks, and exclamation points *within*, not outside, the quotation marks at the ends of sentences.

ACTIVITY 6.4 | *Using Effective Dialogue*

In the following passages, note the underlined indirect dialogue, and write out direct speech that seems appropriate to the speaker and situation.

EXAMPLE: Mrs. Hill sat silently at the front of the room, grading papers. I decided I would just use my study card to get started on the exam. So I cautiously reached down to retrieve the card, which had suddenly become my cheat sheet. I slid it under my leg and began filling in my exam. Then I heard Mrs. Hill's pencil fall to the floor, and she rose from her chair. My heart stopped as she reached my desk. I was asked to rise from my chair. As I stood, I felt as though my knees would buckle beneath me. My cheat sheet fell to the floor. Mrs. Hill, my most admired teacher, now had my test in hand and began shredding it.

Direct dialogue: *"Anita," Mrs. Hill said sternly, "get up from your seat—now!"*

1. It's a cool spring night at Qualcomm Stadium in San Diego, and I am preparing for my most exhilarating start ever, and my last as a pitcher for the all-Marine baseball team. As my teammates and I walk down the long hallway to the field, all I can hear are the cleats clicking on the cement floor. I see the nervous tension on their faces increase as we reach the field. They look like kids at their first big league game. Their mouths fall open as they stand on the field and see thousands of cheering fans filling the stadium. My coach turns to the team and lets us know that we should be calm, that if we relax we will do a good job tonight.

   Direct dialogue: _____

   _____

2. Running down to the bullpen, I can feel the beads of sweat dripping down my face. While I am going through my warm-up pitches, my good friend C. J. gives me a few words of encouragement. He tells me that I should think of this game as any of the past 50 we have played. He says that I should forget about the pressure and just try to have fun like we always do.

   Direct dialogue: _____

   _____

   _____

   _____

HINT

Note that the first comma and the exclamation point are *inside* the quotation marks.

English Review Note

Use caution when changing from direct to indirect dialogue. Edit for word order, tense shifts, pronoun changes, and punctuation.

Including Metaphors and Similes to Add Clarity and Interest

Metaphors and **similes** are figures of speech that compare things.

METAPHOR The ancient, bent oak tree at the wood's edge is the old man of the forest.

SIMILE The ancient, bent oak at the wood's edge looks like an old man.

In both cases, the comparison is between a man and a tree. Notice that the simile uses *like*. Similes also use *as*.

Figures of speech like these can add color and clarity to your writing and focus readers on important parts of your story. Compare the following sets of sentences for a literal description versus a figurative one:

LITERAL   Suddenly, it began to rain hard.

FIGURATIVE   Suddenly, the sky became an open faucet, pouring rain on all of us below.

LITERAL   I will always remember the sight of the man who died in front of me.

FIGURATIVE   The 33-year-old man died right in front of me, a sight that will stay in my memory, like a stain, forever.

LITERAL   She was the biggest woman I had ever seen.

FIGURATIVE   She was huge, like an NFL linebacker.

In the literal versions, the meaning is clear, but the figurative versions take the meaning one step further, adding emphasis, clarity, and color. In fact, metaphors and similes are common in everyday life. Try reading an article in *Sports Illustrated* or listening to a sports broadcast; expressions like "the shot came low, like a heat-seeking missile" or "her speed is her ticket back to the Olympics" are common. In your own writing, try experimenting with metaphors and similes, especially when you revise for style.

As you practice metaphors and similes, be wary of creating **clichés**—figures of speech grown stale from overuse. Avoid clichés like these:

Caught between a rock and a hard place

Seemed to last for an eternity

Sent chills down my spine

Moved like lightning

Reinvented the wheel

Got a handle on the situation

Began to see the light

Felt butterflies in my stomach

Felt his heart pounding like a drum

Stood still as a statue

HINT

For more on metaphors and similes see pp. 498, 500. Beware of clichés—overused figures of speech. For more on clichés, see pp. 499–500.

HINT

Try using images from nature: animals, plants, storms, fire, earthquakes, and so on.

ACTIVITY 6.5 | *Including Metaphors and Similes*

To practice figurative language, for the following literal expressions, create a metaphor or simile that expresses the same thought.

EXAMPLE: Literal: **The sun shone down on the wet street.**

Figurative: *The street had been transformed by the rain into a river of light.*

1. Literal: Bill was angry as he approached the return desk.

   Figurative: _____

2. Literal: Dilated to 9 centimeters, Alice was in terrible pain.

   Figurative: _____

   _____

3. Literal: Asking Elise out on their first date, Eduardo felt awkward and embarrassed.

   Figurative: _____

4. Literal: Earth's atmosphere is degraded daily.

   Figurative: _____

   _____

5. Literal: Professor Davis droned on, once again boring his captive students.

    Figurative: _____

    _____

Analyzing Student Models: Narrative Paragraphs

The student narratives that follow should give you ideas for your own. As you read them, look for narrative strategies that you like, and use them in your own story. Also, read the prereading commentary and marginal annotations, which will help you understand why the stories work well.

➡ *Prereading Exploration for "Sixteen and Mother of Twelve"*

The author, Lani Houston, wrote this narrative for her class members to help them understand one of her important personal insights. To further define her audience, she noted that anyone with military or leadership experience might be interested in her story. Before you jump into the reading, answer these questions:

1. Think about the title. Does it make you want to read on?

2. Read the first and final sentences. What do you think the story will be about?

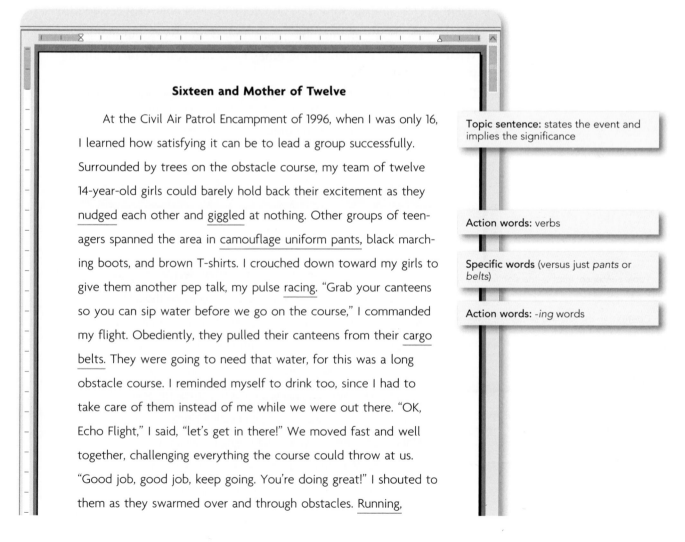

Sixteen and Mother of Twelve

At the Civil Air Patrol Encampment of 1996, when I was only 16, I learned how satisfying it can be to lead a group successfully. Surrounded by trees on the obstacle course, my team of twelve 14-year-old girls could barely hold back their excitement as they nudged each other and giggled at nothing. Other groups of teenagers spanned the area in camouflage uniform pants, black marching boots, and brown T-shirts. I crouched down toward my girls to give them another pep talk, my pulse racing. "Grab your canteens so you can sip water before we go on the course," I commanded my flight. Obediently, they pulled their canteens from their cargo belts. They were going to need that water, for this was a long obstacle course. I reminded myself to drink too, since I had to take care of them instead of me while we were out there. "OK, Echo Flight," I said, "let's get in there!" We moved fast and well together, challenging everything the course could throw at us. "Good job, good job, keep going. You're doing great!" I shouted to them as they swarmed over and through obstacles. Running,

Topic sentence: states the event and implies the significance

Action words: verbs

Specific words (versus just *pants* or *belts*)

Action words: -*ing* words

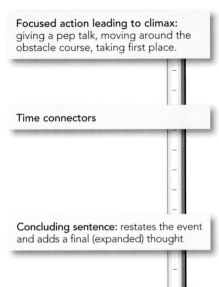

Focused action leading to climax: giving a pep talk, moving around the obstacle course, taking first place.

Time connectors

Concluding sentence: restates the event and adds a final (expanded) thought

climbing wooden walls, crossing rope bridges, and playing Tarzan on a rope swing—my girls tore through that course. Our faces were sweaty and streaked with mud, but we were soon ahead of the other teams, feeling so good that we even started cheering them on. Before we knew it, we had finished the course and taken first place. Echo Flight went on to prove itself time after time in the next few days, finally being awarded Honor Flight of the Encampment. Working hard together, we had achieved our goal, and I had learned that leadership is not about shouting orders or acting tough; it's all about setting an example for others to follow.

—*Leilani Houston*

➤ *Prereading Exploration for "What a Joke!"*

Anna Suarez wrote this story primarily to amuse her classmates and family members. Before reading the paragraph, read the first and final sentences, which tell the essence of the story. Next, think back on your life and answer these questions:

1. Can you recall any memorable prank that didn't work out as planned?

2. What were your feelings at the time? How did you interact with the people involved?

3. Did the misadventure cause you to change your behavior or attitude toward practical jokes as Anna hints that her event did?

4. Summarize the prank that misfired and your reaction to it.

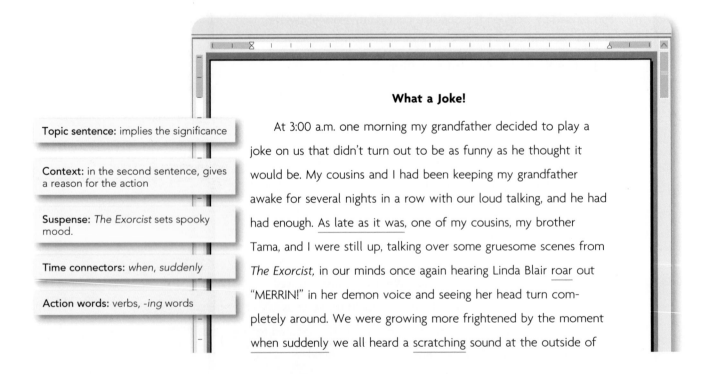

Topic sentence: implies the significance

Context: in the second sentence, gives a reason for the action

Suspense: *The Exorcist* sets spooky mood.

Time connectors: *when, suddenly*

Action words: verbs, *-ing* words

What a Joke!

At 3:00 a.m. one morning my grandfather decided to play a joke on us that didn't turn out to be as funny as he thought it would be. My cousins and I had been keeping my grandfather awake for several nights in a row with our loud talking, and he had had enough. As late as it was, one of my cousins, my brother Tama, and I were still up, talking over some gruesome scenes from *The Exorcist*, in our minds once again hearing Linda Blair roar out "MERRIN!" in her demon voice and seeing her head turn completely around. We were growing more frightened by the moment when suddenly we all heard a scratching sound at the outside of the door and an awful noise that sounded like someone groaning in pain: "Ooohhh-aaaghh!" Inside the room we stared hard at each other, searching for an answer to the frightening noises. "What is it?" my cousin whispered. And then Tama said, "Anna, go find out." "No way," I said. "We all go or no one." Finally, we got the courage to walk to the door, hearing the sounds grow louder as we approached. I was thinking, "Oh my God, I am not dreaming. It is real!" When I finally opened the door, I was shocked to see grandfather. My so-serious, blind grandfather, who never got up at night—this was how he would pay us back for our noise. Toothless, his hair ruffled from sleep, and wearing loose white pajamas, he was standing in front of me, leaning forward to scratch on the door again and continue his joke. Only not being able to see that I had opened the door, he fell forward onto the floor, and I lost my balance as I tried to catch him, falling too. For some reason I decided that he must be having a heart attack and needed help. My brother, who obviously thought something similar, screamed, "Mom, grandpa is dead!" Suddenly, the whole house was up—my aunt and uncle, two sisters, mom and dad—everyone crowding into the hall asking, "What happened? Who's hurt? Is grandfather all right?" I lay on the floor, paralyzed, and grandfather couldn't talk, not because he was hurt, but because he was laughing so hard. The more he laughed, the more we thought he was having some kind of seizure. Dad ended up calling an ambulance before grandfather calmed down enough to say what had happened, to assure everyone that he was really all right, and to apologize for the disturbance. I still think back on this joke that backfired whenever I'm tempted to try one of my own pranks, remembering what kind of disaster can follow a little "harmless fun."

—*Anna Suarez*

Direct dialogue: increases suspense

Revealed thought: builds suspense

Specific words: versus just *pajamas*

Direct dialogue: adds humor

Concluding sentence: includes expanded thought

POSTREADING QUESTIONS FOR PARAGRAPH ANALYSIS: NARRATION

Note: These questions apply to either student model.

1. In the topic sentence, what words name the event, and what words make a limiting statement about it?

2. What words in the concluding sentence link to the topic sentence?

3. What is the expanded thought (p. 50) in the final sentence? Does it end the story smoothly, or does the point seem "tacked on"?

4. Create an action outline of the characters' major movements from place to place, beginning each phrase with an *-ing* word. Limit the outline to eight actions. (For action outlines, see Activity 6.1.)

5. How much time does the story cover?

6. What details about the setting has the writer provided?

7. List any sensory details that you can find. Does this narrative have more or fewer details than you found in the descriptive models in Chapter 5?

8. Name three specific words, and list a more general word for each.

9. Name three active verbs and three *-ing* words the author uses to show characters in motion.

10. Find two instances of showing and two of telling. How does the showing make the story interesting?

11. How does the dialogue (pp. 112–113) add to the story? What does it show about the narrator and the other characters?

12. List at least three time and three space transitions (p. 123). How do the time transitions help readers move through the story?

13. What is your favorite image in this story? Why do you like it?

For more on specific language, see pp. 75–76.

For more on active verbs, see Chapter 24.

WRITING A NARRATIVE PARAGRAPH

Summarizing the Assignment

Building on the descriptive skills you practiced in Chapter 5, create a short narrative of 250 to 300 words that tells the story of a significant event in your life. Your story should include a topic sentence that draws readers in, actions arranged chronologically (by time order) that involve you and another person(s), and a final sentence that refers to the story's point and adds a final, expanded thought. Describe the setting well enough to help your readers follow the events and learn about the characters, but concentrate on narration, or telling and showing what the people are doing, feeling, and thinking. Whereas the dominant impression helped you focus your descriptive paper, the significance will help you focus your narrative. Remember, the story must have a point. How has the event affected your view of yourself? What does the event say about the larger world or your relation to it?

Establishing Audience and Purpose

For more on audience, see Chapter 1.

Choose an audience for this paper, a person or group you think might be interested in your story. You might tell a story that involves family members and so could be meaningful to them. Perhaps you want to relive some special moment with a good friend and think that she would also enjoy the tale. Often, your audience will be people who can identify with your experience because they have lived through something similar. For example, while many people might be interested in and sympathize with the author of "Do unto Others . . ." (pp. 126–131), mothers with several young children might best identify with the story.

You can also get a sense of who your audience is by thinking about what they read. Would your story interest someone who subscribes to *National Geographic* or *Car and Driver*? Your audience should affect the content of your story, the actions you include, your explanations, and your word choices. Your composition instructor is always at least a secondary audience, so also write to show him or her that you are learning narrative strategies.

Your overall purpose may be to inform, persuade, or entertain, but the significance of the story should be clear.

Working through the Writing Assignment

Discovering Ideas

Begin your prewriting by identifying several topics you feel strongly about that involve conflict (person with person, person within him- or herself, person with some external force). The following topics list may help you choose.

> ### POSSIBLE TOPICS: **NARRATION**
>
> - A situation that made you feel good (or bad) about yourself: helping someone, reacting quickly in an emergency, completing a big project
> - A special experience in a group: sports team, band, club, Boy Scouts/Girl Scouts, fraternal organizations (Kiwanis, Rotary, Elks), military, PTA
> - An embarrassing moment: speaking in public, asking for a date, not having money at a restaurant when the bill comes, being caught in a lie
> - A "first" experience: infatuation, love, fight, "A," honor roll, speeding ticket
> - An experience with altering your appearance: tattoo, body piercing, hair coloring, cosmetic surgery, weight loss, bodybuilding
> - An event that made you see yourself or someone else in a new light: realizing that a friend is a bigot, understanding why someone dislikes you, losing respect for a hero, discovering an unlooked-for quality in a person
> - An event that you especially looked forward to: concert, symphony, trade show, sporting event, fashion show, art exhibit, mall opening
> - A time when you experienced great pain: childbirth, broken bone, burn, kidney stone, migraine headache, dislocated shoulder, muscle spasm, heart attack
> - A childhood prank: throwing snowballs at a car, soaping windows, throwing firecrackers, calling strangers on the phone, frightening a friend
> - A moment of triumph: acing the exam, achieving a high GPA, graduating
> - A particularly pleasant (or unpleasant) experience on the job: raise, promotion, decrease in workload, more authority, departure of disliked boss or co-worker, increase in vacation time

For additional narration topics, see Chapter 6 at www. mhhe.com/brannan.

NARRATING A STORY

Recall a conversation you've had or overheard—one with some element of conflict—about conservation, the environment, or the natural world. It might be an argument with a friend about whether camping is fun or awful, a lively class discussion about global climate change, or a disagreement with roommates about recycling. Tell the story of this exchange, using the dialogue to show a relationship between the people you are writing about. What is your story's central point? ●

Brainstorm with others to discover ideas.

If you still have no idea for a story after reading through this list and the additional topics on the book's website, read the student models and the paragraph models in the "Developing Skills" section. Think back over your life. Have you ever been particularly depressed or happy? Have you made any major life changes: moving from one school, city, or country to another; becoming part of a new group; switching careers? If ideas are not coming, talk to others about stories they could tell, or choose a topic from the list and begin one of the prewriting methods listed in Chapter 1.

ACTIVITY 6.6 | WORKING ONLINE: *Use the Narration Writing Tutor*

For additional topic ideas for this assignment, look under Chapter 6 at www.mhhe.com/brannan. And for more narrative writing strategies, download the Narration Writing Tutor.

Prewriting

Asking the journalist's questions is an excellent way to generate ideas for a narrative paper. Here is an example with an event from the topics list: a childhood prank.

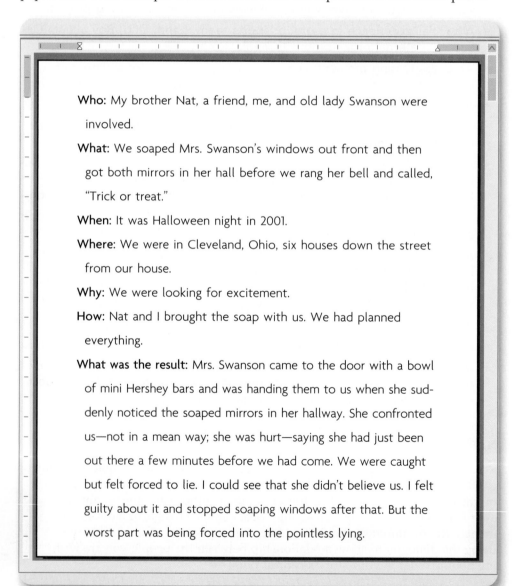

Who: My brother Nat, a friend, me, and old lady Swanson were involved.

What: We soaped Mrs. Swanson's windows out front and then got both mirrors in her hall before we rang her bell and called, "Trick or treat."

When: It was Halloween night in 2001.

Where: We were in Cleveland, Ohio, six houses down the street from our house.

Why: We were looking for excitement.

How: Nat and I brought the soap with us. We had planned everything.

What was the result: Mrs. Swanson came to the door with a bowl of mini Hershey bars and was handing them to us when she suddenly noticed the soaped mirrors in her hallway. She confronted us—not in a mean way; she was hurt—saying she had just been out there a few minutes before we had come. We were caught but felt forced to lie. I could see that she didn't believe us. I felt guilty about it and stopped soaping windows after that. But the worst part was being forced into the pointless lying.

Try several topics before you commit to one.

When using a prewriting technique like this one, you may have better luck writing a little about several topics rather than a lot about your first choice. After you have decided on one event, you can extend your prewriting by asking more specific questions. For example, what were the boys' and Mrs. Swanson's ages? Further details could help set the mood (a cold, rainy evening) and sharpen the setting (details of the hall). If one prewriting method doesn't work, switch to another.

To further focus your prewriting, think about one aspect of your story at a time, setting aside half a page for each and listing memories as they surface. Try gathering material on the following important story elements:

- **Setting:** In narrative, the setting or scene is merely a backdrop against which characters move, so you will seldom go into great detail. However, some details are needed to show the characters in relation to one another and to help set the mood. For example, consider how the darkness and silence of the house in "What a Joke!" (pp. 116–117) add to the children's feelings of fright. Jot down details about physical objects (car, chair, tree) as you recall them, including their size and location, color, sound, and smell. You won't use them all, but it is good to have them to draw on.

- **People:** You and perhaps one other person are important enough to describe in any detail in your event paper. You need to provide only a brief sketch (approximate age, overall physical look, maybe hair or eye color, some article of clothing). Then you can focus on the action and your thoughts and feelings.

- **Dialogue:** While not all narratives include spoken dialogue, most do. Dialogue is a powerful device for showing what people feel and think. You can use it to vary your narrator's voice and to provide information that adds to the story. Try to write down dialogue as accurately as you can.

- **Action:** Without action, narrative dies. The action does not have to be dramatic or violent, though. Remember that mental and emotional action can be compelling as well. However, as you gather ideas, try to recall physical movement. How did you cross the room? Where did the other person sit? Did you lean back on one arm, slouch in your chair, or slice the air with your hand as you emphatically said "No!"?

- **Thoughts and feelings:** As you reflect on the event, try to recall what you thought and felt immediately before, during, and after the action. Often, you will capture only a piece of the thought or feeling you had at the time and then elaborate on it based on your current thoughts and feelings.

- **Significance:** In our personal narratives, we need to discover why the memory is important enough to write about. The meaning may not be clear at first or may be limited to one point, but it is important. The following questions will help you discover your meaning:
    - How did my behavior reflect on who I was at the time?
    - How did my behavior affect who I am now?
    - What did the other person's (people's) behavior indicate about her or him (them)?
    - What were the positive or negative effects of the action?
    - What could have resulted?
    - Have I learned anything about myself, another person, or the world from the event?
    - Has the event changed my behavior, thinking, or feeling?

Get reactions from others on your story.

Whether you have finalized your topic or not, now is a good time to hear from others. Talk to people about your event. If they think it can be shaped into an interesting final story, you may feel more confident in moving ahead.

PREWRITING—SUMMING UP

1. Decide on several events or choose several from the topics list.
2. Use a prewriting technique to get an overview of your events.
3. Choose an event and briefly summarize it.
4. Prewrite to generate ideas for the setting, people, action, and significance.
5. Summarize your story for someone else to see the person's reaction.

JOURNAL / BLOG ENTRY 6.2

Review your prewriting notes, particularly the ones that cover significance. Do you feel that your story has a point yet? Does your material reveal something about you? In a brief paragraph, explain the meaning of your narrative.

Try hinting at the significance of your event in the topic sentence. For more on topic sentences, see pp. 38–41.

Organizing Ideas

The following points will help you shape and focus your material before you start your draft. First, write out at least a rough topic sentence. The topic sentence does not have to reveal the outcome of your story, but it should hint at it and give readers a sense of your direction with a limiting statement. It may state the significance outright. In the following topic sentences, from the student models in this chapter, the topics are underlined once and the limiting statements twice.

A. At the Civil Air Patrol Encampment of 1996, when I was only 16, I learned how satisfying it can be to lead a group successfully.

B. At 3:00 a.m. one morning my grandfather decided to play a joke on us that didn't turn out to be as funny as he thought it would be.

Once you have a rough topic sentence, organize your paragraph chronologically (as the clock moves), beginning close to the high point, or climax, of the action and keeping your buildup to the climax short. For example, a one-paragraph story on the birth of a child should begin on the day of the delivery, leaving out the other 9 months.

Here are two ways to manage time problems in one-paragraph narratives:

Limit the amount of time or number of scenes in your narrative.

1. Limit the time of the event. Many terrific short narratives cover only a few minutes, as do the student models in this chapter. If you try to cover more than a few minutes, be sure to summarize, using time transitions like *the next morning, when we got there,* and *by 8:00.*
2. Stick with one or two scenes in which all the action occurs. For example, in the student model "What a Joke!" the story is set entirely in Anna's room.

Remember to use strong connectors (pp. 54–56). between sentences, as in this shortened list of time and space transitions.

FOR LOCATING OR MOVING IN SPACE

above	east (west, etc.)	in between	over
against	elsewhere	in the distance	surrounded by
alongside	far off (away)	into	there
around	farther on	near	through

FOR MOVING IN TIME

after	first (second, etc.)	next	suddenly
afterward	immediately	now	then
at last	in the meantime	often	time passed
awhile	in the past	once	until
All references to calendar time and events: one day, days ago, tonight, afternoon			
All references to clock time: a few minutes, 12:00 a.m., 3 hours			
All references to regular meals: during breakfast, lunch, dinner			

ORGANIZING—SUMMING UP

1. Write out a rough topic sentence that hints at the outcome or significance of your event.

2. Limit the time span of the story and the number of scenes in it.

3. Cut any unneeded lead-in to the main part of your story.

4. Arrange your narrative material chronologically using an action outline (see p. 108).

5. Review the list of transitions—especially time and space transitions—above and the other connectors on pages 54–56.

Watch out for homonyms—such as "there," "their," and "they're" or "through" and "threw"—or easily confused words, such as "then" and "than."

JOURNAL / BLOG ENTRY 6.3

To help focus your draft, try an action outline that lists the major actions of your event. For a sample action outline, see page 108.

Drafting

With the preliminary work done, you are almost ready to draft. But before plunging in, review the drafting suggestions in Chapter 1. Also keep the following suggestions in mind:

1. Visualize the setting. Close your eyes and try to envision the setting of your story. If the narrative occurs inside, what does the room look like? What kind of furniture is there? How is it arranged? Is it day or night? Warm or cold? Summer or winter? Sometimes it helps to establish a larger frame for the picture before moving in to capture the details. Imagine that you are hovering in a helicopter filming from a hundred feet above the scene. What do you see?

2. Use your "creative memory." Few people can remember everything they want to put into a story. Feel free to fill in the blank spaces of your memory with details and dialogue that could have happened.

3. Summarize action to move readers quickly through your story.

4. Describe a scene in detail when you want the reader to slow down and pay attention, especially when you are close to the climax of your story.

JOURNAL / BLOG ENTRY 6.4

After you have written your first draft, reread it and note the climax. Is it near the end of your story, and do you then wrap up the paragraph within a sentence or two? Explain how the action in your story logically leads up to this climax.

FEEDBACK *Comment on the climax in a classmate's story. Does the climax grow logically from the action, and are setting details clear?*

Revising Drafts

First-Stage Drafts

At this stage, you should focus on content (main story elements: action, climax, resolution, setting, thoughts, and feelings) and organization (arranging and connecting ideas).

Move straight from your topic sentence into the action. For more on topic sentences, see the models in this chapter and pp. 38–41.

1. **Has your narrative paragraph grown too long?** Once you get rolling, it is easy to include interesting side details that nonetheless distract readers and weaken your main point. So find the center of your tale—the high point of the action and its meaning—and then cut whatever doesn't get readers there quickly. Use only a sentence or two to set up a context for the action, and move immediately from the climax to the concluding sentence (or two). Also, limit the time span the narrative covers—a few minutes to a few hours works well for a paragraph.

2. **Is your topic sentence effective?** Sometimes, it is effective to begin a personal narrative with an action sentence like the following: "After finishing a lunch of greasy fries and burgers, I dashed through the parking lot toward room 130." However, this sort of beginning does not give readers (or you) a clear sense of the paper's direction. To focus your brief story, it is usually best to begin with a topic sentence that hints at the climax or states the meaning of the event.

Conflict and movement are crucial to your story.

3. **Does the story have conflict, suspense, climax, and resolution (pp. 107–108)?** For your narrative to work, it must have conflict: person versus person, person versus the external world (forces of nature, animals, machines), or person versus him- or herself (an internal struggle). For the story to have suspense, it must keep readers wondering what will happen next. If the action is well organized, it will move chronologically to a climax, where the action stops. As you reflect on the action in the final sentence (or two), you can create a resolution for the story by highlighting a significant point or meaning.

4. **Have you sketched the setting sufficiently?** In narrative, readers need only a few well-chosen details to visualize a setting—just a sketch will usually do. Remember to use specific words (*Mustang* vs. *car*) and sensory details (sight, sound, touch, smell, taste).

5. **Have you described people sufficiently?** Although narrative emphasizes people's actions, thoughts, and emotions, you should provide some physical details about the main characters. In "What a Joke!" (pp. 116–117),

notice how the brief description of the grandfather adds interest to the tale. You might show how your main characters move—what gestures they make, and how they walk, sit, or stand.

6. **Have you included effective dialogue (pp. 112–113)?** Because dialogue is a powerful device for showing people's thoughts and emotions, it is used frequently in stories. You may not need dialogue in your story, depending on the topic (see the student model "Death Strikes" on pp. 52–53), but your story probably will benefit from it. Check to make sure the dialogue sounds convincing.

7. **Have you revealed your thoughts and feelings?** Narratives become slow and boring when writers "tell" too much of the story rather than showing the action. However, when writers tell about their thoughts and feelings and then show them, stories become more interesting.

8. **Is the significance of the event clear?** Your event may have several meanings to you, but you should focus on one, sharing that insight with your audience. A clear point adds substance to your story and helps readers connect with you, the author.

9. **Is the concluding sentence effective (pp. 49–53)?** Your final sentence should contain a connector (transitional word or repeated word) and clearly indicate the significance of the event. But don't conclude with a cliché or worn expression.

10. **Are sentences within the paragraph well connected?** First drafts of narratives usually need more time and space connectors, especially time transitions. Sentences can also be more strongly linked using synonyms, repeated words, and pronouns. Also, remember that time transitions such as "in the meantime" or "a few moments later" can speed up the pace of the story.

Summarizing actions can link scenes and speed up the pace of the story.

JOURNAL / BLOG ENTRY 6.5

To help you focus on the revision process and alert your instructor to your progress, list three *specific* changes you have made or feel you ought to make in going from your first to second draft. Refer to the first-stage draft questions, answering specifically. Next, in several sentences, state what you like best about your story.

FEEDBACK *Respond to a classmate's story, telling him or her what the strongest feature of the draft is, and then suggest one change.*

Second and Final Drafts
For advice on revising and then editing further drafts of your work, turn to Chapter 4.

Annotated Student Model: "Do unto Others . . ."

To help with your narrative, read through the Annotated Student Model that follows. In examining Chris Potts's drafts, you can profit from her hard work and head off some of the problems that are likely to creep into your own drafts.

As you read, keep in mind that revision seldom occurs in tidy stages. Sometimes, for example, you will edit early in the process of writing a draft and change content later. However, the following draft stages will help focus your revision efforts.

First-Stage Draft

First drafts are for getting words on paper, so, naturally, there will be plenty to change. While many narratives initially leave out important parts of the story, other first drafts include too much. Notice in this first draft how much of the lead-in was not needed.

Total words = 538 (need to focus)

"Come on, Joelle, we need to hurry up," I said, trying to motivate my three-year-old girl toward the car. "Coming, mommy, I gotta get my babies!" Oh, no, I thought, this could take forever, and I don't have forever. I had to get to the bank to pick up some papers for the house. Jordan, her nineteen-month-old sister, looked on, playing with her "babies." She was not getting ready to move any faster than her big sister. "Listen, sweetie, we are in a hurry, like a race. Ready. Set. Go!" Neither of my girls were cooperating today, so I scooped them both up and headed for the garage. After wrestling the girls into their car seats, I slowly backed down the driveway. It was getting more difficult each day to maneuver the car with my ever-increasing midsection—the girls' little brother, 4 weeks till delivery—getting in the way. But we made it into the street and were on our way to the bank. What I hadn't counted on was taking a turn too hard. I flattened a tire. I didn't know what to do since there was no one around to help me, and I couldn't do the job anymore myself. Panic and frustration are a sure-fire recipe for tears, but I tried to stay calm and composed so my girls wouldn't catch my mood. Suddenly, I heard a voice. "Listen I have a cell phone. Do you want to call someone to come pick you up?" As I turned toward the voice, I saw an older guy who looked a lot like my dad. I explained to him that everyone who could help was out of reach and I wasn't sure what I was going to do. As I spoke, I had no control over the tears. "Are you sure you've thought through all your options?" he asked. "How about Triple-A? Do you have any other family or friends who could help?" I just shook my head. "Well, then," he said as he rolled up his sleeves I still no how to fix a flat. If you don't mind me taking a run at it? Show me where the jack and spare are, and I'll see what I can do. "Why don't you wait inside the bank while I put the spare on?" I nodded yes, and opened the door to get the keys. Then I unbuckled the girls and ushered them out of the car. As Joelle jumped out, she called the man "Papa," thinking he might be my dad, but she wasn't sure about it. To really confuse her, the man, said, "Hi, Peanut," which is the name my dad calls her. The girls and I went into the bank, retrieved our papers, and headed to check on the man's progress. "Well, you're back in buisness," he said. "It's just a spare tire. You shouldn't go over 45 miles per hour with it." As he spoke, I offered the cash envelop to him. Then I attempted to utter a profound thank-you. Gratefulness was still caught in my throat, and I was crying again. He said that he didn't want the money in the envelop and added, "You don't have to that, but I will ask you to do a favor for me. The next time you see who needs help, stop and help them." I said "I will" and a few "thank-yous" and we headed our seperate ways.

Second-Stage Draft

First drafts of narratives often have unnecessary details, especially in the beginning, and the topic and concluding sentences often need to be revised. If your draft seems too predictable, you may not have developed much suspense yet or shown the conflict clearly. Double-check dialogue for realism and brevity. Finally, look closely at the setting and people. Are all pieces of your scene adequately described to help readers follow the action?

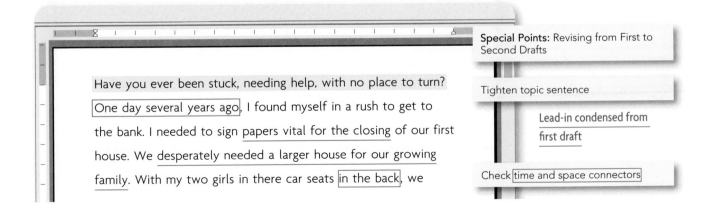

Have you ever been stuck, needing help, with no place to turn? One day several years ago, I found myself in a rush to get to the bank. I needed to sign papers vital for the closing of our first house. We desperately needed a larger house for our growing family. With my two girls in there car seats in the back, we

Special Points: Revising from First to Second Drafts

Tighten topic sentence

Lead-in condensed from first draft

Check time and space connectors

Add material to increase tension/suspense.	neared the parking lot of the bank. I thought we would make it before the bank closed but I hadn't counted on the accident.
Describe physical actions.	Bang! A nasty metallic sound told me what to expect. As I got out
Added: sound, action, specific details	I could see it, yes, the tire was flat. The rim touched the ground. What was I going to do? I ran through my options quickly. My
Show as well as tell.	husbands plane wouldn't land for another hour and a half. My friend Angie had left town with her family that morning. I knew
Examples added to *show* helpless condition	how to change flat, but, I was pregnant. And then what would I do with my daughters in the back seat? Panic and frustration are a sure-fire recipe for tears, but I tried to remain calm and composed so my girls wouldn't catch my mood. Suddenly I heard a voice say, "Listen I have a cell phone. Do you want to call some-
Explaining added to *show* emotion	one to come pick you up?" As I turned toward the voice. I saw an older guy, who looked a lot like my dad. I explained to him that everyone who could help was out of reach and I wasn't
Delete unnecessary material.	sure what I was going to do. As I spoke, I started crying.* "Well, then," he said as he rolled up his sleeves, "why don't you wait
*Unneeded dialogue deleted	inside the bank while I put the spare on. You have a spare, don't you?" I had no words. Gratefulness had swallowed panic and frustration but had gotten caught in my throat as I simply nod- ded yes. The girls and I went into the bank, retrieved our papers,
Specific detail added for clarity	made a cash withdrawal, and headed back outside. The man had just shut the trunk, and was rolling down his sleeves. "You're
Action added	back in buisness," he said with a smile." As he spoke, I offered him the cash envelop. Then I attempted to utter a profound thank-you. Gratefulness was still caught in my throat, and I was crying again. He said that he didn't want the money in the
Conclusion revised to reinforce significance	envelope and added, "You don't have to that, but I will ask you to do a favor for me. The next time you see who needs help, stop and help them." I said, "I will" and a few "thank- yous," and we headed our seperate ways. Later, after I had
Tighten concluding sentence.	returned the favor I understood why he hadn't excepted the money I had offered. *No reward could be as satisfying as the*
Expanded thought added	*good deed itself.*

Third-Stage Draft

By this point, Chris has her draft in good shape. The content is mostly in place, and the organization is effective. Topic and concluding sentences work well, and time and space connectors firmly anchor her reader in the story. Now she will deal with sentence- and word-level problems to polish the draft.

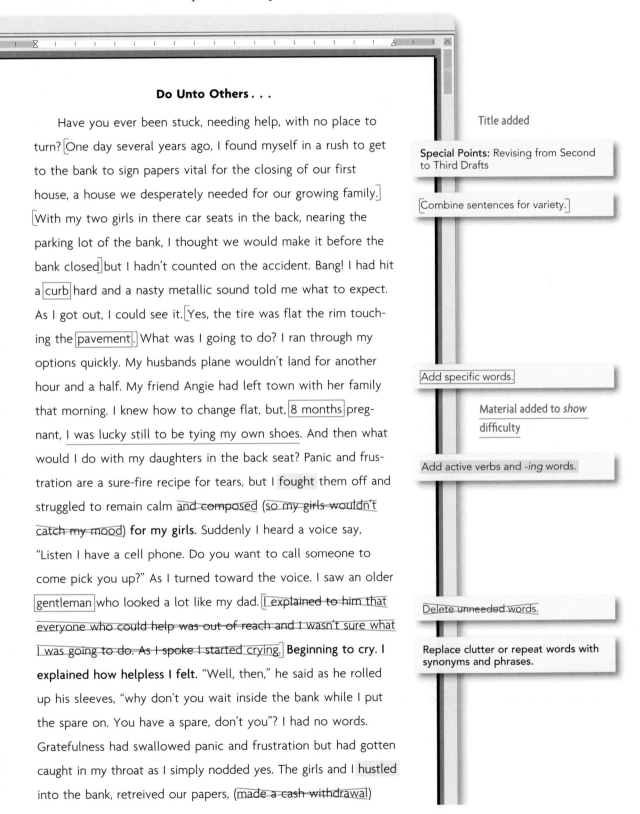

Do Unto Others . . .

Have you ever been stuck, needing help, with no place to turn? One day several years ago, I found myself in a rush to get to the bank to sign papers vital for the closing of our first house, a house we desperately needed for our growing family. With my two girls in there car seats in the back, nearing the parking lot of the bank, I thought we would make it before the bank closed but I hadn't counted on the accident. Bang! I had hit a curb hard and a nasty metallic sound told me what to expect. As I got out, I could see it. Yes, the tire was flat the rim touching the pavement. What was I going to do? I ran through my options quickly. My husbands plane wouldn't land for another hour and a half. My friend Angie had left town with her family that morning. I knew how to change flat, but, 8 months pregnant, I was lucky still to be tying my own shoes. And then what would I do with my daughters in the back seat? Panic and frustration are a sure-fire recipe for tears, but I fought them off and struggled to remain calm and composed (so my girls wouldn't catch my mood) **for my girls.** Suddenly I heard a voice say, "Listen I have a cell phone. Do you want to call someone to come pick you up?" As I turned toward the voice. I saw an older gentleman who looked a lot like my dad. I explained to him that everyone who could help was out of reach and I wasn't sure what I was going to do. As I spoke I started crying. **Beginning to cry. I explained how helpless I felt.** "Well, then," he said as he rolled up his sleeves, "why don't you wait inside the bank while I put the spare on. You have a spare, don't you"? I had no words. Gratefulness had swallowed panic and frustration but had gotten caught in my throat as I simply nodded yes. The girls and I hustled into the bank, retrieved our papers, (made a cash withdrawal)

Title added

Special Points: Revising from Second to Third Drafts

Combine sentences for variety.

Add specific words.

Material added to *show* difficulty

Add active verbs and *-ing* words.

Delete unneeded words.

Replace clutter or repeat words with synonyms and phrases.

withdrew cash, and headed back outside. Our good samaritan had just shut the trunk, and was rolling down his sleeves. "You're back in business," he said with a smile." As he spoke, I offered him the cash envelop, and attempted to utter a profound thank-you, but gratefulness was still caught in my throat, and the tears were in full force again. He (~~said he didn't want the money in the envelope~~) **declined** the envelope **saying** "You don't have to that, but I will ask you to do a favor for me. The next time you see who needs help, stop and help them." I squeaked out an "I will" and a few "thank-yous," and we headed our seperate ways. Later, after I had returned the favor I understood why he hadn't excepted the money I had offered. No reward could be as satisfying as the good deed itself.

Final-Editing Draft

In this last draft, Chris slows her reading to a crawl, editing closely, word by word, line by line. It is a tedious process, but she knows that she still has many errors to correct.

Special Points: Editing Final Drafts

1. **Misspelling**

2. **Sound-alike word**

3. **Missing word(s)**

4. **Wrong word**

5. **Sentence fragment**

6. **Comma splice/run-on**

7. **Faulty capitalization**

8. **Incorrect apostrophe**

Do Unto Others . . .

Have you ever been stuck, needing help, with no place to turn? One day several years ago, I found myself in a rush to get to the bank to sign papers vital for the closing of our first house, a house we desperately needed for our growing family. With my two girls in ~~there[2]~~ their car seats in the back, nearing the parking lot of the bank, I thought we would make it before the bank closed[9c], but I hadn't counted on the accident. Bang! I had hit a curb hard[9c], and a nasty metallic sound told me what to expect. As I got out, I could see it[6]. Yes, the tire was flat[9b], the rim touching the pavement. What was I going to do? I ran through my options quickly. My ~~husbands[8]~~ husband's plane wouldn't land for another hour and a half. My friend Angie had left town with her family that morning. I knew how to change[3] a flat, but, 8 months pregnant, I was lucky still to be tying my own shoes. And then what would I do with my daughters in the back seat? Panic and frustration are a sure-fire recipe for tears, but I fought them off and struggled to remain calm for my girls. Suddenly, I heard a voice say, "Listen[9a], I have a cell phone. Do you want to call someone to come pick you up?" As I turned toward the voice[5], I saw an older gentleman who looked a lot like my dad. Beginning to cry[5], I explained how helpless I felt. "Well, then," he said as he rolled up his sleeves, "why don't you wait inside the bank while I put the spare on? You have a spare, don't you?" I had no words. Gratefulness had swallowed panic and frustration but had gotten caught in my throat as I simply nodded yes. The girls and I hustled into the bank, ~~retreived[1]~~ retrieved our papers, withdrew cash, and headed back outside. Our ~~good samaritan[7]~~ Good Samaritan had just shut the trunk,[10] and was rolling down his sleeves. "You're back in ~~busyness[1]~~ business," he said with a smile. As he spoke, I offered him the cash ~~envelop[4]~~ envelope[10] and attempted to utter a profound thank-you, but gratefulness was still caught in my throat, and the tears were in full force again. He declined the envelope saying, "You don't have to do[3] that, but I will ask you to do a favor for me. The next time you see someone[3] who needs help, stop and help them." I squeaked out an "I will" and a few "thank-yous," and we headed our ~~seperate[1]~~ separate ways. Later, after I had returned the favor[9b], I understood why he hadn't ~~excepted[2]~~ accepted the money I had offered. No reward could be as satisfying as the good deed itself.

—Chris Potts

9a. Comma(s) needed: Introductory word(s)/ phrase/clause

9b. Comma(s) needed: Nonessential word group(s)

9c. Comma(s) needed: Main clauses with coordinating conjunction

10. Unneeded comma

FINAL-DRAFT CHECKLIST: NARRATION

Before you turn in your final draft for a grade, review this checklist. You may find that, as careful as you think you have been, you have still missed a point or two—or more.

- [ ] 1. Has your narrative paragraph grown into an essay?
- [ ] 2. Is your topic sentence effective?
- [ ] 3. Does the story have conflict, suspense, a climax, and a resolution?

For more detailed coverage of revision, see Chapter 4.

English Review Note

Add to the checklist:
Have you . . .
(a) eliminated digressions, details that do not develop your thesis? (b) been consistent in verb tenses? (c) included appropriate and correct transitions? (d) combined sentences effectively, especially adverbial clauses of time?

HINT

Check to see if you need to include a title page. Double space, leave at least a 1-inch margin, and use a 12-point font.

4. Have you sketched the setting fully?

5. Have you described people sufficiently?

6. Have you included effective dialogue?

7. Have you revealed your thoughts and feelings?

8. Is the significance of the event clear?

9. Is your concluding sentence effective?

10. Are all the sentences within the paragraph well connected?

11. Have you used specific language?

12. Are you using active verbs and *-ing* words to describe action?

13. Would a metaphor or simile strengthen your story?

14. Are your sentences varied in length and beginnings?

15. Have you used synonyms for words that are repeated too often?

16. Have you cut unneeded words?

17. Does the paper have an interesting title? Have you checked its capitalization?

18. Have you prepared the paper according to the format expected by your instructor?

19. Have you edited your work closely (including having at least one other person proofread)? Have you checked your Improvement Chart for pattern errors?

20. Have you looked for the following errors: misspellings, sound-alike words, missing words, wrong words, sentence fragments, comma splices/run-ons, faulty capitalizations, incorrect apostrophes, missing commas, and unnecessary commas?

Alternate Writing Assignments

Here are a few more narrative options that may be of interest. For any of the following assignments, be sure to do the following:

- Create a narrative with conflict and tension.
- Choose a story with clear significance or meaning.
- Build a story that shows as well as tells.
- Use effective dialogue.
- Include metaphors and similes to add clarity and interest.

1. **Interview your parents and ask them to relate a story or two from your early childhood that involves you.** You might help them recall a moment by mentioning several possible topics:

    - How they picked your name
    - How they prepared for your arrival in the home

- What life was like during your first 6 months
- When you first crawled, talked, or walked
- When you made the move from a crib to a bed
- Any other significant developmental moment

Retell one of their stories about you as a narrative with a beginning, middle, and end. Arrange the action chronologically, build suspense, detail a setting, and move toward a climax. The significance of your event could involve a realization you have about your parents or parenting in general. Since you will rely on your parents' memories for details, ask plenty of questions and take careful notes.

2. **Role-play someone you have recently disagreed with.** This person could be close to you (father, mother, child, etc.) or someone you don't know well. The point is to get inside the person's skin and then retell the argument from her or his perspective. As you narrate the event, use lots of dialogue, but don't neglect the setting and a brief lead-in to set up the disagreement. What did it stem from, and how serious is it? Remember that you are the other person, so you can only guess at your actual thoughts/feelings. The significance of the event may be how sympathetic you became to the other person's perspective.

3. **Write an extended joke or retell a humorous story that has a point.** For example, you might recall a time when you used poor judgment and suffered from it. Perhaps the "great deal" you got on a $500 used car turned out not to be so hot. Maybe you took 21 credit hours in one semester and learned how stressful academic life can be. Or your first experience with credit cards might have shown you how much fun 20 percent interest rates can be on a $5,000 balance. Follow narrative conventions, organize using topic and concluding sentences, and be sure to make the significance of the event clear.

4. **Create a fictional story starring you or another character.** Your story should have conflict as well as physical, mental, and emotional movement. The story should be brief—only one or two scenes. Since it must have a point, you might avoid a purely action sequence—guns blazing and cattle stampeding—in favor of one that shows something about who people are and what they are worth.

This is probably the hardest of the six alternate assignments.

5. **Interview a grandparent to learn about some significant event in his or her life.** You might ask him or her to show or send you photographs and time travel together, moving back 40 or 50 years to an era that probably seems like ancient history to you. Memorable events in most people's lives include births, engagements, weddings, illnesses, deaths, relocations, and career changes (see the topics list, p. 119). You could write your retelling of the story in the third person (he said/thought, etc.) or assume the identity of the grandparent and write from that first-person perspective.

6. TV and movie writers use storyboards like the one on the following page to map out scenes. **Using any of the previous five assignments, storyboard the paragraph before you write it;** this is a creative kind of prewriting that visual learners in particular can benefit from. Include your storyboard with your final draft.

ACTIVITY 6.7 WORKING ONLINE: *Sharing Stories*

Read stories from students across the country at College Stories—www.collegestories.com—and contribute your own. You can even search by school and read what people at your college are writing about.

Determining the Value of Narration

Getting better at telling stories can help you in many ways. For example, on the job, you might have to defend yourself by narrating a conflict you had with a customer or fellow employee. In school, you might be called on to narrate events in your classes. For instance, in political science, you might be asked to tell the story of the 2008 presidential campaign; in sociology, you might need to illustrate with personal examples a discussion of violence in movies and its effects on teens; and in composition, you might recount an event that helped you see yourself in a different light.

Improving your narrative skills will also enrich your personal life. Knowing more about storytelling can increase your enjoyment of stories and films. Telling your stories in class will help you speak more comfortably in front of people. And as you work through the process of remembering an event, you will reflect on your behavior and the behavior of others, thinking about the meaning of your story and how the events helped make you who you are.

Chapter Summary

1. A narrative tells about events and usually involves people. Narratives have many forms, but when we tell a story, we are usually talking about "someone doing something somewhere for some reason."

2. Narratives involve conflict and suspense: a chronological arranging of actions leading to a high point and having a point.

3. The setting serves as a backdrop for the action.

4. Narratives reveal characters' thoughts and feelings and usually use dialogue.

5. Well-organized narrative paragraphs require topic and concluding sentences. Time and space connectors are essential.

6. Both showing and telling are used to develop stories. Of the two, showing requires the most energy from the writer but has the most power.

7. Specific words and sensory details help build memorable scenes.

8. Figures of speech like metaphors and similes add clarity and color to narratives.

9. Like any writing, a narrative is not complete until it has been revised and carefully edited.

Illustrating through Examples

7

[*What is it about amusement parks that appeals to people in general? What activities appeal to you specifically?*]

KEY TOPICS

- Developing skills and exploring ideas in illustration paragraphs

  - Organizing examples through subtopic sentences

  - Arranging examples by order of importance

  - Linking sentences

  - Developing examples

- Analyzing student models: Illustration paragraphs

- Writing an illustration paragraph

What Are We Trying to Achieve and Why?

Setting the Stage

Suppose a friend asks you what you like best about a local theme park. If you say "the rides" or, more specifically, "wooden roller coasters, like the Timber Wolf," you have given an example. Whenever we make a statement and then follow it with an example to show our meaning, we are illustrating a point. Examples are the building blocks of all writing.

In this chapter, we will build on the narrative/descriptive skills you developed in Chapters 5 and 6, using specific word choices, sensory details, comparisons, and well-connected sentences. And we will go one step further. Instead of focusing on a single place or story, we will work with *several* examples, each introduced by a **subtopic sentence.** In addition to personal examples, we will use our general knowledge of the world and close observation to create a slightly more formal tone.

Linking to Previous Experience

If you worked through Chapters 5 and 6, you have already used examples to express a dominant impression and an event's significance. Also, our own lives are full of examples. When we try to clarify a statement for another person, we usually do so with an example. You might say, "I can't stand my job," and a friend responds, "Why?" If you answer by mentioning that you are often asked to work late, are not paid overtime, and have to work for a lazy boss, you have given specific examples. If you discuss bad jobs in general, you might leave your personal experience out, instead citing typical examples: a rotten boss, low pay, long hours, unpleasant coworkers, and poor work environment. We often give examples to explain ourselves or defend a position, based on what we have read or heard.

As we develop examples in Chapter 7, we will learn to communicate more effectively and to clarify our own thinking.

JOURNAL / BLOG ENTRY 7.1

Think about an occasion in the recent past when you used examples to explain, defend a position, or entertain. Summarize the situation in a sentence or two. Was one example sufficient to achieve your purpose, or were more needed? How much detail did you give? Did you re-create part of a scene using specific language, sensory detail, dialogue, and so on, or did you explain at length, perhaps using comparisons?

FEEDBACK *Read a classmate's entry and tell him or her one example you find especially useful or interesting; explain why it is an effective illustration of the author's point.*

Developing Skills and Exploring Ideas in Illustration Paragraphs

To learn how to use examples effectively, we will practice the following:

1. Using subtopic sentences to introduce each major example
2. Arranging major examples by order of importance
3. Linking all sentences, especially subtopics, with connecting words
4. Developing examples with specific words, details, and explanations

Organizing Examples through Subtopic Sentences

As we have seen, most paragraphs should begin with a topic sentence that tells what the paragraph will be about. When writers develop a paragraph with several major examples, they often use **subtopic** or minor topic sentences, in addition to the topic sentence, to tell what each major example will be about. Each subtopic sentence should begin with a connector word or phrase (shaded in the following examples), state the example (underlined once), and then make a limiting statement about it (underlined twice).

TOPIC SENTENCE   I will never know how I survived my adolescent years.

The topic sentence predicts a paragraph about the writer's dangerous youth.

FIRST SUBTOPIC SENTENCE   Although I was never more than bruised while doing it, jumping onto the tops of boxcars from a low bridge was one of my earliest dangerous stunts.

The first subtopic sentence gives the first major example of a dangerous act: jumping onto boxcars. This sentence would be followed by several more sentences giving details (sights, sounds, smells, etc.) that show what jumping onto boxcars was like.

SECOND SUBTOPIC SENTENCE   More dangerous (and stupider) than train jumping was my 16-year-old's effort at flying a '69 convertible Firebird from an off-ramp.

The second subtopic sentence gives the second major example: "flying" a Firebird. More details would follow to develop the scene: an explanation of how the driver lost control, sensory details, thoughts, and feelings.

THIRD SUBTOPIC SENTENCE   However, the closest I came to death was when I was just 13 and thought the ice on Granite Lake would support me.

The third subtopic sentence gives the third major example: walking on weak ice. More details would follow: the action of walking onto the ice, the sound of ice cracking, and the feeling of being immersed in freezing water.

Many paragraphs focus on only one main example and therefore do not need subtopic sentences.

ACTIVITY 7.1 *Subtopic Sentences*

For the topic sentences that follow, decide on three major examples that could illustrate a paragraph about them; then complete each of the subtopic sentences.

EXAMPLE: Topic sentence: To be a good parent, a person must either be born with or develop several essential personality traits.

Subtopic sentence 1: *The first trait a parent should have is a love of play.*

Subtopic sentence 2: *Another important quality is a vivid imagination.*

Subtopic sentence 3: *However, the most necessary quality for a parent is patience.*

1. Topic sentence: When people lose control of their anger, there are often severe consequences.

   Subtopic sentence 1: One negative effect is _____

   Subtopic sentence 2: Angry people will also _____

   Subtopic sentence 3: The worst result of losing control is _____

   _____

2. Topic sentence: Some people love fall, with the trees glowing brilliant red, orange, and gold, but it is my least favorite season.

   Subtopic sentence 1: Autumn depresses me because _____

   _____

   Subtopic sentence 2: Another reason I don't like fall is _____

   _____

   Subtopic sentence 3: The main reason I dislike this season, though, is that

   _____

Arranging Examples by Order of Importance

The examples in illustration paragraphs may be arranged in several ways: spatially, chronologically, and by order of importance. Of these, the last method works particularly well for emphasizing one example. When ordering by importance—beginning with the least interesting or dramatic example and progressing to the most—you tell readers what to pay special attention to and leave them thinking about your strongest point. Notice how the last subtopic sentence in the example on page 138 signals its importance:

> However, the closest I came to death was when I was just 13 and thought the ice on Granite Lake would support me.

When you think about how to arrange your examples, sometimes the order of importance is obvious, but sometimes it is not. Often, the writer needs to determine whether, for instance, a house burning down is more or less significant than the death of a much-loved pet.

For more on organizing examples, see pp. 152–153.

ACTIVITY 7.2 *Arranging Examples by Order of Importance*

The following sets of examples are ordered randomly. Rearrange them by putting a number in the spaces provided, beginning with what you feel is the least important or dramatic example (1) and progressing to the most (5).

1. Alexander's vacation was a disaster.

   _____ The prices at Disney World were outrageous.

   _____ One of his suitcases was stolen.

   _____ He was mugged in the parking lot.

   _____ The weather was mostly gloomy.

   _____ People were rude at his hotel.

2. Some people invite accidents when they drive.

    _____ They drive drunk.

    _____ They change lanes without signaling.

    _____ They drive too fast in bad weather.

    _____ They race along residential streets with children nearby.

    _____ They slow down to a crawl on the highway to gawk at accidents.

3. Jobs within a restaurant can be ranked according to status.

    _____ Dishwasher

    _____ Manager

    _____ General manager

    _____ Owner

    _____ Wait person

4. The Internet is not an unqualified blessing.

    _____ Some people become Internet addicts, losing the other parts of their lives.

    _____ It allows advertisers into the house in yet another way.

    _____ E-mail and online social networking eat up time.

    _____ Much online information is questionable.

    _____ The Internet gives children access to pornography.

HINT

For more on linking sentences, see Chapter 3.

Linking Sentences

As we saw in Chapter 3, linking sentences within and between paragraphs helps readers follow our ideas more easily. We can make these connections in five ways: transitions, repetition, synonyms, pronouns, and reference to a main idea.

Notice the shaded transitions in the following example. The author has indicated order of importance by using several transitional words ("more" and "closest") and has referred back to boxcar jumping with a repeat word ("jumping") and a synonym ("train"). Also note the reference in each subtopic sentence to danger.

TOPIC SENTENCE	How I survived my adolescent years, I will never know.
SUBTOPIC SENTENCE 1	Although I was never more than bruised at it, jumping onto the top of boxcars from a low bridge was one of my earliest dangerous stunts.
SUBTOPIC SENTENCE 2	More dangerous (and stupider) than train jumping was my 16-year-old's effort at flying a '69 convertible Firebird from an off-ramp.
SUBTOPIC SENTENCE 3	However, the closest I came to death was when I was just 13 and thought the ice on Granite Lake would support me.

As you construct subtopic and concluding sentences in your own paragraphs, use connectors to link examples and signal order of importance.

ACTIVITY 7.3 WORKING TOGETHER: *Linking Sentences*

Working in pairs or small groups, rewrite each subtopic sentence in the three paragraph outlines that follow so that the sentence clearly connects with the example that precedes it. Use any of the transitional words in the lists provided and/or any other connector that works. Circle all connectors.

For a longer list of connectors, see pp. 54–56.

FOR ADDING MATERIAL

again	besides	furthermore	moreover
also	best	in addition	next
and	first	last	one
as well as	further	likewise	worst

FOR GIVING EXAMPLES AND EMPHASIS

above all	for example	it is true	surely
after all	for instance	most important	that is
another	indeed	of course	to illustrate
as an example	in fact	one example	
certainly	in particular	one reason	
especially	in truth	specifically	

EXAMPLE: Topic sentence: A good coach has to know how to relate to his or her players.

Subtopic sentence 1: A coach should be patient.

Rewrite with connectors: (One important quality) in a coach is patience.

Subtopic sentence 2: A coach should be a good listener.

Rewrite with connectors: (Another ability) a coach needs is to be a good listener.

Subtopic sentence 3: A coach should be sympathetic.

Rewrite with connectors: While being a (good listener) is important in coaching, being sympathetic is the (most important trait) of all.

1. Topic sentence: James Hanson is one of the most boring people alive.

   Subtopic sentence 1: He speaks in a monotone.

   Rewrite with connectors: _____

   Subtopic sentence 2: All he ever talks about is football.

   Rewrite with connectors: _____

   _____

   Subtopic sentence 3: Once he has someone cornered, he won't let the person go.

   Rewrite with connectors: _____

2. Topic sentence: Fishing is a relaxing sport for many people.

   Subtopic sentence 1: Tossing a line in the water and reeling it back in is simple.

   Rewrite with connectors: _____

   _____

Subtopic sentence 2: The natural surroundings are pleasant.

Rewrite with connectors: _____

_____

Subtopic sentence 3: A person can get away from routine distractions.

Rewrite with connectors: _____

_____

3. Topic sentence: Urban living has a number of disadvantages.

Subtopic sentence 1: Pollution can be a problem.

Rewrite with connectors: _____

Subtopic sentence 2: Traffic is often frustrating.

Rewrite with connectors: _____

Subtopic sentence 3: The crime rate is often high.

Rewrite with connectors: _____

Developing Examples

As we discussed in Chapter 3, writers develop their points through detailed examples and explanations. Compare the following two excerpts from paragraphs about the problems of owning an older car. Which excerpt seems most interesting and most clearly makes its point? (The subtopic sentences are underlined.)

A. But none of these troubles is more important than unexpected breakdowns, and used cars are more likely than new ones to leave a driver stranded. When the car breaks down, the driver is left without transportation. He or she is going nowhere. This situation is frustrating and can be dangerous, depending on where the breakdown happens.

B. But none of these troubles is more important than unexpected breakdowns, and used cars are more likely than new ones to leave a driver stranded. Imagine driving alone down a deserted country road in the middle of nowhere at midnight when a loud bang from the engine compartment and a horrible grinding noise tells you to pull over fast. You are stuck, going nowhere. It's creepy and cold, and the trees and shrubs crowd up close to the nonexistent shoulder of the road. You can't pull safely off, even if the car would start. Luckily, you have a cell phone, and help will arrive—within the next hour! Being at the mercy of a used car this way is frustrating and sometimes dangerous, and drivers left stuck at a stoplight in the middle of a busy intersection or stalled out on a road trip must wonder just how good that "good" deal was when they decided to buy used instead of new.

Most likely, you decided that version B is more interesting. In version A, the second and third sentences merely repeat the idea of the first sentence, and the final sentence only makes general statements about "frustration" and "danger." In contrast, version B develops the statement about unexpected breakdowns with a "what-if" example that includes action, specific words, sensory details, and explanation. The examples and details help clarify how unpleasant being stranded could be. B's final sentence reinforces the main point of the excerpt, providing several more specific examples.

Specific words, sensory details, and action descriptions help to develop paragraphs. For more on developing body paragraphs, see pp. 42–49.

The two paragraph subtopics that follow are general and repetitious. Rewrite the sentences in each of the subtopics, using more specific examples and details. As you revise them, ask yourself, "What does the writer mean by these statements?" and "What kinds of examples, details, and explanations can I add to make the statements clearer?"

EXAMPLE: Topic: What constitutes a healthy diet?

Subtopic sentence: Low-fat foods are an important part of a healthy diet.

Poorly developed subtopic: Unlike other food, vegetables are low in fat. They will not put weight on a person because they do not contain much fat. Vegetables are low in calories and so do not cause a person to gain weight; therefore, they can keep a person healthy.

Revised subtopic with specific, detailed material:
Most vegetables, such as broccoli, asparagus, and cauliflower, have no fat but plenty of fiber and essential nutrients. In fact, snack-friendly vegetables like carrots and celery have so few calories that a person burns most of those they contain just by chewing. On the other hand, dairy products like whole milk, cheese, and ice cream are loaded with fat and low-density cholesterol, which can clog arteries and cause heart attacks.

1. Topic: What makes a person interesting?

   Subtopic sentence: One way to be interesting is to be a good listener.

   Poorly developed subtopic: A good listener is someone who knows how to listen well. He or she pays attention and tries to hear what a person is saying. Paying close attention, a good listener follows a conversation and does not drift away from what is being said.

   Revised subtopic example with specific, detailed material:

   _____

   _____

   _____

   _____

2. Topic: What fears did I have as a child?

   Subtopic sentence: The most terrifying moments for me came at night.

   Poorly developed subtopic: I especially hated being alone in my dark room. Because the room was so dark, I could too easily imagine things that were not there. Seeing imaginary creatures always frightened me and made me want to be anywhere but in my bedroom.

   Revised subtopic example with specific, detailed material:

   _____

   _____

   _____

   _____

Analyzing Student Models: Illustration Paragraphs

The following model paragraphs will help you write effective illustration papers. "Teaching with Whips" and "Dying to Have Fun" were developed using the "I" voice of personal experience. "Dangers in a Deli" and "Nothing Worthwhile Comes Easy" use the "they" voice, which shifts the readers' focus away from the author.

➡ Prereading Exploration for "Teaching with Whips"

Jeong Yi wanted to share some of his personal experiences with classmates so that they could compare their own education with his and learn about some of the cultural differences between them. Jeong also noted that teachers might be interested in the paper because he discusses using force to make students learn.

1. Having read the chapter introduction and worked through several activities, how many main examples might you expect this paragraph to contain?

    _____

2. What kind of sentence would you expect each major example to begin with?

    _____

Key Points: Building Illustration

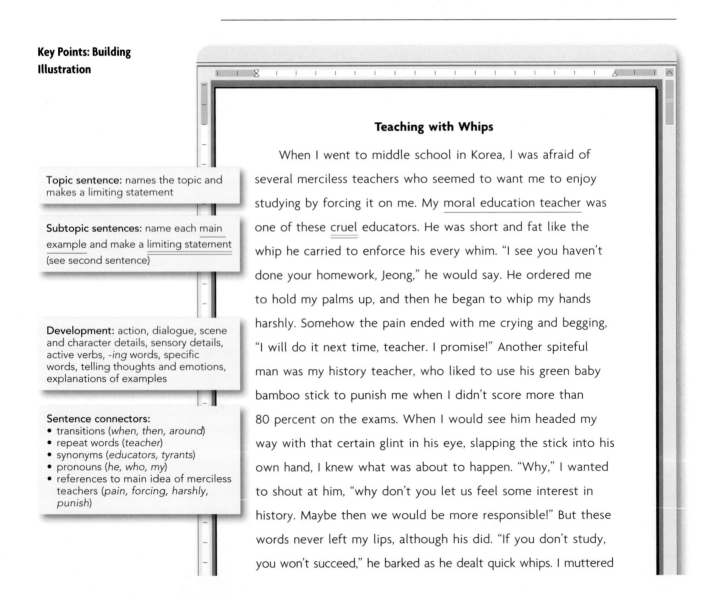

Topic sentence: names the topic and makes a limiting statement

Subtopic sentences: name each main example and make a limiting statement (see second sentence)

Development: action, dialogue, scene and character details, sensory details, active verbs, -ing words, specific words, telling thoughts and emotions, explanations of examples

Sentence connectors:
• transitions (when, then, around)
• repeat words (teacher)
• synonyms (educators, tyrants)
• pronouns (he, who, my)
• references to main idea of merciless teachers (pain, forcing, harshly, punish)

Teaching with Whips

When I went to middle school in Korea, I was afraid of several merciless teachers who seemed to want me to enjoy studying by forcing it on me. My moral education teacher was one of these cruel educators. He was short and fat like the whip he carried to enforce his every whim. "I see you haven't done your homework, Jeong," he would say. He ordered me to hold my palms up, and then he began to whip my hands harshly. Somehow the pain ended with me crying and begging, "I will do it next time, teacher. I promise!" Another spiteful man was my history teacher, who liked to use his green baby bamboo stick to punish me when I didn't score more than 80 percent on the exams. When I would see him headed my way with that certain glint in his eye, slapping the stick into his own hand, I knew what was about to happen. "Why," I wanted to shout at him, "why don't you let us feel some interest in history. Maybe then we would be more responsible!" But these words never left my lips, although his did. "If you don't study, you won't succeed," he barked as he dealt quick whips. I muttered curses with his final blow. The most memorable of all these tyrants was the despised art teacher nicknamed Poisonous Snake. None of the students got along well with him. He seemed to dislike all of us equally. The black tape wrapped around the long, powerful stick that he used so frequently increased all our fear. I could only anticipate the pain I would feel the day I scored poorly on an exam I'd just taken. Burning with anxiety, I thought the only way to prevent these pains would be to study more diligently. If the goal of Poisonous Snake and the rest of my teachers was just to make me study harder, they succeeded. But if they were concerned at all whether or not I learned to like education, then they all failed miserably.

—Jeong Yi

Concluding sentence: restates the topic and adds a final (expanded) thought

➡ Prereading Exploration for "Dying to Have Fun"

Tom Kellogg wrote this paper for himself to think through a tragedy and for people who like the outdoors and can identify with the float trip examples.

1. Are there any pastimes you enjoy that others consider dangerous, exhausting, uncomfortable, or just plain tedious?

2. List one activity that you like, make a limiting statement about it (is it fun or dangerous or exhausting or challenging?), and then write three or four examples to illustrate your statement.

Key Points: Building Illustration

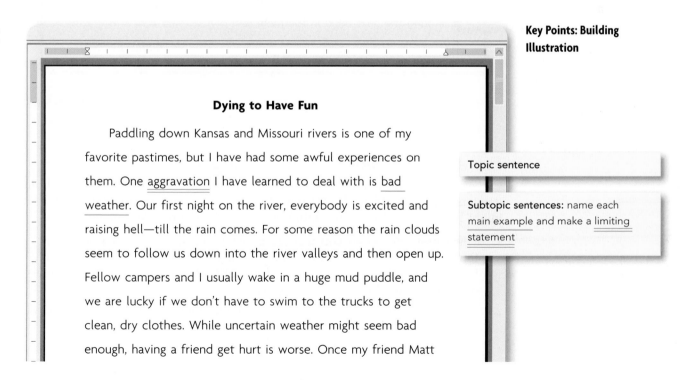

Dying to Have Fun

Paddling down Kansas and Missouri rivers is one of my favorite pastimes, but I have had some awful experiences on them. One aggravation I have learned to deal with is bad weather. Our first night on the river, everybody is excited and raising hell—till the rain comes. For some reason the rain clouds seem to follow us down into the river valleys and then open up. Fellow campers and I usually wake in a huge mud puddle, and we are lucky if we don't have to swim to the trucks to get clean, dry clothes. While uncertain weather might seem bad enough, having a friend get hurt is worse. Once my friend Matt

Topic sentence

Subtopic sentences: name each main example and make a limiting statement

Sentence connectors:
- transitions (*first, while, down into*)
- repeat words (*river*)
- synonyms (*fellow campers*)
- pronouns (*our, everybody*)
- reference to main idea of awful experiences (*bad weather, hurt, purple lump, death*)

Development: action, dialogue, scene and character details, sensory details, active verbs, *-ing* words, specific words, telling thoughts and emotions, and explanation of the examples

Concluding sentence: restates the topic and adds a final (expanded) thought

flipped his canoe in front of mine, and I couldn't stop in time. Matt caught the bow of my canoe in his right eye. The cold, clear spring water of the Current River did not stop the huge purple lump above his eye from swelling. After 10 years of floating, I thought I had experienced all the problems a person could run into on a river until one trip on the Niangua 3 years ago. My partner and I pulled up onto a gravel bar alongside a crowd gathered in a circle. At first I thought they were only having a party. But then I saw my friend Mitch kneeling in the sand, pushing on a man's chest. "What happened?" I asked. "Is there anything I can do?" He shook his head. "It's too late for this guy. No one knows what happened. He just keeled over and stopped breathing." Mitch kept trying, anyway, to jumpstart the man's heart, but it was a losing battle. I walked back to my canoe and sat down on the soggy, vinyl-covered seat cushion, for once not feeling my butt itch from it. A line from the miniseries *Lonesome Dove* ran through my mind: "The best thing you can do with death is just walk away from it." This guy had started out his trip like I had, expecting only to have a good time, ending up having his last time. I thought to myself, "It could just as easily be me lying there." Despite the problems over the years, even the death, I still enjoy floating, but I am more prepared now than ever to deal with the bad times that too often are waiting just around the next bend in the river.

—*Thomas Kellogg*

➤ *Prereading Exploration for "Dangers in a Deli"*

Catherine Denning avoids the "I" voice in this informative paragraph about dangers at her job. She felt that new employees reading an orientation booklet might listen more closely to a more objective, even authoritative, voice.

1. Think of a time when you were responsible for someone else's safety, a time when that person depended on your knowledge and experience. Try to remember a situation in which you alerted someone to possible dangers (perhaps a friend or family member).

2. List several examples of the dangers. Do you think the "I" voice of personal experience or a less informal "they" voice would be better to develop a paragraph explaining the dangers? Why?

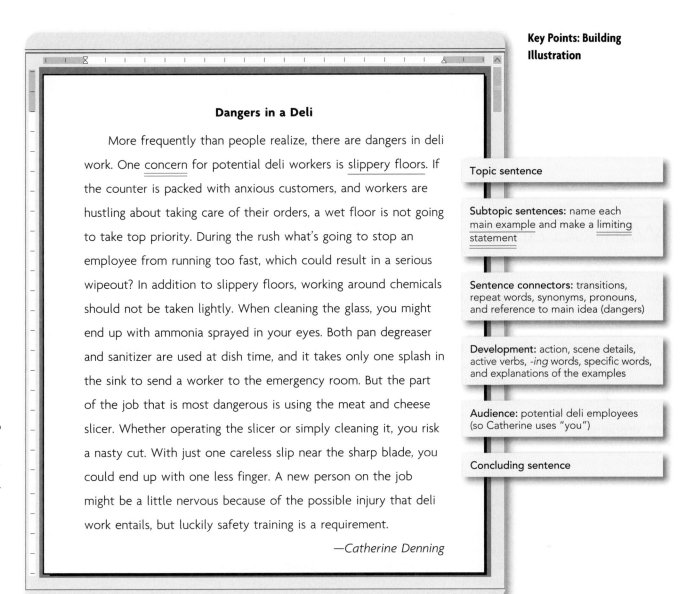

Dangers in a Deli

More frequently than people realize, there are dangers in deli work. One concern for potential deli workers is slippery floors. If the counter is packed with anxious customers, and workers are hustling about taking care of their orders, a wet floor is not going to take top priority. During the rush what's going to stop an employee from running too fast, which could result in a serious wipeout? In addition to slippery floors, working around chemicals should not be taken lightly. When cleaning the glass, you might end up with ammonia sprayed in your eyes. Both pan degreaser and sanitizer are used at dish time, and it takes only one splash in the sink to send a worker to the emergency room. But the part of the job that is most dangerous is using the meat and cheese slicer. Whether operating the slicer or simply cleaning it, you risk a nasty cut. With just one careless slip near the sharp blade, you could end up with one less finger. A new person on the job might be a little nervous because of the possible injury that deli work entails, but luckily safety training is a requirement.

—Catherine Denning

Topic sentence

Subtopic sentences: name each main example and make a limiting statement

Sentence connectors: transitions, repeat words, synonyms, pronouns, and reference to main idea (dangers)

Development: action, scene details, active verbs, *-ing* words, specific words, and explanations of the examples

Audience: potential deli employees (so Catherine uses "you")

Concluding sentence

POSTREADING QUESTIONS FOR PARAGRAPH ANALYSIS: ILLUSTRATION

Note: These questions apply to any of the three preceding student models.

1. In the topic sentence, what words name the topic, and what words make a limiting statement about it?

2. What words in the concluding sentence link to the topic sentence?

3. What is the expanded thought (p. 50) in the final sentence?

4. Copy each of the subtopic sentences, and underline the main example once and the statement about it twice. Circle connectors: transitions, repeat words, synonyms, and pronouns.

5. What words show that the main examples are arranged by order of importance? (See Activity 7.3.)

6. Choose an example and tell how the author's explaining (as opposed to detailing or action description) helps you better understand the author's point.

For more on connectors, see pp. 54–56.

For more on explaining examples, see pp. 42–49.

7. Choose an example and tell how the action description and detailing help you to better understand the author's point (Chapters 5 and 6, pp. 42–43).

8. Name three specific words, and list a more general word for each (pp. 75–76).

9. Name three ways to further develop any example in this paragraph. Consider action, active verbs, dialogue, specific words, sensory details, description of person or setting, revealing thoughts or emotions, and further explanation.

WRITING AN ILLUSTRATION PARAGRAPH

Summarizing the Assignment

In many college-level classes, instructors will want you to use a more academic, formal tone, avoiding "I" altogether.

Write a single paragraph of 250 to 300 words that illustrates a point with several examples. Whereas in Chapters 5 and 6 you focused on a single place or story unified in time, now you will use *several* examples (three or four) to illustrate your point, and you will introduce each of these examples with a subtopic sentence.

You may rely on personal examples and the "I" voice to develop your topic, or you may distance yourself from the material by using the "they" voice of more general knowledge and observation.

Establishing Audience and Purpose

After choosing a topic, decide whom you want to write for (realizing that your composition instructor is always a member of your audience). If, for instance, you choose a topic like great spring break vacations and want to write for friends, you should use examples that will interest them. If many of them are party hounds, then you might show and tell about young people at parties on the beach, in the mountains, or in some other desirable place. But if your readers might be more interested in art galleries, museums, and historical sites, then you could develop examples of these. Writing for a specific audience (pp. 12–14) will help focus your work.

You may have several purposes in mind—to entertain, persuade, or inform—but communicating ideas clearly should take top priority.

Working through the Writing Assignment

Discovering Ideas

Before brainstorming for topics, consider two approaches to the assignment: illustrating with personal experience or with more general knowledge.

- **Personal experience:** This method lets you draw on your own experiences and use the "I" voice, illustrating your examples with brief narrative/descriptive examples, as in the student models "Teaching with Whips" and "Dying to Have Fun."

- **General knowledge:** This approach is a bit more formal, avoiding "I" and favoring the third-person "they" (see "Dangers in a Deli" and the annotated student model). You might write in this voice if you are dealing with a topic from personal experience but one that you would like to distance yourself from (divorce, addiction, death of a loved one). Or you might want to discuss a subject that you have no personal experience with but have knowledge of through talking to people, reading, watching TV, and observing. For example, you may never have played football but still have opinions on what makes a great football game or football player. Your insights can make interesting examples.

The following list is divided to suggest topics that may be more given to an "I" or "they" approach. Many of the topics, however, can be written about using either voice.

POSSIBLE TOPICS: ILLUSTRATION

Topics to develop through personal involvement/experience
(Will use "I" and personal anecdotes to create a relatively informal tone.)

- Things your high school did well (or poorly) to prepare you for college
- Possible benefits of composition or math skills (or any other school subject) in helping you achieve career goals
- Rules at home, work, or school that you hate (or hated) to obey
- Competition with a brother or sister
- Instances when you were independent or courageous or industrious or instances of being dependent or fearful or lazy
- A memorable trip or trips you have taken with family or peers
- A musical or sporting event that was particularly memorable
- Childhood or adult fears or delights or fantasies
- Embarrassing moments while growing up

Topics to develop through observation and accumulated knowledge
(Will usually call for the use of "they," generalized examples, and a more formal tone.)

- Challenges college students have balancing school and other demands (could focus on community college students)
- Qualities or practices of a good (or bad) teacher or student
- Qualities of a good (or bad) parent
- Characteristics of a good role model for children (a parent, teacher, athlete, musical artist, or cartoon or story character)
- Benefits or ill effects of any sport or form of exercise (basketball, swimming, rock climbing, skating, surfing, etc.)
- Foods found in a healthy (or an unhealthy) diet
- Signs of alcohol or other drug abuse
- Advertising on TV (could be: creative or funny or boring or frightening or . . .)
- TV programming (too much sex or violence or profanity or stereotyping or . . .)

HINT

For additional illustration topics, see Chapter 7 at www.mhhe.com/brannan.

English Review Note

If you do not have experience about a particular topic or are unfamiliar with an American English reference, do some online research.

REDUCE YOUR CARBON FOOTPRINT

Write about three or four specific ways you could reduce your carbon footprint. For ideas, visit the Conservation Fund's website: http://www.conservationfund/org/gozero/footprint. ●

Conservation in Context

For additional topic ideas for this assignment, look under Chapter 7 at www.mhhe.com/brannan. And for more illustrative writing strategies, download the Illustration Writing Tutor.

After choosing several possible topics, prewrite (clustering, freewriting, and listing are good choices) to find five or six examples to illustrate each one. Having more examples than you will use lets you choose the strongest when you cut back to three or four. The following topic—problems of community college students—demonstrates how to list and develop examples for an illustration paragraph.

There is no "right" number of examples in a paragraph or essay. The writer uses as many as she or he feels are necessary to fully illustrate the point.

Prewriting

The first step is to come up with **first-level examples** or main examples—kinds of general or typical problems. You should develop six but keep only three or four.

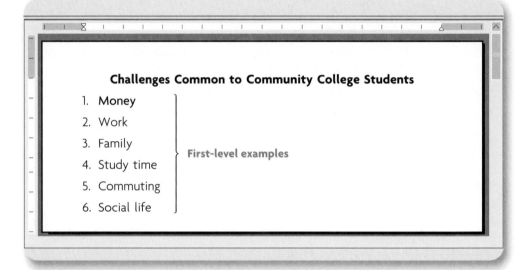

This list includes six main or first-level examples of problems, only three or four of which will be used in the paper. The next step is to develop each main example by answering the question "What exactly do I mean by that?" For the first problem from the list above, you might use **second-level examples** like the following:

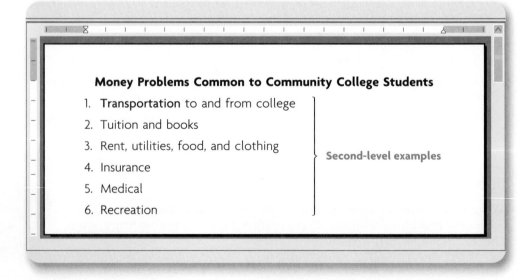

In this second-level list, you answer the question "What do I mean by money problems of community college students?" But can we be even more specific? What if someone wants to know more about transportation expenses? You could create a list of **third-level examples** like the following:

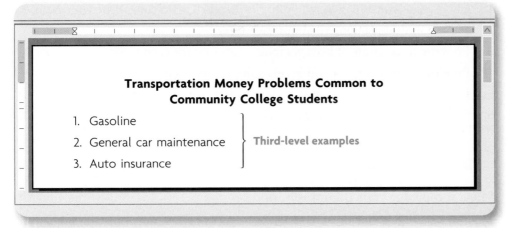

Transportation Money Problems Common to Community College Students

1. Gasoline
2. General car maintenance
3. Auto insurance

} Third-level examples

With each level you clarify and so develop your examples by *limiting* them. This is the same principle we used in Chapter 5 when we practiced moving from relatively general to relatively specific words (pp. 75–76). You can also see this concept using the graphic introduced on page 75.

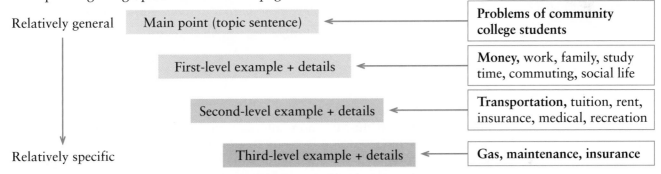

Relatively general

Main point (topic sentence) ← Problems of community college students

First-level example + details ← **Money**, work, family, study time, commuting, social life

Second-level example + details ← **Transportation**, tuition, rent, insurance, medical, recreation

Relatively specific

Third-level example + details ← **Gas, maintenance, insurance**

To build one subtopic in an illustration paragraph, we could use the examples developed in our prewriting lists like this:

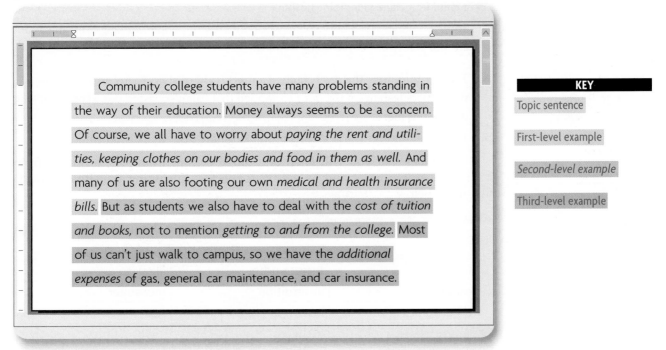

Community college students have many problems standing in the way of their education. Money always seems to be a concern. Of course, we all have to worry about *paying the rent and utilities, keeping clothes on our bodies and food in them as well.* And many of us are also footing our own *medical and health insurance bills.* But as students we also have to deal with the *cost of tuition and books,* not to mention *getting to and from the college.* Most of us can't just walk to campus, so we have the *additional expenses* of gas, general car maintenance, and car insurance.

KEY

Topic sentence

First-level example

Second-level example

Third-level example

HINT

It's best to create material and then prune.

Now readers have a fairly good idea of what we meant when we said that community college students have money problems.

PREWRITING—SUMMING UP

1. Choose several topics from the topics list, or create several of your own.
2. Make a limiting statement about each topic.
3. Prewrite to generate at least six main examples for each topic.
4. Prewrite to generate second-level examples for each main example.
5. List any third-level examples or details that come to mind.
6. Select the topic that most interests you.

JOURNAL / BLOG ENTRY 7.2

Select a topic for your paragraph, and on pages 150–151 follow the prewriting model, which develops challenges common to community college students. Write out six examples that illustrate your topic, and then develop them with second- and third-level examples.

FEEDBACK *Respond to a classmate's use of second- and third-level examples. Which are particularly effective? Which do you have concerns or questions about?*

Organizing Ideas

A topic sentence will guide you as you write the rest of the paper. If you have not yet decided on the "I" (more informal) or "they" (more formal) approach, now is a good time to do so. Here are two pairs of topic sentences, one sentence in each pair using the "I" voice and the other using the "they" voice. Topics are underlined once; statements are underlined twice.

A. Topic = laziness: Although I have become more industrious as an adult, when I was a child I specialized in doing nothing.

B. Topic = laziness: In a busy country like ours, full of people working overtime, there are still plenty of people doing nothing.

A. Topic = smoking: The day I climbed a short flight of stairs to my apartment and stood there leaning on the door so winded that I almost passed out, I knew smoking was hurting me.

B. Topic = smoking: The ill effects of smoking have been well documented.

Remember that you will keep only three or four examples, arranged from least to most important and linked by connectors, including transitional words like those below.

HINT

For more on connectors, see pp. 54–56.

FOR ADDING MATERIAL

again	as well as	furthermore	likewise
also	besides	in addition	moreover
and	further	last	next

FOR GIVING EXAMPLES AND EMPHASIS

above all	especially	in particular	one reason
after all	for example	in truth	specifically
another	for instance	it is true	surely
as an example	indeed	most important	that is
certainly	in fact	of course	to illustrate

ORGANIZING IDEAS—SUMMING UP

1. Write out a rough topic sentence to focus your material.
2. Decide on a formal ("they") or informal ("I") approach.
3. Choose three or four examples to illustrate your topic.
4. Arrange your examples from least to most important.
5. Review the list of transitions and other connectors on pages 54–56.

Review the meanings of these English transition words. Use them correctly in your writing and avoid overusing a particular one.

JOURNAL / BLOG ENTRY 7.3

Write out your working topic sentence. Is it focused enough to help you choose examples? List your five or six examples from least to most important; now cross out two or three of the least interesting ones. What makes your final example the most interesting one to you, and why would it be to your readers?

FEEDBACK *Tell a classmate whether his or her final example is the most interesting—and why or why not.*

Drafting

With the preliminary work done, you are almost ready to draft. But before plunging in, review the drafting suggestions on pages 16–17 and think about the following points:

1. Recognize that you can get quick results by writing each major example at spaced intervals down the page and then starting with the one (probably the last one) that you have the most to say about. Polish your subtopic sentences later.

2. Remember to keep asking the question "What do I mean by what I have just written?" Add examples and details that will clarify each point for your readers.

3. Recognize that your examples do not need to be perfectly balanced, though all should be developed. In fact, your final, most important example may be several sentences longer than the others.

4. To replace "I" in papers using the more formal "they" voice, try pronouns like *their, they, them,* and *those,* and nouns like *people, men, women, young adults, students, consumers, athletes,* and *applicants.*

Try placing each main example on the page before drafting.

Use sensory details: sight, sound, touch, smell, and taste.

Soon after writing your first draft, reread the assignment on page 148 and then skim the draft. Does it fit the assignment? Do you have three or four examples that are arranged by importance? What part of your draft do you like best? What part do you dislike most? Answer in a paragraph.

Revising Drafts

First-Stage Drafts

At this stage, you should focus on content (detailed examples and explanations) and organization (arrangement and connection of ideas).

1. **Have you used three or four examples, or have you developed only one?** Although this assignment calls for three or four examples, don't try to cram five, six, or more into the paragraph. Too many examples mean too little development.

2. **Is your topic sentence effective (pp. 38–41)?** Your topic sentence has two functions: to identify and to limit your topic. Instead of creating an overly general topic sentence ("There are many interesting musical groups"), be specific ("My favorite group of ancient rock and rollers is the Beatles"). You might also use a **forecasting statement,** as in "The Beatles are my favorite vintage rock group because <u>their music is simple yet inventive, and their lyrical themes are largely positive.</u>"
   Be sure to use specific words in your topic sentences.

3. **Have you arranged your main examples either by time or by importance (pp. 139–141)?** Chronological order can work well in illustration paragraphs, but order of importance is more emphatic. Determine which method works best for you, and then follow it consistently. By the way, sometimes you can use both patterns simultaneously, which is fine.

4. **Have you written a subtopic sentence to introduce each main example (pp. 138–139)?** Subtopic sentences can strengthen your paragraph in several ways. These sentences guide your readers, they guide you, and they create emphasis.

5. **Are your main examples adequately developed?** Each main example should be developed with second- and perhaps third-level examples and the details that go along with them. Remember to ask yourself "What do I mean by that?" and to become increasingly specific as you develop each example. Use the elements of vivid scene building where appropriate (specific word choices, sensory details, active verbs, *-ing* words, dialogue, descriptions of setting and people).

6. **Are your examples thoroughly explained?** Each example should not only be vividly presented but also be clearly explained. Often, you must tell readers what an example means or how it connects with your main point. Notice how in "Teaching with Whips" (pp. 144–145) Jeong includes a subtopic sentence of explanation ("He seemed to dislike all of us equally") with his descriptive example of the black stick.

7. **Are your examples relevant (pp. 46–47)?** In first drafts, especially, examples can slip in that might be interesting but that nevertheless distract

In this brief paragraph assignment, forecasting may make the subtopics sound repetitive. You must decide what works best for your topic and audience.

For examples of effective subtopic sentences, see any of the student models in Unit Two.

For more on clarity in examples, see pp. 48–49.

from the main point. For instance, in the student model "Dangers in a Deli," while it is true that deli workers often get along well and have good times on the job, these facts distract from the main point about dangers to watch out for.

8. **Are sentences within the paragraph well connected (pp. 53–59)?** First drafts usually need more transitions for adding material, giving examples, and emphasizing a point. Also, within narrative/descriptive examples, you may need more time and space transitions. For overall coherence, remember to use the other connectors as well: repeat words, synonyms, pronouns, and references to main ideas.

9. **Is your concluding sentence effective?** Your final sentence should use a connector, refer back to the topic sentence, and expand the main idea of the paragraph. While drafting, if you saved an idea that seemed out of place in the body, the idea might make a good expanded thought in the conclusion. For example, it might have been distracting to talk about "good times" in the body of the deli paragraph, but "good times" might work well as a final comment.

Ideas for expanded thoughts in the conclusion will often occur to you while you are drafting. See pp. 16–17.

JOURNAL / BLOG ENTRY 7.5

To help you focus on revision and alert your instructor to your progress, list three specific changes you have made or feel you ought to make in going from your first to second draft. Refer to the first-stage draft questions, answering specifically. Next, in several sentences, say what you like best about your draft.

Second and Final Drafts

For advice on revising and then editing further drafts of your work, turn to Chapter 4, pages 62–72.

Annotated Student Model: "Nothing Worthwhile Comes Easy"

Carefully reading the annotated student model will help clarify questions you have about your own draft.

First-Stage Draft

Bill Ross decided to explain how difficult college can be to those who have never been and those who have attended but forgotten the challenges they faced. He used listing to discover eight major examples, which he then trimmed to four. As you will see, he was not sure what tone to adopt initially, so the first draft skips back and forth between the "I" approach and the more formal "they" approach.

First drafts often give a new direction to your ideas.

   Note: This rough draft of a paragraph is separated into topic and concluding sentences and four subtopics to illustrate the connections among its parts. Because it is a rough draft, it includes errors in grammar, spelling, and punctuation.

Some college students have a difficult time with school and the rest of there lives.

We all want to relax sometimes, but it's hard to have a social life and still get the studying done. And if you are a partier, look out! Its hard to make grades and have fun.

Bills are another problem. Some students have it easy, scholarships or a free ride from there parents, but most community college students, anyway, are working their way through. If you have children, it's even worse. Just think of all bills having a house and family can rack up like mortgage payments, utilities, food, clothing, doctor bills, etc. Stressing out over money makes studying difficult.

Having to work to pay the bills is another problem. Of course, almost all adults have to support themselves but most people aren't running in three different directions at once. With college students trying to study, have some kind of social life and then work forty hours a week, it can be to much.

And then there's the family hassle that students like me have to worry about. I'm a returning student who hasn't been in college for 15 years. Along the way I accummulated a wife and three children, so its especially hard for me. But I am not alone. Just look around in your classes and you will see lots of older students struggling to make it all work out. As much as I love my family, they take the biggest chunk of my time, after work. And you probably know how much a family can just wear you out. By the time my wife and I get the kids to bed, it's hard to hit the books.

College is not easy for most people, but I think it has to be harder for the older returning student with a family.

Margin annotations:

Topic sentence

Refocus of paper will create *material cuts and additions.*

First subtopic

Second subtopic

Third subtopic

Need overall developing of main examples with specific support, details, and explanations

Fourth subtopic

Avoid tone shift from "they" to "I."

Concluding sentence

After completing the first draft, Bill made two important decisions. First, he thought that the "I" voice made him sound like he was merely complaining, so he decided to try for a more objective reporter's voice. Second, he discovered that he wanted to shift the focus of his topic from the experience of college students in general to that of nontraditional students like himself who attend community colleges.

Second-Stage Draft

First-stage drafts of illustration papers often have difficulties with focus and development. Note how much explanation and how many more examples were added to the following draft to help clarify meaning. As you work on your own draft, keep asking, "What do I mean by that last statement, example, or idea?" Also use topic, subtopic, and concluding sentences. Help your readers find their way through your paper with the least difficulty. They will appreciate your efforts.

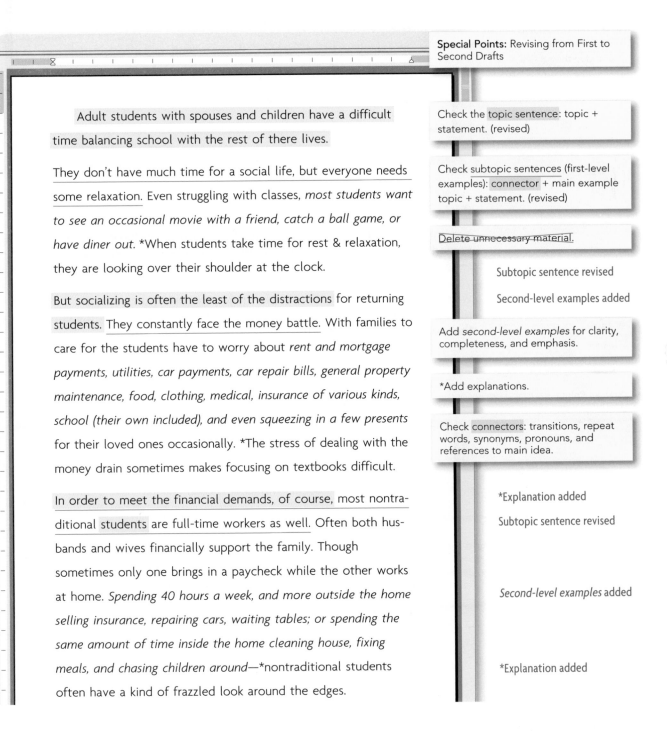

Special Points: Revising from First to Second Drafts

Adult students with spouses and children have a difficult time balancing school with the rest of there lives.

Check the topic sentence: topic + statement. (revised)

They don't have much time for a social life, but everyone needs some relaxation. Even struggling with classes, *most students want to see an occasional movie with a friend, catch a ball game, or have diner out.* *When students take time for rest & relaxation, they are looking over their shoulder at the clock.

Check subtopic sentences (first-level examples): connector + main example topic + statement. (revised)

Delete unnecessary material.

Subtopic sentence revised

Second-level examples added

But socializing is often the least of the distractions for returning students. They constantly face the money battle. With families to care for the students have to worry about *rent and mortgage payments, utilities, car payments, car repair bills, general property maintenance, food, clothing, medical, insurance of various kinds, school (their own included), and even squeezing in a few presents for their loved ones occasionally.* *The stress of dealing with the money drain sometimes makes focusing on textbooks difficult.

Add *second-level examples* for clarity, completeness, and emphasis.

*Add explanations.

Check connectors: transitions, repeat words, synonyms, pronouns, and references to main idea.

In order to meet the financial demands, of course, most nontraditional students are full-time workers as well. Often both husbands and wives financially support the family. Though sometimes only one brings in a paycheck while the other works at home. *Spending 40 hours a week, and more outside the home selling insurance, repairing cars, waiting tables; or spending the same amount of time inside the home cleaning house, fixing meals, and chasing children around—*nontraditional students often have a kind of frazzled look around the edges.

*Explanation added

Subtopic sentence revised

Second-level examples added

*Explanation added

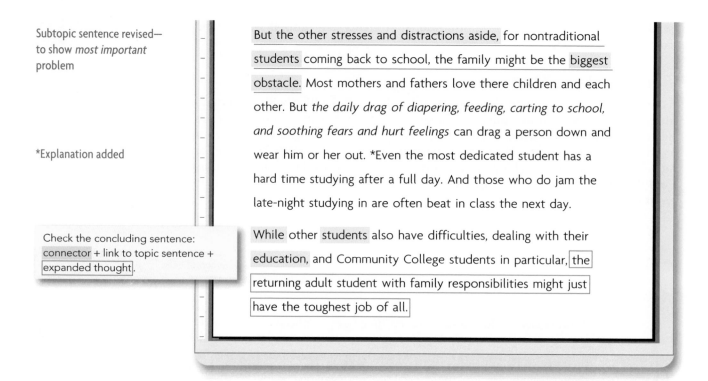

Subtopic sentence revised—to show *most important* problem

But the other stresses and distractions aside, for nontraditional students coming back to school, the family might be the biggest obstacle. Most mothers and fathers love there children and each other. But *the daily drag of diapering, feeding, carting to school, and soothing fears and hurt feelings* can drag a person down and wear him or her out. *Even the most dedicated student has a hard time studying after a full day. And those who do jam the late-night studying in are often beat in class the next day.

*Explanation added

Check the concluding sentence: connector + link to topic sentence + expanded thought.

While other students also have difficulties, dealing with their education, and Community College students in particular, the returning adult student with family responsibilities might just have the toughest job of all.

Third-Stage Draft

You might think the paper is complete by the time you have written a thorough second draft. After all, you have reorganized, deleted material, and added new examples, details, and explanations—shouldn't the paper be done? However, if you want your work to move beyond good to excellent, you usually need to write a third draft. With most of the major concerns taken care of, you can now improve your word choices and sentence variety and get rid of the clutter words that so often slip into rough drafts.

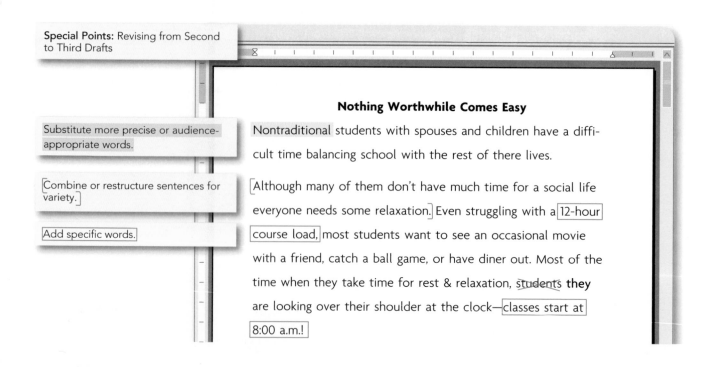

Special Points: Revising from Second to Third Drafts

Substitute more precise or audience-appropriate words.

Combine or restructure sentences for variety.

Add specific words.

Nothing Worthwhile Comes Easy

Nontraditional students with spouses and children have a difficult time balancing school with the rest of there lives.

Although many of them don't have much time for a social life everyone needs some relaxation. Even struggling with a 12-hour course load, most students want to see an occasional movie with a friend, catch a ball game, or have diner out. Most of the time when they take time for rest & relaxation, ~~students~~ **they** are looking over their shoulder at the clock—classes start at 8:00 a.m.!

[But socializing is often the least of the distractions for returning students, as they constantly face the money battle.] ~~Students~~ **Their** families add to the financial worries with **parents** footing the bills for rent or mortgage, utilities, insurance, general property maintenance, food, clothing, medical, car, school (their own included), and even the occasional present for a loved one. The stress of dealing with the money drain sometimes makes focusing on textbooks difficult.

In order to meet the financial demands, of course, most non-traditional students are full-time workers as well. Often both ~~husbands and wives~~ **spouses** financially support the family. Though sometimes only one brings in a paycheck while the other works at home. Spending 40 hours a week, and more outside the home selling insurance, repairing cars, waiting tables; or spending the same amount of time inside the home cleaning house, fixing meals, and chasing children around—non-traditional students often have a ~~kind of~~ frazzled look around the edges.

But the other stresses and distractions aside, for ~~non-traditional students~~ **mom's and dad's** coming back to school, the family might be the biggest obstacle. [As much as most mothers and fathers love there children and each other, the daily routine of diapering, feeding, clothing, carting to school, soothing fears and hurt feelings, explaining, teaching, and just generally loving family members can ~~drag a person down and~~ wear a person ~~him or her~~ out.] Even the most dedicated student has a hard time studying at 2:00 a.m. after a full work and family day. And those who do jam the late-night studying in are easy to spot as they work to keep their heads propped up in class the next day.

While other college students also have difficulties, dealing with their education, and Community College students in particular, the returning adult student with family responsibilities might just have the toughest job of all.

Replace clutter and repeat words with synonyms and phrases.

~~Delete unneeded words.~~

Synonym replaces phrase

Clutter phrase deleted

More appropriate word substituted

Sentences combined, specific words added, redundant expression cut

More accurate word added

Final-Editing Draft

In this last draft, Bill slows his reading to a crawl, editing closely, word by word, line by line, looking especially for the pattern errors he listed on his Improvement Chart. He knows that he still has many errors to correct.

Special Points: Editing Final Drafts

Topic, subtopic, and concluding sentences merged to show a single, complete paragraph

1. **Misspelling**

2. **Sound-alike word**

3. Missing word(s)

4. **Wrong word**

5. **Sentence fragment**

6. Comma splice/run-on

7. **Faulty capitalization**

8. **Incorrect apostrophe**

9a. **Comma(s) needed: Introductory word(s)/ phrase/clause**

9b. **Comma(s) needed: Nonessential word group(s)**

9c. Comma(s) needed: Main clauses with coordinating conjuction

10. **Unneeded comma**

Nothing Worthwhile Comes Easy

Nontraditional students with spouses and children have a difficult time balancing school with the rest of ~~there~~[2] their lives. Although many of them don't have much time for a social life[9a] everyone needs some relaxation. Even struggling with a 12-hour course load, most students want to see an occasional movie with a friend, catch a ball game, or have ~~diner~~[1] dinner out. Most of the time when they take time for rest & relaxation, they are looking over their shoulder at the clock—classes start at 8:00 a.m.! But socializing is often the least of the distractions for returning students[10] as they constantly face the money battle. Their families add to the financial worries[9b] with parents footing the bills for rent or mortgage, utilities, insurance, general property maintenance, food, clothing, medical, car, school (their own included), and even the occasional present for a loved one. The stress of dealing with the money drain sometimes makes focusing on textbooks difficult. !n order to meet the financial demands, of course, most nontraditional students are full-time workers as well. Often both spouses financially support the family[5] ~~T~~though sometimes only one brings in a paycheck while the other works at home. Spending 40 hours a week[10] and more outside the home selling insurance, repairing cars, waiting tables; or spending the same amount of time inside the home cleaning house, fixing meals, and chasing children around—nontraditional students often have a frazzled look around the edges. But the other stresses and distractions aside, for ~~mom's and dad's~~[8] moms and dads coming back to school, the family might be the biggest obstacle. As much as most mothers and fathers love ~~there~~[2] their children and each other, the daily routine of diapering, feeding, clothing, carting to school, soothing fears and hurt feelings, explaining, teaching, and just generally loving family members can wear a person out. Even the most dedicated student has a hard time studying at 2:00 a.m. after a full work and family day. And those who do jam the late-night studying in are easy to spot as they work to keep their heads propped up in class the next day. While other college students also have difficulties,[10] dealing with their education, and C[7] community C[7] college students in particular, the returning adult student with family responsibilities might just have the toughest job of all.

—William Ross

FINAL-DRAFT CHECKLIST: ILLUSTRATION

Before you turn in your final draft for a grade, review this checklist. You may find that, as careful as you think you have been, you still missed a point or two—or more.

1. Is your topic sentence effective?
2. Have you used three or four examples, or have you used only one?
3. Have you clearly arranged your main examples—either by time or by importance?
4. Does a subtopic sentence introduce each main example?
5. Are your main examples well developed and thoroughly explained?
6. Are all sentences well connected?
7. Is your concluding sentence effective?
8. Have you used specific language?
9. Have you chosen active verbs and -ing words to describe action?
10. Have you used a metaphor or simile (see Chapter 6)?
11. Are your sentences varied in length and beginnings?
12. Have you used words so often that they are noticeable?
13. Have you included unneeded words?
14. Have you written an interesting title? Have you checked its capitalization?
15. Have you prepared your paper using the format expected by your instructor?

For more on paragraph revision, see Chapter 4.

Check to see if you need a title page, use double spacing, leave at least a 1-inch margin, and use a 12-point font.

16. Have you edited your work as closely as you know how to (including having at least one other person proofread)? Have you checked your Improvement Chart for pattern errors?

17. Have you looked for these errors: misspellings, sound-alike words, missing words, wrong words, sentence fragments, comma splices/run-ons, faulty capitalizations, incorrect apostrophes, missing commas, and unnecessary commas?

Alternate Writing Assignments

Here are a few more illustration assignment options that may be of interest. For any of these, be sure to do the following:

- Use subtopic sentences to introduce each major example.
- Arrange major examples by order of importance.
- Link all sentences, especially subtopics, with transitional words and other connectors.
- Develop examples with specific words, details, and explanations.

If you are drawing on personal experience, you might review Chapters 5 and 6 for reminders on the dominant impression and significance of the event.

1. Although the chapter assignment asks for several examples, you will often write paragraphs within essays that rely on only one major example. **Rethink any one of the major examples you chose for the chapter assignment, and then develop it further.** Be sure to use plenty of second- and third-level examples. Remember to rework your topic sentence to reflect your narrowing of scope.

2. **After writing the Chapter 7 assignment, rewrite it, shifting the tone.** If you were especially warm and chatty, in the new version use a more distant reporter's voice. If you chose an objective tone, become more personable. Because your audience influences the tone, you may need to redefine your target reader. If, for instance, you wrote to young adults about great vacations and emphasized the partying potential, you may have used personal examples and informal diction. Changing the audience to parents who are interested in their teens' vacation plans would affect the tone and the content of the main examples.

3. **Write a biographical sketch of a person, focusing on a single personality trait and using three or four anecdotes (brief stories) as examples.** For instance, you might characterize your brother as selfish. What three or four instances of selfish behavior can you remember that would show this trait to a reader?

4. **Select a work-related project that you will use on the job.** If you work in retail sales, for example, you could characterize three or four types of customers that a new employee should be able to identify. Maybe you work at a business like Kinko's and can identify several potential problems for a person new to the job. Perhaps you are writing a job evaluation for yourself or another employee and need to supply several examples to justify a statement such as "Jasmine has great communication skills." Give your supervisor or prospective employer several specific examples demonstrating these skills.

5. **Choose a topic that relates to your cultural heritage or to any group with which you closely identify.** Perhaps you are of Irish descent and are interested in the mythology or music of Ireland. Coming from a western European background, you might like Renaissance festivals.

Perhaps you love music and go to concerts every chance you get. What might attract you to a particular concert? What are three reasons that you go to concerts?

6. **Make a fairly specific observation about your college** (such as "The sculptures on X College's quad are a truly bizarre but creative mix of subjects and styles." or "If you're on campus on a Friday night, the best place to be is the Ground Cafe's Poetry Slam.") **and support it with three or four examples.** Before you begin to write, take photographs (like the three shown here) to demonstrate each example, and include them with your paragraph.

Linking to Future Experience

Determining the Value of Examples

Specific examples help us share our experiences, discuss ideas, and plan for the future. Unsupported statements like "I can't stand Shannon," "The Royals are a second-rate ball club," and "This policy will lead the country to ruin" raise questions that well-chosen examples can answer.

Examples also help us understand our own feelings and thoughts. Why do we trust one co-worker and not another? What examples can we give to explain these feelings? When we prepare for an essay exam, we gather as many examples as we can remember. Why is Martin Luther King, Jr. considered a pivotal figure in the civil rights movement in this country? Why do some people believe in the conspiracy theory behind the assassination of President John F. Kennedy? If we can offer specific examples to support our answers, we will probably do well on the exam.

ACTIVITY 7.6 WORKING ONLINE: *Using Examples in Context*

Using your school's Web site as a primary resource, write a paragraph convincing prospective students to attend your school. Use a primary reason and back it up with 3–4 examples. You might consider factors such as campus layout and location, the student body and alumni, the faculty, course offerings or schedules, extracurricular offerings, and so on.

ACTIVITY 7.7 WORKING ONLINE: *Examples Review*

Take the Chapter 7 Review Quiz at www.mhhe.com/brannan.

Chapter Summary

1. Writers use expository writing to communicate ideas, information, and opinions. After making a relatively general statement (topic sentence), they use examples, explanations, and details to develop and clarify that statement.

2. Examples may be based on personal experience or developed through close observation, accumulated knowledge, "what-if" situations, generalized or typical instances, and research.

3. Examples often include narrative/descriptive details, especially examples based on personal experience.

4. Tone is the attitude or feeling authors have toward their subjects and the relationship they want to establish with their audience. Writers vary their tone based on their material and audience.

5. Writers who adopt a more formal tone seldom use *I* and rely heavily for development on close observation, accumulated knowledge, "what-if" situations, generalized or typical instances, logical reasoning, and research.

6. Each major example in an illustration paragraph should be introduced with a subtopic sentence.

7. In expository and persuasive writing, writers often organize examples from least to most important or dramatic.

8. Transitional words and other connectors are needed to link subtopic and concluding sentences to the rest of the paragraph. The transitional phrases *for example* and *for instance* are important in illustration paragraphs.

9. To explain examples, writers limit the category to which the example belongs; they answer the question "What do I mean by that?"

10. Writing is never complete until it has been carefully revised and edited.

Creating and Explaining Groups (Classification)

8

[Have you ever tried to find something in a grocery store and been baffled about where to look? What was the item, and why do you think it was hard to classify into a larger group? If you can remember, mention how and where you eventually found it.]

KEY TOPICS

- Developing skills and exploring ideas in classification paragraphs

  - Using a single organizing principle

  - Choosing an organizing principle

  - Dividing and developing topics

  - Completing the groups

- Analyzing student models: Classification paragraphs

- Writing a classification paragraph

What Are We Trying to Achieve and Why?

Setting the Stage

As a shopper new to a supermarket, if you were looking for, say, strawberries, you would head to the fruit section. If instead the fresh strawberries were shelved next to the cat food, you would have a hard time finding them. In a store that had no signs or that lumped items together randomly there would be chaos, and few people would shop there.

But in reality all major stores use **classification,** a method of organizing their merchandise systematically. As we work through this chapter, we will practice classifying. We will learn to select a logical **single organizing principle (SOP)** to divide topics into groups, which we will then develop through examples, explanations, and details.

Linking to Previous Experience

What experience do you already have with classification? Well, as a shopper, you have a sense of how store managers classify. For example, in grocery stores you will often find items grouped by how they are used (such as cleaning products) or what they are most similar to (such as fruits grouped with vegetables). At home, most of us sort laundry from time to time—socks, underwear, pants, shirts; we classify and group these items by their use (the SOP). If you have ever moved to a new home, you confronted a major classification project. Unless you grouped and labeled items by room, the logical SOP here, you probably had a mess on the other end.

In college, too, classifying with an SOP is common. Most teachers are grouped by discipline (the SOP): history, math, English, and so on. Textbooks are full-length examples of classification, with material divided by topic (the SOP) into units, chapters, and sections.

We depend on our ability to classify and often use the skill unknowingly. For this reason, as valuable as the ability is, we also need to be wary of it. When we categorize things and people in haste, without much thought, we sometimes **stereotype.** Stereotyping oversimplifies complex issues and people, often creating rather than solving problems for us.

Misusing classification can create stereotypes.

JOURNAL / BLOG ENTRY 8.1

List several examples of classifying you have done or seen. Indicate the SOP for each one.

FEEDBACK *Respond to one classmate's classification system's SOP, suggesting an alternate way to organize. For instance, if he or she organizes clothes in a closet by frequency of use, you might name another SOP of organizing by type of clothing (tops, pants, etc.) or by color.*

Developing Skills and Exploring Ideas in Classification Paragraphs

To write a successful classification paragraph, practice the following:

1. Using a single organizing principle (SOP)
2. Choosing an organizing principle
3. Dividing and developing topics
4. Completing the groups

Using a Single Organizing Principle

To group items logically, we need a standard for grouping them, or single organizing principle. For example, a restaurant menu groups items by courses—appetizers, entrées, side dishes, and desserts—listed in the order in which they are usually served. Every item fits into one group or another, and within each group we find only items that are similar to each other—desserts, for example, feature ice cream and pie but not pork chops.

After choosing a topic for this assignment, you will need to choose a single organizing principle, one that will give you appropriate groups for your topic.

ACTIVITY 8.1 *Using a Single Organizing Principle (SOP)*

The following topics are divided into groups based on an organizing principle. Put an "X" next to the category that doesn't belong; then state the SOP.

EXAMPLE: Topic: holidays

Categories: ____ Spring ____ Summer ____ Fall ____ Winter __X__ Christmas

Organizing principle: *seasons of the year*

1. Topic: parties

    Categories: ___ Home ___ Friend's house ___ Park ___ Boring ___ Hotel

    Organizing principle: _____

2. Topic: first dates

    Categories: ___ Relaxed ___ Cheap ___ Tense ___ Exciting ___ Funny

    Organizing principle: _____

3. Topic: love

    Categories: ___ Spouse ___ Child ___ Friend ___ Erotic ___ Parent

    Organizing principle: _____

4. Topic: cooking

    Categories: ___ French ___ Greek ___ Spicy ___ Mexican ___ Vietnamese

    Organizing principle: _____

5. Topic: movie scenes

    Categories: ___ Explosions ___ Gunfire ___ Punching ___ Humor ___ Falls

    Organizing principle: _____

Choosing an Organizing Principle

With many topics, the SOPs we use are obvious. For instance, in buying a car, most of us use price to group cars into bargains, good deals we can afford, and those we only dream about. Asked to classify insurance, most of us would list groups like life, health, and auto.

However, some topics are less predictably grouped. We often have the freedom to choose an SOP based on what interests us and our audience. For instance, you might group children by any of the following: age, creativity, gender, growth rate, health, height, intelligence, math and reading skills, personality, physical abilities, responsibility, weight. Each of these could be a valid standard for classification, depending on your purpose. After you have selected a topic, you also need to decide among several organizing principles.

Topics can be grouped using one of many SOPs.

ACTIVITY 8.2 | WORKING TOGETHER: *Choosing an Organizing Principle*

Working in a group, discuss how a person might choose an SOP. Next, look at the following topics and write three different SOPs for each.

EXAMPLE: Topic: **drivers**

Possible organizing principles:

A. *temperament*   B. *experience*   C. *responsibility*

1. Topic: relatives

   Possible organizing principles:

   A. _____   B. _____   C. _____

2. Topic: leaders

   Possible organizing principles:

   A. _____   B. _____   C. _____

3. Topic: weddings

   Possible organizing principles:

   A. _____   B. _____   C. _____

4. Topic: sports

   Possible organizing principles:

   A. _____   B. _____   C. _____

For more on using detailed examples, see pp. 42–49.

Dividing and Developing Topics

After selecting a topic and an SOP, use the SOP to divide the topic into groups. Then develop each group with detailed examples and explanations. You might start by jotting down your topic, SOP, groups, and examples:

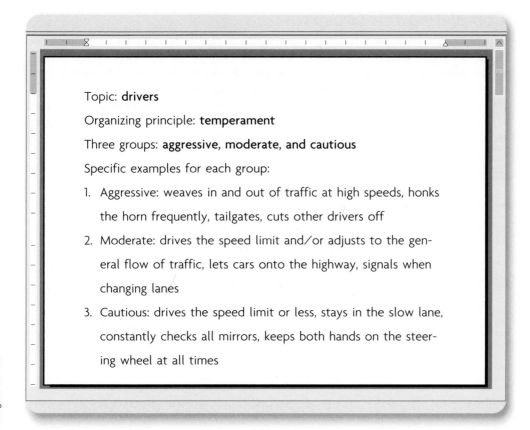

Topic: **drivers**

Organizing principle: **temperament**

Three groups: **aggressive, moderate, and cautious**

Specific examples for each group:

1. Aggressive: weaves in and out of traffic at high speeds, honks the horn frequently, tailgates, cuts other drivers off

2. Moderate: drives the speed limit and/or adjusts to the general flow of traffic, lets cars onto the highway, signals when changing lanes

3. Cautious: drives the speed limit or less, stays in the slow lane, constantly checks all mirrors, keeps both hands on the steering wheel at all times

ACTIVITY 8.3 *Dividing and Developing Topics*

Choose a topic from Activity 8.2, select one of the SOPs you listed, and write out three categories, or groups, that you get from applying the SOP (just as, in the example, "temperament" resulted in "aggressive, moderate, and cautious"). Next, list several examples to show what each category means. You may draw on personal experiences or use more general observations to create your examples.

Topic: _____

Organizing principle: _____

Three groups:

1. _____

2. _____

3. _____

Examples for each group:

1. _____

2. _____

3. _____

Completing the Groups

When classification of a familiar topic yields a small, definite set of groups, we expect all those groups to be mentioned. For example, if you classify the professional team sports in the United States, you should not limit your groups to, say, baseball, football, and basketball but should include hockey and soccer as well. Or, if you classify informational media, you should not list just newspapers, magazines, and television. What else should you include? Omitting obvious categories makes readers think you have not been careful, an impression you want to avoid.

ACTIVITY 8.4 | *Completing the Groups*

Fill in the blanks to complete each list.

1. Places to swim outdoors: pond, lake, river, _____

2. School levels: preschool, kindergarten, _____, middle school, high school, college, graduate school

3. Common gems: rubies, sapphires, emeralds, _____

4. Food groups: meat, fish, poultry; fruits, vegetables; grains; _____

5. Continents: Africa, Asia, North America, South America, Europe, Australia, _____

Analyzing Student Models: Classification Paragraphs

The student models that follow will help you write effective classification paragraphs. Both "Mall Crashers" and "Shopping the Easy Way" are developed through generalized experience, whereas "I Do" includes several personal examples. Either method can work well.

➡ Prereading Exploration for "Mall Crashers"

During a class discussion about types of shoppers, Chanthan Srouch decided to write this paper on nonshoppers. He thought that the members of his writing group and others who frequent malls would enjoy it.

Before reading the paragraph, think about the kinds of people you have seen in a mall who are not shopping but are there for some other reason. List three categories of nonshoppers. After reading, compare your list with the author's categories. What kind of paragraph might you have written on this same topic?

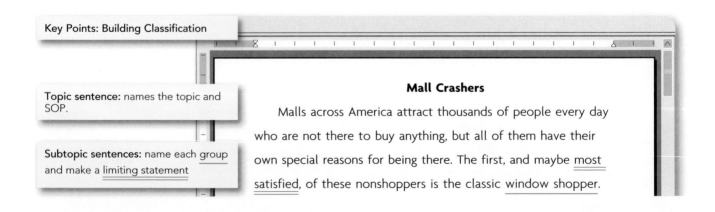

Key Points: Building Classification

Topic sentence: names the topic and SOP.

Subtopic sentences: name each group and make a limiting statement

Mall Crashers

Malls across America attract thousands of people every day who are not there to buy anything, but all of them have their own special reasons for being there. The first, and maybe most satisfied, of these nonshoppers is the classic window shopper.

These people are the ones who only browse, looking at and trying out merchandise, but seldom buying anything. They may try on four pairs of shoes or half a dozen sweaters, but they mostly just leave the salesclerks with no money and plenty of mess. The next nonshoppers, generally teens and young adults, are the ones looking to meet a member of the opposite sex. They can be found cruising the aisles of stores, sometimes pretending to be interested in merchandise; but usually when they are spritzing cologne around or feeling fabric, their eyes are on the attractive man or woman who is really shopping. Standing in a store, sitting on a bench, or sipping a soda in a food court, they are the ones who are not much interested in picking up merchandise, but who would love picking up a date. The remaining nonshoppers, the least happy, are those who accompany the serious shoppers. This group might include friends who are dragged along for company, children who have no choice, or the reluctant spouse of a shopaholic wife or husband. These nonshoppers are easy to spot because they are often the package carriers and protectors. While their determined partners are attacking the sale racks, the poor tagalongs can be seen draped with shirts, pants, and blouses as they obediently follow the leader; or they spend their time pacing back and forth on mall sidewalks, muttering to themselves as they glance back and forth from their watch to the store. As closing time for the mall stores nears, the nonshoppers will be among the last ones to leave, many having achieved their ends, but few carrying any purchases of their own.

—*Chanthan Srouch*

Sentence connectors: transitions (*first, next, when*), repeat words (*shopper*), synonyms (*people, teens*), pronouns (*they, who*), and reference to main idea (shopping: *browse, trying out*)

Development: action, scene and character details, sensory details, active verbs, *-ing* words, specific words, and explanations of the examples

Humor: wordplay (*shopaholic;* "picking up *merchandise*" versus "picking up a *date*")

Concluding sentence: restates the topic and adds a final (expanded) thought

→ *Prereading Exploration for "Shopping the Easy Way"*

Ann Nall works in a local Toys "R" Us and chose it as her topic. She thought that her information would be especially interesting to new parents and to parents in general.

Skim the paragraph. Notice that Ann does not use any personal experiences in the paper. Would they help or seem out of place?

Topic sentence

Development: action, scene and character details, sensory details, active verbs, *-ing* words, specific words, and explanations of the examples

Organization: arranged from oldest to youngest, not by importance

Subtopic sentences: name each group and make a limiting statement

Sentence connectors: transitions (*in no time*), repeat words (*shopper*), synonyms (*customers, parents*), pronouns (*each*), and reference to main idea (shopping efficiency: *clearly marked, guiding shoppers*)

Concluding sentence

Shopping the Easy Way

In order to help customers shop more efficiently in Toys "R" Us, the store is divided into three overall categories: areas for older children, toddlers, and babies. The older children have four major areas—Blue, Pink, R-Zone, and Silver—with piles of toys for everyone. Boys mostly head for the Blue section and items like the GI Joes, Hotwheels, and Legos. In no time at all, the boys can have Lego racetracks assembled on the floor and be racing miniature Batmobiles after the "bad guys." Girls, on the other hand, usually go for the Pink section, where there are Barbies, Cabbage Patch Kids, and tea sets to help them build fantasies and pretend they are older. Both sexes are interested in the video games and bicycles in R-Zone and Silver. The next group of children, the toddlers, has the Red and Green areas. Customers shop in Red to find smaller toys such as Play Dough and building blocks to help their children develop fine motor skills. Large outdoor play sets with swings, slides, and gliders are located in the Green section. For the babies, moms and dads shop in Purple. This part of the store contains most of what parents need to get children through their first year. Each aisle is clearly marked, guiding shoppers to shelves of diapers, formula, bottles, clothes, and many other items. After the baby's immediate needs have been met, the store can still help with important items like baby carriers, car seats, and strollers. Because Toys "R" Us does such a good job of labeling and grouping its merchandise, customers can be sure to find what they need right away, minimizing the wasted time and frustration that often come with shopping of any kind.

—*Ann Nall*

POSTREADING QUESTIONS FOR PARAGRAPH ANALYSIS

Note: Many of these questions apply to either of the preceding models.

1. In the topic sentence, which words name the topic and which name the SOP?

2. What words in the concluding sentence link to the topic sentence?

3. What is the expanded thought (p. 50) in the final sentence?

4. Copy each of the subtopic sentences, and underline the <u>group</u> once and the <u>statement</u> made about it twice. Circle connectors: transitions, repeat words, synonyms, and pronouns (pp. 53–59).

5. What words show that the main examples are arranged by order of importance in "Mall Crashers"? (See Activity 7.3.)

6. Choose an example and tell how the author's explaining (as opposed to detailing or action description) helps you better understand the author's point.

7. Choose an example and tell how the action description and detailing help you to better understand the author's point.

8. Name three specific words and list a more general word for each (pp. 75–76).

9. Name three ways to further develop any example in this paragraph. Consider action, active verbs, dialogue, specific words, sensory details, description of person or setting, revealing thoughts or emotions, and further explanation.

For more on detailing and explaining examples, see pp. 42–49.

WRITING A CLASSIFICATION PARAGRAPH
Summarizing the Assignment

Write a well-developed paragraph of 250 to 300 words that classifies things logically. You must have a topic that can be divided into at least three groups according to a single organizing principle (SOP). As usual, you will begin with a topic sentence—this one containing the topic and SOP—and end with a concluding sentence that expands the main thought. You will also create three or four subtopic sentences and use detailed examples and explanations, in this case to develop each group.

Establishing Audience and Purpose

After you have a topic, choosing an audience will help you focus and develop your ideas. Suppose you want to write about jewelry because you are impressed by its price, beauty, history, and effects on people. For a paragraph, you would have to narrow your focus. If you imagine your reader as someone who would like to buy gifts of jewelry but can't spend too much, you have a possible focus. You could choose price as an SOP, splitting jewelry into expensive, moderately priced, and inexpensive. The information you give would have real meaning for your readers.

You may have several purposes in mind—to entertain, persuade, or inform—but communicating ideas clearly should be your top priority.

You can write in a fairly objective tone, using your general knowledge and avoiding the "I" voice of personal experience, or write from the "I" perspective.

Working through the Writing Assignment

Discovering Ideas

Writing that groups things, information, and ideas can be dull. Classifying certainly helps a customer in a hardware store to locate a number-2-size Phillips head screw; however, nuts, nails, and screws may not make for a fascinating paper. As you explore topics, consider several SOPs, and think about whether they will lead to groups that you can develop with detailed examples and lively explanations. Think about whether you will be able to make a point with the resulting classification. If you don't make a point, you are likely to bore your readers and yourself. For

Having a point to make about your topic will focus your groups and guide the examples.

There are many ways to divide and classify topics from the list.

example, merely talking about a pet parakeet, gerbil, iguana, and guinea pig because they all live in cages (the SOP) might well make the reader respond "So what?"

The items in the following topics list all can be divided in different ways, depending on the SOP you use. For example, you might classify students (a topic in the first item, "People") according to their study habits: studies night and day, prepares most of the time, occasionally cracks a book, and never bothers to buy a book.

POSSIBLE TOPICS: CLASSIFICATION

- **People:** relatives, neighbors, students, drivers, dates, white-collar professionals, blue-collar workers, criminals, friends, enemies, men, women
- **Places:** zoos, parks, sports arenas, rivers, beaches, swimming pools, cemeteries, websites, vacation spots, restaurants, schools
- **Events:** embarrassing moments, funerals, weddings, life stages, parties
- **Services:** dating, moving, pest control, hair styling, bail bonds, landscaping, employment, phone, adoption, counseling, body shops
- **Emotional states:** happiness, enthusiasm, boredom, desire, revulsion, depression, fear
- **Behavior:** kind, cruel, responsible, irresponsible, generous, selfish
- **Personal adornment:** jewelry, makeup, tattoos, piercing, hair coloring
- **Clothing:** shirts, pants, dresses, coats, shoes
- **Expenses:** home, work, school, recreational
- **Academic subjects:** history, math, English, science, art, music, business
- **Career programs:** nursing, welding, paralegal, fashion merchandising
- **Art:** drawing, painting, sculpture, pottery, metal work, photography
- **Musical instruments:** strings, wind, percussion
- **Energy sources:** renewable, nonrenewable
- **Sports:** team sports, individual sports, spectator sports

---

For additional classification topics, look under Chapter 8 at www.mhhe.com/brannan.

ACTIVITY 8.5 | WRITING ONLINE: *Use the Classification Writing Tutor*

For additional topics for this assignment, look under Chapter 8 at www.mhhe.com/brannan. And for more classifying strategies, download the Classification Writing Tutor.

After choosing several possible topics, prewrite to explore SOPs for these topics. For each SOP you explore, you need to determine what groups will result and how you can develop these groups.

Prewriting

One way you can explore SOPs is with focused clusters, such as the following for the topic of weddings:

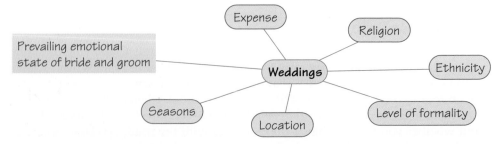

Expense, religion, ethnicity—any of these could be used to classify weddings, so the writer must decide which. Using clustering or another prewriting method, we could develop categories for several of the boxed terms. For example, you could choose "seasons" and list spring, summer, fall, and winter. But then you might ask, "What do I want to say about these kinds of weddings?" If you want to write for, say, a trade magazine that specializes in weddings, you could use "seasons" as the SOP and present information in a businesslike tone. But if your purpose is to entertain and reveal something about your experiences, you might use an SOP like the "prevailing emotional state of the bride and groom."

Here is how Richard Bailey, the author of the student model "I Do," grouped weddings based on the feelings of the bride and groom.

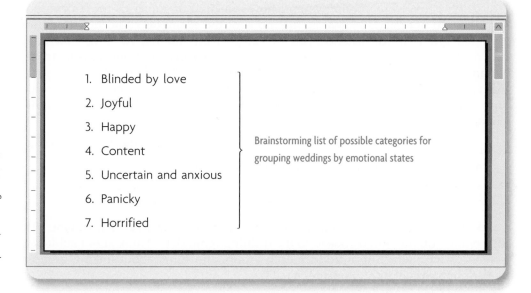

1. Blinded by love
2. Joyful
3. Happy
4. Content
5. Uncertain and anxious
6. Panicky
7. Horrified

Brainstorming list of possible categories for grouping weddings by emotional states

Brainstorming can also help you decide which groups to use. After brainstorming examples for each group in his list, Richard chose three groups: joyful, content, and uncertain/anxious weddings. To see how he developed these groups, turn to the model "I Do," on page 181.

PREWRITING—SUMMING UP

1. Choose several topics from the topics list, or create several of your own.
2. Prewrite to generate several organizing principles.
3. Prewrite to generate categories and examples for each principle.
4. Reflect on your purpose, interests, and audience to choose a topic and an SOP.

JOURNAL / BLOG ENTRY 8.2

List several SOPs for your topic, and then choose one that most interests you. Explain in a few sentences why this SOP interests you more than the others, is appropriate to your topic, and might interest an audience.

Organizing Ideas

To help focus and arrange categories, write a topic sentence, one that states the SOP, with or without using words like *categories, groups, kinds, types, sorts, varieties,*

classes, and *divisions.* Some writers also forecast their groupings. The following topic sentences illustrate these points:

GROUPING WORD MENTIONED	The weddings I have attended over the years fall into several distinct <u>categories</u> based on the emotional state of the bride and groom.
NO GROUPING WORD MENTIONED	The weddings I have attended over the years often reflect the emotional state of the bride and groom.
GROUPINGS FORECASTED	Weddings can be divided into the four following <u>types</u> based on the emotional state of the bride and groom: joyful, content, uncertain, and panicky.

Think about your groupings and how you will organize them. Make sure that they do not overlap—that is, that none of the examples could fit into more than one group. If, for instance, you are categorizing movies, you might include *action/adventures, romantic comedies, westerns,* and *musicals,* but not films starring Orlando Bloom, many of which would fall into the action/adventure category. Also make sure that you don't have more groups than you can effectively develop in a paragraph; three or four are enough. For overall organization, you might choose space, time, or importance:

- **Space:** for a topic requiring physical grouping of objects (books in a library)
- **Time:** for a topic using brief stories to group (stages of your life)
- **Importance:** for a topic using groups that are clearly less and more dramatic (dangerous weather: thunderstorm, blizzard, tornado)

HINT

Follow the same order in the paragraph as in the forecasting statement.

HINT

Try a scratch outline before you draft.

When you have an organization method, try writing a scratch outline. At this point, you might look ahead to the drafting reminders. Think about subtopic sentences with which to introduce each group, and think about linking groups with connectors like the transitions below.

FOR ADDING MATERIAL

again	as well as	furthermore	likewise
also	besides	in addition	moreover
and	further	last	next

FOR GIVING EXAMPLES AND EMPHASIS

above all	especially	in particular	one reason
after all	for example	in truth	specifically
another	for instance	it is true	surely

FOR COMPARING

alike	both	like	resembling
also	in the same way	likewise	similarly

FOR CONTRASTING

after all	dissimilar	nevertheless	though
although	even though	on the contrary	unlike
but	however	on the other hand	whereas

ORGANIZING—SUMMING UP

1. Create a rough topic sentence to focus your material.
2. Eliminate excess categories and any that overlap. Keep three or four.
3. Arrange the categories by space, time, or importance.
4. Try a scratch outline.
5. Review the list of transitions and other connectors.

JOURNAL / BLOG ENTRY 8.3

Jot down your rough topic sentence. Does it contain an SOP? Next list your categories in whichever order you have chosen. In a few sentences, explain why you think this arrangement will work well.

Drafting

With the preliminary work done, you are almost ready to write your first draft. But before plunging in, review the drafting suggestions in Chapter 1 (pp. 16–17). Also, recheck the SOP and groups you have chosen for the following:

- An SOP that effectively classifies your topic
- A clear reason for the classification, one that makes a point about your topic
- An SOP that avoids overlapping categories and makes it possible for you to include all important group members without creating an endless list

JOURNAL / BLOG ENTRY 8.4

Soon after writing your first draft, reread the assignment on page 173, and then skim the draft. Does it fit the assignment? Are there three or four categories in place that are arranged effectively? What part of your draft do you like best? What part do you dislike most? Answer in a paragraph.

Revising Drafts

For detailed help with revising drafts at every stage, turn to Chapter 4 (first-stage drafts: p. 63, second-stage: p. 64, final: p. 66).

Annotated Student Model: "I Do"

Carefully reading the annotated student model will help clarify questions you have about your own draft.

First-Stage Draft

Richard Bailey, who had been to several weddings, picked weddings as his topic and young adults thinking of getting married soon as his audience. After limiting his groups to three—joyful, content, and uncertain/anxious weddings—he wrote a fast draft to get some ideas down on paper.

The groups are in place but need to be developed with detailed examples and further explanation.

Second sentence is <u>unneeded sentence</u>

The second and third subtopic sentences need further focus.

Weddings come in all shapes and sizes but not all of them are happy. <u>I have been to half a dozen over the last 10 years, and I can tell you that some were great, some were so-so, and others were disasters.</u> One of the happiest weddings I have ever been to was my older brother's best friend. He married a terrific woman of about the same age (they were in their forties), and the church was full of teary eyes as they walked down the aisle with some old fifties tune in the back ground. Not all people getting married can be ecstatic. Some fall into another group. These kinds of weddings are with people who have grown up as childhood sweethearts and then they become friends and then they get married. Weddings like these are full of people who already know each other because of the couple's history together the conversation in the church is among people saying the wedding is long overdue. Another bad wedding to be in is the confused and panicky kind. Weddings like this are often between two people who don't belong together in the first place. Sometimes accidents force the issue, sometimes familys pressure people, and sometimes two people just chose the wrong partners. My younger brother's first marriage was this sort, and the problems were obvious even to the wedding guests. His bride's people took one-half of the church and Marks took the other half of the church. The ceremony was over fast. No one seemed sure what was happening and Mark ended up dropping his wife on the floor! As awful as Mark's wedding was and despite high divorce statistics in this country, I will probably get married someday.

Second-Stage Draft

Rough first drafts of classification papers often have difficulties with overall focus, development, and relevant material. Note the explanations and examples added to the following draft to help clarify meaning.

The weddings I have been to over the years can be grouped into several categories based on how the bride and groom feel. When many people think of weddings, they think of deliriously happy young couples. These are the people who can't wait to get the wedding over, and the honeymoon started. I have been to several like this. However, the happiest couple I have ever seen were not young, but in their early forties. Neither Jack nor Fran had any doubt. As they stood at the altar reciting their vows to the sound of some old fiftys tune and the church was full of teary eyes as they completed their vows with a kiss. If not all marrying couple are lucky enough to be overjoyed, there are still many who are happy and content. Often these weddings are between people like my older brother and his wife. Bruce and Julie grew up together, became friends, and then fell in love. Weddings like these are often full of people who already know each other, because of the couple's history together. The conversation in the church is full of people saying stuff like "Well . . . it's about time" and "at last." The worst kind of state for a couple to be in is in confusion and panic. Weddings like this are often between two people who don't belong together in the first place, shouldn't be together, and who will never last. Sometimes accidents force the issue, sometimes familys pressure people, and sometimes two people just chose the wrong partners. My younger brother's first marriage was this sort, and the problems were obvious even to the wedding guests. Evelyns people took one-half of the room and Marks took the other half of the room. No mixing it up between the families. The ceremony was quick and the reception was short. No one seemed sure what was happening, and Mark, who had been drinking too much made matters worse when he dropped Evelyn as he tried to carry her across the threshold. As awful as the panicky marriage can be and despite all the divorces in this country, I expect to get married one day, and I hope that mine lasts.

Special Points: Revising from First to Second Drafts

Check the topic sentence: topic + statement of SOP.

Check subtopic sentences: connector + group + statement.

Delete unnecessary material.

Add material for clarity, completeness, and emphasis.

Check connectors: transitions, repeat words, synonyms, pronouns, and references to main idea.

Transitional word *worst* added to show order of importance

Explanation added

Supporting details and examples added throughout

Explanation added

Check the concluding sentence: connector + link to topic sentence + expanded thought.

Third-Stage Draft

Many of us would call the paper complete after a thorough second draft. But if you want your work to move beyond good to excellent, a third draft gives you that opportunity. With major material and organizational concerns taken care of, you can now improve word choices and sentence variety and delete clutter.

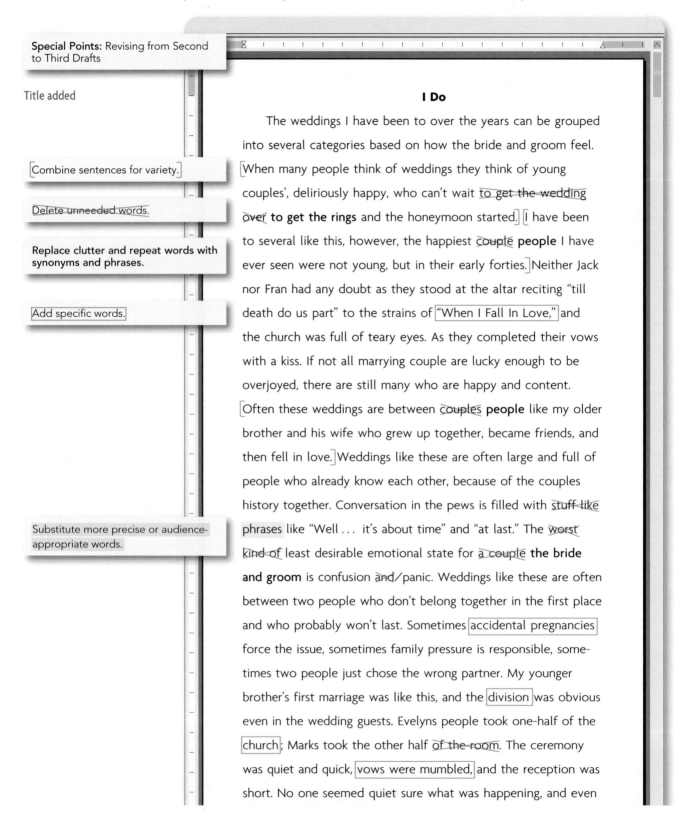

Special Points: Revising from Second to Third Drafts

Title added

Combine sentences for variety.

Delete unneeded words.

Replace clutter and repeat words with synonyms and phrases.

Add specific words.

Substitute more precise or audience-appropriate words.

I Do

The weddings I have been to over the years can be grouped into several categories based on how the bride and groom feel. When many people think of weddings they think of young couples', deliriously happy, who can't wait ~~to get the wedding over~~ **to get the rings** and the honeymoon started. I have been to several like this, however, the happiest ~~couple~~ **people** I have ever seen were not young, but in their early forties. Neither Jack nor Fran had any doubt as they stood at the altar reciting "till death do us part" to the strains of "When I Fall In Love," and the church was full of teary eyes. As they completed their vows with a kiss. If not all marrying couple are lucky enough to be overjoyed, there are still many who are happy and content. Often these weddings are between ~~couples~~ **people** like my older brother and his wife who grew up together, became friends, and then fell in love. Weddings like these are often large and full of people who already know each other, because of the couples history together. Conversation in the pews is filled with ~~stuff like~~ phrases like "Well . . . it's about time" and "at last." The ~~worst kind of~~ least desirable emotional state for ~~a couple~~ **the bride and groom** is confusion ~~and~~/panic. Weddings like these are often between two people who don't belong together in the first place and who probably won't last. Sometimes accidental pregnancies force the issue, sometimes family pressure is responsible, some-times two people just chose the wrong partner. My younger brother's first marriage was like this, and the division was obvious even in the wedding guests. Evelyns people took one-half of the church; Marks took the other half ~~of the room~~. The ceremony was quiet and quick, vows were mumbled, and the reception was short. No one seemed quiet sure what was happening, and even

Mark's ~~who had been drinking too much~~ big attempt to lighten the mood by carrying Evelyn across a threshold at the reception hall fell flat when he stepped on her dress and dropped her. As awful as the panicky marriage can be and despite all the divorces in this country, I expect to get married one day, but I hope that mine lasts!

Final-Editing Draft

In this last draft, Richard reads slowly. He edits closely, word by word, line by line, looking especially for the pattern errors he has listed on his Improvement Chart. He knows that he still has many errors to correct.

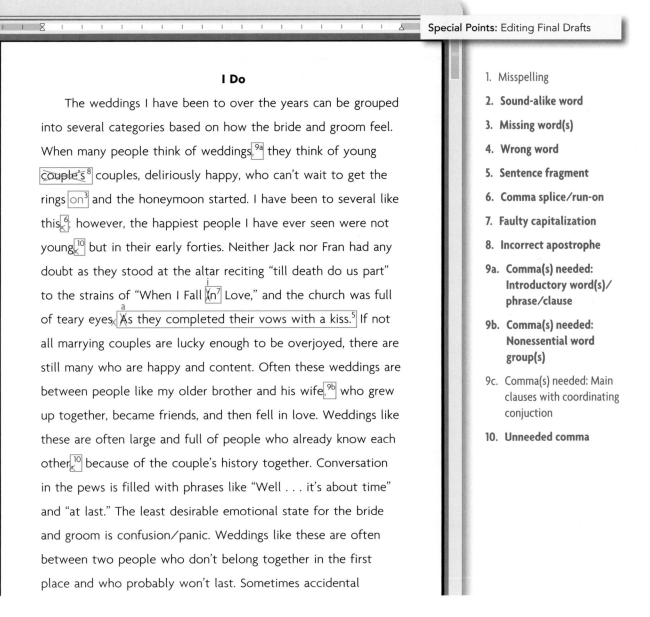

Special Points: Editing Final Drafts

I Do

The weddings I have been to over the years can be grouped into several categories based on how the bride and groom feel. When many people think of weddings, [9a] they think of young couple's [8] couples, deliriously happy, who can't wait to get the rings on [3] and the honeymoon started. I have been to several like this, [6]; however, the happiest people I have ever seen were not young, [10] but in their early forties. Neither Jack nor Fran had any doubt as they stood at the altar reciting "till death do us part" to the strains of "When I Fall in [7] Love," and the church was full of teary eyes, As they completed their vows with a kiss. [5] If not all marrying couples are lucky enough to be overjoyed, there are still many who are happy and content. Often these weddings are between people like my older brother and his wife, [9b] who grew up together, became friends, and then fell in love. Weddings like these are often large and full of people who already know each other, [10] because of the couple's history together. Conversation in the pews is filled with phrases like "Well . . . it's about time" and "at last." The least desirable emotional state for the bride and groom is confusion/panic. Weddings like these are often between two people who don't belong together in the first place and who probably won't last. Sometimes accidental

1. Misspelling
2. **Sound-alike word**
3. **Missing word(s)**
4. **Wrong word**
5. **Sentence fragment**
6. **Comma splice/run-on**
7. **Faulty capitalization**
8. **Incorrect apostrophe**
9a. **Comma(s) needed: Introductory word(s)/ phrase/clause**
9b. **Comma(s) needed: Nonessential word group(s)**
9c. Comma(s) needed: Main clauses with coordinating conjuction
10. **Unneeded comma**

pregnancies force the issue, sometimes family pressure is responsible, and sometimes two people just ~~chose~~[4] choose the wrong partner. My younger brother's first marriage was like this, and the division was obvious even in the wedding guests. ~~Evelyns~~[8] Evelyn's people took one-half of the church[6]; ~~Marks~~[8] Mark's took the other. The ceremony was quiet and quick, vows were mumbled, and the reception was short. No one seemed ~~quiet~~[2] quite sure what was happening, and even Mark's big attempt to lighten the mood by carrying Evelyn across a threshold at the reception hall fell flat when he stepped on her dress and dropped her. As awful as the panicky marriage can be and despite all the divorces in this country, I expect to get married one day, but I hope that mine lasts!

—*Richard Bailey*

For more on revising paragraphs, see Chapter 4.

FINAL-DRAFT CHECKLIST: CLASSIFICATION

Before you turn in your final draft, review this checklist. You may find that, as careful as you think you have been, you still missed a point or two—or more.

- [ ] 1. Have you used a single organizing principle?
- [ ] 2. Have you included all important groups?
- [ ] 3. Do you have a clear reason for your classification?
- [ ] 4. Does your topic sentence name your topic and state the SOP?
- [ ] 5. Have you arranged your groups—usually by time or importance?
- [ ] 6. Does a subtopic sentence introduce each group?
- [ ] 7. Are your main examples relevant, developed, and thoroughly explained?
- [ ] 8. Are all sentences well connected?
- [ ] 9. Does the concluding sentence have an expanded thought?
- [ ] 10. Have you used specific language?
- [ ] 11. Have you used a metaphor or simile?
- [ ] 12. Are your sentences varied in length and beginnings?
- [ ] 13. Have you used synonyms for words that are repeated too often?
- [ ] 14. Have you cut unneeded words?
- [ ] 15. Have you written an interesting title? Have you checked its capitalization?
- [ ] 16. Have you prepared your paper using the format expected by your instructor?

Check to see if you need a title page, use double spacing, leave at least a 1-inch margin, and use a 12-point font.

17. Have you edited your work as closely as you know how to (including having at least one other person proofread)? Have you checked your Improvement Chart for pattern errors?

18. Have you looked for these errors: misspellings, sound-alike words, missing words, wrong words, sentence fragments, comma splices/run-ons, faulty capitalizations, incorrect apostrophes, missing commas, and unnecessary commas?

Alternate Writing Assignments

Here are a few more classification assignment options that may be of interest. For any of these assignments, be sure to do the following:

- Establish a single organizing principle that includes all logical groupings.
- Announce this principle in your topic sentence.
- Introduce each main grouping with a subtopic sentence.
- End with a concluding sentence that restates and expands the main idea.

1. **Describe or upgrade a classifying system at your job.** Secretaries and other office personnel file information according to an SOP (often alphabetically); restaurant personnel group food, beverages, and menu items; people in retail sales arrange counters, aisles, and departments. Look closely at what you or someone else does at your job, and then either simply describe the classification system or suggest a more efficient method. Consider this a business document and adjust your tone accordingly.

2. **Write a classification paragraph with a humorous intent.** You might focus on events of a certain type—say, family gatherings—and classify them ranging from warm and wonderful encounters to pitched battles. You might choose behaviors of some type—say, those that children use to try to manipulate their parents—and classify them ranging from screaming tantrums to kisses and avowals of love. Or you might choose some type of restrictions that you find annoying—say, questionable rules—and classify them according to how seriously they need to be taken.

3. **Write a classification paragraph involving a field you are considering a career in.** For example, engineering could divide into mechanical, electrical, civil; teaching could split into preschool, elementary, middle school, high school, and college. If you are headed for certification in a field like HVAC or fire science, you could categorize the job elements or opportunities within it. Your goal in this assignment is to increase your knowledge of the field.

4. **Write a classification paragraph in which you divide your life to date into stages, to gain insights into who you are.** You might use as an organizing principle one of the following: productivity, freedom, responsibility, risk taking, or socializing. For

example, a person could choose degree of freedom as an SOP and group life stages into nearly absolute freedom, much freedom, not much freedom, and almost no freedom.

5. **Write a classification paragraph based on the three photos shown on this and the previous page.** You can see the three families enjoying themselves through different activities (the SOP): bicycling, camping, and building a snowman. Comment on these activities as ways to bring a family closer, and include some personal examples.

6. CLASSIFYING ON CAMPUS

Conservation in Context

Do a little research and write a classification paragraph describing the different ways your campus classifies the things it disposes of. For instance, the college might offer different recycling bins for paper and for cardboard, with another one for glass bottles and yet another for plastics. Maybe there is even a composting system for food waste, so food is separated from other types of trash. Or you could focus on the way that you classify disposing of items; what do you do with old clothes? with batteries? with your broken cell phone? ●

| **ACTIVITY 8.6** | WORKING ONLINE: *Classification Review* |

OLC

Take the Chapter 8 Review Quiz at www.mhhe.com/brannan.

Linking to Future Experience

Determining the Value of Classification

College assignments often require classifying. For example, in a history class, you might be asked to group the causes of the Civil War by the aspect of American life they related to (the SOP)—that is, to group them into economic, social, political, and other causes. In a biology class, you might be asked to classify a plant by how it reproduces (the SOP). At home, on the job, and in school, classifying is valuable, helping us to simplify and make sense of the world. As you classify and examine groups in a college essay or in a social situation, be careful not to stereotype or oversimplify.

Chapter Summary

1. Classification groups things by a single organizing principle (SOP).
2. We classify information, people, places, events, and objects to simplify our lives, making ideas more comprehensible and accessible.

3. Writers choose an SOP based on the topic and on their own and their audience's interest in the topic.

4. Classification should include all obvious groups without creating an endless list.

5. Writers should always have a reason for classifying.

6. Writing that classifies may use any of the three basic organizing strategies but frequently uses order of importance.

7. Each category should be introduced with a subtopic sentence.

8. Each category should be developed with detailed examples and explanations.

9. Writing is never complete until it has been carefully revised and edited.

Recognizing Causes, Explaining Effects

9

[*What are some causes or effects of global climate change?*]

KEY TOPICS

- Developing skills and exploring ideas in cause or effect paragraphs

    - Discovering causes and effects

    - Developing causes and effects

    - Choosing real causes and effects

    - Thinking critically, avoiding oversimplification

- Analyzing student models: Cause or effect paragraphs

- Writing a cause or effect paragraph

What Are We Trying to Achieve and Why?

Setting the Stage

As the 21st century unfolds, people around the globe are growing more aware of frightening changes in the earth's environment, changes that are accelerating. Most of the world's scientists agree that the earth is slowly warming, due to both natural processes and the activity of people. If we continue to pour carbon dioxide into the atmosphere from power plants like the one pictured on the preceding page, from industrial production, from the cars we drive, and even from the operation of our own homes, what might be the result? Will the glaciers and ice sheets at both poles continue to melt? If so, will animals like the polar bear in the accompanying photograph be driven into extinction? What other results might we expect—will sea levels rise, drowning coastal cities and island countries the world over; will hurricanes continue to increase in frequency and intensity; will arid areas become deserts and fertile farmland become a dustbowl, leading to massive starvation? Or is there something we can do to prevent these results and produce different ones?

When we ask these sort of questions, we are speculating about **causes** and **effects,** the focus of Chapter 9.

Linking to Previous Experience

People constantly face problems that need solutions. For instance, you are stuck in your driveway because the car won't start. Or in your house, you suddenly heard a splashing sound from the bathroom—it was the toilet. Now your car won't start, and the toilet won't stop. What's causing the problems? How will you fix them? What results (effects) can you expect if you tear into them with a hammer and a wrench? Maybe you should call Dad, your older sister, or a plumber? Solving problems and anticipating outcomes are basic survival skills that we all have practiced from the earliest age.

Within this text, we have already worked with cause and effect. In Chapter 5, when you established a dominant impression (effect), you needed to show what elements brought about (caused) the feeling. Chapter 6's personal narrative was full of cause-and-effect relationships. The significance of the event (effect) was created (caused) by the people and their actions. In Chapter 7, you made a statement (often the effect) and then used examples (causes) to illustrate it. And the categories of Chapter 8 were often developed with cause-and-effect examples.

As we move ahead in this text, we will continue to see cause and effect operating as part of other writing patterns.

JOURNAL / BLOG ENTRY 9.1

When have you recently used cause/effect thinking to understand a situation, solve a problem, or predict an outcome? Perhaps your in-laws came for the weekend. What effects did they have on your household? Maybe you just received a brand new MasterCard with a $5,000 limit. If you don't cut it in two, what effects might you predict? Summarize two situations, and tell the causes and/or effects for each.

FEEDBACK   *What other possible causes or effects might you suggest for situations listed by your classmates?*

Developing Skills and Exploring Ideas in Cause or Effect Paragraphs

To learn to write effective cause/effect paragraphs, you need to practice the following:

1. Discovering causes and effects
2. Developing causes and effects
3. Choosing real causes and effects
4. Thinking critically, avoiding oversimplification

Discovering Causes and Effects

Most events have more than one cause and more than one effect, even when these added causes and effects are not obvious to us. For example, we might think that a student did poorly on an algebra exam because he didn't study enough. This is likely a primary, or main, cause, but perhaps there are other significant reasons, which we could explore with a list like the following:

QUESTIONS FOR EXPLORING CAUSES

-   **Primary:** What causes would certainly bring about the event?
-   **Secondary:** What causes might reasonably bring about the event?
-   **Contributing:** What causes might play a role by creating or adding to another cause?
-   **Immediate:** What is the cause closest in time that produced the event?
-   **Distant:** What causes might be separated from the event by time or space?
-   **Hidden:** What causes might not be readily apparent?
-   **Minor:** What causes might be involved in a lesser way (and in some cases be mistaken for significant ones)?

Applying these questions to the failed algebra exam, we might come up with this list:

-   **Primary:** insufficient studying
-   **Secondary:** argument with parents the night prior to the test
-   **Contributing:** work demands cutting into study time
-   **Immediate:** answering only half the problems
-   **Distant:** not grasping arithmetic concepts from earlier grade levels
-   **Hidden:** undiagnosed attention deficit disorder
-   **Minor:** student nearby whistling throughout the exam

Now we can see that there are many reasons for poor grades, and we would pick the ones best suited to our purpose, interest, and audience. Notice that what might be only a secondary reason for one person might be a primary reason for another. For example, the argument might have upset the student so much that he could not think clearly during the exam. Also, a distant or hidden cause might be crucial to the effect, so you must decide which causes or effects are most significant.

You could use a similar series of questions to explore effects ("What effects would this event have?" and so on).

There are often several primary causes and effects. Whether a cause is primary or secondary is often the writer's judgment.

In a small group, discuss one of the following topics, brainstorming for causes or effects. The Questions for Exploring Causes may help you discover ideas. Next, list six possible causes or effects. Then decide which three are most likely, and tell why you eliminated the others.

EXAMPLE: Topic: being elected valedictorian of your graduating class

Possible causes:

1. *Having overall highest GPA*	2. *Making A's on all final exams*
3. ~~*Having a parent as a dean*~~	4. ~~*Getting early computer training*~~
5. *Having good study habits*	6. ~~*Being rewarded by parents for A's*~~

Reasons for cutting causes: *Number 3 is not likely because GPA, not the dean, determines the valedictorian. Causes 4 and 6 could contribute to student success but are not as significant as causes 1, 2, and 5.*

1. Topic: requiring all high school students to take a course that educates about addictive substances

Possible causes:

1.	2.
3.	4.
5.	6.

Reasons for cutting causes: _____

_____

2. Topic: switching careers in midlife

Possible causes:

1.	2.
3.	4.
5.	6.

Reasons for cutting causes: _____

_____

_____

_____

3. Topic: marrying while still teenagers

Possible effects:

1.	2.
3.	4.
5.	6.

Reasons for cutting effects: _____

_____

_____

4. Topic: watching too much television

Possible effects:

1.	2.
3.	4.
5.	6.

Reasons for cutting effects: _____

_____

_____

Developing Causes and Effects

After choosing likely causes or effects for your topic, you will develop them with detailed examples and clear explanations. You may use the "I" voice of personal experience or the more formal "they" approach. Examples can be developed through specific words, sensory details, active verbs, -ing words, and dialogue. You will need a subtopic sentence to introduce each cause or effect.

ACTIVITY 9.2 *Developing Causes and Effects*

Choose a topic from Activity 9.1 and develop one of its causes or effects with examples, details, and explanations. You can use personal experience, as in the following example, or general knowledge. After deciding how you will develop this cause or effect, write a subtopic sentence that includes the cause or effect and makes a statement about it. Then develop it in several sentences.

EXAMPLE: Topic: **watching too much television**

Possible effect: *Too little time for studying causes poor grades.*

Subtopic sentence: *When I was a sophomore in high school, my grades took a nosedive when my parents gave me a TV for my room.*

Subtopic developed: *It was great to have some privacy to watch TV and not have to fight with my older brother over who got to see what program. But I started watching the tube nonstop from the time I got home from school till bedtime. After failing three out of five classes, even I saw a problem, and my parents took the set till my grades improved.*

Topic from Activity 9.1: _____

Possible cause or effect: _____

Subtopic sentence: _____

_____

Subtopic developed: _____

_____

_____

_____

Choosing Real Causes and Effects

People are often wrong about causes and effects because they judge too quickly, assuming that, just because two actions are closely related in time, one causes or is an effect of the other. For example, children who hear thunder and see rain follow might conclude that thunder causes rain. Or a motorist caught in slow highway traffic might conclude that the driver in front of him is the problem when, in fact, the slowdown is caused by gawkers ahead who are staring at a stalled car. When we slow down and think critically, we are more likely to find the real causes and effects of an event.

ACTIVITY 9.3 *Choosing Real Causes and Effects*

For each topic, put an X in front of the cause and the effect that seem *least* reasonable. Next, explain why you think the cause or effect is unlikely.

1. Topic: becoming addicted to alcohol

Causes	**Effects**
_____ Having parents who are heavy drinkers	_____ Losing a job
_____ Having friends who are heavy drinkers	_____ Losing friends
_____ Suffering from overstress	_____ Leading a happier life
_____ Liking the taste of beer	_____ Becoming malnourished
_____ Being genetically predisposed	_____ Developing cirrhosis of the liver

Unlikely cause: _____

_____

Unlikely effect: _____

2. Topic: overusing pesticides and herbicides on a lawn

Causes	**Effects**
_____ Being ignorant of the problem	_____ Killing some plants and animals that aren't pests
_____ Being indifferent to the problem	_____ Polluting water
_____ Having no laws restricting use	_____ Eradicating insect pests and weeds
_____ Wanting a beautiful lawn	_____ Polluting soil
_____ Reacting to environmentalists	_____ Making animals and people sick

Unlikely cause: _____

_____

Unlikely effect: _____

3. Topic: attending the funeral of someone you never liked

Causes	**Effects**
_____ Fulfilling a family obligation	_____ Feeling good about the decision
_____ Trying to meet new people	_____ Feeling horribly bored

———— Acting kindly toward the family	———— Making family members happy
———— Fulfilling a moral obligation	———— Reassessing feelings toward the deceased
———— Fulfilling a work obligation	———— Realizing deceased was a saint

Unlikely cause: _____

Unlikely effect: _____

_____

Thinking Critically, Avoiding Oversimplification

When people look for a quick explanation or solution to a problem, they often oversimplify. For instance, when you see a young person driving a $50,000 car, you might conclude that she has lots of money. But there are several other likely explanations: She is leasing the vehicle, or she is driving her parents' car, or she has a 5-year loan and barely makes the payments. To write and think critically, we often need to slow down, asking the question "Is this the only or best explanation possible?"

ACTIVITY 9.4 *Thinking Critically*

Read the following oversimplified statements, and list five other likely causes or effects.

1. When the earth's temperature rises a few more degrees, people will just enjoy milder winters.

   Other effects of global warming:

   A. _____

   B. _____

   C. _____

   D. _____

   E. _____

2. If the driving age were raised to 18, there would be fewer accidents.

   Other causes of accidents:

   A. _____

   B. _____

   C. _____

   D. _____

   E. _____

3. If a person switches careers in midlife, he is probably failing at his job.

   Other causes of a career change:

   A. _____

   B. _____

   C. _____

D. _____

E. _____

4. People exercise mainly to feel good about themselves.

   Other effects of exercise:

   A. _____

   B. _____

   C. _____

   D. _____

   E. _____

5. Rap music makes people behave violently.

   Other effects of rap music:

   A. _____

   B. _____

   C. _____

   D. _____

   E. _____

Analyzing Student Models: Cause or Effect Paragraphs

The following models will help you write cause or effect paragraphs. "Making the Promise Last" is developed through generalized experience, whereas "The Thousand-Dollar Lesson" and "Building Memories" focus on personal examples. As with any writing models, do not simply reproduce the authors' work; instead, apply the principles you discover to your own writing.

➤ Prereading Exploration for "Making the Promise Last"

In discussions with group members, Gebdao Kaiwalweroj found that they agreed with her that early marriage can lead to problems. They shared stories from which she drew some specific examples for her paper. For a target audience, Gebdao chose young people considering early marriage.

Though this paper is not a formal argument, part of the author's purpose is persuasion. Before reading further, for perspective on the issue, list four possible *positive* effects on young adults of marrying right out of high school.

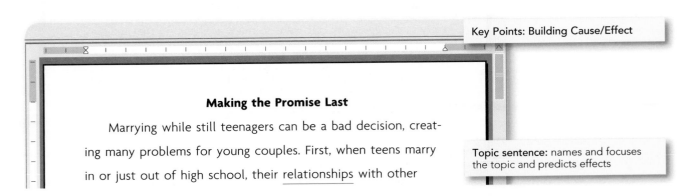

Key Points: Building Cause/Effect

Making the Promise Last

Marrying while still teenagers can be a bad decision, creating many problems for young couples. First, when teens marry in or just out of high school, their relationships with other

Topic sentence: names and focuses the topic and predicts effects

Subtopic sentences: name each effect and make a <u>limiting statement</u>

Sentence connectors: transitions (*first, when, now*), repeat words (*couple*), synonyms (*teenagers, newlyweds*), pronouns (*many, themselves, who*), and reference to main idea (marriage problems: *die out, cut off, stress*)

Development: action, scene and character details, sensory details, active verbs, *-ing* words, specific words, and explanations of the examples

Qualifying: words used to soften a statement (*often, can, maybe, some, may*)

Concluding sentence: restates the topic and adds a final (expanded) thought.

people often <u>change drastically</u>. Instead of spending time with their individual former friends, newlyweds often find that their spouse does not like some or all of their friends, so the husband or wife has to choose—"them or me." Even when the old friends are accepted, many times friendships die out because a married couple's interests can be so different from a single person's. While some young couples continue to go to the same parties, concerts, and vacation spots, many more find themselves having to try to have fun with each other's in-laws instead. As the years pass, another problem begins as young couples often find themselves becoming increasingly cut off from the rest of life and dependent on one another. They have already been seeing less of old friends, many of whom are off at college or trade school or simply doing other things, but after that first baby arrives, the young couple's life becomes really isolated. A new baby also has the effect of making their life hard. If they had been thinking about more school, with the new load of bills, forget it. The newest priority becomes baby food and diapers. When the normal stress of raising a baby is added to life goals put aside and relaxation time vanishing, many young marriages begin to crumble. Now the couple experiences one of the worst effects of hasty marriage—divorce. Even without the added tension of a baby, many young adults, who are still finding out who they themselves are, soon learn in their time living together that they are not right for each other. If a child is involved, then the baby's life and the parents' lives are inevitably changed for the worse. The childless couple may split, finding a better life for themselves one day, but divorce with a baby heaps extra bills for separate maintenance and guilt on the parents. While some early marriages work out well, so many end poorly that maybe teens should wait until they know and can take care of themselves better before they stand at an altar and promise to take care of someone else.

—*Gebdao Kaiwalweroj*

➡ Prereading Exploration for "The Thousand-Dollar Lesson"

In this essay, Lucas Eimers writes for an audience of young adults who have gotten a speeding ticket or two and who have had trouble with their car insurance.

Before reading the paragraph, think about this question: If you were to write about speeding, would you focus on causes or effects? Which do you think would make a more interesting paper? Why? Since Lucas tells about the effects of speeding, focus on causes, listing four of them.

Key Points: Building Cause/Effect

The Thousand-Dollar Lesson

While traveling last spring, I learned about the miserable consequences of speeding. My first unpleasant experience was actually getting the ticket. I knew I was in trouble from the moment I saw the red flashing lights in my rearview mirror and looked down at the speedometer to see the needle on 85. I thought I might be able to talk my way out of it until I saw the Clint Eastwood look-alike Texas highway patrol officer step up to my window. "All right, boy, let me see your license and proof of insurance," he drawled, cutting off my "Gee-I-didn't-realize-I-was-going-that-fast" line. The officer seemed to enjoy every second it took him to write that ticket out, and with an evil smirk he handed it to me, saying, "Have a nice day." I'm pretty sure he was the only one having fun. The next problem was paying the ticket. I didn't want it on my record because it would crank up my insurance rates, so I knew it would cost plenty, and it did. The ticket was only 75 dollars, but it cost 300 to have it "disappear" from my record. Yet as bad as that expense was, the next effect was worse. My parents had been paying my insurance because I was still living at home and going to college. However, after they learned of my ticket, they decided to stop helping me with the coverage. They reasoned that if I had enough money to speed, then I had enough money to pay for my own insurance. I never quite figured out their logic, but I got their point. A thousand dollars for a year's premiums is an expensive lesson. Having to cover the insurance on top of the ticket led to the worst consequence of all—work, work, work! I picked up additional hours at the golf course where I work, but that was not enough. So I turned to my parents, who were willing to help, they said, with

Topic sentence: names and focuses the topic and predicts effects

Subtopic sentences: name each effect and make a limiting statement—for example, "My first unpleasant experience was actually getting the ticket."

Sentence connectors: transitions (*first, next, however*), repeat words (*speeding*), synonyms (*cost, expense*), pronouns (*it, my, who*), and reference to main idea (speeding problems: *miserable, unpleasant, work*)

Development: action, scene and character details, sensory details, active verbs, *-ing* words, comparisons, specific words, and explanations of the examples

Concluding sentence: restates the topic and adds a final (expanded) thought

smiles that reminded me of the Texas highway patrol officer. There were plenty of odd jobs for me to do on the weekends around the house: painting the shed, staining the deck, washing the windows, cleaning out the garage. . . . My folks were very creative and have given me lots of this kind of "help." Before this last year I thought I knew what kind of trouble speeding could cause me, but I know now, and I am more inclined to think about the consequences of everything I do now before I act.

—*Lucas Eimers*

POSTREADING QUESTIONS FOR PARAGRAPH ANALYSIS

Note: These questions apply to both student models.

1. Which words in the topic sentence name the topic, limit it, and predict cause or effect?

2. What words in the concluding sentence link to the topic sentence?

3. What is the expanded thought (p. 50) in the final sentence?

4. Copy each of the subtopic sentences, and underline the <u>cause or effect</u> once and the <u>statement</u> made about it twice. Circle connectors: transitions, repeat words, synonyms, and pronouns.

5. What words show that the main causes or effects are arranged by order of importance (see Activity 7.3) or in another way?

6. Choose a cause or effect and tell how the author's explaining (as opposed to detailing or action description) helps you better understand the author's point.

7. Choose a cause or effect and tell how the action description and detailing help you better understand the author's point.

8. Name three specific words and list a more general word for each (pp. 75–76).

9. Name three ways to further develop any cause or effect in this paragraph. Consider action, active verbs, dialogue, specific words, sensory details, description of person or setting, revealing thoughts or emotions, and further explanation.

For more on connectors, see pp. 54–56.

For more on detailing and explaining examples, see pp. 42–49.

WRITING A CAUSE OR EFFECT PARAGRAPH

Summarizing the Assignment

Write a single paragraph of 250 to 300 words that explains the reasons (causes) something happens or the results (effects) that follow from it. While writers often develop their work with both causes and effects, to keep your paragraph focused, choose either causes *or* effects. Include a focused topic sentence that predicts causes or effects, use three or four well-developed major examples (causes or effects), and end with a sentence that links to the topic sentence and adds a final (expanded) thought about it.

Establishing Audience and Purpose

One of the best ways to focus this paper is through audience and purpose. Aside from your instructor, consider who else might be interested in your topic—for example, your parents, a good friend, or a group to which you belong. If you chose as your topic the causes of poor grades in college, you could write for students who are not doing well in school. They might be interested in your insights, and you would then have a purpose: to inform these students and perhaps help them improve their academic performance. At a more general level, a cause or effect paper has one or more of the following purposes:

- To understand a situation
- To solve a problem
- To predict an outcome
- To entertain
- To persuade

Targeting an audience will help focus your material. For more on audience profiling, see pp. 12–14.

Working through the Writing Assignment

Discovering Ideas

There are many possibilities for this assignment; you can write about any of the following:

- Behaviors (Why do some people become anorexic?)
- Ideas or concepts (What is the basis for your views on physical beauty?)
- People (What lasting effects has your grandmother had on your family?)
- Places (What brought Crater Lake into being?)
- Objects (What are the effects of having a bird feeder in your backyard in the winter?)
- Animals (What effects does your new Great Dane puppy have on your household?)

Your topic can center on an event, person, place, object, or animal.

Discussions about causes and effects concern actions and interactions. Thus, many cause or effect papers have as their topic events (things that happen).

The following topics list will help you with ideas for the assignment. As you skim the topics, remember that you will focus on causes *or* effects. However, for each topic you consider, think about both causes and effects to discover which approach would be more interesting to you.

POSSIBLE TOPICS: CAUSES OR EFFECTS

- Taking a child to a museum (zoo, ball game, pool, movie) for the first time
- Having parents choose a spouse for their child
- Becoming a parent (grandparent)
- Making the football (basketball, baseball, soccer) team

For more cause-and-effect topics, look under Chapter 9 at www.mhhe.com/brannan.

- Making a personal commitment to reduce your carbon footprint
- Learning to cook
- Limiting TV viewing to 1 hour per day
- Graduating from high school (college)
- Dropping out of high school
- Enrolling a 4-year-old in preschool
- Joining the military after high school graduation
- Riding your bicycle to school & work instead of driving
- Raising the driving age to 18
- Requiring counseling before a couple can divorce

ACTIVITY 9.5 WORKING ONLINE: *Use the Causal Analysis Writing Tutor*

For additional topic ideas for this assignment, look under Chapter 9 at www.mhhe.com/brannan. And for more cause-and-effect strategies, download the Causal Analysis Writing Tutor.

Once you have several topics in hand, explore their causes and effects more systematically, through brainstorming methods such as focused clustering and listing. This will help you to make a final choice, to decide whether you will write about causes or effects, and to discover possible examples for developing your paragraph.

Create a list for *both* causes and effects.

Prewriting

Listing is a particularly effective strategy. The Questions for Exploring Causes (p. 188) can help with ideas. Brian Peraud, the author of the model on pages 205–206, chose the topic "taking a child somewhere" and then focused it with his own experience of taking his daughter to the zoo.

BRIAN'S LIST OF QUESTIONS

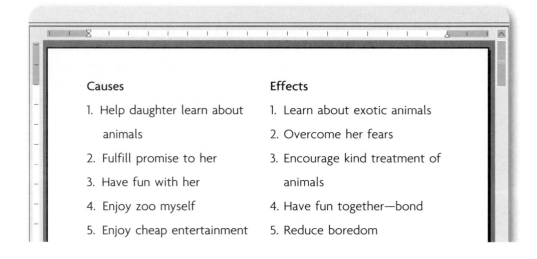

Causes	Effects
1. Help daughter learn about animals	1. Learn about exotic animals
2. Fulfill promise to her	2. Overcome her fears
3. Have fun with her	3. Encourage kind treatment of animals
4. Enjoy zoo myself	4. Have fun together—bond
5. Enjoy cheap entertainment	5. Reduce boredom

6. Escape from house	6. Teach her about larger world
7. Enjoy good weather	7. Increase environmental awareness

PREWRITING—SUMMING UP

1. Choose several topics from the list, or create several of your own.
2. Prewrite to create a cause list and an effect list for each.
3. Brainstorm to discover examples for the causes and effects.
4. Choose a topic, and choose to write about either causes or effects to focus your paragraph.

JOURNAL / BLOG ENTRY 9.2

Tell why you chose your topic and focus—causes or effects. What is your purpose (to inform, entertain, or persuade), and who is your audience? List several examples with details that you can use to develop your causes or effects. Are these examples drawn from personal experiences ("I" tone) or from general knowledge ("they" tone)?

For more on tone, see Chapter 20.

Organizing Ideas

To help focus and arrange your main examples, write a rough topic sentence that states the topic and focus and predicts either causes or effects. You can say directly that you will deal with causes or effects. For causes, use a word like *reasons, explanations, problems,* or *factors* or a phrase like *to bring about* or *to create.* For effects, use a word like *results, outcome, consequences, occurrences,* or *solutions* or a phrase like *what follows* or *what happens to.* Also, you can more specifically **forecast** the causes or effects you will explain. The following topic sentences show the different approaches (the topic is underlined once; the words predicting effects are underlined twice):

EFFECTS WORD INCLUDED	Taking my daughter to the zoo last Sunday had three important consequences.
EFFECTS FORECASTED	Our trip to the zoo last Sunday taught my daughter a lot about exotic creatures, helped her to overcome her fears of large animals, and helped us grow closer together.
NO EFFECTS WORD OR FORECASTING	Before our trip to the zoo last Sunday, I would not have believed so many positive experiences could come from one place.

After writing a topic sentence, look again at your list of causes or effects and make decisions, limiting your list to three or four points. Think about how these points might best be organized (by time or order of importance), and write a working outline. Brian crossed out several effects and then combined 2 with 3 and 4 with 5 to arrive at a manageable working outline with three points:

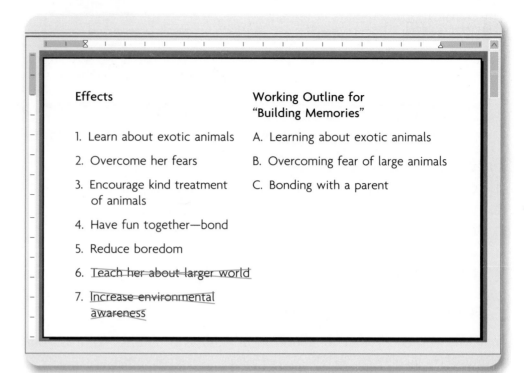

Effects	Working Outline for "Building Memories"
1. Learn about exotic animals	A. Learning about exotic animals
2. Overcome her fears	B. Overcoming fear of large animals
3. Encourage kind treatment of animals	C. Bonding with a parent
4. Have fun together—bond	
5. Reduce boredom	
6. ~~Teach her about larger world~~	
7. ~~Increase environmental awareness~~	

HINT

For more on connectors, see pp. 54–56.

You will introduce each cause or effect with a subtopic sentence linked to the paragraph by connectors like the transitions listed below. Before drafting, review this list.

FOR ADDING MATERIAL

again	as well as	furthermore	likewise
also	besides	in addition	moreover
and	further	last	next

FOR GIVING EXAMPLES AND EMPHASIS

above all	especially	in particular	one reason
after all	for example	in truth	specifically
another	for instance	it is true	surely
as an example	indeed	most important	that is
certainly	in fact	of course	to illustrate

FOR SHOWING CAUSE AND EFFECT

accordingly	because	hence	then
and so	consequently	since	therefore
as a result	for this reason	so	thus

FOR SUMMARIZING AND CONCLUDING

finally	in conclusion	in short	that is
in brief	in other words	largely	to summarize

ORGANIZING—SUMMING UP

1. Create a rough topic sentence to help focus your material.

2. Decide on the main causes or effects (only three or four). To do this, combine closely related causes/effects, delete unneeded ones, and add any that are needed.

3. Arrange the main causes/effects either by importance or chronologically.

4. Create a working outline.

5. Review the list of transitions (and remember the other connectors).

JOURNAL / BLOG ENTRY 9.3

Write out your working topic sentence. Does it mention causes or effects? Now list your main causes or effects. Does chronological order or order of importance seem the best arrangement for the material? Why?

Drafting

With the preliminary work done, you are almost ready to write your first draft. But before plunging in, review the drafting suggestions in Chapter 1 (pp. 17–19). As you write, be sure to do the following:

1. Qualify where needed, using terms like *often, many, sometimes, usually, frequently, seldom, might, could,* and *possibly.*

You can avoid oversimplifying your topic by using qualifying words. See pp. 485–487.

2. Include important causes or effects.

3. Remember that the fact that one event occurs before another does not mean one event causes the other.

4. Complete all thoughts so readers can see the cause/effect relation. If, for instance, you said that because your parents were on vacation you almost lost your job, a reader might be confused. However, if you explained that your folks usually wake you in the morning so you won't be late for work, you would clarify the causal connection.

Complete all points or thoughts.

JOURNAL / BLOG ENTRY 9.4

Soon after writing your first draft, reread the assignment on pages 196–197, and then skim the draft. Does it fit the assignment? Are there three or four causes or effects, and are they arranged effectively? What part of your draft do you like best? What part least? Answer in a paragraph.

FEEDBACK *Comment on the organization and effectiveness of a classmate's causes or effects in his or her draft. Then respond to a comment you receive.*

Revising Drafts

For help with revising first, second, and final drafts, turn to Chapter 4, pages 63–67.

Annotated Student Model: "Building Memories"

Carefully reading the annotated student model will help clarify questions you have about your own draft.

First-Stage Draft

Brian Peraud chose parents with school-age children as an audience. He wrote a fast draft based on his working outline.

Topic sentence needs focus.

Second sentence is unneeded.

Main effects are in place but need to be developed with detailed examples and further explanations.

I had a great time with my daughter the other day. The drive over to the zoo took longer than it should have, but that didn't keep us from having a good time. First, we both learned more about foreign animals like lions and elephants. Katy learned that they live in families called prides and the females do almost all the hunting. Then the female lions bring home the food to the head of the pride and the other lions. Another good thing about our trip together was that it helped my daughter overcome fear of big animals. When she was 3, she was knocked down by a dog, and she has been nervous around dogs since. Being close to calm animals like the elephants, made her feel more relaxed. She enjoyed seeing the mother caring for her new baby. After we had been at the zoo for awhile, Katy was relaxed enough to help me feed a giraffe. It was fun watching my little girl feed the animal. The giraffe was so tall and she was so small. She held the grass out to it standing so high above the ground. As the tongue curled around the grass, Katy squealed, yet she fed the giraffe even more. Another good thing about our trip was spending play-time together. It was fun to run around, laughing at the prairie dogs and creeping up on the peacocks shimmering in the sunlight. We both had our hands slimmed by the baby goats, and Katy got a big kick out of seeing me butted from behind. We had to keep up our strength by eating. This gave us an excuse to eat all the junky zoo food we could get our hands on: hotdogs, cheese nachos, and rainbow bomb pops. This trip to the zoo helped me realize how important it is to keep building happy memories.

Second-Stage Draft

Rough first drafts of cause or effect papers often have difficulties with overall focus, development, and relevant material. Note the explanations and examples added to this draft to help clarify meaning.

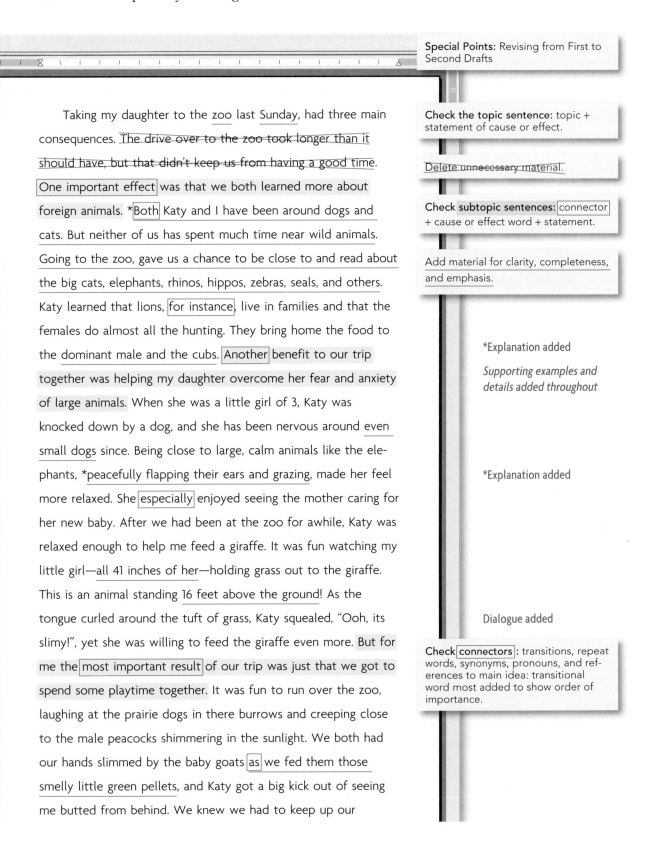

Special Points: Revising from First to Second Drafts

Check the topic sentence: topic + statement of cause or effect.

Delete unnecessary material.

Check subtopic sentences: connector + cause or effect word + statement.

Add material for clarity, completeness, and emphasis.

*Explanation added

Supporting examples and details added throughout

*Explanation added

Dialogue added

Check connectors: transitions, repeat words, synonyms, pronouns, and references to main idea: transitional word most added to show order of importance.

Taking my daughter to the zoo last Sunday, had three main consequences. ~~The drive over to the zoo took longer than it should have, but that didn't keep us from having a good time.~~ One important effect was that we both learned more about foreign animals. *Both Katy and I have been around dogs and cats. But neither of us has spent much time near wild animals. Going to the zoo, gave us a chance to be close to and read about the big cats, elephants, rhinos, hippos, zebras, seals, and others. Katy learned that lions, for instance, live in families and that the females do almost all the hunting. They bring home the food to the dominant male and the cubs. Another benefit to our trip together was helping my daughter overcome her fear and anxiety of large animals. When she was a little girl of 3, Katy was knocked down by a dog, and she has been nervous around even small dogs since. Being close to large, calm animals like the ele-phants, *peacefully flapping their ears and grazing, made her feel more relaxed. She especially enjoyed seeing the mother caring for her new baby. After we had been at the zoo for awhile, Katy was relaxed enough to help me feed a giraffe. It was fun watching my little girl—all 41 inches of her—holding grass out to the giraffe. This is an animal standing 16 feet above the ground! As the tongue curled around the tuft of grass, Katy squealed, "Ooh, its slimy!", yet she was willing to feed the giraffe even more. But for me the most important result of our trip was just that we got to spend some playtime together. It was fun to run over the zoo, laughing at the prairie dogs in there burrows and creeping close to the male peacocks shimmering in the sunlight. We both had our hands slimmed by the baby goats as we fed them those smelly little green pellets, and Katy got a big kick out of seeing me butted from behind. We knew we had to keep up our strength by eating. This gave us an excuse to eat all the junky zoo food we could get our hands on: hot dogs, cheese nachos, rainbow bomb pops, $\boxed{\text{and}}$ a wad of cotton candy that would have choked a hippo. $\boxed{\text{Besides being great fun,}}$ our trip helped me again to realize how important it is in any relationship—but especially for a parent and child—to keep building happy memories.

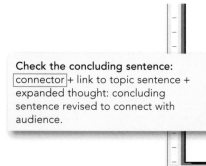

Check the concluding sentence: $\boxed{\text{connector}}$ + link to topic sentence + expanded thought: concluding sentence revised to connect with audience.

Third-Stage Draft

This draft gave Brian the opportunity to polish his work at the word and sentence level, and to move his draft beyond good to excellent. Notice in particular how he has added more specific words to clarify images.

Special Points: Revising from Second to Third Drafts

Title added

Delete unneeded words.

Substitute more precise or audience-appropriate words.

Combine sentences for variety.

Add specific words.

Replace clutter and repeat words with synonyms and phrases.

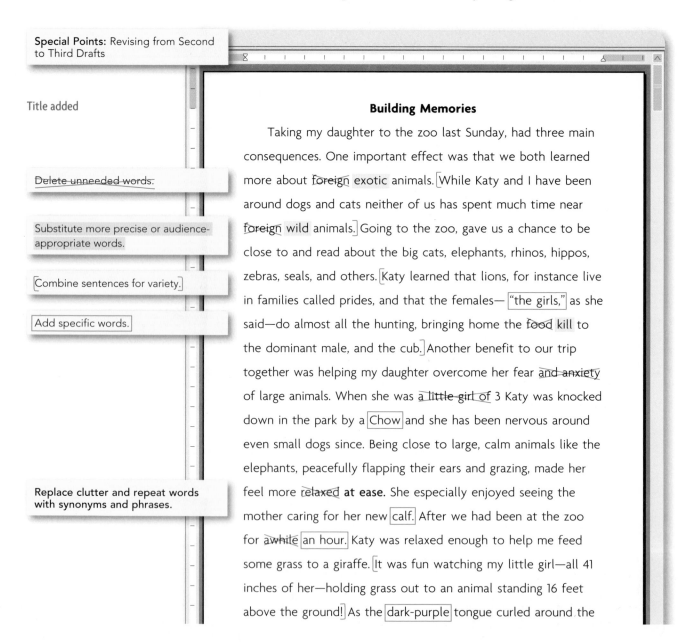

Building Memories

Taking my daughter to the zoo last Sunday, had three main consequences. One important effect was that we both learned more about ~~foreign~~ exotic animals. While Katy and I have been around dogs and cats neither of us has spent much time near ~~foreign~~ wild animals. Going to the zoo, gave us a chance to be close to and read about the big cats, elephants, rhinos, hippos, zebras, seals, and others. Katy learned that lions, for instance live in families called prides, and that the females— $\boxed{\text{"the girls,"}}$ as she said—do almost all the hunting, bringing home the ~~food~~ kill to the dominant male, and the cub. Another benefit to our trip together was helping my daughter overcome her fear ~~and anxiety~~ of large animals. When she was ~~a little girl of~~ 3 Katy was knocked down in the park by a $\boxed{\text{Chow}}$ and she has been nervous around even small dogs since. Being close to large, calm animals like the elephants, peacefully flapping their ears and grazing, made her feel more ~~relaxed~~ **at ease.** She especially enjoyed seeing the mother caring for her new $\boxed{\text{calf.}}$ After we had been at the zoo for ~~awhile~~ $\boxed{\text{an hour.}}$ Katy was relaxed enough to help me feed some grass to a giraffe. It was fun watching my little girl—all 41 inches of her—holding grass out to an animal standing 16 feet above the ground! As the $\boxed{\text{dark-purple}}$ tongue curled around the tuft of grass in her hand, Katy squealed, "Ooh, its slimy!" yet she was willing to feed the giraffe even more. For me the most important result of our trip was just that we got to spend some playtime together. It was fun to run over the zoo, laughing at the little prairie dogs in there burrows and creeping close to the male peacocks shimmering blue-green in the sunlight. We both had our hands slimmed by the baby pygmy goats, as we fed them those smelly little green pellets, and Katy got a big kick out of seeing me butted from behind. To keep up our strength, we just had to eat all the junky zoo food we could get our hands on: hotdogs, cheese nachos, rainbow bomb pops, and a wad of cotton candy that could have choked a hippo. Besides being great fun, our trip to the zoo helped me again to realize how important it is in any relationship—but especially for a parent and child—to keep building happy memories.

Final-Editing Draft

By this point, Brian's draft is in great shape, and he can shift into low gear, moving slowly, line by line, looking for each error in grammar, spelling, and punctuation, and using his Improvement Chart to help find pattern errors.

Special Points: Editing Final Drafts

Building Memories

Taking my daughter to the zoo last Sunday[10] had three main consequences. One important effect was that we both learned more about exotic animals. While Katy and I have been around dogs and cats,[9a] neither of us has spent much time near wild animals. Going to the zoo[10] gave us a chance to be close to and read about the big cats, elephants, rhinos, hippos, zebras, seals, and others. Katy learned that lions, for instance[9b] live in families called prides[10] and that the females—"the girls," as she said—do almost all the hunting, bringing home the kill to the dominant male[10] and the cubs. Another benefit to our trip together was helping my daughter overcome her fear of large animals. When she was 3,[9a] Katy was knocked down in the park by a Chow[9c]

1. **Misspelling**
2. **Sound-alike word**
3. **Missing word(s)**
4. Wrong word
5. **Sentence fragment**
6. Comma splice/run-on
7. Faulty capitalization
8. Incorrect apostrophe
9a. **Comma(s) needed: Introductory word(s)/ phrase/clause**
9b. **Comma(s) needed: Nonessential word group(s)**

**9c. Comma(s) needed:
Main clauses with
coordinating
conjunction**

10. Unneeded comma

and she has been nervous around even small dogs since. Being close to large, calm animals like the elephants, peacefully flapping their ears and grazing, made her feel more at ease. She especially enjoyed seeing the mother caring for her new calf. After we had been at the zoo for an hour⁵, Katy was relaxed enough to help me feed some grass to a giraffe. It was fun watching my little girl—all 41 inches of her—holding grass out to an animal standing 16 feet above the ground! As the dark-purple tongue curled around the tuft of grass in her hand, Katy squealed, "Ooh, ~~its²~~ it's slimy!", yet she was willing to feed the giraffe even more. But for me the most important result of our trip was just that we got to spend some playtime together. It was fun to run all³ over the zoo, laughing at the little prairie dogs in ~~there²~~ their burrows and creeping close to the male peacocks shimmering blue-green in the sunlight. We both had our hands ~~slimmed¹~~ slimed by the pygmy goats¹⁰ as we fed them those smelly little green pellets, and Katy got a big kick out of seeing me butted from behind. To keep up our strength, we just had to eat all the junky zoo food we could get our hands on: hot dogs, cheese nachos, rainbow bomb pops, and a wad of cotton candy that could have choked a hippo. Besides being great fun, our trip to the zoo helped me again to realize how important it is in any relationship—but especially for a parent and child—to keep building happy memories.

—Brian Peraud

For more on revising paragraphs, see Chapter 4.

FINAL-DRAFT CHECKLIST: CAUSE/EFFECT

Before you turn in your final draft, review this checklist. You may find that, as careful as you think you have been, you still missed a point or two—or more.

- [ ] 1. Have you listed the three or four most important causes or effects?
- [ ] 2. Is your topic sentence effective?
- [ ] 3. Have you arranged your causes or effects by importance or time?
- [ ] 4. Does a subtopic sentence introduce each cause or effect?
- [ ] 5. Are your main examples relevant, developed, and thoroughly explained?

6. Are all sentences well connected?

7. Does the concluding sentence have an expanded thought?

8. Have you used specific language?

9. Have you used a metaphor or simile?

10. Are your sentences varied in length and beginnings?

11. Have you used synonyms for words that are repeated too often?

12. Have you cut unneeded words?

13. Have you written an interesting title? Have you checked its capitalization?

14. Have you prepared your paper using the format expected by your instructor?

15. Have you edited your work closely (including having at least one other person proofread)? Have you checked your Improvement Chart for pattern errors?

16. Have you looked for errors involving the following: misspellings, sound-alike words, missing words, wrong words, sentence fragments, comma splices/run-ons, faulty capitalization, incorrect apostrophes, missing commas, and unnecessary commas?

Check to see if you need a title page, use double spacing, leave at least a 1-inch margin, and use a 12-point font.

Alternate Writing Assignments

These assignments show some other ways we use cause-and-effect analysis and may help you find a topic. For any of these assignments, be sure to do the following:

- Choose either causes or effects, and mention your focus in the topic sentence.

- Beware of oversimplifying and underexplaining.

- Introduce each main cause or effect with a subtopic sentence.

- End with a concluding sentence that expands the main idea of the paper.

1. **Write a letter of complaint dealing with a situation, service, or product.** For example, think of a time when you were dissatisfied with some service (lawn care, car repair, haircut) or product and discuss the outcome (effects). You might focus your effects merely on reporting, say, the stalling of your car after a tune-up or mention in detail what you will do about the poor service if it is not remedied (call the Better Business Bureau, sue, go to small claims court).

2. **Write about the causes or effects of a trend in society.** For example, you might have noticed an increase in young women smoking and speculate on why (advertising targeting young women, schools cutting back on health education, role models who smoke). Or you might have noticed a decrease in attendance at concerts or sporting events. What is causing it? What might be the results? Consider trends affecting entertainment, sporting events, employment, education, interpersonal relationships, consumer products, child care, health care, and other areas.

3. **Write about the long-term effects someone has had on you.** Think about a person who has been important in your life—a teacher, coach, boss, parent, or child—and tell about the effects he or she has had on you. For instance, you might discuss how your child helped you learn

patience, humility, and appreciation for the little things in life. Or you may remember a coach who was a tyrant—overly demanding, belittling, verbally abusive—and who caused you to consciously avoid such behavior.

4. **Choose a problem and find solutions to it.** Think about a problem that has troubled you recently. For example, tuition costs might be hard for you to meet. How did you or will you handle this difficulty? You might continue to work part- or full-time, pick up more hours, ask for a loan from a parent or friend, apply for a bank loan, apply for a Pell grant, or buy 10 more lottery tickets and hope. The solutions will be the effects generated by the problem.

5. WRITE ABOUT EFFECTS ON OUR PLANET

Select what might seem to be a small cause and look for dramatic effects in the world around us. When you build your chain of effects, think about how each action affects the one that follows it. For instance, many imported species of plants and animals have ravaged their new environment. In the late 1800s, rabbits were introduced into Australia but rapidly decimated the local animal population by eating so much of the vegetation. Common dandelions have caused many lawn lovers to pour herbicides onto their grass, and when the chemicals run off or seep into the water table, another chain of destruction begins.

Conservation in Context

You might want to use the two photos on page 208 to write a paragraph on effects that begin with people overusing pesticides and herbicides. Toxic runoff pours from a drainage pipe in the first illustration; fish have been killed by it in the second. What other effects might come about from this pollution? Think of other animals—large and small—that live in the river and the animals that depend on them as a food source. Also consider how the poisoned water might affect people who use the river for drinking water and recreation. ●

Linking to Future Experience

Determining the Value of Causal Thinking

We also see cause and effect at work in every course we take. In a nursing class, students must understand the possible causes of a patient's wheezing and the effects of different ways of treating this symptom. In an interior design class, students must solve the problem of making a tiny room appear larger, determining what will have the effect of creating a spacious impression. In an economics class, the professor asks students to predict the effect on mortgage loans of raising the prime interest rate. Learning causal thinking will help you in college classes, but aside from earning good grades, you will develop a more critical frame of mind. The world is complex, and its people multifaceted. As you practice clear causal thought, you will see the world more clearly and make more reasoned judgments.

 **ACTIVITY 9.6** WORKING ONLINE: *Causes or Effects of Stress*

 At HelpGuide.org (http://www.helpguide.org/mental/stress_signs.htm) you can choose from a variety of articles about the causes or effects of stress. After reading two or three, write a paragraph summarizing your findings. OPTIONAL: Try mixing writing patterns by incorporating a brief personal narrative about specific causes or effects of stress in your own life.

ACTIVITY 9.7 WORKING ONLINE: *Causes and Effects Review*

Take the Chapter 9 Review Quiz at www.mhhe.com/brannan.

Chapter Summary

1. Writing about cause and effect forces us to think about reasons and outcomes. It helps us explore the "why" behind events, ideas, people, places, and objects.

2. Using cause-and-effect thinking can help us solve problems.

3. Events are complex, rarely having only one cause or only one effect.

4. Closeness in time or space of one thing to another does not necessarily mean that there is a causal connection between the two.

5. Without closely considering causes and effects, we risk oversimplifying.

6. Writers often decide which causes/effects are most important and best to include, based on their topic, interest, and knowledge and the interest of readers.

7. Writers should complete all ideas; they should not expect readers to make any but obvious connections.

8. A topic sentence for a cause/effect paragraph should name and focus the topic and predict either causes or effects.

9. Each major cause or effect should be introduced by a subtopic sentence.

10. Each sentence in a paragraph should be clearly linked, with subtopic and concluding sentences the most well connected of all.

11. Writing is never complete without careful revising and editing.

Explaining Activities: Doing or Understanding Them (Process Analysis)

10

[*If you have never handled a telescope, do you think you could follow instructions telling how to focus one? What makes instructions, or steps in a process, easy to follow? What makes them unclear or confusing?*]

KEY TOPICS

- Developing skills and exploring ideas in process-analysis paragraphs

  - Listing all necessary steps

  - Explaining steps thoroughly

  - Defining all terms

  - Avoiding monotonous sentence patterns

- Analyzing student models: Process-analysis paragraphs

- Writing a process-analysis paragraph

What Are We Trying to Achieve and Why?

Setting the Stage

In the photos on the previous page, a family prepares to focus their telescope on a full moon. But before they can focus the image, they will have to follow a few steps: loosening lock knobs, using the viewfinder to target the moon, tightening the lock knobs, and then adjusting the focus knob. When we try to explain or understand an activity, we are involved in **process analysis,** the focus of Chapter 10.

Process analysis can help us do or understand something. An explanation of how to focus a telescope—how to physically turn knobs and make fine adjustments—is an example of process analysis that enables *doing*. An explanation of how the telescope works—how the lenses and mirrors reflect and refract light, for instance—is a process analysis that furthers *understanding*.

Linking to Previous Experience

We live in a world filled with processes. In nature alone, we can see thousands of processes operating daily, from the cycle of rainfall and evaporation to the transformation of caterpillars into butterflies. We busily pursue our daily routines, seldom thinking about the steps needed to complete them—until something makes them difficult (say, having an arm in a sling) or until we need to learn a new routine or explain one to someone.

School, too, has given you experience with learning to do and understand processes. When you solved problems in algebra class, listing the steps, or learned about photosynthesis in biology, you used and honed your process-analysis skills.

JOURNAL / BLOG ENTRY 10.1

List two activities that you are familiar with, and write out six steps a friend could follow to complete or understand each. Were six steps enough? Too many? What words in your steps might need to be explained further?

FEEDBACK *Ask a question about each of a classmate's two processes. Which is more interesting to read about—and why?*

Developing Skills and Exploring Ideas in Process-Analysis Paragraphs

To learn to write effective process papers, you need to practice the following:

1. Listing all the necessary steps
2. Explaining the steps thoroughly, giving reasons and warnings

3. Defining all the terms

4. Avoiding monotonous sentence patterns

Listing All Necessary Steps

When we try to understand or perform an activity, we need to know all the important steps. If any are missing, we won't be able to follow the process. Consider, for example, this list of steps for changing a flat tire:

1. Jack up the car.

2. Take the tire off.

3. Put the spare on.

4. Jack the car down.

5. Put away the jack.

Is this enough information for someone who has never changed a tire before? Or would we need a few more steps, like these?

1. Make sure you are on a level surface.

2. Locate the jack, lug wrench, and spare tire.

3. Check to see if the spare is sufficiently inflated.

4. Locate the correct jacking point.

5. Block the wheel across from the flat tire.

6. Set the parking brake.

7. Break the lug nuts free.

8. Position the spare tire within arm's reach.

9. Raise the car slowly several inches higher than needed to remove the flat.

10. Check to make sure the car is stable.

11. Remove the lug nuts, leaving the top nut for last.

12. Remove the wheel.

13. Put on the spare.

14. Finger tighten the lug nuts in a crosswise fashion.

15. Lower the car till the tire touches the ground.

16. Fully tighten the lug nuts.

17. Fully lower the jack and pull it away.

18. Unblock the opposite wheel.

19. Put the tire, jack, and lug wrench away.

Just as we need complete steps to understand or perform an activity, so do our readers. When you are not sure how much your readers know, include *more* information.

ACTIVITY 10.1 *Listing All Necessary Steps*

Pick one of the following processes and, in the space on the following page, list all the steps the stated audience would need to complete it.

1. Process (to perform): how to build a campfire

   Audience: 18-year-old who has never built a campfire

2. Process (to perform): how to housebreak a puppy

   Audience: 10-year-old who has never had a pet

3. Process (to perform): how to buy a used car

   Audience: 16-year-old who has just gotten her driver's license

4. Process (to understand): childbirth

   Audience: First-time expecting parents

Explaining Steps Thoroughly

Beyond listing the steps necessary to complete a process, we must explain the steps fully. An instruction such as "locate the correct jacking point" might only further confuse if readers don't know what "jacking point" means. If we clarify by stating that it is one of four spots on the vehicle reinforced to bear the car's weight and either list the spots or include a picture, then readers would more likely be able to accomplish the step.

Aside from clarifying meaning, we must often explain the "why" behind a step for curious readers. For instance, why would a person changing a tire want to remove the top lug nut last? If we explain that it is to keep the wheel centered so it won't slip off from a side, we satisfy readers' curiosity, making them more likely to follow our suggestions.

Also, include warnings whenever not following a step could cause problems. For example, we might warn readers not to fully tighten the lug nuts on a tire while the vehicle is suspended because they risk knocking the car off the jack.

Keep in mind that one clarification may make another one necessary.

ACTIVITY 10.2 | Giving Reasons and Warnings

Look at the steps you wrote for a process in Activity 10.1, and decide which need to be clarified for the stated audience. Identify each step needing clarification and rewrite the step in the space provided so that it includes an explanation, reason, or warning.

Process: _____

Audience: _____

Explanation(s)/reason(s): _____

_____

_____

_____

_____

_____

_____

Warning(s): _____

_____

_____

_____

_____

Defining All Terms

Process analysis calls for clearly defining all terms. Just because a word is familiar to you does not mean that everyone knows it. For example, would you expect someone who has never changed a tire to be able to identify a lug wrench or wheel block? Further, could you expect the person to know how to set the wheel block? Because you cannot know whether readers understand all your terms, you should define any that you think might be a problem for them.

HINT

For more on defining terms, see Chapter 15.

ACTIVITY 10.3 | WORKING TOGETHER: *Defining All Terms*

Again using the process from Activity 10.1, work in small groups to list which terms each of you *probably* and *possibly* needs to define for the stated audience. Next, explain why you separated the "possibles" from the "probables." Remember, there is no sure way to predict readers' knowledge, so you must use your best judgment on when to define terms.

EXAMPLE

Process: *earthquake*

Audience: *seventh-grade earth science class*

Probable terms to define: *plate tectonics, seismic activity, crust, magma, faults, Richter scale, seismograph, epicenter*

Possible terms to define: *shock, aftershock, earth's core*

Why we separated the terms: *The probable terms to define are common in the scientific community, and many adults would know them, but most 12- and 13-year-olds would not. The possible terms to define are more familiar and likely to be understood through the context of the discussion.*

Process: _____

Audience: _____

Probable terms to define: _____

_____

Possible terms to define: _____

Why we separated the terms: _____

_____

_____

_____

_____

_____

_____

_____

_____

_____

Avoiding Monotonous Sentence Patterns

Have you ever found yourself reading a process explanation—say, instructions for assembling a bookcase or learning to factor in algebra—and exclaiming, "Hey, this is exciting! I can't wait to read more"? If not, it is because most process instructions try to be straightforward; their purpose is to get a job done, not entertain. However, even the driest subject can be made more (or less) readable through the sentence structures used. Consider the following paragraph excerpt on putting up a wall shelf:

DRAFT: MONOTONOUS SENTENCES

> First, I gather all my supplies. Second, I set them within reach. Third, I begin to attach the shelf brackets to the wall. Fourth, I pencil in each hole in the mounting brackets against the wall. I do this so I can drill in the correct spots. Fifth, I choose a bit one size smaller than the bracket screws. Sixth, I drill holes about half the length of the screws. I do this to help the screws grip more firmly. Seventh, I screw the brackets into the wall. Eighth, I begin the steps for attaching the shelf.

If your response is "clear but boring writing," then why not combine sentences to vary length and delete the monotonous string of beginnings—*first, second, third,* and so forth?

REVISED: VARIED SENTENCES

> Once I have gathered all of my supplies, I set them within reach and begin the process of attaching the shelf brackets to the wall. First, I place the mounting brackets on the marks that I previously measured for the height of the shelf, and then I pencil in each bracket hole so I can drill in the correct spots. With a bit the next size smaller in diameter than the bracket screws, I drill holes about one-half the length of the screws (the smaller holes help the screws grip the wall more firmly and eliminate the problem of making holes too big for the screws). Now I line up the brackets with the holes and screw the brackets into the wall, being careful not to overtighten the screws so I don't pull them out of the soft drywall. With the brackets secure on the wall, it's time to attach the shelf.

The revised paragraph is more readable and therefore more interesting. Also, these revisions made it possible to include more explanations, so the paragraph is also more informative.

For additional ways to achieve variety and improve writing, see Chapter 19.

ACTIVITY 10.4 | *Avoiding Monotonous Sentence Patterns*

Read the following paragraph of ten short sentences. Then rewrite it on a separate piece of paper, combining some sentences to vary sentence beginnings and length. Begin with a topic sentence. Feel free to add information or explanations that would strengthen the paragraph. Consult Chapter 19 or try to combine sentences using some of the following words:

because, although, as, if, since, when, where, while, and, but, so, or, for, nor, yet, who, which, that, first, second, third, last, next, then, now, after, as a result, later, soon, before, especially

Process: how to guarantee that you will get a ticket after being pulled over for speeding

Audience: a younger brother or sister

Monotonous version:

First, act like you are trying to hide something. Second, avoid eye contact with the officer. Third, loudly protest that you weren't speeding. Fourth, refuse to show your driver's license. Fifth, throw your license at the officer. Sixth, accuse the officer of harassing you. Seventh, accuse the officer of just trying to fill a ticket quota. Eighth, try to bribe the officer. Ninth, swear at the officer. Tenth, act like you want to punch the officer.

Analyzing Student Models: Process-Analysis Paragraphs

The following model paragraphs will help you write process papers. "A Boy's Best Friend" and "Recipe for a Red-Hot Sunday" are how-to-do paragraphs; "Staying Alive," the annotated model, is a paragraph about a process to be understood.

Process papers that tell how to do something often use the word *you*, referring to the reader. In addition to being directly stated, *you* is implied in commands ("Keep the heat at 350 degrees"—meaning *you*, the reader, must keep the heat at 350). Another approach is to use *I* throughout. "A Boy's Best Friend" uses *I*, and "Recipe for a Red-Hot Sunday" uses *you*. "Staying Alive" largely avoids both *I* and *you*, an approach that is common in writing about processes to be understood.

➤ Prereading Exploration for "A Boy's Best Friend"

Steve Oh chose a topic from his childhood in rural Korea. He knew the topic—how to make a slingshot—would be manageable and might appeal most to young men who had similar childhood experiences of making "weapons" for fun and as a way to gain some control over their environment.

Do you remember as a child making anything that was particularly special to you? On a separate piece of paper, list one thing that you made along with six or more steps that went into it.

Topic sentence: names the topic and predicts how-to-do process

Subtopic sentences: name each major step and make a limiting statement.

Development: action, scene and character details, sensory details, active verbs, -ing words, and specific words; also, explanations of the examples

Sentence connectors: transitions (*though, also, finally*), repeat words (*slingshot*), synonyms (*treasure, prize*), pronouns (*it, he*), and reference to main idea (make one: *collecting, to obtain, to construct*)

Warnings: "I didn't want to lose an eye . . ."

Concluding sentence: restates the topic and adds a final (expanded) thought

A Boy's Best Friend

Living in the country as a child, I longed for a slingshot to play and hunt with, and finally decided I would make one. Collecting the materials for my treasure, though, did not come easy. It required the most perfectly forked branch from an oak tree, a square of leather to hold the stone, and a piece of rubber band. Any old rubber band would not do, though; it had to be surgical tubing, light brown and hose shaped, for the power I wanted. To obtain this rarity, I biked half an hour into town to the drugstore, after begging the money from my older brothers. My brothers also helped me find the best-shaped and healthiest-looking branch from a nearby forest. Because the only leather I could find was my dad's belt, I secretly cut off a two-inch length from the end of it, praying that he would not notice. Finally, I was ready to construct my prize. With instructions from my brothers, I sawed the three ends of the oak branch to form a capital Y, each section approximately 6 inches long. Next, I peeled away the rough brown bark and sanded it with a medium grade of sandpaper until it was smooth as silk. Using the Korean equivalent to a pocketknife, on the side of the Y facing away from me, I carved notches roughly 1/8 inch deep and 1/4 inch wide about 1/2 inch from the tips. Then I wrapped the ends of the rubber band around the notches, being extra careful to tie the bands securely. (I didn't want to lose an eye if the tubing slipped from the branch when I had the slingshot fully drawn back!) With my knife I drilled a small hole in the ends of the leather patch, slipped one inch of the tubing through each hole, folded it over, and tied it together with a square knot so it, too, would not slip. My slingshot was complete. I pulled back the band to test it, let it go, and heard the best "Snap!" I could have hoped for. My childhood dream was realized, and I was ready to chase after those terrible little sparrows that had been ruining our rice crop.

—Steve Oh

➤ Prereading Exploration for "Recipe for a Red-Hot Sunday"

Jeff Coburn decided to write about the only dish he knows how to make. He doesn't much enjoy cooking and writes for readers who feel the same way but might appreciate a quick dish for a party. As you read, decide if the ingredients are clear and the explanations complete.

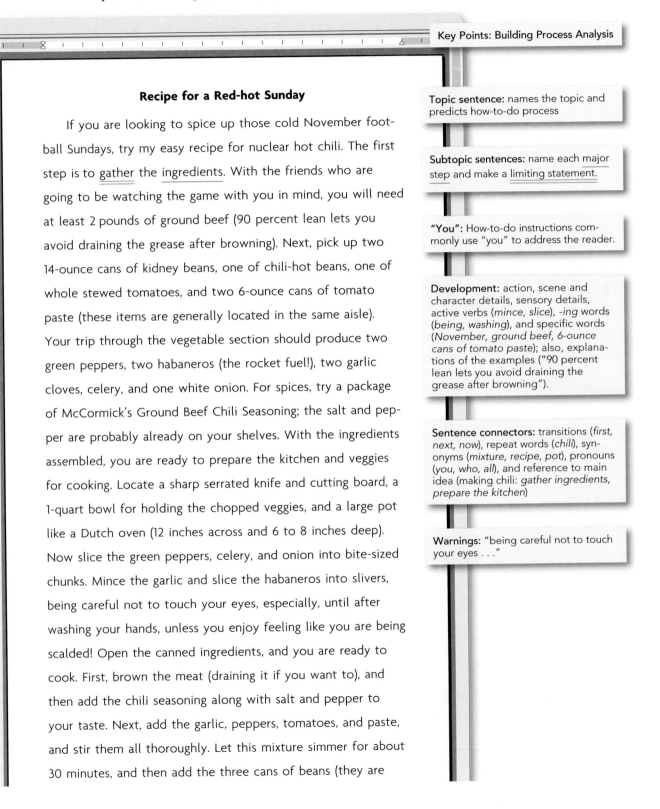

Key Points: Building Process Analysis

Recipe for a Red-hot Sunday

If you are looking to spice up those cold November football Sundays, try my easy recipe for nuclear hot chili. The first step is to gather the ingredients. With the friends who are going to be watching the game with you in mind, you will need at least 2 pounds of ground beef (90 percent lean lets you avoid draining the grease after browning). Next, pick up two 14-ounce cans of kidney beans, one of chili-hot beans, one of whole stewed tomatoes, and two 6-ounce cans of tomato paste (these items are generally located in the same aisle). Your trip through the vegetable section should produce two green peppers, two habaneros (the rocket fuel!), two garlic cloves, celery, and one white onion. For spices, try a package of McCormick's Ground Beef Chili Seasoning; the salt and pepper are probably already on your shelves. With the ingredients assembled, you are ready to prepare the kitchen and veggies for cooking. Locate a sharp serrated knife and cutting board, a 1-quart bowl for holding the chopped veggies, and a large pot like a Dutch oven (12 inches across and 6 to 8 inches deep). Now slice the green peppers, celery, and onion into bite-sized chunks. Mince the garlic and slice the habaneros into slivers, being careful not to touch your eyes, especially, until after washing your hands, unless you enjoy feeling like you are being scalded! Open the canned ingredients, and you are ready to cook. First, brown the meat (draining it if you want to), and then add the chili seasoning along with salt and pepper to your taste. Next, add the garlic, peppers, tomatoes, and paste, and stir them all thoroughly. Let this mixture simmer for about 30 minutes, and then add the three cans of beans (they are

Topic sentence: names the topic and predicts how-to-do process

Subtopic sentences: name each major step and make a limiting statement.

"You": How-to-do instructions commonly use "you" to address the reader.

Development: action, scene and character details, sensory details, active verbs (*mince, slice*), *-ing* words (*being, washing*), and specific words (*November, ground beef, 6-ounce cans of tomato paste*); also, explanations of the examples ("90 percent lean lets you avoid draining the grease after browning").

Sentence connectors: transitions (*first, next, now*), repeat words (*chili*), synonyms (*mixture, recipe, pot*), pronouns (*you, who, all*), and reference to main idea (making chili: *gather ingredients, prepare the kitchen*)

Warnings: "being careful not to touch your eyes . . ."

Concluding sentence: restates the topic and adds a final (expanded) thought

precooked, so you don't want to overcook them to mush).

That's it. You're done. Now just let the pot simmer till you

hear the doorbell ring, and get set for a good, hot game.

—Jeff Coburn

POSTREADING QUESTIONS FOR PARAGRAPH ANALYSIS

Note: These questions apply to either of the preceding student models.

1. Which words in the topic sentence name the topic and predict a how-to-do process?

2. What words in the concluding sentence link to the topic sentence?

3. What is the expanded thought (p. 50) in the final sentence?

4. Copy each subtopic sentence, and underline the major step. Circle connectors: transitions, repeat words, synonyms, and pronouns.

5. What transitional words show that the steps are arranged chronologically (Chapter 6)?

6. Choose part of a major step in the process and tell how the author's explaining (as opposed to detailing or action description) helps you better understand one of the author's reasons or warnings.

7. Choose part of a major step and tell how the action description and detailing help you to better understand the author's point.

8. What warning(s) does the author include?

9. Name three specific words and list a more general word for each (pp. 75–76).

10. Name three ways to further develop any step in this paragraph. Consider action, active verbs, dialogue, specific words, sensory details, description of person or setting, revealing thoughts or emotions, and further explanation, including reasons and warnings.

For more on connectors, see pp. 54–56.

For more on using examples, see Chapter 7 and pp. 42–49.

WRITING A PROCESS-ANALYSIS PARAGRAPH

Summarizing the Assignment

Write a paragraph of 250 to 300 words that explains a process or activity. Rather than give three or four examples to illustrate a point, as in Chapter 7, now your paragraph should enable your readers to do or understand something. So, instead of saying "Home-cooked meals are far superior to restaurant food" and then explaining why, you might say, "Anyone can make a great home-cooked meal if he can read a cookbook and has an hour for preparation time."

Because you want an audience to be able to follow your instructions, specific examples, clear explanations, and well-defined terms are especially important. Paragraphs will be arranged chronologically (as the clock moves), with information grouped into several major steps introduced with subtopic sentences.

Establishing Audience and Purpose

Which of the following two process explanations is easier for you to understand?

A. Most pelecypods move by extending the slender, muscular foot between the valves. Blood swells the end of the foot to anchor it in the mud or sand, and then longitudinal muscles contract to shorten the foot and pull the animal forward. In most bivalves, the foot is used for burrowing, but a few creep. Some pelecypods are sessile.

B. Most creatures like clams and oysters move by extending a slender, muscular part of their bodies called a foot. The foot is often smaller than a person's little finger and works a bit like a rubber band. As the animal stretches the foot from between its two shells, it digs into the sand with one end, and then moves its body forward as the "rubber band" contracts. Most of these creatures use their foot for burrowing, but a few can move across the ground. Some are permanently fixed in one spot.

You will probably find version B easier to follow because specialized terms from version A (*pelecypods, valves, bivalves, sessile*) have been simplified. Whenever you write process explanations, you should know your audience so that you can define words that might be unfamiliar to them or use simpler terms and fully explain concepts that might be difficult.

You may have several purposes—to entertain, persuade, or inform—but explaining the process clearly should take top priority.

Working through the Writing Assignment

Discovering Ideas

Look for something that you know well or want to know more about. We work, go to school, play sports, have families, and belong to organizations—all of which involve processes. Keep the need for manageability in mind as you choose a topic. For instance, explaining how a space shuttle is built would be far too broad, but discussing the installation of heat-shielding tiles on the nose might work well.

The HINT reads:

This topics list may help you find and limit a topic. Remember, you want to write a paper to enable readers to do or understand something.

POSSIBLE TOPICS: PROCESS ANALYSIS

How To:

- Make your house more energy efficient
- Break a bad habit (smoking, drinking, unhealthy eating)
- Ski moguls, pitch a tent, or get up on a surfboard
- Get along with a neighbor you don't like
- Handle an embarrassing moment in public
- Become more aware of environmental problems and solutions
- Do something with a musical instrument (hold it, clean it, tune it), or explain how a musical instrument works
- Lose (or gain) weight, or explain how the body loses or gains weight
- Plan a great vacation
- Condition yourself for a demanding sport

- Fix a broken vacuum (or any other appliance/machine), or explain how an appliance/machine works
- Deal with an angry customer or handle a "rush"
- Reduce boredom on the job
- Create a good excuse for tardiness or absence
- Balance your schedule as an athlete and student

For additional process topics, see Chapter 10 at www.mhhe.com/brannan.

ACTIVITY 10.5 WORKING ONLINE: *Use the Process Analysis Writing Tutor*

For additional topics for this assignment, look under Chapter 10 at www.mhhe.com/brannan. Download the Process Analysis Writing Tutor for more helpful strategies in process writing.

In thinking about how you will approach potential topics, keep in mind these two important points:

1. **Limit your topic.** Choose a small part of a larger process, or select only major points in a larger process. For example, don't try to instruct someone on how to play guitar; help her learn a scale, a chord, or a strumming method.

2. **Remember that you are writing a process, not an illustration, paper.** For example, if your topic is housebreaking a pet, your topic sentence might be something like "Housebreaking a puppy requires patience, planning, and time," *not* "Several funny things happened to our household while we were housebreaking Fluffy."

Once you have tentatively decided on a topic, you need to decide whether you will be writing about a process for readers to do or to understand.

Decide on an approach—to do or to understand.

Prewriting

Listing can work well at various points in the process of discovering ideas. Suppose that you choose to write about aquariums and decide to take a to-do approach. You might use listing to generate more specific ideas for possible topics:

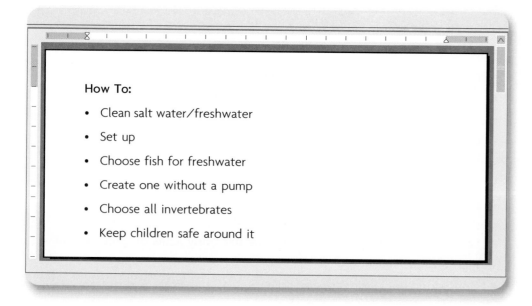

How To:
- Clean salt water/freshwater
- Set up
- Choose fish for freshwater
- Create one without a pump
- Choose all invertebrates
- Keep children safe around it

Because processes involve steps, listing is especially useful in developing ideas for a process-analysis paragraph. Suppose you choose a to-understand approach and plan to explain how an aquarium functions. You might create a list of steps like the following:

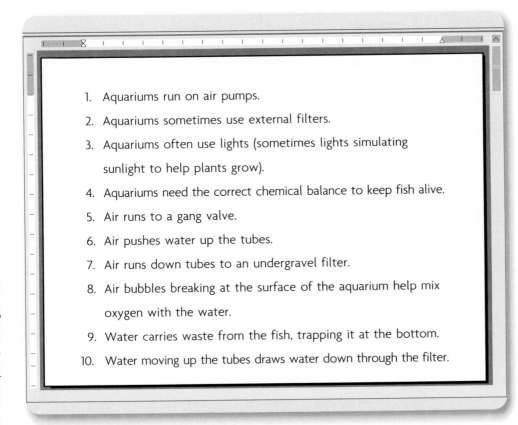

1. Aquariums run on air pumps.

2. Aquariums sometimes use external filters.

3. Aquariums often use lights (sometimes lights simulating sunlight to help plants grow).

4. Aquariums need the correct chemical balance to keep fish alive.

5. Air runs to a gang valve.

6. Air pushes water up the tubes.

7. Air runs down tubes to an undergravel filter.

8. Air bubbles breaking at the surface of the aquarium help mix oxygen with the water.

9. Water carries waste from the fish, trapping it at the bottom.

10. Water moving up the tubes draws water down through the filter.

HINT

List steps in the process before you begin a draft.

With a list of steps in hand, you can now delete, add, and arrange material.

PREWRITING—SUMMING UP

1. Decide on several possible topics, of your own or from the topics list.

2. Think about how to write about your topic in terms of a real process—one involving steps—not general explanation.

3. Limit the process enough for a one-paragraph paper.

4. Decide on a to-do or to-understand approach to the assignment.

5. Pick an audience.

6. Prewrite for a list of steps needed to explain your process.

JOURNAL / BLOG ENTRY 10.2

List your topic, approach (to do or to understand), audience, and steps. In a paragraph, answer the following questions: Is the topic limited enough? Based on your target audience, what steps may not be needed? What steps might you need to add?

Organizing Ideas

As always, a topic sentence is vital to focus your work. Here are several that could introduce a paragraph explaining how an aquarium functions:

A. An aquarium is a simple closed environment carefully designed to keep fish alive.

B. Have you ever wondered how it is possible for fish to survive in such a small space as an aquarium?

C. The watery world that captive fish survive in depends on two primary elements in a working system: an air pump and an undergravel filter.

Notice that all three topic sentences mention the topic (aquariums) and predict a process and that sentence C also forecasts two important points.

The next step in organizing is to make sure steps are arranged chronologically, delete any unnecessary steps, and add steps where needed. Guided by sentence C, you might modify your list in this way:

Steps 2–4 are deleted because they are not essential to the discussion of the undergravel filter and air pump. Steps 8 and 10 have been switched for a more logical order.

1. Aquariums run on air pumps.
2. ~~Aquariums sometimes use external filters.~~
3. ~~Aquariums often use lights (sometimes lights simulating sunlight to help plants grow).~~
4. ~~Aquariums need the correct chemical balance to keep fish alive.~~
5. Air runs to a gang valve.
6. Air runs down tubes to an undergravel filter.
7. Air pushes water up the tubes.
8. Water moving up the tubes draws water down through the filter. (was step 10)
9. Water carries waste from the fish, trapping it at the bottom.
10. Air bubbles breaking at the surface of the aquarium help mix oxygen with the water. (was step 8)

HINT

Arrange material by time (or by order of importance). Subtopic sentences may be useful for ordering and clarifying your steps.

Now you must decide whether to group the steps. Many simple process explanations are clear enough without grouping, but complex explanations need the clarity that grouping steps under subtopic sentences provides. The mention in the aquarium topic sentence of the air pump and undergravel filter suggests the need to organize the steps into two groups.

One common grouping in process analysis is the **preliminary step,** or the gathering of supplies. This grouping is important in writing about processes like tearing apart a carburetor, hanging a picture, or preparing a dish. Notice how it is handled in "Recipe for a Red-Hot Sunday."

Before you draft, review the following lists of transitions and those on pages 54–56, and think about other connectors—repeat words, synonyms, and so on—you might use.

FOR MOVING IN TIME

after	first (second, etc.)	next	suddenly
afterward	immediately	now	then
at last	in the meantime	often	time passed
awhile	in the past	once	until

FOR ADDING MATERIAL

again	as well as	furthermore	likewise
also	besides	in addition	moreover
and	further	last	next

FOR GIVING EXAMPLES AND EMPHASIS

above all	especially	in particular	one reason
after all	for example	in truth	specifically
another	for instance	it is true	surely

FOR SHOWING CAUSE AND EFFECT

accordingly	because	hence	then
and so	consequently	since	therefore
as a result	for this reason	so	thus

ORGANIZING—SUMMING UP

1. Create a rough topic sentence to help focus your material.
2. Eliminate steps not essential to the process.
3. Add needed steps.
4. Arrange the steps chronologically.
5. Use subtopic sentences as needed to group and clarify the steps.
6. Review the list of transitions and other connectors.

JOURNAL / BLOG ENTRY 10.3

Write out your working topic sentence. Does it clearly indicate that your paragraph is about a process? List your steps in chronological order. Should you group steps? If so, write subtopic sentences, naming the major groupings. What words might you need to explain to your reader?

Drafting

With the preliminary work done, you are almost ready to draft. But before moving ahead, review the drafting suggestions on pages 17–19. As you write, be sure to do the following:

1. Explain how some activity occurs or is performed.
2. Include needed steps so as not to lose your readers.
3. Explain the why behind steps, and give warnings of what to avoid.
4. Define any word that you think might puzzle your readers. You can often place the definition within parentheses following the term in question.
5. Write complete sentences, being sure to include all necessary words. Not this: "Grab a tomato and rinse off," but this: "Grab a tomato and rinse *it* off."
6. Decide whether you will use *you* or *I* in giving instructions or if you will largely avoid both. Be careful not to switch back and forth between the two.

Be consistent with pronoun use.

JOURNAL / BLOG ENTRY 10.4

Soon after writing your first draft, reread the assignment on page 220. Then look carefully at your draft, and in a paragraph answer the following questions: Does it fit the assignment? Have you written a series of steps, probably grouped under subtopic sentences? What part of your draft do you like best? What part least?

FEEDBACK   *Tell a classmate what you like best about his/her draft; then recommend one change, giving the reasoning behind your critique.*

Revising Drafts

For help with revising first, second, and final drafts, turn to Chapter 4, pages 63–67.

Annotated Student Model: "Staying Alive"

Carefully reading the annotated student model will help clarify questions you have about your own draft.

First-Stage Draft

Carla Schumann wrote about one of her hobbies, keeping freshwater fish. To help focus the paragraph, she picked as her audience people who do not know much about keeping fish as pets but who might like to.

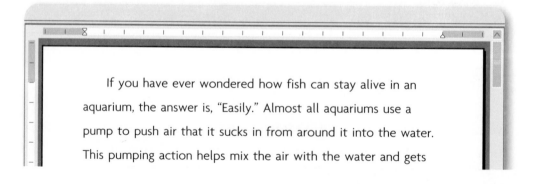

If you have ever wondered how fish can stay alive in an aquarium, the answer is, "Easily." Almost all aquariums use a pump to push air that it sucks in from around it into the water. This pumping action helps mix the air with the water and gets rid of fish waste. You can see how the air travels first thru one or two small tubes that are attached to the pump and end up in the water. The tubes can run directly into the water but are usually connected to a valve that splits the air into separate channels. Then the plastic tubing runs down to the undergravel filter. After the air is pushed down through the risers to the bottom of the aquarium, it immediately moves upward, making it rise up the tube. As the water rises, the water nearest the undergravel filter is drawn through the gravel and filter on the bottom of the tank. This pulls all the junk out of the water and traps it within the gravel and under the filter, so the water stays clear and the bacteria down enough for the fish to live. As the water comes from the risers, it splashes around on the surface of the water in the aquarium, which in turn speeds up the mixing of oxygen into the water. This process of air mixing with water keeps the tank clean and the fish lively.

Need more specific words

Avoid shift to *you* in process to be understood.

Need to define and explain more thoroughly

Missing a step

Second-Stage Draft

When drafting process explanations, we often leave out steps or include unneeded ones, as is the case with Carla's first draft. Other common difficulties are under-explaining steps and not defining important terms. Role-playing your audience and/or having another person read the draft will help you with these problems.

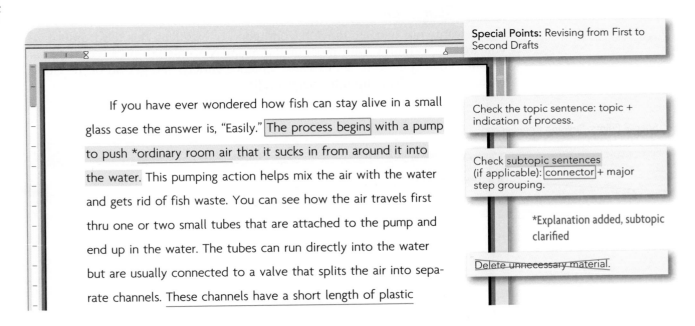

If you have ever wondered how fish can stay alive in a small glass case the answer is, "Easily." The process begins with a pump to push *ordinary room air that it sucks in from around it into the water. This pumping action helps mix the air with the water and gets rid of fish waste. You can see how the air travels first thru one or two small tubes that are attached to the pump and end up in the water. The tubes can run directly into the water but are usually connected to a valve that splits the air into separate channels. These channels have a short length of plastic

Special Points: Revising from First to Second Drafts

Check the topic sentence: topic + indication of process.

Check subtopic sentences (if applicable): connector + major step grouping.

*Explanation added, subtopic clarified

Delete unnecessary material.

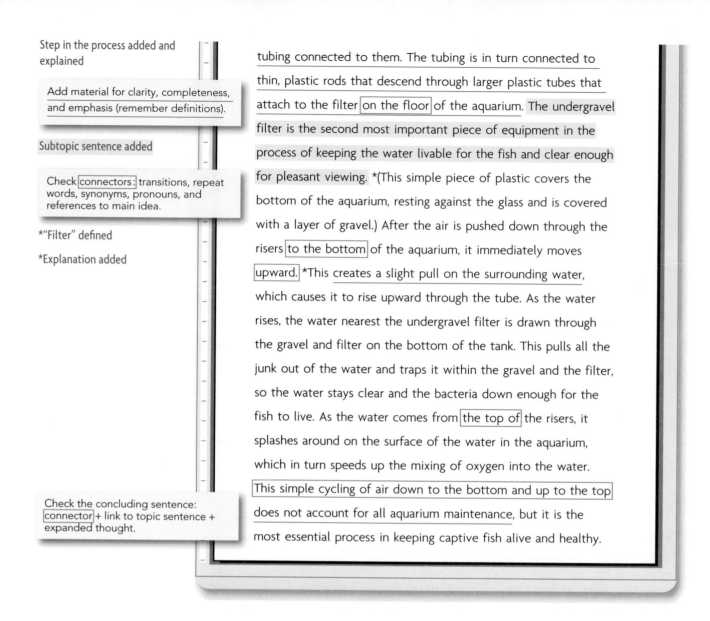

Step in the process added and explained

Add material for clarity, completeness, and emphasis (remember definitions).

Subtopic sentence added

Check connectors: transitions, repeat words, synonyms, pronouns, and references to main idea.

*"Filter" defined

*Explanation added

Check the concluding sentence: connector + link to topic sentence + expanded thought.

tubing connected to them. The tubing is in turn connected to thin, plastic rods that descend through larger plastic tubes that attach to the filter on the floor of the aquarium. The undergravel filter is the second most important piece of equipment in the process of keeping the water livable for the fish and clear enough for pleasant viewing. *(This simple piece of plastic covers the bottom of the aquarium, resting against the glass and is covered with a layer of gravel.) After the air is pushed down through the risers to the bottom of the aquarium, it immediately moves upward. *This creates a slight pull on the surrounding water, which causes it to rise upward through the tube. As the water rises, the water nearest the undergravel filter is drawn through the gravel and filter on the bottom of the tank. This pulls all the junk out of the water and traps it within the gravel and the filter, so the water stays clear and the bacteria down enough for the fish to live. As the water comes from the top of the risers, it splashes around on the surface of the water in the aquarium, which in turn speeds up the mixing of oxygen into the water. This simple cycling of air down to the bottom and up to the top does not account for all aquarium maintenance, but it is the most essential process in keeping captive fish alive and healthy.

Third-Stage Draft

If you want your work to move beyond good to excellent, this third draft gives you that opportunity. With most of the major concerns taken care of, you can now improve your word choices and sentence variety, and get rid of the clutter phrases that so often slip into rough drafts.

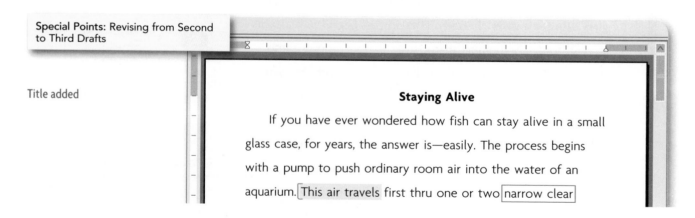

Special Points: Revising from Second to Third Drafts

Title added

Staying Alive

If you have ever wondered how fish can stay alive in a small glass case, for years, the answer is—easily. The process begins with a pump to push ordinary room air into the water of an aquarium. This air travels first thru one or two narrow clear plastic tubes that are attached to the pump, and end up in the water. The tubes can run directly into the ~~water~~ aquarium, but are usually connected to what is called a "gang valve" that splits the air into several outlets. These outlets have a short length of plastic tubing connected to them and the tubing in turn is connected to thin hollow plastic rods that descend through larger plastic tubes called risers ~~connected~~ attached to the undergravel filter on the floor of the aquarium. The undergravel filter is the second most important piece of equipment in the process of keeping the water livable for the fish and clear enough for pleasant viewing. (This simple piece of slotted plastic covers the bottom of the ~~aquarium~~ tank from side to side, resting against the glass, and is covered with a one- to two-inch layer of gravel.) After the air is pushed down thru the risers to the bottom of the aquarium, it immediately ~~rises~~ bubbles upward, causing the surrounding water to rise ~~upward~~ through the tube. As some water moves toward the surface that water nearest the bottom of the tank is slowly drawn downward through the gravel layer and undergravel filter. This continual movement of water pulls all the fish waste and excess food out of the water, trapping it within the gravel and under the filter, keeping the water clear and the bacteria level low enough for the fish to survive. As the water emerges from the top of the risers, it agitates ~~splashes around on~~ the surface of the water in the aquarium, in turn speeding up the absorption of needed oxygen into the water. This simple cycling of air down ~~to the bottom and up to~~ the top does not account for all aquarium maintenance (other chores include regular feeding, examining fish for illnesses, scraping algae, water changes) but it is the most essential process in keeping captive fish alive and healthy.

You used to connect with reader in topic sentence.

You removed to cut pronoun shift in body

Add specific words.

Substitute more precise or audience-appropriate words.

Combine sentences for variety.

Replace clutter and repeat words with synonyms and phrases.

~~Delete unneeded words.~~

Parentheses used to add definition

Final-Editing Draft

Carla's draft is now in good shape, and she can shift into low gear, editing slowly, line by line, looking for each error in grammar, spelling, and punctuation, especially for the pattern errors listed in her Improvement Chart.

Audience: People who might want to begin keeping fish as a hobby

1. **Misspelling**

2. Sound-alike word

3. Missing word(s)

4. **Wrong word**

5. Sentence fragment

6. Comma splice/run-on

7. Faulty capitalization

8. Incorrect apostrophe

9a. **Comma(s) needed: Introductory word(s)/ phrase/clause**

9b. **Comma(s) needed: Nonessential word group(s)**

9c. **Comma(s) needed: Main clauses with coordinating conjuction**

10. **Unneeded comma**

Parentheses used to add definition

Word italicized for emphasis

Staying Alive

If you have ever wondered how fish can stay alive in a small glass case,[10] for years, the answer is—easily. The process begins with a pump to push ordinary room air into the water. The air travels first thru[1] through one or two narrow clear plastic tubes that are attached to the pump,[10] and end up in the water. The tubes can run directly into the water,[10] but are usually connected to what is called a "gang valve," which splits the air into several outlets. These outlets have a short length of plastic tubing connected to them,[9c] and the tubing in turn is connected to thin hollow plastic rods that descend through larger plastic tubes called risers,[9b] attached to the undergravel filter on the floor of the aquarium. The undergravel filter is the second most important piece of equipment in the process of keeping the water livable for the fish and clear enough for pleasant viewing. (This simple piece of slotted plastic covers the bottom of the aquarium from side to side, resting against the glass, and is covered with a 1- to 2-inch layer of gravel.) After the air is pushed down through the risers to the bottom of the aquarium, it[4] the air immediately bubbles upward, causing the surrounding water to rise through the tube. As some water moves toward the surface,[9a] that water nearest the bottom of the tank is slowly drawn downward through the gravel layer and undergravel filter. This continual movement of water pulls all the fish waste and excess food out of the water, trapping it within the gravel and under the filter, keeping the water clear and the bacteria level low enough for the fish to survive. As the water emerges from the top of the risers, it agitates the surface of the water in the aquarium, in turn speeding up the absorption of needed oxygen into the water. This simple cycling of air down and up does not account for *all* aquarium maintenance (other chores include regular feeding, examining fish for illnesses, scraping algae, water changes),[9c] but it is the most essential process in keeping captive fish alive and healthy.

—*Carla Schumann*

FINAL-DRAFT CHECKLIST: PROCESS ANALYSIS

Before turning in your final draft, review this checklist. You may find that, as careful as you think you have been, you still missed a point or two—or more.

☐ 1. Have you chosen a process—either to do or to understand?

☐ 2. Do you have an effective topic sentence?

☐ 3. Have you listed the steps needed to complete or understand the process?

☐ 4. Have you arranged your main examples by time (or, if appropriate, by importance)?

☐ 5. Is there, if needed, a subtopic sentence to introduce each grouping of steps?

☐ 6. Have you explained clearly and given reasons, warnings, and definitions?

☐ 7. Are all sentences well connected?

☐ 8. Does the concluding sentence have an expanded thought?

☐ 9. Have you used specific language?

☐ 10. Have you used a metaphor or simile?

☐ 11. Are your sentences varied in length and beginnings?

☐ 12. Have you used synonyms for words that are repeated too often?

☐ 13. Have you cut unneeded words?

☐ 14. Have you written an interesting title? Have you checked its capitalization?

☐ 15. Have you prepared your paper using the format expected by your instructor?

☐ 16. Have you edited your work closely (including having at least one other person proofread)? Have you checked your Improvement Chart for pattern errors?

☐ 17. Have you looked for errors involving the following: misspellings, sound-alike words, missing words, wrong words, sentence fragments, comma splices/run-ons, faulty capitalization, incorrect apostrophes, missing commas, and unnecessary commas?

For more on revising paragraphs, see Chapter 4.

Check to see if you need a title page, use double spacing, leave at least a 1-inch margin, and use a 12-point font.

Alternate Writing Assignments

Here are some additional process topics that may be of interest. For any of these assignments, be sure to do the following:

- Write practical instructions for doing a task, or simply explain how something is done or functions.

- List and explain steps, and, where appropriate, give warnings.

- Define any terms that might be unfamiliar to your audience.

- Use a topic sentence, link sentences, and conclude with an expanded thought.

1. **Write a how-to-do paper for a child.** Pick an age group—say, 4 to 6 or 10 to 12—and then give age-appropriate instructions for completing a task. For example, how would you explain to a 5-year-old how to "straighten up"

his room? Do you expect him to put every toy in its place? Are all clothes to be neatly folded and hung or shelved? Or would this be expecting too much? For a very young child, a more realistic goal might be getting the big toys into one box and the small toys into another.

2. **Write a humorous process paper telling someone how to fail at something.** For example, advise someone how to flunk a composition class, lose a job, or break off a relationship the wrong way. Or you could describe something that you have done poorly, giving all the "steps" that ultimately led to disaster. For example, perhaps you mishandled a breakup by taking your significant other to a restaurant to give him or her the news, hoping the public location would reduce the tension, and then watched as your move backfired.

3. **Help a reader to annoy someone.** We all have people in our lives who irritate us and whom we would like to irritate in turn. You might have a next-door neighbor who deserves to hear you mow the lawn several times a week around midnight. If your process for annoying involves only one activity, be sure to detail how to perform it step by step. If you have several evil ideas in mind, consider arranging them from least to most dramatic.

4. **Give someone how-to-do advice on getting a job.** Choose a job you know something about, perhaps your current one. How did you prepare yourself to get the job? Did you write a cover letter and résumé, or did you simply walk in? How did you handle the interview? What advice might you give on researching a company, rehearsing or dressing for an interview, or presenting oneself to a prospective employer?

5. **As a to-do or to-understand paper, discuss the planning of a special occasion.** Perhaps you have organized a family holiday celebration, a graduation, or a birthday party. Be sure to consider your audience when you explain your steps and to warn the reader of potential problems in the planning.

6. **In a written paragraph, describe the visual process (how to help a choking person) shown on this poster.** You'll have to use more specific language than the poster designer because your audience will not have access to the visual aid. Why do you think visuals are so useful for explaining certain processes?

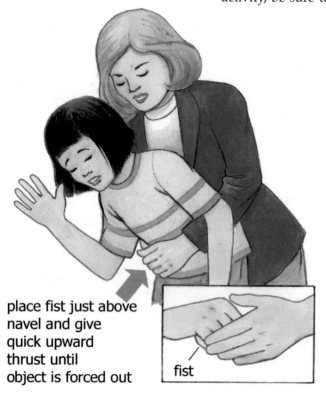

place fist just above navel and give quick upward thrust until object is forced out

fist

7. EXPLAIN ONE MULTI-STEP ACTION THAT WILL HELP THE ENVIRONMENT

Conservation in Context

Using the to-do approach, explain this action to fellow students. You might walk them through how to set up online bill payment, how to start composting, how to go about choosing a good hybrid vehicle, or how to conserve energy or save water at home. Avoid preaching to your audience; keep the information practical and the tone instructive and supportive. ●

Determining the Value of Process Analysis

Process description is useful in many ways. For example, while you rely on cause-and-effect analysis to decide that the car won't start because the battery is dead, you need process skills to charge or replace the battery. On the job, you may regularly learn new procedures and explain procedures to fellow workers. In school, also, you often explain processes in detail; for example, students training to be dental assistants must detail every step of the preparation for a root canal. Process skills also help us satisfy our curiosity. We wonder about the vast reaches of space and the beginning of existence; we are also curious about the smallest processes, down to the subatomic level. Learning to examine, understand, and do is an essential survival skill, and it is one of the traits that makes us human.

ACTIVITY 10.6 WORKING ONLINE: *Process Analysis Review*

 Take the Chapter 10 Review Quiz at www.mhhe.com/brannan.

Chapter Summary

1. Writers use process analysis to examine an activity so that others might understand or perform it.

2. Knowing how to understand, explain, and do is a basic survival skill.

3. Writing for a specific audience is critical in process analysis.

4. Process instructions require a complete list of steps.

5. Each step or suggestion must be explained clearly and thoroughly.

6. Wherever needed, warnings must be provided.

7. Clarifying terms is essential. When readers might not understand a term, a definition should be given.

8. Sentences should be varied to avoid monotonous sentence patterns.

9. Most process instructions are organized chronologically.

10. Grouping steps using subtopic sentences is often necessary.

11. The topic sentence should state the topic and predict a process explanation.

12. Writing is never complete until it has been carefully revised and edited.

Exploring Similarities and Differences (Comparison or Contrast)

11

[*What similarities and differences do you see between these two photographs? Make a list of each.*]

KEY TOPICS

- Developing skills and exploring ideas in comparison/contrast paragraphs
  - Making a meaningful comparison or contrast
  - Making an interesting comparison or contrast
- Developing topics thoroughly
- Using transitions and other connectors
- Analyzing student models: Comparison or contrast paragraphs
- Writing a comparison or contrast paragraph

What Are We Trying to Achieve and Why?

Setting the Stage

Whenever we notice similarities or differences between two people, places, events, objects (such as the two photographs in this chapter opener), or ideas, we are comparing or contrasting—the assignment for Chapter 11. With **comparison,** the focus is on similarities. (In both photos, a doctor uses a stethoscope to check a patient's heart.) With **contrast,** it is on differences. (One image shows a real medical exam, while the other shows a child playing.)

Linking to Previous Experience

We all have a wealth of experience with comparing and contrasting. From the 3-year-old child comparing two video covers and picking the one that most resembles her much-loved *Aladdin* film, to the young couple comparing and contrasting houses as they search for a first home, people compare and contrast daily. On the job, we discover important similarities and differences as quickly as possible. If the new boss begins to seem like the tyrant from a former job, you might soon be looking for other work. In school, you are asked to compare and contrast historical figures like George Washington and Thomas Jefferson, Ulysses S. Grant and Robert E. Lee, and Elizabeth I and Mary Queen of Scots. And in this text, you have practiced comparison/contrast in several ways, including by using metaphors and similes.

JOURNAL BLOG / ENTRY 11.1

Summarize several recent instances in which comparison/contrast was used, either by you or by someone else (friend, teacher, news anchor). What was being compared/contrasted: two people, places, or events? What was the reason: to inform, entertain, or persuade? Did the comparison/contrast achieve its purpose?

FEEDBACK   *Tell a classmate which of his or her comparison/contrast examples is most interesting to you, noting why.*

Developing Skills and Exploring Ideas in Comparison/Contrast Paragraphs

To learn to write effective comparison or contrast papers, you need to practice the following:

1. Making a meaningful comparison or contrast
2. Making an interesting comparison or contrast
3. Developing topics thoroughly
4. Using transitions and other connectors

Making a Meaningful Comparison or Contrast

In all of your writing projects, you need to establish a purpose and point. Lacking either, you are likely to wander all over the landscape. Can you determine the writer's point from the following outline?

Topic sentence: Ford and Chevy pickup trucks have a lot in common.

- Fords have engines, and so do Chevies.
- Fords have four wheels, and so do Chevies.
- Fords have beds in the back, and so do Chevies.
- Fords have cabs in the front, and so do Chevies.
- Fords have windshield wipers, and so do Chevies.
- Fords come in many colors, and so do Chevies.

Concluding sentence: I think you can see that Ford and Chevy pickups are similar.

If you said, "Yes, I see what the writer is trying to say—many times over—but so what?" your reaction is understandable. Merely listing similarities is not enough. You must have a point if you want to interest readers. The Ford–Chevy comparison could be focused in ways like the following:

- Ford and Chevy trucks are so similar that price should decide which you buy.
- Although Ford and Chevy trucks are similar in many ways, Ford has a better warranty.
- Although Ford and Chevy trucks are similar in many ways, Chevies have a better maintenance record.

ACTIVITY 11.1 WORKING TOGETHER: *Making a Meaningful Comparison or Contrast*

Working in groups, brainstorm to uncover several similarities and differences for each of these topics. Next, on your own, write three statements that give the topic a point. Then compose a topic sentence based on one of the statements. Be sure to indicate in the topic sentence that you intend to compare or contrast.

EXAMPLE

Topic: jogging versus bicycling

Pointless topic sentence: Both jogging and bicycling are forms of aerobic exercise.

Points that could be made about this topic:

A. _Jogging is worse for a person's body than bicycling._

B. _Bicycling is more dangerous than jogging._

C. _Bicycling requires more dedication than jogging._

Possible topic sentence: _Although jogging is a convenient and inexpensive form of exercise, it is far harder on a person's body than bicycling._

_____ (paragraph of _contrast_)

HINT

For more on topic sentences, see pp. 38–42.

1. Topic: men versus women

   Pointless topic sentence: Men are a lot different from women.

   Points that could be made about this topic:

   A. _____

   B. _____

   C. _____

   Possible topic sentence: _____

   _____

   _____ (paragraph of _____)

2. Topic: college classes versus high school classes

   Pointless topic sentence: Both college classes and high school classes require homework.

   Points that could be made about this topic:

   A. _____

   B. _____

   C. _____

   Possible topic sentence: _____

   _____

   _____ (paragraph of _____)

3. Topic: infatuation versus love

   Pointless topic sentence: Infatuation is different from real love.

   Points that could be made about this topic:

   A. _____

   B. _____

   C. _____

   Possible topic sentence: _____

   _____

   _____ (paragraph of _____)

Making an Interesting Comparison or Contrast

It is easy to settle for a topic's obvious similarities or differences. For instance, in comparing a rowboat to a canoe, you might easily list similarities: both carry people on water, require muscle power to move, can be used for fishing, are easy to transport, and are found on lakes and rivers. However, choosing an obvious comparison often leads to boring reading.

To minimize a dull approach, try this: If two topics seem alike, contrast them. If they seem different, compare them. Making a point about the rowboat–canoe comparison—say, that rowboats are superior for fishing—we could then list interesting differences to support that claim: Rowboats are more stable, provide more room for casting, hold more gear, and are easier to anchor in moving water.

HINT

Avoid obvious comparisons.

ACTIVITY 11.2 *Making an Interesting Comparison or Contrast*

For each of the following paired topics, create a list of similarities and differences, decide which list would make the more interesting paragraph, and then write a topic sentence that makes a point.

EXAMPLE

Topic: winter versus summer

DIFFERENCES		SIMILARITIES
Winter	**Summer**	**Winter and Summer**
Cold	Hot	Extreme temperatures
Snow	Rain	People need shelter
Plants sleep	Plants awake	Some pleasant days
Short days	Long days	School break
Animals scarce	Animals plentiful	Drought

More interesting list: *similarities*

Topic sentence: *Although there are some obvious differences between winter and summer, the weather extremes affect people in much the same way.*

1. Topic: high school versus college

DIFFERENCES		SIMILARITIES
High School	**College**	**High School and College**

More interesting list: _____

Topic sentence: _____

_____

2. Topic: beach vacation versus mountain vacation

DIFFERENCES		SIMILARITIES
Beach	**Mountain**	**Beach and Mountain**

More interesting list: _____

Topic sentence: _____

_____

_____

3. Topic: river versus lake

DIFFERENCES		SIMILARITIES
River	Lake	River and Lake

More interesting list: _____

Topic sentence: _____

_____

4. Topic: smoking cigarettes versus standing in a burning house

DIFFERENCES		SIMILARITIES
Smoking Cigarettes	Standing in Burning House	Smoking Cigarettes and Standing in Burning House

Most interesting list: _____

Topic sentence: _____

_____

Developing Topics Thoroughly

To make comparisons interesting, explain them clearly and develop detailed, layered examples (pp. 42–49). For instance, to expand the winter–summer comparison from the example in Activity 11.2, we first write down the topic sentence:

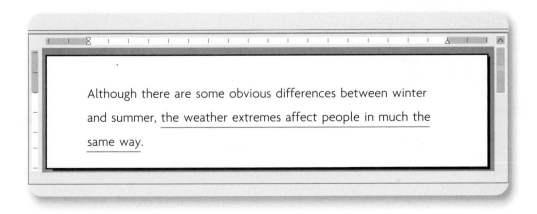

Although there are some obvious differences between winter and summer, the weather extremes affect people in much the same way.

To develop this topic sentence, which predicts a comparison paragraph, we need a list of main examples to show how "weather extremes affect people." We then need a list of second-level examples in order to develop these main examples.

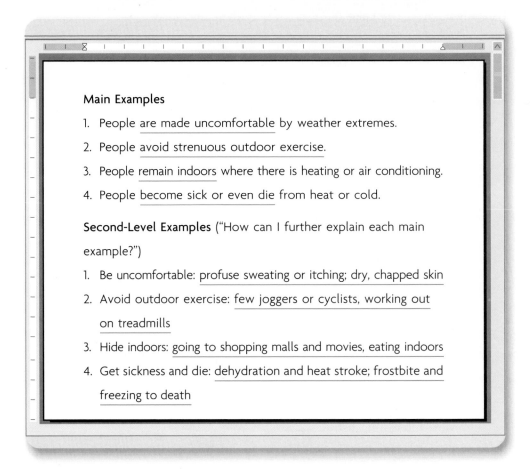

Main Examples

1. People are made uncomfortable by weather extremes.
2. People avoid strenuous outdoor exercise.
3. People remain indoors where there is heating or air conditioning.
4. People become sick or even die from heat or cold.

Second-Level Examples ("How can I further explain each main example?")

1. Be uncomfortable: profuse sweating or itching; dry, chapped skin
2. Avoid outdoor exercise: few joggers or cyclists, working out on treadmills
3. Hide indoors: going to shopping malls and movies, eating indoors
4. Get sickness and die: dehydration and heat stroke; frostbite and freezing to death

These examples are good material with which to *begin* a comparison paragraph. While drafting, we would add other examples and supporting details—for instance, how hot? 105 degrees; how cold? 20 degrees below zero.

ACTIVITY 11.3 *Developing Topics Thoroughly*

Pick a topic from Activity 11.2 and, using a prewriting method like listing, create several main supporting examples. Next, list at least one second-level example for each main example.

Topic from Activity 11.2: _____

Topic sentence from Activity 11.2: _____

_____

Main examples:

1. _____ 3. _____

2. _____ 4. _____

Second-level examples:

1. _____

2. _____

HINT

For help developing examples, see pp. 42–49.

3. _____
   _____

4. _____
   _____

English Review Note

Learn these transition words and copy them correctly into your writing assignment. For example, write "on the other hand" and not "in the other hand."

Using Transitions and Other Connectors

As you will see later in the chapter, there are two ways to organize comparisons/contrasts. Transitions like the ones listed and other connectors are important in either organization. They signal the switch from one part of a comparison or contrast to another.

FOR COMPARING

alike	both	like	resembling
also	in the same way	likewise	similarly

FOR CONTRASTING

after all	dissimilar	nevertheless	though
although	even though	on the contrary	unlike
but	however	on the other hand	whereas
difference	in contrast	otherwise	yet
differs from	in spite of	still	

ACTIVITY 11.4 *Using Transitions and Other Connectors*

Complete each sentence with a suitable transitional word.

1. I liked going to camp when I was young, _____ I missed my family a lot.

2. _____ living on my own has its advantages, it _____ has its downside.

3. _____, living with a roommate can be a problem.

4. _____, many people prefer to live on the Plaza.

5. _____ all the preelection promises, I still don't expect much government reform.

6. The helicopter, _____, is superior to the plane in at least two respects.

7. Most of my friends don't like museums, _____ I do.

8. _____ Carlo, Tony is energetic and enjoys being around people.

9. Bruce thinks I prefer electric guitar. _____, I would rather hear acoustic.

10. Eleanor is going to medical school _____ her mother did.

HINT

For more on connectors, see pp. 53–56.

Analyzing Student Models: Comparison or Contrast Paragraphs

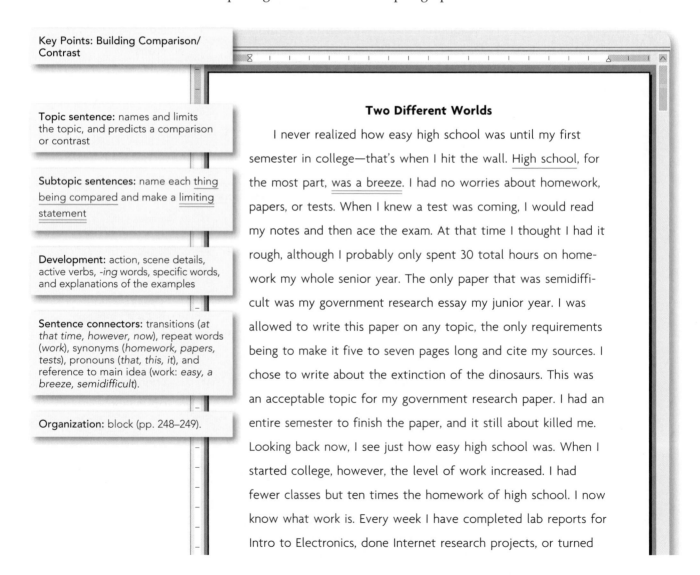

HINT

See "Organizing Ideas," pp. 248–250.

The following model paragraphs will help you write comparison or contrast papers. "Two Different Worlds" shows **block organizing,** in which the writer first gives all of the examples, or points of comparison or contrast, for one of the two things being compared/contrasted and then all of those for the other thing. "Breakin' Through" and "The Joy of Simple Living," the annotated paragraph, illustrate **point-by-point organizing,** in which the writer discusses the two things being compared/contrasted together, point by point.

➡ *Prereading Exploration for "Two Different Worlds"*

Dave Harrison decided to contrast the work demands in high school and those in college for an audience of college-bound high school seniors.

To find a topic for your paper, think about your own expectations of what college would be like versus what it is like.

1. What surprises have you had so far?
2. Have you changed your views about education, other people, or yourself since you started? If so, list your views before and after, and consider exploring the differences in a paragraph of contrast.

Key Points: Building Comparison/Contrast

Topic sentence: names and limits the topic, and predicts a comparison or contrast

Subtopic sentences: name each thing being compared and make a limiting statement

Development: action, scene details, active verbs, *-ing* words, specific words, and explanations of the examples

Sentence connectors: transitions (*at that time, however, now*), repeat words (*work*), synonyms (*homework, papers, tests*), pronouns (*that, this, it*), and reference to main idea (work: *easy, a breeze, semidifficult*).

Organization: block (pp. 248–249).

Two Different Worlds

I never realized how easy high school was until my first semester in college—that's when I hit the wall. High school, for the most part, was a breeze. I had no worries about homework, papers, or tests. When I knew a test was coming, I would read my notes and then ace the exam. At that time I thought I had it rough, although I probably only spent 30 total hours on homework my whole senior year. The only paper that was semidifficult was my government research essay my junior year. I was allowed to write this paper on any topic, the only requirements being to make it five to seven pages long and cite my sources. I chose to write about the extinction of the dinosaurs. This was an acceptable topic for my government research paper. I had an entire semester to finish the paper, and it still about killed me. Looking back now, I see just how easy high school was. When I started college, however, the level of work increased. I had fewer classes but ten times the homework of high school. I now know what work is. Every week I have completed lab reports for Intro to Electronics, done Internet research projects, or turned out papers for my writing class. On top of doing my lab reports, I spend from 6 to 8 hours a week doing the labs. Late nights are not uncommon anymore. Some nights I have been known to stay up till two in the morning, and sometimes I never sleep, period. Adjusting to the workload from high school to college has been a shock, and I have learned that if a student wants to learn and do well in school, he or she has to be committed.

—David Harrison

> **Concluding sentence:** restates the topic and adds a final (expanded) thought.

➡ *Prereading Exploration for "Breakin' Through"*

Comparison and contrast papers are a great opportunity to reflect on a person's life, as Gina Rizzo did in this paragraph, in which she contrasted her "roaring twenties" and late twenties. She wrote for members of her writing group, who she felt would be interested since they were entering their twenties.

To generate possible topics, think back on your own life.

1. List one or two things you have done that surprised you, times when you behaved in a way that was indifferent, lazy, selfish, or cruel—or perhaps involved, active, generous, or kind.

2. If you have ever felt like a different person than you are now, write a short description of that person, and consider pursuing the topic in a paragraph of contrast.

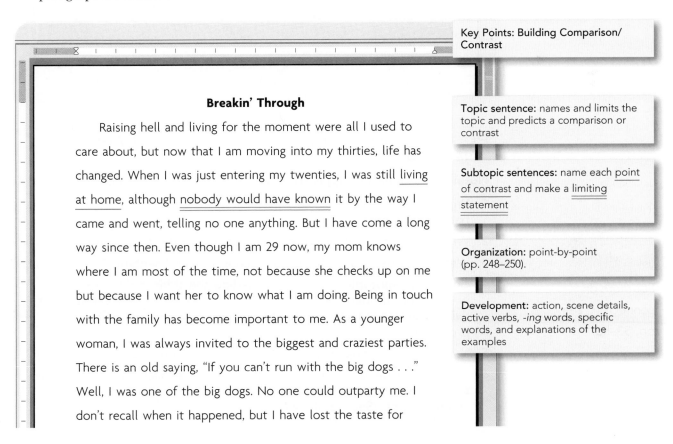

Key Points: Building Comparison/ Contrast

Breakin' Through

Raising hell and living for the moment were all I used to care about, but now that I am moving into my thirties, life has changed. When I was just entering my twenties, I was still <u>living at home</u>, although <u>nobody would have known</u> it by the way I came and went, telling no one anything. But I have come a long way since then. Even though I am 29 now, my mom knows where I am most of the time, not because she checks up on me but because I want her to know what I am doing. Being in touch with the family has become important to me. As a younger woman, I was always invited to the biggest and craziest parties. There is an old saying, "If you can't run with the big dogs . . ." Well, I was one of the big dogs. No one could outparty me. I don't recall when it happened, but I have lost the taste for

> **Topic sentence:** names and limits the topic and predicts a comparison or contrast

> **Subtopic sentences:** name each <u>point of contrast</u> and make a <u>limiting statement</u>

> **Organization:** point-by-point (pp. 248–250).

> **Development:** action, scene details, active verbs, *-ing* words, specific words, and explanations of the examples

Sentence connectors: transitions (*despite, however, although*), repeat words (*I*), synonyms (*self, woman, big dogs*), pronouns (*myself, nobody, anything*), and reference to main idea (contrast: *changed, come a long way, difference*).

drinking altogether. Somewhere down the road my body started rejecting the soothing liquid that I had begun to rely on too much. I don't go to the big or crazy parties anymore. My friends have quit inviting me, which is just as well. I don't much feel like partying that way now. I would rather remember my life instead of just hearing about it. Maybe the most important difference between my younger self and the woman of today is how I think about time. I used to live only in the present, never planning ahead, never saving money. I bartended for a living, so my money was spent just like I made it, one day at a time. I didn't plan vacations; I would decide the day before, and off I'd go, hopping another red-eye to Las Vegas. I would go anywhere I could afford with the money I had in my pocket. However, times have changed. I actually have a savings account now, and I just bought a plane ticket for my coming vacation two months in advance! Being more responsible with money ought to help me get a few more wants out of life, not just my needs. As I look back over my roaring twenties, I see a lot that makes me shake my head at myself, but I have realized that nobody comes into the world fully grown. We just have to inch forward, a bit at a time, hoping for the best.

—Gina Rizzo

Concluding sentence: restates the topic and adds a final (expanded) thought

POSTREADING QUESTIONS FOR PARAGRAPH ANALYSIS

Note: These questions apply to either of the preceding student models.

1. Which words in the topic sentence name the topic and predict a comparison or contrast?
2. What words in the concluding sentence link to the topic sentence?
3. What is the expanded thought (p. 50) in the final sentence?
4. Copy each subtopic sentence. Underline the <u>thing being compared or point of comparison or contrast</u> once and the <u>statement</u> about it twice. Circle connectors: transitions, repeat words, synonyms, and pronouns.
5. List three transitional words that show comparison or contrast (p. 241).
6. Choose an example and tell how the author's explaining (as opposed to detailing or action description) helps you better understand the author's point. (See pp. 42–49.)

For more on connectors, see pp. 53–56.

7. Choose an example, and tell how the action description and detailing help you better understand the author's point.

8. Name three specific words and list a more general word for each.

9. Name three ways to further develop any example in this paragraph. Consider action, active verbs, dialogue, specific words, sensory details, description of person or setting, revealing thoughts or emotions, and further explanation.

WRITING A COMPARISON OR CONTRAST PARAGRAPH

Summarizing the Assignment

Write a paragraph of 250 to 300 words that compares or contrasts two people, places, events, objects, or ideas. While writers often develop their work with both comparison and contrast, to stay focused, pick either comparison or contrast. Also, choose a block or point-by-point method of arrangement; then develop the topic with detailed examples and clear explanations.

Begin the paragraph with a sentence that names the two things being compared or contrasted, indicates a comparison or contrast, and makes a limiting statement about the topic. Each major example should begin with a subtopic sentence, and the final sentence should make a clear point.

Establishing Audience and Purpose

What point do you want to make about your topic, and for whom? As we saw in Activity 11.1, it is all too easy to write a meaningless comparison or contrast. If, however, you choose a topic that you care about and present it to others whom you want to know about it, you will probably find a point. Consider how the student writers in this chapter chose examples with their audience in mind. Most college-bound high school seniors would be interested in Dave Harrison's discovery about the college workload, and many young adults would be interested in Gina Rizzo's life changes. Finding a point and an audience to tell it to will make your work easier and more enjoyable.

You may write with several purposes—to entertain, persuade, or inform—but explaining the similarities or differences should be your top priority.

Working through the Writing Assignment

Discovering Ideas

You can write about many topics, including two people, places, or events. Or you might pick two objects—say, an oak tree and a rose—and think about their relationship to one another. Perhaps, as in "Breakin' Through," you will compare one period of your life with another. The topic choices are limited only by your imagination and what you can develop in a single paragraph.

However, resist the impulse to choose a topic too quickly. Look for one that you care about, and think of how to develop it in a way that will interest readers. If you want to discuss a German shepherd and a Labrador retriever, surprise your readers by contrasting the animals. Because a dog and a cat seem so different, try comparing them. But, while an "apples-and-oranges" comparison can make a creative paper, be careful in choosing your subjects. For example, a TV and a blender have little in common. A paper comparing them would be a stretch.

HINT

Search for an interesting topic, and try for a surprising slant on it. However, choose subjects that can reasonably be compared.

POSSIBLE TOPICS: COMPARISON OR CONTRAST

- **Pets:** dog/cat, fish/turtle, parakeet/boa constrictor
- **Cars:** Camry/Taurus, SUV/van, Miata/MG
- **Consumer services:** MCI/Sprint, two cable providers, Yahoo/Web Crawler
- **Cultural traditions:** wedding: Italian/Jewish; funeral: Irish/Japanese
- **Family members:** brother/sister, mother/father, aunt/uncle
- **Food:** Korean/Thai, Creole/Italian, German/French, ballpark/movie theater
- **Homes:** childhood/current, house/apartment, mobile home/fixed home
- **Locations:** town/city, United States/other country, East Coast/Midwest
- **Stages of education:** kindergarten/high school, elementary school/college, high school/college
- **Groups:** football team/soccer team, marching band/choir, athletes/debate team
- **Jobs:** mowing lawns/waiting tables, military/civilian, clerical/manual labor, part-time/full-time
- **Energy sources:** fossil fuels (coal, oil, gas)/renewables (wind solar, geothermal, etc.)
- **Working conditions:** current/past, indoors/outdoors, stress level for job A/for job B

ACTIVITY 11.5 WORKING ONLINE: *Use the Comparison/ Contrast Writing Tutor*

For additional topic ideas for this assignment, look under Chapter 11 at www.mhhe.com/brannan. Download the Comparison/Contrast Writing Tutor for more strategies in comparing and contrasting.

Prewriting

After picking a topic, decide on a point for your paper. A general cluster can help with this. For example, if you chose a topic like town versus city living, you could begin with the question "What comes to mind when I think about both towns and cities?" and then write a cluster like the following:

Now you can list both differences and similarities:

DIFFERENCES		SIMILARITIES
Town	City	Town and City
Quieter/peaceful	Noisier	Both can be noisy
Fewer people	More crowded	People can be a problem in both
Friendlier people	Less friendly	People can be helpful in both
More living space	Less living space	Can be room enough in both
Less crime	More crime	Some crime in both
Lower cost of living	Higher cost of living	People cope with expenses in both
Lower salaries	Higher salaries	People earn an income in both
Fewer activities	More activities	Many similar activities

Listing both differences and similarities will help you see which are more interesting to you. The author of this chapter's annotated model, "The Joy of Simple Living," chose differences for her paragraph, focusing on three main examples to contrast her experiences with towns and cities.

PREWRITING—SUMMING UP

1. Pick several topics, of your own or from the topics list, and decide on one that will interest you and an audience.

2. Prewrite, including by listing, to find both similarities and differences.

3. Check your lists for focus and a point.

4. Choose either to compare or to contrast.

JOURNAL / BLOG ENTRY 11.2

List differences and similarities for the two things you will discuss. Which list will lead to the more interesting paper? Who besides your instructor might like to read about your topic? Why would the audience be interested? How will you limit the subject so it can be developed in a single paragraph?

Organizing Ideas

Write a topic sentence that includes the topic, your point, and an indication of contrast or comparison. To show how two things are alike, use words like *same, similar, alike, resembling, both,* and *also.* To show how two things are different, use words like *different, unlike, dissimilar, opposite, although,* and *whereas.* If your rough topic sentence reads something like "Towns are different from cities," you probably have not yet decided on a point. Go back to your prewriting lists, and see if the examples suggest a point.

From the town–city list, you might come up with one of these topic sentences:

A. City living offers cultural advantages that cannot be found in small towns.

B. Although cities have many cultural advantages, small towns offer a sense of community that a city cannot easily duplicate.

C. Although small towns often have a strong sense of community, cities offer more economic opportunities.

D. For raising a family, a small town is better than a city in several ways: more room, more peace and quiet, and friendlier people.

Notice that each topic sentence indicates the topic (the two subjects—towns and cities) and the focus of the topic (the underlined words) and also tells the reader to expect a paragraph of contrast. Sentence D includes a forecasting statement (the shaded words) as well.

To organize a comparison/contrast paper, you need to pick either block or point-by-point arrangement:

- **Block method:** First state all points of comparison or contrast for one of the two subjects and then, midway through the paragraph, state all the points for the second subject, in the same order.

- **Point-by-point method:** State the first point for one subject and then the other, then the next point for one subject and then the other, and so on until you have stated all the points.

Although both methods are effective for paragraphs, longer essays are more likely to use the point-by-point method so readers don't have to try to keep in mind points from one part as they read the points in a later part.

Here are examples of the two methods:

Small Town versus City

Block	Point by Point
Topic sentence:_____	Topic sentence:_____
I. Small town 1. Space for the children to play 2. Peaceful for the whole family 3. Relationships with the neighbors	**I. Space for the children to play** A. Small town B. City
	II. Peaceful for the whole family A. Small town B. City
II. City 1. Space for the children to play 2. Peaceful for the whole family 3. Relationships with the neighbors	**III. Relationships with the neighbors** A. Small town B. City
Concluding sentence: _____	Concluding sentence: _____

In the block organization, the first half of the paragraph discusses three points about small town living, and the second half discusses the same three points about city living. In the point-by-point organization, the three points are discussed one at a time in relation to both town and city.

To show how these methods actually work, we can use material from "The Joy of Simple Living," the annotated model. (The author herself used the point-by-point method; that example has been excerpted, and the block example adapted.) Notice that the two paragraphs have the same topic sentences and the same concluding sentences.

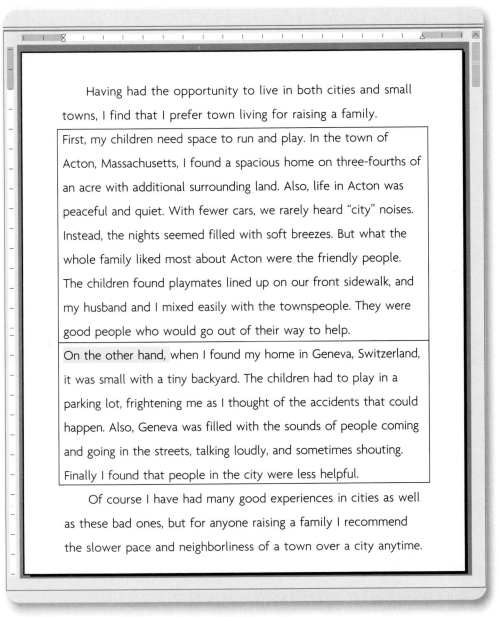

BLOCK
ARRANGEMENT

Having had the opportunity to live in both cities and small towns, I find that I prefer town living for raising a family.

First, my children need space to run and play. In the town of Acton, Massachusetts, I found a spacious home on three-fourths of an acre with additional surrounding land. Also, life in Acton was peaceful and quiet. With fewer cars, we rarely heard "city" noises. Instead, the nights seemed filled with soft breezes. But what the whole family liked most about Acton were the friendly people. The children found playmates lined up on our front sidewalk, and my husband and I mixed easily with the townspeople. They were good people who would go out of their way to help.

On the other hand, when I found my home in Geneva, Switzerland, it was small with a tiny backyard. The children had to play in a parking lot, frightening me as I thought of the accidents that could happen. Also, Geneva was filled with the sounds of people coming and going in the streets, talking loudly, and sometimes shouting. Finally I found that people in the city were less helpful.

Of course I have had many good experiences in cities as well as these bad ones, but for anyone raising a family I recommend the slower pace and neighborliness of a town over a city anytime.

POINT-BY-POINT
ARRANGEMENT

Having had the opportunity to live in both cities and small towns, I find that I prefer town living for raising a family.

First, my children need space to run and play. In the town of Acton, Massachusetts, I found a spacious home on three-fourths of an acre with additional surrounding land. On the other hand, when I found my home in Geneva, Switzerland, it was small with a tiny backyard. The children had to play in a parking lot, frightening me as I thought of the accidents that could happen.

Also, life in Acton was more peaceful and far quieter. With fewer cars, we rarely heard "city" noises. Instead, the nights seemed filled with soft breezes. In contrast, Geneva was filled with the sounds of people coming and going in the streets, talking loudly, and sometimes shouting.

What the whole family missed most, however, were the friendly people of Acton. The children found playmates lined up on our front sidewalk, and my husband and I mixed easily with the townspeople. They were good people who would go out of their way to help. In contrast, I found that city residents were less helpful.

Of course I have had many good experiences in cities as well as these bad ones, but for anyone raising a family I recommend the slower pace and neighborliness of a town over a city anytime.

Usually arrange points by order of importance.

With either method, use subtopic sentences to name the things being compared or contrasted. And whichever organizing method you choose, you need to decide how to order your points. These are usually ordered by importance, but occasionally spatially or chronologically.

When switching from one subject to the other or moving from one point to the next, remember to use transitions (pp. 54–56).

ORGANIZING—SUMMING UP

1. Create a topic sentence to focus your material.
2. Limit points of comparison or contrast to three or four.
3. Arrange the points by importance (occasionally by space or time).
4. Pick either block or point-by-point organization.
5. Use a subtopic sentence to introduce each subject or point.
6. Review the lists of transitions and other connectors.

JOURNAL / BLOG ENTRY 11.3

Write out your topic sentence. Does it mention two subjects, tell whether you will compare or contrast, and express an opinion/reason for making the comparison or contrast? Now list three or four points of comparison or contrast by order of importance, following either a block or point-by-point format.

Drafting

Before you begin drafting, review the drafting suggestions in Chapter 1 (pp. 16–17). In writing, be sure to do the following:

1. Choose either comparison or contrast.

2. Include all the points, or main examples, for one subject that you have for the other, and develop each point with at least one detailed example.

3. Be sure your paper makes a point. The topic and concluding sentences can help clarify why the subject has meaning for you.

4. Include transitions to help your readers keep track of your comparisons or contrasts.

JOURNAL / BLOG ENTRY 11.4

Soon after writing your first draft, reread the assignment on page 245, and then skim the draft. Does it fit the assignment? Have you compared **or** contrasted? Have you introduced each subject or point with a subtopic sentence? What part of your draft do you like best? What part least? Answer in a paragraph.

FEEDBACK *Share your draft with at least two other people—classmates, your instructor, someone at the writing center. Comment on your blog or in your journal about specific feedback you received, and note how you will incorporate some of it into your revisions.*

Revising Drafts

For help with revising first, second, and final drafts, turn to Chapter 4, pp. 63–67.

Annotated Student Model: "The Joy of Simple Living"

Carefully reading the annotated student model will help clarify questions you have about your own draft.

First-Stage Draft

Ana Maria Sauer had moved with her family many times and decided that small towns were better places for raising children than cities. So she chose a paragraph of contrast for an audience of parents who might be considering a move.

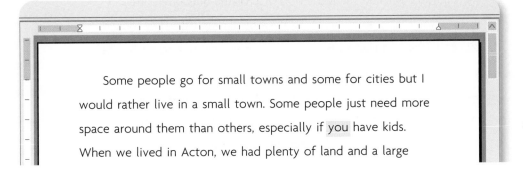

Some people go for small towns and some for cities but I would rather live in a small town. Some people just need more space around them than others, especially if you have kids. When we lived in Acton, we had plenty of land and a large

Avoid this use of *you.*

Need to develop examples with more specific supporting examples and details

Need more connecting words to move between town and city points

house. There was a ton of room for the kids to play, and I loved watching them playing games in the neighborhood. In Geneva we were cramped. There wasn't much room in our house and the children ended up playing in the streets, with all the problems that meant. Life in Acton was quieter than in Switzerland. We weren't bothered by car noises. Instead, we heard the sounds of the wind moving through the treetops. But, in Geneva we heard way too much racket. People shouted and cars raced their engines on a regular basis which disturbed all our sleeping. I think that I most missed the good friends and even acquaintances I made in Acton. Maybe we were just lucky to find such a good group, but the townsfolk were almost always friendly and willing to help. In Geneva people seemed to want to ignore you. They were standoffish, and none of us really made any lasting relationships. Cities are depressing places and I'm glad we will be moving once again; you guessed it, back to Acton.

Second-Stage Draft

First drafts are often underdeveloped and unfocused. Notice how Ana Maria strengthened her paragraph.

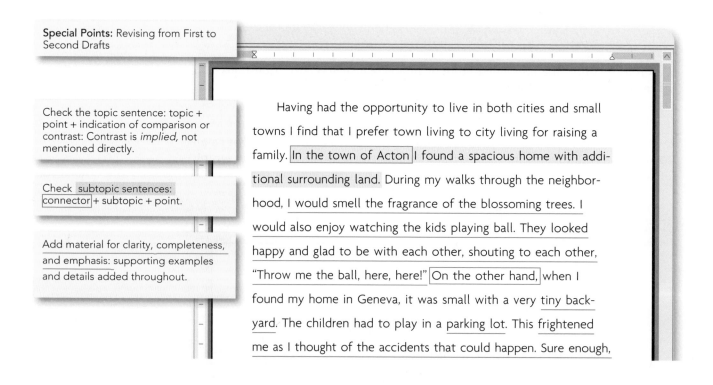

Special Points: Revising from First to Second Drafts

Check the topic sentence: topic + point + indication of comparison or contrast: Contrast is *implied,* not mentioned directly.

Check subtopic sentences: connector + subtopic + point.

Add material for clarity, completeness, and emphasis: supporting examples and details added throughout.

Having had the opportunity to live in both cities and small towns I find that I prefer town living to city living for raising a family. In the town of Acton I found a spacious home with additional surrounding land. During my walks through the neighborhood, I would smell the fragrance of the blossoming trees. I would also enjoy watching the kids playing ball. They looked happy and glad to be with each other, shouting to each other, "Throw me the ball, here, here!" On the other hand, when I found my home in Geneva, it was small with a very tiny backyard. The children had to play in a parking lot. This frightened me as I thought of the accidents that could happen. Sure enough, one day my daughter Anina came weeping and crying to me. Making me long for are safe home in Acton. Also, life in Acton was more peaceful and far quieter, with so few cars, we rarely heard "city" noises. Instead, the nights seemed filled with soft breezes the wind whispering through the treetops. In contrast, Geneva was filled with the noises of people killing time in the streets, talking loudly and sometimes shouting. Sirens, backfiring, and racing engines disturbed all our sleep, especially my daughter Sandra's. What the whole family missed most, however, were the friendly people of Acton. The kids easily found playmates and my husband and I also found friends. They were good people who would go out of their way to help. Once when I locked my keys in car, one of the people I barely knew took me home, waited for me to locate my spare key, and then drove me back to my car. In contrast, I found that people in the city were less helpful. Once when my battery died, none of the people I asked for help would bother. I ended by calling a tow service and I lost a day waiting for them to come get my car. Of course I have had many good experiences in cities as well as these bad ones, but for anyone raising a family I recommend the slower pace and neighborliness of a town over a city any time.

Dialogue added

Delete unnecessary material.

Subtopic sentences revised

Check connectors: transitions, repeat words, synonyms, pronouns, and references to main idea: transitional words *in contrast* and others added.

Check the concluding sentence: connector + link to topic sentence + expanded thought: expanded thought

Third-Stage Draft

Rather than call a second draft complete, we can focus on word choices, sentence variety, and concision—polishing a good draft to make it a great one.

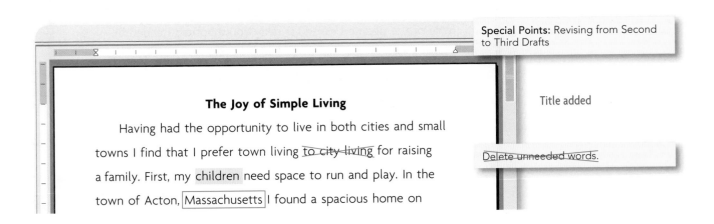

Special Points: Revising from Second to Third Drafts

The Joy of Simple Living

Having had the opportunity to live in both cities and small towns I find that I prefer town living ~~to city living~~ for raising a family. First, my children need space to run and play. In the town of Acton, Massachusetts I found a spacious home on

Title added

Delete unneeded words.

Clutter phrase deleted

Substitute more precise or audience-appropriate words.

Add specific words.

Clutter phrase deleted

Combine sentences for variety.

Replace clutter and repeat words with synonyms and phrases.

More appropriate words substituted

Sentences combined and specific words added

Synonym replaces phrase

three-fourths of an acer with additional surrounding land. During my leisurely walks through the neighborhood in spring, I would smell the fragrance of the blossoming apple trees, and enjoy watching the children playing ball. They looked happy and glad to be with each other with their flushed faces, shouting to each other, "Throw me the ball, here, here!" On the other hand when I found my home in Geneva, Switzerland, the house it was small with a very tiny backyard. The children had to play in a parking lot frightening me as I thought of the accidents that could happen. Sure enough, one day my daughter Anina came weeping and crying to me with her knee bleeding. Making me long for are safe home in Acton. Also, life in Acton was more peaceful and far quieter, with so few cars, we rarely heard "city" noises. Instead, the nights seemed filled with soft breezes the wind whispering lullabies through the treetops. In contrast, Geneva was filled with the noises sounds of people coming, and going in the streets, talking loudly and sometimes shouting. Sirens from police cars and ambulances, backfiring from cars and motorcycles, and racing engines disturbed all our sleep, especially my daughter Sandra's. What the whole family missed most, however, were the friendly people of Acton. The children found playmates lined up on our front sidewalk and my husband and I mixed easily with the townspeople. They were good people who would go out of their way to help. Once when I locked my keys the car in the grocery store parking lot, one of the people a neighbor I barely knew took me home, waited for me while I rummaged around to locate my spare key, and then drove me back to my car. In contrast, I found that people in the city were more detached, less helpful. Once when my battery died while I was parked downtown, none of the people I asked for help would bother. I ended by calling a tow service and I lost a day waiting for them to come get my car. Of course I have had many good experiences in cities as well as these bad ones, but for anyone raising a family I recommend the slower pace and neighborliness of a town over a city any time.

Final-Editing Draft

At this point, Ana shifted into low gear, moving slowly line by line, to find errors in grammar, spelling, and punctuation that she knew were still there. She used her Improvement Chart to locate pattern errors.

Special Points: Editing Final Drafts

The Joy of Simple Living

Having had the opportunity to live in both cities and small towns,[9a] I find that I prefer town living for raising a family. First, my children need space to run and play. In the town of Acton, Massachusetts,[9b] I found a spacious home on three-fourths of an ~~acer~~[1] acre with additional surrounding land. During my leisurely walks through the neighborhood in spring, I would smell the fragrance of the blossoming apple trees,[10] and enjoy watching the children playing ball. They looked happy with their flushed ~~faces'~~[8] faces, shouting to each other, "Throw me the ball, here, here!" On the other hand,[9a] when I found my home in Geneva, Switzerland, it was small with a tiny backyard. The children had to play in a parking lot,[9b] frightening me as I thought of the accidents that could happen. Sure enough, one day my daughter Anina came crying to me with her knee bleeding,[5] ~~M~~making me long for ~~are~~[2] our safe home in Acton. Also, life in Acton was more peaceful and far quieter[6] ~~W~~with so few cars, we rarely heard "city" noises. Instead, the nights seemed filled with soft breezes,[9b] the wind whispering lullabies through the treetops. In contrast, Geneva was filled with the sounds of people coming[10] and going in the streets, talking loudly and sometimes shouting. Sirens from police cars and ambulances, backfiring from cars and motorcycles, and racing engines disturbed all our sleep, especially my daughter Sandra's. What the whole family missed most, however, were the friendly people of Acton. The children found playmates lined up on our front sidewalk,[9c] and my husband and I mixed easily with the townspeople. They were good people who would go out of their way to help. Once when I locked my keys in[3] the car in the grocery store parking lot, a neighbor I barely knew took me home, waited for me while I rummaged

1. **Misspelling**
2. **Sound-alike word**
3. **Missing word(s)**
4. **Wrong word**
5. **Sentence fragment**
6. **Comma splice/run-on**
7. Faulty capitalization
8. **Incorrect apostrophe**
9a. **Comma(s) needed: Introductory word(s)/ phrase/clause**
9b. **Comma(s) needed: Nonessential word group(s)**
9c. **Comma(s) needed: Main clauses with coordinating conjuction**
10. **Unneeded comma**

around to locate my spare key, and then drove me back to my car. In contrast, I found that people in the city were more detached, less helpful. Once when my battery died while I was parked downtown, none of the people I asked for help would bother. I ended by calling a tow service,[9c] and I lost a day waiting for them to come get my car. Of course I have had many good experiences in cities as well as these bad ones, but for anyone raising a family I recommend the slower pace and neighborliness of a town over a city any time[4] anytime.

—Ana Maria Sauer

For more on revising paragraphs, see Chapter 4.

Edit for (1) correct use of superlative forms of adjectives and adverbs; (2) the distinction between "few" and "a few," and "fewer" and "less"; (3) word order with "just as."

Check to see if you need a title page. Double space your paper, leave at least a 1-inch margin, and use a 12-point font.

FINAL-DRAFT CHECKLIST: COMPARISON OR CONTRAST

Before turning in your final draft, review this checklist. You may find that, as careful as you think you have been, you still missed a point or two—or more.

1. Have you chosen to write either a comparison *or* a contrast?
2. Does your topic sentence name and limit the topic, and predict a comparison or contrast?
3. Have you chosen a block or point-by-point method of arrangement?
4. Have you arranged your main points of comparison or contrast effectively?
5. Have you written a subtopic sentence to introduce each subject (block arrangement) or point (point-by-point arrangement)?
6. Have you detailed and explained three or four examples?
7. Are points of comparison or contrast and examples linked with transitions and other connectors?
8. Does the concluding sentence have an expanded thought?
9. Have you used specific language?
10. Have you used a metaphor or simile?
11. Are your sentences varied in length and beginnings?
12. Have you used synonyms for words that are repeated too often?
13. Have you cut unneeded words?
14. Have you written an interesting title? Have you checked its capitalization?
15. Have you prepared your paper using the format expected by your instructor?
16. Have you edited your work closely (including having at least one other person proofread)? Have you checked your Improvement Chart for pattern errors?

17. Have you looked for errors involving the following: misspellings, sound-alike words, missing words, wrong words, sentence fragments, comma splices/run-ons, faulty capitalization, incorrect apostrophes, missing commas, and unnecessary commas?

Alternate Writing Assignments

Here are some additional comparison/contrast topics that may be of interest. For any of these assignments, be sure to do the following:

- First consider both similarities and differences.
- Have a reason for your comparison or contrast.
- Either compare or contrast.
- Develop each of your subjects equally.
- Use transitions and other connectors.

1. **Compare or contrast a period in your life, such as early childhood, with the same period in the life of someone you know well.** To prepare, you could talk to an older family member (a parent or grandparent, an aunt or uncle) about his or her life growing up. Here are some points to compare or contrast:

   - Location: town/city, state
   - Home
   - School
   - Work
   - Friends
   - Recreation
   - Hopes/aspirations
   - Worries/fears

   Encourage the person to tell stories related to any of these points or other points. You may decide to focus on just one of the suggested points.

2. **Compare or contrast yourself with someone from another country or culture.** To prepare, interview a student you know from writing class or elsewhere, asking about his or her home and culture and how they compare to yours. Points you might ask about include the following:

   - Country/area in the country
   - Form of government
   - School
   - Recreational activities
   - Music
   - Hopes/fears
   - Clothing
   - Dating
   - Friends
   - Sports

3. **Write a paper that contrasts a stereotype with your own view.** You might briefly describe the stereotype and then develop three or four specific points on which the stereotype differs from your own experience or general knowledge. Here are some stereotypes:

   - Teenagers are bad automobile insurance risks.
   - Men want sex while women want love.
   - Heavy metal music is just loud noise.
   - Anyone with a high GPA must be a nerd.
   - High school and college athletes don't care much about academics.

4. **For a comparison paper, create a profile of yourself that matches a job you would like.** Lay out the necessary skills for the job, and then show how

you are well suited for it. You might locate an actual job description—from your current employer, for instance, or from your school career center. Or you can make up your own description, including for a fantasy job. Perhaps you have always wanted to be a special assistant to Steven Spielberg, or a philosopher king—a ruler of your own country or maybe even of the universe. Match your imagined qualifications with those needed for the job.

5. **Examine the photos above and write either a comparison or contrast paragraph on them.** Before you choose an approach, list similarities and differences to help find the most interesting slant on your subjects. Next, decide on a point for your paper. For example, you might want to comment on the value of music in social gatherings or how personal style changes from one generation to the next.

6. COMPARE OR CONTRAST TWO SPECIFIC NATURAL SPACES

Conservation in Context

You might compare the local public park to the campus sculpture garden or contrast two different beaches on the Jersey shore. As an alternative, contrast the condition of one space over two periods of time. For instance, you might write about your garden, which was once well taken care of but now languishes while you write paragraphs about it. Or you might write about a nearby lake that was only recently cleaned up. ●

Linking to Future Experience

Determining the Value of Comparison and Contrast

Comparison/contrast skills help us every day to avoid making poor choices, like buying overripe bananas or avocados at the supermarket. In larger, more important ways, too, we need to compare and contrast critically to live a happier life. If we judge correctly from the start, we are more likely to avoid that unsuitable college, dead-end job, or unhappy marriage.

Developing the habit of comparing also improves our thinking and makes us more open to new experiences. Seeing similarities between an unfamiliar activity and an activity we already practice—say, between ice-skating and roller-skating—we might be more likely to try the new activity. As we move into the wider world of human experience, we can see how similar people are across ethnicities in our own country and across nationalities around the world. Learning to compare, to see ourselves in other people, can help us become more tolerant human beings.

ACTIVITY 11.6 WORKING ONLINE: *Comparing Web Sites*

In a paragraph, compare or contrast two social networking sites, such as Facebook and MySpace. Remember to focus your comparison or contrast around a central point.

ACTIVITY 11.7 WORKING ONLINE: *Comparison-Contrast Review*

Take the Chapter 11 Review Quiz at www.mhhe.com/brannan.

Chapter Summary

1. Comparison and contrast are the discovering of similarities and differences between two people, places, events, objects, or ideas.

2. Through comparison and contrast, we explore and evaluate unfamiliar things in the light of those we already know. Analogy, metaphor, and simile are forms of comparison.

3. Comparisons should be meaningful and interesting and made between two topics that are similar enough to be compared.

4. Two ways to organize comparison/contrast are block and point by point.

5. Transitional words and other connectors are needed to introduce new points of comparison/contrast and shifts from one subject to the other.

6. Points are frequently arranged by order of importance but can be ordered spatially or chronologically.

7. Subtopic sentences are useful for introducing new points of comparison/contrast.

8. The topic sentence should name the topic, make a statement about it, and predict a comparison or contrast.

9. The concluding sentence should begin with a connector, link to the topic sentence, and expand the main point of the paper.

10. Writing is never complete until it has been carefully revised and edited.

Building Essays

3

BRANNAN

Introducing the Essay

12

[*List five processes, skills, or techniques from earlier chapters that have prepared you for writing the college essay. How might you apply one or more of them in this chapter? What will likely be challenging about writing in a longer form?*]

KEY TOPICS

- What is an essay?
- Writing introductory paragraphs
- Crafting thesis sentences
- Developing introductions
- Avoiding weak introductions

- Writing body paragraphs
- Writing concluding paragraphs
- Avoiding weak conclusions
- Creating coherence
- Selecting a title

Linking to Previous Experience

What Is an Essay?

Although we worked through many challenging single-paragraph assignments in Unit Two, the essay may still seem intimidating. In truth, though, an essay is largely an expanded paragraph, written for the same reasons (to entertain, inform, or persuade) and complete with parts you already know: an introduction, body, and conclusion. Transitioning from writing paragraphs to writing essays is a matter of applying skills learned in a smaller setting to a larger one. The learning curve might remind you of driving on the highway after practicing on back roads or of climbing a small mountain after practicing on your gym's climbing wall.

While essays may have dozens of body paragraphs—and others to introduce and conclude them—many are relatively brief, as are the ones in this unit. While we write short essays of five to six paragraphs, we will practice all the strategies for discovering, organizing, and developing ideas we learned earlier in the term, and we will learn about an important focusing statement—the **thesis.**

Body Paragraph
Topic **sentence:** topic + statement
Body sentences • Subtopic sentence 1: connector, subtopic, statement • Development: examples, details, explanations • Subtopic sentence 2: connector, subtopic, statement • Development: examples, details, explanations • Subtopic sentence 3: connector, subtopic, statement • Development: examples, details, explanations
Concluding **sentence** • Connector • Link to topic sentence • Summary • Expanded thought

Essay

Essay
Introductory **paragraph** • Hook • Development • Thesis: topic + statement
Body paragraph 1 • Topic sentence: connector, subtopic, statement • Development: examples, details, explanations • Summary sentence (optional)
Body paragraph 2 • Topic sentence: connector, subtopic, statement • Development: examples, details, explanations • Summary sentence (optional)
Body paragraph 3 • Topic sentence: connector, subtopic, statement • Development: examples, details, explanations • Summary sentence (optional)
Concluding **paragraph** • Connector • Link to thesis • Summary • Development (expanded thought)

Essay Form

In Chapter 3, we saw that a body paragraph and an essay have many similarities. Both should begin with a controlling point, support that point with detailed examples and explanations, and end decisively. The illustration on this page shows how body paragraphs and essays are related.

The body paragraph often begins with a **topic sentence** (main point) while the essay begins with a **paragraph** that usually contains a thesis sentence (main point), often positioned as the *last* sentence in the paragraph. Notice in the illustration on the preceding page how the first arrow shows this relationship. Topic and thesis sentences are comparable, except that because essays are more fully developed, the thesis may need to allow for the fuller treatment of a subject.

As we saw in Chapter 7, body paragraphs that develop several primary examples begin each example with a **subtopic sentence** to introduce the main point. Similarly, body paragraphs in essays usually begin with a **topic sentence** to predict the main point. Both subtopic and topic sentences are then developed with detailed examples and explanations.

Body paragraphs end with one or two sentences while brief essays end with one paragraph, as the fifth arrow indicates. In both cases, a writer finishes by referring back to the paper's main point—found in the topic or thesis sentence. Body paragraphs sometimes summarize with a few words while essays often use a sentence or more.

See the second, third, and fourth arrows in the preceding illustration.

Student Models: Paragraph and Essay

To see how a paragraph might grow into an essay, let's compare paragraph and essay student models, both of them versions of "Dangers in a Deli," especially noting the beginnings, endings, and development.

Paragraph Model

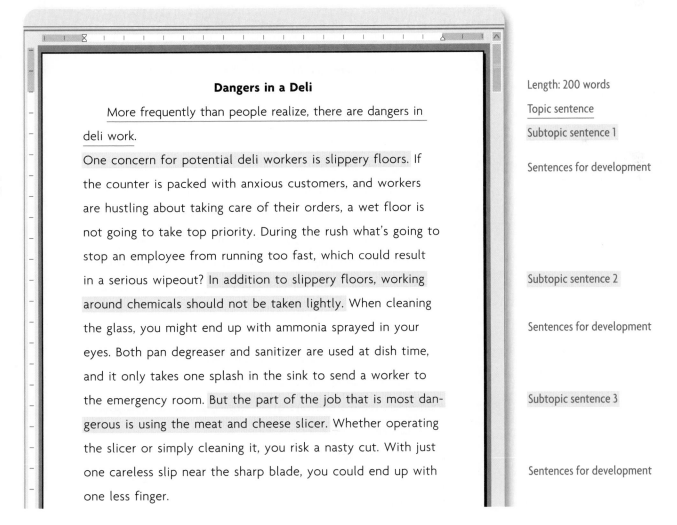

Dangers in a Deli

More frequently than people realize, there are dangers in deli work.

One concern for potential deli workers is slippery floors. If the counter is packed with anxious customers, and workers are hustling about taking care of their orders, a wet floor is not going to take top priority. During the rush what's going to stop an employee from running too fast, which could result in a serious wipeout? In addition to slippery floors, working around chemicals should not be taken lightly. When cleaning the glass, you might end up with ammonia sprayed in your eyes. Both pan degreaser and sanitizer are used at dish time, and it only takes one splash in the sink to send a worker to the emergency room. But the part of the job that is most dangerous is using the meat and cheese slicer. Whether operating the slicer or simply cleaning it, you risk a nasty cut. With just one careless slip near the sharp blade, you could end up with one less finger.

Length: 200 words

Topic sentence

Subtopic sentence 1

Sentences for development

Subtopic sentence 2

Sentences for development

Subtopic sentence 3

Sentences for development

Concluding sentence

A new person on the job might be a little nervous because of the possible injury that deli work entails, but luckily safety training is a requirement.

—Catherine Denning

Essay Model

Hook: First sentence arouses curiosity.

Length: 575 words

Essays require an introductory paragraph.

Sentences for development

Thesis sentence

Topic sentence 1

Sentences for development

Topic sentence 2

Dangers in a Deli

Would you like to keep all of your body parts intact today? How about your eyesight, how much do you value it, or that brain that keeps your body functioning? With all of the activity in a deli, employees rushing about, impatient customers pressuring you to hurry, and management barking orders, accidents can happen when you least expect them. Smashing your head on a slippery tile floor, splashing caustic chemicals into your eyes, and slicing off fingers are just a few of the dangers you can encounter. If you don't want to end up in the emergency room on your first day here, you need to be aware of the potential dangers in working at a deli.

One common hazard for deli workers is slippery floors. Often, especially during the lunch rush, the place gets jammed. Anxious customers crowd into one another and lean over the stainless steel counter in your face to call out three more changes to their already late orders. Trying to manage the rush, employees hustle about, carrying checks, prepping sandwiches, carting plates back and forth. When scurrying from the salad case to the register, you might not notice that freshly mopped floor, and before you know it, you are crashing into a wall and banging your head on the slick, hard tile. And if you don't trip yourself up, there are always other employees to run into you, which can also cause a serious wipeout.

Besides the slippery floors, workers also need to be cautious around chemicals. Even when business is slow, it is easy enough to be careless: for example, when cleaning the grease and handprints off all the glass, you might suddenly spray yourself in the face with ammonia. But it gets worse when the rush begins, and the owner goes into his panic mode: "Get these dishes done! Now, now— we're filling up!" You might think you have a good grip on that slippery platter, until it slips out of your hands and splashes into a sink full of pan degreaser and sanitizer. It only takes one faceful of that hot, soapy water to send a worker to the emergency room.

But the part of the job that is most dangerous is using the meat and cheese slicer. Whether operating the slicer or simply cleaning it, you risk a nasty cut. The shiny circular blade on the machine is as sharp as a surgeon's scalpel, and you will be using it all the time, your hand just inches away from the cutting edge. Everyone knows the kind of damage that can happen; everyone is extra careful, but then business picks up or someone is just too tired to pay attention. The blade doesn't know the difference between a piece of ham and four fingertips. Just one careless slip and you could end up with one less finger.

Cuts, chemicals, concussions, and other dangers—with all these ways to be injured, a new person on the job might feel a little nervous. But deli work doesn't always make you feel anxious and frazzled; in fact, it can be enjoyable. Whether you are talking to interesting customers or spending time with friends, the deli is usually a fun place to work. It can even be a great place for keeping your mind off problems at home or that algebra exam on Friday. Although accidents can happen, you are a lot less likely to have one if you keep the worst of the hazards in mind.

—*Catherine Denning*

Sentences for development

Topic sentence 3

Sentences for development

Essays require a concluding paragraph with a connector, link to thesis, summary, and development.

English Review Note

Reading and analyzing paragraph models is a good way to learn what is expected of writers in academic English.

As you compare the paragraph and essay models, you might notice the chief differences between them: **length, introduction,** and **conclusion.**

- **Length:** You can increase length in two ways: by adding examples and by developing them. The deli paragraph of **200** words grew into an essay of **575** words not by using more main examples but by developing those already there.

- **Introduction:** Whereas the deli paragraph is introduced by a sentence, which serves to focus what follows, the deli essay is introduced by a

In developing a paragraph into an essay, you might change the expanded thought.

paragraph, which does that and much more. Specifically, the essay's thesis (main point) is similar to the paragraph's topic sentence, *and* the author has added a **lead-in sentence** to "hook" readers, along with several more sentences to maintain the readers' interest and lead into the thesis.

- **Conclusion:** Rather than ending with a single sentence, the deli essay uses a concluding paragraph. The lead sentence includes a connector, a brief summary of the essay's main points, and a link to the thesis. Instead of merely trailing off, the author finishes decisively with an expanded thought. Note that the expanded thought has changed in the essay, from safety training to good times.

As we move ahead in Chapter 12, you will learn how to transform simple paragraphs into more complex essays.

Writing Introductory Paragraphs

If you began some of your one-paragraph papers with two or three sentences you then trimmed back, you have already written partial introductory paragraphs. In the context of these shorter papers, full-fledged introductions would have been distracting to readers. Now, however, you can develop these sentences and arrange them for greater interest and force.

Introductory paragraphs serve an important function: engaging readers' interest. If a reader is disappointed by or disinterested in the first few sentences of an essay, why should he or she continue? You can make your introductions interesting and well focused by including the following parts:

- **Hook:** one sentence (first sentence in the introductory paragraph)
- **Development:** three or four sentences (middle sentences)
- **Thesis:** one sentence (often the last sentence in the introductory paragraph)

Crafting Thesis Sentences

The **thesis sentence** is the most important part of your introduction. By naming the topic and making a statement about it, the thesis sentence guides readers through the essay, just as a topic sentence guides them through a paragraph. If you are expanding a paragraph from Unit Two, your topic sentence, essentially unchanged, may serve as your thesis sentence. However, if in expanding the paragraph you are adding points or changing a main example, you may need to rewrite your topic sentence so that it further focuses your essay. Even if you are not making such changes, you might still want to polish the wording. Compare the topic and thesis sentences from the paragraph and essay versions of "Dangers in a Deli":

TOPIC SENTENCE   More frequently than people realize, there are dangers in deli work.

THESIS SENTENCE   If you don't want to end up in the emergency room on your first day here, you need to be aware of the potential dangers in working at a deli.

Clearly, both sentences express the same point; however, the thesis targets an audience more precisely (potential deli employees) and uses a more specific phrase (*emergency room*) for emphasis.

Position the thesis as the last sentence in your first paragraph to keep yourself and your readers oriented.

Writers may use several sentences to express their thesis, locate it outside the introduction, or, occasionally, only imply rather than state it. For example, when arguing to a potentially resistant audience, a writer might delay the thesis. However, to keep both yourself and your readers oriented in your essay, it helps to make the thesis the last sentence in the first paragraph.

When you write a thesis sentence, be sure to do the following:

1. Limit the topic.

2. Make a clear statement about the topic.

3. Refine the statement by explaining it clearly and using specific words, action words, and sensory details.

Limiting the Thesis Sentence

A thesis sentence should be midway between general and specific—general enough to need focused examples to illustrate it, and specific enough to need only as many of those examples as the writer intends to give. The Language Line from Chapter 5 can help us see the general-specific range and locate the thesis:

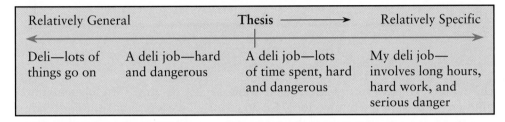

Relatively General		Thesis ⟶	Relatively Specific
Deli—lots of things go on	A deli job—hard and dangerous	A deli job—lots of time spent, hard and dangerous	My deli job—involves long hours, hard work, and serious danger

HINT

For more on general and specific language, see Chapter 5.

Often, the writer begins with a fairly general thesis and, in part through trial and error, discovers the focus needed to sufficiently limit it. Notice how the following thesis sentence becomes increasingly focused until it could guide the drafting of "Dangers in a Deli":

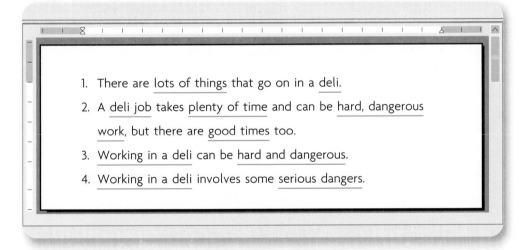

1. There are lots of things that go on in a deli.

2. A deli job takes plenty of time and can be hard, dangerous work, but there are good times too.

3. Working in a deli can be hard and dangerous.

4. Working in a deli involves some serious dangers.

Like a topic sentence, a thesis sentence can include a **forecasting statement.** Thus, the example could be expanded as follows:

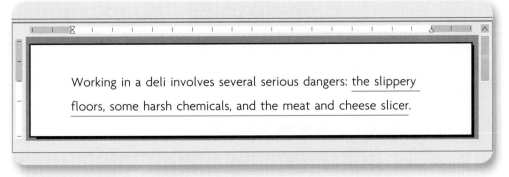

Working in a deli involves several serious dangers: the slippery floors, some harsh chemicals, and the meat and cheese slicer.

HINT

Forecasting an essay's main points can be an effective addition to a thesis sentence.

Making a Clear Statement about the Topic

Sometimes, the thesis sentence might be limited enough, but the statement it makes about the topic isn't clear. The problem may be in the wording of the sentence or the thinking behind it. Consider the following thesis:

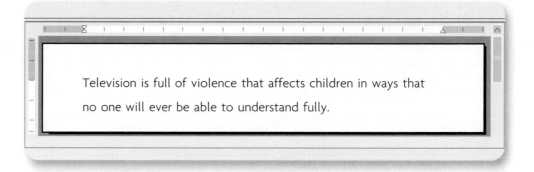

Television is full of violence that affects children in ways that no one will ever be able to understand fully.

The writer evidently wants to discuss some aspect of how TV violence affects children—a reasonably limited topic for an essay. However, as this thesis sentence is phrased, it's not clear where the essay is going. There are two possible directions, and the writer needs to revise the thesis to indicate one or the other:

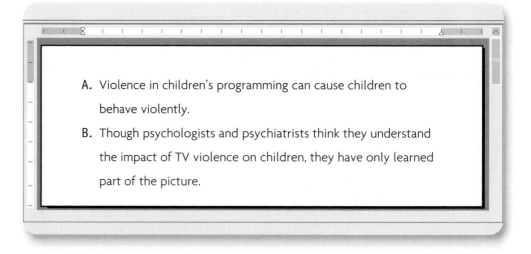

A. Violence in children's programming can cause children to behave violently.

B. Though psychologists and psychiatrists think they understand the impact of TV violence on children, they have only learned part of the picture.

Aside from the thesis that goes astray through faulty wording or thinking, there is the thesis that meanders, like a lazy, old river until it finally arrives at the end—sort of. Consider the following example:

HINT

Watch out for the meandering thesis sentence.

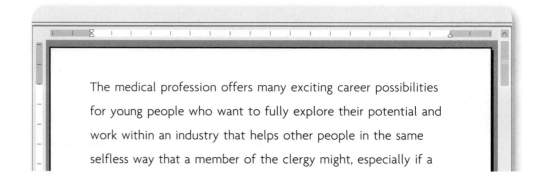

The medical profession offers many exciting career possibilities for young people who want to fully explore their potential and work within an industry that helps other people in the same selfless way that a member of the clergy might, especially if a person decides to go into an area that some would avoid

because of unpleasant working conditions or patients who suffer

too much, areas like respiratory therapy or geriatric care.

Besides being too long for a thesis (or most any other) sentence, this example includes too many ideas—though most are worthwhile and could be useful elsewhere in the essay.

How long is too long or too short for a thesis sentence? While there is no set rule, a medium-length sentence of 15 to 30 words generally works well. Some thesis sentences can be quite short for dramatic impact; others run to 40 words or more. As long as your thesis is clear, the word count should not be an issue.

A thesis sentence that is well crafted can *imply* its focus; what is important is that it not *hide* it. For example, an essay dealing with effects might use either of these thesis sentences:

Thesis sentences are often between 15 and 30 words long.

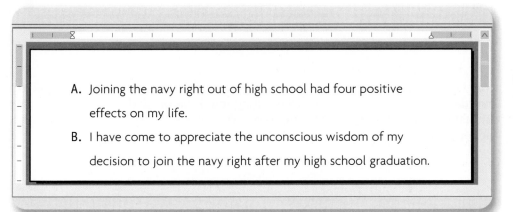

A. Joining the navy right out of high school had four positive effects on my life.

B. I have come to appreciate the unconscious wisdom of my decision to join the navy right after my high school graduation.

Thesis sentences may artfully *imply* the focus of an essay.

Version A clearly states the topic and even uses the word "effects." But version B also clearly states the topic while implying that the essay will develop effects. Contrast these two thesis sentences with the following one:

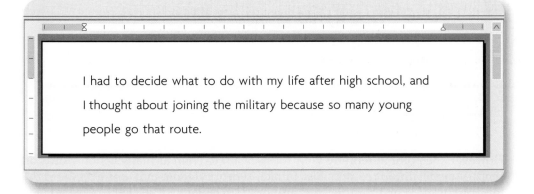

I had to decide what to do with my life after high school, and I thought about joining the military because so many young people go that route.

Undecided, or "waffling," thesis sentences like this make it difficult for readers to know where the essay is headed.

Polish thesis sentences
through **specific
words, action words,**
and **sensory details.**

Polishing the Thesis Sentence

Few of us will immediately hit upon the perfect thesis sentence and then go tearing into an essay. Instead, we will most likely need to work on the thesis, revising it for clarity and style, often using **specific words, action words,** and **sensory details** to make it more interesting.

With the deli essay, we can see one example of a writer upgrading her thesis:

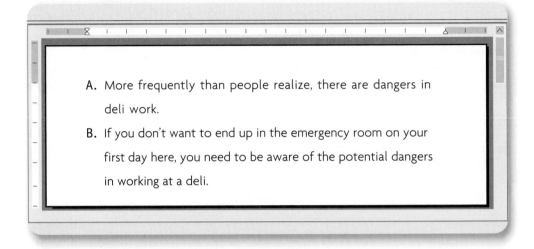

A. More frequently than people realize, there are dangers in deli work.

B. If you don't want to end up in the emergency room on your first day here, you need to be aware of the potential dangers in working at a deli.

Version B, aside from more directly addressing readers, includes the **specific words** *emergency room* to show where they might be headed if they do not pay attention to the information in the essay. The next two example sentences add action words and sensory details:

Added action word

Added sensory details, action
words, specific words

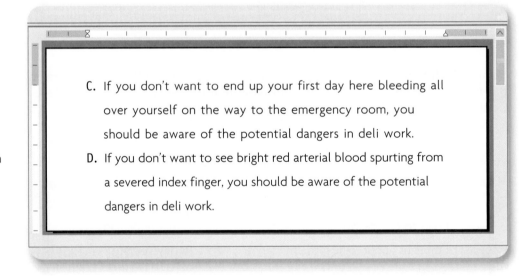

C. If you don't want to end up your first day here bleeding all over yourself on the way to the emergency room, you should be aware of the potential dangers in deli work.

D. If you don't want to see bright red arterial blood spurting from a severed index finger, you should be aware of the potential dangers in deli work.

However, the point in refining your thesis is not to cram as many action words or sensory details into it as possible. In fact, sensory details may not even be right for your topic. For example, the author of "Dangers in a Deli" polished her thesis sentence without including these action words and sensory details. The point is to look critically at your work with an eye to making a passable thesis sentence a powerful one.

ACTIVITY 12.1 *Polishing Thesis Sentences*

Revise the following rough thesis sentences, underlining any specific words, action words, or sensory details that you add.

    EXAMPLE: Rough thesis: A sense of humor has been useful to me.

    Revised thesis: *Being able to laugh at myself in embarrassing situations has saved me from some depressing moments.*

1. Rough thesis: Winter is hard on the world.

   Revised thesis: _____

   _____

Use your imagination, have some fun, and remember that even small additions can be real improvements.

2. Rough thesis: I know how to make my wife (husband, girl/boyfriend) happy.

   Revised thesis: _____

   _____

   _____

3. Rough thesis: There is one kind of party that is sure to attract the police.

   Revised thesis: _____

   _____

4. Rough thesis: Buying gifts that will be well received is not easy since you need to pick the right gift.

   Revised thesis: _____

   _____

5. Rough thesis: Extreme sports fall into several different categories.

   Revised thesis: _____

   _____

   _____

Developing Introductions

With a clear thesis sentence to end the introduction, you have a strong start to your essay. To lead readers to that thesis, use any of the following methods:

STRATEGIES FOR INTRODUCTIONS

    1. Description

    2. Narration

    3. Comparison/contrast

    4. Cause and effect

    5. Definition

    6. Persuasion

Some writers prefer to begin an essay draft with only a thesis, composing the introduction later.

These methods are often combined.

7. Question(s)

8. Background information/history (including why the topic is important to you)

9. Startling information

10. Reversal

11. Combination of several methods

To see these methods in action, read through the following introductions for "Dangers in a Deli." Notice that these different introductions can each lead to the same thesis sentence. The thesis sentence is shaded, and the "hook," or lead-in sentence, discussed in the next section, is underlined.

Note: In these introductions, you will see the word *you*. It is appropriate in this situation because the author is directly addressing readers. However, *you* is frequently overused in student writing; use it only in contexts in which you are sure it is appropriate.

Methods for Developing Introductory Paragraphs

There are at least ten basic methods for developing introductory paragraphs:

For more on *you* and pronoun shift problems, see Chapter 25.

1. **Description:** Create a series of vivid images— perhaps three or four. Consider these images as quick snapshots rather than a continuous story. Use one sentence for each image, and develop each with actions, specific words, and sensory details (sight, sound, and touch, especially).

Irritated customers shouting orders, pans clanging together, shirts soaked through with sweat—another shift at the deli is well under way. Employees are racing to keep up with the orders. Ben is slicing bread too fast for safety, the bread knife barely missing his palm as he opens one loaf after another. Ellen slips on a wet spot on the tile floor and jams her wrist against a wall. Ramon mutters, "Damn it!" as he scalds himself in the sink. A delicatessen in a lunch rush can be a hectic, nerve-wracking place. If you don't want to end up in the emergency room on your first day here, you need to be aware of the potential dangers in working at a deli.

2. **Narration:** Tell a brief story.

Shawn came into the restaurant cracking jokes, kidding customers and fellow employees alike, and generally having a good time. Everyone liked him right away and could see that he would be fun to have around. But in the middle of his third day on the job, during the lunch rush, we lost him for good. I was taking an order at table seven, when all the loud talking, jostling, and eating stopped abruptly. Everyone in the restaurant heard Shawn scream as he lost the first joint of his little finger to the meat slicer. He learned the hard way how dangerous this job can be. If you too don't want to end up in the emergency room on your first day here, you need to be aware of the potential dangers in working at a deli.

3. **Comparison/contrast:** Compare or contrast your topic with something your readers would be familiar with. You might also compare through a metaphor or simile.

Although I have never been on a cattle ranch, I think I know what it feels like to be caught in the middle of a stampede. I don't usually think of my customers as cows (though some do eat like animals), but in the middle of a lunch rush in our deli, with the restaurant packed from the front door to the counter and frustrated people calling out orders, you too might feel like you are about to be trampled. The pressure during a rush from customers and management alike can cause employees to move faster than what is safe. If you don't want to end up in the emergency room on your first day here, you need to be aware of the potential dangers in working at a deli.

Let's talk about Allen, a fictitious new employee at the deli, who is not paying much attention to his trainer as she talks about procedures and hazards on the job. He halfway listens as she tells him about how fast he will be expected to move in about an hour, when the lunch rush hits. "Right, yeah, OK," he says, paying more attention to Will Smith's rap in his headphones. An hour passes, people begin flooding in, and Allen begins to panic. Trying to carry a tray full of salads too quickly, he slips on the tile floor and lands flat on his back, knocking himself unconscious. Unless you are careful, you could be Allen. If you too don't want to end up in the emergency room on your first day here, you need to be aware of the potential dangers in working at a deli.

4. Cause and effect: Explain causes leading to or effects leading from the topic. Or create a fictional scenario—what might happen relating to your topic.

Self-preservation is an instinct that tries to keep animals out of harm's way, and it works pretty well for most of them, except for some humans. These are the people—maybe you know some like this—who refuse to listen to good advice or even to warnings that might save them from much misery. On the other hand, when a reasonable person has the opportunity to learn about job hazards that might endanger her, she listens, that good old self-preservation instinct kicking in. In this restaurant a new employee has to be careful. If you don't want to end up in the emergency room on your first day here, you need to be aware of the potential dangers in working at a deli.

5. Definition: Briefly define some concept important to your topic.

There is no reason that you have to be hurt today. No sane person enjoys pain, and few people can afford the recovery time that serious injury on the job requires. All new employees at this restaurant get a careful orientation that includes warnings on how to avoid accidents. Intelligent people pay attention. If you don't want to end up in the emergency room on your first day here, you need to be aware of the potential dangers in working at a deli.

6. Persuasion: Appeal to your readers' self-interest by showing them what they have to gain by reading your essay.

Would you like to keep all of your body parts intact today? How about your eyesight, how much do you value it, or that brain that keeps your body functioning? With all of the activity in a deli, employees rushing about, impatient customers pressuring you to hurry, and management barking orders, accidents can happen when you least expect them. Smashing your head on a slippery tile floor, splashing caustic chemicals into your eyes, and slicing off fingers are just a few of the dangers you can encounter. If you don't want to end up in the emergency room on your first day here, you need to be aware of the potential dangers in working at a deli.

7. Question(s): Ask your readers several questions that relate to your thesis.

8. Background informa-tion: Give information or history about your topic that would help orient your readers or show them why the topic is important to you.

As a deli manager I like to keep my fellow employees healthy, and as a reasonably good-hearted human being, I don't like to see people suffer. During our peak hours we only run five employees in the front and back of the house, even though we usually need more. In order for the operation to work, everyone has to do his or her job efficiently and with some enthusiasm. If even one person just gets the slows or, worse, is injured, the rest of the crew suffers. To help the restaurant, your fellow workers, and yourself, listen closely to this orientation. You can keep yourself out of the emergency room on your first day here, if you are aware of the potential dangers in working at this deli.

9. Startling information: Give facts or statistics that might seem unusual or dramatic to your readers. Or create graphic examples that would cause an emo-tional response in your readers.

A day rarely passes without some kind of accident in our deli. Most of the time the problem is small and the hurt to a person slight. But who wants even a little pain? It is bad enough to deal with small glass cuts and scalds from hot coffee, but when business picks up, the big accidents follow. New employees especially run the risk of breaking a wrist or slicing off a body part. If you don't want to end up in the emergency room on your first day here, you need to be aware of the potential dangers in working at a deli.

10. Reversal: Begin your introduction moving in one direction, but switch direction as you approach your thesis sentence.

Working in a deli can be great fun. Employees dress casually, no suits and ties here. Most of us are young adults with plenty happening in our lives. I enjoy listening to Felipe brag about his date last night (knowing that at least half of what he says is a lie) and watching Gabrielle and Nathan pester each other over nothing, like sister and brother. Also, when business picks up, it is a good feeling to work closely as an effi-cient team, depending on one another as we get the job done. But the work is not all play. There are real, serious hazards in this business. If you don't want to end up in the emergency room on your first day here, you need to be aware of the potential dangers in working at a deli.

11. Combination: Focus on any one introductory paragraph method to get started, but then include other meth-ods, as many of the paragraphs above do. For example, number 10 uses description within the reversal strat-egy. Number 9 includes a question, description, and cause/effect. Number 8 explains in part through cause and effect. Almost all paragraphs, including introductions, are developed through examples.

There are many interesting ways to write introductory paragraphs, and the approach you choose depends on your topic, purpose, and audience. If you are writing, for example, how-to instructions for assembling a swing set, you might avoid the more colorful narrative/descriptive methods, favoring instead a sim-ple listing and defining of parts. If, however, you are persuading a group of teens not to smoke, you might begin with a story to capture their attention. Your tone (formal/informal), word choices, and explanations in the essay body depend on the context in which you are writing, and these choices begin in your introduction.

Remember, too, that lively, interesting introductions rarely just fall from the sky. You must bring beginnings to life. So apply the same prewriting methods to this paragraph that you do to the body of the essay: Plan on clustering, listing, freewriting, and so forth to discover ideas.

ACTIVITY 12.2 *Creating Interesting Introductions*

Pick one of the thesis sentences you created for Activity 12.1. For three different introductory paragraphs, write five to seven sentences leading to this thesis.

Review the ten methods listed on pages 272–274, and remember that you can combine several.

1. List the method number(s): _____

   Begin the introductory paragraph: _____

   _____

   _____

   _____

   _____

   Thesis sentence: _____

   _____

2. List the method number(s): _____

   Begin the introductory paragraph: _____

   _____

   _____

   _____

   _____

   Thesis sentence: _____

   _____

3. List the method number(s): _____

   Begin the introductory paragraph: _____

   _____

   _____

   _____

   _____

   Thesis sentence: _____

   _____

Hooks

If the introduction as a whole is important to draw readers in, then its lead sentence, the **hook,** is especially so. The first sentence should "hook" the fish, your readers, arousing their interest and encouraging them to forge ahead. In creating hooks, keep these points in mind:

1. Do not state the obvious.

2. Do say something that will interest readers.

Looking back at "Dangers in a Deli," note how the author, Catherine Denning, managed her hook:

> Would you like to keep all of your body parts intact today? How about your eyesight, how much do you value it, or that brain that keeps your body functioning?

Catherine wrote this essay with an audience of newly hired deli employees in mind. While most people are presumably interested in keeping all their "body parts intact," the new employee who will soon be operating the slicer might feel like paying special attention. Notice that the hook is phrased as a question and that it begins to answer a question most readers ask: "Why should *I* read this essay?" Also note that the hook extends into the next sentence. For our purposes, we will talk about the hook as the first sentence, realizing that it can be more than one sentence and that it should blend easily into the rest of the introduction.

METHODS FOR CREATING HOOKS

1. Ask a question.
2. Begin with a line of dialogue.
3. Begin with a quotation.
4. Make a startling statement.
5. Present an unusual fact.
6. Use a vivid image.
7. Create a comparison (possibly a metaphor or simile).
8. Use a combination of methods.

A hook can be created by combining several methods.

Hooks, like the rest of the introduction up to the thesis sentence, are largely interchangeable, often overlapping pieces that can vary as much as a writer's imagination allows. For example, Catherine could have begun her essay with any of the following sentences:

DIALOGUE   "Aaggh! Help, I just splashed sanitizer in my eyes!"

VIVID IMAGE   Irritated customers shouting orders, pans clanging together, shirts soaked through with sweat—another shift at the deli is well under way.

COMPARISON   Although I have never been on a cattle ranch, I think I know what it feels like to be caught in the middle of a stampede.

In contrast, here are three sentences that would make poor hooks:

POOR HOOKS   Everybody has to have some kind of job or another.

    I have a job in a deli.

    Accidents can happen to people when they are at work.

Obvious statements make poor hooks.

Such obvious statements arouse no curiosity; in fact, they would likely discourage readers from enjoying what might be an interesting essay.

ACTIVITY 12.3 | *Polishing Hooks*

Choose one of the introductory paragraphs that you wrote in Activity 12.2, and revise the first sentence to create a more interesting hook.

First sentence of one paragraph from Activity 12.2: _____

_____

Your revision of the hook: _____

_____

ACTIVITY 12.4 | *Creating Interesting Hooks*

Revise the following boring hooks, using three of the methods suggested above or some of your own.

1. Topic of essay: The day I won the lottery

   Boring hook: Sometimes good things happen to people.

   Interesting hooks:

   Version 1: _____

   _____

   Version 2: _____

   _____

   Version 3: _____

   _____

2. Topic of essay: Causes of a divorce

   Boring hook: Sometimes marriages don't work out.

   Interesting hooks:

   Version 1: _____

   _____

   Version 2: _____

   _____

   Version 3: _____

   _____

3. Topic of essay: How difficult returning to college can be for nontraditional students

   Boring hook: A college education can be very valuable.

   Interesting hooks:

   Version 1: _____

   _____

   Version 2: _____

   _____

   Version 3: _____

   _____

Avoiding Weak Introductions

Introductions can go wrong in various ways—sometimes several at the same time. Try to avoid the following problems:

1. **Beginning with obvious statements.** One boring sentence likely breeds another, and this often predicts an uninteresting essay. Consider this dull opener: "It was a day like any other day, with weather, people moving

about, and cars going from one place to another. The weather was not particularly hot or cold, the people were not extraordinary, and the cars were not really moving all that fast either." Remember that your reader is wondering, "Why should I read this essay?"

2. **Stating that you are getting ready to write an essay about something.** Here are two examples to avoid: "In this essay I will tell you about . . ." and "The first part of my essay will discuss . . . and the next paragraph will say . . . ."

3. **Apologizing for what you may not know.** Avoid beginning your essay with any of these openers: "Although I do not know much about this topic . . ." and "There are experts who know a lot more about this subject than I do . . ." and "I managed to find out a little bit about this subject, and so I can say something about it." Writers are asking readers for their time. If you begin by telling readers that you don't have much worth saying, why should they waste time reading your work?

4. **Needlessly repeating information.** Consider this opening: "Some students have problems with their schoolwork. When they do their work, it is often difficult for them. The homework and in-class work is hard to complete, and so many students—as hard as they work—find that they have a lot of trouble getting the work done." By now, readers have gotten the point— and are probably sleeping on it.

5. **Using clichés and worn expressions.** Think about these tired phrases: "Caught between a rock and a hard place," "after what seemed like an eternity," and "with butterflies in my stomach." If a fresh figure of speech doesn't occur to you, use a literal phrase. Say, for example, "caught in a difficult situation" in place of the first cliché.

6. **Writing overly long or overly short introductions.** Introductions should be in proportion to the rest of the work. A book, for instance, might use a whole chapter, while an essay of fifteen pages might need only a paragraph or two. Our brief essay introductions will be well developed in five to seven sentences—about a hundred words.

For more on effective repetition, see Chapter 20.

For more on clichés and worn phrases, see Chapter 20.

ACTIVITY 12.5 WORKING TOGETHER: *Recognizing and Revising Weak Introductions*

Working in a group, decide which five of the following six introductory paragraphs are ineffective. Explain why each is ineffective. Then rewrite one of them, using a method listed or one of your own. Optional: Share your group's revisions with the larger class; see what different choices groups have made.

1. Credit cards can be a real problem for anyone, especially college students. In this essay I will first discuss how much of a problem they can be, and then I will provide some solutions to this situation. Before I am through, I will show—in paragraph four to be exact—how irresponsible it is of the credit card companies to scatter their cards around so that anyone can get one. In my conclusion I will tell readers where to go to get more information on the problem.

2. Some people argue that IMing contributes to bad writing. After all, they say, look at how people dash off those notes, and look at all the obvious errors in them. However, IM can actually make people better writers.

3. Many Americans insist on driving new vehicles, even if they do cost an arm and a leg. These people seem to think that new is automatically better, but I think half the time the supposed new technology is just re-creating the wheel. Who needs electric windows when a crank will do the same job? Who needs a $500 antenna that pops up and down like a

jack in the box? My old '96 Toyota pickup truck with its 115,000 miles is still as good as gold and better than most of the new products on the market. I prefer driving an older vehicle for several good reasons.

4. I don't know a lot about professional sports, but it seems to me that the players make an awful lot of money. Take for instance professional baseball players. They make a ton of money. Why I think I remember reading about a month ago how some pitcher signed a $5,000,000 contract! This seems like too much money for someone who just throws a baseball. And, even though I am no authority, I'll bet it's even worse for football and basketball. I think these guys make even more! All these high salaries are bound to have negative effects on professional sports.

5. Most people want to be happy. They want to feel good about themselves and the world around them. They like to wake up in the morning feeling good, go through the day without many problems, and then come home at night to a relaxing sleep. People don't want a lot of anxiety in their lives; they prefer to be stress free. But not everyone is lucky enough to have a good life. And if a person is not lucky, he needs to take responsibility on his own shoulders, to carry the weight of his own life. The fact is that happiness is not something that just happens for most people; they have to work for it.

6. "Dammit, Jack," the shift manager yelled at me, "that's the third time you burned those fries tonight! Get your head together or get a new job!" I stood there looking at my feet on the greasy tile floor, hating to take it, but apologizing anyway to keep my job. Around me rang out all the noise of a McDonald's Friday night: ovens beeping, warmers buzzing, pans clanging, deep fat fryer popping, Vera calling back for more Big Macs, kids crying up front from waiting too long in this so-called fast-food restaurant. That's when I finally decided I had had enough. I had to get a new life. The way I've chosen to escape from McDonald's is to enroll in college, and this first semester has been full of challenges for me.

Ineffective paragraphs: _____

Reasons that each introduction is weak: _____

_____

_____

_____

One weak introduction rewritten: _____

_____

_____

_____

_____

_____

_____

CREATING INTRODUCTORY PARAGRAPHS—SUMMING UP

1. Write out a working thesis sentence.
2. Skim the introductory paragraph methods, the methods for writing a hook, and the tips for avoiding weak introductions.

Some writers prefer to draft using only a thesis for focus and then create an introduction after the body is complete.

3. Prewrite using one or more of the introductory paragraph methods.

4. Draft your introduction.

Writing Body Paragraphs

Introductory paragraphs take the first step of attracting and then focusing a reader, but then the writer must follow through, keeping the essay interesting. We do this in the **body paragraphs,** where we present most of our information.

Essay body paragraphs begin with a topic sentence, as did the Unit Two assignments, and sometimes end with a summarizing sentence, similar to our Unit Two concluding sentence. Also, you will sometimes find a subtopic sentence useful, depending on how many points you want to develop in the paragraph. Whereas our former body paragraphs were around 300 words, now we will reduce the length to 100–200 words, around five to eight sentences.

Here are the three main parts of body paragraphs:

- **Topic sentence:** connector + topic + statement (first sentence)
- **Development:** four to six sentences (middle sentences)
- **Summary sentence** (optional): restatement of paragraph's main idea (last sentence)

Topic and Summary Sentences in Body Paragraphs

Topic sentences develop the thesis, offering the *more specific* points or examples from which the essay will grow. Within each topic sentence, it is important to name and focus the point or example and to include a link to the preceding paragraph—a transition or other connector.

Notice how the topic sentence in the following paragraph uses several connectors (boxed) to link to the previous paragraph and to link this main example (slicer) to the thesis, the dangers of deli work.

In an essay expanded from a paragraph, the subtopic sentences in the paragraph become topic sentences.

Always use strong connectors between body paragraphs. To review methods for coherence, see pp. 53–59.

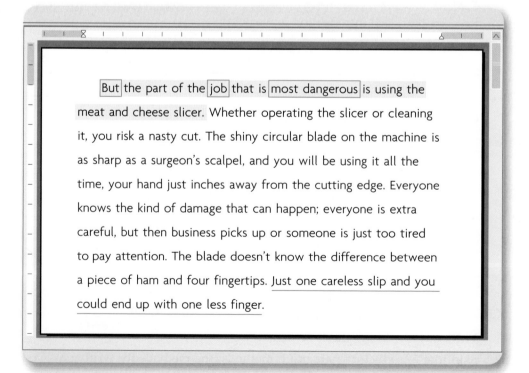

But the part of the job that is most dangerous is using the meat and cheese slicer. Whether operating the slicer or cleaning it, you risk a nasty cut. The shiny circular blade on the machine is as sharp as a surgeon's scalpel, and you will be using it all the time, your hand just inches away from the cutting edge. Everyone knows the kind of damage that can happen; everyone is extra careful, but then business picks up or someone is just too tired to pay attention. The blade doesn't know the difference between a piece of ham and four fingertips. Just one careless slip and you could end up with one less finger.

To conclude longer body paragraphs, writers sometimes create a **summary sentence** like the one underlined in the preceding paragraph. These sentences can be useful because they reinforce and clarify an author's message. However, in short paragraphs, they can become repetitive, boring readers. You must judge for yourself when summary sentences will be effective in your essays.

Developing Body Paragraphs

Whether expanding a single-paragraph assignment or beginning an essay from scratch, you need to develop your main points, which you can do by using detailed examples and explanations (see pp. 42–49) and asking yourself, "How can I more clearly show my readers what I am saying?"

By comparing a major example (subtopic) from the paragraph version of "Dangers in a Deli" with the corresponding body paragraph in the essay version, we can see how one writer used details and explanations to make her paragraph grow:

Summary sentences can be useful in body paragraphs.

Development of ideas relies on examples, details, and explanations.

Subtopic sentence

Author explains what she means by "slippery floors" by naming things and giving details.

Author also uses action words to support the main idea of danger.

Single-Paragraph Subtopic	**Essay Body Paragraph**
One concern for potential deli workers is slippery floors. If the counter is packed with anxious customers, and workers are hustling about, taking care of their orders, a wet floor is not going to take top priority. During the rush what's going to stop an employee from running too fast, which could result in a serious wipeout?	One common hazard for deli workers is slippery floors. Often, especially during the lunch rush, the place gets jammed. Anxious customers crowd into one another and lean over the stainless steel counter in your face to call out three more changes to their already late orders. Trying to manage the rush, employees hustle about, carrying checks, prepping sandwiches, carting plates back and forth. When scurrying from the salad case to the register, you might not notice that freshly mopped floor, and before you know it, you are crashing into a wall and banging your head on the slick, hard tile. And if you don't trip yourself up, there are always other employees to run into you, which can also cause a serious wipeout.

Topic sentence

Author uses process analysis to show how workers manage the rush.

Author uses cause and effect to show what happens when workers rush.

Notice how the single-paragraph subtopic of 57 words grew to an essay body paragraph of 121 words. The author held in mind her main idea of danger—specifically, slippery floors—and, through prewriting, found more detailed examples and explanations, which she developed using the patterns of process analysis and cause and effect.

To generate more ideas for your body paragraphs, use your favorite prewriting methods.

Essays grow through many patterns of development.

Remember that, unlike writing in some other languages, English writing begins with a strong and direct statement. While you may refer back to this main idea in body paragraphs or your conclusion, you do not need to repeat it multiple times for emphasis.

In Unit Two, where we focused on individual patterns of development, we saw that patterns could be combined. In Unit Three, we will see even more clearly that substantial, artful development comes through combining many of these patterns:

- **Description:** using vivid details to show something about a subject
- **Narration:** telling a brief story to make a point about a subject
- **Illustration:** giving examples to illustrate some point
- **Classification/division:** grouping a subject or breaking it into parts
- **Cause/effect:** telling what actions affect a subject or what effects flow from it
- **Process analysis:** telling how a subject works
- **Comparison/contrast:** showing how a subject is like and unlike similar subjects
- **Definition:** telling the essential characteristics of a subject
- **Persuasion:** trying to move someone to agreement or action

ACTIVITY 12.6 *Developing Body Paragraphs*

Revise the following underdeveloped body paragraphs, using several **patterns of development, detailed examples,** and **explanations.** Topic sentences are shaded. Remember that you can use description and narration to create images and show people acting in a setting. Try for paragraphs of six to eight sentences.

1. Another problem with people who drink and drive is that they often can't be trusted. Sometimes they say they haven't been drinking at all. Other times they say they have had only one drink when it's clear they have had more. Frequently, they go to a party saying that they will not drink at all. Right.

   Revision: _____

   _____

   _____

   _____

   _____

   _____

   _____

2. However, the most annoying habit my younger brother has is fooling with the TV while we are all trying to watch it. Channel surfing is his specialty. He has many ways of sneaking the constant channel changing in. If there is a commercial, watch out. If you leave the room for a snack, it's all over.

   Revision: _____

   _____

   _____

   _____

   _____

3. In addition to the other signs of wealth in this country, when I first entered a supermarket, I found the abundance almost dazzling. Americans have more of everything than we have in Russia. The aisles seemed endlessly stocked with anything a person might need.

Revision: _____

_____

_____

_____

_____

Arranging Body Paragraphs within Essays

To organize body paragraphs within essays, we use much the same logic that we used to organize subtopics within single-paragraph papers. A writer might choose any of these organizational patterns:

- **Spatial:** describing a place or other subject from front to back, side to side, top to bottom, and so on. If you were writing an essay (or part of one) describing a house as seen from a boat in the water, you might focus the first body paragraph on the dock and boathouse, the next on the yard, and the third on the house itself.

- **Chronological:** relating a series of actions in their order of occurrence. In writing personal narrative, fiction, or process analysis, you order your paragraphs chronologically—for example, Little Red Riding Hood first packed her basket of goodies, then walked into the woods, then met the wolf, then walked to her grandmother's house, and so on.

- **Order of importance:** arranging from least to most dramatic (or most to least). Much expository and persuasive writing uses this method. For example, in "Dangers in a Deli," the three body paragraphs go from least to most dangerous—from falls to chemical hazards to losing a finger.

Remember, also, that you may follow one of these patterns within a body paragraph, as we did in Unit Two. Although "Dangers in a Deli" uses least to most for overall arranging, within the body paragraphs the author relies more on time order, moving from slow to fast business while the clock ticks and customers arrive, as in this body paragraph:

For more on these patterns, see pp. 53, 84–89, 115–117, 122–123, 139–140, and 144–147.

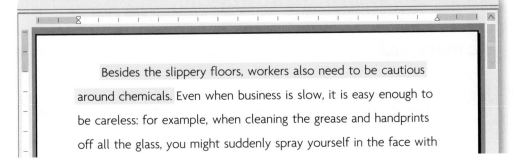

Besides the slippery floors, workers also need to be cautious around chemicals. Even when business is slow, it is easy enough to be careless: for example, when cleaning the grease and handprints off all the glass, you might suddenly spray yourself in the face with

TIME ORDER

Topic sentence

ammonia. But it gets worse when the rush begins, and the owner goes into his panic mode: "Get these dishes done! Now, now— we're filling up!" You might think you have a good grip on that slippery platter, until it slips out of your hands and splashes into a sink full of pan degreaser and sanitizer. It only takes one faceful of that hot, soapy water to send a worker to the emergency room.

Using Outlines

Another aid in organizing essays is the **outline.** Our paragraph assignments from Unit Two often required short lists, but because essays are more complex, more detailed outlines can help you keep them on track. A formal sentence outline is probably not needed for short essays, but outlining primary examples and several supporting points is useful, as in the following example:

INFORMAL WORKING OUTLINE: "DANGERS IN A DELI"

Thesis	If you don't want to end up in the emergency room on your first day here, you need to be aware of the potential dangers in working at a deli.
Topic sentence	I. One common hazard for deli workers is slippery floors.
Supporting examples	A. Lunch rush
	B. Hurrying employees
	C. Fall on tile floor
Topic sentence	II. Besides the slippery floors, workers also need to be cautious around chemicals.
Supporting examples	A. Slow business still dangerous—ammonia
	B. Owner panicking
	C. Platter splashing into sink—degreaser and sanitizer
Topic sentence	III. But the part of the job that is most dangerous is using the meat and cheese slicer.
Supporting examples	A. Operating or cleaning—dangerous
	B. Sharp blade
	C. People too tired—accident

However you outline, write your thesis where you can refer to it often, and list at least the main examples with supporting examples and details.

ACTIVITY 12.7 | WORKING ONLINE: *Outlining and Using Journalists' Questions*

To practice prewriting and organizational techniques in essay writing, do one or both of the activities under Activity 12.7 at www. mhhe.com/brannan.

Writing Concluding Paragraphs

Even more than introductions, conclusions can pose problems for essay writers. How do you leave readers feeling that the promise made in the thesis sentence has been met and that the essay is decisively completed?

One way to provide a satisfying ending is to *plan* a concluding paragraph. Though many longer works use several paragraphs or even a chapter to conclude, you need only five to seven sentences (a hundred words or so) for your short essays. You can make these sentences interesting by using the familiar strategy of the expanded thought.

As you draft the concluding paragraph, be sure to create strong links to the introductory paragraph, and include the following elements:

- **Lead sentence:** one sentence (connector + link to thesis)
- **Summary:** one sentence or less
- **Development:** three or four sentences (often containing expanded thought)

Writing Lead Sentences and Summaries

Just as introductory and body paragraphs have a lead sentence (the hook and the topic sentence, respectively), so do concluding paragraphs. This first sentence of the conclusion includes a connector and often touches on the thesis. It may also give a brief summary of the essay's main points. Alternately, the summary might be in the second sentence. Notice that in "Dangers in a Deli" the lead sentence includes the summary:

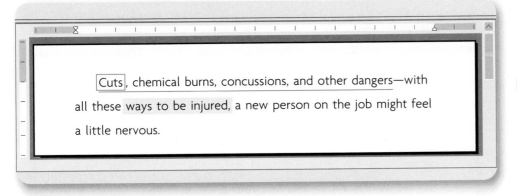

Cuts, chemical burns, concussions, and other dangers—with all these ways to be injured, a new person on the job might feel a little nervous.

The author could have saved the summary for a second sentence:

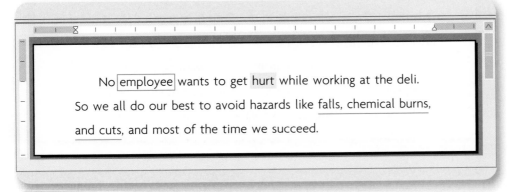

No employee wants to get hurt while working at the deli. So we all do our best to avoid hazards like falls, chemical burns, and cuts, and most of the time we succeed.

The beginning of a concluding paragraph eases readers out of the main stream of the writer's ideas and into his or her final comments, which wrap up the essay.

HINT

The conclusion should fulfill the promise made in the thesis sentence.

HINT

Introductions and conclusions should be tightly linked.

Statement about topic is shaded.

Connector is boxed.

Summary is underlined.

HINT

Effective writing leads readers carefully into the final thoughts.

Developing Conclusions

After leading readers into the concluding paragraph, rather than meander for half a dozen empty, repetitive sentences, end your essay decisively. You can do this with the following strategies, most of which are already familiar:

STRATEGIES FOR CONCLUSIONS

1. **Frame:** return to the image, comparison, story, and so on from the introductory paragraph.
2. **Expanded thought:**
    A. Express an emotion.
    B. Give a judgment, opinion, or evaluation.
    C. Show how something has affected your behavior or outlook on life.
    D. Ask a related question.
    E. Make a reflective statement.
    F. Suggest a course of action.
3. **Combination of above methods**

When you "frame" an essay, you return to the introduction and the method you used there (description, narration, comparison/contrast, and so on), extending that content. For example, here is an introduction for "Dangers in a Deli" that uses a **narrative** approach:

Introduction with a Narrative Frame

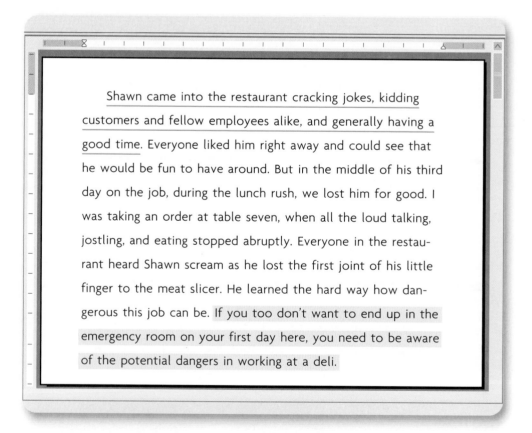

Thesis

Shawn came into the restaurant cracking jokes, kidding customers and fellow employees alike, and generally having a good time. Everyone liked him right away and could see that he would be fun to have around. But in the middle of his third day on the job, during the lunch rush, we lost him for good. I was taking an order at table seven, when all the loud talking, jostling, and eating stopped abruptly. Everyone in the restaurant heard Shawn scream as he lost the first joint of his little finger to the meat slicer. He learned the hard way how dangerous this job can be. If you too don't want to end up in the emergency room on your first day here, you need to be aware of the potential dangers in working at a deli.

We can frame the essay by writing a conclusion that extends the narrative like this:

Conclusion with a Narrative Frame

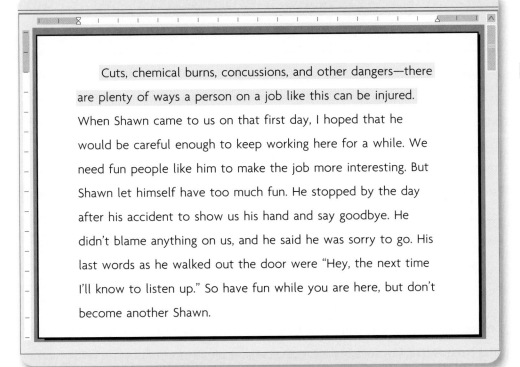

Lead and summary

Cuts, chemical burns, concussions, and other dangers—there are plenty of ways a person on a job like this can be injured. When Shawn came to us on that first day, I hoped that he would be careful enough to keep working here for a while. We need fun people like him to make the job more interesting. But Shawn let himself have too much fun. He stopped by the day after his accident to show us his hand and say goodbye. He didn't blame anything on us, and he said he was sorry to go. His last words as he walked out the door were "Hey, the next time I'll know to listen up." So have fun while you are here, but don't become another Shawn.

Concluding Paragraphs with Expanded Thoughts

Another effective way to capture readers' attention one last time is to offer an **expanded thought.** With this strategy, you take your audience one closely related step beyond the ideas in your body paragraphs, broadening your topic. You have probably already used this strategy in the final sentence of a one-paragraph paper, but now you can develop it. The following conclusions for the deli essay show different ways to use an expanded thought, with methods often overlapping. Lead and summary sentences are shaded.

Cuts, chemical burns, concussions, and other dangers—there are plenty of ways for a person to get hurt on this job. I worried about it for the first month I was here, especially after I saw several other workers get hurt. But I learned that I could work safely if, when the restaurant began to speed up and people started moving fast, I kept myself at about 75 percent of my maximum speed. I can still get out the orders and keep everyone satisfied without pushing myself into an accident. Nowadays I don't need to worry much about getting hurt. I just pace myself, watch what I'm doing, and have a good time.

1. **Personal emotion:** Let your reader know how you feel about your topic. What emotional response has it created in you?

Lead and summary sentences combined

Cuts, chemical burns, concussions, and other dangers—with all these ways to get injured, a new person on the job might feel a little nervous. But deli work doesn't always make you feel anxious and frazzled; in fact, it can be enjoyable. Whether you

2. **Judgment:** Evaluate your topic or express an opinion.

are talking to interesting customers or spending time with friends, the deli is usually a fun place to work. It can even be a great place for keeping your mind off problems at home or that algebra exam on Friday. Although accidents can happen, you are a lot less likely to have one if you keep the worst of the hazards in mind.

3. **Outlook or behavior change:** Show how your outlook on life or behavior has changed as a result of your experience with the topic.

Cuts, chemical burns, concussions, and other dangers—there are plenty of ways for a person to get hurt on this job. Before I came to work here, I used to jump right into an activity without much thought of the consequences. Frying up a skilletful of bacon, chasing a soccer ball downfield, mowing the lawn—I used to rush through them all. But now I think twice. I don't want to burn myself with hot grease, sprain an ankle, or lose part of my foot under the mower. And I have found that being more cautious hasn't taken anything from me; instead, it lets me participate more fully in everything. Fingers crossed, from now on I won't be standing around on crutches on the sidelines of anything I want to do in life.

4. **Question(s):** Ask one or more questions that might grow from your topic.

With all these ways to be injured on the job, a person might wonder about working at a deli at all. Why should people put themselves in such a risky situation? The truth is that few jobs are altogether safe. A librarian can fall off a ladder and break a leg as easily as a waiter can slip and fall on a wet tile floor. The only sure way to reduce the chance of injury on the job is to follow the advice lots of parents give their children when they approach streets: stop, look, and listen. Slow down to live longer.

5. **Reflective statement:** Tell readers something your topic suggests beyond the points made in the body paragraphs. Think of some larger application to the world around you.

Lead and summary sentences separated

With all these ways to be injured on the job, a person might wonder about working at a deli at all. After all, no one wants to be cut, burned by chemicals, or knocked unconscious. But the truth is that no matter how careful a person might be, accidents cannot always be avoided. The world is an uncertain place, full of dangers. We like to think we can control our lives and protect ourselves absolutely. However, because this is not possible, perhaps it's best always to hope for, plan for, and work toward the best while preparing for the worst.

6. **Call to action:** Suggest that your readers or someone else act on the information you have presented.

Lead and summary sentences separated

New employees and old hands alike can have an accident when they get too tired. Falls, scalds, and cuts are not uncommon in the deli as a result. Your best option to protect yourself is to listen to your trainer on your first few days at the job. Sure, some of the advice will sound obvious—"Don't put sharp knives into a sinkful of soapy water"—but the time you stop paying attention is the time you will start hurting. So during your training period listen carefully, watch closely, and read all the instructions thoroughly for operating equipment safely. We want to keep you on the job, not put you in the hospital.

ACTIVITY 12.8   *Determining an Expanded Thought*

For each of the following essays, write the thesis sentence and then, in your own words, the final expanded thought.

> **EXAMPLE:** "Dangers in a Deli" (pp. 264–265)

Thesis sentence: *"If you don't want to end up in the emergency room on your first day here, you need to be aware of the potential dangers in working at a deli."*

Expanded thought: *Working in a deli is not all danger and unpleasantness. The job can be fun.*

1. "The Jobs from Hell" (pp. 299–300)

    Thesis sentence: _____

    _____

    Expanded thought: _____

    _____

2. "A Skill beyond Price" (pp. 304–305)

    Thesis sentence: _____

    _____

    Expanded thought: _____

    _____

3. "I'll Park. You Get the Tickets—Hurry!" (pp. 319–320)

    Thesis sentence: _____

    _____

    Expanded thought: _____

    _____

ACTIVITY 12.9   *Creating Interesting Conclusions*

Choose an introductory paragraph from Activity 12.2, and brainstorm to uncover several main examples for an essay that could grow from it. Next, write two concluding paragraphs for the essay. In one, use a frame; in the other, use one or more of the methods for writing an expanded thought.

You might combine the lead and summary sentences.

1. Concluding paragraph using frame:

    Lead sentence: _____

    _____

    Summary sentence: _____

    _____

    Development: _____

    _____

    _____

_____

_____

_____

2. Concluding paragraph using expanded thought (method number(s): _____

Lead sentence: _____

_____

Summary sentence: _____

_____

Development: _____

_____

_____

_____

_____

Avoiding Weak Conclusions

Even knowing how to write strong final paragraphs, we sometimes stumble. Here are some common problems to avoid:

1. **Under- or oversummarizing (and repeating).** Some form of summary is used in almost all conclusions: The longer and more complex the essay, the longer and more detailed the summary might be. However, in brief essays, readers do not need much repetition of main points. A sentence or less is enough. Here is how the author of the deli essay might have oversummarized for a weak conclusion:

   > As you can see, there are plenty of dangers around a deli. It is all too easy for a person to slip and get hurt on a wet floor. And there are chemical hazards as well. Also, even experienced employees might have a serious problem with the meat and cheese slicer, so everyone needs to be extra careful around it. Because people can be seriously and permanently injured by falls, chemical burns, and cuts, they should be alert on the job at all times.

Avoid oversummarizing in conclusions.

2. **Telling readers that you are getting ready to end your essay.** While you should connect your conclusion to the rest of your essay, avoid doing it with statements like these: "Well, as you can see, my essay is just about wrapped up," "In conclusion, my thesis sentence has already told you . . . ," and "In the essay you have just read, I have tried to show . . . ."

3. **Moving into an unrelated or too loosely related topic.** Remember that an expanded thought should grow naturally from the body of the essay, an extension of the thesis. It should not move into a different topic. The following concluding paragraph for our deli essay shows this problem:

   > Cuts, chemical burns, concussions, and other dangers—with all these ways to be injured, a new person on the job might feel a little overwhelmed. But, you know, life is full of danger. People get hurt all the time. Why once when I was

mowing a lawn, I wasn't paying attention and sliced off the front of my right tennis shoe. I learned a lesson from that scare—watch what you're doing when operating dangerous equipment, especially lawn mowers!

Clearly, the emphasis has shifted from the deli to lawn mowing.

4. **Overgeneralizing.** Expressing opinions and evaluating can be effective concluding strategies. However, it is important to qualify statements, so you don't claim more than you can prove. Avoid assertions like these: "And so you can see no one has a good reason for watching a lot of television," "Any student who tries hard can make good grades," and "Everybody loves football."

5. **Apologizing.** Apologizing is an ineffective concluding strategy, as is illustrated by these examples: "Although I do not know much about this topic, I have tried to show you . . . ," "Even though there are experts who know a lot more about this subject than I do . . . ," and "Although I am still kind of fuzzy about this topic, I hope you have learned something from my essay . . . ." You should appear confident in the conclusion. If you have serious doubts about the essay, why not revise it?

6. **Using clichés and worn expressions.** Beware of clichés like these: "There were butterflies in my stomach," "All I had left was the shirt on my back," and "No one could ever fill her shoes." If a fresh figure of speech does not come to mind, use a literal phrase—for example, "I was nervous" in place of the butterfly cliché.

7. **Making your conclusion too long or too short.** Conclusions should be written in proportion to the rest of the work. Our brief essays can support a final paragraph of five to seven sentences—about a hundred words or so.

For more on qualifying, see pp. 376, 485–487.

For more on clichés and worn phrases, see Chapter 20.

ACTIVITY 12.10 *Recognizing and Revising Weak Conclusions*

Note: In each paragraph, lead and summary sentences are shaded.

Decide which five of the following six conclusions are ineffective. In each case, explain why it is ineffective. Next, on the lines that follow, rewrite any *one* of them, using a frame, one of the six methods for creating an expanded thought, or a method of your own.

1. Thesis: Rebuilding a carburetor is difficult, but with the right instructions most people can do it.

With all of the complicated steps in rebuilding a carburetor, from initially removing it to reinstallation, you might have trouble with it like I did. I got lost in the process myself several times, and I'm not sure that I included all the steps you will need to get the job done right. But I hope that I explained clearly enough and remembered the really important warnings that you ought to follow if you don't want a big mess on your hands. If you think you can rebuild that carburetor now, then all I can say is "Good luck!"

2. Thesis: My two older brothers are as different as two people can be.

With two brothers whose personalities are this different—one a whirlwind, the other a couch potato—a person might think that I would have a favorite. But that is not the case. I love both of my brothers equally, and I find many activities that we can share—though usually two's company, three's a crowd.

3. Thesis: One way to group friends is by how long you have known them.

   Friends are important in every person's life. There are potential friends, recent friends, and long-time friends, all of whom have their places in the overall category of friends. Potential friends might become friends someday if circumstances are right. Recent friends might be good friends, but they don't have a real track record yet. They might not hold up as good friends over the long haul. But long-time friends have proven themselves time and time again. A person knows that he can depend on long-time friends because they have been around for quite awhile and have shown their loyalty, support, and friendship many times over. For my money, the best and most valuable friends are long-time friends.

4. Thesis: A mother is much more than just the woman who carries a baby to term.

   All of these qualities are necessary for a woman to be a truly great mother. Mothers must be able to maintain their children on a daily basis, care for them when they are sick, teach and model behavior, and, most important, love them even when they are being unlovable. A friend of mine gave her baby up for adoption and was worried that when the child grew older, he might think his birth mother had abandoned him. I reassured my friend that adoptive mothers can do a terrific job of raising children and that she had made the right decision. At seventeen my friend is too young to take on the responsibility of raising a child. Giving the baby to a responsible, more mature, and financially stable parent was a wise choice.

5. Thesis: Lying to loved ones is a bad idea because it is ultimately self-destructive.

   Telling even small "white" lies is dangerous in a relationship, much less the big lies that are the instant death of friendship. The guilt and worry over being caught often lead to a slow but undeniable distancing from our spouse, significant other, child, or friend. And this is, perhaps, the greatest damage done. Once the lies begin, they become easier to tell, but not easier to deal with. Instead of creating new, fun memories, we spend too much energy trying to make the stories we have told mesh. Lies take us away from the ones we love a little bit at a time. Instead of many shared memories in the house of our relationships, we have few . . . and then fewer. Even if the ones we love never catch us in the Big Lie, we can still trap ourselves, finally, in an empty room of our own making.

6. Thesis: While driving in their cars, people should use cell phones only for urgent business or emergencies.

> Accidents like the ones just mentioned are the most important reason not to overuse cell phones, but wasting money, missing out on the world, and being inconsiderate to passengers are also important reasons. Cell phones are a nuisance. They don't really have any place in cars and ought to be outlawed. How in the world did people survive, after all, ten years ago (and five thousand years before that) without these obnoxious little time eaters? There is no good reason to yak away on a cell phone when people are never any farther away from a stationary phone than a 5-minute drive.

Ineffective paragraphs: _____

Reasons the conclusions are weak: _____

_____

One weak conclusion rewritten: _____

_____

_____

_____

_____

_____

_____

CREATING CONCLUDING PARAGRAPHS—SUMMING UP

1. Look over your thesis sentence and the main points in your body paragraphs.
2. Review the discussion of writing a lead sentence and summary.
3. Draft a lead sentence and summary that link to your thesis sentence and main points.
4. Review the methods for expanding a thought and the ways of avoiding weak conclusions.
5. Decide on a frame and/or an expanded thought.
6. Prewrite, focusing on a frame or method for expanding a thought.
7. Draft the rest of your conclusion.

Review examples or ideas you cut from body paragraphs to see if one might work as an expanded thought.

Creating Coherence

In Unit Two, we learned how critical it is to create coherence by linking words within and between sentences, especially between subtopics. Essays also require strong connectors, especially *between* paragraphs.

Pay special attention to linking paragraphs.

1. **Transitions:** using linking words in various categories, including:
   - Locating or moving in space: *above, against, around, behind, below, on, in*
   - Moving in time: *after, at last, awhile, first, next, now, often, then*
   - Adding material: *again, also, and, in addition, furthermore, as well as*
   - Giving examples: *for example, for instance, another, one reason, in fact*
   - Comparing: *alike, also, both, in the same way, similarly*
   - Contrasting: *in contrast, although, but, differs from, even though, however*
   - Cause/effect: *and so, as a result, because, consequently, since, so, then*
   - Summarizing/concluding: *finally, in brief, in other words, in short*
2. **Repetition:** repeating a significant word from a preceding sentence
3. **Synonyms:** using a word equivalent to one in a preceding sentence
4. **Pronouns:** using words like *he, she, they, that, this*
5. **Reference to a main idea:** reminding readers of some important point in a preceding sentence

The following concluding paragraph illustrates these coherence methods.

For a longer list of transitions and more on coherence methods within paragraphs, turn to pp. 53–59.

KEY
Transitions
Repetition
Synonyms
Pronouns
Reference to main idea

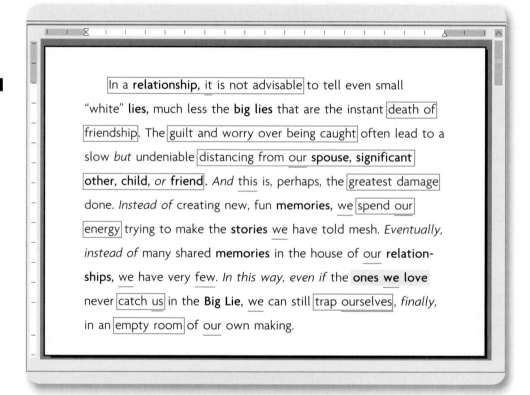

In a **relationship**, it is not advisable to tell even small "white" **lies**, much less the **big lies** that are the instant death of friendship. The guilt and worry over being caught often lead to a slow *but* undeniable distancing from our **spouse, significant other, child,** *or* **friend**. *And* this is, perhaps, the greatest damage done. *Instead of* creating new, fun **memories**, we spend our energy trying to make the **stories** we have told mesh. *Eventually, instead of* many shared **memories** in the house of our **relationships**, we have very few. *In this way, even if* the **ones we love** never catch us in the **Big Lie**, we can still trap ourselves, *finally,* in an empty room of our own making.

Selecting a Title

The title is your first opportunity to impress readers, and most of us would like to have them think, "Hmm . . . interesting, I wonder what this is about?" Creating an engaging title represents a last bit of attention to an essay, and this effort inclines readers to think that the rest of the work is developed with equal care.

STRATEGIES FOR CREATING A GOOD TITLE

1. Keep the title relatively short—around one to eight words.

2. Link the title to your main idea, central point, or dominant impression.

3. Create an image: Use a metaphor/simile, specific words, action words, and/or sensory details.

4. Ask a question.

5. Make a play on words.

6. Refer to something that your readers might know about and find interesting.

This list of reminders will help you create an interesting title when you are putting the finishing touches on your essay. For more on titles, see pp. 59–60.

Linking to Future Experience

You will write essays of some sort in most of your college classes; as you advance to more complex writing assignments in higher-level courses, you can always refer back to Chapter 12 of this text and review the shape and purpose of an essay. Different instructors (and subject areas) will require you to write in different forms and in a variety of lengths, but the lessons learned here provide a solid foundation for approaching future templates. As you get more comfortable writing in any form, you will find you can bend more rules and experiment more with combining patterns. The remaining chapters in Unit Three will help you expand paragraphs into essays, revise essays, write definition and persuasive essays, and use research in your papers.

ACTIVITY 12.11 WORKING ONLINE: *Essay-Writing Review*

Take the Chapter 12 Review Quiz at www.mhhe.com/brannan.

Chapter Summary

1. An essay is a group of related paragraphs that develop an overall point.

2. Like a single body paragraph, an essay requires an introduction, development, and a conclusion.

3. The most obvious differences between a single-paragraph paper and an essay are that the essay is longer and has full paragraphs to introduce and conclude it.

4. Introductory paragraphs usually consist of a hook, development, and a thesis.

5. Thesis sentences are like topic sentences except that they may be slightly more general because the essay that follows a thesis will include more complex examples, details, and explanations than found in a paragraph.

6. There are many methods for developing interesting introductions, including using one of the patterns of development, such as narration, comparison/contrast, questions, or background information.

7. Body paragraphs often begin with topic sentences and sometimes end with summary sentences.

8. Concluding paragraphs consist of a lead sentence, a summary, and development.

9. Concluding paragraphs may be developed in several ways, including using a frame and/or an expanded thought.

10. Essays should be both unified (all material is relevant) and coherent (all sentences are clearly linked).

11. A title is an important finishing touch, and there are strategies for creating interesting titles.

Expanding Paragraphs into Essays

13

[*Here a family is changing the look of their home. Perhaps they have gained a new member or feel pressed for space. Rather than abandoning their home, they have decided to expand it. When have you made improvements or additions to something you already owned (or had previously made) instead of buying a new one? Write a paragraph recalling this experience.*]

KEY TOPICS

- Illustrating through examples (illustration)
- Analyzing student models: Illustration essays
- Creating and explaining groups (classification)
- Analyzing student models: Classification essays
- Recognizing causes, explaining effects (cause/effect)
- Analyzing student models: Cause/effect essays

- Explaining, doing, and understanding activities (process analysis)
- Analyzing student models: Process-analysis essays
- Explaining similarities and differences (comparison and contrast)
- Analyzing student models: Comparison/contrast essays
- Writing an essay

What Are We Trying to Achieve and Why?

In this chapter, you will develop a paragraph assignment from Unit Two into an essay. Like the people working on their house on the previous page, you may be happy with your paragraph as a small unit, but now you can increase its size, developing the ideas and adding details to make it more interesting. Some of you may also be using this chapter to build your essay from scratch.

Linking to Previous Experience

Find out more about layered examples on pp. 42–49.

You can also investigate two additional essay strategies—**definition** in Chapter 15 and **argument** in Chapter 16.

For a more complete discussion of illustrating with examples, turn to Chapter 7.

Having worked through Chapter 12, you probably have a clear sense of essay form and have reminded yourself of the primary ways of developing ideas: through detailed examples and explanations. In this chapter, you will see models for essays that follow patterns of development introduced in Unit Two—illustration, classification, cause/effect, process analysis, and comparison/contrast. For each pattern, there are two models, one of which has been expanded from a paragraph model in Unit Two. These models will give you ideas for your own essay. By analyzing them carefully and by comparing essays with the corresponding paragraphs in Unit Two, you will gain a better sense of how to create effective essays, from paragraph papers or from scratch.

As you read these essays, pay close attention to their introductions and conclusions, noting how other student writers use these important sections of the paper effectively. Also note the use of specific and layered examples throughout.

Whether or not you are coming to this chapter with a paragraph to expand, review the chapter from Unit Two on the specific pattern of development (process analysis, classification, etc.) that your essay will follow.

Illustrating through Examples (Illustration)

Using examples to illustrate a point or clarify an idea is the heart of all writing, so you will find examples used in all of the patterns of development. Here, however, we focus specifically on **illustration** as the main pattern of development.

As you learned in Chapter 3, examples come in two basic varieties: those drawn from our own lives—**personal examples**—and those drawn from outside our personal experience, including facts, statistics, and information from print sources. If you made a statement about your own family—say, that they are very involved in sports—you would probably choose personal examples to show that involvement. But if you wanted to speak in general terms about American families' enjoyment of sports, you would rely not on your personal experience but on your observations and general knowledge.

Developing an essay through examples is much like developing a paragraph through examples. You make a statement or give an example and then ask yourself, "What exactly do I mean by that?" and "How can I make myself more clear?"

Analyzing Student Models: Illustration Essays

The following two models, "The Jobs from Hell" and "Teaching with Whips," will help you write illustration essays. Both authors rely on personal experience to develop their examples, and so they frequently use the pronoun "I."

Look closely at the introductory and concluding paragraphs; introductions and conclusions are major parts of essays, and most of us and need more experience with them. Also, to see how a paragraph might grow into an essay, compare the essay version of "Teaching with Whips" with the paragraph version in Chapter 7 (pp. 144–145).

→ *Prereading Exploration for "The Jobs from Hell"*

Eric Latham decided on an audience of young adults between the ages of 16 and 25, thinking they might be especially interested in his examples and main point.

1. Before reading the essay, look at the thesis and title. Do they give a clear idea of what to expect in the body of the paper? Why or why not?
2. Think about any unpleasant jobs you have had (or have). What makes them so miserable?
3. If you have been as unlucky as Eric and can remember three, four, or more bad jobs, list them, and then give several examples of what you most disliked about them. If you have had only one marginal job, give examples from it. If you are lucky and have had only good work experiences, list those. These ideas may help you find a topic for your essay.

To see a model using the more formal "they" approach, see "Dangers in a Deli" in Chapter 7.

Record these prereading responses in your journal or on your blog.

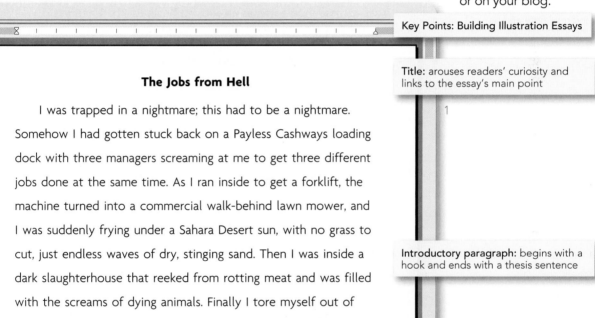

Key Points: Building Illustration Essays

The Jobs from Hell

I was trapped in a nightmare; this had to be a nightmare. Somehow I had gotten stuck back on a Payless Cashways loading dock with three managers screaming at me to get three different jobs done at the same time. As I ran inside to get a forklift, the machine turned into a commercial walk-behind lawn mower, and I was suddenly frying under a Sahara Desert sun, with no grass to cut, just endless waves of dry, stinging sand. Then I was inside a dark slaughterhouse that reeked from rotting meat and was filled with the screams of dying animals. Finally I tore myself out of the nightmare and sat up in bed, realizing with a start that all these images came from the rotten jobs I have worked in my life.

My first miserable work experience was at Payless Cashways when I was fifteen. I remember walking through the automatic doors on day one, excited, confident, and ready to learn. Soon I *did* learn—all about angry customers who expected me to know everything about every item in the store and how to fix every broken door hinge, light, window, and toilet they were having problems with. Then the manager began overloading me with work. Twenty hours a week was too much for a freshman in high school, so that was the first "good" job to go by the wayside.

Title: arouses readers' curiosity and links to the essay's main point

1

Introductory paragraph: begins with a hook and ends with a thesis sentence

2

Body paragraphs: begin with a topic sentence, which names the subtopic and makes a limiting statement about it— and may end with a summary sentence

Development: uses specific examples, action, scene and character details, sensory details, active verbs (*trapped*), *-ing* words (*stinging, rotting*), and specific words (*Payless Cashways*); tells thoughts and emotions; explains the examples ("Twenty hours a week was too much for a freshman in high school . . .")

3

Sentence connectors: guide readers: transitions, repeat words, synonyms, pronouns, and reference to main idea

When I was a senior, I found another job, this one at Dr. Lawn, that, at first, looked promising. The job paid well, but I had to mow lawns for six to eight hours a day in the July heat, with temperatures running into the nineties. One day on the job I grew sick to my stomach and feverish and literally collapsed in back of a walk-behind mower. My manager would not let me go home because we had come in a car pool, and if I had left, it would have affected the other five people working. When I finally made it home, my dad found that I had a 105-degree fever, and we both decided that no job was worth my health.

4

Style points: increase readability. Italicizing words (paragraph 2: *did*) and using dashes (paragraph 2) can create emphasis. Contractions can add an informal note and prevent stilted writing (paragraphs 4, 5)

These other bad experiences aside, the worst job I have ever had was in my sophomore year when I applied for work at Fritz's Meat House. At the time twelve dollars an hour sounded like great money, so I was as anxious to begin as I had been at Payless. However, I soon found out how disgusting the work was. The store was absolutely gross, filled with rotting meat from days ago, hanging pig carcasses waiting to be chopped, and an overflowing grease bin. The bin was located on the bottom floor of the two-story building, and all the animal parts ended up in it—chicken heads, legs, and feathers; pig feet; cow ribs; and gray intestines slippery from blood and yellow fatty tissue. Well, the bin didn't empty itself. It was my treat to empty that lovely stinking mess with a huge ladle, which I did for one week, averaging twelve-hour days. Needless to say, I soon found that the money wasn't worth it.

5

Concluding paragraph: restates the thesis, briefly summarizes, and adds a final (expanded) thought

I am happy no longer to be stuck in the nightmare of these bad jobs. I am working myself away from them. After sitting out from school for a year and realizing that life was not going to shower me with opportunities unless I got an education, I decided to go back. As hard as this first year back at JCCC has been, I know that graduation is not that far away. With my AA in computer science, I'll head for KU and a four-year degree. Fingers crossed, I'm saying goodbye forever to the jobs from hell.

—*Eric Latham*

➡ *Prereading Exploration for "Teaching with Whips"*

Jeong Yi wanted to share some personal experiences with classmates so that they could compare their own education with his and learn something of the cultural differences between them. Jeong also thought that teachers might be interested in the essay because of his comments on the use of force to motivate students.

Before reading the essay, think about the issue of corporal punishment in school. Some people say schools in the United States would maintain better discipline and turn out more academically prepared students if physical punishment were used. How do you feel about this issue?

HINT

Record prereading responses in your journal or on your blog.

HINT

To see this essay as a paragraph, turn to Chapter 7, pp. 144–145.

Teaching with Whips

When I went to middle school in Korea, I feared a beating almost every day of my life. I was not worried about fellow students or even outside gang members hurting me, the way many young people in America are. And I did not cause trouble in school, so misbehavior was not the reason for my punishment. Instead, I often did not perform academically up to many of my teachers' high expectations. My low grades meant whippings. There were several merciless teachers in particular who seemed to want me to "enjoy" studying by forcing it on me.

As a new middle school student, I was surprised by my first painful encounter with my moral education teacher, a short fat man who carried a short fat whip to enforce his every whim. His manner of speaking somehow did not make it seem urgent for me to thoroughly complete all the homework. Then one day he noticed that I was not prepared and made an example of me to show the class how harsh he could be to defiant students. "I see you haven't done your homework, Jeong," he said, his angry red face shaking. Straining with fear, the class was dead quiet, wondering what was going to happen at that frightful moment. "Jeong, stand up!" he ordered. His chalk-dusty hands held my two shaky little hands palms up and aimed at them as if they were targets. The punishment ended with me crying and begging, "I will do it next time, teacher. I promise!"

Another spiteful man was my history teacher, who liked to use his green baby bamboo stick to punish students who didn't score more than 80 percent on the exams. Many of us had felt our skin rip from that skinny bamboo rod. And when I would

1

2

3

see him headed my way with that certain glint in his eye, slapping the stick into his own hand, I knew what was about to happen. "Why," I wanted to shout at him, "why don't you let us feel some interest in history? Maybe then we would be more responsible!" But these words never left my lips, although plenty of words left his. "If you don't study, you won't succeed," he barked as he dealt quick whips. I muttered curses with his final blow.

4   None of the teachers seemed to understand that my test scores did not necessarily reflect how much I studied, and this was especially true of my cruel art teacher. Nicknamed Poisonous Snake, he was hated by all the students. His face was always red, like a drunken man's, and he seemed unable to smile. I never received a kind word or look from him. Instead, he gave me intimidating glares with his narrow, slanted eyes. He carried a black-taped wooden stick, which was bigger and more frightening than any of the other teachers' weapons, and it never left his hand. As he used the stick in other classes, the whacking sound echoed through the silent and empty halls. I could only anticipate the pain I would feel the day I scored poorly on an exam. Burning with anxiety, I knew the only way to prevent these pains would be to study more diligently.

5   Having had to endure the anxiety, pain, and humiliation of corporal punishment from my teachers, I was finally convinced to study. Yet early on I realized that even when I studied hard I could not satisfy the teachers in some of my classes. All the focus was on test grades—performance—and my efforts put into studying never were acknowledged. Teachers should realize that forcing students is not the only or the best way to persuade them to study and that some students are not going to do well in some subjects. What is the value of a few "A's" on a report card when the knowledge can be forgotten so quickly? Why not help students to really enjoy learning so that they can motivate themselves for a lifetime of education?

—Jeong Yi

THINKING ABOUT THE MODEL

1. How has this essay evolved from the paragraph on page 144? Give three specific examples.

2. Annotate the **Key Points** in the margin, using "The Jobs from Hell" as an example.

POSTREADING REVIEW: KEY ELEMENTS OF ILLUSTRATION ESSAYS

Here are several important points—illustrated by the preceding student models—to keep in mind for your own illustration essay:

1. Organize by beginning each body paragraph with a topic sentence (pp. 138–139).

2. Arrange your examples by order of importance (or time) (p. 139).

3. Use clear connectors between sentences and paragraphs (pp. 293–294).

4. Develop your examples through details and explanations (pp. 42–49).

Creating and Explaining Groups (Classification)

We often need to classify or divide ideas or objects into groups, and to do so effectively, we use a **single organizing principle (SOP),** a standard for classification. For example, when people pack their belongings in preparation for a move, they group them logically—according to what room things are going to be in. They don't group them according to, say, shape—the plates together with CDs and a Frisbee.

Many essay topics, too, are usefully developed through classification. With an essay-length paper, the rules for classifying paragraphs that you saw in Chapter 8—using only one principle for classifying, avoiding overlapping groups, and including all important groups—become even more essential.

For a more complete discussion of classifying, turn to Chapter 8.

Analyzing Student Models: Classification Essays

The following two models will help you write classification essays. Notice that each essay makes the SOP clear in the thesis sentence, so that the readers know the basis for dividing and classifying the topic. "A Skill beyond Price" discusses groups that the author created himself, while "Shopping the Easy Way" uses a preestablished system for categorizing. Either approach can work well.

To see how a paragraph might grow into an essay, compare this version of "Shopping the Easy Way" with the paragraph version in Chapter 8 (p. 172).

To aid your own writing, look closely at the introductory and concluding paragraphs in these models.

➤ *Prereading Exploration for "A Skill beyond Price"*

Ho-Chul chose reading as a topic because he strongly believes that it is a key to a successful, happy life. The people he most wants to address are those who do not read much or see any special value in it—some of his fellow students, in particular.

1. How important do you feel reading is?

2. Do you read often or only occasionally?

3. Do you think that college students today value reading more or less than their parents' generation? Why?

Record your prereading responses in your journal or on your blog.

Title: arouses readers' curiosity and
links to the essay's main point

Introductory paragraph: begins with a
hook and ends with a thesis sentence
that specifies the SOP

Body paragraphs: begin with a topic
sentence, which names the subtopic
and makes a limiting statement about it

Development: uses specific examples,
details, active verbs (*sort*), -*ing* words
(*warning*), and specific words (*Borders*);
tells thoughts and emotions; explains
the examples ("However, there is
much to be gained from required
reading . . .")

A Skill beyond Price

Frequently it is said, "No one reads anymore." I have read
this observation in newspapers and magazines and heard it on
television commentaries. And I have heard teachers at my college complain that their students do not even read the work
assigned in their textbooks, much less read for pleasure. But I
wonder if this is true. The students I spend most of my time
around seem to be reading constantly, and not always just their
homework. Reading is a skill beyond price, and I see people
profiting from it daily as they move through various types of
reading based on the person's purpose.

The first category can be called required reading. Most people have some kind of regular required reading. At home we sort
through mail to find which pieces may be valuable and which are
a waste. At work many people have to read office communica-
tions, and even service and manual labor jobs post memos and
warning notices that employees should read if they want to
profit or keep themselves from harm. Of course, students are surrounded by books that they are expected to read and prove that
they know on exams. Sometimes we resent the have-to part of
this kind of reading, and sometimes just the word "required"
makes us want to put it aside. However, there is much to be
gained from required reading, and I have often seen that the
book that one person drags himself through is happily embraced
by another person.

More pleasant for most people is the reading that they
choose for leisure and entertainment. Some people enjoy
short stories and novels—literature, westerns, romances, mysteries and detective stories, and/or science fiction. Huge
bookstores like Borders and Barnes & Noble are filled with
people relaxing with their favorite new story. Others prefer
magazines that keep them informed about the world, such
as *Newsweek* and *National Geographic,* about their profession,
or about some special interest or hobby. People read daily

newspapers, comic books, and letters from friends. Many people find inspiration in the Bible and other religious publications. The World Wide Web offers chat rooms, listservs, and e-mail, all of which allow people to read and write for fun and knowledge. The greatest difference between reading in this category and that which is required seems to be freedom, the choice to read or not.

The category of reading that is the most helpful for many people and the most enjoyable for me is the practical information found in how-to books and magazines. After reading this kind of material, people can immediately apply the knowledge to their everyday lives. For instance, they can learn how to cook delicious food, how to make a beautiful garden, how to take photographs well, and how to decorate a house attractively. Because people have a personal interest, a clear goal, in practical reading, they can concentrate on it more than with much required reading. And I have noticed that, as with some required reading, how-to books can be interesting and fun for many people, moving these books into the more-preferred leisure/entertainment category.

People read for many reasons, and if they achieve their goal in any category of reading, then it can be said that they have profited. Even the least-preferred type of reading, that which is required, can be beneficial in many ways. It seems to me that people are still much involved with words and pages in books, magazines, and electronic sources, and how could this be otherwise since reading is the foundation of civilization? We may not like to do some kinds of reading, but all the knowledge that exists outside of one person and the people he or she can immediately speak to is contained within books. The Internet, which my generation is growing up with, is a vast library that offers a wealth of words to any who will pause to view them. I think truly that we are still in a reading world.

—Ho-Chul Sung

Sentence connectors: guide readers: transitions, repeat words, synonyms, pronouns, and reference to main idea

4

Style points: increase readability. Rhetorical questions can involve the reader (paragraph 5). A short sentence after several longer ones can create emphasis (paragraph 5: "I think truly that we are still in a reading world")

5

Concluding paragraph: restates the thesis, briefly summarizes, and adds a final (expanded) thought

Prereading Exploration for "Shopping the Easy Way"

Ann Nall works in a local Toys "R" Us and decided that it would make a good topic for her classification paper. She thought that new parents might appreciate the information she offers, especially on items in the baby section.

1. If you have ever been in a Toys "R" Us or another toy store, how did you find your way around?
2. What single organizing principle seems logical to apply to a toy store? Present one or more methods for dividing and grouping merchandise in a toy store.

Record your prereading response in your journal or on your blog.

Shopping the Easy Way

1   Have you ever entered a toy store and been confused by the masses of toys and cluttered aisles of seemingly endless options? Sometimes you may know exactly what you are looking for but spend half an hour just trying to find the right area to start the real search. Other times you may have only a general idea of what you want, but you still hope to see everything the store has to offer so that special gift does not pass you by. When people are overwhelmed by shelves crammed so full of toys that they cannot tell one from the other and put their lives in danger as they stumble over merchandise lying haphazardly on the floor, they are not having a pleasant shopping experience. However, Toys "R" Us is nothing like this. To help customers shop more efficiently, Toys "R" Us is neatly divided into three overall categories: areas for older children, toddlers, and babies.

2   The older children have four major areas—Blue, Pink, R-Zone, and Silver—with piles of toys for everyone. Boys mostly head for the Blue section and items like the GI Joes, super-heroes, Hotwheels, and Legos. In no time at all, the boys can have Lego racetracks assembled on the floor and be racing miniature Batmobiles after the "bad guys." Girls, on the other hand, usually go for the Pink section, where there are dozens of different Barbies, complete with friends—Ken, Skipper, Stacie, Kelly, Teresa, Kira—Cabbage Patch Kids, and tea sets that help the girls build fantasies as they pretend they are older. Both sexes enjoy the video games and bicycles in the

R-Zone and Silver. Although it may seem like gender stereotyping to some, the Blue and Pink sections, especially, do help both children and parents get to the merchandise they are most interested in.

3 The next group of children, the toddlers, has the Red and Green areas. Toys in these sections are larger than those in the older children's area and do not have as many small pieces, so the toddlers are less likely to choke. Customers shop in Red to find smaller toys such as Play Dough and building blocks to help their children develop fine motor skills. Also Red offers a variety of musical instruments, from simple shakers like maracas and tambourines to the more complicated guitars and electronic keyboards. Large outdoor play sets, made primarily of plastic, and traditional metal swing sets complete with slides and gliders are located in the Green section.

4 For the smallest children, moms and dads shop in Purple, and it surprises many parents that Toys "R" Us offers so much for infants. This part of the store contains most of what parents need to get children through their first year. Each aisle is clearly marked, guiding shoppers to shelves of diapers, wipes, bottles, formula, clothes, rattles, teething toys, eating utensils (mostly spoons), and . . . well, you name it. After the baby's immediate needs have been met, the store can still help with important items like baby carriers, car seats, and strollers.

5 Shoppers are often confused by disorganized toy stores, but organizing merchandise the way Toys "R" Us does helps people readily find what they need for children of different ages. There are other places to shop for your children—Kmart, Wal-Mart, Target, K B Toys—but finding what you want in these stores can be an ordeal. As frustrating as shopping of any kind can be, with the general confusion, noise, poor service, tight schedules, and money concerns, why not try to make the venture as painless as possible? Good organization is the key to a pleasant and productive shopping experience.

—Ann Nall

1. How has this essay evolved from the paragraph on page 172? Classify three types of changes the writer has made.
2. Annotate the **Key Points** in the margin, using "A Skill beyond Price" as an example.

POSTREADING REVIEW: KEY ELEMENTS OF CLASSIFICATION ESSAYS

Here are several important points—illustrated by the preceding student models—to keep in mind for your own classification essay:

1. Use a single organizing principle (pp. 167–168).
2. Avoid overlapping categories (pp. 175–177).
3. Include all important members of the group (p. 170).
4. Have a reason for the classification (p. 173).

Recognizing Causes, Explaining Effects (Cause/Effect)

For a more complete discussion of causes and effects, turn to Chapter 9.

When we explore the reasons for and outcomes of an event, we are dealing with the concept of **cause and effect.** For example, if a tree falls on a house, what might have caused it? High winds are a likely immediate cause, but perhaps there are other reasons: Insects, disease, or drought may have weakened the tree, contributing to the fall. Beyond learning why the tree fell, the homeowner will want to know about the consequences. What will this event mean in terms of the costs of the cleanup, the inconvenience, and the ultimate appearance of the house?

In an essay using this pattern of development, you want to focus on the causes or effects that are likely and significant and to exclude those that are not. Take care to avoid oversimplifying; it's rare that an event has only one clear source or outcome.

Analyzing Student Models: Cause/Effect Essays

In these models, look closely at the introductory and concluding paragraphs, important parts of essays.

The first student model, "My Friend Who Gave Up on Life," discusses likely causes of a tragic event, while the second, "The Thousand-Dollar Lesson," deals with the effects of a questionable pastime. Essays are often developed with both causes and effects, but to help focus your brief essay, you should probably choose either causes *or* effects.

To see how a paragraph might grow into an essay, compare the essay version of "The Thousand-Dollar Lesson" with the paragraph version in Chapter 9 (pp. 195–196).

➤ Prereading Exploration for "My Friend Who Gave Up on Life"

While we often write for a larger audience, sometimes we do write primarily for ourselves. That is the case for Julie Hammond's introspective essay, which she wrote to reflect on a friend's death and in a small way come to terms with her grief.

If you have lost a loved one or had some other tragedy enter your life, undoubtedly you have been concerned with the "why" behind the event. Take a moment to write down an unpleasant or painful event in your life and speculate about its causes. Try to list four or more probable causes.

My Friend Who Gave Up on Life

On July 14, 1996, at midnight, I was sound asleep when suddenly the phone rang. It was my friend Austin. His voice was soft and shaky as he told me that our friend had committed suicide. The shock of the information was hard for me to take, especially at such a late hour, and I didn't want to grasp what I had heard. "OH NO!" rang through my mind over and over; I didn't know what to do or think. I sat alone in the darkness of my room with tears streaming down my cheeks. The thought of Sam following through with his drunken promises made me sick, and still to this day I wonder what could have caused my friend to decide his life was not worth living.

Nobody can really know what causes a suicide, but one of Sam's problems was depression. His life seemed always to be falling apart. When he was younger, it wasn't so bad, but as he moved into his teens, he began having problems with his family, friends, and school. He couldn't even get his car to run right. School officials started calling home about his absences, and he began acting up in classes, one time getting suspended. Most of his friends didn't know how to handle the "new" Sam, and a lot of them just stopped seeing him. His family wasn't much help either, always nagging at him to straighten up. In his parents' eyes he was just another teenager going through a stage. And after the drinking began, his folks grew even harder on him.

By sixteen Sam was definitely an alcoholic, which must have pushed him closer to the end. Alcohol was a way for him to escape a world going wrong. School, friends, family—everyone seemed to be deserting him. His family could see that he had a drinking problem. Their solution was to stick him in rehab and figure that should take care of it. When he returned, he would be OK for a while. But it didn't take long for him to start drinking

Key Points: Building Cause/ Effect Essays

1

Title: arouses the readers' curiosity and links to the essay's main point

Introductory paragraph: begins with a hook and ends with a thesis sentence that predicts a cause or an effect essay

2

Body paragraphs: begin with a topic sentence, which names the subtopic and makes a limiting statement about it

3

Development: uses specific examples, details, active verbs (*rang*), *-ing* words (*streaming*), and specific words (*alcoholic*); tells thoughts and emotions; and explains the examples ("Those three years looked like a prison sentence to Sam . . .")

Sentence connectors: guide readers: transitions, repeat words, synonyms, pronouns, and reference to main idea

and acting up. This set his family off, and they began yelling at him that he better shape up or else. He never did, so they just sent him away again. Those of us who were left of Sam's friends should have been listening more carefully. When he was drunk, Sam began saying that he was going to kill himself. I guess deep down inside I thought he might do it someday, but I didn't know what to do about it.

4 The drinking was bad enough, but it led to another serious problem for Sam, probation. In the last year he was drunk all the time; he never seemed to take a night off. And for some reason he always seemed to get caught. Finally, he was stuck with three years of probation. We used to talk about it, and he told me how trapped he felt. The school didn't want him, his family thought he was hopeless, he couldn't keep a job, and now the probation people were hounding him, making him take drug tests that he couldn't pass and watching his every move. Those three years looked like a prison sentence to Sam, and he said he figured that it would just get worse. If it wasn't his mom and dad, it was the law; someone was just waiting to lock him up for good.

Style points: increase readability. Capitalizing letters (paragraph 1) and using a dash (paragraph 3) can create emphasis. A semicolon can create sentence variety and emphasis (paragraph 4). A metaphor or simile can add interest and clarity (paragraph 4: "like a prison sentence")

5 I'm not sure if it was the probation that pushed him over, any one reason, all of them combined, or some others that I will never know. When a friend dies this way, people want to know why. Everyone talks about it, trying to figure it out. What caused the suicide; what could we have done to stop it? All of the friends Sam had left heard him talk about killing himself, and no one said they believed him. But I wonder how many of my friends are like me, inside still thinking that they really did believe he might just do it. When a friend dies, don't we all share the blame?

Concluding paragraph: restates the thesis, briefly summarizes, and adds a final (expanded) thought

—Julie Hammond

Record your prereading response in your journal or on your blog.

➡ *Prereading Exploration for "The Thousand-Dollar Lesson"*
Lucas Eimers chose an audience of young adults, particularly ones who have received speeding tickets and as a result have had trouble with their auto insurance. Before reading ahead, consider the topic of speeding tickets.

1. If you wrote an essay on this subject, would you prefer to write about causes or effects?
2. What topics do you think might be better handled as causes, on the basis of the topic itself and readers' likely interest?
3. What topics might be better handled as effects?
4. List four possible reasons a person might speed.

To see this essay as a paragraph, turn back to Chapter 9, pp. 195–196.

The Thousand-Dollar Lesson

Sometimes you just have to drive fast, even when you know you are breaking—maybe even shattering!—the speed limit. It feels great to be on an eight-lane interstate, the traffic sparse, the day clear and dry, and the pedal to the metal. My '85 Camaro can handle the speed. I push her up to ninety (well, a hundred) all the time, and she floats over the pavement like she's riding on some kind of sci-fi antigrav. Other drivers just seem to drift past my windows as I change a lane here and there, leaving even the long-haul truckers in the dust. I wish we had an autobahn like Germany so I could drive as I want to, but we don't, and I guess I have finally found that out. While traveling last spring, I learned about the miserable consequences of my favorite pastime.

My first unpleasant experience was actually getting the ticket. I knew I was in trouble from the moment I saw the red flashing lights in my rearview mirror and looked down at the speedometer to see the needle on eighty-five. I knew that I had been driving that slow for at least five minutes, so even though the posted limit was seventy, I thought I might be able to talk my way out of it. But then I saw the Clint Eastwood look-alike Texas highway patrol officer step up to my window. "All right, boy, let me see your license and proof of insurance," he drawled, cutting off my "Gee-I-didn't-realize-I-was-going-that-fast" line. The officer seemed to enjoy every second it took him to write that ticket out, and with an evil smirk he handed it to me, saying, "Have a nice day." I'm pretty sure he was the only one having fun.

The next problem was paying the ticket. I didn't want it on my record because it would crank up my insurance rates, and I knew taking care of the ticket would cost plenty. It did. First I had to call all my friends to dig up a lawyer who could make the ticket "disappear" without making what was left of my bank account disappear too. The ticket turned out to be only seventy-five dollars, but the lawyer cost three hundred. Everyone said I got off cheap, and I believe them, but ouch!

4   As bad as that expense was, the next effect was worse. My parents had been paying my insurance because at the time I was still living at home and going to college. However, after they learned of my ticket, they decided to stop helping me with the coverage. They reasoned that if I had enough money to speed, then I had enough money to pay for my own insurance. I never quite figured out their logic, but I got their point. A thousand dollars for a year's premiums is an expensive lesson.

5   Having to cover the insurance on top of the ticket led to the worst consequence of all—work, work, work! I picked up extra hours at my job on the golf course, but that was not enough. So I turned to my parents, who were willing to help, they said, with smiles that reminded me of the Texas highway patrol officer. There were plenty of odd jobs for me to do on the weekends around the house: painting the shed, staining the deck, washing the windows, cleaning out the garage. . . . When I got tired of manual labor, they would let me cart my younger sister around town, babysit, and help her with her homework. My folks were very creative and have given me lots of this kind of "help."

6   The expense and extra work aside, I know that a high-speed accident is the most serious possible consequence of my fast driving. And I don't want to end up with pieces of my car and me (or others) scattered along a highway somewhere, looking like a broken up 737. I think I've learned my lesson. I can't always follow my impulses, even when everything says, "Go, go, go!" As I consider career choices now that I am in college, I have more decisions to make, and I know they should be practical ones. I have always wanted to be a pro golfer, but my parents have questioned the wisdom of this goal. Well, I still have my Camaro; maybe it's not too late to drive a NASCAR (just joking).

—Lucas Eimers

THINKING ABOUT THE MODEL

1. How has this essay evolved from the paragraph on page 195? What are some effects of lengthening its form?

2. Annotate the **Key Points** in the margin, using "My Friend Who Gave Up on Life" as an example.

POSTREADING REVIEW: KEY ELEMENTS OF CAUSE/ EFFECT ESSAYS

Here are several important points—illustrated by the preceding student models—to keep in mind for your own cause/effect essay:

1. Explore all the likely causes and effects (pp. 188–190).

2. Develop causes or effects thoroughly (pp. 190–191).

3. Choose only the real causes and effects (pp. 191–192).

4. Avoid oversimplifying by thinking critically (pp. 192–193).

Explaining Activities, Doing Them, Understanding Them (Process Analysis)

HINT

Process analysis includes steps, reasons, and warnings. For a more complete discussion of process analysis, see Chapter 10.

When we explain an activity so that someone can perform or understand it, we are doing **process analysis.** For example, in building a house there are many steps: clearing the ground, pouring the foundation, framing the walls, putting on the roof, and much more. An experienced builder would be able to tell us about each step in the process. The explanation would probably include definitions of new words, warnings about dangers, and reasons, for example, that one step comes before another or why one material is used and not another.

The builder could give us a detailed explanation so that we might understand the process, or he could give specific instructions so we could perform some part of it. You may take either of these approaches in your essay, writing about a **process to perform** or a **process to understand.** In either approach, you will find that breaking down an activity into steps and explaining each one clearly are powerful tools for learning about what you thought you already knew.

Analyzing Student Models: Process-Analysis Essays

The following two models will help you write process-analysis essays. The first, "Jokers Wild," promotes playing practical jokes as an amusing and worthwhile pastime. The author uses humor in writing about a process to understand. The second, "A Boy's Best Friend," in which we see the author as a boy, explains a process to perform.

To see how a paragraph might grow into an essay, compare the essay version of "A Boy's Best Friend" to the paragraph version in Chapter 10 (p. 218).

➤ *Prereading Exploration for "Jokers Wild"*

As a practical joker, Michael Feldman decided to explain the process of playing a practical joke. And as a nontraditional student returning to college after years on the job, he decided to simultaneously comment on how hard so many people work in our society. For this **process-to-understand** essay, he chose to describe the general

HINT

Record your prereading responses in your journal or on your blog.

process, rather than any one particular joke. His target audience is young, hard-working adults who might themselves be inclined to play a prank on friends.

If you have ever played a joke on or deliberately surprised someone—anything from making a crank phone call to setting up a surprise party—how did you go about it? List six steps that you followed to surprise the person.

Key Points: Building Process Analysis Essays

Title: arouses readers' curiosity and links to the essay's main point

Introductory paragraph: begins with a hook and ends with a thesis sentence that predicts a process-analysis essay

Body paragraphs: begin with a topic sentence, which <u>names</u> the subtopic and makes a <u>limiting statement</u> about it

Development: uses specific examples, details, warnings, active verbs (*back-fires*), -ing words (*playing*), and specific words (*gerbil*); tells thoughts and emotions; explains the examples ("If you are shy or introverted, practical jokes may not work for you because . . .")

Organization: is arranged chronologically (as the process unfolds in time)

Jokers Wild

The world needs an antidote to seriousness. Too many people are bogged down in the day-to-day grind of making a living and taking care of all their RESPONSIBILITIES. Childhood seems to end about the time we get our driver's licenses and can haul ourselves to work. It's either school or work or, for many of us, both. We can't always take the vacations we want—sometimes it's even hard to get a weekend—and between studying, working, and taking care of the people in our lives, we get kind of dried out and wrinkly, like grapes turned into raisins. But there is one partial remedy for this condition, playing pranks. If you have a general understanding of the ground rules for playing pranks on friends, everyone can survive, and most will even have a good time.

The <u>first step</u> is to <u>know yourself</u>. If you are shy or introverted, practical jokes may not work for you because you may suddenly, sometimes unpleasantly, find yourself in the spotlight when/if you are discovered. If you are reasonably outgoing and think you can stand the attention, you may still have problems if the prank backfires. For example, when your friend breaks her favorite desk lamp trying to escape from the gerbil you put in her desk drawer, you may find yourself buying a new lamp and apologizing profusely, on both knees if necessary.

If you are the right sort for pranking, the next important point is to know your victim. While casual friends make fairly good targets, good friends are often a better choice. First, you know where they work and play, so you can pick a good spot to lay the trap for that singing telegram or surprise birthday party. Second, and more important, if the joke really blows up in your face, a good friend is less likely to hit or sue you. A casual friend, for instance, might not be as tolerant if he discovers the identity of the person who anonymously had a truckload of gravel dumped on his driveway.

With a target and suitable prank picked out, you can begin to think about execution—of the plan, not the person. The first rule here is no dangerous jokes. If, for example, you want to drop water on someone, don't put it in a metal bucket over someone's door. Physical pain is not funny, at least to the sufferer. Next, remember that timing is critical. The singing stripper that you have visit a friend at a party might go over well with everyone there, but send her to the church picnic, and you have problems. In general, if you remember that you still have to live around your victim after the joke has passed, your sense of self-preservation should tell you when to quit.

No advice on playing pranks would be complete without a few words on the aftermath, or dealing with the fallout. Your primary concern is how well it went over. If all went well, everyone chuckled, and there were no hard feelings, terrific. Then you can accept the credit for the general good times. However, if the response was mixed or poor, and you want to escape, you have several options, depending on how many people are in on the joke (you can't really rely on anyone not to blab over time). First, admire the idea behind the prank but wish that whoever did it had used a little better judgment. Second, inconspicuously offer an airtight alibi. Third, shift the blame to another friend who is also known to play pranks. Maybe he or she will appreciate your attempt to save yourself, knowing that he or she would do the same thing in your place.

Playing practical jokes can be fun for everyone—well, almost everyone—if the joker is temperamentally suited, knows his or her victim well, chooses a suitable prank, and can deal with the aftermath. As busy as we grownups have become, we still need to take a break sometimes and lift our faces up from the grindstone. Whether we are planning a surprise birthday party or having someone call a friend who has just "won" the lottery, well-played jokes can help relieve the stress of too-serious lives. And as long as we have a good friend who can stand us (and another friend or two to take the blame), we will have all the opportunities we need. Happy pranking!

—Michael Feldman

4

Sentence connectors: guide readers: transitions, repeat words, synonyms, pronouns, and reference to main idea

5

Style points: increase readability. Capitalizing letters and using a dash (paragraph 1) can create emphasis. The pronoun *you* is often used in process explanations. Puns can add humor (paragraph 4: "execution"). Parentheses can add variety and allow for a brief digression (paragraph 5). Fragments can create emphasis (paragraph 6: "Happy pranking!")

6

Concluding paragraph: restates the thesis, briefly summarizes, and adds a final (expanded) thought

Record your prereading responses in your journal or on your blog.

To see this essay as a paragraph, turn back to Chapter 10, p. 218.

➡ Prereading Exploration for "A Boy's Best Friend"

For his **process-to-perform** essay, Steve Oh chose a manageable topic from his childhood in rural Korea. He thought his essay might appeal most to young men in any culture who had similar childhood experiences, of making "weapons" for fun and as a way to gain some control over their environment.

Do you remember as a child making anything that was particularly special to you? Write down one thing that you remember making, and list six steps that went into it.

A Boy's Best Friend

1 Living in the country as a child, I did not have plastic army men or fluffy dolls as toys. There were no mass-produced playgrounds with red-painted swing sets, climbing bars, and miniature castles for children to enjoy. My toys came mostly from my rural surroundings and always kept me fully content. To this day, high-tech video games and talking robots could never compare to the precious toys of my youth. The one I longed for the most was a slingshot. If I wanted one to hunt the sparrows that were always attacking our rice crop, I knew that I would have to make it myself.

2 Collecting the materials for my treasure, though, did not come easy. It required a piece of rubber band, the most perfectly forked branch from an oak tree, and a square of leather to hold the stone. Any old rubber band would not do, though; it had to be surgical tubing, light brown and hose shaped, for the power I wanted. To obtain this rarity, I biked half an hour into town to the drugstore, after begging the money from my older brothers. The shopkeeper carefully measured off the 24 inches of hose that I needed, not giving me an inch more. When I returned home, I pleaded with my older brothers until they finally agreed to help me find the right branch in the nearby forest. We chose an oak for the sturdiest wood, and they sawed off the best-shaped, healthiest-looking branch for me. Next, I needed a piece of leather to hold the stones, but the only leather I could find was my dad's belt. My brothers were not about to risk angering my father, so I snuck into his closet by myself and secretly cut

off a two-inch length from the end of his belt, praying that he would not notice.

Finally, I was ready to construct my prize. With instructions from my brothers, I sawed the three ends of the oak branch to form a capital Y, each section approximately 6 inches long. Next, I peeled away the rough brown bark and sanded it with a medium grade of sandpaper until it was silky smooth. Using the Korean equivalent to a pocketknife, on the side of the Y facing away from me, I carved notches roughly 1/8 inch deep and 1/4 inch wide about 1/2 inch from the tips. Then I wrapped the ends of the rubber band around the notches, being extra careful to tie the bands securely. (I didn't want to lose an eye if the tubing slipped from the branch when I had the slingshot fully drawn back!) With my knife I drilled a small hole in the ends of the leather patch, slipped one inch of the tubing through each hole, folded the tubing over, and tied it together securely with string so it, too, would not slip. My slingshot was complete. I pulled back the band to test it, let it go, and heard the best "Snap!" I could have hoped for.

Growing up in a quiet little town, I had enormous fun making my own toys and using them to "fight in the cause of justice." Chasing a flock of hateful sparrows with my sling-shot, as seldom as I actually hit one, is a boyhood experience I would never erase. Thinking back to my simpler life, I some-times feel confused today. Surrounding me are my computer, fax machine, cordless phone, television, and stereo—products of technology and my new city life. At one time I was con-tent with almost nothing, just a few toys I had made with my own hands. But now I am hardly content with an apartment full of adult toys, needing more and more to be satisfied. I have gained many things in growing up, but I fear that I have lost the boy who knew how to be happy with nothing more than a slingshot.

—*Steve Oh*

THINKING ABOUT THE MODEL

1. How has this essay evolved from the paragraph on page 218? Describe what you think the author's process was like, expanding the paper into this longer form.

2. Annotate the **Key Points** in the margin, using "Jokers Wild" as an example.

POSTREADING REVIEW: KEY ELEMENTS IN PROCESS-ANALYSIS ESSAYS

Here are several important points—illustrated by the preceding student models—to keep in mind for your own process-analysis essay:

1. List all the necessary steps (p. 213).

2. Explain the steps thoroughly, giving reasons and warnings (p. 214).

3. Define all the terms (pp. 215–216).

4. Avoid monotonous sentence patterns (pp. 216–217).

Explaining Similarities and Differences (Comparison and Contrast)

Comparing and contrasting ideas, people, and things is the process of discovering similarities and differences among them. Topics often lend themselves to either approach. For example, we could *contrast* the players at a football game to the cheerleaders. The football team is entirely male while the cheerleading squad is mostly female. One group wears pads, helmets, and spiked shoes while the other wears light clothing and tennis shoes. Those in one group have serious, almost grim, expressions while those in the other are smiling and enthusiastic. One group is riveted on the action on the playing field while the other is turned outward and upward toward the crowd.

We could also *compare* the two groups. Both are the focus of the spectators' attention, both consist of athletes, both work as teams whose members depend on one another for success, both have leaders, both have organized plays or routines, and both are working toward the goal of winning the game.

Longer essays often explore both comparisons and contrasts. However, to keep your brief essay focused, you would do better to choose either comparison or contrast, as in the student model essays that follow.

For more on comparison and contrast, see Chapter 11.

Analyzing Student Models: Comparison/Contrast Essays

The first model, "I'll Park. You Get the Tickets—Hurry!" focuses on differences between watching movies at home and in a theater. The second, "Break on Through to the Other Side," also focuses on differences, this time between two stages of the author's life. The first model uses **block organization;** the second uses **point-by-point organization.**

To see how a paragraph might grow into an essay, compare the essay version of "Breakin' Through" with the paragraph version in Chapter 11 (p. 243).

In these models, look closely at the introductory and concluding paragraphs, important parts of essays.

➤ Prereading Exploration for "I'll Park. You Get the Tickets—Hurry!"

HINT

Record your prereading response in your journal or on your blog.

Hugh Edwards picked a topic he thought most people could identify with—watching movies at home versus going to a movie theater. Of the many ways to compare and contrast movies at home and movies out, Hugh chose to contrast the *experience*, focusing on the extent to which he finds it relaxing in each case.

Think about your own movie-going experiences, and then list ways in which watching a movie at home is preferable to going to the movies. How many of your examples matched the author's?

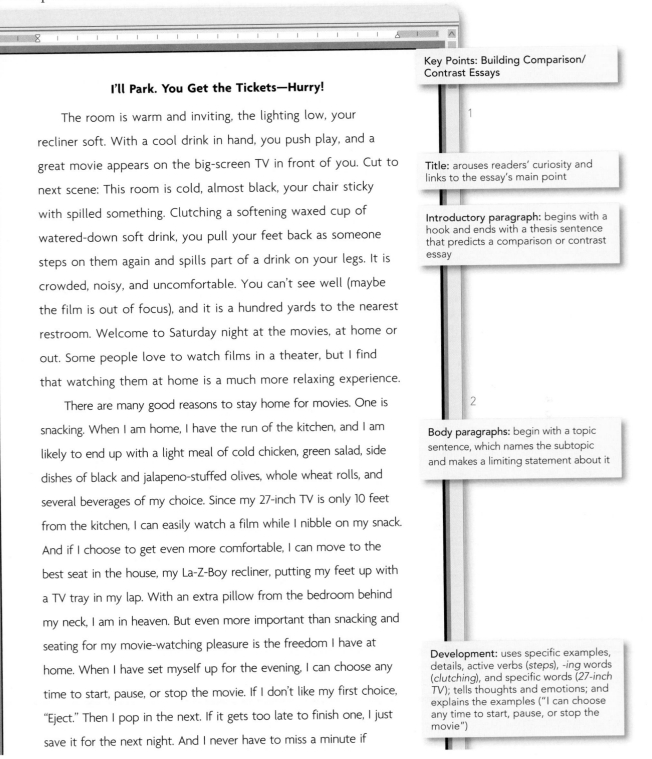

I'll Park. You Get the Tickets—Hurry!

The room is warm and inviting, the lighting low, your recliner soft. With a cool drink in hand, you push play, and a great movie appears on the big-screen TV in front of you. Cut to next scene: This room is cold, almost black, your chair sticky with spilled something. Clutching a softening waxed cup of watered-down soft drink, you pull your feet back as someone steps on them again and spills part of a drink on your legs. It is crowded, noisy, and uncomfortable. You can't see well (maybe the film is out of focus), and it is a hundred yards to the nearest restroom. Welcome to Saturday night at the movies, at home or out. Some people love to watch films in a theater, but I find that watching them at home is a much more relaxing experience.

There are many good reasons to stay home for movies. One is snacking. When I am home, I have the run of the kitchen, and I am likely to end up with a light meal of cold chicken, green salad, side dishes of black and jalapeno-stuffed olives, whole wheat rolls, and several beverages of my choice. Since my 27-inch TV is only 10 feet from the kitchen, I can easily watch a film while I nibble on my snack. And if I choose to get even more comfortable, I can move to the best seat in the house, my La-Z-Boy recliner, putting my feet up with a TV tray in my lap. With an extra pillow from the bedroom behind my neck, I am in heaven. But even more important than snacking and seating for my movie-watching pleasure is the freedom I have at home. When I have set myself up for the evening, I can choose any time to start, pause, or stop the movie. If I don't like my first choice, "Eject." Then I pop in the next. If it gets too late to finish one, I just save it for the next night. And I never have to miss a minute if

Key Points: Building Comparison/Contrast Essays

1

Title: arouses readers' curiosity and links to the essay's main point

Introductory paragraph: begins with a hook and ends with a thesis sentence that predicts a comparison or contrast essay

2

Body paragraphs: begin with a topic sentence, which names the subtopic and makes a limiting statement about it

Development: uses specific examples, details, active verbs (*steps*), -*ing* words (*clutching*), and specific words (*27-inch TV*); tells thoughts and emotions; and explains the examples ("I can choose any time to start, pause, or stop the movie")

Body paragraphs often benefit from order of importance organizing.

3

Organization: uses block for overall arrangement and order of importance and chronological order within body paragraphs

Sentence connectors: guide readers: transitions, repeat words, synonyms, pronouns, and reference to main idea

4

Style points: increase readability. Using a series, rather than separate sentences, makes writing more concise (par. 2: "cold chicken, green salad, side dishes of . . ."). Short sentences create emphasis (par. 2: "One is snacking"). A colon can create emphasis (par. 1)

Concluding paragraph: restates the thesis, briefly summarizes, and adds a final (expanded) thought

another cold beverage or the bathroom calls. The most relaxing part of my home-viewing evening, though, is no people problems. My roommate is almost never around, so I have the apartment to myself. The only noises I don't want to hear come from the neighbor down below, and I just crank the volume up a notch to take care of him.

In contrast, too often when I see a movie out, I run into problems that kill my fun. First, half the time I spend ten minutes waiting in line to get junky movie-house food: popcorn with something that resembles butter, stale nachos with melted Cheese Whiz, and Jujubes that want to yank out my fillings. With this "feast" in hand, spilling popcorn as I go, I have to search for a seat in the dark and usually find one too close to the screen, too far away from it, or at a bad angle. Then comes the balancing act where I usually manage to dump at least a handful of popcorn in my lap to sit on for the next two hours, mystery butter and all. And once I am in my seat, if the theater is crowded and the movie is exciting, I am trapped. In the first place I don't want to walk over people to get to the aisle; it's embarrassing. In the second place there is no pausing the film. Who wants to miss the best scene when that half gallon of Coke finally cycles through, and it's bathroom or bust? Even though I don't like to pop back and forth from my seat to the lobby, it seems like everyone else in my row does. It always caps off my night out at the movies to have people yakking in my ear, blocking my view of the screen, and stepping on my toes on their way out. "Sorry, pal, this is the last time."

Watching a movie at a theater can be downright unpleasant. Because we have less control over our surroundings, we have to put up with more annoyances than we would ever stand for in the security of our own homes. But despite the potential aggravations, there are some good reasons for abandoning the La-Z-Boy. First, if you want to see the newest releases, you have to go out. Second, some films, like those with great special effects, are made to be viewed on a huge screen. And finally, seeing movies out can be a good social experience—and a safe first date.

—Hugh Edwards

➡ Prereading Exploration for "Break on Through to the Other Side"

Comparison and contrast papers can help us reflect on our lives, perhaps to gain some perspective on them. Gina Rizzo chose to divide her twenties into her "roaring twenties" and late twenties and to contrast the two for her writing group, students just entering their twenties. Gina felt that young adults moving into the years she had just lived through might be interested in her experiences and how they had shaped her recent decisions.

1. Think back on your own life. Have you ever done anything that surprised yourself? Were you unexpectedly indifferent, lazy, selfish, or cruel (or involved, active, generous, or kind)?

2. If you have ever felt like a different person than you are now, even briefly, describe that person, and consider pursuing the topic in an essay of contrast.

Record your prereading responses in your journal or on your blog.

To see this essay as a paragraph, turn back to Chapter 11, pp. 243–244.

Break on Through to the Other Side

Raising hell and living for the moment were all I used to care about. I could see through glassy eyes, somewhat clearly, all the way from one day till the next morning. Then, when I would roll out of bed hungover and crawl toward the bathroom, I would remind myself how much fun I was having. These were the good old days, the days of my roaring twenties. I had some fun, learned a little, and came through, surprisingly, with few visible battle scars. But now that I am moving into my thirties, life has changed.

When I was just entering my twenties, I was still living at home, although nobody would have known it by the way I came and went, telling no one anything. But I have come a long way since then. Despite my being twenty-nine now, my mom knows where I am most of the time, not because she checks up on me but because I want her to know what I am doing. Being in touch with the family has become important to me.

As a younger woman, I was always invited to the biggest and craziest parties. There is an old saying, "If you can't run with the big dogs . . . ." Well, I was one of the big dogs. No one could outparty me. I don't recall when it happened, but I have lost the taste for drinking altogether. Somewhere down the road my body started rejecting the soothing liquid that I had begun to rely on too much. I don't go to the big or crazy parties anymore.

1

2

3

My friends have quit inviting me, which is just as well. I don't much feel like partying that way now. I would rather remember my life instead of just hearing about it.

4   Another important difference between my younger self and the woman of today is how I think about time. I used to live only in the present, never planning ahead, never saving money. I bartended for a living, so my money was spent just like I made it, one day at a time. I didn't plan vacations; I would decide the day before, and off I'd go, hopping another red-eye to Las Vegas. I would go anywhere I could afford with the money I had in my pocket. However, times have changed. I actually have a savings account now, and I just bought a plane ticket for my coming vacation two months in advance! Being more responsible with money ought to help me get a few more wants out of life, not just my needs.

5   As I began to think more about a future, maybe the most dramatic change came over me when I finally decided to stop playing follow the leader. Like lots of young people I wanted to be in there doing what everyone else was doing. For me that included becoming a Deadhead after my first Grateful Dead concert. The other Deadheads became my family, and we followed our leaders around the country, living the Dead life, pushing ourselves to the limit, right up to the end on that warm night in August when Jerry Garcia died. His death stopped me short. "Is this what I want?" I asked myself. "Do I also want to 'break on through to the other side'?" I decided no. It was time to make another kind of break, this time with the pack. I was ready to become an individual, to take some responsibility as I'd need to do if I expected to survive as an adult. Among other changes I made, the Deadhead has become a college student.

6   As I look back over my roaring twenties, I see a lot that makes me shake my head at myself: the hiding from my family, the hard partying, the child's sense that there is no tomorrow. But I realize, too, that nobody comes into the world fully grown. Infant, child, teen, adult—we move through stages, learning a little or a lot as we go. I am satisfied with what I have learned so far, and the wild-child-who-was helped to get me here. I hope now that I am on the right path, the one that leads to a long, peaceful,

and happy life. But no one can know. We can only think and plan and work for the best. Probably the only thing I can be sure of is that the woman of thirty-nine will be as different from me today as I am from the nineteen-year-old—and as much the same.

—*Gina Rizzo*

THINKING ABOUT THE MODEL

1. How has this essay evolved from the paragraph on pages 243–244? Compare or contrast the two versions, focusing on what meaningful aspects of it have stayed the same or changed.

2. Annotate the **Key Points** in the margin, using "I'll Park—You Get the Tickets" as an example.

POSTREADING REVIEW: KEY ELEMENTS IN COMPARISON/CONTRAST ESSAYS

Here are several important points—illustrated by the preceding student models—to keep in mind for your own comparison/contrast essay:

1. Make a meaningful comparison or contrast (p. 236).
2. Make an interesting comparison or contrast (pp. 237–239).
3. Develop each point of comparison or contrast thoroughly (pp. 239–240).
4. Use transitions and other connectors (pp. 54–56).

POSTREADING QUESTIONS FOR ESSAY ANALYSIS

Note: These questions apply to all model essays in this chapter.

1. Where is the thesis located? What is the topic, and what statement limits it?

2. Why is the hook effective? Which of the hooks discussed in Chapter 12 has the author used?

3. What method(s) from Chapter 12 has the author used to develop the introductory paragraph (pp. 272–274)? Why might the introduction interest the audience stated in the prereading exploration?

4. Why might the lead sentence (p. 285) in the concluding paragraph be effective?

5. What method(s) from Chapter 12 has the author used to develop the concluding paragraph (pp. 285–288)? What is the expanded thought? Why might the conclusion interest the target audience? (Think of how the conclusion links with the introduction.)

6. For each topic sentence, what are the topic, the limiting statement, and the connecting words?

7. How are the body paragraphs arranged: chronologically or by order of importance? What connector words reveal this?

8. Choose a paragraph in which the author explains an example clearly. How does the explanation help you to understand the paragraph's main point?

For more on hooks, see pp. 275–277.

For more on connecting sentences, see pp. 53–59.

9. Why do you think any one paragraph is well written? Consider topic sentences, connecting words, sensory details, specific words, action description, dialogue, metaphors/comparisons, sentence variety, and clear explanations.

10. What are five instances of specific language?

WRITING AN ESSAY

Summarizing the Assignment

Whether you are expanding a paragraph already written or starting with a new topic, the goal is the same: to write a clear, well-organized, and well-developed essay of approximately 500 to 600 words. To do this, you should focus your topic with a thesis sentence, which you will then expand with two to four body paragraphs, each beginning with a focused topic sentence. Because introductory and concluding paragraphs are such crucial parts of essays, you should pay close attention to them.

Establishing Audience and Purpose

For more on introductions and conclusions, see Chapter 12.

Writing to a specific audience helps focus material.

We all are experienced in speaking to different audiences—don't we, for example, speak differently to a close friend than to someone we have just met at work? When it comes to writing, though, we sometimes forget about shaping what we say for our audience; we feel almost as if we are writing for ourselves. However, precisely because we are removed from our audience, and don't have their reactions as immediate feedback, it is especially important that we keep them in mind. Do they understand? Are they interested? Are we offending someone? Choose an audience who might care about your message, and visualize them as you write. By keeping a specific audience in mind, you will often be better able to select ideas, explanations, and even individual words. The result will be a more focused, and thus more interesting, essay.

You may have several purposes—to entertain, inform, or persuade—but clearly communicating ideas should take priority.

Working through the Writing Assignment

Discovering Ideas

Any of the prewriting methods we have worked with this semester (clustering, listing, freewriting, etc.) can be useful for uncovering a topic for your essay or for expanding examples from a former paragraph. For topics lists appropriate to specific patterns of development, see the following pages:

To review prewriting techniques, turn to Chapter 1.

1. Illustration: p. 149
2. Classification: p. 174
3. Cause and effect: pp. 197–198
4. Process analysis: pp. 221–222
5. Comparison and contrast: p. 246

You may find that the examples you used in your paragraph assignment are right for your essay and simply need to be developed, or you may want to change or add an example, group, cause, or step. However, check with your instructor before making major changes in content. He or she may want you to work with the main example of your paragraph for practice with artful development.

Organizing Ideas

A thesis sentence is essential to keep an essay on track, so you should write one at the top of your paper before beginning to draft. The topic sentence from a paragraph assignment may work as your thesis, but, again, you may need to revise it, particularly if you have added or dropped major examples. Remember, too, that topic sentences are just as important in your essay body paragraphs as they were in your one-paragraph papers.

To arrange your body paragraphs overall, use either time or order of importance. Whichever method seems most appropriate for your topic, include transitions and other connectors throughout the essay—but especially between paragraphs.

Thesis and topic sentences are the keys to solid organization.

Use connecting words between sentences and paragraphs. See pp. 54–56 for more on connectors.

Drafting

As you develop examples, remember the principle of **layering,** first discussed in Chapter 3, by which you add sufficient examples, details, and explanations to help readers see exactly what you mean. In this excerpt from the illustration essay "The Jobs from Hell," we can see how the author layered meaning:

> When I was a senior, I found another job that, at first, looked promising. Dr. Lawn paid well, but I had to mow lawns for six to eight hours a day in the July heat, with temperatures running into the nineties. One day on the job I grew sick to my stomach and feverish and literally collapsed in back of a walk-behind mower. My manager would not let me go home because we had come in a car pool, and if I had left, it would have affected the other five people working. When I finally made it home, my dad found that I had a 105-degree fever, and we both decided that no job was worth my health.

What does Eric mean by "sick"? His stomach ached, he had a 105-degree fever, and he collapsed on the job. Why did he become ill? He had to mow lawns for six to eight hours a day in ninety-degree heat. Why was his illness a special problem? His boss wouldn't let him go home. As you ask and answer questions about your own examples, more material will come to you, and your paragraphs will grow.

To see how you might develop a former paragraph assignment, notice how Jeong Yi made a subtopic in his illustration paragraph, "Teaching with Whips," into a body paragraph in the essay he later wrote. The added material has been shaded:

Asking questions about your statements will help you develop them.

Single-Paragraph Excerpt: 71 Words (complete paragraph on p. 144)

> My moral education teacher was one of these cruel educators. He was short and fat like the whip he carried to enforce his every whim. "I see you haven't done your homework, Jeong," he would say. He ordered me to hold my palms up, and then he began to whip my hands harshly. Somehow the pain ended with me crying and begging, "I will do it next time, teacher. I promise!"

Essay Body Paragraph: 157 Words (complete essay on pp. 301–302)

> As a new middle school student, I was surprised by my first painful encounter with my moral education teacher, a short fat man who carried a short fat whip to enforce his every whim. His manner of speaking somehow

did not make it seem urgent for me to thoroughly complete all the homework. Then one day he noticed that I was not prepared and made an example of me to show the class how harsh he could be to defiant students. "I see you haven't done your homework, Jeong," he said, his angry red face shaking. Straining with fear, the class was dead quiet, wondering what was going to happen at that frightful moment. "Jeong, stand up!" he ordered. His chalk-dusty hands held my two shaky little hands palms up and aimed at them as if they were targets. The punishment ended with me crying and begging, "I will do it next time, teacher. I promise!"

Jeong developed this paragraph through further explanation, examples, and details. You can do the same if you ask the critical question "What do I mean by what I just said?" and answer it with a specific audience in mind.

Linking to Future Experience

Revising Drafts

In Unit Two, we revised body paragraphs for content and organization. In addition to revising body paragraphs, we now need to pay attention to introductory and concluding paragraphs:

- Does your introductory paragraph have a strong hook? Have you developed the paragraph with three to five sentences to interest readers? Is there a thesis sentence stating the main point of the essay?

- Does your concluding paragraph have a lead sentence with a connector and link to your thesis? Have you summarized main examples? Does the paragraph frame the essay and/or expand the thesis?

If you take time to revise your essay in several stages, dealing first with larger issues of content and organization and then working toward style and editing concerns, you will produce a superior final draft.

Chapter 14 covers step-by-step suggestions on revising, editing, and proofreading your drafts.

Alternate Writing Assignments

For additional writing assignments, turn back to the chapter in Unit Two featuring the specific pattern of development.

WRITE AN ESSAY ON A GREEN TOPIC

Expand one of the Conservation in Context paragraph assignments from Unit Two into an essay. See pages 91, 119, 149, 184, 208, 232, or 258 for possibilities. Consider submitting your essay to a college publication, such as a newspaper or newsletter. ●

ACTIVITY 13.1 WORKING TOGETHER: *Revising Collaboratively*

After you have drafted an essay that is an expanded version of an earlier paragraph assignment, trade papers with a classmate or two; include your original paragraph as a reference point for your peer editor(s). After reading and making notes on each other's essays, discuss the experience of expanding each paragraph into an essay and how successful each workshopper's process has been. Balance your response between praise for what is working well and questions about what might be improved. Now, try to give each other at least two specific revision suggestions. You can do this activity at any stage of the drafting process—first draft, second, or even final.

ACTIVITY 13.2 WORKING ONLINE: *Process Analysis Review*

Take the Chapter 10 Review Quiz at www.mhhe.com/brannan.

Chapter Summary

1. Many body paragraphs can be developed into essays. When these body paragraphs are developed into essays, their topic sentences become thesis sentences, subtopic sentences become topic sentences, and concluding sentences become concluding paragraphs.

2. Illustration essays use examples to clarify a point. The examples can be based on personal experience or on general knowledge.

3. Classification essays arrange their material around a single organizing principle (SOP).

4. Cause and effect essays focus on events and answer in-depth the questions "What made this happen" and "What will be the results of this event?"

5. Process analysis helps people understand how to do or how to understand a process or activity.

6. Comparison and contrast essays pair familiar points with unfamiliar ones to help a reader better understand unfamiliar topics.

7. Several patterns of development are often used together to develop an essay topic.

8. Writing essays requires a clear sense of purpose—a goal to be accomplished for a specific audience and one that follows a writing process of discovery, organization, drafting, revising, editing, and proofreading.

Revising Essays

[*In a paragraph, describe your current revision process, answering several of these questions: How long do you spend revising a paper? Do you like trading papers with other students; why or why not? Have you ever used a writing center as a resource—and if so, how helpful was it? What do you find most challenging about revising? Do you have a "good revision" success story?*]

KEY TOPICS

- Revising essays
- Revising first-stage drafts
  - Common first-stage draft issues
- Revising second-stage drafts
  - Common second-stage draft issues
- Editing
  - Common editing problems
- Proofreading

Revising Essays

We revise essays in much the same way we revise paragraphs—slowly, carefully, and critically. To produce that final polished draft, we must believe that we *can* improve an essay, that there are clear steps to follow, and that it is worth the effort to do so. This chapter will review many points you practiced in Unit Two and help take you from that first rough collection of ideas through the final proofreading that results in superior work.

Revising First-Stage Drafts

With your first draft in hand, you can begin to tighten the essay. Be prepared to revise for content and organization. An example or two may not be working, so you may need to add and delete details. Whenever the connection between an example and the thesis is unclear, you need to further clarify. Look closely at your introductory and concluding paragraphs. Are they doing their job well? At this point, if you like what you have but feel your examples are geared toward a different audience than the one you had selected, you might redefine your audience. If you develop a writer's attitude toward revision—that it may be painful but it is necessary—then your work can only improve.

Remember that in revising first drafts, the overall focus is on **content** (the substance of the examples, clarity of explanations, and kind of details) and **organization** (thesis and topic sentences, arrangement of paragraphs, unity, and coherence). You can attend to spelling errors and questionable words when revising later drafts.

For more on revising on your own or within a group, see pp. 63–72.

Common First-Stage Draft Issues

☐ **1. Do you use several major examples to illustrate your thesis?**

Use enough examples to develop your main point. Resist settling for one or two major examples when three or four would better illustrate your thesis.

Longer essays may have more body paragraphs, but our essays (500 to 600 words) should have two to four. If you have written, say, six to eight body paragraphs, you probably have not developed each one fully, or you are moving into a lengthier essay.

☐ **2. Is your thesis sentence effective (pp. 266–271)?**

Your thesis sentence should name the topic and make a clear statement about it. The sentence may also include a forecasting statement. If your working thesis sentence is unclear or too general, the essay may be headed for trouble.

Unless you have a good reason to locate it elsewhere, put the thesis sentence at the end of your introduction.

You can make a focused thesis sentence even more effective through **specific words, action words,** and **sensory details.**

☐ **3. Is the hook of your introductory paragraph effective (pp. 275–277)?**

The first sentence should arouse readers' interest and connect with your target audience.

Grammar, spelling, and punctuation are low priorities in revising first drafts.

Check with your instructor on the length range of your assignment.

Be sure that both you and at least one other reader can easily predict where the essay is going based on the thesis sentence.

Material sometimes will be arranged by both time and importance, which is fine.

For more on developing body paragraphs, see pp. 281–283; for more on using narrative and descriptive elements, see Chapters 5 and 6.

Make sure the hook, does not include an obvious statement or worn expression.

4. **Is your introductory paragraph well developed (pp. 266–280)?**

Introductions in short essays should be around five to seven sentences. Be sure that you develop your paragraph using one or several of the methods listed in Chapter 12 or one of your own.

Make sure, too, that you avoid problems leading to weak introductions. There are so many effective ways to begin an essay that settling for something so-so is a shame.

5. **Are your body paragraphs logically arranged by space, time, or importance (pp. 283–284)?**

In expository and persuasive writing, you will probably organize your body paragraphs by order of importance or, less often, chronologically. Whichever method you pick, be consistent and begin body paragraphs with transitions signaling that order.

6. **Do you introduce each body paragraph with a topic sentence? If relevant, do you include a summary sentence?**

While not all essay body paragraphs begin with topic sentences, many do. In your essays, for clarity and focus, each body paragraph should contain a topic sentence related to the thesis. Usually, it is the first sentence in the paragraph. Remember: Topic sentence = transition or other connector + topic + statement.

You may sometimes find a summary sentence useful for wrapping up a body paragraph, particularly if the paragraph is fairly long. For more on topic and summary sentences in essays, see page 280.

7. **Are your body paragraphs well developed?**

All paragraphs in an essay should be necessary, appropriate to a specific audience, and well developed. Also, each body paragraph should illustrate one main idea, using detailed examples and explanations. Remember to be specific, layering examples and explanations so that one sentence adds to the next. Ask yourself, "What do I mean by that statement? How can I make it more clear?"

Develop your work where appropriate through sensory details, active verbs, *-ing* words, dialogue, revealed thoughts and emotions, and descriptions of settings and people.

8. **Are sentences within and between paragraphs well connected?**

All sentences in your essay should be smoothly linked, and strong connections are especially important between paragraphs. Remember to use **transitional words** (words like *first, next, for example,* and *another*) and other connectors: **repeat words, synonyms, pronouns,** and **reference to main idea.** (For more on sentence connectors see pp. 54–56, 293–294.)

9. **Is your concluding paragraph effective?**

Check your concluding paragraph for these three parts:

- **Lead sentence:** one sentence (connector + link to thesis)
- **Summary:** one sentence or less
- **Development:** three or four sentences (frame and/or expanded thought)

The first sentence of your conclusion should connect with the last body paragraph and the essay's thesis, and your main points or examples should be summarized in that sentence or a separate sentence (but avoid oversummarizing). Make the rest of your conclusion interesting by using the methods in Chapter 12 or one of your own. Check for problems that result in weak conclusions (pp. 290–293).

JOURNAL / BLOG ENTRY 14.1

List three changes you have made or feel you ought to make from your first to second draft. Refer to the first-stage draft questions, answering them specifically—for example, "Question 4: I decided that my introduction was weak, so I rewrote it, using method 9 from Chapter 12." Next, in several sentences, state what you like best about the revised draft.

FEEDBACK *Trade drafts with a classmate, and, in several sentences, state what you like best about his or her revised draft.*

Revising Second-Stage Drafts

If your draft is fairly complete at this stage—with most of your concerns about content and organization under control—you can focus on revising words and sentences.

Common Second-Stage Draft Issues

1. **Do you use specific language?**

   Your essay will include both general and specific language, but specific words create the sharpest images. Instead of *shoes*, try *alligator cowboy boots with three-inch heels.*

2. **Do you include sensory details (pp. 77–78)?**

   Sensory details, useful in expository and persuasive essays, are often linked to specific words. In "Sixteen and Mother of Twelve" (pp. 115–116), the author appeals to our sense of sight—*camouflage uniform pants, black marching boots,* and *brown T-shirts*—and our sense of touch—*sweaty faces.* Of course, all spoken dialogue creates a sound impression, but linked to active verbs, the sound can become more dramatic, as in "What a Joke!" (pp. 116–117)—*when Linda Blair roars out, MERRIN!*

3. **Do you choose the most "active" verbs to describe action (pp. 478–479, 508–509)?**

   Verbs are important in conveying action, but some verbs do not convey action well (*be, do, have,* and *make* are common culprits). Consider these pairs of sentences:

   A. Thunder could be heard on the lake.

   B. Thunder shook the lake.

   C. I moved my head around to my left toward the shore.

   D. I jerked my head around to my left toward the shore.

Review the verbs in your own draft to see if any can be replaced with more active, interesting ones.

For more on specific language, see pp. 75–77.

For more on passive voice, a problem in sentence A, see pp. 563–564.

English Review Note

Writing multiple drafts is part of the process of academic writing. Even professional writers will submit many revisions before a final piece is ready for publication.

For more on metaphors and similes, see pp. 498–500.

For more on sentence variety, see Chapter 19, for variety in openers, pp. 462–472.

For more on unnecessary repetition, see pp. 481–483, 503–504.

4. **Do you use any *-ing* words?**

Present participles and progressive verb tenses (*-ing* words used as adjectives) show action while helping you vary your sentences. Consider these sentence pairs:

A. My girls made it through all the obstacles.

B. Running, climbing wooden walls, crossing rope bridges, and playing Tarzan on a rope swing, my girls tore through that course.

C. In loose white pajamas, grandfather was in front of me to scratch on the door.

D. Wearing loose white pajamas, grandfather was standing in front of me, leaning forward to scratch on the door again.

B and D use *-ing* words to create more vivid images. Revise your own sentences, adding *-ing* words wherever needed.

5. **Do you experiment with comparisons like metaphors or similes?**

Metaphors and similes can create fresh, sometimes startling images by comparing two seemingly dissimilar things that have something in common. Consider these two descriptions:

A. Thunder shook the lake, and I could see the water move.

B. Thunder shook the lake as if it were a glass of water, vibrating, ready to fall off of some gigantic rock and shatter on the ground.

Comparing the lake to a glass of water is a fresh image (versus a cliché), and the fragile nature of a glass that can be smashed helps set the mood for the tragedy later in the story. If you think that sentence B has more power, then review the sentences in your own draft to see if any literal description might benefit from a metaphor or simile.

6. **Are the sentences in your essay varied in length?**

Writing can be more or less interesting based on the structure of sentences alone. After polishing word choices, check the length of sentences (counting the words can help). If you find more than four sentences in a row of roughly the same length, either combine two or divide a long one.

7. **Are the beginnings of your sentences varied?**

If even two sentences in a row begin with the same word, such as *the,* change an opening or combine sentences to break up the pattern. Also, look for too many similar openings. For example, you might notice that you started eight out of twenty sentences with the word *As.* It is easy to change a word or combine sentences to increase the readability of the essay.

8. **Do you avoid repeating a word so often that it becomes noticeable?**

While some repetition is useful, too much becomes boring. Consider the following two sets of sentences:

DRAFT: TOO REPETITIVE — There were many people on the lake waiting to put their boats in the water there at Hillside Lake on that tragic July afternoon. In my boat on the lake, I felt hot and sticky from waiting on the humid lake water as I frantically maneuvered my small aluminum boat closer to the ramp by the lakeshore.

REVISED — There were many people in the water waiting to put their boats on their trailers at Hillside Lake on that tragic July afternoon. I felt hot and sticky waiting on the lake, frantically maneuvering my small aluminum boat closer to the ramp.

Revise your own sentences, cutting nonessential words.

9. **Do you avoid words that serve no purpose?**

Everyday speech is full of unneeded words, but writing should not be. Cluttered writing can bore and confuse; concise writing, in contrast, involves readers and clarifies ideas. Compare the following two sentences:

CLUTTERED   The meat hotdogs, long and thin, sizzle with a sizzling sound as they cook, roasting, and drip their meaty juices off the end of the wooden stick.

CONCISE   The hotdogs sizzle as they cook and drip their juices off the end of the stick.

Revise your own sentences, cutting unneeded words.

For more on unneeded words, see pp. 484–489.

JOURNAL / BLOG ENTRY 14.2

Skim the questions on revising second-stage drafts, looking for three ways to improve your paper (or three points you think might be a problem). After you have revised your paper, list three changes you made. Be specific in your response and refer to the questions by number.

Editing

With your essay almost complete, now is the time to edit it closely, by yourself and with others. Use the following checklist as a guide:

- Misspelled words
- Sound-alike words
- Missing words
- Wrong words
- Sentence fragments
- Comma splices/run-ons
- Faulty capitalization
- Incorrect apostrophes
- Missing comma(s)
  - Introductory words/phrases/clauses
  - Nonessential word groups
  - Main clauses with coordinating conjunction
- Unneeded commas
- Verb tense shifts
- Faulty pronoun agreement
- Faulty pronoun reference

HINT

Editing the practice essay excerpts on the next page will help you with your own revision. For three more Editing Reviews, see Chapter 14 at www.mhhe.com/ brannan.

ACTIVITY 14.1   *Editing: Practice in Context*

For practice, choose one of the following editing review paragraphs and read it slowly, trying to catch the common mechanical errors in the checklist above.

EDITING REVIEW
14-1

The corrected version of
this excerpt is on p. 131 in
"Do Unto Others . . . ."

Panick and fustration our a sure fire recipe, for tears but I fought them of and strugled too remain calm, for my girls. Suddenly I hear a voice, say "Listen I have a cell phone, do you want to call someone to come pick you up". As I turned toward the voice I saw an older gentleman, who looked a lot like my dad. Begining to cry I explained how helples I felt.

EDITING REVIEW
14-2

The corrected version
of this excerpt is on
pp. 348–349 in
"Finding Home."

Another important part of true Home is that people can relax their. When we feel safe we can begin to feel at ease in are surroundings. If famly members our considerat of one another they will give each other the space each need they will give each other the time, and opportunity to unwind in, whatever, way works best for each. Some listens to music some watches TV and, some just appreciates laying down on a couch. A true Home encourages relaxation. At the end of a busy stressful day out "there" we all needed to escape the pressure's of being productive.

"Your'e a dummy and so's your Old Lady and Old Man!" These were fighting words for me as a child and I ended up rolling around in the dirt more than once with the kids from school who said them. Growing up with hearing impaired parents in sixties if I was not fighting some kid in an alley it seems

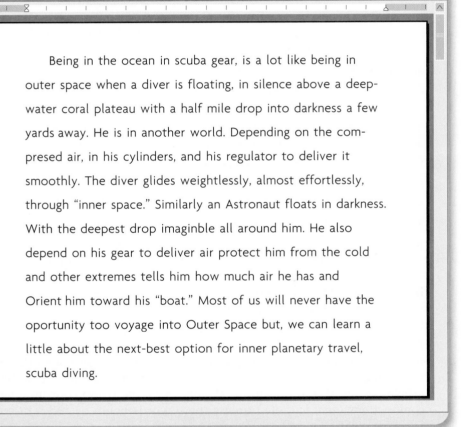

like I was trying to explain to some other child that my family was normal, we just didnt talk much which words. Back then most people didnt no much about the deaf comunity and even, today I, often see people turn, and gawk at the hearing impaired when they are signing each other. Maybe knowing more about the deaf will make them seem less strange to the hearing world.

The corrected version of this excerpt is on p. 350 in "Deaf, Not Dumb."

Being in the ocean in scuba gear, is a lot like being in outer space when a diver is floating, in silence above a deep-water coral plateau with a half mile drop into darkness a few yards away. He is in another world. Depending on the compresed air, in his cylinders, and his regulator to deliver it smoothly. The diver glides weightlessly, almost effortlessly, through "inner space." Similarly an Astronaut floats in darkness. With the deepest drop imaginble all around him. He also depend on his gear to deliver air protect him from the cold and other extremes tells him how much air he has and Orient him toward his "boat." Most of us will never have the oportunity too voyage into Outer Space but, we can learn a little about the next-best option for inner planetary travel, scuba diving.

EDITING REVIEW 14-4

The corrected version of this excerpt is on pp. 362–363 in "Get Wet."

If you caught all but two or three errors, congratulations—you are a careful editor! If you missed more than five or six, try slowing down. The following are tips for finding and fixing errors.

Common Editing Problems

1. **Misspelled words:** Use your spell checker first, and then try to find at least one other reader who is a fairly good speller. Remember, too, that the dictionary can help.

HINT

For help with spelling and sound-alike words, see Chapter 28.

2. **Sound-alike words** (*there/their/they're, to/too, then/than, your/you're,* and so forth): Keep adding these word mistakes to your Improvement Chart, and review them regularly. You probably have only a few soundalike word problems, but unless you memorize the words, you may continue repeating the mistakes endlessly.

3. **Missing words:** Read slowly. Sometimes, reading a sentence backward can help, and covering the sentence that follows the one you are editing can keep you from jumping ahead too quickly.

4. **Wrong words:** Be suspicious of words that sound too "writerly." If you often refer to a thesaurus to find words, you might be using them incorrectly. Smaller, more common words are frequently the best choices, though occasionally new vocabulary (when used correctly!) can add something specific and useful to a discussion. When your readers alert you to *possible* poor selections, work with a dictionary to make the final decisions.

For more on achieving clarity through small words, see pp. 491–492.

5. **Sentence fragments (pp. 546–551):** Remember two common types of fragments:

| PHRASE | Running to the store for bread and a six-pack of Coke. (The word group lacks a subject and a verb and is not a complete thought.) |
| SUBORDINATE CLAUSE | Because he is the kind of man we want for mayor. (The word group has a subject and verb, but the subordinating word *because* makes it an incomplete thought.) |

You can correct most fragments by joining them to another sentence or adding words to make them complete sentences.

6. **Comma splices/run-ons:** These errors happen when two sentences are joined incorrectly with only a comma or with no punctuation at all:

| COMMA SPLICE | The cement is freezing, it instantly numbs my feet. |
| RUN-ON | The cement is freezing it instantly numbs my feet. |

Remember, there are at least five ways to fix these.

For more on comma splices and run-ons, see Chapter 23.

    Note: In dialogue, be careful to avoid this kind of comma splice: "Roxanne shouted, 'Get out of here, nobody cares about you anyway!'" Instead write: "Roxanne shouted, 'Get out of here! Nobody cares about you anyway!'" People frequently speak in short sentences and in fragments. You can show this in your dialogue.

7. **Faulty capitalization (pp. 600–601):** Capitalize proper nouns—the names of specific, unique people, places, and things. In your titles, capitalize most words, even little ones like *is* and *one.* But do not capitalize articles (*a, an, the*), prepositions (*to, on, of, in,* etc.), and coordinating conjunctions (*and, but,* etc.) unless these words begin or end a title or follow a colon.

8. **Incorrect apostrophes (pp. 599–600):** Use apostrophes to show ownership or mark the omission of a letter in a contraction: "Maria's calculator isn't working."

9. **Missing commas:** These three categories govern perhaps half of our common comma mistakes:

A. Use a comma to mark where a word group at the front of a sentence ends and a main clause begins (cue words: *because, as, if, when,* etc.).

    EXAMPLE   If I finish my paper early, I will watch *The Matrix Reloaded* on DVD.

B. Use commas to enclose a <u>nonessential</u> word group within a main clause or to set it off after a main clause (cue words: *who/which,* etc.).

   EXAMPLE *The Matrix Reloaded,* which <u>follows</u> *The Matrix,* <u>uses</u> more computer animation and special camera effects than the previous film.

C. Use commas between main clauses joined by a coordinating conjunction (*and, but, or, so, yet, for, nor*).

   EXAMPLE Neo <u>gains</u> more powers in this sequel, and <u>he</u> <u>uses</u> them outside of the Matrix against the machines.

10. **Unnecessary commas:** As you learn the handful of rules that help with comma placement, you will move away from the old standby "I put commas where I hear pauses." Using your ear helps with punctuation—but only about half the time. Try to avoid unneeded commas such as those in the following examples:

   INCORRECT I went to Burger King for lunch, and then to McDonald's for dinner. (Your ear might tell you to pause, but a comma is not needed unless the two word groups you are joining with *and* are complete sentences.)

   CORRECT I went to Burger King for lunch and then to McDonald's for dinner.

   INCORRECT I eat three 13-ounce bags of potato chips every day, because I want to have a heart attack. (You might naturally pause before *because,* but it begins an essential clause that explains *why* the subject eats so foolishly and should not be set off with a comma.)

   CORRECT I eat three 13-ounce bags of potato chips every day because I want to have a heart attack.

11. **Faulty pronoun reference and agreement:** Pronouns must refer to a specific noun, and they must agree with that noun in number:

   REFERENCE ERROR Florence was talking to Abby when *she* saw the accident. (Clarify *she* reference: *she* = Abby.)

   AGREEMENT ERROR *Each* of the players want a raise. (*All . . . want . . .*)

After editing on your own, don't be reluctant to seek help. Every writer benefits from critical input. You will undoubtedly spend class time editing collaboratively, but don't stop there. Look for help from your family, friends, instructor, and writing center—all valuable resources to help you improve your work.

See pp. 596–597 for more on finding and correcting unnecessary commas.

For more on pronoun problems, see Chapter 25.

JOURNAL / BLOG ENTRY 14.3

By now, your draft should have all the important details in place, words carefully chosen, and sentence flowing smoothly. Review your Improvement Chart to focus on pattern errors, and then *slooowly* edit your paper, word by word, line by line. List at least three errors from the editing review list that you found in your draft, and then write out the corrections.

FEEDBACK *Exchange final drafts with a classmate and give editing suggestions, using the checklist on p. 333.*

Proofreading

Proofreading is the last polishing step in preparing your paper. After you have closely edited your draft, catching mechanical errors, you will print out what could be your final copy. But before turning it in for a grade, you need to make a few last checks.

HOW TO PROOFREAD AND PREPARE YOUR FINAL MANUSCRIPT

1. Check for typographical errors such as misspelled, run-together, and omitted words. Often, when fixing errors in the editing stage, we slip up in small ways on the keyboard. **Be sure to spell check once again.**

2. If necessary, prepare a title page.

3. Check the following carefully: font size (12 point), line spacing (double space), margins (1 inch), and capitalization of title (see "Common Editing Problems," number 7).

4. Spell check any additional required material, such as outlines and audience profiles.

5. Staple or paper clip your pages. Avoid putting the paper in a plastic sleeve, which most instructors consider a nuisance.

JOURNAL / BLOG ENTRY 14.4

Reflect for a moment on your work in producing this essay. Now write a page telling your instructor (and, if on a blog, your classmates) what challenges you faced. What strategies have you learned that you will apply to your next writing assignment?

FEEDBACK   *Comment on a classmate's reflective remarks; relate to his or her experience, providing a comparison or contrast.*

FINAL-DRAFT CHECKLIST: ESSAYS

- [ ] 1. Have you used several major examples to illustrate your thesis?
- [ ] 2. Is your thesis effective?
- [ ] 3. Is the hook of your introductory paragraph effective?
- [ ] 4. Is your introductory paragraph well developed?
- [ ] 5. Are your body paragraphs arranged by space, time, or importance?
- [ ] 6. Have you introduced each body paragraph with a topic sentence?
- [ ] 7. Are your body paragraphs well developed?
- [ ] 8. Are sentences well linked within and between paragraphs?
- [ ] 9. Is your concluding paragraph effective?
- [ ] 10. Have you used specific words, sensory details, active verbs, and *-ing* words?
- [ ] 11. Have you tried a comparison like a metaphor or simile?
- [ ] 12. Are your sentences varied in length and beginnings?
- [ ] 13. Have you avoided repeating words too often and including unneeded words?

14. Have you written an interesting title? Have you checked its capitalization?

15. Have you edited your work closely (including having at least one other person edit)? Have you checked your Improvement Chart for pattern errors?

16. Have you looked for errors involving the following: misspellings, sound-alike words, missing words, wrong words, sentence fragments, comma splices/run-ons, faulty capitalization, incorrect apostrophes, missing commas, unnecessary commas, and faulty pronoun reference and agreement?

17. Have you prepared your paper according to the format expected by your instructor?

HINT

Check to see if you need a title page. Be sure you have double spaced, left at least a 1-inch margin, and used a 12-point font.

ACTIVITY 14.2 WORKING ONLINE: *Putting a Professional Essay to the Test*

Find an online article that is of interest to you. It might be about sports, fashion, or movies. You might begin your search on ESPN.com, *Cosmopolitan* magazine (www.cosmopolitan.com/), or *Entertainment Weekly* (www.ew.com). Once you've read the article, answer the following questions: Is there a hook? Is there a clear thesis statement? Are all the body paragraphs fully developed? Does the author use concrete details? Does the author use sensory details? Is there a strong conclusion? If you feel the article could use help in any area, write a description of what *you* would revise if you were the magazine's editor.

ACTIVITY 14.3 WORKING ONLINE: *Revising Essays Review*

Take the Chapter 14 Review Quiz at www.mhhe.com/brannan.

Chapter Summary

1. Revising essays requires patience and time.

2. Having a clear sense of audience helps writers make decisions as they revise.

3. Writers often revise as they write, stopping to change a word or add a comma, but first drafts should focus mainly on organization and development.

4. As focus, organization, and content are established, writers should spend more time with style and mechanics.

5. Editing requires a slow reading and rereading of a paper, word by word, concentrating on a few potential errors each time.

6. Other people can help you in all stages of the revision process, including editing.

7. Keeping an Improvement Chart (see the back of this book) and editing with pattern errors in mind will improve your editing results.

8. Proofreading the final polished and printed copy of your essay is the last step in the revision process.

English Review Note

Create an ESL rubric together with your instructor, a tutor, or a writing lab assistant. Make use of the Improvement Chart in the back of this book.

Defining Terms, Clarifying Ideas

15

[*How would you define* **energy**? *How many different definitions can you think of for this single word? What associations do you have with it?*]

KEY TOPICS

- Developing skills and exploring ideas in definition essays
  - Defining with synonyms
  - Defining by negation
  - Defining with comparisons
  - Defining formally
  - Creating extended definitions
- Analyzing student models: Definition essays
- Writing a definition essay

What Are We Trying to Achieve and Why?

Setting the Stage

Most of us will immediately recognize this object: a box. We probably view the word *box* as uncomplicated, its meaning clear. But how simple is it?

In a dictionary, we find a number of definitions. Do we mean "a container typically constructed with four sides perpendicular to the base and often having a lid or cover"? How about "a square or rectangle" or "a compartment in a theater"? If we were British, we might mean "a gift or gratuity." *Box* is also a verb, so we might mean "to slap or hit," as in "box his ears." If we were collecting sap for making maple syrup, we might mean "to cut a hole (in a tree)," or if we were painting, we might mean "to blend (paint) by pouring alternately between two containers." Or maybe we just want to put a few old clothes in storage—"to box them up."

Does *box* still seem simple? Whenever we try to limit the meaning of a word, to clarify it and separate it from other meanings, we are **defining,** the focus of Chapter 15. As we move through the chapter, you will see how you can use brief definitions with expanded definitions based on the patterns of development from Unit Two to develop definition essays.

For more on the patterns of development, see pp. 9–10, 346–347, 355.

Linking to Previous Experience

In our own lives, we define daily. At home, your 6-year-old son wants to know what you mean by *responsibility,* so you tell him about the jobs people have, providing several examples. At work, the waiter you are training knows nothing about wine, so you find yourself defining *cabernet* and *chardonnay.* In school, you might have to define terms like *democracy, republican,* and *free enterprise.* Whenever we explain a word with another word, a phrase, a comparison, or an example, we are defining.

In this text, we have used definition in every chapter. In Chapter 6, Lani Houston uses narration to reveal what *leadership* means to her; in Chapter 8, Chanthan Srouch defines *mall crashers* by classifying three groups; in Chapter 11, Dave Harrison uses contrast to help define the meaning of *hard work* in college. All the patterns of development that we have worked with in this course are forms of definition.

Also, each pattern depends on examples, and as we develop them, we answer the question "What exactly do I mean by that word or statement?" This, too, is definition.

Finally, definition ties to the essential concept of the Language Line, introduced in Chapter 5.

JOURNAL / BLOG ENTRY 15.1

Have you recently defined something or heard someone else (a friend, newscaster, teacher, etc.) doing so? What was being defined—a technical term like *website,* a job like *veterinary technician,* or an abstraction like *beauty*? Was the definition intended to entertain, inform, or persuade? Did the definition

When we define, we *limit* the meaning of a term, making it more specific.

accomplish its purpose? In a paragraph, summarize the definition and tell what its purpose was and whether that purpose was accomplished.

FEEDBACK   *Read a classmate's definition and ask two questions about the word and how it was used or defined, according to the writer. What other patterns are at work so far in the writer's definition?*

Developing Skills and Exploring Ideas in Definition Essays

This section will help you to thoroughly define terms and to write definition essays. There are a variety of approaches to developing brief definitions (through synonyms, negation, comparisons, or formal definition) and extended definitions (through various patterns of development—description, narration, illustration, etc.).

Defining with Synonyms

See p. 355 for a list of methods for developing definition essays.

One method for developing a definition is to use a **synonym**—a word that is roughly equivalent in meaning to the one being defined. For example, if you say, "Granddad is feeling cantankerous today," you could substitute *grouchy* or *disagreeable*. However, if you used *angry*, you would be saying something different—intensifying his irritable mood. Words often have subtle shades of meaning, so writers must take care when choosing substitutes. Keep in mind also that, to be useful, the synonym should be more familiar to readers than the word being defined.

| ACTIVITY 15.1 | WORKING TOGETHER: *Defining with Synonyms* |

Using a dictionary, find two synonyms (one can be a phrase) for each <u>underlined</u> word in the following sentences. Next, with group members use a dictionary to help you come up with an inaccurate synonym—a word whose meaning is near that of the original but in some way alters it. Then explain why this word is different from the original. See if each member of the group can suggest a different inaccurate synonym.

EXAMPLE: Because Jason won't listen to others, I would call him a <u>maverick</u>.

Synonyms: *dissenter, independent in thought and action*

Inaccurate synonym: *radical*   Reason: *Radical suggests "extreme" behavior, and Jason can be independent without being extreme (although he might be extreme too).*

1. Nobody trusts Mark anymore; he's a <u>weasel</u>.

   Synonyms: _____

   Inaccurate synonym: _____ Reason: _____

   _____

2. Sonya spends too much time making decisions, <u>vacillating</u> continually.

   Synonyms: _____

   Inaccurate synonym: _____ Reason: _____

   _____

Choose a synonym that is more familiar than the word being defined.

3. Angelina's accident <u>ruined</u> her Subaru.

Synonyms: _____

Inaccurate synonym: _____ Reason: _____

_____

4. Isabella's <u>premonition</u> about her uncle's death was correct.

Synonyms: _____

Inaccurate synonym: _____ Reason: _____

_____

5. Medical researchers are worried that the avian flu will <u>mutate</u> and trigger a pandemic.

Synonyms: _____

Inaccurate synonym: _____ Reason: _____

_____

Defining by Negation

Another way to narrow a word's meaning is through **negation.** When you negate, you say what the word is not and then what it is or what you will argue it is in your essay. For example, you might say, "*Marriage* is not just a legally binding contract between two people in love; it is a deeply felt personal lifelong commitment." Or you might say, "Being *loyal* is not just supporting a person when everyone else does; it is sticking by the person when almost no one else will."

Defining by negation is especially useful when an audience might disagree with your definition (persuasive writing, for instance, often uses negation). Even when a reader doesn't view your definition differently, the word may simply have close shades of meaning that you wish to clarify. For instance, you might say, "Emily is assertive, not aggressive" or "Jack is a person with opinions but not an opinionated person."

HINT

A writer's definition of a term can be a personalized definition that the writer argues for.

ACTIVITY 15.2 | *Defining by Negation*

Using either a dictionary or your own knowledge, work to write a one- or two-sentence definition by negation for the following terms. Remember to include both what the term is not and what it is.

EXAMPLE

Landscaping: *Landscaping is not just the activity of planting shrubs, trees, and so on around a property; it is a skilled profession that requires a great deal of horticultural knowledge and an art that demands a sense of esthetics.*

1. Hip-hop: _____

_____

_____

2. Work: _____

_____

HINT

A semicolon can effectively divide two main clauses in a sentence of negation.

3. Environmentalism: _____

_____

4. Teenager: _____

_____

_____

5. Vacation: _____

_____

Defining with Comparisons

Brief definitions can be given using **metaphors** and **similes,** figures of speech that compare things. A metaphor makes the comparison indirectly by simply substituting one thing for another; a simile makes it directly by including the word *like* or *as.* In explaining how water moves up through a tree, here is how we could use each approach:

METAPHOR   Phloem and xylem are pathways for carrying nutrients—river channels in the main trunk, becoming streams in the branches and trickles in the leaf stems.

SIMILE   Phloem and xylem are like pathways for carrying nutrients . . .

Here are two tips for using metaphors and similes: First, compare the term being defined to something readers would know and accept as an accurate comparison. Second, avoid clichés, such as "Websites are sprouting like weeds."

HINT

For more on figures of speech and clichés, see pp. 498–503.

ACTIVITY 15.3 | *Defining with Comparisons*

In a sentence, create a brief metaphor or simile for the following terms.

EXAMPLE

A prison is *like a moon, spinning in space, a separate world for the unwilling colonists, cut off from the mother planet a short space fight away.*

Dating is *a minefield from which few leave without wounds.*

_____

1. Depression is _____

2. Freedom is _____

3. Alzheimer's is _____

4. A rain forest is _____

5. The subway is _____

Defining Formally

Another way to define is with a **formal definition,** such as those found in dictionaries. Formal definitions are often a good jumping-off point for developing definition essays.

To create a formal definition, put your term in a group or category and then add examples, details, and explanations that separate it from other members of the group. A formal definition therefore has three parts:

Term	Group or category	Examples: details explanations
Beagle	Breed of hound	Short legs; drooping ears; white, black, and tan markings
Aerobics	System of physical conditioning	Designed to enhance circulatory and respiratory efficiency; involves vigorous sustained exercise—jogging, swimming, cycling, and so on
Culture shock	Mental and emotional condition	Characterized by the confusion and anxiety that occur when a person is suddenly exposed to an alien culture or milieu

Examples and details separate a term from other members of its group.

In writing out a formal definition, use a verb like *is* or *means* to link a term with its group and identifying features—for example, *A beagle is a breed of hound with short legs, drooping ears, and white, black, and tan markings.*

Here are three common problems in writing formal definitions:

1. **Vague, general groups and details**

   - If you indicated the group as "kind of animal" instead of "breed of hound," readers would miss an essential defining element—a beagle is a dog.

   - If you omitted the details "short legs" and "white, black, and tan markings," a bloodhound might also fit the description.

2. **Circular defining** (using a term to define itself)

   - You tell readers little if you say, "Aerobics is a form of aerobic exercise."

3. ***Where*** and ***when*** **replacing categories**

   - Readers lose information if you say, "Culture shock is *when* a person is confused and anxious after coming in abrupt contact with a culture different from her own." Instead of *when*, give the category: "mental and emotional condition."

If this method looks familiar, it may be because we have used it throughout this book, beginning with the Language Line in Chapter 5 and the discussion in Chapter 7 of developing paragraphs by becoming increasingly specific with examples, details, and explanations.

ACTIVITY 15.4 *Defining Formally*

Using a dictionary, write out a one-sentence formal definition of each of the following terms. You may quote directly or put the definition in your own words. Underline the group or category each term falls into, and include specific examples, details, and explanations.

EXAMPLE

Aerobics is ___*a system of physical conditioning designed to enhance*___ *circulatory and respiratory efficiency through vigorous sustained exercise, such as jogging.*

1. Affirmative action is _____

   _____

   _____

2. A bat mitzvah is _____
   _____
3. A piñata is _____
   _____
   _____
4. Kwanzaa is _____
   _____
5. Global warming is _____
   _____

The patterns of
development in
Unit Two include:
description,
narration, illustration,
comparison/contrast,
classification, cause/
effect, and process
analysis.

Creating Extended Definitions

Sometimes, particularly when dealing with complex terms, you need to extend a definition to essay length. For definition essays, you will use not only brief definitions but also several of the patterns of development from Unit Two. That is, you create extended definitions by mixing several patterns. Notice how such mixing, which characterizes well-developed professional writing, is used to help define the term *scuba* in the following paragraph from "Get Wet," the chapter's annotated student model:

Process analysis
Comparison

Cause and effect
Process analysis

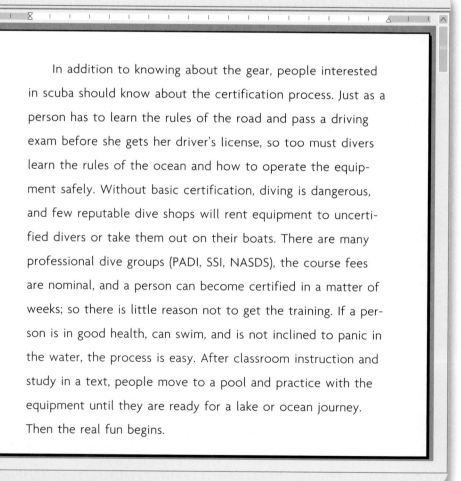

In addition to knowing about the gear, people interested in scuba should know about the certification process. Just as a person has to learn the rules of the road and pass a driving exam before she gets her driver's license, so too must divers learn the rules of the ocean and how to operate the equipment safely. Without basic certification, diving is dangerous, and few reputable dive shops will rent equipment to uncertified divers or take them out on their boats. There are many professional dive groups (PADI, SSI, NASDS), the course fees are nominal, and a person can become certified in a matter of weeks; so there is little reason not to get the training. If a person is in good health, can swim, and is not inclined to panic in the water, the process is easy. After classroom instruction and study in a text, people move to a pool and practice with the equipment until they are ready for a lake or ocean journey. Then the real fun begins.

ACTIVITY 15.5 | WORKING TOGETHER: *Creating Extended Definitions*

With group members, choose one of the terms from the list below, brainstorm, and then define the term in four different ways, using each of the following patterns of development. You might assign one or two types of definition per member and split up, then regroup to finish the exercise.

1. **Comparison/contrast:** showing how the term is like/unlike similar terms

2. **Classification/division:** putting the term into a group or separating it from others like it

3. **Cause/effect:** telling what actions can affect the term and what effects can flow from it

4. **Process analysis:** telling how some part of the term works

Include specific examples and details. Don't be surprised if a pattern incorporates several others—for instance, if description and narration occur within a comparison.

Terms to choose from (or choose from the Topics List, p. 353):

dating   teenager   vegetarianism   ideal vacation   greed

cheap   workaholic   hero   carbon footprint   sexual harassment

EXAMPLE: Term to define: **pregnancy**

1. Comparison and/or contrast: *In my first trimester I felt like I was terminally seasick and permanently at sea. I threw up constantly, was dizzy and bumping into walls, and was confined to my "cabin" so much I longed to be anywhere else.*

2. Classification/division: *Pregnancy can be divided into three stages: the first, second, and third trimesters.*

3. Cause/effect: *Not only was I sick for the first six months of my pregnancy, but I watched in horror as my weight climbed through the ceiling. By my eighth month I weighed fifty-five pounds more than I had before and looked like a walrus.*

4. Process analysis: *I knew my baby needed the food I was shoveling in. I watched as the embryo grew, beginning as a few cells; developing a head, arms, and legs; and finally transforming into a beautiful child. Protected in other ways by the placental wall, he would still starve to death without the nutrients flowing through the umbilical cord. I had a duty to feed my baby, and, oh brother, did I ever!*

Analyzing Student Models: Definition Essays

As you read through the following essays—"Finding Home," "Deaf, Not Dumb," and "Get Wet"—look for the ways of defining we have discussed: synonyms, negation, metaphors/similes, formal definitions, and the patterns of development. Also note that none of the essays examines its topic exhaustively. When you write your essay, you will need to decide how to focus it.

➡ *Prereading Exploration for "Finding Home"*

April Griffin defines the concept of *home*. Because home is a universal concept, her potential audience is huge, but she narrowed it by specifying families that do not support one another as much as they should.

Record prereading responses in your journal or on your blog.

1. Reflect for a moment on the meaning of home. How do you define this concept?

2. List three things you see as an important part of an ideal home.

Key Points: Building Definition Essays

1

Title: arouses readers' curiosity and links to the essay's main point

Introductory paragraph: begins with a hook and ends with a thesis sentence

2

Body paragraphs: begin with a topic sentence that names each main example and makes a limiting statement about it

3

Finding Home

"Welcome to Our Happy Home." Perhaps you have read this phrase in an entryway or hanging over a doorway. I know that I have seen the welcome many times when entering my friends' and family members' homes. What makes the home happy? Is it the house, decorated in warm, inviting colors, furnished with all the modern conveniences, or is it the people who live inside? I believe a home is not defined by the physical structure but by the people who live in it. Home is a place where a person feels safe, relaxed, and loved.

The most basic requirement of a home is that a person can feel safe there. Of course physical safety is essential—protection from the weather, animals, and people—but there are also emotional and mental securities. It is hard to feel comfortable in a home surrounded by people who attack each other in small ways. "What do you have to be so down about?" "You'll never make the team." "He's too good for you." These kinds of comments make a person feel small and uncertain. And it can be just as bad when a person's ideas are belittled. "You don't know what you're talking about." "That's a stupid thing to say." Buildings with families that behave this way are more houses than homes, places where people stay out of habit and need but not because they feel secure.

Another important part of a true home is that people can relax there. When we feel safe, we can begin to feel at ease in our surroundings. If family members are considerate of one another, they will give each other the space each needs; they will give each other the time and opportunity to unwind in whatever way works best for each. Some listen to music, some watch TV, and some just appreciate lying down on a couch. A true home encourages relaxation. At the end of a busy, stressful day out "there," we all need to escape the pressures of being productive. If we can find this room in our homes, we can recover our perspective and gather energy again to face a new day. A home in which a person can relax is a home in which she can stay sane.

But to me what most defines a home is love. In a loving home people do not just avoid hurting one another and then leave each other alone. They try to involve themselves in each other's lives. If someone has had a hard day at work or school, and she looks depressed or frustrated, people in a caring family talk to her, share their thoughts and feelings, and try to help her out of her bad mood. In a loving home people know what matters to each of the others and what activities each is involved in. In contrast is the house or apartment empty except for one person who wants no one else in his life, or the house shared with another person, not with love but for convenience.

A real home is not just a place where a person can safely hang her hat and be left alone. A real home consists of people—no matter what structure they live in—who try to create a loving environment. A house, apartment, cabin, wigwam, or grass hut—all can be true homes. A church group, sports team, or group of friends—all can be families, and where they gather can be a home. As long as a person is loved, he can feel at home in any place or with any group. One part of a definition from *The American Heritage College Dictionary* calls a home "the center or heart of something." What better thing comes from the heart than love?

—April Griffin

Development: uses specific examples, action, dialogue, active verbs (*attack*), *-ing* words (*loving*), and specific words (*American Heritage*); tells thoughts and emotions; and explains the examples ("And it can be just as bad when a person's ideas are belittled"). Uses brief definitions: synonyms (*house = home*), negation (par. 1), and patterns of development (cause/effect and comparison/contrast, par. 2)

4

Sentence connectors: guide readers: transitions, repeat words, synonyms, pronouns, and reference to main idea

Style points: increase readability. Using questions and the pronouns *you* and *we* to *intentionally* speak to the audience can involve your readers (par's. 1 and 3). Dashes can set off lists in sentences (par. 2) and provide emphasis (par. 5). Imagined dialogue can create variety (par. 2)

5

Concluding paragraph: restates the thesis, briefly summarizes, and adds a final (expanded) thought

➤ Prereading Exploration for "Deaf, Not Dumb"

Bruce Hayworth has a clear purpose in this essay about the hearing impaired. He thought that people who have little experience with the deaf could use the information he provides, but he particularly wanted to speak to fellow college students.

1. Name a group you are part of that is little understood and possibly misrepresented.

HINT

Record prereading responses in your journal or on your blog.

2. Consider racial or ethnic minorities, groups drawn together by a common interest (heavy metal, knitting, books), or cliques in high school. List one group and three inaccurate statements you have heard made about it.

Key Points: Building Definition Essays

Title: arouses readers' curiosity and links to the essay's main point

1

Introductory paragraph: begins with a hook and ends with a thesis sentence

Body paragraphs: begin with a topic sentence that names each main example and makes a limiting statement about it

2

Development: uses specific examples, action, dialogue, active verbs (*gawk*), -*ing* words (*hearing*), and specific words (*Japan*); tells thoughts and emotions; explains the examples ("There are many degrees of partial hearing loss . . ."). Creates brief definitions, including through synonyms (*hearing impaired = deaf*) and negation (the title), and extended definitions through patterns of development (process analysis and comparison/contrast, par. 3)

Sentence connectors: guide readers: transitions, repeat words, synonyms, pronouns, and reference to main idea

3

Style points: increase readability. Using exclamations can arouse interest (par. 1). Proper nouns can be represented by initials after the first mention, for economy (*ASL*, par. 3). Similes can be implied (ASL signers compared to mimes, par. 3). Rhetorical questions (statements disguised as questions that produce a predictable response from readers) can engage readers (par. 5)

Deaf, Not Dumb

"You're a dummy, and so's your old lady and old man!" These were fighting words for me as a child, and I ended up rolling around in the dirt more than once with the kids from school who said them. Growing up with hearing-impaired parents in the sixties, if I was not fighting some kid in an alley, it seemed like I was trying to explain to some other child that my family was normal. We just didn't talk much with words. Back then most people didn't know much about the deaf community, and even today I often see people turn and gawk at the hearing impaired when they are signing to each other. Maybe knowing more about the deaf will make those in the hearing world see them as less strange.

Everyone knows that *deaf* means the inability to hear, but not everyone knows what causes it or to what degree it can affect people. First, not all hearing-impaired people have profound or complete hearing loss. There are many degrees of partial hearing loss, with some occurring progressively as people get older. Those who have been able to hear somewhat from birth are more likely to articulate well, while those completely deaf from birth have problems speaking clearly. Hearing loss might be caused by congenital nerve damage or by diseases like meningitis, rubella, and chicken pox, especially in early childhood. Worldwide there are 300 million people with some form of hearing impairment.

Many, though not all, of these people communicate through some form of sign language. In the United States most of the deaf learn American Sign Language (ASL), which differs from sign used in other countries like England or Japan. ASL communicates primarily through gestures and signs made with the hands and arms but also frequently adds the fingerspelling of words, using letters from the English alphabet. Signing is visual, often theatrical, and can be beautiful, depending on how skilled the signer is. People express their personalities in how they sign. Some are reserved,

---

their signing and body language economical. Others are expansive, exaggerating their gestures and body language to make the "listener" laugh. Some signers can be as entertaining as professional mimes, and even nonsigners can follow and enjoy the story.

ASL serves the deaf community well, but their most serious communication problems are in the hearing world. Few hearing people sign, so most of the hearing impaired have learned to read lips, but this has its limitations. Often only part of the message gets across because the speaker says the words too quickly or turns away, requiring the deaf person to frequently ask for clarification or miss the point. When, for instance, this noncommunication happens often enough in a classroom, the hearing students sometimes think the deaf student is unintelligent, rather than merely missing the words spoken so clearly to those who can hear. If hearing-impaired students have enough difficulties in a classroom that cannot or will not understand them, their education suffers, which affects their future employment prospects and so the rest of their lives.

The deaf have many difficulties to overcome to compete in the larger world of those who hear. Maybe knowing something about the causes of hearing impairment, how widespread it is, how the deaf "speak," and how they can be helped or hurt by the hearing, will make the general public more sensitive to this minority. In the same way that we might go out of our way to be courteous to a nonnative speaker, say, a visitor from Russia or Thailand, we should do so for the hearing-impaired. Sometimes we do need to slow our lips down or at least allow them to be seen. Being willing to write and read notes can also help, and learning a little basic ASL is a way to welcome the nonnative "speaker" into our hearing world. In a society as privileged as ours, is a moment's worth of consideration for those who have so much to offer too much to ask?

—Bruce Hayworth

> **Concluding paragraph:** restates the thesis, briefly summarizes, and adds a final (expanded) thought

POSTREADING QUESTIONS FOR ESSAY ANALYSIS

Note: These questions apply to either "Finding Home" or "Deaf, Not Dumb."

1. Where is the thesis located? What is the topic, and what statement limits it?

2. Why is the hook effective? Which of the Chapter 12 hooks (pp. 275–277) has the author used?

3. What introductory paragraph method(s) from Chapter 12 (pp. 266–279) has the author used to develop the essay's opening? Why might the introduction interest the audience stated in the prereading exploration?

4. Why might the lead sentence in the concluding paragraph be effective?

5. What concluding paragraph method(s) from Chapter 12 (pp. 285–293) has the author used to develop the essay's close? What is the expanded thought? Why might the conclusion interest the target audience?

6. What patterns of development or brief definition strategies has the author used (pp. 342–347, 355)? How did any three of these help you further understand the term being defined?

7. For each topic sentence, what are the topic, the limiting statement, and the connecting words? (For more on connecting sentences, see pp. 53–59 and 293–294.)

8. How are the body paragraphs arranged: chronologically or by order of importance? What connector words reveal this?

9. Choose a paragraph in which the author has explained an example clearly. How does the explanation help you understand the paragraph's main point?

10. Why do you think a given paragraph is well written? Consider topic sentences, connecting words, sensory details, specific words, action description, dialogue, metaphors/comparisons, sentence variety, and clear explanations.

11. What are five instances of specific language?

See p. 285 for a review of lead and summary sentences.

Consider how the conclusion links with the introduction.

WRITING A DEFINITION ESSAY
Summarizing the Assignment

This assignment asks you to define a word as completely as possible within a 500- to 600-word essay. The word may name a physical object, place, activity, group, or person. Or it may name a **concept**—an abstraction not knowable through the senses. Concepts include ideas, emotions, and qualities; words like *freedom, love,* and *goodness* name concepts. A major goal for this assignment is for you to *consciously* work with patterns of development from Unit Two. This work will help your writing become more diverse and interesting.

Your paper will consist of about five or six paragraphs, three or four of which will be in the body. Because introductory and concluding paragraphs are such crucial elements in essays, you should work hard on them. You should also, of course, begin each body paragraph with a strong topic sentence.

Establishing Audience and Purpose

Writing effective definitions depends on understanding your readers and what they need or want to know about your term. For example, a writer might *over*explain *aerobic exercise* if he forgot that his target reader commonly rides her bicycle one hundred miles each week. Or a writer could easily *under*explain a complicated term and quickly confuse readers. For example, if a biology major wrote the formula

$$6CO_2 + 12H_2O \xrightarrow{\text{light}} C_6H_{12}O_6 + 6O_2 + 6H_2O$$

and began talking about light and chemical energy, carbon dioxide, and chlorophyll without first explaining that he was defining *photosynthesis*

See Chapters 5–11 and 16 for more on other patterns of development.

and giving a general description of photosynthesis, most readers would rapidly be lost.

Furthermore, if a writer has no sense of readers' understanding of the term, how can she know when negation might be useful, what synonyms might work best, or what metaphor or simile readers might respond to? Having a clear sense of audience will help you choose material your readers will be interested in and understand.

As usual, you may have several purposes—to entertain, persuade, or inform—but defining clearly should be the top priority.

Working through the Writing Assignment

Discovering Ideas

As you search for topics, remember the distinction between abstract and concrete terms: **Abstract terms** cannot be known through the senses whereas **concrete terms** have weight, texture, color, and so forth. A rose is concrete; grab one quickly, and you may feel the prick of its thorns. You might define *rose* as a concrete term and develop an extended definition around it, but you could also treat it as a specific example illustrating a more abstract term, say, *beauty* or *symmetry*. The topics list gives suggestions for both concrete and abstract terms, with most of the abstractions in the concepts group.

Whether you choose a term from the list or one of your own, a good way to begin prewriting is to look up the term in a dictionary. If your term has multiple meanings, select one meaning, to focus your essay. To further focus the essay, ask yourself, "What part of this subject am *I* most interested in; what part is an *essential*, defining element; what part would my *audience* care about?"

Focus on only one meaning of your term.

Search for an essential, defining element of your term.

For additional definition topics, look under Chapter 15 at www.mhhe.com/brannan.

POSSIBLE TOPICS: DEFINITION

- **Family:** mother, father, brother, sister, uncle, aunt, grandmother, grandfather, husband, wife, son, daughter

- **Occupations:** nurse, lawyer, architect, engineer, accountant, minister, salesperson, coach, counselor, teacher, musician, carpenter

- **Fields:** welding, paralegal work, nursing, dental hygiene, fashion merchandising, travel

- **Groups:** sports teams, choir, debate team, Girl Scouts, Shriners, clubs (gun club, book club), PTA, Democrats, Republicans, gang, minority

- **Places:** zoos, parks, sports arenas, beaches, cemeteries, websites, retail stores, restaurants, libraries, schools (any kind)

- **Activities:** dating, shopping, driving, moving, playing sports (baseball, hiking, diving), traveling

- **Behavior:** kind, cruel, responsible, irresponsible, truthful, deceptive, generous, selfish, charitable

- **Personal adornment:** jewelry, makeup, tattoos, piercing, hair coloring, hair styling, fingernail polishing

- **Illnesses/dysfunctions:** AIDS, smallpox, diphtheria, malaria, measles, mumps, chicken pox, cancer, meningitis, alcoholism, cirrhosis

- **Concepts:** marriage, divorce, family, capital punishment, emotional states (love, hate, envy, joy, depression), beauty, good, evil, home, addiction, music, employer, employee, co-worker, bore, leader, follower, man, woman, art, education, work, play, slang, intelligence, sex appeal, fashion, self-esteem, discrimination, virtual reality

Conservation in Context

DEFINE A GREEN TERM

Write an extended definition of one of the following words or phrases, helping readers to see the term in relation to a global, local, or personal conservation commitment: *environmentalism, ecology, organic food, green, nature, climate change, global warming, conservation, carbon credits, endangered species, deforestation, rain forest, coral reef, water, resources, recycling, Earth Day, car pool, national park, beach, litter, energy* (see photos on p. 340), *Kyoto Treaty.* ●

Prewriting

After you have chosen several terms, explore them by using any of the prewriting methods from Chapter 1 together with the methods for developing brief and extended definitions:

METHODS FOR DEVELOPING DEFINITION ESSAYS

1. **Brief definitions**
   - Synonyms (similar words)
   - Negation (not that, but this)
   - Comparisons (metaphor/simile)
   - Formal (grouping and detailing)

2. **Extended definitions:** patterns of development
   - Narration: telling a brief story to make a point about the term
   - Description: using vivid details to show something about the term
   - Illustration: giving examples to make a point about the term
   - Comparison/contrast: showing how the term is like and unlike other, similar terms
   - Classification: putting the term into a group or separating it from others like it
   - Cause/effect: telling what actions can affect the term and what consequences can flow from the term
   - Process analysis: telling how some part of the term works

For example, using the questioning prewriting method, you can ask questions that apply the brief definition methods to your term. For the term *scuba*, you could ask questions like these:

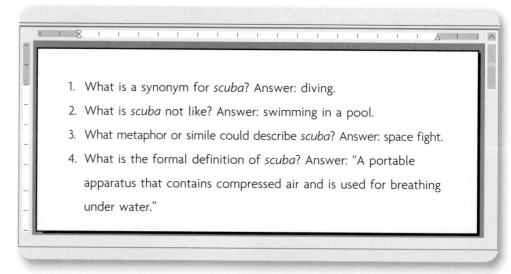

1. What is a synonym for *scuba*? Answer: diving.

2. What is *scuba* not like? Answer: swimming in a pool.

3. What metaphor or simile could describe *scuba*? Answer: space fight.

4. What is the formal definition of *scuba*? Answer: "A portable apparatus that contains compressed air and is used for breathing under water."

Or you can combine clustering with the patterns of development for extended definitions:

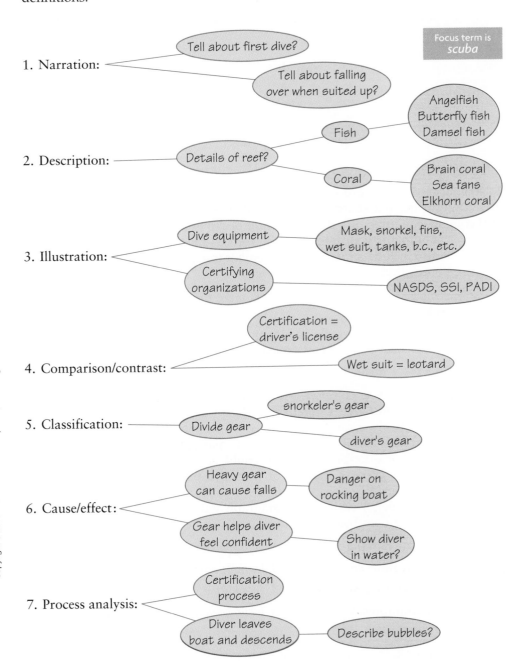

1. Narration: — Tell about first dive? / Tell about falling over when suited up?

Focus term is *scuba*

2. Description: — Details of reef? — Fish — Angelfish / Butterfly fish / Damsel fish / Coral — Brain coral / Sea fans / Elkhorn coral

3. Illustration: — Dive equipment — Mask, snorkel, fins, wet suit, tanks, b.c., etc. / Certifying organizations — NASDS, SSI, PADI

4. Comparison/contrast: — Certification = driver's license / Wet suit = leotard

5. Classification: — Divide gear — snorkeler's gear / diver's gear

6. Cause/effect: — Heavy gear can cause falls — Danger on rocking boat / Gear helps diver feel confident — Show diver in water?

7. Process analysis: — Certification process / Diver leaves boat and descends — Describe bubbles?

Because one goal of the definition essay assignment is to use several patterns, thinking about all of them during your initial brainstorming, as illustrated above, can move you quickly into a substantial first rough draft.

PREWRITING—SUMMING UP

1. Choose several topics from the list, or choose several of your own.
2. Consider defining a concept rather than a concrete term.
3. Try both questioning and clustering, using the methods discussed previously.
4. Decide on a purpose and point for your definition essay.

HINT

To see how the author of "Get Wet" used the material gathered from questioning and clustering in his essay, turn to pages 362–364.

┌──────────────────────────────
JOURNAL / BLOG ENTRY 15.2

Write a paragraph telling why you have chosen your term. What about it makes you want to explore it further? Who do you think will be interested in reading your essay, and what do you want to tell them about the term? What words in your definition will you need to explain?

Organizing Ideas

To stay focused as you proceed, write out a **thesis sentence.** Remember to name the term and make a statement about it that lets readers know a definition is forthcoming. You might use the word *define* or *definition* (as in "one way to define XYZ is . . .") or follow your term with the verb *is* or *means* (see sentence C below). You might also include a forecasting statement (see sentence C). Here are sample thesis sentences from the chapter models:

A. Maybe knowing more about the deaf will make those in the hearing world see them as less strange.

B. Most of us will never have the opportunity to voyage into outer space, but we can learn a little about the next best option for inner planetary travel, scuba diving.

C. Home is a place where a person feels safe, relaxed, and loved.

Because an essay is complex, you should create a rough outline that lists your major points and give several supporting examples for each.

You will probably arrange your body paragraphs by time or, more often, order of importance. However, a single body paragraph might differ from the overall pattern. For example, the essay could be arranged from least to most important, but one process-analysis or narrative paragraph might be ordered chronologically.

Remember to begin each body paragraph with a topic sentence linked by connectors like the ones below:

- **Locating or moving in space:** *above, against, around, behind, below, on, in*
- **Moving in time:** *after, at last, awhile, first, immediately, next, now, often, then*
- **Adding material:** *again, also, and, in addition, furthermore, as well as*
- **Giving examples:** *for example, for instance, another, one reason, in fact*
- **Comparing:** *alike, also, both, in the same way, similarly*
- **Contrasting:** *in contrast, although, but, differs from, even though, however*
- **Showing cause/effect:** *and so, as a result, because, consequently, since, so, then*
- **Summarizing/concluding:** *finally, in brief, in other words, in short, to summarize*

ORGANIZING—SUMMING UP

1. Create a rough thesis sentence to focus your material.
2. Limit body paragraphs to three or four.
3. Create a rough outline.
4. Arrange body paragraphs by time or order of importance.
5. Plan on using a topic sentence to introduce each body paragraph.
6. Review the list of transitions.

Resist the temptation to include a formal definition in your thesis in this overworked way: "As stated in *Webster's Dictionary,* home is . . . ."

To review outlines, see pp. 14–16, 284.

For more on connectors, see pp. 54–56 and pp. 293–294.

JOURNAL / BLOG ENTRY 15.3

Write out your thesis sentence. Does it state the term and indicate that a definition will follow? Create a rough outline, and list each developmental pattern you will use. Do you have enough material to thoroughly define your term?

FEEDBACK *Workshop your thesis sentences in small groups. What specific advice did you give others? What feedback did you receive?*

Drafting

With the preliminary work finished, you are almost ready to write a first draft. But before moving ahead, take a moment to review the drafting suggestions in Chapter 1 (pp. 16–17), and then do the following:

1. Remember that negation may be useful in your introductory paragraph (see "Finding Home," pp. 348–349).

2. Insert synonyms and phrase definitions in sentences, using commas, parentheses, or dashes (see "Get Wet," pp. 358–364).

3. With body paragraphs, use a single pattern of development or, as the model essays in this chapter do, mix several. But be sure to rely on specific, detailed examples.

4. Be sure to include information that touches on the essential nature of your term, and tell your readers that the information is essential.

5. Be sure to give your first draft a clear point, so that your writing will have energy and interest. The essays in this chapter can hold an audience's attention partly because each writer is interested and has a point to make. One writer has an opinion on what a good home is, another encourages people to be more sensitive to the needs of the hearing-impaired, and the third is excited about scuba diving.

HINT

Refer to pp. 266–271 when critiquing thesis statements.

JOURNAL / BLOG ENTRY 15.4

Does your first draft fit the assignment, including using *several* patterns of development? Does it focus on a single meaning of the term? Are all paragraphs developed with detailed examples and clear explanations? Are topic sentences in place? What parts of the draft do you like best, what parts least? Answer in a paragraph.

FEEDBACK *Workshop your definition essay with a trusted classmate. For revising from first- to second-stage drafts, focus on the special points listed on page 360; for revising from second- to third-stage drafts, see page 362.*

Revising Drafts

To review the detailed lists for revising drafts, turn to Chapter 14.

Annotated Student Model: "Get Wet"

If you read through the following drafts thoughtfully, you will learn many ways to improve your own definition essay.

For more on questions
related to the PODs,
see pp. 346–347 and
354–355.

First-Stage Draft

For this essay, Kyle Jennings chose an audience of people who are interested in scuba diving but have not yet tried it. He assumed that they would know a little about the sport and that they may have been snorkeling, so they would be familiar with terms like *mask, fins,* and *snorkel.* He helps define the sport by discussing several crucial elements and reveals the essence of scuba diving in his conclusion.

Having gathered material through prewriting methods including questions related to the patterns of development, Kyle wrote the following working thesis and working outline and then wrote his first draft.

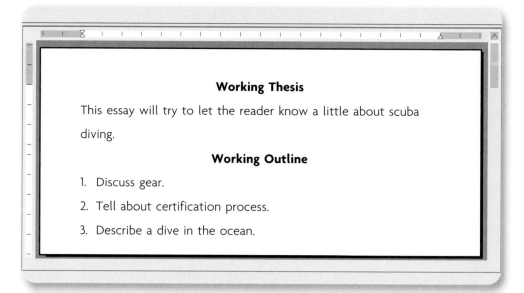

Working Thesis

This essay will try to let the reader know a little about scuba diving.

Working Outline

1. Discuss gear.

2. Tell about certification process.

3. Describe a dive in the ocean.

Begins comparison — 1

First draft lacks several patterns, examples, details, and explanations.

Creates working thesis

Lists some equipment — 2

Tells about certification — 3
process

A Definition of Diving

Being in the ocean in scuba gear is a lot like being in outer space. In the ocean you are weightless just like in space, and you depend on specialized gear to keep you safe. An astronaut has a helmet and breaths air; a diver has a face mask and breaths compressed air from special tanks on his back. Both situations often involve the people being in darkness. This essay will try to let the reader know a little about scuba diving.

A snorkeler needs a face mask, swimming fins, and a snorkel. But a diver also wears a wet suit, heavy cylinder of air for breathing with an attached regulator, weight belt, diving vest, gauges for monitoring air and time, and a compass. If this seems like a lot of equipment, it is. It's a pain to haul around and expensive.

The next thing to know about scuba is certification. Divers need to learn the rules of the ocean and how to operate the equipment. Without basic certification diving is dangerous, and only a few money-starved dive operations or so-called resort dive operations will take uncertified divers out on their boats. There are many professional dive groups, and a person can become certified in a matter of weeks; so there is little reason not to get the training. If a person is in good health and can swim, the process is easy. You just splash around in a pool for a few weeks, and then you are ready for open water, which becomes more interesting.

4 Picture yourself on a dive boat out in the ocean on your way down for that final checkout dive. You jump into the ocean and feel good. You are part of the water world with all the gear that feels so uncomfortable on land. But now it's different. In the water the gear makes you feel like a fish. Down you go, clearing the pressure, trailing bubbles, till you hang a few feet above the reef. Stretching in every direction are forests of tall, jagged corals. Brain coral of all sizes dot the sandy bottom with sea fans around. Scattered throughout the water are salt-water fish: brown and white damsels; orange and white clowns; butterfly fish; green and blue angels. You are overwhelmed and glad you shelled out the cash to get here.

5 Scuba is a great sport that everyone should try. It's a sport for all ages, from twelve to seventy. Once you are in the water, it doesn't take a lot of strength to get around; your equipment does the work for you, so the young and old both can do it. Also diving is a good sport because it brings people together. Because everyone helps one another on and off with gear and talks about things they saw on the dive, they become friendly. It's not uncommon to go out to a restaurant or bar with a new-found dive buddy after the boat docks. Diving is a wonderful sport that no one should miss.

Side annotations:

4 Describes process of ocean dive

Uses fish simile

Uses examples and descriptive details

Overuses *you*

Rough conclusion lacks summary and single focus.

Second-Stage Draft

Most first drafts are underdeveloped, lacking sufficient concrete, specific examples, details, and explanations. And they can also be unfocused. Kyle's first draft is strong, with most of the basic ideas from his prewriting in place, but he knew he had material to add, as well as some problems connecting paragraphs.

1. **Introduction:** hook, engaging support sentences, thesis
2. **Body paragraphs:** topic sentence with connector
3. **Overall development:** examples, details, explanations; brief definitions and extended definitions using patterns of development
4. **Conclusion:** connector, summary, expanded thought

Introduction reworked, adding descriptive details to strengthen comparison

Thesis revised

Topic sentence added

Classification added

Comparison added

Examples of equipment added with explanations

Cause and effect added

A Definition of Diving

1   Being in the ocean in scuba gear is a lot like being in outer space. When a diver is floating in deep water, he is in another world. He depends on the compressed air in his cylinders and his regulator to deliver it smoothly. The diver swims weightlessly through "inner space." Similarly an astronaut floats in darkness with the deepest drop imaginable all around him. He also depends on his gear to deliver air, protect him from the cold and other extremes, tell him how much air he has, and orient him toward his "boat." Most of us will never have the opportunity to go into outer space, but we can learn a little about the next best option for inner planetary travel, scuba diving.

2   To understand something about scuba as a sport, we can take a look at some of the gear. Basic diving equipment can be divided into two categories. The first is gear for a snorkeler, and the second is gear for a diver. A snorkeler or breath-hold diver needs a face mask, swimming fins, a snorkel, and sometimes a wet suit, depending on the temperature of the water. The wet suit is a skin tight coverall of rubber used to keep warmth in. Putting one on is a pain. It is much like squeezing into a really tight leotard that stretches from the neck to the ankles. A scuba diver most often wears a wet suit of varying degrees of thickness (there is a dry suit for really cold water), and in addition to the snorkelers' gear wears a heavy cylinder (or tank) of air with an attached regulator for delivering the air, weight belt, diving vest, gauges for monitoring amount of air and time underwater, and a compass. If this seems like a lot of equipment, it is. And until a

diver gets into the water, the diver is overloaded, uncomfortable, and prone to falling down. A complete set of scuba equipment is expensive (more than a thousand dollars), but many certified divers own only snorkeling gear and rent the rest.

In addition to knowing about the gear, people interested in scuba diving should know about the certification process. Just as a person has to learn the rules of the road and pass a driving exam before she gets her driver's license, so too must divers learn the rules of the ocean and how to operate the equipment safely. Without basic certification diving is dangerous. Few reputable dive shops will rent equipment to uncertified divers or take them out on their boats. There are many professional dive groups (PADI, SSI, NASDS), and the course fees are nominal. Also a person can become certified in a matter of weeks; so there is little reason not to get the training. If a person is in good health, can swim, and is not inclined to panic in the water, the process is easy. After classroom instruction and study in a text, divers move to a pool and practice with the equipment until they are ready for a lake or ocean journey. Then the real fun begins.

The most exciting part of scuba diving, naturally, is being in the water. The pool may have seemed fascinating at first, but it pales by comparison to open water, especially the waters of a reef. Teetering on the dive boat, all gear in order, the diver "strides" out and splashes into the ocean, and the diver feels in her element. The equipment she is wearing makes her part of the environment, like she belongs, something of a fish. Down the diver sinks, clearing the pressure in her ears, trailing bubbles, equalizing buoyancy till she is floating, weightless, above the reef. Stretching in every direction are forests of tall, jagged corals. Light-brown brain coral ranging in size from basketballs to boulders dot the pale sandy bottom with purple sea fans rocking at their feet. Scattered throughout the coral are the cousins of all those captive saltwater aquarium fish: brown and white damsels; orange- and white-striped clowns; yellow butterfly fish; lime-green and blue angels. The new diver hovers, amazed by the beauty of inner space, eager to see more.

3 Transition added to topic sentence

Comparison added

Examples added

Explanation added

4 Topic sentence added

You pronoun replaced

Gender pronoun *he* shifted to *she*

Examples, details, action words added

Brief summary added 5

> Scuba is a wonderful sport that only requires the right equipment and proper training to open a new world to the diver. It is a safe sport for all ages, and one that brings people together. Because a number one rule in diving is to pair up before going under, people meet quickly. They help each other with their gear. Then they dive together and share their experiences back on board. "Did you see the size of that lobster?" "How about those amber jacks?" "The mantas looked like flying saucers!" This is the essence of scuba diving: people cooperating and sharing their excitement as they explore the new world of inner space.

Conclusion rewritten to focus the point—sharing

Third-Stage Draft

With most of the organizational and material concerns out of the way, Kyle focused more in this draft on style points. He paid close attention to word choices and sentence patterns and tried to punctuate more for emphasis.

> **SPECIAL POINTS TO CHECK IN REVISING FROM SECOND TO THIRD DRAFTS**
> 1. Add specific words.
> 2. Substitute more precise or audience-appropriate words.
> 3. Combine sentences for variety.
> 4. **Replace clutter and repeat words with synonyms and phrases.**
> 5. Delete unneeded words.

Get Wet

1

Being in the ocean in scuba gear is a lot like being in outer space. When a diver is floating in silence above a deep-water coral plateau, with a half-mile drop into darkness a few yards away, he is in another world. Depending on the compressed air in his cylinders and his regulator to deliver it smoothly, the diver glides weightlessly, almost effortlessly, through "inner space." Similarly, an astronaut floats in darkness with the deepest drop imaginable all around him. He also depends on his gear to deliver air, protect him from the cold and other extremes, tell

Title revised

More specific words added

Sentences combined for variety

More precise words substituted

him how much air he has, and orient him toward his "boat." Few of us will have the opportunity to voyage into outer space, but we can learn a little about the next best option for inner planetary travel, scuba diving.

To understand something about scuba (self-contained underwater breathing apparatus) as a sport, we can take a look at some of the gear. Basic diving equipment can be divided into two categories: gear for a snorkeler and gear for a diver. A snorkeler or breath-hold diver needs a face mask, swimming fins, a snorkel, and sometimes a wet suit, depending on the temperature of the water. The wet suit is a skin-tight coverall of neoprene rubber (rubber filled with millions of bubbles of nitrogen) used to keep warmth in. Putting one on is a pain. It is much like squeezing into a really tight, thick leotard that stretches from the neck to the ankles. A scuba diver most often wears a wet suit of varying degrees of thickness (there is a dry suit for really cold water), and in addition to the snorkelers' gear wears a heavy cylinder (or tank) of compressed air with an attached regulator for delivering the air, weight belt, diving vest, gauges for monitoring amount of air and time underwater, and a compass. If this seems like a lot of equipment, it is. And until a diver gets into the water, ~~the diver~~ **she** is overloaded, uncomfortable, and prone to falling down. A complete set of scuba equipment is expensive (more than a thousand dollars), but many certified divers own only snorkeling gear and rent the rest.

In addition to knowing about the gear, people interested in scuba ~~diving~~ should know about the certification process. Just as a person has to learn the rules of the road and pass a driving exam before she gets her driver's license, so too must divers learn the rules of the ocean and how to operate the equipment safely. Without basic certification diving is dangerous, and few reputable dive shops will rent equipment to uncertified divers or take them out on their boats. There are many professional ~~dive groups~~ **scuba organizations** (PADI, SSI, NASDS), the course fees are nominal, and a person can become certified in a matter of weeks; so there is little reason not to get the training. If a person is in good health, can swim, and is not inclined to panic

2   Term defined in parentheses

Sentences combined for variety

More specific words added

Synonym replaces overused words.

3

Unneeded word deleted

Sentences combined for variety

Synonym replaces overused word.

Synonym replaces overused
word.

in the water, the process is easy. After classroom instruction and study in a text, ~~divers~~ **people** move to a pool and practice with the equipment until they are ready for a lake or ocean journey. Then the real fun begins.

4   The most exciting part of scuba diving, naturally, is being in the water. The pool may have seemed fascinating at first, but it pales by comparison to open water, especially the clear waters of a reef. Teetering at the end of the dive boat, all gear in order, the diver "strides" out and splashes into the ocean. Immediately, she feels in her element. The equipment she is wearing makes her part of the marine environment, ~~like she belongs~~, something of a fish. Down the diver sinks, clearing the pressure in her ears, trailing bubbles, equalizing buoyancy till she is floating, weightless, a few feet above the reef. Stretching in every direction are forests of tall, jagged staghorn and elkhorn corals. Light-brown brain coral ranging in size from basketballs to boulders dot the pale sandy bottom with green and purple sea fans rocking at their feet. Scattered throughout the ~~coral~~ **seascape** are the cousins of all those captive saltwater aquarium fish: sassy brown and white damsels; orange- and white-striped clowns; yellow butterfly fish; stately lime-green and blue angels. The new diver hovers, amazed by the beauty of inner space, eager to see more.

More precise locator phrase
added

Sentence divided for
emphasis

More specific words added

Redundant phrase removed

Synonym replaces overused
word.

5   Scuba is a wonderful sport that only requires the right equipment and proper training to open a new world to the diver. It is a safe sport for all ages and one that brings people together. Because a number one rule in diving is to pair up before going under, people meet quickly. They help each other with their gear, dive together, and share their experiences back on board. "Did you see the size of that lobster?" "How about those amber jacks?" "The mantas looked like flying saucers!" This is the essence of scuba diving: people cooperating and sharing their excitement as they explore the new world of inner space.

—Kyle Jennings

Sentences combined for
variety

Alternate Writing Assignments

The following assignment options may help you focus your definition essay. For any of these assignments, be sure to do the following:

- Review brief definitions and the patterns of development, and use several methods to develop your essay.
- Have a point for your definition, and make the point clear to your reader.
- Touch on the essential nature of what you are defining.
- Write to a specific audience.
- Review Chapter 12's methods for creating introductions and conclusions.
- Create a controlling topic sentence for each body paragraph.

ASSIGNMENT OPTIONS

1. **Write an essay defining the term** *home* **in a way that either adds to or differs from the definition in "Finding Home" (pp. 348–349).** Perhaps, for example, you don't agree with April Griffin's feeling that a home requires more than one person. Brainstorm for ideas based on your personal experience, and if you plan to disagree with points from "Finding Home," consider using negation in your introduction to show how your definition will differ from the author's.

2. **Write a definition essay that treats a term—for example, a person, place, or activity—as the best or worst of its kind.** For instance, you might discuss a person and tell what makes for a terrific or terrible boss, leader, co-worker, parent, child, grandparent, athlete, or neighbor. Or you could choose a place like an amusement park, stadium, or beach or an activity like a vacation, sporting event, or date. You may include personal experiences, perhaps using narration as one method of development.

3. **Write an essay defining a term important in a career you are interested in or defining the career itself.** For example, if you are thinking about graphic design as a career, you might want to know more about terms like *hosting*, *frame*, *HTML*, *DPI*, *splash page*, or *bandwidth*. Or you might want to learn about the education required, employment prospects, or potential salary. If you research the career, remember to limit your findings to three or four significant points.

4. **Write a definition essay on one word that best describes you.** You might know immediately what that word is—*hardworking*, *athletic*, *lazy*, *funny*, or *loyal*—or you might struggle with two or three before you pin it down. If you are not sure yourself, try asking a good friend or family member. One of them may surprise you with the defining word. Another approach is to imagine a setting and audience. If you were in a job interview and asked to define yourself in a word, what would you say? How would you support your definition? Presuming you want the job, you would, of course, select your word with care.

5. **Write an extended definition that reacts to some term regularly applied to you individually or as a representative of a group.** For example, perhaps your friends have often called you "out of control" just because you love high-risk activities like free climbing, hang gliding, skydiving, and bungee jumping. If you agree with them, write an essay that clarifies what "out of control" means in your life. If you disagree, either define "out of control" at length or offer another term to describe your lifestyle, and then develop it through definition.

   Another approach to this assignment is to agree or disagree with a term someone applies to you as a member of a group. For example, you may be tired of hearing generation Xers referred to as "politically apathetic," the Irish as "alcoholics," or feminists as "radical." As in the preceding option, define the term at length as you see it, or define an alternative term that better describes your group.

6. Can images help define a word? **Using these photos as a guide, define the word** *dream.* How might each photo define it? How do these different definitions relate to each other? What does *dream* mean to you, personally? What more general associations—positive or negative—do people have with the word? (As an alternative, choose the word *change* and find or take three photographs that embody various meanings of this word.)

Linking to Future Experience

Determining the Value of Definition

Words that are clear to us because we have been familiar with them for years are not always clear to others. If you talk about rebuilding an engine, using terms like *overhead cam, stroke, compression,* and *valve clearance,* mechanics understand without a second thought, but the uninitiated soon become lost. You need to define your terms. Also, murky meanings can create serious problems. Think of the trouble that vague language like "employer will contribute to moving costs" might cause in an employment contract. A clear definition can help satisfy all parties.

Finally, writing out definitions helps us understand our own ideas. Novelist E. M. Forster said, "How can I know what I think until I see what I say?" Defining allows us to examine significant words carefully so we can be sure we know our own mind.

 ACTIVITY 15.6 WORKING ONLINE: *Defining a Word Search*

How does Google or Yahoo "define" your word? See what the first twenty-five hits are. In a paragraph or two, discuss the term from the point of view of a web browser, or explain your browser's preferences to an audience of your peers. Feel free to use humor in this exercise.

ACTIVITY 15.7 WORKING ONLINE: *Exploring the OED*

As a college student, you have free online access to the most comprehensive and reputable dictionary in the English language—the *Oxford English Dictionary*. Go to your college library's website (ask a librarian if you need assistance) and explore the origins and history of the word you chose to write about. If you're still working on your essay, consider including some of your *OED* findings in your paper.

ACTIVITY 15.8 WORKING ONLINE: *Definition Review*

Take the Chapter 15 Review Quiz at www.mhhe.com/brannan.

Chapter Summary

1. Definition is the act of limiting and clarifying the meaning of a word, of separating it from other, similar terms.

2. We define daily at home, school, and work.

3. Brief definitions—synonyms, negation, comparisons, and formal definitions—are often part of a paragraph or essay being developed with a single pattern.

4. Brief definitions may be a single word or a short phrase, often enclosed by commas, parentheses, or dashes.

5. Definition essays often use brief definitions and extended definitions based on several patterns of development.

6. Definition depends on thoroughly explained and detailed examples.

7. Transitional words and other connectors are especially important in bridging the gap between paragraphs.

8. Definition essays can be organized chronologically but are frequently arranged by order of importance.

9. A thesis sentence is the first step in focusing an extended definition essay.

10. Outlining is a valuable organizing technique.

11. Topic sentences are an essential part of a coherent body paragraph.

12. Writing is never complete until it has gone through several revisions and careful editing.

HINT

Across the curriculum, you will use both brief and extended definitions in exams and papers.

Writing Persuasively (Argument)

16

[*In both of these photographs, a person is making an argument. Write a paragraph describing what you think the political figure or family member is trying to convince someone to believe or do. Provide at least three reasons behind this argument.*]

KEY TOPICS

- Developing skills and exploring ideas in persuasive essays
  - Defining the issue
  - Presenting reasons and providing support
  - Connecting with the audience
  - Avoiding errors in logic
  - Countering opposition
- Analyzing student models: Persuasive essays
- Writing a persuasive essay

What Are We Trying to Achieve and Why?

Setting the Stage

Both of these pictures involve **persuasion**—the attempt to convince someone to accept an idea or policy (as with Barack Obama giving a speech) or to take some action, such as helping to clean a room.

This chapter will focus especially on a form of persuasion known as **argument.** By *argument,* we don't mean raised voices and fists pounding on the table, but rather a reasoned exchange of ideas between people with different opinions on an issue. Our goal is to discover an issue (an arguable topic), frame a position on the issue, explore it through **reasons** backed by **evidence,** expand the argument with several patterns of development, and, finally, influence an **audience** to accept or at least respect our position on the issue.

Linking to Previous Experience

Trying to get what we want from others is basic human nature. As babies, persuasion begins when we learn that food will come if we cry loudly enough. During childhood, we quickly learn what strategies we can use on our parents to get the things we want. We appeal to them unconsciously on all three levels that operate in more formal argumentation: mind, heart, and self. "If we're going to get the bike, now's the time because it's on sale for 50 percent off" (appeal to the parents' minds with a bargain); "I need a new bicycle because the brakes on my old one are shot, and I might get hurt" (appeal to the parents' hearts); and "You promised that if I did well this term in school you would buy the bike" (appeal to their sense of you as hardworking and of themselves as fair). We work on (and are worked on by) our family members, friends, significant others, fellow employees, employers, teachers, and even the police officer about to write us a speeding ticket. Sometimes we succeed, and sometimes we don't.

Many of you have already written papers that are at least partly persuasive. When you created a dominant impression in describing a place, for example, you chose details that would encourage readers to feel what you wanted them to. When you narrated a story, you manipulated plot, dialogue, and description to interest the audience. In establishing causes and effects, you may have influenced your readers to change a behavior to avoid negative consequences. In short, much of what you have written this semester has had a persuasive element, but now persuasion becomes your main goal.

JOURNAL / BLOG ENTRY 16.1

What persuading have you tried recently or seen others try? Maybe you wanted to see one film and a friend, another. Perhaps you tried to talk your boss into giving you a raise, time off, or a shift change. Maybe you watched a teacher try to persuade her class to find value in some subject. Summarize a situation when you used persuasion. Explain your purpose, your strategy, the reasons you gave, and how successful you believe your argument was.

FEEDBACK *Get thoughts from peers on how persuasive your argument seems, and offer comments in return. Discuss what you think makes a convincing argument.*

Developing Skills and Exploring Ideas in Persuasive Essays

The activities in this section will show you what you need to do to write an effective persuasive essay, as summarized in the following points. Remember that you are trying to persuade not only those who are neutral on your issue but also those who disagree with you; dealing with that "opposition" is a large part of effective persuasion.

1. Define the issue and clarify terms.
2. Present reasons and support.
3. Connect with the audience.
4. Avoid errors in logic.
5. Qualify assertions.
6. Counter opposing reasons and audience objections.

Defining the Issue

Many arguments fail because the writer has not defined the issue clearly for readers. Consider the following thesis sentence:

Minors who break the law should get the same treatment that adults do.

Does "minors" mean anyone from age 3 to 17? And what exactly does "get the same treatment that adults do" mean? Someone reading this thesis sentence might imagine the writer arguing that, say, a 5-year-old caught stealing a candy bar should have to appear in court on a misdemeanor charge or that a 13-year-old caught joyriding in a stolen car should be locked up with adult criminals. Presumably, the writer would not take these positions, but her unfocused thesis sentence implies that she would.

Because arguments can easily be misinterpreted, writers must carefully define—limit and clarify—their issue and all terms. Limiting is also important for another reason: issues that are too broad cannot be supported, especially within the confines of a brief essay.

ACTIVITY 16.1 *Defining the Issue*

The following thesis sentences are unfocused and might be misinterpreted by readers. Rewrite each of them to limit and clarify the issue, as well as any unclear terms. Write out a thesis that you think you could support in your own argument.

EXAMPLE

Unfocused issue: Children should be able to leave school whenever they want to.

Focused issue (thesis): *Students who have parental consent should be allowed to quit school by the age of sixteen.*

1. Unfocused issue: Birth control should be available to anyone who wants it.

   Focused issue (thesis): _____

   _____

2. Unfocused issue: Pharmaceutical companies have too much influence over doctors' decisions.

   Focused issue (thesis): _____

   _____

3. Unfocused issue: Playing sports is bad for young people.

   Focused issue (thesis): _____

   _____

4. Unfocused issue: People should be protected from television violence.

   Focused issue (thesis): _____

   _____

5. Unfocused issue: Everyone should value the environment more.

   Focused issue (thesis): _____

   _____

Presenting Reasons and Providing Support

After focusing an issue, writers must present reasons and evidence to support their position. **Reasons** are the main points made about the issue; **evidence** supports those points. For example, to argue that fireworks should be outlawed, you could list reasons like the following:

1. Fireworks hurt people.
2. Fireworks cause property damage.
3. Fireworks annoy many people.

Unsupported, these reasons are not very convincing. If, however, you add specific evidence, an argument begins to take shape. For instance, to support reason 1, you could offer the statistic that last year 17,000 people were injured by fireworks. Next, you could add an example that the red-hot wires from sparklers burn people. And you might continue with an anecdote about the time a younger brother shot someone in the face with a Roman candle.

Here are several forms of evidence, most of which we have already worked with, that are useful for developing arguments:

1. **Facts/statistics:** commonly accepted truths in words and numbers
2. **Authorities:** information from people who are generally recognized as experts in their field
3. **Examples:** specific illustrations
4. **Anecdotes:** brief stories
5. **Scenarios:** "what-if" situations, speculating about causes and effects
6. **Logical interpretations:** explanations of how the reasons and evidence support the thesis

As you explore your argument, you will probably find several sound reasons to support your position and will develop a body paragraph around each. However, occasionally, one reason is so strong that a whole argument may rest on it. In this case, the rest of the essay will be evidence to support the reason and/or refutation of the opposition's reasons.

English
Review Note

Your writing for academic assignments should be assertive and confident in tone; take care your argument is neither too aggressive nor too subtle.

An anecdote is a brief story, first- or second-hand. See Chapter 6 for more on narration.

ACTIVITY 16.2 | WORKING TOGETHER: *Presenting Reasons and Providing Support*

Discuss with group members each of the following topics, looking closely at the thesis and the reason given to support the thesis. Then try to support each reason with *three* pieces of acceptable evidence.

EXAMPLE: Topic: Outlawing fireworks

Thesis: Fireworks should be prohibited in this country.

Reason: Many children are injured by them each year.

Evidence:

- Fact: *Last year there were 17,000 injuries nationally on July 4th.*
- Authority: *Dr. Horace Caruthers, director of the Johns Hopkins Trauma Center, has stated that bottle rockets alone are responsible for hundreds of eye injuries on July 4th.*
- Example: *Even relatively harmless fireworks like sparklers can cause severe burns when children grab the glowing wires in their hands or step on them with bare feet.*
- Anecdote: *When my younger brother was 9 years old, he shot me in the face with a Roman candle.*
- Scenario: *Imagine your 11-year-old son teased into holding and throwing lit cherry bombs or M-80s. Now imagine how you would feel if his hearing were damaged or his fingers were blown off, or if he were blinded.*
- Logical interpretation: *Because children get caught up in the moment and so often don't think of consequences, they will continue to be injured by fireworks.*

1. Topic: Freedom of choice in high school curriculum

   Thesis: High school students should be allowed to choose more of their own curriculum.

   Reason: If students are more interested in their studies, they will perform better.

   Evidence:

   - _____
     _____
     _____
   - _____
     _____
     _____
   - _____
     _____
     _____

HINT

Assign one group member as the secretary; he or she can take notes while everyone brainstorms.

2. Topic: Teachers accepting late homework

   Thesis: Teachers should accept late homework from students with legitimate excuses.

   Reason: Students who have worked hard on homework assignments are demoralized and angered when they cannot turn them in for credit.

   Evidence:

   * _____

     _____

     _____

   * _____

     _____

     _____

   * _____

     _____

     _____

3. Topic: Changing sports teams' names

   Thesis: Professional sports teams that feature names related to Native Americans should change them.

   Reason: Many Native Americans understandably feel demeaned by such team names.

   Evidence:

   * _____

     _____

     _____

   * _____

     _____

     _____

   * _____

     _____

     _____

4. Topic: Fourth amendment rights of subway passengers versus the need for security checks

   Thesis: Police should have the right to search any large bag or suspicious-looking package carried by New York City subway passengers.

   Reason: Police need to guard against potential dangers to other riders.

   Evidence:

   * _____

     _____

     _____

- _____
  _____
  _____
  _____
- _____
  _____
  _____
  _____

Connecting with the Audience

How can you connect with your readers in order to persuade them? We have already discussed one way: through a careful presentation of ideas, with a well-defined issue and clear reasons effectively supported by evidence. However, there are two other important strategies to consider: **presenting yourself well** and **influencing readers' emotions.** As the figure below shows, in persuasive writing, you need to think about each of the three interrelated parts of communication—the text, the writer (you), and the reader.

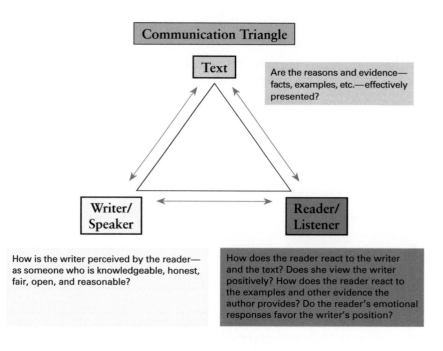

Communication Triangle

Text

Are the reasons and evidence—facts, examples, etc.—effectively presented?

Writer/Speaker

Reader/Listener

How is the writer perceived by the reader—as someone who is knowledgeable, honest, fair, open, and reasonable?

How does the reader react to the writer and the text? Does she view the writer positively? How does the reader react to the examples and other evidence the author provides? Do the reader's emotional responses favor the writer's position?

English Review Note

Persuasive writing is often required to exit developmental and ESL writing classes. This rhetorical mode incorporates many of the patterns explored in Chapters 5–11.

Most of us respond positively to those whom we see as reasonable, fair, and honest. In writing, we create this impression of ourselves—our **persona**—by what we say and how we say it. If our persona is a good one, it advances our argument; if not, it hinders it. For example, if you were to argue that drivers over age 70 should take an annual physical and driving exam, which of the following statements would create a more positive persona?

A. Old farts shouldn't be on the road any longer if they can't handle a grown-up's responsibility. They don't deserve to drive, and I hate it whenever I'm stuck near one in traffic.

B. Though many of our senior citizens have driven responsibly for years, when through no fault of their own the aging process diminishes their capacity to drive safely, in order to protect them and others, we ought to ask them to take an annual physical and driving exam.

Clearly, version A creates an unsympathetic persona, and readers might suspect the writer's motives for proposing a driving exam. In contrast, version B shows a writer who seems to respect the older driver and proposes an annual exam only because it would serve the greater good.

Along with considering persona, a writer should consider the potential emotional responses of readers and choose examples that cause them to respond favorably. Which of the following two paragraphs promoting a driving exam for the elderly would be more likely to influence an audience including people with seniors in their family?

A.   Like I said, these old fogies have got to go. They aren't capable anymore, they get in the way, and they cause accidents. Blue hairs and other semigeriatric cases belong more in wheelchairs than automobiles. If they have a hard time getting out to buy their Geritol without driving, let the city foot the bill for taxis or let their families do the driving. However we get them off the road, the sooner the better.

B.   Neither of my grandfathers wants to endanger anyone, and they both have to get from place to place just like everyone else. But their failing physical and mental health made them unsafe drivers, so they finally stopped driving, luckily before anyone was seriously injured. As a result, my folks and I and the rest of our family are pitching in to shuttle our grandparents around. It is inconvenient. And family members are annoyed by the chore on occasion. But this "chore" has the benefit of bringing us more often in contact with each other. I see all of my grandparents more frequently now than before they stopped driving. The family profits because we are sharing a task that is right. Our older generation took care of their children and their children's children in their time. Now it is our time to take care of them.

Most of us would probably choose paragraph B because it evokes a more sympathetic emotional response. Effective argumentation requires a clear sense of your audience so that you can shape your persona and choose effective emotional appeals.

ACTIVITY 16.3 | WORKING TOGETHER: *Connecting with the Audience*

Discuss with group members the Communication Triangle and the appeals of persona and emotion. Next, revise *one* of the following paragraphs (on a separate sheet of paper), making the persona more positive and trying for emotional appeals that might influence the stated audience. Consider including yourself in the audience, as in the paragraph on elderly drivers, and using pronouns like *we*, *us*, and *our*.

1. Issue and position: Schools should enforce dress codes.

    Audience: Public high school students

    It should be obvious to anyone that these high school students ought to be wearing uniforms. Just look at what they are doing to one another in their own schools! They beat each other up for a pair of sneakers and form packs like animals to hunt each other down. And teachers have to suffer from it too. If they are not risking their lives breaking up knife fights in the halls, they are having to beg the students to stop admiring each other's new sunglasses and pay attention to the lesson. I know that some students are going to whine about personal identity and freedom, but who ever said school was supposed to be a democracy after all?

2. Issue and position: People should only use cell phones for urgent business while driving.

   Audience: Owners and frequent users of cell phones

   > Phones have no business in cars. Aside from the rare emergency call, people just yak away while they buzz down the highway, paying little attention to the traffic and other drivers around them. And what are these pressing conversations that can't wait five minutes till the driver gets to his or her destination? "Hi, Judy, remember to bring the potato salad to Jan's on Friday." "Hello, dear, would you be sure to defrost the hamburger for dinner?" "Bill, it's killin' me. I gotta know the name of the lead in *The Hulk*." Cell phone addicts are a menace on the road as they weave in and out of traffic, speed up, slow down, and cut off other drivers as the phone freaks swerve to make almost-missed exits. My request to cell phone owners is this: "Shut up. Even your friends don't want to hear from you that much."

3. Issue and position: Andrea Hoffman wants a raise from eight to nine dollars an hour at Family Tree Nursery.

   Audience: Andrea's immediate supervisor

   > Dear Mr. T. Ightwad:
   >
   > I have been working at this dive for a year now, and I've made it to work most of the time. When I'm here you can ask anyone—well, you better ask Glen or Annette—and they will tell you I work hard. Whenever you need someone to come through for you with overtime or weekend work, I am right there sometimes, and I stayed late twice last year. Besides, I need the money. I took two classes at the community college last year, and my books were almost a hundred dollars (what a rip-off!). I really do like working at the nursery all right, and I'll probably stick around for awhile, so I hope you will consider giving me the raise that I really do deserve.
   >
   > P.S. No hard feelings if you don't give me what you owe me. Besides I know where you park your Lexus. Ha, ha, just kidding.

Avoiding Errors in Logic

Logical reasoning—the way you connect your reasons to your evidence—is another important part of persuasive writing. If readers don't think what you are stating makes sense, even if you have plenty of good evidence, they are not likely to believe you. Below are some common **logical fallacies,** or errors in logic.

LOGICAL FALLACIES

1. **Oversimplifying complex issues:** As discussed in Chapter 9, events rarely have only one cause or effect. When you reduce a complex issue in this way, ignoring other significant causes and effects, you have oversimplified. Beware of words and phrases like *simply, just a case of, always, never,* and *every.*

   Example: "Sexual harassment in the workplace is just a case of too many sexually frustrated men acting like schoolboys." *Is* sexual frustration a cause or the only cause of sexual harassment at work?

See Chapter 9 for more on causes and effects.

2. **Reducing a complex situation to two sides or solutions,** only one of which is acceptable: More oversimplifying, this either/or thinking clouds issues and lessens options for compromise.

    Example: "If we outlaw guns, only outlaws will have guns." Gun control legislation wouldn't prohibit police officers, gun collectors, or hunters from having guns.

3. **Overgeneralizing** from limited evidence: This fallacy involves drawing a conclusion too broad to be supported by the evidence.

    Example: "Because eight fans were trampled to death at the Pearl Jam concert in Denmark in 2000, people who don't want to die should stop going to Pearl Jam concerts." This event was a tragedy, but 49,992 fans made it out alive, and subsequent concerts have gone off without a hitch.

4. **Drawing an unwarranted conclusion:** Whereas overgeneralizing involves drawing a conclusion too broad for the evidence, this fallacy involves drawing an incorrect conclusion.

    Example: "That little boy's face is dirty, and his clothes are old; his parents must not care much about him." This conclusion is incorrect if, for example, the boy was outside playing, and his parents dressed him in old clothes for that purpose.

5. **Confusing time order with cause:** Just because a possible cause precedes an event does not mean it is a real cause.

    Example: "Emily always chats with her math instructor before exams, and she always makes A's on them, so her schmoozing is paying off." Perhaps Emily studies diligently.

6. **Using a faulty analogy:** As we have discussed in several chapters, comparisons through metaphor, simile, and analogy are useful support, but they can be carried only so far as evidence in an argument. Analogies relied on too heavily as proof often break down.

    Example: "Of course we should execute people convicted of murder. We shoot mad dogs to protect people from them, don't we?" Dogs are not people, and the punishment of one is not valid support for applying the punishment to the other. Think of carefully selected analogies as useful support, but as only one piece of evidence among many.

7. **Attacking a person,** not an argument: Sometimes when people cannot present their own reasons and evidence persuasively or refute those of the opposition, they resort to name-calling and trying to defame the opponent. This tactic, frequently used in political campaigns, is known as "mudslinging."

    Example: "How can anyone want to reelect a governor like Jackson, who has been divorced three times and still sees a therapist twice a month?"

8. **Running with the crowd:** This fallacy relies on a common human trait, the herd impulse. People often feel more comfortable doing what others have done or are doing. The logic goes, "If so-and-so is doing it, then it must be right."

    Example: "I guess I shouldn't use the TV as a baby-sitter so much, but all the people I know do, and their kids don't seem ruined." Even though many people may be doing something, it still may not be a good idea.

Writers often succumb to fallacies like these when they allow their emotions to replace more critical judgment. Also, we hear fallacies so regularly from other people and from advertisements that faulty logic can become second nature.

Qualifying can reduce
logical fallacies.
Qualify where needed,
but be careful not to
over-qualify. For more
on qualifying, see
pp. 485–486.

One way to avoid fallacies is to **qualify** statements where needed:

TOO BROAD Sexual harassment in the workplace is just a case of too many sexually frustrated men acting like schoolboys.

QUALIFIED One reason behind sexual harassment in the workplace is that <u>some</u> men let their sexual frustration rule their behavior around their female co-workers.

Writers qualify statements based on how much evidence they have. In general, the less qualified an assertion, the more evidence is needed to support it.

Here are some qualifying words: *seems, appears, apparently, could be, can, may, maybe, perhaps, likely, often, sometimes, seldom, usually, frequently, most, many, few.*

ACTIVITY 16.4 *Avoiding Errors in Logic*

Identify the logical fallacy or fallacies in each of the following sentences. Then rewrite the sentence so that it still makes a point but does not have errors in logic. Where relevant, include evidence (as defined on page 371) and qualify statements.

EXAMPLE: Vegetarian diets must be bad for people because one of my friends got sick when she tried to go vegan.

Fallacy: _Overgeneralizing_

Revised sentence: _If vegetarians don't handle their diets carefully, especially taking into account the body's need for protein, they are likely to become sick._

1. Because in football people learn to get back up after they've been knocked down, and this is an important lesson in life, children should play football.

   Fallacy: _____

   Revised sentence: _____

   _____

2. Requiring automobile manufacturers to produce either hybrid gas/electric or totally electric cars is the only way to save this country's air quality.

   Fallacy: _____

   Revised sentence: _____

   _____

   _____

3. If we do not pass a law making English the national language, soon our country will be divided into a dozen "minicountries," each speaking its own language.

   Fallacy: _____

   Revised sentence: _____

   _____

   _____

4. That self-confidence DVD I bought paid off; I watched it every night last week, and, when I talked to my boss, I got the raise!

Fallacy: _____

Revised sentence: _____

_____

5. We could win the war on drugs if the United States would wipe out all the coca leaf production in South America.

Fallacy: _____

Revised sentence: _____

_____

6. Now that I'm in college, most of my friends drive after drinking a few beers, and none of them has ever had a problem, so I've decided it's all right to drink and drive.

Fallacy: _____

Revised sentence: _____

_____

Countering Opposition

Because issues have at least two sides, there is more to argument than presenting reasons. You must deal with the opposition's major reasons and also with objections that readers might have to your own reasons. When you show that you know the other side of the issue and can answer the reader's question "Yes, but did you think of this?" you increase your credibility and strengthen your position.

Writers handle opposing reasons and objections to their reasons by first acknowledging them, in some cases **conceding** points that are true, and then **refuting** them, showing how they are wrong. Refutation often involves giving more evidence (such as facts and examples), further clarifying your reasons, and showing how opposing reasons or objections are poorly defined, incomplete, or illogical (knowing logical fallacies can help here).

Avoid attacking the character of the opposition—for example, "Pro-choice advocates have no feeling for murdered babies"—or insulting your readers. Refutation should be tactful, aimed at persuading, not forcing agreement from, the audience.

ACTIVITY 16.5 WORKING TOGETHER: *Countering Opposition*

In pairs or a small group, choose one of the following thesis statements, and assume you are going to argue for it based on the reasons favoring it. Discuss reasons for opposing the thesis, and then list three of those reasons. Next, brainstorm for ways to refute the reasons you listed. You might need to concede a point, offer evidence as defined on page 371, explain your reasoning, and show how an opposing reason is poorly defined, incomplete, or illogical.

EXAMPLE: Thesis: Doctors should be allowed to assist patients who are terminally ill and in great pain to commit suicide.

Reasons Favoring Assertion	Reasons Opposing Assertion
1. Patient's free will	1. *Sanctity of life*
2. Compassion for patient	2. *Possibility of cure*
3. Compassion for family	3. *Depressed patients making bad decisions*

Refuting Opposing Reasons

1.   Sanctity of life: *While it is true that many people think of human life as sacred, as a society we allow the taking of life in several ways: executions, warfare, and abortion. Perhaps there are justifiable reasons for taking human life.*

2.   Possibility of cure: *There are some cases that might warrant this wait-and-see attitude, but shouldn't that be the doctor's area of expertise? For the rest of the suffering patients, holding out futile hope is cruel. If a terminally ill patient is riddled with cancer and is gasping out her last few months, it is pretty obvious there's not going to be a miracle cure for her.*

3.   Depressed patients making bad decisions: *There is truth here, but the doctor should decide. If a patient is clinically depressed, he should be protected from himself. But some bleak outlooks on life are justified. If the patient is judged competent by a psychiatrist and still wants to die because the patient is in great physical pain, he should be allowed to.*

1.   Thesis: Elderly family members who are having difficulty maintaining their homes should be encouraged to sell them and move to assisted-living quarters.

Reasons Favoring Assertion	Reasons Opposing Assertion
A. Homes can be dangerous.	A.
B. Homes can be too demanding.	B.
C. Homes can be isolating.	C.

Refuting opposing reasons: _____

_____

_____

_____

2.   Thesis: For most busy people, jogging is an excellent choice of aerobic exercise.

Reasons Favoring Assertion	Reasons Opposing Assertion
A. Jogging is convenient.	A.
B. Jogging is inexpensive.	B.
C. Weather seldom interferes.	C.

Refuting opposing reasons: _____

_____

_____

_____

3. Thesis: The benefits of eating only organically grown food outweigh the drawbacks.

Reasons Favoring Assertion	Reasons Opposing Assertion
A. Organic food has fewer health hazards.	A.
B. Organic food is more nutritious.	B.
C. Organic food often tastes better.	C.

Refuting opposing reasons: _____

_____

_____

_____

_____

Analyzing Student Models: Persuasive Essays

As you read the following student essays, look for the argument strategies we practiced in the skills section: defining the issue and clarifying terms, presenting reasons and support, connecting with the audience, avoiding logical fallacies (including through qualifying), and countering opposing reasons and objections. Also, try to role-play the stated audience, and see if you are persuaded by the authors. If you are not, ask yourself why the argument failed, and use the answer to improve your own essay.

▶ Prereading Exploration for "Just Say No"

Marisa Youmbi wrote about children's TV viewing habits because she has to deal with the issue regularly in her household. She thought that her essay would interest parents of school-aged children, especially single parents and dual-earner parents, since many of them are also wrestling with the issue.

How do you feel about TV? Is it a blessing in your life? Do you watch much yourself? Do you watch more than you think you should? List three reasons why TV might be a blessing and three why it might be a curse.

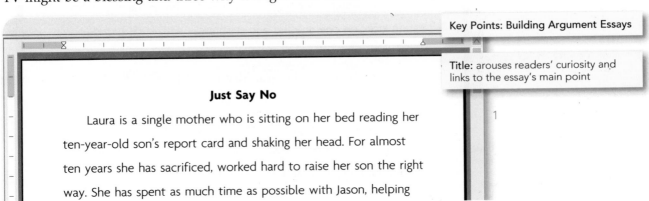

Key Points: Building Argument Essays

Title: arouses readers' curiosity and links to the essay's main point

Just Say No

Laura is a single mother who is sitting on her bed reading her ten-year-old son's report card and shaking her head. For almost ten years she has sacrificed, worked hard to raise her son the right way. She has spent as much time as possible with Jason, helping him with his homework, but she can't do everything, and she has often turned to the TV to babysit when she has had work to do. Now she reads the teachers' comments again: "Jason does not do his homework." "Jason needs to pay more attention in class." She knows that TV is not solely responsible for the D's and F's, but she also knows that four hours a night of TV is too much. Like many parents Laura has a hard decision to make: Should she fight the battle with the idiot box again or just give up?

One of many good reasons for a parent to limit a child's TV intake is to keep the child physically healthy. Most kids are by nature active; they want to be up and doing things. Whether they are out on a soccer field or just tearing around in the house, they want to Go. But TV reaches out for them (all of us really). It casts a spell like one of the fantasy witches from one of their cartoons. I can almost see the green smoke bubbling out of the set and curling around my son's head as he sprawls out on the couch, mesmerized by the flashing lights, music, and action in front of him. "Peter?" I call his name. "Peter, are you in there?" He might as well be drugged for all the response I sometimes get. When children spend hours each day in a trance, they are not exercising. They are learning couch potato habits that will affect what they can and want to do for the rest of their lives.

Besides the health issue, children suffer from too much exposure to the wrong messages on TV. There has been much debate about whether violence on television influences children to behave in aggressive or violent ways. Some say that TV violence allows kids to release frustration and anger in the fantasy acts of cartoon characters, instead of punching their brothers and sisters, so at least some TV violence is good for children. Perhaps. But when I watch my own children, nieces, and nephews practice karate kicks on one another and slash away with stick swords after seeing the same behavior on TV, it makes me suspicious. Aside from the violent behavior that kids at least model after their cartoon heroes, there are all kinds of sexual, racial, and ethnic stereotypes shaping kids' views of themselves and others. My daughter does not now look like Barbie and never will. Why should she feel this is an image to live up to?

What most disturbs me about excessive television for children is the negative effect it has on their learning. Of course there is a lot of good programming—on the Discovery Channel, Animal Planet, Nickelodeon, Travel, and so on—that exposes children to new ideas. But the truth is that most kids are more attracted to the action/role-playing programs than to a History Channel documentary on the life of Lincoln. When children are unsupervised, they can easily spend four to six hours a day—the national average—watching junk, which leaves little time for homework or other learning activities. Schools practically beg parents to spend time with their children reading and helping with math and other course work. How can this happen when TV has captured the audience? And schoolwork is not all that suffers. Don't we as parents want to involve our children in other learning activities like music, dance, and sports?

Television is a mixed blessing. In small doses it does not have to have the negative effects on our children's health, behavior, and learning that it often has in large amounts. In fact most of us enjoy watching TV ourselves and with our family; and, let's face it, we often need the break from the kids that the box can provide. But, as tiring as it can be, we need to keep fighting the TV battle with our kids. We need to monitor what they watch and how much. Children cannot see very far down the road. They want what they want when they want it, regardless of the consequences. It is part of our job as parents to protect them from themselves.

—Marisa Youmbi

> **Style points:** increase readability. Using rhetorical questions (disguised statements) and the pronouns *we, us,* and *our* to *intentionally* speak to the audience can involve your readers (pars. 4 and 5). Dashes can be used for emphasis (par. 4). Imagined dialogue can create variety (pars. 1 and 2). Short sentences can be emphatic ("Television is a mixed blessing")

> **Concluding paragraph:** restates the thesis, briefly summarizes, and adds a final (expanded) thought

➤ *Prereading Exploration for "Something for Nothing?"*

Matt Smith discusses another family issue: allowances. Drawing on personal experience, Matt directs his argument toward middle- and lower-income parents who want to give their children allowances but are debating whether to have them earn the money. Because he defines his audience as already favoring allowances, Matt can avoid complicating his argument and make it more focused.

Authors of arguments make various assumptions, with which readers—depending on their values, knowledge, and experiences—might agree or disagree. As readers' responses to your assumptions can help or hurt your arguments, you should assume with care. How do you feel about the author's assumption that money can be a strong motivator for young people from "six to sixteen," perhaps more powerful than pleasing a parent or helping the family, and more effective than being deprived of something they value?

Record your prereading response in your journal or on your blog.

Title: arouses readers' curiosity and links to the essay's main point

1

Introductory paragraph: begins with a hook and ends with a thesis sentence

2

Body paragraphs: begin with a topic sentence that often contains a reason supporting the position taken, naming the reason and making a limiting statement about it—and may end with a summary sentence

3

Development: uses specific examples, action, dialogue, active verbs (*shout*), *-ing* words (*helping*), specific words (*six to sixteen*), and qualifiers (*most, some*); tells thoughts and emotions; explains the examples ("households run on people power"); anticipates opposing reasons and objections (par. 4); and uses synonyms (*allowance* = *money*), negation (par. 4), and patterns of development (narrative, par. 1; cause/effect, pars. 1–5)

Sentence connectors: guide readers: transitions, repeat words, synonyms, pronouns, and reference to main idea

Something for Nothing?

"Josh, congratulations, you don't have to work anymore if you don't want to. You just come in whenever you please, and I'll keep writing you a paycheck every month for at least the next ten years. What do you say?" I don't know about you, but if I were Josh, I'd be thanking the Lord and not planning on many more visits to the job site. Paying a child an allowance is not quite the same as an employer paying an employee wages; but there are some similarities, and a child is likely to react like most adults would on hearing he is about to get something for nothing— take the money and run. Parents who believe in allowances for their children should consider making their children work for the money.

One good reason for <u>expecting children to work for extra spending money</u> is that <u>most families need the help</u>. While there are plenty of wealthy folk in this country, most of us are not, and households run on people power. Both of my parents worked when I was growing up, so neither had a lot of extra time to keep the house running smoothly. They still carried a lot of the load, but my brothers and sister and I were expected to wash dishes, vacuum, do laundry, carry out the trash, rake leaves, and mow the lawn—all the routine chores—especially if we wanted an allowance. I remember my youngest brother at six helping us rake leaves. He was proud to be a "big kid," and we all got along pretty well together.

Another point in favor of children's working in return for their allowance is the motivation factor. Most parents expect their children to help out around the house, whether they give the children an allowance or not. A lot of the minimal jobs are supposed to be "understood"— putting toys away, keeping clothes on hangers, putting books back on shelves, making up a bed, and so on. But by the time children are six or so, many parents begin leaning pretty hard on them to do the daily chores. I have seen adults shout at their kids, call them names, and spank the youngest ones for not doing their jobs. I say, rather than making kids mind by punishing them, why not reward them for doing what they should? Earned allowances can be a positive motivator for young people from six to at least sixteen, especially when they can buy whatever they want with the money.

The most important reason for tying allowances to performance is that it gives children an early clear view of the real world. People have to work and produce for a living, almost everyone. Whatever we want to call it—a paycheck, grades on a report card, praise from someone we respect, or an allowance—the world turns on people's putting out effort and being rewarded, sometimes, for it. Why shouldn't children learn this lesson early in life? If they learn it well, maybe they will carry it through to other areas as they grow older, areas like good performance at work and school. I know that some might think a ten-year-old shouldn't have to think of the pressures of the "real world," that kids should be allowed just to be kids. But I am not talking about slave labor here, just a regular routine of chores that kids can reasonably be expected to handle in any day, without taking too much time from their schoolwork or probably even from their TV watching.

Expecting children to do some work for what they are given just makes sense to me. Aside from the reasons of helping the family, positive motivation, and teaching a realistic view of the world, I think that helping children learn to work and see the benefit in it instills values in children. Too many kids are going bad today, trying to take the easy way out—cheating in school, scraping by at low-status jobs they hate, drifting off into a cloud of drugs. Maybe as simple a decision by a parent early in a child's life as teaching the youngster to earn what he gets, that the world owes him nothing, maybe this lesson will help send a son or daughter off onto the road to success.

—Matt Smith

4

> **Style points:** increase readability. Using rhetorical questions (disguised statements) and the pronouns *we* and *us* to *intentionally* speak to the audience can involve your readers (pars. 2 and 4). Dashes can be used to separate a list (par. 4). Imagined dialogue can create variety (par. 1). Short sentences can be emphatic (What do you say?)

5

> **Concluding paragraph:** restates the thesis, briefly summarizes, and adds a final (expanded) thought

POSTREADING QUESTIONS FOR ESSAY ANALYSIS

Note: These questions apply to either "Just Say No" or "Something for Nothing?"

1. Where is the thesis located? What is the issue, and what statement limits it? Does the thesis sufficiently clarify the author's issue and position? In which other paragraphs does the author reiterate his or her thesis?

2. Why is the hook effective? Which of the Chapter 12 hooks has the author used (pp. 275–277)?

3. What method(s) from Chapter 12 has the author used to develop the introductory paragraph (pp. 271–275)? Why might the introduction interest the audience stated in the prereading exploration?

4. Why might the lead sentence in the concluding paragraph be effective (p. 285)?

5. What method(s) from Chapter 12 has the author used to develop the concluding paragraph (see pp. 286–290)? What is the expanded thought? Why might the conclusion interest the target audience? Think of how the conclusion links with the introduction.

6. For each topic sentence, what are the reason, the limiting statement, and the connector words? (For more on connecting sentences, see pp. 53–59 and 293–294.)

7. How are the body paragraphs arranged: chronologically or by order of importance? What connector words reveal this organization?

8. Where has the author acknowledged an opposing reason or objection to his or her reasons? Has the author refuted or weakened the opposing reason or objection? How?

9. What are three instances of qualifying (*most, sometimes, often*) (pp. 378, 485)?

10. What are three places in the essay where the author tries to connect with his or her audience? Consider use of the pronouns *we, us,* and *our;* mentions of shared experiences or values; and emotional appeals (pp. 374–376).

11. Why do you think any one paragraph in the essay is well written? Consider elements like patterns of development, appeals, topic sentences, connecting words, sensory details, specific words, action description, dialogue, metaphors and other comparisons, sentence variety, and clear explanations.

For more on refutation, see pp. 379–381.

WRITING A PERSUASIVE ESSAY
Summarizing the Assignment

In this assignment, you will tackle an **issue** (a debatable topic), taking a clear position and defending it in an essay of 500 to 600 words. There are many potential issues to write on. You might choose one that requires some research, such as drug testing in the workplace or selective admission policies in universities, or stick with one that you know about from personal experience or general knowledge, as the students who wrote the model essays did.

Plan on a paper of five or six paragraphs, three or four of which will be in the body. Because introductory and concluding paragraphs are such crucial elements in essays, you should pay special attention to them. You should also, of course, introduce each body paragraph with a strong topic sentence, which in most cases will give a reason for your position.

If you want or need to do research, see Chapter 18.

Establishing Audience and Purpose

Argument is, arguably, the writing that requires the most sensitivity to **audience.** Because you are asking something from your readers besides understanding—to think or act differently—you can expect your job as writer to be tougher. After all, how do you react when people call to ask you for your time or money? How anxious are you to pull out your wallet or prolong a conversation with telemarketers?

When considering an audience in persuasive writing, you should ask questions like "How resistant are they to my position? What can I expect to accomplish in my argument? How far can I move them to action or agreement?" Maybe you will decide that the best you can do is talk them out of throwing a rock at you. In short, within your general persuasive purpose, you need to decide more specifically how far you will try to move your audience. Because of the importance of audience, successful argument depends on giving and supporting reasons readers will find convincing, countering opposing reasons and objections to your reasons, and generally showing that you are a credible writer.

Working through the Writing Assignment

Discovering Ideas

In exploring issues for this assignment, look to your own life for inspiration. We all lead lives full of potential topics for argument, particularly when we react to situations we are unhappy with. At home, perhaps you would like more help with the housework. Who can you persuade to help? At school, you may need an extension on a class project. How do you move your instructor to grant it? At work, you know that you deserve a raise. How will you talk your boss into it?

You may also choose a topic because you want to learn more about it, perhaps something about which you have strong feelings but not clearly thought out reasons. For example, perhaps you oppose disciplining children by spanking but are not sure what ways might be better. This essay will give you a chance to find out those better ways.

As you brainstorm, remember that a topic is not necessarily an issue but that, with a little thought, most topics can become issues. Consider this example:

TOPIC   When husbands and wives divide chores in a marriage, men often do the yard work.

This statement is merely a topic because it is not arguable. It is a truth with which no reasonable person can disagree. However, we can frame it as an issue like this:

ISSUE   Men ought to do most or all of the yard work in a marriage.

Now we have a potential argument because some people will disagree with the statement, offering reasons to prove their point. The following list may help you choose an issue. Although the issues are framed as assertions, many will need to be further focused with your interests and audience in mind.

POSSIBLE ISSUES: PERSUASION

Issues from Family Life

- Parents ought to control their children's access to television.
- Parents should use methods other than spanking to discipline their children.
- High-schoolers should be allowed to set their own curfews.
- Dividing household chores along gender lines is a bad idea.
- Parents should remove handguns from their house.

Issues from Personal Life

- Your parents should pay for any one of the following for you: your college tuition, a car, auto insurance, a vacation.

For additional issues for this assignment, look under Chapter 16 at www.mhhe.com/brannan.

- One of your friends should change a behavior toward you or others—for example, his or her anger, caustic humor, selfishness, or indifference.
- A friend should stop or reduce some self-destructive behavior—for example, drinking, smoking, overeating, binging and purging, gambling, or couch potatoitis.
- A police officer pulling you over for speeding should not give you a ticket.
- Your best friend (wife, husband, boy- or girlfriend, son, daughter) and you should communicate more openly about issues that annoy you both.

Issues from School

- College students should be able to base their GPA on the last 50 percent of their education.
- Teachers should be more lenient on any of the following: tardiness, absences, or late homework (persuade one of your teachers).
- Colleges should provide more support services for nonnative speakers.
- Campus security should be required to issue one-dollar fines to any smoker who throws a cigarette on the ground.
- Your college ought to provide free day care to students with young children.

Issues from the Workplace

- Your company should change any form of discrimination in hiring, such as according to age, gender, or race.
- Women should react more strongly to sexual harassment on the job.
- Employee X should be fired (or promoted).
- Your company should provide on-site day care.
- Your company should allow four-day workweeks.

Issues from the Community

- By age seventy, people should be required by law to pass an annual physical and driving exam to prove that they can competently handle their vehicles.
- People should become involved with their community by volunteering.
- Parental consent should be required for minors to obtain birth control.
- People should use cell phones in their cars only for emergencies.
- Penalties in your state should be more severe for fathers delinquent on child support payments.

Conservation in Context

ISSUES FROM THE GLOBAL COMMUNITY

Choose one of these green issues to write your essay about:

- There should be a specific incentive to (or a penalty not to) separate recyclables from trash.
- The United States should sign the Kyoto Treaty and show a commitment to conserving world resources.
- Stores should only sell energy-efficient lightbulbs.
- Cell phone companies should offer a financial incentive to consumers to return their used phones so they can be properly recycled or disposed of.

- A specific development project in your community should be rethought because it will be a major source of pollution.

- A large local company (or your college) should encourage carpooling to help reduce emissions. ●

ACTIVITY 16.6 | WORKING ONLINE: *Use the Persuasion Writing Tutor*

Under Chapter 16 at www.mhhe.com/brannan you can find more topics for this assignment. For additional argument strategies, download the Persuasion Writing Tutor from the site.

Prewriting

First, check to be sure you have an issue, and not merely a topic. The test is whether you have a statement with which people might reasonably disagree. For instance, if your topic is only children, and you say, "Only children have a different experience growing up than children with brothers and sisters," you have just a topic—a factual statement. But if you say, "Only children are less prepared for life than children who have brothers and sisters," you have an issue—more specifically, an assertion that takes a position on the issue.

Next, make lists of reasons favoring and opposing your position on the issue. For instance, if on the topic of elderly drivers you assert, "Drivers over seventy should be required to pass an annual physical exam and driving test to keep their driver's license," you can then brainstorm lists of reasons favoring and opposing the assertion:

Creating a for/against list of reasons is an essential prewriting strategy for persuasive essays.

Reasons Favoring Assertion	Reasons Opposing Assertion
1. Injury to older drivers	1. Discrimination against elderly
2. Injury to other people	2. Unfair treatment of elderly
3. Inconvenience to other motorists	3. Unnecessary law
4. Failing mental abilities	4. Transportation problems the elderly face
5. Failing physical abilities	5. Infringement on civil liberty

If you are going to argue for the position, the reasons favoring it can become points you will make, and the reasons opposing it points you will argue against. How do you choose which points to use; that is, how do you focus your lists?

You can focus your lists in two ways: by defining an audience and by finding supporting evidence. Erica Hood, who wrote the annotated student model, chose as her audience mostly urban drivers with older family members who could be at risk behind the wheel. With these readers in mind, Erica decided to include

Knowing your audience will help you choose reasons to support and refute your argument.

the opposing reasons "discrimination" and "transportation problems." She found evidence to support her refutation of these opposing reasons: The increased risk because of failing physical and mental health would enable her to refute the point about discrimination, and the existence of alternative means of transportation for seniors would help her refute the point about transportation problems.

As you gather ideas for your argument, select the reasons to support and refute that are most appropriate in light of your audience and evidence.

PREWRITING—SUMMING UP

1. Choose several topics from the lists, or choose several of your own.
2. Focus the topic as an issue.
3. Create lists of favoring and opposing reasons.
4. Select favoring and opposing reasons based on your evidence and audience.
5. Develop several reasons with evidence.

JOURNAL / BLOG ENTRY 16.2

Who would oppose your position on this issue, and what is one reason they would give? How will you refute it—with one of your reasons or by showing how the reason is faulty? Perhaps the logic is flawed or poorly supported by evidence.

For some common fallacies, see pp. 376–377.

Organizing Ideas

Before moving ahead, write out your thesis, stating your issue and position. When you draft your essay, you may simply imply the thesis or frame it as a question (see "Just Say No," pp. 381–383), but for now, state it directly. Most of you will put the thesis in the last sentence of the first paragraph. Remember to **qualify** and focus the thesis, and consider including a word like *should*, *ought to*, or *must* to clarify your position. Here are two thesis sentences from the chapter models:

A. Parents who believe in allowances for their children should consider making their children work for the money.

B. Not testing the competency of older drivers annually could be a dangerous oversight.

There are two related mistakes to avoid in the introduction in general and the thesis in particular: inappropriate use of *you* and alienating the audience. Because you are asking an audience to change an attitude or behavior, you can easily sound critical of them. To avoid communicating this impression (even if, in fact, it is true), do not use *you* and do include yourself in the audience if possible. Contrast thesis sentence A above with this alternative:

> Unless *you* want to keep raising lazy kids who don't much care about *you* or their family, *you* ought to wise up and make the kids do their fair share around the house to earn their allowance, rather than continuing to spoil them.

As you can see, the original version of this thesis is far more likely to draw the audience of parents into the essay.

The best arrangement for the body is probably order of importance, in which you present your reasons from least to most strong. One good way to organize is to build your body paragraphs around single reasons. Each body paragraph can then also deal with the relevant opposing reasons or objections. Alternately, you may create a separate paragraph to refute all opposing reasons together (see the annotated student model for a separate-paragraph refutation). Because essays are complex, you

Avoid alienating your audience at the outset; qualify and clarify thesis sentences.

An Argument against Older Drivers

Older drivers can have a hard time of it on the road. Their reflexes slow down, their eyesight deteriorates, and their hearing goes. Although some can handle their cars competently, many are accidents waiting to happen. For everyone's safety, including their own, older drivers should be willing to take a test each year to see if they are still able to drive safely.

My first point is that elderly drivers are often in poor health. They have trouble moving, their joints ache, getting in and out of a car is a problem, and they neither see nor hear well. Getting behind the wheel is dangerous if these senses are impaired. When traffic is heavy, people need to see the cars all around them and hear if someone leans on the horn. Even drivers in good health with all their senses intact can drift out of their lane and only be brought back to reality by a loud horn honk.

Reflex time also slows down as people get older. This creates other difficulties and problem for drivers. There are many situations where people have to react quickly while driving like when an ambulance wants by or when a car slows down drastically in front of a person. In order to help out their slow reaction time, many old folks slow down, but slower driving can be as dangerous as fast driving. During rush hour when cars are racing past, you can see the older driver, poking along at forty miles an hour. This can cause accidents.

As people age, many catch illnesses that lead to dangerous driving. My older grandfather on my mother's side has Alzheimer's, and the disease began lowering his competency long before he stopped driving. No one in our family knew that he had Alzheimer's, and he was driving on the very day that he was diagnosed. I am not trying to discriminate against the elderly. However, when a driver frequently endangers himself, putting himself at risk and others, steps must be taken to ensure everyone's safety.

1 First draft contains reasons but lacks several counters and specific examples as evidence.

Working thesis

2 Topic sentence unfocused

3

Needs further qualifiers throughout

4

Disclaimer

We all want to protect our grandparents and ourselves from harm. To do this we need to support an annual driving exam and physical checkup for older drivers. Some might oppose such a law on the grounds that once an older driver loses their license, they become housebound. But in the city there are busses and taxis. In rural areas, people can carpool, and family members can take care of their grandparents by driving them. If people want to protect and care for their grandparents' needs, they can insist on more and better public transportation. Our lawmakers can accomplish this.

Elderly drivers are creating problems for everyone in society because they have such a hard time driving. Their failing health puts them in danger too. Although seniors will certainly be inconvenienced and so will their family members who have to cart them around, there really is no alternative. When a person is a proven menace, through no fault of his or her own, that person must give up certain privileges for the greater good.

Begins to refute counterreason

Conclusion needs work to improve persona.

Second-Stage Draft

First drafts of arguments are often underdeveloped, lacking enough reasons, opposing reasons, evidence, details, and explanations. There may also be difficulties with **emotional appeals** and the writer's **persona**. Erica knew that her first draft was solid but needed more material, a stronger connection with her audience, and a more effective introduction and conclusion. This second draft addresses these concerns.

PERSUASION: SPECIAL POINTS TO CHECK IN REVISING FROM FIRST TO SECOND DRAFTS

1. **Introduction:** hook, engaging support sentences, <u>thesis</u> (clear issue and position)

2. **Body paragraphs:** topic sentence with connector

3. **Overall development:** reasons: evidence (detailed examples, clear explanations, facts/statistics, anecdotes, scenarios, authorities)

4. **Appeals of persona and emotion:** including connecting with audience through *we, us,* and *our*

5. **Counterreasons and objections:** pointing out logical fallacies

6. Qualifiers

7. **Conclusion:** connector, summary, expanded thought

An Argument against Older Drivers

Last year my grandfather drove through the back of the garage and into the garden behind it. Of course, this can happen to anyone, but since his reflexes are so slow, half his car went through the garage wall before he was able to stop. Maybe my grandfather should no longer be driving, but once people in America take a driving test, they are usually turned loose until the day they die. Not testing the competency of older drivers annually—especially by age seventy—could be a dangerous oversight.

We all know that eyesight and hearing almost always worsen as people age. For various reasons some older people don't like to admit it. Driving is dangerous if these senses are impaired. When a solid wall of cars stops during rush hour, a driver better be able to see it, and when a semi blows its horn announcing that it is changing lanes, a driver better be able to hear it. Sometimes eye wear or even surgery cannot correct vision enough for the elderly to drive safely. And sometimes hearing aids are turned off or their batteries are low. These are just two reasons why people over seventy should take driving tests every year.

Reflex time also slows as people get older. This creates other difficulties and problems for drivers. My grandfather might not have caused as much damage to his car or garage if he had reacted faster. There are many situations where people have to react quickly while driving. Sometimes an emergency vehicle needs by. And then there are times when a car abruptly slows in front of another. Also, a hazard like a piece of lumber or truck tread might appear on the highway, or a child might run out into the road. In order to compensate for their slow reaction time, many elderly reduce their overall speed, but slower driving can be as dangerous as fast driving. During rush hour when cars are racing past, that old car with someone's grandmother in it who is barely able to see over the steering wheel, poking along in the high-speed lane, can cause accidents.

As people age, many contract debilitating illnesses that can lead to dangerous driving. My older grandfather on my mother's

---

1 Introduction revised with personal anecdote to connect with audience

   Qualifiers added throughout

   Thesis revised to clarify age group of drivers

2 Topic sentence revised

   Further explaining added.

   Reiterates thesis

3

   Personal example added as specific evidence and link to reader

   Examples added as evidence

   Specific details added to example

4 Reveals personal response to help shape persona

side has Alzheimer's, and the disease began lowering his competency long before he stopped driving. No one in our family knew that he had Alzheimer's, and he was driving on the very day that he was diagnosed. It frightens me to think that he might not have been able to find his way back home while driving or, worse, become disoriented and had a high-speed accident. I am not trying to discriminate against older drivers. My own young adult age group is often, and sometimes justifiably, bashed for reckless driving. However, when a driver frequently endangers himself, putting himself at risk and others, even though it is not through his own fault, steps must be taken to ensure everyone's safety.

5   We all want to protect our grandparents and ourselves from harm. To do this we need to support an annual driving exam and physical checkup for older drivers. Some might oppose such a law on the grounds that once an older driver loses his license, he becomes housebound, unable to take care of his needs. But in the city there are busses and taxis and in some cities the subway. In rural areas, people can carpool, and family members can take care of their elderly by driving them. If we as citizens and children of our grandparents seriously want to protect our grandparents and care for their needs, we can insist on more and better public transportation. Our lawmakers can accomplish this.

6   Neither of my grandfathers wants to endanger anyone, and they both have to get from place to place just like everyone else. But their failing health made them unsafe drivers, so they finally stopped driving, luckily before anyone was seriously injured. As a result, my folks and I and the rest of our family are pitching in to shuttle our grandparents around. It is inconvenient. And family members are annoyed by the chore on occasion. But this "chore" has the benefit of bringing us more often in contact with each other. I see all of my grandparents more frequently now than before they stopped driving. The family profits because we are sharing a task that is right. Our older generation took care of their children and their children's children in their time. Now it is our time to take care of them.

Margin annotations:

More explaining as evidence

Evidence added—persona

Thesis implied

Pronouns added to identify with audience: *we, us, our*

Facts added as evidence

Conclusion revised to increase persona and appeals to readers' emotions

Third-Stage Draft

With most of the organizational and material concerns out of the way, Erica could focus more on style. In this draft, notice how she improved her word choices and sentence patterns.

PERSUASION: SPECIAL POINTS TO CHECK IN REVISING FROM SECOND TO THIRD DRAFTS

1. Add specific words.
2. Substitute more precise or audience-appropriate words.
3. Combine sentences for variety.
4. **Replace clutter and repeat words with synonyms and phrases.**
5. Delete unneeded words.

Should Our Grandparents Be Driving?

Last year my seventy-five-year-old grandfather drove through the back of the garage and into the garden behind it. Of course, an accident like this can happen to anyone, but since his reflexes are so slow, half his car went through the garage wall before he was able to stop. Maybe my grandfather should no longer be driving, but once people in America take a driving test at sixteen, they are usually turned loose until the day they die. Not testing the competency of older drivers annually could be a dangerous oversight.

We all know that eyesight and hearing almost always worsen as people age, even though some older people don't like to admit it. ~~Driving~~ **Getting behind the wheel** is dangerous if these senses are impaired. When a solid wall of cars stops on I-435 during the 5:30 rush hour, a driver better be able to see it. When a semi blows its air horn announcing that it is changing lanes, a driver better be able to hear it. Sometimes eye wear or even surgery cannot correct vision enough for the elderly to drive safely. And sometimes hearing aids are turned off or their batteries are low. ~~These~~ Poor eyesight and hearing are just two reasons why people over seventy should take driving tests every year.

Annotations (right margin):

1 — Title revised to correct negative tone—*our* added

More specific words added

More precise words substituted

2 — Sentences combined for variety

Phrase replaces overused word.

Sentence divided for emphasis

More precise words substituted

Sentences combined for variety

3

Redundant phrase removed

Sentences combined for variety using colon with list

More specific words added

[Reflex time also slows as people get older, creating ~~other difficulties and~~ another problem for drivers.] My grandfather might not have caused as much damage to his car or garage if he had reacted faster. [There are many situations where people have to react quickly while driving: when an emergency vehicle needs by, when a car abruptly slows in front of another, when a hazard like a piece of lumber or large chunk of truck tread appears on the highway, or when a child runs out into the road chasing a ball.] In order to compensate for their slow reaction time, many elderly reduce their overall speed, but slower driving can be as dangerous as fast driving. During rush hour when cars are racing past at seventy-five miles per hour, that old Chrysler with someone's grandmother in it who is barely able to see over the steering wheel, poking along at forty in the high-speed lane, can cause accidents.

4

As people age, many contract debilitating illnesses that can lead to dangerous driving. My grandfather on my mother's side has Alzheimer's, and the disease began lowering his competency long before he stopped driving. No one in our family knew that Grandpa Miller had Alzheimer's, and he was driving on the very day that he was diagnosed. It frightens me to think that he might not have been able to find his way back home ~~while driving~~ or, worse, become disoriented and had a high-speed accident. I am not trying to discriminate against ~~older drivers~~ **the elderly.** My own young adult age group is often, and sometimes justifiably, bashed for reckless driving. However, when a driver frequently endangers himself ~~putting himself at risk~~ and others, even though it is not through his own fault, steps must be taken to ensure everyone's safety.

Unneeded phrases removed

Synonym replaces overused word.

Sentences combined for variety

5

Gender pronouns alternated

[If we want to protect our grandparents and ourselves ~~from harm~~, we need to support an annual driving exam and physical checkup for ~~older drivers~~ **the elderly.**] Some might oppose such a law on the grounds that once an older driver loses her license, she becomes housebound, unable to take care of her needs. But in the city there are busses and taxis and in some cities the subway. In rural areas, people can carpool, and family members can take care of their elderly by driving them. If we as citizens and children of our ~~grandparents~~ **older generation** seriously want to protect our grandparents and care for their needs, we can insist on more and better public transportation. Our lawmakers can accomplish this.

Neither of my grandfathers wants to endanger anyone, and they both have to get from place to place just like everyone else. But their failing physical and mental health made them unsafe drivers, so they finally stopped driving, luckily before anyone was seriously injured. As a result, my folks and I and the rest of our family are pitching in to shuttle our grandparents around. It *is* inconvenient. And family members are annoyed by the chore on occasion. But this "chore" has the benefit of bringing us more often in contact with each other. I see all of my grandparents more frequently now than before they stopped driving. The family profits because we are sharing a task that is right. Our older generation took care of their children and their children's children in their time. Now it is our time to take care of them.

6

—Erica Hood

Alternate Writing Assignments

The following alternate assignments may help you discover topics for persuasive writing. For any of these assignments, be sure to do the following:

- Review the points in the skills section.
- Define your issue and position clearly for a specific audience.
- Create a chart of reasons favoring and opposing your position.
- Review the Communication Triangle.
- Review methods for creating introductions and conclusions (see Chapter 12).

1. **Write an argument that refutes a newspaper or magazine editorial.** Find an editorial you disagree with at state.com, nytimes.com, or another online publication (a local or school paper is fine). As you read through the editorial you chose, list reasons and evidence the author gives in support of his or her position. Also note opposing reasons and objections the author deals with. Do any of the opposing reasons give you ideas for supporting your position? Try challenging some of the author's evidence, the way he or she interprets it, or the conclusions drawn from it.

2. **Write an advertisement for a product, service, or place, persuading an audience to buy it.** There are a zillion possibilities: a brand of running shoes, a concert, a brand of frozen yogurt, an online dating service, a place to live, or a great vacation spot, to name a few. You might model your ad on one that you think is effective. You can include a picture or describe a film clip that reinforces your message. Remember to deal with concerns and objections the audience might have, including price, quality, dependability, availability, and safety. You might mention a competing product and show how yours is superior. Feel free to use emotional appeals, as most advertisers do, but remember that logical fallacies can hurt your credibility. Evidence is useful even in the sales world.

HINT

See the essay "Abortion, Right and Wrong," pp. 675–677, for help with alternate assignment #3.

3. **Write an argument to persuade a highly resistant audience to listen to and perhaps respect an opposing point of view.** In essence, you will play the role of an arbitrator, trying to bring one side on an issue closer to the other. For example, you might help a pro-life group understand that being pro-choice does not necessarily imply favoring abortion.

   Here are some other possibilities: the NRA and pro–gun control groups, tobacco companies and antismoking groups, loggers or ranchers and environmentalists, pharmaceutical companies and animal rights activists, and pro–nuclear energy supporters and supporters of renewable resources. Try showing the group what they have in common with the other side, dispelling misconceptions they might have about the other side and showing how they can profit from reduced friction.

4. **Write an argument asking for more tolerance toward a group with which you or others are associated that is misunderstood or in some way discriminated against.** For instance, in high school, you or others may have belonged to a social group that was derided by more mainstream groups. Perhaps you are overweight and have felt discriminated against as a result. You may have spent time in prison or know someone who has. Maybe you have a physical or mental disability or spend time with a person who has one. How will you persuade a target audience to become more tolerant? Try dispelling stereotypes and showing the ordinary human side of the marginalized person. Let your reader see how the behavior of the mainstream population can help or hurt fellow human beings.

5. **Persuade the editor-in-chief of your college newspaper to run several antismoking ads, shown below.** You might use several appeals to your audience, including these: The college has a moral obligation to discourage

self-destructive behavior in its students; the college should try to reduce the hazard and annoyance to nonsmoking students of secondhand smoke; and the college would look better without ash containers and cigarette butt litter. Anticipate probable objections and opposing reasons, such as discrimination against smokers, the expense of writing the ads, paternalism by the college in policing student behavior, and exaggeration of the threat to nonsmokers from secondhand smoke.

Alternate Approach: Use one of the ads on the preceding page as a starting point, and expand it into an argument essay aimed at a specific person—a roommate, a loved one, and so on—that he or she should stop smoking. Be sure to qualify your argument, keeping in mind that most ads, while very persuasive, rely to some extent on oversimplification or other fallacies. Consider why you chose one ad over the other.

Linking to Future Experience

Determining the Value of Persuasion

Clearly, people influence one another, and those who are good at it profit. Persuasive skills help us negotiate purchases, land jobs, and meet significant others. But knowing persuasive strategies can also help us resist the professional persuaders—politicians, salespeople, advertisers, and others—and make reasoned rather than manipulated decisions. The process of examining and building arguments can help us think more clearly.

Further, as people living in a society, we need to think carefully about the many issues that unite and divide us. Should abortion remain legal? Do we support capital punishment? Do we need stricter gun control laws? Should sex education be taught in schools? Through argument, we can arrive at reasoned positions on these issues, in the process helping to shape the society in which we want to live.

ACTIVITY 16.7 WORKING ONLINE: *Persuasion Review*

Take the Chapter 16 Review Quiz at www.mhhe.com/brannan.

Chapter Summary

1. Persuasion means moving someone to accept or consider an idea or to perform an action.

2. Argument is formal persuasion that tries to move a target audience, using reasons supported by evidence and refuting opposing reasons.

3. Persuasive speaking and writing are a regular part of our daily lives.

4. Argumentation requires a clearly defined issue and position.

5. An argument benefits from the writer's developing not only logical appeals (in the form of clearly presented evidence) but also emotional appeals and a positive persona.

6. Arguments should avoid errors in logic, including oversimplifying and underqualifying.

7. Writers can connect with an audience by showing that they are part of it; that they understand what readers need to know; and that they share in their beliefs and concerns.

8. Insulting or trying to intimidate readers is a poor persuasive strategy.

9. Argument essays are frequently arranged by order of importance.

10. Writing is never complete until it has been revised and edited.

Taking Essay Exams

17

[*Do you get anxious before or during written exams? In a paragraph, explore either the possible causes of these feelings or the effects (positive or negative) they might have on your performance.*]

KEY TOPICS

- Developing skills and exploring ideas in writing for essay exams

  - Analyzing the question

  - Writing relevant, specific responses

  - Writing essay-exam introductory paragraphs

  - Writing essay-exam concluding paragraphs

  - Writing a complete essay-exam response

- Analyzing student models: Essay-exam responses

- Writing an essay-exam response

What Are We Trying to Achieve and Why?

Setting the Stage

The photo on the previous page shows a familiar scene—a class of students taking an exam. We have all lived through this situation, sometimes with only mild anxiety, other times in a state of panic. In college, one of the most common exam types is the in-class essay; it requires analysis, synthesis, and evaluation—all under the pressure of the ticking clock. Helping you use this pressure to your advantage, gain confidence, and prepare yourself for tackling written exams (in and out of class) is the purpose of Chapter 17.

Two important aspects of essay examinations distinguish them from our other assignments this semester:

- **Process limitations:** To be successful on in-class essays, you must be particularly well prepared because you have to write quickly, with little time for revision. Although most instructors consider time constraints when they evaluate responses, they still expect a well-written essay.

- **Audience:** For perhaps the first time this term, you will be consciously writing to your teacher. Knowing the material and knowing what your instructor expects will help you succeed.

Linking to Previous Experience

Even if you have not taken an essay exam before, you have taken multiple-choice, matching, and fill-in-the-blank tests. Essay exams require much the same preparation and come in several familiar forms, including short-answer (a paragraph), long-answer (an essay), and take-home exams. To develop a paragraph- or essay-length response, use the composition skills you have practiced all semester: unearthing ideas, organizing, drafting, and revising/editing, as time permits. Sometimes a single pattern is called for, such as comparison/contrast. Often, however, you will use several patterns together, as you have throughout *A Writer's Workshop*, particularly in Unit Three.

As in most writing, you will be dealing with a target audience you want something from—in this case, a superior grade. So keep your instructor in mind as you explain, illustrate, and define.

Preparing for the Exam

When studying for a written exam, consider some or all of the following techniques:

- Carefully study the material on a weekly basis.
- Take thorough notes.
- Ask questions in class.
- Participate in class discussions.
- Annotate your text.
- Memorize key terms.
- Link related ideas.
- Create practice questions.

How well, in general, have you done on essay exams? Do you have strategies for preparing? Which of the strategies listed on the preceding page do you usually follow to prepare? What is one change you could make in your preparation habits?

FEEDBACK *Share additional exam prep strategies—ones you currently use or want to try—with your classmates. Make a collective list of good ideas.*

Developing Skills and Exploring Ideas in Writing for Essay Exams

Although we all are experienced in answering test questions, we can always improve. In addition to developing preparation strategies, you can practice the following when actually taking the exam:

1. Analyze the exam question.
2. Write relevant, specific responses.
3. Write brief but effective introductions.
4. Write brief but effective conclusions.

Analyzing the Question

To succeed on essay exams, you must first understand the questions being asked. This seems easy enough—until a vaguely written or complicated question comes along. Consider this question from an American history exam:

> In brief, relate the economic conditions of the South in the years immediately preceding the Civil War.

What exactly does "relate" mean, and what is the professor's purpose in asking the question? Most likely, you are expected simply to summarize the economic conditions in the South at that time. However, you might also be expected to show a causal link between these conditions and the outbreak of the war.

Sometimes verbs of command like *relate, discuss, examine,* and *explore* are open to interpretation. When in doubt, ask your instructor for clarification.

The following essay question is more precise but requires analysis—that is, it gives directions that are specific if you know how to interpret them:

> The causes that led to the War between the States are complicated. While many have been taught that the main issue was slavery, we have learned otherwise in this class. List the three most important factors leading to the Civil War, but focus on the one that seems to be the most significant (as we have discussed it in class). Include the names of people prominent in each of the causes and tell something about their contribution toward the ultimate declaration of war.

The key phrase "list the three," combined with "factors" or "causes," indicates that causes are important and that you will structure the response in three body paragraphs. "Focus on the one . . ." suggests least-to-most organization, with the most attention given to the last, most significant, reason (which the question tells us is *not* slavery). Within each paragraph, you would not only *explain* the cause,

To analyze an essay question, try noting key words and phrases (here boxed).

giving at least one specific example, but also *identify* at least one important person and *summarize* ("tell") what the person did to help bring about war.

When analyzing an essay question, circle key words and phrases that tell you what to write about, how to write about it, and how many parts should be included. The following box lists common phrases used in essay questions along with the general category of question—that is, the pattern of development—they signal.

PHRASES USED IN ESSAY QUESTIONS

General Category	Phrases to Look for in Essay Questions
1. Description	Create a verbal picture of XYZ.
	Describe XYZ.
2. Narration	Trace the beginning of XYZ.
	Tell how XYZ happened.
3. Illustration	Give several examples of XYZ.
	Discuss/explore/explain XYZ.
4. Division/classification	Divide XYZ.
	Group or categorize XYZ.
5. Cause/effect	What caused/were some reasons for/were some factors in XYZ?
	What were the results/consequences/effects of XYZ?
6. Process analysis	Explain (list the steps in) how XYZ works.
7. Comparison/contrast	Explain the similarities and differences between XY and YZ.
8. Definition	Explain the meaning of XYZ.
	Identify XYZ.
9. Persuasion	Argue in favor of XYZ.
	Take a stand on XYZ.
	Show how XY is better than YZ.
	Defend the position of XYZ.
10. Summary	In brief, tell how XYZ works.
	Sketch out (the beginning of) XYZ.
	Give the main points of XYZ, and briefly discuss them.

ACTIVITY 17.1 WORKING TOGETHER: *Analyzing the Question*

In a group, analyze the following essay questions. Circle the key words, indicate the general category of question, and then explain how students are expected to respond. Include how many parts the answer should have and how to organize it—if the question gives you these hints.

EXAMPLE

History: Compare and contrast the major advantages and the major disadvantages of the North and the South as they began the Civil War.

Consider such factors as population size, economy, geography, political structure, and the military.

General category: *comparison/contrast*

To complete the response: *Students are expected to explain similarities and differences between the North and the South as they began the Civil War that might have helped them win or made it harder for them to win. Students should focus on the five points listed. The essay might be structured by either the block or the point-by-point method.*

1. History: Explain who Pocahontas was and what she contributed to the history of the United States. Be sure to mention all figures prominent in the Pocahontas myth and to explain how this romantic myth evolved from the reality.

    General category: _____

    To complete the response: _____

    _____

    _____

    _____

2. Business: Explain the process of balancing a ledger.

    General category: _____

    To complete the response: _____

    _____

    _____

    _____

3. Biology: Explain the principal components of the eukaryotic cell and how they function. Consider dividing your explanation into these three parts: the outer membrane, the components in the cytoplasm, and the nucleus.

    General category: _____

    To complete the response: _____

    _____

    _____

    _____

4. Computer science: Discuss similarities and differences among the human brain, a library, and a computer in terms of how they store information, retrieve it, and present it so people might work with it.

    General category: _____

    To complete the response: _____

    _____

    _____

    _____

Writing Relevant, Specific Responses

When writing an exam response, you are not likely to fool your instructor into thinking that you know the material if you don't. So answer the question as directly and specifically as possible. Stay within any length requirements, and avoid responses that meander or are "padded."

You can make sure your response is relevant and specific by including a topic (or, in a longer essay, thesis) sentence that rephrases the exam question and forecasts an answer to it.

Of the following two responses to an exam question, which is likely to score well, and which sounds like the student is going under?

AMERICAN HISTORY EXAM QUESTION: Explain in a paragraph why Abraham Lincoln is particularly well suited to be an American hero. Give specific examples to illustrate your answer.

Irrelevant first sentence and unfocused topic sentence

Several reasons listed but not explicitly linked to essay question

Response full of empty phrases and several factual inaccuracies

Why not just say "slaves"?

The quote is inaccurate and has nothing to do with the question

A. This is a good question that more people should ask instead of just taking it for granted that Abraham Lincoln is some kind of saint or something. There really are very good reasons why most people think of Lincoln as an important figure in history, mostly because of the many things he did while he was president of our country. He accomplished many great deeds. For example, he helped to free African Americans, <u>who were brought to this country against their will and who up until this point in time were bound to work for the white majority for no pay and with no civil rights</u>. Also, Lincoln was president during the Civil War, which started around 1860 and continued until approximately 1865. And he is famous for writing things like the Gettysburg Address, which begins, "Four score and seven years ago our ancestors made a new nation on this continent for all people to be free and equal." Many people think that the Gettysburg Address is one of the most well-written pieces of writing in this country's history and that the person who wrote it had to be a genius. There is no doubt about it. Abraham Lincoln is a great man and our country is lucky to have had him for a president once upon a time.

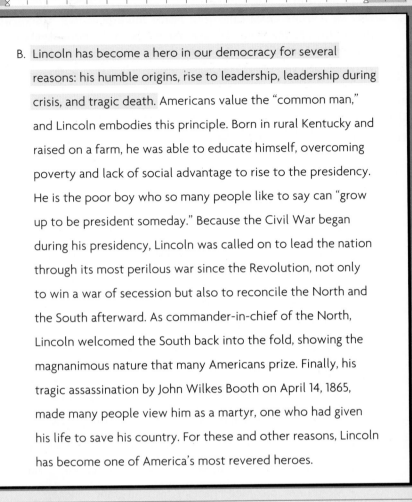

B. Lincoln has become a hero in our democracy for several reasons: his humble origins, rise to leadership, leadership during crisis, and tragic death. Americans value the "common man," and Lincoln embodies this principle. Born in rural Kentucky and raised on a farm, he was able to educate himself, overcoming poverty and lack of social advantage to rise to the presidency. He is the poor boy who so many people like to say can "grow up to be president someday." Because the Civil War began during his presidency, Lincoln was called on to lead the nation through its most perilous war since the Revolution, not only to win a war of secession but also to reconcile the North and the South afterward. As commander-in-chief of the North, Lincoln welcomed the South back into the fold, showing the magnanimous nature that many Americans prize. Finally, his tragic assassination by John Wilkes Booth on April 14, 1865, made many people view him as a martyr, one who had given his life to save his country. For these and other reasons, Lincoln has become one of America's most revered heroes.

Clear topic sentence with forecasting statement

While we may have written exam responses like that in version A, we usually knew that they would not score well. Instead of answering the question of why Lincoln is considered an American hero, version A talks about several of Lincoln's accomplishments in office but then fails to connect them with the point of the question. Also, the author tries to "fill up the space" with empty expressions, repetition, and irrelevant information. To further damage his credibility, the author misquotes part of the Gettysburg Address and reports the beginning date of the Civil War inaccurately. When answering exam questions, if you are unsure about a fact, it is best not to include it.

ACTIVITY 17.2 | WORKING TOGETHER: *Writing Relevant, Specific Responses*

First, analyze the exam question on the next page, circling key terms. Next, read the one-paragraph response that follows the essay question, and then discuss with group members how to improve it. Look for unneeded repetition and "filler" material, missing examples and details, and elements not linked to the topic sentence. Now, drawing from the following information, write a scratch outline, and then draft a one-paragraph response

to the question. Include part of the exam question in your topic sentence, and forecast the four points you have chosen.

AMERICAN HISTORY EXAM QUESTION: Name and explain four reasons why the Civil War, next to the Revolutionary War, has been the most significant war in the history of the United States. Give specific examples to illustrate your answer.

Information from Which to Write a One-Paragraph Response

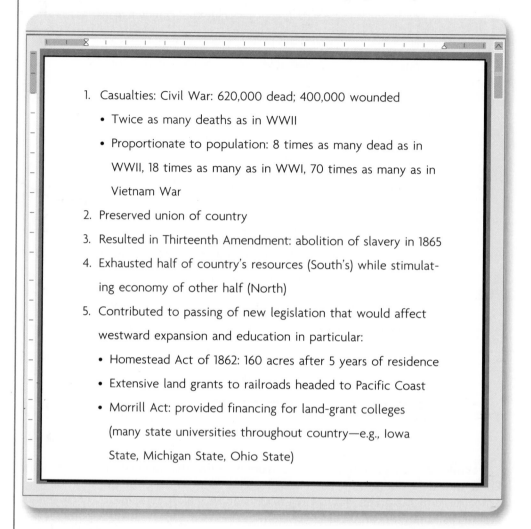

1. Casualties: Civil War: 620,000 dead; 400,000 wounded
   - Twice as many deaths as in WWII
   - Proportionate to population: 8 times as many dead as in WWII, 18 times as many as in WWI, 70 times as many as in Vietnam War
2. Preserved union of country
3. Resulted in Thirteenth Amendment: abolition of slavery in 1865
4. Exhausted half of country's resources (South's) while stimulating economy of other half (North)
5. Contributed to passing of new legislation that would affect westward expansion and education in particular:
   - Homestead Act of 1862: 160 acres after 5 years of residence
   - Extensive land grants to railroads headed to Pacific Coast
   - Morrill Act: provided financing for land-grant colleges (many state universities throughout country—e.g., Iowa State, Michigan State, Ohio State)

Poor Response

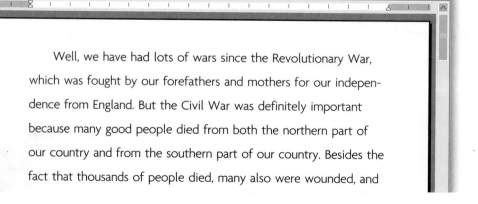

Well, we have had lots of wars since the Revolutionary War, which was fought by our forefathers and mothers for our independence from England. But the Civil War was definitely important because many good people died from both the northern part of our country and from the southern part of our country. Besides the fact that thousands of people died, many also were wounded, and lots of the wounded died from their injuries at some later point in time. Hospitals back then weren't as good as they are today, and many soldiers died from infections and just plain bleeding to death. Even though lots of good doctors (good for what they knew back then, I mean) tried hard on both sides to save the soldiers, because of poor facilities, infection, and lack of medical supplies, the doctors often failed, and so the soldiers died. Another result of the Civil War, also called the War between the States, the War of Secession, and the War of the Rebellion, depending on what part of the country you are from, was that the African Americans who were living in this country against their will as slaves were freed by a proclamation from Abraham Lincoln, who was president then.

Writing Essay-Exam Introductory Paragraphs

The introductory paragraph for an essay-length response should be brief—usually three to five sentences, or less than 100 words. Its purpose is to involve your professor in the response and to show that you know the material. When you write your introduction, be sure to do the following:

1. As with any introductory paragraph, begin with a hook, continue with material to interest your audience, and then state your thesis.

2. Remember to use the exam question in your thesis and to use a forecasting statement for clarity.

Here is one possible introductory paragraph for an essay response to the exam question from Activity 17.2:

Limit introductions to three to five sentences.

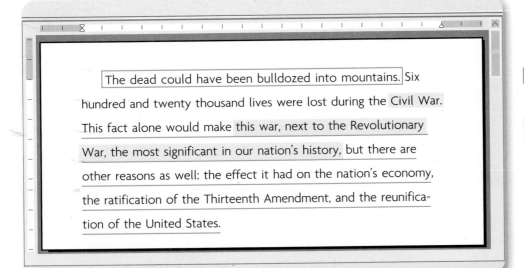

The dead could have been bulldozed into mountains. Six hundred and twenty thousand lives were lost during the Civil War. This fact alone would make this war, next to the Revolutionary War, the most significant in our nation's history, but there are other reasons as well: the effect it had on the nation's economy, the ratification of the Thirteenth Amendment, and the reunification of the United States.

Hook

Restatement of exam question

Forecasting statement

Review introductions in Chapter 12 and then return to your paragraph response from Activity 17.2. Assuming that you were going to develop that paragraph into a full-length essay, write an introductory paragraph for it of three to five sentences that would interest a history professor. Be sure to forecast the focus of the essay.

Writing Essay-Exam Concluding Paragraphs

Like introductions, conclusions for essay-exam responses should be kept to three to five sentences, or less than 100 words. You can use them to show that you understand the significance of your answer. Teachers hope to see evidence of students' ability to make connections, and conclusions are a good place to link your response to other important concepts covered in the text and/or by your instructor. When you write your conclusion, do the following:

1. Begin with a connector and brief summary, and then move into an expanded thought that reacts to the information you have presented.

2. Include a point your instructor has stressed, perhaps a relevant fact or quotation that shows you know more than what you have discussed in the body.

Here is one way to conclude an essay response to the exam question from Activity 17.2:

Limit conclusions to three to five sentences.

Transition and summary

Expanded thought, stressed by instructor

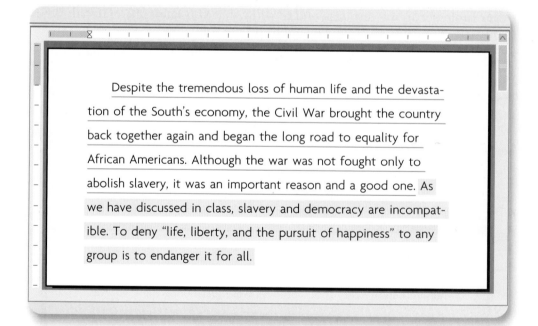

> Despite the tremendous loss of human life and the devastation of the South's economy, the Civil War brought the country back together again and began the long road to equality for African Americans. Although the war was not fought only to abolish slavery, it was an important reason and a good one. As we have discussed in class, slavery and democracy are incompatible. To deny "life, liberty, and the pursuit of happiness" to any group is to endanger it for all.

| **ACTIVITY 17.4** | *Writing Essay-Exam Conclusions* |

Review conclusions in Chapter 12, and then write a three- to five-sentence paragraph to conclude your response in Activity 17.2. Include a connector, link to thesis, summary, and expanded thought—some reflective comment that connects the essay question to something else in the history class or in the larger world. You might include a fact or quotation.

Writing a Complete Essay-Exam Response

A good way to study for and practice writing essay exams is to create and then try to respond to your own questions based on main points in your textbook. Your response can take the form of an outline with supporting examples and then perhaps a rough essay draft to see if you know enough to answer in depth.

In the following activity, the exam question is based on material from this textbook.

ACTIVITY 17.5 WORKING TOGETHER: *Writing a Complete Essay-Exam Response*

Turn back to Chapter 6, Telling Your Own Story, and review the information on narrative elements in the "Prewriting" section. Then, with group members, analyze the following question, circling key words and deciding how to organize a response. After this discussion, write an outline and then an essay response. One person might draft while the rest add wording, or you might each write separate drafts.

Your essay should be concise, use only relevant examples, and be written within 45 minutes. Include a brief introduction that would appeal to your audience (your composition instructor), body paragraphs focused around each narrative element, and a conclusion with an expanded thought. Ask your instructor to review the narrative material with the class, and then include in your final paragraph a point that your teacher has stressed.

EXAM QUESTION: We have learned many important elements that make up personal narrative. List and define three that you think are particularly important, and explain why you think so. Illustrate your response with specific examples from the text, and perhaps include personal experiences as well.

Analyzing Student Models: Essay-Exam Responses

While reading the following models, notice how the authors used a range of information from their textbooks—facts, statistics, names, dates, and brief quotations.

The first student essay, "Clinging by Their Fingers," which answers a U.S. history question, includes many dates and names. The second essay, "Natural Selection," defines an important concept in biology, relying on explanations and examples. The annotated student process model defines concepts basic to photography, using process analysis to explain. In addition to process analysis, patterns of development you will see in the models include description, narration, illustration, cause/effect, comparison/contrast, and definition.

HINT

Use facts, statistics, names, dates, and brief quotations in your answers.

➡ *Prereading Exploration for "Clinging by Their Fingers"*

Adam Fletcher wrote this essay to answer a question in his class on U.S. history to 1877. He had the luxury of choosing among several questions, as well as the time to revise, because this was a take-home exam.

Before reading the essay, circle the key terms in the exam question, and discuss or write on separate paper what you think Adam's history professor expected in a response.

QUESTION: The colonizing of the New World was not rapid or easy. In fact, there were many disasters that led some to abandon the effort altogether. Summarize British efforts at establishing colonies in the New World, beginning with the attempts of Sir Humphrey Gilbert and Sir Walter Raleigh in 1578.

1

Introductory paragraph: begins with a
hook and ends with a thesis sentence
that rewords the exam question and
forecasts what the essay will cover

Body paragraphs: begin with a topic
sentence that names the main example
and makes a limiting statement about it

2

Development: uses specific examples,
including facts, statistics, dates,
names, and quotations; uses active
verbs (*struggled*), *-ing* words (*dying*),
and specific words (*swampy*); explains
the examples ("George Popham . . .
was bad tempered, alienated the
Native Americans, and could not
hold his group together"). Uses **brief
definitions** and synonyms (*settlers =
colonists*), and **patterns of development** (illustration and cause/effect,
par. 3).

3

Style points: Dashes can create
emphasis (par. 3). A series saves space
and can increase clarity ("starvation,
illness, injury . . . ," par. 1). An appositive phrase saves space when defining
and adds clarity ("George Popham, the
president . . . ," par. 4).

4

Clinging by Their Fingers

Huddled together in tiny dark windowless shacks, the first English settlers in the New World struggled to survive the winter. Having little experience with rough living conditions, planning poorly, and often being led by those unqualified for the job, the colonists in most of the early settlements suffered terribly, many dying their first year from starvation, illness, injury, and conflicts with Native Americans. Beginning with the "lost colony" of Gilbert and Raleigh, and progressing through the Massachusetts Bay Company, early English attempts at colonizing the New World met with disaster.

Sir Humphrey Gilbert and his half-brother, Sir Walter Raleigh, were the first adventurers to try colonizing America. Obtaining permission from Queen Elizabeth in 1578 to "inhabit and possess" any land in the New World not claimed by a "Christian ruler," they both tried and failed several times. Gilbert, after two attempts, was drowned in passage, and Raleigh had to abandon two more colonies in 1585. Raleigh's final attempt was in 1587 with the infamous "lost colony," settled by more than a hundred people on Roanoke Island, near the coast of North Carolina. It vanished without a trace within three years.

After Gilbert and Raleigh, colonization efforts stopped until 1607, when James I allowed two companies, the London and Plymouth, to try again, but neither, at first, met with success. The London Company financed the first attempt (to be called Jamestown), which from the start ran into problems. On the four-month voyage across the Atlantic thirty-nine Englishmen died. Not knowing any better, the survivors located Jamestown near swampy ground that bred mosquitoes and malaria. Instead of pre-paring for winter by planting and storing enough food, the mainly gentlemen settlers searched for gold. As a result many starved to death during the winter, and others died from disease. By 1608 only thirty-eight colonists were alive. Although Jamestown began to prosper after 1630, between 1607 and 1624 eighty percent of the colonists—thousands of men, women, and children—died.

The Plymouth Company had even worse luck than the London Company. The merchants of the Plymouth group tried to settle a colony in Maine in 1607, without success. One problem was poor leadership. George Popham, the president of the plantation, was bad tempered, alienated the Native Americans, and could not hold his group together. Expecting a warm, tropical winter, the colonists were not prepared for the extreme cold of Maine. After many died during their first winter, the colony was abandoned. The Plymouth Company next granted land to the small group of Pilgrims and others who sailed on the *Mayflower*, arriving at Plymouth in 1620. They too were decimated by illness and starvation, losing half of their people during the first winter.

The last large group of early English settlers, the Massachusetts Bay Company, also got off to a shaky start. A group of 400 Puritans who founded Salem, Massachusetts, arrived in America in 1628. Their first winter was not much better than that of the Plymouth colony. Half the Puritans died. However, they were met in 1630 by a fleet of eleven ships and 700 new settlers who were far better supplied and prepared for their new life than any previous colonists had been. Even so, 200 of the new arrivers starved to death during the first winter. In 1631, with more supply ships landing, the Massachusetts Bay Colony received the reinforcements and materials it needed to prosper.

Colonizing the New World was no easy task. In the nearly fifty years that it took for the settlements to finally gain a secure foothold, thousands of English men, women, and children died in a world that must have seemed to many of them a nightmare. Some were motivated by greed, some by religion, others by a sense of adventure, but, incredibly, they kept coming, as new immigrants still do today.

—*Adam Fletcher*

5

> **Sentence connectors:** guide readers: transitions, repeat words, synonyms, pronouns, and reference to main idea

6

> **Concluding paragraph:** restates the thesis, briefly summarizes, and adds a final (expanded) thought

➡ *Prereading Exploration for "Natural Selection"*

Emma Perez wrote this essay to practice for a final exam in an introductory biology course. Even though it was written for her professor, a biologist, to explain concepts, Emma mainly relied on ordinary, nontechnical language and examples. As you read, see how well you can follow her explanations. Important concepts do not necessarily require obscure or "big" words.

QUESTION: Explain Charles Darwin's theory of natural selection, and discuss two weaknesses in it that science has since resolved.

Title: arouses readers' curiosity and
links to the essay's main point

1

Introductory paragraph: begins with a
hook and ends with a thesis that
rewords the exam question and forecasts what the essay will cover

2

Body paragraphs: begin with a topic
sentence that names the main example
and makes a limiting statement about it

3

Development: uses specific examples,
including facts, names, dates, and
quotations; uses active verbs (*win*), *-ing*
words (*fueling*), and specific words
(*Darwin*); explains the examples ("the
creature with the most favorable
variation will ultimately win this
contest . . ."); and uses **brief definitions**
and synonyms (*beneficial = favorable*),
and **patterns of development** (illustration and cause/effect, par. 3)

4

Natural Selection

"Charles Darwin effected the greatest of all revolutions in
human thought," wrote Sir Julian Huxley, "greater than Einstein's
or Freud's or even Newton's. . . ." This praise refers to Darwin's
theory of evolution, which is a cornerstone for the biological
sciences. At the heart of this theory is the concept of natural
selection, which, with the exception of two points, convincingly
explains organic evolution.

First, Darwin said, all organisms show variation, meaning that
no two creatures are identical. No mouse is exactly like another
even from the same litter; no person is an exact replica of
another. Organisms differ in height, weight, color, intelligence,
behavior, personality, and in many other ways. He cited the breeding of domesticated animals and cultivated plants as instances of
human beings taking advantage of inherited variations to shape a
species. If people can engineer the selection of desirable traits,
then so can nature, and so the term "natural selection."

Next, Darwin discussed the struggle within a species that
favors creatures with beneficial variations. He noted that all living
things reproduce more of themselves than the original parents.
Even a slowly reproducing species like the elephant can produce
millions of descendants from a single pair given enough time, and a
plant species like an elm tree produces tens of thousands of seeds
each season. If all offspring survived, the species would crowd
itself into extinction. However, it is clear that not all or even most
offspring survive, especially when resources become scarce.
Members of a species must compete for limited resources, as
when two elm seedlings compete for the same nutrients in the soil
or two lions struggle for the same gazelle. Because *variation* exists,
the creature with the most favorable variation will ultimately win
this contest for limited resources and pass its characteristics down
to succeeding generations, and so the term "survival of the fittest."

Finally, to explain the emergence of new species, Darwin
said that when the environment of a species changes, members

of the species will gradually change as their variations allow them to exploit the new resources, as did the Galápagos finches, for example. Over time, as the members of a species diverge more widely, they eventually become a new species.

Science has come to accept Darwin's theory of natural selection as he explained it in 1859, but since that time two points have been further clarified. Darwin knew that characteristics could be passed from one generation to the next, but he did not know how it was done. The science of genetics has accounted for the "how" of traits being passed on. Darwin also did not know of the concept of mutation, by which a gene carrying a variant trait could be created and passed along, thus fueling natural selection. Although he noted that isolation of a species, as in the Galápagos, contributed to speciation, Darwin did not give it the weight that biologists do today, who call it an "essential element" in the development of a new species.

Beneficial variations (genetic mutations), competition among members of the same species, reproduction, and time are the ingredients of the natural selection (and evolution) recipe. Darwin's theory has stood the test of time and is now almost universally accepted among scientists. Over the years some have criticized Darwin's work on the grounds that it is merely a theory, as in a nonscientist's guess. But as we have discussed in class, Darwin's theory is as close to fact as science gets most of the time and belongs with the other "mere" theories that the world runs on, such as the "theory" of numbers or gravity.

—Emma Perez

> **Sentence connectors:** guide readers: transitions, repeat words, synonyms, pronouns, and reference to main idea

5

> **Style points:** Ellipsis points save space ("Newton's. . . ." par. 1). A series saves space and can increase clarity ("height, weight, color . . . ," par. 2). An appositive phrase saves space and adds clarity ("a theory, as in a nonscientist's guess," par. 6). Quotation marks can be used to treat a word ironically ("theory," par. 6)

6

> **Concluding paragraph:** restates the thesis, briefly summarizes, adds a final (expanded) thought, and emphasizes a point discussed in class

POSTREADING QUESTIONS FOR ESSAY ANALYSIS

Note: You can use these questions to analyze either "Clinging by Their Fingers" or "Natural Selection" and apply them to your own essays as well.

1. Name the thesis sentence—the topic and the statement that limits it. Does the author include part of the exam question in the thesis?

2. Why is the hook effective? Which of the Chapter 12 hooks (pp. 275–277) has the author used?

3. What method(s) from Chapter 12 has the author used to develop the introductory paragraph (pp. 271–275)? Would the introduction be effective for the instructor who is the audience? Why or why not?

For more about
lead and summary
sentences, see p. 285.

4. Why might the lead sentence in the concluding paragraph be effective?

5. What method(s) from Chapter 12 has the author used to develop the concluding paragraph (pp. 286–290)? What is the expanded thought? Why might the conclusion interest the target audience? Think of how the conclusion links with the introduction.

6. What patterns of development has the author used? Tell how two of these help answer the essay question.

7. For each topic sentence, name the topic, the limiting statement, and the connector words (see pp. 53–59 and 293–294).

8. How well does the author seem to have used information from his or her text to answer the exam question? Comment on statistics, dates, specific names, and quotations. Does any information seem "dropped in," perhaps related to but not specifically supporting the answer to the exam question?

9. Explain why you think one paragraph is well written. Consider topic sentences, connecting words, specific words, clear examples and explanations, effective use of various patterns of development, action description, and sentence variety.

WRITING AN ESSAY-EXAM RESPONSE
Summarizing the Assignment

This assignment asks you to write an essay of 500 to 600 words in response to an exam question. The question may come from your instructor, yourself, the topics list, or another class (nursing, psychology, etc.). This last is perhaps the best choice, as it will help you prepare for an actual exam or simply better learn the material. If you don't have an exam coming up, you might ask an instructor from another class to create a question for you to use as a study guide or to answer for extra credit.

Plan on studying information from a text, making a detailed outline, and then writing your essay *in class* within one period, just as you would for an actual timed essay exam. You will include a brief introduction and conclusion and several body paragraphs. Because this is an in-class project, preparation is critical to your success.

Establishing Audience and Purpose

Your instructor is, of course, the audience for an essay-exam response, and your purpose is to show him or her what you know. Here are several points to keep in mind as you brainstorm for material:

1. Remember that your instructor's goal in giving the exam is to see what you have learned and how you can apply it. Not everything you have studied will be on the exam, so part of your preparation ought to involve finding out what the exam will focus on.

2. Recognize that your writing does not have to be eloquent, but it does have to be clear and specific. Make sure you will be able to show how your examples fit together and how they help answer the question.

3. Keep tone in mind. Most instructors—even if their classrooms are usually informal and relaxed—expect a fairly formal, academic voice on an essay exam.

Working through the Writing Assignment

Discovering Ideas

Almost all of your material for this essay will come from one of your textbooks and your class notes. Therefore, you should plan on studying outside of class even if the essay exam is open book. Trying to piece together a strong answer from several chapters you are not familiar with while the minutes tick away is a discouraging experience.

The following topics list may help you create your own exam question, or you may simply want to choose and answer one. Most of the questions contain cues to help you develop and organize the answers.

POSSIBLE TOPICS: ESSAY EXAMS

- Biology: Describe the seven major categories in the taxonomic classification system of Carolus Linnaeus.
- HVAC: Name and explain the five factors that must be controlled in providing heating, ventilation, and air conditioning for human beings.
- Sociology: Define the term *social stratification*, and explain the systems it is based on, giving a specific example for each.
- Music: Define the term *harmony*, and explain how it relates to chord progressions.
- Nursing: Explain how the AIDS virus suppresses a human being's immune system, and discuss several common effects of the virus.
- Accounting: Explain the four basic steps in the process of balancing the general ledger of a small company that uses a cash-based accounting system.
- Chemistry: List and explain the three physical states of matter, and then classify the three forms that matter is found in.
- Photography: Explain the relationship between aperture diameter and shutter speed in controlling the amount of light entering a lens. Next, describe three photo shoots where the light varies significantly, and explain what settings to use for f-stop and shutter speed to achieve the effect you hope for.
- Hospitality management: Explain the differences and similarities among the red wines of France, Italy, and the United States.
- Fire science: Explain what is meant by class "A," "B," and "C" fires. Then describe what kind of fire extinguishers are effective on them, and explain the rating system used to determine how large a fire each extinguisher can control.

GREEN EXAM TOPICS

- ENVIRONMENTAL SCIENCE: Define the term *ecosystem* and develop several examples with specific details.
- FORESTRY: Define *timber management*, and explain the process. Be sure to include the three factors a forest manager must take into account when he or she first analyzes a new forest, and include the major problems the manager is likely to encounter.
- BOTANY: Describe the water cycle. Include specific examples that illustrate the terms *precipitation, transpiration, percolation, runoff,* and *evaporation.*

Conservation in Context

- BUSINESS: Many companies are now partnering with green or carbon-neutral organizations to do cause-based marketing. Name and explain three key challenges large corporations face as they seek to make their business more environmentally friendly. Once greener, what are three benefits these companies could look forward to? ●

Preparing for an Exam out of Class

No matter how hard you study each week, reviewing for an exam may seem an overwhelming task. Here are some points to keep in mind:

1. Recognize that you don't have to know every fact and detail. Your instructor will usually help focus your studying by indicating key pages in the text, handing out study sheets, and offering practice (or actual) essay questions.

2. If you feel uncertain about some aspect of the exam, ask questions in class or talk to your instructor. She may be able to clarify any conceptual problems and give you some further direction for studying.

3. If you don't have a study guide with trial questions, create your own questions. To figure out what text material to write questions on, look at chapter headings, subheadings, introductions, conclusions, and summary boxes, and words in **boldface** and *italics*.

4. In your notes, look for points that appear several times; these are probably points your instructor sees as significant.

5. As you study, drill yourself on key terms and ideas, learning not only definitions but also spellings. It is important to be able to link ideas, so while reviewing, try to cross-reference main points. You might also memorize a few short quotations that seem useful.

6. Whether reviewing your text or your notes, use annotation and then outlining and summarizing.

7. After you have studied as much as your time and energy permit, try to relax. If you can avoid "cramming" late into the night, you will be more rested and better able to think clearly during the exam. To minimize pre-test jitters, use this relaxation technique: Mentally put yourself in your usual seat in the classroom; visualize the room, the students, and the teacher; and imagine that you are taking the test and doing great.

Preparing for an Exam in Class

After arriving in class for the exam, do the following:

1. Listen carefully to instructions, and then ask your teacher to clarify any point you are unsure of.

2. Skim the whole exam to be sure you understand the questions and their point value. Look to see how much time is left. Decide how much time to spend on each question, based on its point value; jot these times by the questions, and try to stick to them.

3. Analyze each question (as in Activity 17.1). Circle key words and phrases, notice the command verbs (*define, contrast, evaluate,* etc.), and decide how many parts the answer should have. If the question is confusing, ask your instructor to clarify it.

4. If you have no idea how to answer a question, especially a question with a high point value, don't give up on it. But do move on to the other questions; one of them may jog your memory.

5. As you write, check the time to make sure that you are not getting too caught up in one question.

Know the terminology of your discipline.

Annotate, outline, and summarize. See Chapter 2 for tips on effective reading.

Plan on less than the regular length of your class session to write your responses.

Use your time efficiently: skim the exam, and then monitor your time.

Prewriting

After circling key terms in the exam question, you may need to prewrite to shake loose a few ideas. Clustering and listing can be particularly helpful. For example, when Doug Cunningham, the author of the annotated student model, got the following question, he circled key terms and then listed possible topics for his response:

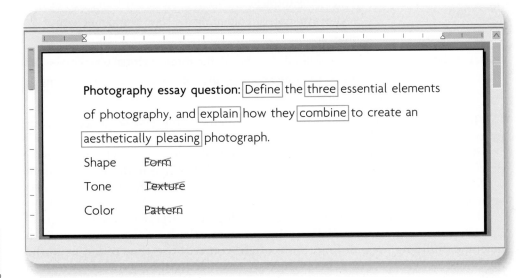

Photography essay question: Define the three essential elements of photography, and explain how they combine to create an aesthetically pleasing photograph.

Shape — Form

Tone — Texture

Color — Pattern

The time you take up front will save you time and trouble when you write. When he listed the terms, Doug realized that his instructor had classed *form, texture,* and *pattern* as subcategories of the first three terms and that these first three were therefore the essential elements.

PREPARING AND PREWRITING—SUMMING UP

1. Prepare for the exam out of class: Review, create practice questions, and ask your instructor to help focus your efforts.

2. Prepare for the exam in class: Skim the exam, ask questions, and plan your time.

3. Analyze each question for key terms and command verbs.

4. Prewrite on paper to uncover ideas.

Take time to prewrite on separate paper if you are not sure of your main ideas.

JOURNAL / BLOG ENTRY 17.2

Briefly explain your essay question. What does it ask you to do? What are the key terms? Have you found enough material in your textbook and class notes to answer the question? What point or points that your instructor has stressed will you include in your response?

Organizing Ideas

Now write a thesis sentence that includes key terms from the essay question. (Other parts of the introductory paragraph can also include wording from the question.) Often your thesis will forecast what your essay will cover, as do

Include key terms from the essay question in your thesis.

the second and third of these effective thesis statements drawn from the student models in this chapter:

NO FORECASTING
At the heart of this theory is the concept of natural selection, which, with the exception of two points, convincingly explains organic evolution.

PARTIAL FORECASTING
Beginning with the "lost colony" of Gilbert and Raleigh and progressing through the Massachusetts Bay Company, early English attempts at colonizing the New World met with disaster.

COMPLETE FORECASTING
When skillfully combined, the three essential elements—shape, tone, and color—can produce aesthetically pleasing pictures

To maximize clarity, make the thesis statement the last sentence of your introductory paragraph.

If an essay question seems in some way ambiguous or unclear, you may need to make sure you have correctly interpreted it. When in doubt, you might write out a preliminary thesis statement and ask your professor whether it is appropriate.

How you arrange the body paragraphs depends largely on the essay question. You may organize spatially if the question calls for description, say, of a machine, building, or painting. More often, you will use time order, as in the model essay "Clinging by Their Fingers," or an order that shows progression of thought, as in "Natural Selection." Sometimes order of importance is called for, as in the annotated student model. So look to the question for guidance, and if you see cues like "compare and contrast" or "describe the process of," your knowledge of the patterns of development will help you organize the essay.

If you are not allowed to bring a prewritten outline to class, write a **scratch outline** (see the annotated student model). Include the main point of each body paragraph and one or two supporting examples. If there are several questions to answer, you might start by skimming the exam and jotting down a scratch outline for each item.

Remember to begin each body paragraph with a topic sentence linked to the preceding paragraph by connectors like transitions.

Prepare a scratch outline. For more on outlining, see pp. 14–15.

ORGANIZING—SUMMING UP

1. Analyze the essay question, and use parts of it in your thesis.
2. Be alert to the possible need to interpret the question.
3. Look to the question to help organize your response.
4. Write a scratch outline.
5. Plan on using a topic sentence to introduce each body paragraph.
6. Review the list of transitions on pages 54–56 and 293–294.

JOURNAL / BLOG ENTRY 17.3

Write your thesis sentence. Does it use key terms from the essay question? Make a rough outline that includes your major points and supporting examples. Be specific with names, dates, facts, and statistics.

Drafting

With an outline in hand, you are ready to draft. Leave wide margins ($1\frac{1}{2}$ inches), and skip lines so you can revise as time permits. Don't be too concerned with style, but do try to write clear sentences that connect to one another. Also try to develop your ideas fully—using specific names, dates, facts, statistics, and quotations as relevant—and to connect them to your thesis. Consider using numbered lists; they can save you time.

While drafting, keep the audience in mind. What points has your instructor stressed? Where would she want you to clarify an idea or define a term, and where wouldn't she? Are you using the language of the discipline and an academic tone?

To improve your essay score, consider also these two time-related strategies:

1. Reserve a few minutes to revise and edit. You may not be able to revise much, but sometimes even clarifying one main example can help a lot. Try to correct errors in spelling, especially of key terms, and major grammar and punctuation problems.

2. Be aware that you might still get partial credit for writing an outline of any points you did not cover because time ran out.

Try to reserve time for brief revision and editing. Out of time? Outline.

Here are some tips for dealing with several other concerns you may have during essay exams:

- **Having an anxiety attack, feeling like you know nothing on the exam:** If you attended class regularly and reviewed even a little, you undoubtedly know *something* on the exam. Take a few deep breaths and refocus. If necessary, leave the class for a moment, with your instructor's permission, to clear your head. Come back to the exam, skim the questions again, find one that you can say something about, and begin an answer.

- **Worrying about other students completing their essay first:** Often finishing early means that the student did *not* do well. Use every available minute to write and revise your responses.

- **Worrying about time running out:** Remind yourself that you have skimmed the exam, planned time for each question, and tracked your progress. You can outline any uncompleted part.

- **Wondering whether to use information you're uncertain about:** If you are not reasonably sure of facts, statistics, quotations, and so on, leave them out.

- **Wondering what to do about a question when no ideas are coming:** Sometimes you simply cannot remember the information needed to answer a question. When this happens, it's best to move forward, returning if time allows.

JOURNAL / BLOG ENTRY 17.4

Does your draft answer all parts of the exam question? Is each paragraph centered around a topic sentence? Have you used detailed examples with names, dates, facts, statistics, and quotations as needed? Have you avoided "padding"? Are your introduction and conclusion brief but interesting and clear? What part of the draft do you like best, and which least? Why?

FEEDBACK *Trade draft answers with a classmate and go through the questions in this entry together.*

Revising Drafts

To review detailed checklists for revising drafts, turn to Chapter 14.

Annotated Student Model: Exam Response

The two drafts that follow will help you with drafting and the minimal revising essay exams allow.

First Draft

Doug Cunningham wrote this response to a question from his photography instructor. Doug knew that he would not need to explain basic concepts or terms in photography, as his instructor is an expert in the field. But Doug did need to explain concepts and terms that related to his understanding of the course material. He brought to class a brief outline with his thesis sentence and knew what he wanted to say in the introduction and conclusion.

Including question and
circling key terms

Thesis with key terms
included and forecasting
points

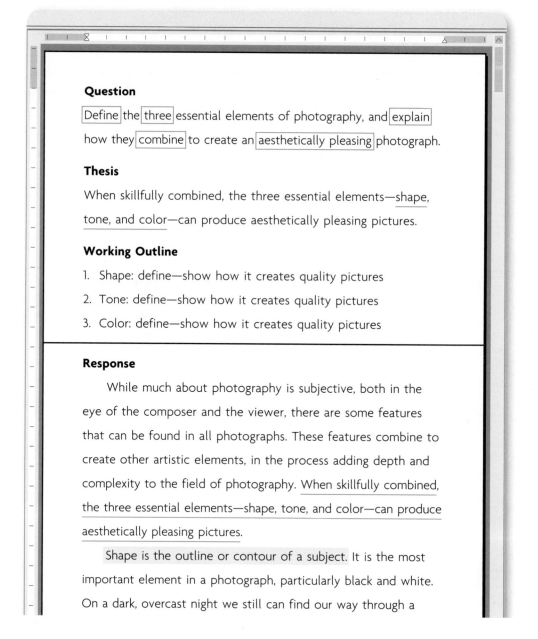

Question

Define the three essential elements of photography, and explain how they combine to create an aesthetically pleasing photograph.

Thesis

When skillfully combined, the three essential elements—shape, tone, and color—can produce aesthetically pleasing pictures.

Working Outline

1. Shape: define—show how it creates quality pictures
2. Tone: define—show how it creates quality pictures
3. Color: define—show how it creates quality pictures

No title

Brief introduction

Thesis incorporates key word
in question.

Clear topic sentence

Definition essential to
question

Response

While much about photography is subjective, both in the eye of the composer and the viewer, there are some features that can be found in all photographs. These features combine to create other artistic elements, in the process adding depth and complexity to the field of photography. When skillfully combined, the three essential elements—shape, tone, and color—can produce aesthetically pleasing pictures.

Shape is the outline or contour of a subject. It is the most important element in a photograph, particularly black and white. On a dark, overcast night we still can find our way through a landscape because we can see the shape of the tree trunk, bush, or car in front of us. In photography the size and placement of shapes within a frame help create balance and draw a viewer's eye to one point or another. Striking images can be formed using silhouettes (a darkened shape with few, if any, features recognizable). One reason shapes handled in this way are so interesting is because they simplify what the viewer sees. Without other visual cues, the eye focuses on the central shape.

Specific examples

Unneeded definition

The second essential element in a photograph is tone, the contrast between light and dark portions of a picture. Tone gives definition to shape. Without the contrast between light and dark, shapes appear flat; in fact, they are silhouettes. The photographer who chooses black and white film specializes in shape and tone, in the absence of color. Black and white pictures may contain very little tonal difference or may run the full range of the light/dark spectrum. Photographs that use tone effectively can create depth and mood, in some instances more effectively than in color. In general, darker images tend to create darker moods, giving a picture a sense of "mystery or menace." On the other hand, lighter tones can give a feeling of "freedom, space, and softness." Experienced photographers work with tonal qualities of film to cause emotional responses, and they are careful not to clash meaning with tone, for example, shooting a joyous wedding in dark, somber shades.

Clear topic sentence

Definition essential to question

No defining of terms instructor knows

Explaining supported by specific example

Color is the last essential element in photography and is linked to tone. Together they give depth and substance, or form, to shapes in a picture. Color, like tone, affects a viewer's emotional response to an image. Bright, warm colors—reds, oranges, yellows—can convey a sense of liveliness and fun; cooler colors—blues, purples, greens—can create a more quiet, reflective tone. Handling color in photography is another matter of selection rather than just pointing the lens at any jumble of colored objects and clicking the shutter. The most aesthetically pleasing color images try for a single dominant color with other colors harmonizing. To achieve harmony in a photograph, the photographer composes a picture using colors closely related on the color wheel, for instance, shades of blue and green as they merge with the bordering yellow

Clear topic sentence

Cause-and-effect development

Explaining link to "aesthetic" point in question

Specific examples given

and purple. When too many muted or too many bold colors are combined within the same frame, the image can become confusing, with shapes "flattening," which damages the feeling of depth.

These three essential features—shape, tone, and color—come together to produce form, texture, and pattern, all of which together can produce beautiful pictures. However, as we have discussed in class, there are few unbreakable rules for combining these basic features of photography. Sometimes, for instance, a photographer wants to use many primary colors to deliberately create a sense of confusion. Some of the strongest images ever recorded on film break many of the "rules," and, after considering their artistic options, people should learn to trust their own subjective response to an image.

—Doug Cunningham

Conclusion contains brief summary, expanded thought, and link to classroom instruction.

First Draft with Minor Revisions and Editing

In-class essays cannot be substantially revised. However, you should save some time to clarify main points, cut unneeded material, and edit. If you have double-spaced and left wide margins, you can add a few words or brief explanation within your essay as needed. For longer additions, use notes: Insert a superscript number at the relevant point in the text and then write the information in a note keyed to that number and included in a notes section at the end of your essay.

SPECIAL POINTS TO CHECK IN REVISING ESSAY-EXAM RESPONSE

☐ Introduction: hook, engaging support sentences, thesis (includes key terms from question)

☐ Body paragraphs: topic sentence with connector

☐ Overall development: detailed examples, clear explanations, patterns of development (all supporting the essay's thesis)

☐ Conclusion: connector, summary, expanded thought

Author never added title. Would it help to have one? What might you suggest?

While much about photography is subjective, both in the eye of the composer and the viewer, there are some features that can be found in all photographs. These features combine to create other artistic elements, in the process adding depth and complexity to the field of photography. When skillfully combined, the three essential elements—shape, tone, and color—can produce aesthetically pleasing pictures.

Shape is the outline or contour of a subject. It is the most important element in a photograph, particularly black and white.[1] On a dark, overcast night we still can find our way through a landscape because we can see the shape of the tree trunk, bush, or car in front of us. In photography the size and placement of shapes within a frame help create balance and draw a viewer's eye to one point or another. Striking images can be formed using silhouettes (a darkened shape with few, if any, features recognizable) with varying degrees of backlighting to create full or semisilhouettes. One reason shapes handled in this way are so compelling is because they simplify what the viewer sees. Without additional visual cues, the eye focuses on the central shape.

The second essential element in a photograph is tone, the contrast between light and dark portions of a picture. Tone gives definition to shape. Without the contrast between light and dark, shapes appear flat; in fact, they are silhouettes. The photographer who chooses black and white film specializes in shape and tone, in the absence of color. Black and white pictures may contain very little tonal difference or may run the full range of the light/dark spectrum. Photographs that use tone effectively can create depth and mood, in some instances more effectively than in color. In general, darker images tend to create darker moods, giving a picture a sense of "mystery or menace." On the other hand, lighter tones can give a feeling of "freedom, space, and softness." Experienced photographers work with tonal qualities of film to cause emotional responses, and they are careful not to clash meaning with tone, for example, shooting a joyous wedding in dark, somber shades.

Color is the last essential element in photography and is linked to tone. Together they give depth and substance, or form, to shapes in a picture. Color, like tone, affects a viewer's emotional response to an image. Bright, warm colors—reds, oranges, yellows—can convey a sense of liveliness and fun; cooler colors— blues, purples, greens—can create a more quiet, reflective tone.

[1]Note added

Unneeded defining eliminated

Explaining added to show full knowledge of silhouettes

Handling color in photography is another matter of selection rather than just pointing the lens at any jumble of colored objects and clicking the shutter. The most aesthetically pleasing color images try for a single dominant color with other colors harmonizing. To achieve harmony in a photograph, the photographer composes a picture using colors closely related on the color wheel,[2] for instance, shades of blue and green as they merge with the bordering yellow and purple. When too many muted or too many bold colors are combined within the same frame, the image can become confusing, with shapes "flattening," which damages the illusion of depth.

These three essential elements—shape, tone, and color—come together to produce form, texture, and pattern, all of which together can produce beautiful pictures. However, as we have discussed in class, there are few unbreakable rules for combining these basic features of photography. Sometimes, for instance, a photographer wants to use many primary colors to create a feeling of confusion. Some of the strongest images ever recorded on film break many of the "rules," and, after considering their artistic options, people should learn to trust their own subjective response to an image.

—*Doug Cunningham*

Notes

1. The reason is that shape occupies the most space within a frame and draws a person's attention immediately, even in the absence of tone and color.
2. Note on the color wheel: Photographers should be aware of the primary and secondary colors, of how they mix with, complement, and contrast with one another to create pleasing images (and other effects).

[2]Note added

Alternate Writing Assignments

The following essay questions are based on *A Writer's Workshop* and may work for you if you have not found a topic from another discipline. For any of these assignments, be sure to do the following:

- Review the points in the "Developing Skills" section.
- Prepare by active reading: questioning, annotating, summarizing, and outlining.
- Construct a thesis sentence with key terms from the essay question.
- Know how you will begin and end your essay.
- Use specific examples and explain concisely.

1. **Question:** Drawing on information in Chapter 1, list and define the seven methods for discovering ideas. Next, choose any two that you have used this semester, and tell why they have been effective for you. Use specific examples from the text to illustrate the methods, but also use examples from your own writing experiences this term.

2. **Question:** Drawing on information from Chapter 1, define what it means to revise a text. Next, explain the process of group revision, categorizing the information by help the writer can give the reader and help the reader can give the writer. Illustrate your response with personal examples.

3. **Question:** Using the information in Chapter 3, list and define the four elements of support found in body paragraphs. Rely primarily on the text for examples.

4. **Question:** Drawing on information from Chapter 5, define the concept of "general versus specific language." Illustrate your response with examples from the text. Then compare the concept with the concept of "increasing specificity," discussed in Chapter 3.

5. **Create your own essay question** and then answer it in an essay of 500 to 600 words. You might want to create a question that involves an interest

outside of school and that requires some reading and learning. For example, look at the photo of lightning on the previous page. Perhaps you are curious about lightning: what causes it, what it consists of, and what its effects can be. After reading about the subject, you could fashion an essay-exam question and then answer it on the basis of your reading. If you choose this option, you will become your own teacher—a fine goal for anyone.

Note: You are likely to have some initial difficulty in focusing the question and making it interesting enough to want to answer. For help with this, review the general categories of questions on page 406 and the topics list questions on page 419. Instead of putting your essay question simply in terms of "listing and explaining," you might want to incorporate comparing and contrasting, evaluating, taking a position, or one of the other general categories. As an example, consider how question A is improved on in question B:

A. Question: Define the term *lightning* and explain its effects.

B. Question: Define the term *lightning*, explaining the process by which it is generated, categorizing the types, explaining its most damaging effects, and explaining how people might protect themselves from lightning injury.

For additional help with researching your topic, see Chapter 18, Writing a Research Essay.

Linking to Future Experience

Determining the Value

Being able to perform well on essay exams will obviously benefit you in school. In the workplace, too, there are many writing situations that require people to quickly organize and draft a response. Examples of such responses include lawyers' reports to their clients, nurses' ward reports, police officers' accident reports, and office workers' project reports. Being able to produce readable writing quickly is a real-world asset.

The process of preparing for an essay exam is also valuable. How often have you thought that you understood a concept until you had to explain it to an audience? Preparing for an essay exam—memorizing material, questioning ideas, making connections, and drawing conclusions—is one good way to explore a topic to ensure that you truly understand it.

Finally, learning to remain calm under stress, or to calm yourself, will give you an ability you can use repeatedly, in school and out.

ACTIVITY 17.6 | WORKING ONLINE: *Creating an Exam Question*

Go to www.slate.com and read an article (one that is at least two pages long) that interests you; then devise an essay exam question you might ask if you were the instructor and this was the course material. Then describe (in a few sentences) what you expect students to accomplish in their responses and which patterns of development they should use. Note: A useful handout on essay exam strategies is available at http://www.unc.edu/depts/wcweb/handouts/essay-exams.html.

ACTIVITY 17.7 | WORKING ONLINE: *Essay-Exam Review*

To be sure you feel comfortable with the meanings of various direction words in essay questions, take the Chapter 17 Review Quiz at www.mhhe.com/brannan.

Chapter Summary

1. Successfully taking an essay exam requires out-of-class preparation: an active review of textbooks and class notes that includes annotating, summarizing, outlining, anticipating questions, and, often, writing practice responses.

2. Responses can be improved by in-class preparation: skimming the exam for an overview, figuring out how much time to allow for each question, analyzing the questions, outlining, and tracking time while drafting.

3. In-class essay exams differ from out-of-class writing assignments in several ways, including the expert audience (your instructor), limited revision time, and shorter introductions and conclusions.

4. Like other major writing projects, essay-exam responses call for the use of the writing process: prewriting, organizing, drafting, and whatever revising and editing time allows.

5. Essay-exam responses usually involve several patterns of development and rely on clear explanations and detailed examples, often with names, dates, facts, statistics, and quotations.

6. Analyzing the essay question and answering all its parts are crucial to a successful essay-exam response.

7. The thesis sentence should contain key terms from the essay question and will often forecast what the essay will discuss.

8. Introductions and conclusions should be brief but clear and targeted to the instructor as the audience.

9. Transitional words and other connectors are important in linking paragraphs.

10. An overall organizational pattern may be suggested by the essay question.

11. Revising and editing, even briefly, will improve the essay-exam response.

Writing a Research Essay

18

[What does writing a research essay mean to you? How would you go about finding information about a topic? Do you prefer researching online or in printed texts? Why?]

KEY TOPICS

- Developing skills and exploring ideas in writing research essays

  - Quoting sources selectively and accurately

  - Integrating quotations from sources smoothly

  - Paraphrasing and summarizing ideas carefully

- Avoiding plagiarism

- Citing sources within your essay

- Preparing a Works Cited page

- Writing a research paper (continued at www. mhhe.com/brannan.)

What Are We Trying to Achieve and Why?

Setting the Stage

Writing research essays is a common academic task, one with which most of us already have some experience. In fact, the research paper is simply an extension of what you have been doing as you worked through the assignments in Units Two and Three of this text—developing a focused idea with detailed examples and clear explanations. However, research requires you to go one step farther. Instead of relying entirely on your own personal experience and general knowledge, now you will find out what other people have to say, and you will use their ideas to help explain your own. In Chapter 18, you will learn how to find, select, use, and document information as you craft a well-developed, source-supported essay.

Linking to Previous Experience

Most of us have written essays that relied on sources outside our personal experience. In high school, you might have written research essays or taken short-answer or full essay exams requiring you to present information—facts, statistics, names, dates, and so forth. If you have worked through Chapter 17, you have likely learned how to include textbook sources in an answer to an essay-exam question. Also, throughout *A Writer's Workshop*, you have worked on focusing and developing ideas, the basis of all writing. Finally, you have had to bring together ideas—a task that research requires—as you combined the patterns of development in essays for different purposes.

See pp. 9–10 for brief descriptions of the patterns of development.

Developing Skills and Exploring Ideas in Writing Research Essays

The following skills will help you write effective research essays:

- Quoting sources selectively and accurately
- Integrating quotations from sources smoothly
- Paraphrasing and summarizing ideas from sources
- Avoiding plagiarism
- Using in-text citations for all sources that you quote, summarize, or paraphrase
- Preparing a Works Cited page

Quoting Sources Selectively and Accurately

One useful method for bringing ideas from sources into your essay is quotation. **Quoting** a source means placing the author's words within quotation marks and then acknowledging the author by name, either within the sentence or within parentheses, usually at the end of the quotation. You should not use quotations merely to fill up space. Rather, you should include quotations when you have good reasons for doing so, as in the following:

- The author's wording is particularly memorable. A well-turned phrase often includes metaphors, similes, and other figures of speech.

See pp. 498–502 for more on figures of speech.

- The material is loaded with statistics, names, dates, and percentages and so would be difficult to reword.
- The author of the quotation would be recognized by and be significant to the audience.

One other point to remember as you quote a source is to do so accurately. You are bound by convention to reproduce each word, punctuation mark, and even error as it appears in your source. If you want to economize by cutting part of a quotation, indicate the missing words with **ellipsis points**—three spaced periods—as in the following example:

"Like much of Mars, the butterscotch plain is . . . pretty dull."

When you need to add a word or two to clarify a point within a quotation or make it fit grammatically within your sentence, use **brackets** [ ], as in the following example:

"Like much of Mars, the butterscotch [meaning yellow] plain is . . . pretty dull."

If you notice an error within a quotation, you can show readers that it is not your mistake by writing the word *sic* within brackets after the error, as in this example:

"Like much of Mars, the butterscotch plane [sic] is . . . pretty dull."

Integrating Quotations from Sources Smoothly

When you quote a source, be sure to include information in your lead-in so that readers are not left to guess at the significance of the quotation. The following examples show how you might leave readers confused by a quotation or help them understand your meaning by introducing and explaining the idea:

Quotation Not Introduced

Oliver Norton says, "It's dustier than the road to death, drier than Dorothy Parker's martinis, colder than the devil's kiss."

Quotation Explained

The author, Oliver Norton, explains how hostile the environment is on Mars with these images: "It's dustier than the road to death, drier than Dorothy Parker's martinis, colder than the devil's kiss."

In addition to clearly introducing and explaining the significance of a quote, writers can vary the verbs they use to introduce quotations by using words in the following list:

says	offers	continues	remarks	argues	claims
explains	gives	adds	tells	maintains	challenges
states	mentions	expands on	reveals	asserts	admits
comments	discusses	points out	presents	denies	acknowledges

If you want to use a quotation that would be longer than *four* lines when reproduced in your essay, you should put it in **block quotation** form by indenting it ten spaces from the left margin, double-spacing between lines, and omitting quotation marks around the information:

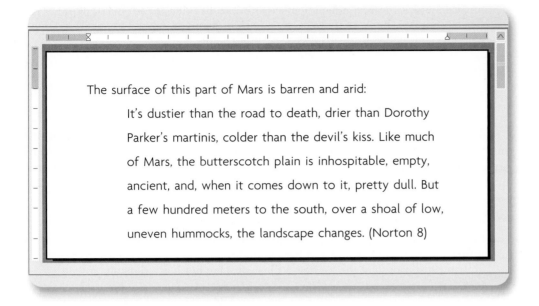

The surface of this part of Mars is barren and arid:

> It's dustier than the road to death, drier than Dorothy
> Parker's martinis, colder than the devil's kiss. Like much
> of Mars, the butterscotch plain is inhospitable, empty,
> ancient, and, when it comes down to it, pretty dull. But
> a few hundred meters to the south, over a shoal of low,
> uneven hummocks, the landscape changes. (Norton 8)

Note the author's last name and the page number in parentheses following the quotation. Full publication information would be provided in a Works Cited list at the end of the essay.

Paraphrasing and Summarizing Ideas Carefully

Two more methods for bringing ideas from sources into an essay are paraphrasing and summarizing. When you **paraphrase,** you put a passage into your own words, changing *both* the source's words and the arrangement of those words. Because you keep most of the main ideas from your source, a paraphrase is about the same length as the original. When you **summarize,** you reword the original text but keep only main points, leaving out supporting points, casual commentary, and most examples. Summaries are generally much *shorter* than the original. When you paraphrase or summarize, you must read a text closely and understand it well enough to report it accurately.

Read the following paragraph, written by Oliver Norton for *National Geographic,* and the paraphrase and summary that follow.

Original Text

Landscapes like this are changing the way geologists look at Mars. They've long been fascinated by the planet's distant past. Now they're getting ever more excited by the mysterious processes shaping its present—thanks in large part to the planet's apparent iciness. Martian ice is not a novelty in itself; for years geologists have expected to find it frozen into the soil at mid and high latitudes. The excitement comes from a growing suspicion that the ice doesn't just sit there but has a dynamic role to play. That it moves from place to place around the globe. That it reshapes the texture of the surface. And that it may sometimes produce fleeting traces of liquid water. (Norton 8)

Paraphrase

Oliver Norton states that geologists are becoming more interested in recent forces shaping the planet Mars because the scientists are beginning to suspect that ice in the soil helps change the landscape. Norton says that geologists, who have studied Mars for many years, have known about ice there for a long time and supposed that it might be found in the planet's soil in middle and upper latitudes. However, the scientists didn't realize that the ice might alter the surface of Mars. Now they theorize that the ice might liquefy in small amounts and that as it travels it erodes surfaces. (8)

Summary

Scientists have recently begun to suspect that ice on Mars may liquefy in small amounts and that as the ice moves, it changes the face of the planet (Norton 8).

Three problems commonly occur when writers use paraphrase and summary: misinterpreting the source's ideas, omitting an idea or adding one that should not be there, and using too many of the author's words and a word arrangement that is too similar to the original.

Original Text

Martian ice is not a novelty in itself; for years geologists have expected to find it frozen into the soil at mid and high latitudes. The excitement comes from a growing suspicion that the ice doesn't just sit there but has a dynamic role to play. (Norton 8)

Misinterpretation that Leaves Ideas Out

The author says that finding ice on Mars was not a surprise to geologists, who thought it would be all over the place. But now they are interested because they are sure the ice affects the planet's surface (Norton 8).

Notice that the original text says geologists thought the ice would be in a specific location, in the soil and at "mid and high latitudes." Also, the scientists are *guessing* at the dynamic function of ice; they are not "sure," as the distorted paraphrase claims. It is often difficult to report accurately what one of your sources intends, so it is important to read your material several times until you are sure you understand it.

ACTIVITY 18.1 WORKING TOGETHER: *Paraphrasing and Summarizing Effectively*

Read aloud the original text below, taken from the article on Mars by Oliver Norton, and read the paraphrase. Then discuss in small groups to determine and tell how, specifically, the paraphrase distorts it.

Original Text

Water will stay liquid only if it's warm enough and at high enough pressure. Drop the temperature, and it will freeze; drop the pressure, and it will vaporize. Physics seems to say that Martian midlatitudes are far too cold for liquid water to persist for any length of time at the surface. (Norton 15)

Distorted Paraphrase

Oliver Norton discusses the physical properties of liquid when he notes that it will flow when it's warm and disappear when there is too little air pressure on it. Physicists are sure that Mars is too cold for water to be there.

_____

_____

_____

Avoiding Plagiarism

Another common problem in research writing is **plagiarism**—the theft of someone else's words or ideas. Sometimes people consciously represent another person's work as their own, deliberately plagiarizing. This is a serious academic offense that can result in a failing grade for an essay or for the entire course. But more often inexperienced writers either fail to document words or ideas from their sources or reword carelessly. Consider the following example of accidental plagiarism:

Original Text

Then in the 1970s this Mars too was killed. Orbiting spacecraft—first Mariner 9 and then the two Viking missions—showed there was much more to the Martian surface than craters. Mariner 9 saw volcanoes twice as tall as any on Earth. There were canyons as deep as the Earth's deepest ocean trenches. (Norton 14)

Accidental Plagiarism

In the 1970s this Mars too was destroyed. Orbiting spaceships, the first being Mariner 9 and then two Viking ships, were able to show there was a lot more to the surface of Mars than craters. Mariner 9 showed volcanoes two times as tall as any on Earth. Also there were canyons as deep as the Earth's trenches (Norton 14).

Even though the author of the plagiarized paragraph cited Norton, because the author included too many of the source's words in the same order and with the same sentence structures, this paragraph is unacceptable. To avoid accidentally plagiarizing, keep these two suggestions in mind:

1. If you use more than two or three of the source's words in a row, use quotation marks (remember, however, that quotations must be justified).

2. Carefully read the passage you will cite, and then *look away from it* as you "translate" the information into your own words. It is difficult to avoid plagiarizing if you shift your eyes back and forth between your source's words and your own.

Here is one way to eliminate plagiarism by paraphrasing and selective quoting:

Plagiarism Eliminated

The author tells of the changing views scientists have had of Mars, including the shift "in the 1970s [when] this [image of] Mars too was killed." Whereas scientists had thought that the surface of Mars was largely riddled with craters and little more, they learned otherwise. Several space ventures, Mariner 9 and Viking, discovered volcanoes higher than any of Earth's and canyons to match those of our deepest ocean trenches (Norton 14).

Although it is critical to acknowledge your sources—their *ideas* as well as their exact words—some ideas and information are so widely known that they are considered to be everyone's property, or **common knowledge.** You do not need to cite the source of common knowledge. For example, most educated people know that the Holocaust took place in World War II, that there are seven continents, and that the United States was attacked by terrorists on September 11, 2001.

ACTIVITY 18.2 *Avoiding Plagiarism*

Read the following original text, taken from the article on Mars by Oliver Norton, and compare it with the plagiarized paraphrase. Then rewrite the paragraph, "translating" Norton's words, quoting selectively, and changing the word arrangement.

For more on avoiding plagiarism, visit www. mhhe.com.brannan.

Original Text

Today Mars looks a lot more like a globe of ice than it ever has before. But it also looks like something shucking that ice away, something moving on, something undergoing change. Whatever else Mars turns out to be, it won't be a useless, changeless lump in the universe. (Norton 30)

Plagiarized Version

Nowadays the planet Mars looks much more like a globe of ice than ever. Yet it also seems like something that is shucking that ice away, something moving along, a thing is changing. The author says that Mars won't turn out to be a useless, unchanging lump in the universe (Norton 30).

Plagiarism Eliminated

_____

_____

_____

_____

Citing Sources within Your Essay

After choosing information to quote, summarize, or paraphrase, you must credit the author of the information within your essay. You do this to direct readers to a **Works Cited** page, on which you list all sources used in the essay. If the author of the information you are citing is well known to your audience or has impressive credentials, you should state his or her name in the sentence that introduces the information, as in "Mark Twain once said, ..." You may also place the author's last name in parentheses near the source material in your paragraph, most often at the end of a sentence. Remember that you must cite summaries and paraphrases as well as direct quotations.

The following examples follow the MLA (Modern Language Association) format for citing sources within text:

Author Mentioned in Your Text
When the author's name is mentioned within your sentence, leave the name out of the parenthetical citation:

> Professor Davis explains that vampires have left a profound mark on literature (125).

Author Not Named in Your Text
Include the name of the author within the parenthetical citation at the end of the sentence if you have not used the name in your own text:

> Some literary experts maintain that vampires have left a profound mark on literature (Davis 125).

Two- or Three-Author Source
Include the names of all the authors:

> *The Lord of the Rings* trilogy is the cornerstone of fantasy fiction (Senter, Harris, and Hogan 66).

HINT

You must cite summaries and paraphrases as well as quotations.

More Than Three Authors

Include the first author's last name and then use the Latin abbreviation *et al.,* meaning "and others":

> As we become familiar with the literature of vampires, we will see the relationship many politicians have with society (Davis et al. 5).

Corporate Author

A work may be attributed to an institution rather than a person:

> The best way to protect the land is to involve the people who live there (Nature Conservancy 32).

Unknown Author

When the author is unknown, use the whole title of the work, if it is short, or the first significant words in the title, within quotation marks:

> The best way to protect the land is to involve the people who live there ("Saving the Land" 32).

Source without Page Numbers

If you are citing a website or other type of source without page numbers, include only the author's name (or, if there is no author, an abbreviated form of the site's title) in your internal citation:

> More campuses are exploring alternative energy options and encouraging students to buy efficient lightbulbs (Jameson).

Author of Several Works

If you use more than one work by the same author, include the first significant words from the title of each source within quotation marks, and include the author's last name:

> The Japanese Samurai was akin to the medieval European knight ("History," Halligan 77).

Several Sources Giving the Same Information

Include both sources, separated by a semicolon:

> Celtic music has undergone a rebirth in recent years (Broomfield 21; Russell 9).

Indirect Source

When using a quotation that your source has taken from someone else, use the words *qtd. in,* short for "quoted in." In this example, Williams has quoted Antle:

> As Jay Antle has remarked, "Storm chasing is not for the faint hearted" (qtd. in Williams 321).

Preparing a Works Cited Page

To help readers locate sources used in an essay, writers following the MLA format create a Works Cited page, which lists in alphabetical order all of the sources quoted, summarized, or paraphrased in the essay. Note that you do not include all sources you have looked at, just the ones you have used. The Works Cited page comes on a separate page after the conclusion of your essay. Follow these guidelines when creating your Works Cited page:

To see a model Works Cited page, turn to p. 447. For help creating a Works Cited page, use the Bibliomaker at www.mhhe.com/brannan.

GUIDELINES FOR CREATING A WORKS CITED PAGE

1. Center the words "Works Cited." However, do not underline them or use quotation marks around them.
2. Alphabetize the authors by last name.
3. Begin each name at the left margin.
4. Indent each line beneath the name within an entry by five spaces.
5. Double-space all lines in and between the author entries.

The following examples will help you build your Works Cited page. (For more information on citing sources, visit the MLA website at http://www.mla.org.

Books

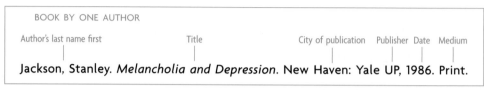

BOOK BY ONE AUTHOR

Author's last name first — Title — City of publication — Publisher — Date — Medium

Jackson, Stanley. *Melancholia and Depression.* New Haven: Yale UP, 1986. Print.

The second line of each entry is indented five spaces. All lines are double-spaced.

Book by Two or Three Authors

Hershman, Jablow, and Julian Lieb. *Manic Depression and Creativity.*

Amherst: Prometheus, 1998. Print.

Chappelle, Sean, Maria Cox, and Steven Fenton. *As the Last Rain Forest Falls.*

New York: McGraw-Hill, 2003. Print.

Book by More Than Three Authors

Rose, Michelle, Margo Schnipper, Russel Binelli, and Michael Cohen. *The*

Myth of the Bermuda Triangle. New York: Harper, 1999. Print.

The abbreviation *et al.,* meaning "and others," may be used after the first author's name, replacing the other author names.

More Than One Book by the Same Author

Martin, Melanie. *Raising Children the Easy Way.* Fort Worth:

Harcourt, 2001. Print.

——. *When Time-Out Is No Longer Enough.* Fort Worth: Harcourt, 2002. Print.

Note: Three hyphens substitute for the author's name.

Book with an Editor

Bellenir, Karen, ed. *Mental Health Disorders Sourcebook.* Detroit:

Omnigraphics, 1996. Print.

Work in an Anthology

Dinesen, Isak. "Sorrow-Acre." *The Norton Anthology of Short Fiction.* Ed.

R. V. Cassill. 4th ed. New York: Norton, 1990. Print.

Encyclopedia Article

Turk, Alexander. "Paleontology in the Twentieth Century." *The New*

Encyclopaedia Britannica: Micropaedia. 15th ed. 2002. Print.

Periodicals

MAGAZINE ARTICLE: WEEKLY

Author's last name first   Title   Name of publication   Date   Page numbers   Medium

Caruthers, Faith L. "Where Is Osama Now?" *Newsweek* 7 Feb. 2003: 44–48. Print.

Magazine Article: Monthly

Lamb, Bertrand. "Learning to Talk to Your Teen." *Parenting* May 2004:

120–23. Print.

Journal Article with Consecutive Paging over Several Issues

Sturbenz, Michael. "Alzheimer's: The Earliest Onset." *Journal of Applied*

    vol. #   page #s

Psychology 64 (1999): 840–47. Print.

Journal Article with New Paging in Each Issue

Walsh, Catherine. "Perspectives: Suicide of Author Michael Dorris."

    vol. # issue #   page #

America. 176.16 (1997): 7. Print.

Newspaper Article

Cowley, Frank. "Kudzu: Meet Your New Neighbor." *New York Times* 14 Jan.

    ed.   pages continue

2001, late ed.: C2+. Print.

Editorial or Unsigned Letter to the Editor

"No Child Left Behind, and No School District Left Funded." Editorial.

    Free Press News 4 Sept. 2003: A12. Print.

Note: A = section.

Only include
an edition of a
newspaper when there
are multiple editions
of the same issue.

Electronic Sources

Only list a website's URL (address) if readers would be unable to find the source's location without one.

Website

    date created   date accessed

"Depression." 4 Jan. 1999. *Mayo Clinic Health Information.* Web. 24 Mar. 2000.

Journal Article Accessed through Subscription Database

Camarillo, Albert M. "Cities of Color: The New Racial Frontier in California's

    name of journal   print pub info   subscription database

Cities." *Pacific Historical Review* 76.1 (2007): 1–28. ProQuest. U of

host library   date of access

Michigan, Ann Arbor, MI. Web. 1 May 2008.

Article from an Online Magazine

    article title   magazine   date published   date accessed

Matlin, Chadwick. "The Carbon Olympics." Slate.com. 29 Apr. 2008. Web. 1 May

2008.

Article from an Online Newspaper

name of online newspaper

Hollander, Sophia. "A Sisterhood Lays a Foundation in Football." *New York Times*
date published   date accessed
on the Web 13 May 2008. Web. 28 Jun. 2008.

Blog Entry

entry in quotation marks   blog title   date posted

Sullivan, Andrew. "The War on Nature." The Daily Dish. Web. 27 Apr. 2008.

E-mail

Bronson, Carter. "Getting Out the Vote." E-mail to Danny Alexander.

22 Jan. 2008.

Other Sources

Interview

Williams, Carmaletta. Personal interview. 4 Dec. 2004.

Film or Video

The Lord of the Rings: The Two Towers. Dir. Peter Jackson. Perf. Elijah

Wood, Ian McKellen, and Viggo Mortensen. Wingnut Films, 2003.

Television Program

"Living Dinosaurs." Narr. Lance Gunderson. Dir. Maureen Fitzpatrick. The

Learning Channel. 7 Nov. 2004.

Television Episode

"Boys of Summer." Writer David Simon. Dir. Joe Chappelle. *The Wire.*

HBO. 10 Sept. 2006.

Music Recording

Dayne, Taylor. *Soul Dancing.* Arista, 1993.

Podcast

Maynard, Thane. "Flying Lemurs." *The 90 Second Naturalist.* WVXU Cincinnati,

Dec. 2007. 10 May 2008.

ACTIVITY 18.3 WORKING ONLINE: *Using Bibliomaker*

At www.mhhe.com/brannan, use the Bibliomaker tool to help format your citations in MLA and other styles.

Conservation in Context

RESIST THE URGE TO PRINT ONLINE SOURCES

Take down the URL and all pertinent information when you first decide to use the website as a source; remember that you can always access an online document later, from anywhere with on online connection, if you note how to find it again. This is yet another small way to save paper (and money) as you write. ●

WRITING A RESEARCH PAPER
Summarizing the Assignment

This assignment asks you to choose a topic and develop an essay of about three pages that uses information you find in books, magazines, and newspapers and on the Internet to support your thesis. You will rely on outside sources for most of the information in the essay, but you may also include personal experience if it helps to develop your ideas. Your instructor will tell you how many sources he or she wants you to use, but three to five can be adequate for a short research essay. This assignment, more than any other this semester, requires careful planning and efficient use of your time.

For a full walk-through of this writing assignment, visit Chapter 18, Research Writing Assignment at www.mhhe.com.brannan. The following topics and features are included:

- Establishing Audience and Purpose
- Working through the Writing Assignment
- Topics List: Research
- Prewriting for a Research Paper
- Questions to Ask When Evaluating Sources
- Organizing Ideas
- Drafting a Research Paper
- Revising a Research Paper

Annotated Student Model: "Why Do I Feel This Way?"

In the following sample paper, student writer Olivia Lutz's purpose is to communicate information about clinical depression for an audience that needs the knowledge—people who suspect that someone in their life may be afflicted with the illness. Notice that she develops her ideas largely through causes and effects, carefully introducing and then explaining her sources.

Olivia Lutz

Professor Brannan

English 106

October 7, 2008

Why Do I Feel This Way?

Depression is the most common of all psychological disorders, affecting nearly everyone occasionally. However, when a person is unable to conduct his or her life normally, depression becomes a problem requiring treatment. According to the World Health Organization, 121 million people across the globe suffer with this debilitating illness, including over 17 million Americans; this cost the United States a shocking $43 billion in 1992 from decreased work productivity ("Mental"). Not only does depression hurt the economy; clinical depression kills. Each year 15 percent of those who are severely depressed may commit suicide (Nemeroff 44). Regardless of its severity, about a third of the people with depression don't know they have it, and two-thirds don't seek treatment ("Depression" 1). After studying the suicide of successful author Michael Dorris, Catherine Walsh believes that "human beings—no matter what their accomplishments or level of self-awareness—are vulnerable" and can slide into depression (7). What causes this illness, what are its effects, what forms does it take, and what does it feel like to be in the grips of depression?

People have studied the causes of mental disorders for centuries and are still finding new information about depression almost daily. In the earliest Greek medical texts, depression or "melancholia" was associated with the "four-element theory," which maintained that physical and mental health corresponded with the four basic elements of fire, air, earth, and water, seen in people as the four "humors" of blood, phlegm, yellow bile, and black bile (Alexander 30). Melancholia was thought to result from excessive black bile (Alexander 32). During medieval times scholars made further progress in the study of depression. A sixth-century Byzantine physician, Alexander of Tralles, went beyond the four-element theory of causes for medical conditions, realizing that depression is centered in the brain (Alexander and Selesnick 60). Researchers have made many advances in the study of depression since these early observations. Today we understand that this illness may have many causes—biological, psychological, and genetic—and that high stress and traumatic events can trigger it (Bellenir 161).

Annotations in margins:

Your name, professor's name, course name, and date double-spaced at left margin

Last name and page number in upper-right corner

Title centered

Introduction begins weaving sources into text.

Using author's name to introduce quotation

Combining quotation with summary

Thesis with forecasting statement

Topic sentence

Paragraph arranged by time

Topic sentence

Science has also learned that biochemical changes in the brain can cause psychological diseases, such as depression. This illness is generally linked with the depletion of serotonin, a molecule that certain brain cells use to communicate with each other. Having too little serotonin negatively affects the hypothalamus, which controls our appetite, libido, and sleep, and the amygdala, which affects our emotions. Depressed patients with low serotonin levels have the greatest risk for suicide (Nemeroff 46).

Defining terms, summarizing source, and explaining effects

Topic sentence

The effects of depression can be hard to detect since everyone experiences them occasionally. Symptoms can be slow thinking, somberness, apathy, loneliness, insecurity, and low interest in normal daily activities. People suffering from depression will often become indecisive, slow their speech, abandon interests, cry frequently, neglect themselves, become inhibited, and, in severe cases, attempt suicide. Appearance, also, usually reflects a person's descent into depression. People with this disorder can look unattractive, aged, expressionless, and sloppy in their grooming and dress (Hershman and Lieb 35–36). In order for a doctor to diagnose a person with depression, the patient must show some of these symptoms nearly every day for at least two weeks.

Source with two authors

Topic sentence

If a person is diagnosed as clinically depressed, the next step is to find out how severe the condition is. The mildest form is called seasonal affective disorder or SAD. Short spurts of depression related to changes in a person's life are common traits of SAD, and these cases are usually not treated. Bipolar disorder, also called manic-depressive disorder, is a more severe form and is characterized by recurrent cycles of depression and mania, extremely low and high periods that seriously affect judgment. Another type of depression, dysthymia, can last two years or longer but is not usually disabling, and some sufferers can have short periods of feeling normal. However, dysthymia can make people feel like their lives are hardly worth living, as one person suffering from the illness wrote: "Lately I've felt like a shell of a person, just barely getting through the day. I just barely get out of bed, then I just sit by the TV and watch my day go by" (qtd. in Jackson 3). This person had a normal life only while around people, but days without company were spent entirely in bed. The worst form of depression is major depression. The symptoms are severe, such as overwhelming grief and mood disturbance, and can last for more than two weeks at a time ("Depression" 1).

Paragraph arranged by importance—"the worst"

Symptoms of depression can be mild or severe; however, even if symptoms are not obvious to others, a person with depression may be struggling on the inside. The French composer Hector Berlioz once wrote:

Useful block quotation to emphasize author's final point

> It is difficult to put into words what I suffered—the longing that seemed to be tearing my heart out by the roots, the dreadful sense of being alone in an empty universe, the agonies that thrilled through me as if the blood were running ice-cold in my veins, the disgust with the living, the impossibility of dying. . . . (qtd. in Jamison 19)

Block quote indented ten spaces and double-spaced

Quoting source within source

Even with all the advances we have made in the study of depression, the number of people suffering from this illness is rising. If we want to help ourselves and our loved ones to remain mentally healthy, we should know the signs of depression, even though sometimes we may have to look closely to see them. The silent sufferers who mask their symptoms and deny even to themselves that they have an illness may be the ones who need our help the most.

Works Cited

Alexander, Franz G., M.D., and Sheldon T. Selesnick, M.D. *History of Psychiatry: An Evaluation of Psychiatric Thought and Practice from Prehistoric Times to the Present*. New York: Harper, 1966. Print.

Bellenir, Karen, ed. *Mental Health Disorders Sourcebook*. Detroit: Omnigraphics, 1996. Print.

"Depression." 4 Jan. 1999. *Mayo Clinic Health Information*. Web. 24 Mar. 2000.

Hershman, Jablow, and Julian Lieb. *Manic Depression and Creativity*. Amherst: Prometheus, 1998. Print.

Howells, John G., ed. *World History of Psychiatry*. New York: Brunner/Mazel, 1975. Print.

Jackson, Stanley. *Melancholia and Depression*. New Haven: Yale UP, 1986. Print.

Jamison, Kay. *Touched with Fire*. New York: Free Press, 1993. Print.

"Mental Health." 19 Sept. 2008. *World Health Organization*. Web. 2 Oct. 2008.

Nemeroff, Charles B. "The Neurobiology of Depression." *Scientific American*. 278.6 (1998): 42–49. Print.

Walsh, Catherine. "Perspectives: Suicide of Author Michael Dorris." *America*. 176.16 (1997): 7. Print.

Double-space all lines within and between author entries.

Do not italicize or put quotation marks around words "Works Cited."

Indent each line beneath name within entry by five spaces.

Finish each entry with period.

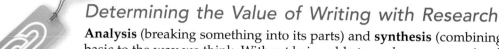

Linking to Future Experience

Determining the Value of Writing with Research

Analysis (breaking something into its parts) and **synthesis** (combining ideas) are basic to the way we think. Without being able to *analyze*, say, a recipe for German chocolate cake to determine its ingredients, you wouldn't be able to *synthesize* the ingredients—put them together—to make that tasty treat. When you analyze and synthesize the ideas you discover through research, you improve your critical thinking skills, which will help you succeed in and out of college. Research has the added benefit of increasing your knowledge as you read and analyze the articles you use in your essays. Lastly, being able to cite respected authorities increases your credibility with readers and listeners.

Conservation in Context

WRITE A RESEARCH ESSAY ABOUT AN ENVIRONMENTAL ISSUE

Draw on one of the Conservation in Context paragraph assignments in Chapters 5–11 or essay assignments in Chapters 15 and 16. Consider using the following resources:

Envirolink: http:..envirolink.org

Environmental Protection Agency: http:..www.epa.gov

WWW Virtual Library: Earth Science: http:..www.vlib.org.EarthScience.html ●

Chapter Summary

1. Research essays use print and other sources to develop a topic.
2. Sources must be analyzed (taken apart) and synthesized (put together).
3. Evaluate sources for currency, accuracy, completeness, objectivity, and credibility.
4. Weave sources into your paper using *selected* quotations, summaries, and paraphrases.
5. Introduce and explain all sources—especially quotations.
6. Use block quotations when the text would appear in your paper as five or more lines.
7. To avoid accidental plagiarizing, when you use more than two or three words in a row from a source, put them in quotation marks. Also, look away from your source when summarizing or paraphrasing.
8. Information that is common knowledge does not need to be cited.
9. When you cite authors within your essay using MLA format, either include the author's name in the introduction to the quotation, paraphrase, or summary, or place the author's last name along with a page number from the work within parentheses at the end of your sentences.
10. All sources used in a paper must be identified on a Works Cited page.
11. Focus your research efforts with a research question or rough thesis sentence.
12. Write a rough outline to help you manage your sources.
13. Include parenthetical citations even in your rough drafts.
14. Edit your final draft carefully, several times.

Polishing Style

4

BRANNAN

Creating Sentence Variety

19

[*Which of these two photographs attracts your attention more—and why?*]

KEY TOPICS

- Varying the length of sentences
- Varying the types of sentences
- Coordinating words in sentences
- Subordinating words in sentences
- Varying sentences with questions, commands, and exclamations

- Varying the beginnings of sentences
- Varying sentence beginnings with adverbs
- Varying sentence beginnings with phrases
- Inverting sentences

What Are We Trying to Achieve and Why?

Looking at the two images on the preceding page, most of us will find our eyes drawn to the football fans rather than the soldiers. Unlike the soldiers—who are identical in uniform and expression—these people are dressed (or undressed) in a variety of clothes, and each behaves differently: smiling, cheering, gesturing. Contrast attracts and holds our attention. Because there are clear differences among the fans, our eyes fix on one person and then another, seeing something new each time. In general, we want contrast and difference in our lives, at least in small doses. We want to hear new stories from friends or newspapers, and we want to spend time with a variety of people. Few of us want to wear the same clothes or eat the same lunch every day.

The same principle holds true in writing. Sentence after sentence constructed the same way, stretching through a paragraph and then into an essay, will, like the company of soldiers on the facing page, tend to lose readers' interest, no matter how exciting the ideas might be. Chapter 19 provides suggestions for involving readers in your ideas by structuring sentences in a variety of ways.

In this chapter, we will work on the following strategies that will help you with sentence variety: varying length, type, openers, and word order.

Varying the Length of Sentences

Sometimes when reading over a draft, we may find that our sentences are too similar in length. Whether they are all short, medium, or long, too many sentences of the same length strung together can become monotonous.

What is your reaction to the following paragraph?

> Music brings simple enjoyment. It also affects our lives in many ways. One song can bring out specific memories. It can change a person's mood from happy to sad. Music is so much more than just a rhythmic combination of sounds. It is a marvelously powerful experience. It is universal in cultures. Music bridges the cultural gap. It brings people closer together. Can you think of a society where music was or is not a part of people's lives?

If you think the paragraph feels "choppy," you are right. The ten sentences are too similar in length, creating a start-stop feeling, not unlike being in a car with someone learning how to use a clutch. We could revise the paragraph by combining sentences to vary their length and make them flow smoothly:

> Besides the simple enjoyment that music brings, it also affects our lives in many ways. It is amazing how hearing one song can bring out specific memories and how it can change a person's mood from happy to sad or vice versa. Music is so much more than just any rhythmic succession or combination of sounds. It is a marvelously powerful experience that is universal in cultures, bridging the cultural gap, bringing people closer together. Can you think of a society where music was or is not a part of people's lives?

The revised version has only five sentences, but notice the variety in length: 15, 27, 14, 19, and 17 words, respectively. The object in varying sentence length is not to jump from long to short to medium in some preset pattern. It is simply to interrupt a string of sentences that are similar in length with a longer or shorter sentence. A good rule of thumb is to alter the length of the third or fourth sentence in a series of sentences that have roughly the same word count.

For more on sentence parts, read ahead in this chapter.

ACTIVITY 19.1 *Combining Sentences for Variety in Length*

To reveal what you already know about sentence variety, revise the following paragraph (using separate paper, your journal, or a computer file) to increase its readability by combining sentences. Aim for a mix of sentence lengths, but don't eliminate all the shorter ones. A short sentence, especially following several longer ones, can draw readers' attention. You may need to drop or add words as you combine.

"If you use a little imagination, Aaron," his mother said, "this bathtub can be an ocean full of adventure." This sounded like a good idea to Aaron. He climbed into the tub. Then he pretended to head out across the vast ocean in search of pirates. He also looked for valuable sunken treasure. Mother began washing him and lathering his hair. Soapsuds fell into the water. They became islands to sail his ship around. Mother washed his hair. Then she said, "OK, time for a rinse." Aaron didn't mind this time. He pretended to swim under his ship. There he would look at all the ocean creatures. He saw a school of huge blue whales. He saw a giant octopus squirting a cloud of black ink. He saw hundreds of pink jellyfish trailing long, stinging tentacles.

Varying the Types of Sentences

Another way to create sentence variety is by using the four following sentence types:

SIMPLE	Aaron likes ice cream.
COMPOUND	Aaron likes ice cream, *so* he eats a lot of it. (two independent clauses joined by a coordinating conjunction)
COMPLEX	Aaron likes ice cream *because* it tastes sweet. (at least one subordinate clause joined to an independent clause)
COMPOUND–COMPLEX	Aaron likes ice cream because it tastes sweet, so he eats a lot of it. (two independent clauses and a subordinate clause)

You can use two strategies to vary the types of sentences you create: **coordination** and **subordination**. When you create a compound sentence, you join relatively equal, or **coordinate,** sentence parts with one of seven words called **coordinating conjunctions** (*and, but, or, so, yet, for, nor*), as in the compound sentence above (or omit the conjunction and use a semicolon). When you **subordinate** sentence parts, you tell readers that one part of the sentence is less important than another, as in the complex sentence above. Both coordination and subordination help you create sentence variety and express your thoughts in sophisticated ways.

For more on coordination and subordination, see Chapter 22.

Coordinating Words in Sentences

As you can see in the previous example, a compound sentence has at least two equal parts, each a separate simple sentence joined by a coordinating conjunction (*and, but,* etc.). You can use compound sentences to reduce the number of simple sentences (as in Activity 19.1). However, you do not always need to create a *complete* compound sentence. In fact, often you can use two-part subjects, verbs, and other words to add variety to your sentence structures and eliminate unneeded words. For example, you might combine two simple sentences into a complete compound sentence *or* create a compound subject:

SIMPLE SENTENCES	My grandmother lived into her nineties.
	My grandfather also lived into his nineties.
COMPOUND SENTENCE	My grandmother lived into her nineties, and my grandfather also lived into his nineties. (Compound sentences have a comma before the coordinating conjunction.)
COMPOUND SUBJECT	My grandmother and grandfather lived into their nineties. (Compound subjects do *not* have a comma before the coordinating conjunction.)

Or you might combine sentences with a two-part verb as in the following:

SIMPLE SENTENCES	Jody smashed the ball over the left field fence.
	She triumphantly rounded the bases to home.
COMPOUND SENTENCE	Jody smashed the ball over the left field fence, and she triumphantly rounded the bases to home.
COMPOUND VERB	Jody smashed the ball over the left field fence and triumphantly rounded the bases to home. (Compound verbs do *not* have a comma before the coordinating conjunction.)

When revising for sentence variety, you will sometimes write complete compound sentences and sometimes only compound subjects, verbs, and other words. Remember to use a comma before the coordinating conjunction in a compound sentence but *not* with a compound subject or verb.

HINT

See Chapter 27 for more on comma rules.

ACTIVITY 19.2 WORKING TOGETHER: *Combining Sentences Using Coordination*

With a partner, combine the following sets of sentences first as compound sentences separated by a comma and *and* or *but*. Next, reduce the compound sentence by using either a two-part subject or a two-part verb, cutting any unneeded words, making necessary changes in words, and removing the comma. For number 6, check each other's work to make sure you are both using coordination correctly.

EXAMPLE

Simple sentence: Muhammad Ali was a great fighter in his day.

Simple sentence: Sugar Ray Leonard was also a great fighter in his day.

Compound sentence: *Muhammad Ali was a great fighter in his day, and Sugar Ray Leonard was also a great fighter in his day.*

Compound subject: *Muhammad Ali and Sugar Ray Leonard were great fighters in their day.*

1. Simple sentence: My best friend won a lot of money in Las Vegas.

   Simple sentence: I also won a lot of money in Las Vegas.

   Compound sentence: _____

   _____

   Compound subject: _____

   _____

2. Simple sentence: Beth approached the counter at Best Buy.

   Simple sentence: She asked for a refund on her DVD player.

   Compound sentence: _____

   _____

   Compound verb: _____

   _____

3. Simple sentence: Jack learned a lot from his DWI conviction.

   Simple sentence: He has given up drinking altogether.

   Compound sentence: _____

   _____

   Compound verb: _____

   _____

4. Simple sentence: The wedding plans had seemed headed for disaster.

   Simple sentence: They finally came together.

   Compound sentence: _____

   _____

   Compound verb: _____

   _____

5. Simple sentence: This century people will explore our solar system.

   Simple sentence: After that they will colonize the planets.

   Compound sentence: _____

   _____

   Compound verb: _____

   _____

6. Write three sentences of your own that are either compound or that
   contain a two-part subject or verb (use commas correctly).

   A. _____

   _____

   B. _____

   _____

   C. _____

   _____

Subordinating Words in Sentences

Aside from coordination, you can also achieve sentence variety through **subordination**—that is, making one part of a sentence less important than another. Subordination helps writers deal with shades of meaning and complex ideas, often by setting information off with commas, parentheses, and dashes.

We will focus here on the **complex sentence** (a simple sentence plus one or more subordinate clauses), using **adjective** (or relative) and **adverb clauses.**

Adjective Clauses—Nonessential

Adjective clauses, also called **relative clauses,** are usually easy to spot because most begin with one of these relative pronouns: *who, which,* and *that.* An adjective clause tells something about the noun or pronoun it follows. Notice the under-lined clauses in the following two sentences:

A. Jason, *who* is really a very bright guy, is flunking out of college.

B. Jason has a drug problem, *which* keeps him from focusing on his studies.

The "who" clause in sentence A adds information about the noun "Jason": that he is "a very bright guy." The "which" clause in sentence B explains one effect of the noun "problem": that it is hurting Jason's schoolwork.

When adjective clauses are used in this way, they are said to be **nonessential** because the meaning of the main part of each sentence would be the same with-out the clauses. In both examples, if we remove the relative clauses, the main clauses would still communicate the central idea. Note that *commas* are used to set off these subordinate clauses. (For more on punctuating nonessential clauses, see pp. 590–592.)

It is usually best to position "which" clauses next to a single noun or pro-noun rather than expecting them to describe several words or ideas. Look at this example:

AMBIGUOUS   Jason has a drug problem and is also dyslexic, which keeps him from focusing on his studies. (Is it the drug problem, the dyslexia, or both that are affecting the studies?)

Be sure not to repeat a subject in an adjective clause. *Do not* say, "Jason, he is a very bright guy, is flunking out of college," or "Jason, who is a very bright guy, he is flunking out of college." Instead, write, "Jason, who is a very bright guy, is flunking out of college."

The three common relative pronouns are *who, which,* and *that.*

ACTIVITY 19.3   *Combining Sentences with Nonessential Adjective Clauses*

Combine the following sets of sentences by crossing out the unneeded noun or pronoun in the second sentence and replacing it with either *who* or *which.* Use *who* to refer to people and *which* to refer to animals or things. Use a comma to set off these subordinate clauses.

EXAMPLE: Eric refused to talk with anyone at the party except Simone. ~~He~~ had been treated for clinical depression last year.

Combined: *Eric, who had been treated for clinical depression last year, refused to talk with anyone at the party except Simone.*

1.   AIDS is still spreading worldwide. It is a debilitating and often fatal disease.

   Combined: _____

   _____

2.   Al Gore has been a tireless advocate for worldwide action to reduce global warming. He won the Nobel Prize in 2007 for his work with climate change.

Combined: _____

_____

3. Brown recluse spiders have a dangerous and painful bite. They have a violin shape on their heads and backs.

   Combined: _____

   _____

4. Tiger Woods makes a fortune through endorsements. He is one of the finest golfers in the world.

   Combined: _____

   _____

5. A classical guitar uses nylon strings. It has a wider neck than other acoustic guitars. The nylon strings give the instrument a more mellow tone.

   Combined: _____

   _____

6. Write three sentences of your own. Each sentence should contain a nonessential adjective clause. Remember to use commas, and be sure that the "which" clause refers to only one noun.

   A. _____

   _____

   B. _____

   _____

   C. _____

   _____

For more on essential and nonessential clauses, see Chapter 21.

Adjective Clauses—Essential

As we have seen, when adjective clauses are not essential to the meaning of the main part of a sentence, we use commas to set them off. However, they can also be **essential;** that is, if we left the clause out, the meaning in the main part of the sentence would be unclear or distorted.

Compare the following two sentences:

A. Senator Smithers, *who* has the backing of several major campaign donors, will challenge the incumbent governor.

B. A politician *who* has the backing of several major campaign donors will challenge the incumbent governor.

Because Senator Smithers is named in sentence A, there can be no doubt about who will challenge the governor; therefore, the relative clause "who has the backing . . ." becomes nonessential and is set off with commas. However, in sentence B, we do not know who will have the opportunity to run for governor until we read the relative clause. We ask the question "Who gets to run for the office?" and we answer it with the essential clause—the politician "who has the backing of several major campaign donors."

Distinguishing between nonessential and essential clauses can be difficult and often depends on the author's intent. In general, the pronoun *that* (not *which*) is used in essential clauses (though *which* is sometimes used). We will continue to use *who* to refer to people.

ACTIVITY 19.4 *Combining Sentences with Essential Adjective Clauses*

Combine the following sets of sentences by crossing out the unneeded noun or pronoun in the second sentence and replacing it with either *who* or *that*. Use *who* to refer to people and *that* to refer to animals or things. Remember that the adjective clause should follow the noun or pronoun in the first sentence that it identifies or limits. Also, do *not* use a comma to set off these subordinate clauses because they are essential to the meaning of the sentence.

> **EXAMPLE:** The Wii is an innovative gaming system. ~~It~~ can detect movement in three dimensions.
>
> Combined: *The Wii is an innovative gaming system that can detect movement in three dimensions.*

1. A grant allowed Wales to build a national botanical garden. The grant was given by the Millennium Commission.

   Combined: _____

   _____

2. J. K. Rowling is an author of children's books. She became phenomenally popular in the past few years with her Harry Potter series.

   Combined: _____

   _____

3. Blast fishing is a self-destructive habit. Blast fishing destroys the reefs needed to support the fish, wiping them out and destroying people's livelihood.

   Combined: _____

   _____

4. Martin Luther King Jr. was a highly influential civil rights leader. He won the Nobel Peace Prize in 1964.

   Combined: _____

   _____

5. The tickling sensation turned out to be a cockroach. I felt it on the back of my neck.

   Combined: _____

   _____

6. Write three of your own sentences that contain an essential adjective clause (remember that essential clauses do *not* need to be set off with commas):

   A. _____

   _____

English Review Note

Remember, do not write "A politician who he has the backing of several . . ." because the relative pronoun replaces the subject when you combine sentences.

HINT

To avoid confusion, review the *nonessential* clauses from Activity 19.3.

B. _____
_____
C. _____
_____

Review the meanings of subordinating conjunctions, especially *although,* and *since.* Compare *even though* and *even if.*

Adverb Clauses

Another form of complex sentence you can use for sentence variety combines an **adverb clause** with a main clause. Adverb clauses, like single adverbs, answer the questions *when, where, why, how,* and *to what extent* something was done. Here is a brief list of **subordinating conjunctions,** which begin adverb clauses (for a more complete list, see p. 512):

> SUBORDINATING CONJUNCTIONS
>
> | after | because | since | when |
> |---|---|---|---|
> | although | before | though | where |
> | as | if | until | while |

Consider these two examples:

COMMA NEEDED Because Jeremy stayed out too late last night, he slept through his 8:00 class.

NO COMMA Jeremy slept through his 8:00 class because he stayed out too late last night.

We ask the question "*Why* did Jeremy miss his 8:00 class?" and answer it with the adverb clause "because he stayed out too late last night." Like adjective clauses, adverb clauses are subordinate to or dependent on a main clause to complete their meaning. Standing alone, they are fragments, but combined with main clauses, they add variety to your sentences. (See pp. 549–551.)

Notice that adverb clauses, like single adverbs and adverb phrases, can be easily repositioned in a sentence to suit the writer's meaning and word flow. You should use a comma to set off adverb clauses that begin a sentence, but you do *not* usually need to use a comma to set them off when they come after the main clause.

Adverb clauses are generally easy to move around.

For more on adverb clauses, see pp. 522–523.

ACTIVITY 19.5 *Combining Sentences with Adverb Clauses*

Choosing from the list of subordinating conjunctions, combine the following sets of sentences by adding a subordinating conjunction to the *second* sentence in each pair. Write two versions, the first with the adverb clause beginning the sentence and the second with the clause ending the sentence. Be careful with the comma.

EXAMPLE: I had never seen such a huge alpine lake. I visited Lake Tahoe.

Adverb clause beginning sentence: *Before I visited Lake Tahoe, I had never seen such a huge alpine lake.* (comma needed)

Adverb clause ending sentence: *I had never seen such a huge alpine lake before I visited Lake Tahoe.* (comma not needed)

1. I can now get to work on time. The city has finally synchronized its stoplights along major thoroughfares.

   Adverb clause beginning sentence: _____

   _____

   Adverb clause ending sentence: _____

   _____

English Review Note

Do not use subordinating conjunctions and coordinating conjunctions in the same sentence, e.g. "Because Jeremy stayed out too late last night, so he slept through class."

2. The mudslides will soon begin. It does not stop raining in northern California.

   Adverb clause beginning sentence: _____

   _____

   Adverb clause ending sentence: _____

   _____

3. Beijing prepared to receive the crowds. The world headed toward the 2008 Olympics.

   Adverb clause beginning sentence: _____

   _____

   Adverb clause ending sentence: _____

   _____

4. Air pollution will become manageable. Automobile manufacturers finally eliminate gasoline-powered engines.

   Adverb clause beginning sentence: _____

   _____

   Adverb clause ending sentence: _____

   _____

5. The government cites a 19th-century land-use law to invade rancher's property and exploit "mineral rights." Most western ranchers protest it.

   Adverb clause beginning sentence: _____

   _____

   Adverb clause ending sentence: _____

   _____

6. Write three sentences of your own that contain an adverb clause.

   A. _____

   _____

   B. _____

   _____

   C. _____

   _____

HINT

Remember to use a comma with adverb clauses only when they *begin* a sentence.

Varying Sentences with Questions, Commands, and Exclamations

We can also create sentence variety by occasionally using the following types of sentences: **interrogative** (asks a question), **imperative** (makes a command), and **exclamatory** (expresses strong emotion). We use **declarative** sentences, or statements, most often in writing, but occasionally mixing one or more of the other three types can make our work more interesting.

Questions

You will usually use two kinds of questions: the **rhetorical question,** which is a disguised statement, and the question that you ask and then answer.

A rhetorical question looks like this: "Do we really want our 10-year-olds addicted to crack?" No sane person would respond with a yes. The question is actually a statement: "We do not want our 10-year-olds addicted to crack." Rhetorical questions, often used in persuasive writing, encourage readers to agree with the writer's view. Here is an excerpt from the Chapter 16 argument essay "Just Say No":

> Schools practically beg parents to spend time with their children reading, learning math, and helping with other course work. How can this happen when TV has captured the audience? And schoolwork is not all that suffers. Don't we as parents want to involve our children in other learning activities like music, dance, and sports?

Both rhetorical questions evoke a predictable response in the reader. The question that a writer asks and then answers, on the other hand, does not call for agreement from the reader but promises further information. Here is an example from the Chapter 15 definition essay "Finding Home":

> What makes the home happy? Is it the house decorated in warm, inviting colors, furnished with all the modern conveniences, or is it the people who live inside? I believe a home is not defined by the physical structure but by the people who live in it. Home is a place where a person feels safe, relaxed, and loved.

After posing questions, the author gives more information. These kinds of questions are particularly useful in introducing paragraphs and developing ideas within them.

Commands and Exclamations

Questions create variety in a text by encouraging a more active response from readers than declarative sentences do. Command and exclamation sentences work in much the same way. Even a mild **command** asks for action from the reader: "Preheat the oven to 350 degrees." If people have to perform, they tend to pay more attention. Commands are used frequently in process-analysis writing.

Exclamations, as expressions of strong emotion, tell readers to pay special attention, that a sentence is particularly important: "You did *what*? You smashed the car!" Exclamations are a way of raising your voice in print. However, used too often, exclamations can give your writing a feeling of forced enthusiasm. A general rule of thumb might be to use no more than one or two per page of text, except in special circumstances.

The following two versions of the same paragraph include questions, commands, and exclamations. Remember that people's opinions of the use of these types of sentences differ. Which version do you favor, A or B?

Think of your own reaction in class when questions are being asked and polite commands given.

A. You notice the tulip tree that had been growing at a furious rate for 6 years has suddenly started to wither! What is the cause? Is it too much water, too much shade, rampant leaf spot, some new parasite, perhaps an insect colony attacking the roots? What is the solution? All too often there is none. The experts at the nursery tell us: "Pray for a long stretch of dry weather, and keep your fingers crossed." And we say, "Right, thanks, I guess," and try not to watch that favorite tree as the leaves continue to turn brown and the branches, the flow of sap stopped, become brittle, lifeless sticks.

B. You notice the tulip tree that had been growing at a furious rate for 6 years has suddenly started to wither. You wonder if the cause might be too much water, too much shade, rampant leaf spot, some new parasite, or perhaps an insect colony attacking the roots. All too often there is no solution. The experts at the nursery talk about hoping the ground will dry out. We are left trying not to watch that favorite tree as the leaves continue to turn brown and the branches, the flow of sap stopped, become brittle, lifeless sticks.

ACTIVITY 19.6 | WORKING TOGETHER: *Creating Variety with Questions, Commands, and Exclamations*

Choose one of the following topics, brainstorm, and then write a paragraph of five to seven sentences that includes a question, a command, an exclamation, or all three. You might use either a rhetorical question or a question that you ask and answer. The command sentence may be mild, as in giving process instructions, or it might be part of dialogue, as in the landscaping example above. When you've finished a draft, trade paragraphs with a classmate and discuss how sentence variety is (or could be) used in each.

Topics

1. An embarrassing moment: speaking in public, asking for a date, not having your wallet or purse in a restaurant when the bill arrives, being caught in a lie

HINT

For more on using narration, see Chapter 6.

HINT

Try to use an exclamation sentence that feels natural rather than forced.

2. A "first" experience: being infatuated, falling in love, fighting, getting an A, making the honor roll, getting a speeding ticket

3. A moment when another person badly frightened you: thief in your house, someone on the street, stalker, phone caller, friend, family member

4. An unpleasant moment as a consumer: returning defective merchandise, being overcharged in billing, suspecting car mechanics of pulling a fast one

Varying the Beginnings of Sentences

In addition to varying the length and type of sentences, you can vary sentence beginnings. English sentences usually begin with a subject, but if you write a group of sentences that all begin with subjects, your writing will feel monotonous. Look at this version of the paragraph we used in Activity 19.1:

A. This sounded like a good idea to Aaron. He climbed into the tub. He pretended to head out across the vast ocean in search of pirates. He also looked for valuable sunken treasure. Mother began washing him and lathering his hair. Soapsuds fell into the water. They became islands to sail his ship around. Mother washed his hair. She said, "OK, time for a rinse." . . .

In version A, aside from similar sentence lengths, all nine sentences begin with subjects. After we combine a few sentences and supply several different sentence beginnings, the paragraph reads like this:

B. This sounded like a good idea to Aaron, so after he climbed into the tub, he pretended to head out across the vast ocean in search of pirates and valuable sunken treasure. Mother began washing him and lathering his hair. When the soapsuds fell into the water, they became islands to sail his ship around. After his hair was washed, mother said, "OK, time for a rinse."

As a general rule, it is best to interrupt the subject-first pattern after three or four sentences. You can vary sentence beginnings by using adverbs, phrases, and clauses.

Varying Sentence Beginnings with Adverbs

Adverbs give more information about verbs, adjectives, and other adverbs by answering the questions *when, where, why, how,* and *to what extent.* Most adverbs end in -ly, so they are easy to spot: *noisily, swiftly, sadly.* Single adverbs can be positioned in several places in a sentence, including at the start. Notice the following sentences:

A. Florence swiftly climbed the rope to the top of the tent.

B. Florence climbed the rope swiftly to the top of the tent.

C. Florence climbed the rope to the top of the tent swiftly.

D. Swiftly, Florence climbed the rope to the top of the tent.

When you make a style choice such as shifting an adverb, you should do so because the positioning best suits the meaning and rhythm of the sentence. If, for instance, you wanted to emphasize "swiftly," you would place it at the begin-ning or end of the sentence.

You might also use two adverbs to open a sentence:

Swiftly and gracefully, Florence climbed the rope to the top of the tent.

While some writers omit the comma after single adverbs beginning sentences, most often the comma is used, and paired adverbs always take a comma.

ACTIVITY 19.7 | *Creating Variety in Sentence Beginnings with Adverbs*

Rewrite the following sentences with the adverb or adverb pair at the begin-ning. Remember to use a comma following the adverb or adverb pair.

EXAMPLE: Sonya dragged herself slowly out of bed.
Slowly, Sonya dragged herself out of bed.

1. The wrecking ball effortlessly leveled the building.

   _____

   _____

2. These corporations have ruthlessly enriched themselves by impoverish-ing people in dozens of countries.

   _____

   _____

3. Juan's best friend shouted at him and angrily left the party.

   _____

   _____

4. Aunt Diana slowly and patiently explained to her 5-year-old niece why the frog could not sleep under the pillow.

   _____

   _____

5. The winds from the storm blew violently and continuously until 4:00 a.m.

   _____

   _____

6. Write three sentences of your own that begin with one or more adverbs.

   A. _____

   _____

   B. _____

   _____

   C. _____

   _____

Varying Sentence Beginnings with Phrases

Most often, the sentence parts that can help you to vary your sentence beginnings are phrases. A **phrase** is a group of related words lacking a subject or a verb. Phrases can be placed in various positions within a sentence, including the beginning. We will work with five phrase types: prepositional, participial (present/past), absolute (present/past), infinitive, and appositive.

Prepositional Phrases

Prepositional phrases are the workhorses of your paragraphs—you can scarcely write a sentence without one—and they are easy to spot once you know a few cue words. Every prepositional phrase begins with a preposition (often a word that tells location) and ends with a noun or pronoun (*in* the ocean, *after* you). These phrases can function as either adjectives or adverbs to describe other words in a sentence, and a phrase functioning as an adverb can be moved from one place to another.

COMMON PREPOSITIONS

above	behind	in	over
across	below	of	to _
at	by	on	with

Single prepositional phrases often begin sentences:

<u>Above the door</u> you will find the house key.

Together, the three words "above the door" tell *where* the key is located, so the phrase functions as an adverb. Notice that we could shift the phrase to the end of the sentence: "You will find the house key *above* the door."

When using two or more prepositional phrases to begin a sentence, set them off with a comma:

<u>Above the door</u> <u>on the north side</u> <u>of the house</u>, you will find the house key.

HINT

For more on prepositions and a longer list of them, see pp. 510–511.

HINT

When a single prepositional phrase begins a sentence, the comma is optional.

English Review Note

Include a subject in every sentence. The noun in the prepositional phrase is not the subject. For example, in "Above the door, <u>you will find the house key</u>" the word *door* is not the subject; the word *you* is.

ACTIVITY 19.8 *Combining Sentences with Prepositional Phrases*

Combine the following sentences by cutting the unneeded words at the beginning of the *second and third* sentences. Reposition the remaining prepositional phrases at the beginning of the first sentence. Remember to use a comma.

> **EXAMPLE:** You will find the reference section. ~~It is~~ on the first floor. ~~The floor is~~ of the library.
>
> *On the first floor of the library, you will find the reference section.*

1. I witnessed a terrible four-car pileup. The accident was at the intersection. The intersection was of 85th and Metcalf.

   _____

   _____

2. I watched the hotel under construction rise to completion seemingly overnight. I watched through a hole. The hole was in a wooden fence.

   _____

   _____

3. A government coalition has finally begun a recovery program for the sandhill crane. It was after 10 years. The years were full of heated debate.

_____

_____

4. John Wayne holds a special place. That place is in the hearts of fans. They are fans of the mythic West.

_____

_____

5. A single determined cricket kept Brian awake far into the night. The cricket was outside a bedroom window. The window was on the north side of the house.

_____

_____

6. Write three sentences of your own that begin with at least two prepositional phrases. Be sure to use a comma.

A. _____

   _____

B. _____

   _____

C. _____

   _____

Participial Phrases—Present Tense

Participial phrases consist of a participle—a verb form with an *-ing* ending in the present tense or an *-ed, -en,* or *-n* ending in the past tense—and words that describe a noun or a pronoun. As single-word openers, present participles can be effective:

Singing, Andrew enjoyed the sound of his voice echoing in the shower.

Who is singing? Andrew. The participle tells readers about a noun. We might want to add an adverb to create a brief phrase:

Singing happily, Andrew enjoyed the sound of his voice echoing in the shower.

To give even more information, we could include a prepositional phrase:

Singing happily and with great volume, Andrew enjoyed the sound of his voice echoing in the shower.

Participial phrases can be used at the beginning, in the middle, or at the end of a sentence and usually come directly before or after the noun or pronoun they are describing. A participial phrase placed next to a word that it does not describe is called a **misplaced** or **dangling modifier.** Confusing and sometimes amusing sentences can result, as in the following:

CONFUSING   Singing happily, the shower echoed with the sound of Andrew's voice.

While it is true that pipes can sometimes make a ringing sound, it is not likely that Andrew's voice would be coming from them.

Beware of misplaced and dangling modifiers (see pp. 582–584).

ACTIVITY 19.9 | *Combining Sentences with Participial Phrases (Present Tense)*

Combine the following sets of sentences by changing the first part of the *second* sentence into a participial phrase. Locate the verb in the *second* sentence, and then convert it into a present participle by adding *-ing*. Next, cross out any unneeded noun or pronoun, and attach the resulting participial phrase to the front of the first sentence. Use a comma.

> EXAMPLE: Lori daydreamed of the warm sands and tropical weather of Fort Lauderdale. She smiled at the thought of Spring Break.
>
> *Smiling at the thought of Spring Break, Lori daydreamed of the warm sands and tropical weather of Fort Lauderdale.*

1. Mountaintop coal mining is heavily practiced in the Appalachians. This type of mining scars the landscape and pollutes waterways.

   _____

   _____

2. Richard screamed "Aaggh!" when he grasped what felt like a handful of wriggling snakes. He reached blindfolded into the box.

   _____

   _____

3. Crosby, Stills, Nash, and Young surprised many people by not just being alive but still being fine musicians. They jammed hard for three straight hours.

   _____

   _____

4. The boys threw down their icy snowballs and tore down the alley. They tried to escape from an angry driver with a dented door.

   _____

   _____

5. Isabella ignored the speed limit in several places. She hoped to catch the 8:00 ferry to Victoria.

   _____

   _____

6. Write three of your own sentences that begin with a present participial phrase. Remember to use a comma.

   A. _____

   _____

   B. _____

   _____

   C. _____

   _____

Participial Phrases—Past Tense

Just as with the present participle, the **past participle** can help you vary sentence beginnings. Past participles of regular verbs are formed by adding an *-ed* or a *-d* to the end of the verb (play = play*ed*, frighten = frighten *ed*, excite = excite*d*). The past participles of irregular verbs are not formed in a consistent way but often end with "-t" or "-n".

Single-word participles can be effective sentence openers:

Overjoyed, Samantha made a beeline for the bank with her 3000-dollar tax refund.

Who is overjoyed? Samantha. The participle tells us about a noun. Or we might give even more information by adding two prepositional phrases:

Overjoyed by the size of her check, Samantha made a beeline for the bank with her 3000-dollar tax refund.

As with the present participle or present participial phrase, be sure to set off the past participle or past participial phrase with a comma, and avoid creating dangling or misplaced modifiers by keeping the participle next to the noun or pronoun that it modifies.

See Chapter 24 for a list of past participles for irregular verbs.

A participial phrase functions as an adjective. Distinguish between present and past participles that are used as adjectives.

ACTIVITY 19.10 | *Combining Sentences with Participial Phrases (Past Tense)*

Combine the following sets of sentences by changing the *second* sentence into a past participial phrase. Cross out the subject (noun or pronoun) and helping verb (*am, was, were*), and attach the resulting participial phrase to the front of the first sentence. Be sure to use a comma.

EXAMPLE

I basked like a walrus on the cement at the pool's edge. I was chilled after a dip in the cool water.

Chilled after a dip in the cool water, I basked like a walrus on the cement at the pool's edge.

1. The soil left behind after mountaintop mining isn't very fertile, but it can be used to grow grapes. The soil is composed largely of fragmented rock.

   _____

   _____

2. Mitch promised himself that he would actually buy textbooks next term. He was disappointed by his semester grades.

   _____

   _____

3. Mark could barely sleep for a week. Mark was excited by the opportunity to intern at Channel 9 News.

   _____

   _____

4. One of the bank tellers actually tried to eat some paper money. The teller was locked in the vault for 48 hours.

_____

_____

5. Tens of thousands of people have donated money to help preserve their environment. The people are impressed by the Nature Conservancy's plan to protect wilderness and wildlife by owning and leasing the land.

_____

_____

6. Write three sentences of your own that begin with a past participial phrase. Remember to use a comma.

A. _____

_____

B. _____

_____

C. _____

_____

Absolute Phrases

The **absolute phrase** is closely related to the participial phrase and consists of a noun or pronoun placed in front of a participle. In the following examples, the nouns are boxed and the endings of the participles are shaded:

ABSOLUTE PHRASES WITH PRESENT PARTICIPLES

A. The winds around it causing severe turbulence, the plane tossed its passengers about like loose bales of hay.

B. Its brown moss–covered fur blending with the surrounding foliage, a three-toed sloth is difficult to spot.

ABSOLUTE PHRASES WITH PAST PARTICIPLES

A. Our expectations shattered, we left New York and headed back to Philadelphia.

B. The tips of his skis pointed straight downhill, Eric started his run for the bottom of the mountain.

Absolute phrases modify the main clause they are attached to and are always set off with commas, whether at the beginning, middle, or end of a sentence.

Note that you could turn any of the absolute phrases above into stand-alone sentences by adding a helping verb like *is, are, was,* or *were*—for example, "The winds around it *were* causing severe turbulence" or "The tips of his skis *are* pointed straight downhill." When creating absolute phrases, writers deliberately leave the helping verb out to create variety in sentence structure, rather than stringing a series of simple sentences together.

If a phrase can be turned into stand-alone sentences by adding a helping verb, it is an absolute phrase.

ACTIVITY 19.11 *Combining Sentences with Absolute Phrases (Past and Present Tense)*

Combine the following sets of sentences by changing the *second* sentence into an absolute phrase. Cross out any unneeded helping verb (*am, are, was, were*), and attach the resulting absolute phrase to the front of the first sentence. Be sure to use a comma.

> EXAMPLE: The singer croaked out a few measures before she gave up. Her throat ~~was~~ aching from laryngitis.
>
> *Her throat aching from laryngitis, the singer croaked out a few measures*
>
> *before she gave up.*

1. Ellen greeted her friends at Union Station. Her hand was waving frantically.

   _____

   _____

2. Frank let himself dream for a moment about world unity. The flags from dozens of countries were rippling together in front of the UN building.

   _____

   _____

3. Skyscrapers collapsed weeks after the earthquake. Their internal support was weakened.

   _____

   _____

4. Monika wondered, "Since when does being nine months pregnant make me communal property?" Her stomach was constantly patted by people she hardly knew.

   _____

   _____

5. Write three sentences of your own that begin with an absolute phrase. Remember to use a comma.

   A. _____

   _____

   B. _____

   _____

   C. _____

   _____

Infinitive Phrases

Infinitive phrases, which can appear in various positions within a sentence, are another way to vary sentence beginnings. Infinitives are easy to spot because they always consist of the word *to* and the present tense form of a verb (*to love, to laugh, to run*). Infinitives can function as nouns, adjectives, and adverbs, but here we will concentrate on their use as adverbs, telling *why, where, when, how,* and *to what degree or extent.*

Here is a two-word infinitive opener:

To think, Rachel needed quiet.

Why did Rachel need quiet? To think. The infinitive works as an adverb. Notice that we could also position the infinitive at the end of the sentence: "Rachel needed quiet to think." We can also add another adverb:

To think deeply, Rachel needed quiet.

To give even more information, we could include a prepositional phrase:

To think deeply about her future, Rachel needed quiet.

Infinitive phrases used at the beginning of sentences, like participial phrases, sometimes are not clearly attached to the word they modify. Be careful not to construct sentences like the following:

To think deeply about her future, the television must be turned off, or Rachel will be distracted.

While the television can be entertaining, it does not generally have much on its mind.

HINT

Beware of misplaced and dangling modifiers.

ACTIVITY 19.12 | *Introducing Sentences with Infinitive Phrases*

Complete each of the following infinitive phrases by attaching a main clause of your choosing. Be careful not to follow the infinitive immediately with a verb like *is* or *was*, which would turn the infinitive into a subject rather than a phrase that describes another word in the sentence. Be sure to use a comma.

EXAMPLE: To approach the president in public,

Not this: To approach the president in public is a dream of mine.

But this: To approach the president in public, *people must first be cleared by the Secret Service.*

1. To scale the last 2,000 feet of the mountain, _____

   _____

2. To create community-owned power sources, _____

   _____

3. To enjoy the concert, _____

   _____

4. To beat the heat on a scorching summer day, _____

   _____

5. To adjust to a new culture, _____

   _____

6. Write three sentences of your own that begin with infinitive phrases. Be careful to create infinitives that describe rather than infinitives that act as subjects, and be sure to use a comma.

A. _____

_____

B. _____

_____

C. _____

_____

Appositive Phrases

The **appositive phrase,** a word group (like this one) that renames a noun or pronoun, also helps with sentence variety. *Nonessential* appositives are set off by a comma wherever they occur in a sentence: beginning, middle, or end.

Here is a brief opening appositive:

A bodybuilder, Arnold Schwarzenegger had greater ambitions.

What was Schwarzenegger? A bodybuilder. The appositive phrase tells about a noun. Notice that the phrase could follow the subject: "Arnold Schwarzenegger, a bodybuilder, had greater ambitions." We could also add several other descriptive words:

A former award-winning bodybuilder, Arnold Schwarzenegger had greater ambitions.

For even more information, we could add a prepositional phrase:

A former award-winning bodybuilder of international fame, Arnold Schwarzenegger had greater ambitions.

To stuff in about as much information as the opening of a sentence will bear, we could include an essential relative clause as well:

A former award-winning bodybuilder of international fame who won the Mr. Olympia title seven times, Arnold Schwarzenegger had greater ambitions.

ACTIVITY 19.13 | *Combining Sentences with Appositive Phrases*

Combine the following sets of sentences by crossing out the unneeded subject and verb in the *second* sentence and attaching the remaining appositive phrase to the front of the first sentence. Circle the word or phrase that serves as a synonym in the appositive phrase. Remember to use a comma.

EXAMPLE: Tae kwon do is practiced by many Americans who want to stay physically fit. It is a Korean martial art.

A Korean (martial art,) tae kwon do is practiced by many Americans who want to stay physically fit.

1. Rap is misunderstood by many people. It is a musical style that focuses on the beat.

   _____

   _____

2. My grandmother is still overjoyed to welcome a new grandchild into the world. She is a woman who has given birth to ten of her own children.

   _____

   _____

3. The coach demanded maximum performance but earned maximum respect. He was a man who did not much like teenagers.

   _____

   _____

4. Frank's Toyota pickup is just beginning to look middle-aged. It is a vehicle with 100,000 miles on it.

   _____

   _____

5. Minnesota is the fourth leading producer of wind energy in the country. It is generating clean energy and money for state residents.

   _____

   _____

6. Write three sentences of your own that begin with an appositive phrase. Be sure to use a comma.

   A. _____

   _____

   B. _____

   _____

   C. _____

   _____

Inverting Sentences

Another method for creating variety in sentence structure is to change the way the sentence parts are usually ordered, a process called **inversion.**

The typical arrangement of words in English sentences is subject, verb, object, as in "Mark hit the ball." However, sometimes writers alter the pattern. When you ask questions—"Where is your brother?"—you put the verb ahead of the subject. And when you begin a sentence with a word like *there* or *here,* you push the subject farther into the sentence: "There are dark clouds overhead" and "Here rests an old friend."

To vary sentence openers, you can shift a prepositional phrase or phrases to the front part of the sentence and then move the subject closer to or all the way

English Review Note

Distinguish between direct question order and inverted sentences.

to the end of the sentence. Shifting the subject closer to the end can give it more emphasis. Compare the following pairs of sentences:

A. The terrified kitten fell from the third-story window of the apartment building.

B. From the third-story window of the apartment building fell the terrified kitten.

A. The welcoming sight of a campground was at the end of the road.

B. At the end of the road was the welcoming sight of a campground.

When we move the subjects to the ends of the sentences, in version B, the readers' focus shifts to the "terrified kitten" and the "welcoming sight" of the campground.

ACTIVITY 19.14 | *Creating Sentence Variety through Inversion*

In the following sentences, underline the subject once and the verb twice. Next, invert the sentences, moving the prepositional phrases to the beginning and switching the positions of the subjects and verbs.

> EXAMPLE: Two innocent bystanders cowered in the middle of the angry crowd.
> In the middle of the angry crowd cowered two innocent bystanders.

1. A rattlesnake slithered into a hole in the ground.

   _____

   _____

2. A fundamental truth about human nature lies at the heart of this story.

   _____

   _____

3. A police officer patrolled underneath the elevated rail.

   _____

   _____

4. Then a flood of winter-melt water comes surging down the Platte River.

   _____

   _____

5. Great white sharks often lurk in the deep, cold water of Monterey Bay.

   _____

   _____

6. Write three inverted sentences of your own. Follow the pattern of the previous six sentences, and begin with at least one prepositional phrase.

   A. _____

   _____

   B. _____

   _____

   C. _____

   _____

Note that in an inverted sentence you do *not* need to set off the introductory prepositional phrase with a comma.

Review the chapter summary, and skim back through the methods for creating sentence variety. Now (on separate paper) revise the following student narrative paper. Think in particular about restructuring the paragraph to vary sentence lengths, types, and beginnings. You will need to add or drop a few words, but keep the organization and content largely intact.

For more on effective narration, see Chapter 6. For more on revision, see Chapters 4 and 14.

The Clown Princess

My daughter Monique is four. She is the most comical child I know. Sometimes I have a bad day. She will find a way to make me laugh. I remember one day I was in the kitchen cooking. All of a sudden, I heard the television volume go up. The volume went up in the living room. Monique had put in her favorite noncartoon movie. The name of the movie is *Hope Floats.* My son was there. His name is Marquise. Baby Mariah was there too. They were also watching the movie. Next, I heard Monique run to her room. I wondered what on earth she was doing. A few minutes later she made her dramatic entrance. She was decked out in high-heels and a purple boa. She also had on a purple skirt. She held a fuzzy purple fan. On her head was a bright fuchsia hat with a purple feather. But the articles that got the most attention were her Marilyn Monroe elbow-length white gloves. She also had a strand of fake pearls. Now was the time for her favorite song. The song was from the movie. Sandra Bullock sang to her sad daughter "I Just Want to Get Next to You." Monique sang the same song to Mariah and Marquise. "I can make a gray sky blue. I can make it rain whenever I want to. I can make a ship sail on dry land. I can make a castle out of a single grain of sand. But the reason I'm so sad and blue is because I can't get next to you." Monique fluttered her hands. She wiggled her fingers to show rain falling. She dipped her hands up and down to pantomime ocean waves. She pinched her fingers together. She pretended she was holding a grain of sand. She strummed an imaginary banjo during the rest of the song. She sang, "ohh-ohh, wooo." Her song was finished. With a bow, she ever so politely said, "Oh thank you very much." I watched smiling from the kitchen. Then she blew a kiss. She waved good-bye to her brother and sister. She made her exit to her room. Mariah and Marquise may still be too young to appreciate how much joy their older sister brings into the house. My little clown princess can always brighten our day with her silly, fun ways.

ACTIVITY 19.16 | WORKING ONLINE: *Analyzing Sentence Variety*

Go to Entertainment Weekly's website at www.ew.com and read a review of any film, music album, TV show, or book. Then write a paragraph describing how the writer uses (or fails to use) sentence variety, giving specific examples from the article. Look for the following: compound sentences, complex sentences, opening words and phrases, and verbs or adjectives in a series.

ACTIVITY 19.17 | WORKING ONLINE: *Chapter Review*

Take the Chapter 19 Review Quiz at www.mhhe.com/brannan.

Linking to Future Experience

Get your instructor's attention—and keep it—by using sentence variety in all of your papers. Audience is one of the most important considerations in writing; you can show you've made readers a priority by keeping your paper's rhythm interesting. But don't be disappointed if teachers fail to comment on this stylistic skill. Well-varied sentences often serve to illuminate the other good things about your paper, not the variety itself. Varying sentence structure and length can make your descriptions more engaging, stories more dramatic, and arguments more powerful. Keep variety in mind as you plan oral presentations, too; you'll notice that all the best speakers make use of it.

VARIETY IN EVERYDAY LIFE

Want more variety in your wardrobe? Instead of buying new clothes, have a clothing swap with friends and recycle what you don't wear. Wish you had a Wii instead of an X-Box? Trade gaming systems with a friend for a few weeks. (Bonus: in both cases, you'll save money.) Write a paragraph exploring other ways you might recycle or reuse material goods in creative ways. Next, revise your paragraph, making sure you have used a variety of sentence structures. ●

Conservation in Context

Chapter Summary

1. Writers create sentence variety by varying the length, types, and beginnings of sentences.

2. Sentences in a paragraph should be a mix of lengths: short, medium, and long. Three or four sentences in a row may be roughly the same length, but the next one should be shorter or longer.

3. Sentences can be compound, with a subject and verb on both sides of a coordinating conjunction (*and, but, so, or, for, nor, yet*): "I like 7-Up, and I drink a quart a day." A comma comes before the conjunction.

4. Sentences may contain several parts connected by *and*, such as a compound subject: "Jim and I both like 7-Up." Or they can contain a compound verb: "I like 7-Up and drink a quart a day." Compound subjects and verbs are *not* separated by a comma.

5. You can subordinate ideas in a sentence in many ways, including with adjective clauses, which are often introduced by *who, which,* or *that.*

6. You can also subordinate information in a sentence with an adverb clause: "Because I was late, I missed the last ferry." When the clause begins the sentence, it is set off with a comma. When it ends the sentence, it is not usually set off with a comma.

7. Sentences may begin with adverbs (*-ly* words: happi*ly*).

8. Using occasional questions, commands, and exclamations is another way to create sentence variety.

9. Phrases create sentence variety and can be especially useful in varying sentence beginnings. Most phrases should be set off with a comma.

   A. Prepositional phrase: "In the drawer next to the file cabinet, you will find the hammer."

   B. Participial phrase (present): "Slipping on the wet tile, Maria wrenched her back."

   C. Participial phrase (past): "Thrilled by his good fortune, Dale carried the trophy home."

   D. Absolute phrase (present): "His train leaving ahead of schedule, Vito missed his ride."

   E. Absolute phrase (past): "Their foundations weakened, buildings collapsed in the earthquake."

   F. Infinitive phrase: "To run a marathon, Keith had to train for a year."

   G. Appositive phrase: "Beautiful but aggressive birds, blue jays swarmed my feeders last winter."

10. Inverting sentences can create variety and help to emphasize the subject: "In the deep, cold water of Monterey Bay often lurk great white sharks."

Choosing the Most Effective Word

[*Contrast the two different ways this woman is dressed and consider why she chose each outfit for each setting. What might happen if she dressed in the suit to meet friends or wore jeans to a job interview?*]

KEY TOPICS

- Using specific and concrete language
- Writing concisely

- Choosing language for tone
- Using figures of speech

What Are We Trying to Achieve and Why?

Like the young woman in the photos (on the previous page) who dresses differently for different situations, you can express similar thoughts in your writing in a variety of ways, depending on the circumstances. When you choose different words and different ways of arranging them based on the subject, your feelings about it, and your audience's likely reaction to it, you are adjusting your **writing style.** If your style is appropriate to the context, your work stands a better chance of being well received. This chapter offers some advice on how to select the most specific, concrete, concise, and artful expressions possible with which to communicate your ideas.

English Review Note

Avoid translations. Work with a good dictionary in hand.

Using Specific and Concrete Language

Choosing Specific Words

One of the most important elements of style is the choice of general versus specific words to express ideas. Language consists of words that are either relatively general or relatively specific, and each type has an appropriate place in your writing. More general words belong to larger categories, and more specific words to smaller categories. We have already seen this concept illustrated as a "Language Line" like this one:

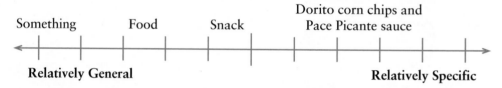

If a friend asks you to go to the store to pick up "something," what will you come back with? If your friend says "food," do you need to know more? If your friend really has a preference, he should be more specific: "a large bag of Dorito Spicy Sweet Chili corn chips and a jar of hot Pace Picante sauce." When writers want to create a clear image, they choose the most specific words possible, particularly concrete nouns and verbs. By narrowing the group to which the word belongs, you can more clearly communicate your meaning.

First drafts are often filled with general language. When revising for word choice, you should search your vocabulary, sometimes supplementing your search with a dictionary or thesaurus (a book containing synonyms of words), for the word that conveys the most precise meaning. Besides nouns like "food" from the previous example, we often choose verbs that lack strength, as in the following sentences:

HINT

When using a thesaurus, choose words you know.

DRAFTED WITH WEAK VERBS

A. Jennifer <u>made</u> an attempt to say she was sorry.

B. Lilah <u>is</u> sleepy as she gets into the van.

C. Sam <u>does</u> hard work when he <u>gets</u> the products up on the shelves.

These sentences are clear enough, but because of bland verbs they lack punch.

REVISED WITH STRONG VERBS

A. Jennifer <u>stuttered</u>, "I . . . I . . . I'm sorry."

B. Lilah's eyelids <u>droop</u> as she <u>fumbles</u> her way into the van.

C. Sam <u>struggles</u> with the 50-pound bags of dogfood as he <u>hoists</u> them onto the shelves.

As you revise, be especially alert to forms of the verbs *be, do, have, make,* and *get,* all of which can cause your sentences to lose energy.

Along with using general nouns and verbs, writers sometimes fall into the "very, really, extremely" habit. They say, "It's very hot out," "She's really smart," and "He is extremely mean." Typically, four out of five of these empty intensifiers in a draft should simply be eliminated, and often they can be replaced with more precise words. In the examples above, *scorching*, *brilliant*, and *brutal* would convey the meaning more effectively.

Other overly general words that add little to your writing are *thing, nice, pretty, handsome, good looking, good, bad, interesting, fun, great, young, old, happy,* and *sad.* This sentence contains nothing but vague words:

HINT

Be, do, have, make, and *get* are often weak verbs.

> A very nice young man, who used to be happy but now is sad, no longer has much fun and has few interesting things to say.

DRAFTED WITH VAGUE WORDS

Notice how much clearer and more effective this version is:

> John Kelley, a sophomore in high school, used to be optimistic and happy but was devastated when his parents were divorced. He no longer talks to even his closest friends about his feelings and has become a virtual recluse.

REVISED WITH SPECIFIC WORDS

ACTIVITY 20.1 *Revising for Specific Word Choice*

Revise the following sentences to make them clearer and more interesting by substituting specific words for general ones. Pay particular attention to the subjects and verbs, but also look for other vague words such as *very*, and either delete or replace them.

EXAMPLE: The person's child ~~very~~ often got into her lap.

Revised: *Anita's three-year-old daughter often crawled up into her mother's lap.*

1. Someone made contact with an object, and it went over some part of a fence somewhere out there.

   _____

   _____

2. A person moved very quietly toward an animal standing near some vegetation.

   _____

   _____

3. A man was occupying himself in a boat on a really small body of water.

   _____

   _____

4. At the place where the big machines do jobs, one that pushes earth around had a problem with the gas flow and quit running.

   _____

   _____

5. In a building full of interesting books and other great things, some young people made conversation in extremely quiet voices.

   _____

   _____

6. Some time ago the structure was damaged in a natural disaster.

_____

_____

7. Feeling the situation was hopeless, the nice person made an attempt to control himself but had to sit down and let his emotions get out.

_____

_____

Choosing Concrete Words

English Review Note

Try to use and recycle vocabulary gleaned from readings and class discussions.

Just as you can choose specific words to clarify ideas and images, you can favor concrete over abstract terms. **Abstractions** are ideas, qualities, emotions, and processes—expressed in terms like *equality, friendship, happiness,* and *evolution,* general terms that we understand through specific examples. When you think of *friendship,* for instance, you probably picture a group of people talking and laughing. Without specific examples, abstract terms can be hard to understand.

To help illustrate abstract terms, we rely not only on specific words but also on concrete ones. Concrete terms we know through our senses: sight, sound, touch, smell, and taste. You can hold a can of Sprite, for example, feeling its coolness and slick aluminum sides. You see that the can is green, feel that it weighs about 12 ounces, and taste the sweet soda in it. Popping the top, you hear it; splashing the liquid into a glass, you see and hear the bubbles rising. *Sprite* is clearly a concrete term. So is *handshake,* whereas *friendship* is not. *Tears* are concrete, but *sorrow* is not.

Abstractions are needed for thinking and communicating because they establish large ideas quickly. You can then illustrate them with specific, concrete examples.

Your writing will be more compelling when you rely on concrete, specific words to develop more abstract terms. Compare the following paragraphs, the first with most of the abstract terms underlined. Which paragraph seems most vivid? Which one best communicates the concept of intense activity?

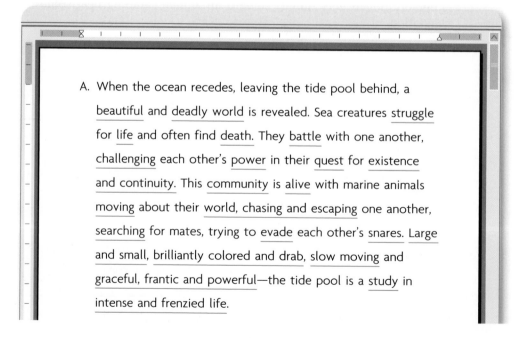

A. When the ocean recedes, leaving the tide pool behind, a beautiful and deadly world is revealed. Sea creatures struggle for life and often find death. They battle with one another, challenging each other's power in their quest for existence and continuity. This community is alive with marine animals moving about their world, chasing and escaping one another, searching for mates, trying to evade each other's snares. Large and small, brilliantly colored and drab, slow moving and graceful, frantic and powerful—the tide pool is a study in intense and frenzied life.

B. But when the tide goes out, the little water world becomes quiet and lovely. The sea is very clear and the bottom becomes fantastic with hurrying, fighting, feeding, breeding animals. . . . Starfish squat over mussels, and limpets attach their million little suckers and then slowly lift with incredible power until the prey is broken from the rock. And then the starfish stomach comes out and envelops its food. Orange and speckled and fluted nudibranchs slide gracefully over the rocks, their skirts waving like the dresses of Spanish dancers. And black eels poke their heads out of crevices and wait for prey. . . . Hermit crabs like frantic children scamper on the bottom sand. . . . Here a crab tears a leg from his brother. The anemones expand like soft and brilliant flowers. . . .

Chances are, you prefer paragraph B, in which author John Steinbeck uses concrete, specific examples to illustrate abstract ideas. Try the same strategy in your own writing.

ACTIVITY 20.2 | WORKING TOGETHER: *Revising for Concrete Words*

In a small group, read through the preceding paragraph B, discuss the differences between concrete and abstract terms, and then underline all the concrete terms.

Writing Concisely

Another quality to strive for when revising for style is **concision**—saying what you mean with no wasted words. In the rush of getting ideas down, writers often include everything that pops into their minds, so first drafts often include repetitive passages like this:

> Let me tell you for a moment about what it means to communicate clearly to other people in words when you are going to a job interview where you hope to find work. Some kinds of advice are more worth listening to than others, and I have always thought the best sort of advice that one person can give to another is the kind of suggestions that get straight to the point.

WORDY PASSAGE

To revise for concision, we need to eliminate unneeded repetition, imprecise words, and stalling phrases. In short, get to the point:

> Communicating clearly will help you do well in a job interview.

REVISED FOR CONCISION

By shrinking the wordy passage from 73 words to 11, we increase economy and clarity. The point is not to cut all repetition—writers often use it for emphasis—and not merely to write short sentences. Focus on removing words that interfere with your meaning. In revising for economy and clarity, reduce or eliminate the following:

- Redundant expressions
- Empty and padded phrases
- Excessive qualifiers and emphasizers
- Unnecessary examples, details, and explanations
- Inflated clauses and phrases

Revising to Eliminate Redundant Expressions

Redundant expressions are unnecessary words that repeat an idea already expressed, as in this example:

> Currently today, as we gather and come together as a group of unemployed people who are out of work, although our numbers are few and there are not many of us, we can still push for decent jobs.

Eliminating the redundant phrases gives us a clearer, more concise sentence:

> Today as we who are unemployed gather, although we are only a few people, we can still push for decent jobs.

Here are several pairs of words and phrases to watch for as you revise:

REDUNDANT PAIRS

adequate enough	gather together	proceeded to go
circle around	heavy in weight	red in color
climb up	hopes and wishes	return again
continue on	if and when	small in size
cooperate together	important essentials	square in shape
each and every one	intentionally try	sum total
few in number	link together	terrible tragedy
first and foremost	old antiques	true facts
free gift	past history	

ACTIVITY 20.3 *Eliminating Redundant Expressions*

Using the preceding chart, revise the following sentences to eliminate redundant expressions.

EXAMPLE: ~~In this day and age each and~~ every one ~~of us~~ today has the right to affordable health care ~~that is inexpensive enough that no one is left without it~~.
Revised: *Everyone today has the right to affordable health care.*

1. If everyone in this country would cooperate together, we could overcome our past history of failure to meet the needs of our poor.

_____

_____

Be careful not to cut any important ideas.

2. Although Horace is small in stature, he is aggressive, and he skates well enough and with sufficient skill to be on the team.

_____

_____

3. If we return again to the auto show for the presentation on energy-efficient cars, we are guaranteed to get a free gift this time.

_____

_____

4. Scaling back the space program would be a terrible tragedy for humanity and all the people living on earth because space research continues to make critically essential discoveries that affect everyone's life on the planet.

_____

_____

5. Heavy in weight but mostly full of liquid water, watermelons are best eaten when their pink color deepens to a red color.

_____

_____

6. Everyone on the committee, meaning all the people who are discussing the issue, continues to circle around the first and foremost problem.

_____

_____

7. Missing her children terribly, Margaret had fond hopes and wishes to gather them together again once more on Christmas Eve to celebrate as they once had.

_____

_____

ACTIVITY 20.4 | WORKING ONLINE: *Eliminating Redundancies*

At www.mhhe.com/brannan, click on "Eliminating Redundancies" under Chapter 20. Come up with an alternate way to revise each example sentence.

Revising to Reduce Empty and Padded Phrases

Writers can also bog readers down with empty or padded phrases. **Empty words** and **phrases** contribute no (or very little) meaning to a sentence, so they can—and should—usually be dropped without altering it.

COMMON EMPTY WORDS AND PHRASES

absolutely	certain	in kind	really
actually	character of	in terms of	situation of
area of	definitely	kind of	sort of
aspect of	element of	manner	thing
awfully	extremely	nature of	type of
basically	factor	quite	very

Padded phrases are stock expressions that use more words than needed to make the point—for example, *due to the fact that,* which simply means *because:*

A. Due to the fact that we are understaffed, no one goes home early.

B. Because we are understaffed, no one goes home early.

Because is a simple, concise replacement for the padded phrase.

COMMON PADDED PHRASES	CONCISE SUBSTITUTES
at the present time, at this point in time, at the present moment, in this day and age	now, today
during that time, in the time when, in those days	then, when
at all times	always
despite (regardless of) the fact that	although
due to the fact that, the reason is because, for the reason that, considering the fact that	because
located close by	near
in the event that	if
by means of	by
form a consensus of opinion	agree
a large number of	many
few in number	few
aware of the fact that	know
refer back	refer
in the final analysis	finally
sufficient amount of	enough
make contact with	contact, meet
for the purpose of	for
in a situation in which, in the event that	when, if
is in a position to, has the opportunity to	can
it is important (crucial/critical) that	must
there is a chance that	may
during the time that	while
all of a sudden	suddenly

ACTIVITY 20.5 *Reducing Empty and Padded Phrases*

Revise the following sentences by crossing out the empty and wordy phrases and substituting more concise ones from the preceding list.

EXAMPLE: ~~Considering the fact that~~ summer is almost over, we will ~~actually~~ ~~very~~ soon be back in school ~~again~~.

Revised: _Because summer is almost over, we will soon be back in school._

1. If the committee would form a consensus on this one issue, we could, in the final analysis, be out of this situation of constant debate and all go home.

_____

_____

2. Some of the team members may not be aware of the fact that there is a chance the coach has an ulcer.

_____

_____

3. Located close by I-435 and Nall is a jogging trail that a large number of people run on daily considering the fact that they need exercise.

_____

_____

4. It is absolutely essential that Sheila and Maureen make contact with their supervisor despite the fact that it is after working hours.

_____

_____

5. In a situation in which CO_2 and other greenhouse gases continue to rise, the earth will warm by several degrees, which is a sufficient enough increase in heat to cause catastrophic coastal flooding.

_____

_____

6. At this point in time, currently, it is the consensus of opinion among many political commentators that Adriana Ramirez, a kind of eloquent speaker, may become a candidate for senator.

_____

_____

Removing Excessive Qualifiers and Emphasizers

Even when you have thoughtfully trimmed redundant and empty expressions from your work, unnecessary qualifiers and emphasizers may remain. **Qualifiers**—words such as *often, usually,* and *frequently*—are important in writing, especially in persuasion, because they help soften your tone and keep you from overstating your case. But when qualifiers are overused, they clutter a text and make writers seem insecure. Consider the following sentences:

A. In my opinion, we should probably lower the drinking age to maybe 18 or possibly 19 because, for the most part, young adults are responsible enough to choose when, where, and how much they drink, most of the time, except for when they are not being responsible, which they are not, admittedly, some of the time.

B. We should lower the drinking age to 18 because most young adults are responsible enough to choose when, where, and how much they drink.

Sentence A bogs the reader down with qualifiers such as "in my opinion" and "probably," whereas B is direct and concise yet still qualifies sufficiently by keeping the qualifier "most."

For more on qualifying, see p. 378.

COMMON QUALIFIERS

almost	for the most part	maybe	often	seldom
apparently	frequently	might	perhaps	sometimes
can	in my opinion	more or less	possibly	try
could be	may	occasionally	seemingly	usually

Emphasizers such as *of course, clearly,* and *obviously* are also needed in writing because they help direct readers' attention to important points. However, cluttering a text with too many emphasizers can make a writer sound arrogant. Consider these sentences:

A. As everyone knows, 18-year-olds are obviously considered adults in the eyes of the law, and as anyone can plainly see, the simple fact that 18-year-olds have to assume adult responsibilities means that, of course, they should be, inevitably, allowed to legally drink.

B. Because 18-year-olds are considered legal adults and have to assume adult responsibilities, they should be allowed to drink.

Sentence A overemphasizes, distracting and possibly irritating readers, whereas B is direct and concise yet still makes its point.

COMMON EMPHASIZERS

all	crucial	invariably	undoubtedly
always	definitely	never	unequivocally
certainly	everyone can see that	obviously	unmistakably
clearly	every time	of course	unquestionably
critical	inevitably	plainly	vital

ACTIVITY 20.6 *Removing Unneeded Qualifiers and Emphasizers*

In the following sentences, cut qualifiers and emphasizers wherever you feel there are too many of them. You may need to add words or restructure a sentence, but keep the main ideas intact.

EXAMPLE: When enough time has passed, most people ~~inevitably~~ forget the broken campaign promises of politicians and, ~~unquestionably, as anyone can see~~, will ~~certainly~~ reelect them.

Revised: *When enough time has passed, most people forget the broken campaign promises of politicians and reelect them.*

1. Although it seems to me that most people would like to feel safe in their homes, keeping loaded handguns at their bedside, for most people, might not be the very best possible solution to their safety concerns, in my opinion.

_____

_____

2. Jailing people for smoking marijuana might just possibly waste taxpayers' money, may be an injustice to some of those imprisoned, and could drain some of the resources for dealing with at least a few of the serious crimes.

_____

_____

3. Most people who love one another might find it helpful in their relationship to try to communicate as often as they can stand to about issues that they are not likely to agree on, unless they don't think they

can talk about a really tough issue, in which case it might be all right for them to skip it occasionally.

_____

_____

4. It should be obvious to any clear thinker that state lotteries are legalized gambling and that supporting the system will inevitably lead to greater state involvement in gaming, with racetracks and, undoubtedly, riverboat gambling in the near future.

_____

_____

5. I think that everyone will agree that parents should definitely be held responsible for their children's education, and the way to deal with this critical issue, obviously, is to withhold tax credits from all parents who allow their children to fail subjects in school.

_____

_____

Removing Unnecessary Examples, Details, and Explanations

Another way writers can be wordy is by including more **examples, details,** and **explanations** than necessary. First drafts can be wordy because writers lose sight of their audience, forgetting what readers already know or want to know about a subject.

Consider the following paragraph response written to remind an *adult* of steps to take before mailing a letter:

> Look closely at the front of the envelope, in the general area of the center, to see if you have remembered to write the proper and complete address where you want the letter to go. Remember to put the person's, company's, school's, or any other institution's name at the top of the outgoing address; and then on the very next line under the first line, put the street address with numbers first, that is, before the name of the street, road, boulevard, or drive. Then on the bottom line, under the middle line, write out the destination, beginning with the city and progressing through the state and possibly country if you are sending the letter out of the United States. Also be sure to write out all the numbers of the zip code (those numbers that help the post office route your mail properly). When you have accomplished this task, repeat it in more or less the same way as you check your return address, which should be in the upper left corner of the envelope you want to mail. Find a stamp that you have to lick or one that already has adhesive on the back, lick or in some other way, possibly using a sponge, dampen the stamp that needs to be wet in order for it to stick; and then affix it to the upper right corner of the envelope. The final step is to seal the envelope, which you can do again by licking or using the same sponge, or you might have envelopes that already have adhesive on them if you are lucky. Now seal it, and you are finished with the job.

For more on using examples effectively and efficiently, see Chapter 7.

If this process paragraph seems too long, it is because the writer has lost sight of what the audience needs and wants to know. Here is a concise revision:

> Address the envelope properly, include your return address, stamp the envelope, and seal it.

The longer version might be the rough draft of an explanation to children who have never before addressed an envelope. However, even for this audience, the writer should cut much of the unnecessary explanation and many of the examples. As you draft, you should be open to new ideas and include specific examples, but during revision, you should prune any that are not essential.

ACTIVITY 20.7 | WORKING TOGETHER: *Removing Unneeded Examples, Details, and Explanations*

In a small group, read the following paragraph aloud, and revise it to remove unneeded examples, details, and explanations. The purpose of the paragraph is to *briefly* explain to an adult how to light a charcoal fire. As you read, ask yourself and each other, "How much of this information would I need to start a charcoal fire?"

To successfully light a charcoal fire for grilling, there are four basic steps, but there is a lot to know about each one. First off, what kind of grill do you have? If it is a gas or electric grill, you have an easy task. Just turn it on. If, on the other hand, you have a small Weber or other type of grill that has to use the kind of fuel you can buy in almost any supermarket, meaning charcoal, then the process becomes more complicated. Do you want to buy matchless charcoal or the kind of charcoal that requires charcoal starting fluid and a match or some other lighting device? Of course, there are several brands of charcoal, but if you choose the kind that requires fluid and a match, then pay for the bag, take it to your car, drive home, and take the charcoal out onto your deck or patio or driveway or wherever you plan to do your grilling. After you get there, open the bag with a knife or a pair of scissors or maybe you can just pull that little string that hangs down. Next, cover the bottom of the grill on the inside with some kind of fire-resistant material like aluminum foil and pour the briquettes (small pieces of charcoal that are sort of square and rough around the edges) out of the bag so that the charcoal covers the bottom of the grill. Now pour just enough fluid on the briquettes so that a film of the liquid covers most of the top at least. Now you are ready to work the charcoal into a pile that has roughly the shape of a pyramid, meaning a pile about 6 inches high at the pointed top tapering down to a kind of round-shaped bottom. The final step is to stand back at least at arm's length and, using a match, lighter, or a piece of paper that you have rolled up and lit with a match or lighter, carefully light the edge of the pile of charcoal. Be sure to stand back immediately so that you won't run the risk of having the flames leap up and possibly scorch your hand or arm or even your face.

Reducing Inflated Clauses and Phrases

The last important method for writing more concisely is to reduce clauses to phrases and phrases to single words where appropriate.

REDUCING PHRASES TO SINGLE-WORD MODIFIERS

A. Hannah ran to answer the phone in an eager way.

Hannah eagerly ran to answer the phone.

B. The wolf could not blow down the house built of bricks.

The wolf could not blow down the brick house.

C. Most people appreciate the beauty of a sunset.

Most people appreciate a sunset's beauty.

REDUCING CLAUSES TO PHRASES OR SINGLE-WORD MODIFIERS

A. Ernest Hemingway, who is a well-known writer, was a big-game hunter.

Ernest Hemingway, a well-known writer, was a big-game hunter.

B. The man who is wearing a red vest is my grandfather.

The man wearing a red vest is my grandfather.

C. Elephants, which are the largest land animals, may weigh 5 tons.

Elephants, the largest land animals, may weigh 5 tons.

D. The painting that is hanging in the library is from the nineteenth century.

The painting hanging in the library is from the nineteenth century.

E. The wolf could not blow down the house that was built of bricks.

The wolf could not blow down the house built of bricks (or brick house).

F. Eleanor has a dance style that is graceful.

Eleanor has a graceful dance style.

Eleanor dances gracefully.

G. While she waited in the lobby, Paula occupied herself by counting roses on the wallpaper.

Waiting in the lobby, Paula occupied herself by counting roses on the wallpaper.

ACTIVITY 20.8 *Reducing Clauses and Phrases*

Revise the following sentences by reducing the underlined clauses to phrases and phrases to single-word modifiers.

1. The journalist who was interviewing Kevin Bacon seemed interested in Bacon's childhood.

_____

2. Labor Day, <u>which is a well-deserved national holiday,</u> falls on the first Monday in September.

3. <u>Because the summer drought is deepening,</u> lawns are beginning to die.

4. Ethanol is not a biofuel that helps <u>in</u> a significant <u>way</u> to reduce global warming gases.

5. Madeline had always wanted <u>a couch covered in leather.</u>

6. Many people are attracted to the style and performance <u>of a sports car.</u>

7. <u>After he had visited Kenya,</u> Lutz flew back home to Germany.

Choosing Language for Tone

Beyond eliminating nonessential words, writers need to consider other elements of language that affect the **tone** of their work, that is, the attitude they reveal toward the subject and audience. Consider the following sentences and the circumstances in which you would be likely to hear or say them:

A. Because Charley was busted by his butthead boss gettin' out the door, he was stuck on the line burning orders till 10:00.
B. Because Charley was caught leaving the restaurant by the shift manager, he had to cook until 10:00.
C. Because his employer discovered that he was departing the restaurant, Charles was required to prepare entrees until 10:00 p.m.

Sentence A is the most informal, and sentence C is the most formal: there are reasons for classifying these sentences in this way.

- **Informal:** Sentence A uses several slang words (*busted, butthead, burnin' orders*), drops letters (*gettin'*), and uses the word *boss* instead of a more formal term like *supervisor.*

- **Midrange:** Sentence B substitutes mainstream American English diction like *caught* for *busted* and *cook* for *burning orders*. The writer has also chosen the more specific words *shift manager* instead of *boss.*

- **Formal:** Sentence C uses longer words: *discovered* for *caught, departing* for *leaving, required* for *had,* and *entrees* for *food.* Also *Charley* has become *Charles.*

As writers, we choose our tone based on our topic and audience and how we feel about both. We speak informally when excited, rushed, or relaxing with friends. Informal writing uses slang, colloquialisms, idiomatic expressions, contractions, and personal pronouns, and it often uses shorter words or abbreviations.

Sentence B is typical of the style many college students use in their academic work. College writing uses fewer contractions, informal idioms, and personal pronouns; it eliminates slang, uses more subordination in sentences, and may choose longer words.

Sentence C has the most formal style, one used in the academic community and in many professions, including law, science, medicine, and business.

The style and tone of your writing are largely determined by your sentence structure and vocabulary. In the next few pages, we will learn some strategies for controlling tone.

Revising Unneeded Big Words

Formal writing uses more multisyllable words than does informal writing. Sometimes larger words are needed to express a complicated idea, but sometimes not. Often writers fall into a habit of picking a larger word when a smaller one will do—for example, *terminate* instead of *end*. This habit can produce writing that sounds pretentious and is difficult to read, as in this example:

> A continuous regimen of nutritional intake of the electronic medium
> most revered by the masses can effect a deleterious transformation in
> the organ responsible for a human being's cerebration, producing
> intellectual obesity.

Your response is probably "huh?" Stringing multisyllable words together generally produces writing that is hard to understand. The previous example is an extreme form of "thesaurus" writing—exotic word hunting—and it obscures rather than clarifies meaning.

Here is a revised version:

> A steady diet of television can make the brain flabby.

Your choice of words depends on your **writing context,** and sometimes you will have good reasons to use some "big" words. If you are writing for an audience knowledgeable in a certain field—say, doctors, mechanics, or restaurant managers—you will often use specialized terms that they understand, though the terms might be unfamiliar to others. People writing for a medical audience would not need to define terms like *otoscope* or *platelets*, for example. Sometimes you might choose a longer word for variety (*additionally* in place of *also* or *and*). However, in general, favoring more common—and often smaller—words will make your writing clearer.

In the following passage, how many words of more than one syllable did the writer, Joseph Ecclesine, need to express himself?

> Small words move with ease where big words stand still—or worse, bog down
> and get in the way of what you want to say. There is not much, in all truth,
> that small words will not say—and say quite well.

ACTIVITY 20.9 | WORKING ONLINE: *Revising Unneeded Big Words*

Revise these sentences by "translating" the unneeded big words into more everyday language. Consult www.dictionary.com or www. thesaurus.com to look up the exact meaning of each unneeded word, or to seek more straightforward alternatives. As you revise, be sure to keep the basic meaning of the sentence the same.

EXAMPLE: The Boy Scouts gathered their paraphernalia and prepared themselves for the coming arduous adventure into the wilderness.

Revised: *The Boy Scouts gathered their gear and prepared for their backpacking trip.*

1. Shannon attempted to purchase an automobile yesterday but did not succeed.

   _____

2. Those who obtain a proficiency with computers can anticipate increased marketability.

   _____

3. The facade of the edifice is deteriorating with rapidity.

   _____

4. Andrea received an equitable remuneration for her laborious toil.

   _____

5. Chen hypothesized that the communiqué in his mail receptacle contained abominable information.

   _____

Avoiding Slang and Colloquial Expressions

Just as using a lot of multisyllable words affects your tone, so does using slang and colloquial expressions. **Slang terms** are typically short-lived, colorful words invented by groups to express meanings members understand but outsiders often do not. Examples include *sweet, freaked out, bling,* and *wired.*

Colloquial terms are similar to slang but are typically understood by a wider audience—for example, words like *kid* for "child" or *hang out* for "spend time with."

Slang and colloquialisms are appropriate for informal situations. However, academic writers almost never use slang and use colloquial terms only on occasion, to vary their tone.

HINT

If you want to achieve a relatively formal tone, replace all slang and most colloquialisms with more standard words.

ACTIVITY 20.10 WORKING TOGETHER: *Translating Slang*

In small groups, choose any five of the terms below and discuss their meaning. Together, for each, write a sentence using the term as slang and then another sentence replacing the term with more formal language. You may need several words to convey your meaning, perhaps by describing a scene, and you may find that your interpretation of a slang word varies from that of others in your group.

EXAMPLE: When I told my grandmother about the car wreck, she freaked out.

Revised: *When I told my grandmother about the car wreck, she hugged me and began sobbing.*

EXAMPLE: Ethan was busted for stealing a car.

Revised: *Ethan was arrested for stealing a car.*

SLANG AND COLLOQUIAL EXPRESSIONS

a drag	busted	dumped on	hot	sweet
airhead	chill	flame	laid back	threads
babe	chill out	freaked out	my bad	totaled
bling	cool	gig	psyched out	tripping
blown away	cop	go postal	ride	wasted
boost	digits	hassle	rip off	wicked
bummed	diss	hit on	stressed out	wired

1. Slang version: _____

    Revision: _____

2. Slang version: _____

    Revision: _____

3. Slang version: _____

    Revision: _____

4. Slang version: _____

    Revision: _____

5. Slang version: _____

    Revision: _____

ACTIVITY 20.11 *Revising Colloquial Expressions*

Revise the following sentences by replacing the colloquial expressions with more formal language.

EXAMPLE: Tony was in a bind.

Revised: *Tony had a problem.*

1. Dale's boss keeps giving him the runaround.

    _____

2. "Did you catch the *Friends* rerun last night?"

    _____

3. "I think that it's time to hit the road."

    _____

4. "Sarah, you're driving me up a wall with that racket!"

    _____

5. "If you're not careful, Rachel will try to pull another fast one on you."

    _____

Controlling Denotation and Connotation

Words have objective, literal meanings found in dictionaries, called **denotation,** but they also have more subjective, figurative meanings that people associate with them, called **connotation.**

Denotative meanings are usually easier for a writer to pin down. When you look up the word *flag* in a dictionary, for example, you might find this definition: "a piece of cloth, usually rectangular, of distinctive color and design, used as a symbol, a standard, a signal, or an emblem." Because a nation's flag is a symbol, however, it evokes different images and emotional responses from different people. For instance, the American flag arouses feelings of patriotism and a sense of national belonging in many Americans. It has positive associations—and connotations—for them. However, within the United States and abroad, there are those who see the flag as a symbol of oppression. To them, the flag has negative connotations.

To control your tone, be aware of the potential connotations words have for an audience. In persuasive writing, try to avoid the temptation to choose words that evoke a negative rather than a positive response. For example, how would you like to be characterized by a writer: as assertive or pushy? Most of us would prefer the more positive connotations of *assertive*.

For more on definition, see Chapter 15.

ACTIVITY 20.12 | *Revising for Connotation*

Review the following terms and consider their connotations. Next, arrange each word group in a roughly ascending order from most negative to most positive.

EXAMPLE: restless, hyperactive, frantic, energetic, active

Reordered from most negative to most positive: *frantic, hyperactive, restless, active, energetic*

Relatively Negative   Relatively Positive

1. Quiet, reserved, shy, timid, withdrawn, reclusive

   _____

2. Frightened, apprehensive, hysterical, nervous, panicked

   _____

3. Odor, fragrance, stench, scent, smell

   _____

4. Thrifty, stingy, frugal, cheap, miserly

   _____

5. Slender, lean, thin, skinny, gaunt, emaciated

   _____

6. Innocent, childlike, unsophisticated, naïve, childish

   _____

Eliminating Biased Language

Sometimes writers unintentionally insult a reader because they don't realize the implications of their words. Without thinking, we convey negative impressions about race, religion, ethnicity, age, gender, social class, physical and mental abilities, body shape, and sexual orientation. To avoid both offending readers and implying that we are either insensitive or unaware, we must choose our words carefully. For example, writers sensitive to **gender bias** in language avoid using career and social stereotypes and pronouns that exclude women.

Career and social stereotypes take several forms, but in general they imply that men belong in one role or profession and that women belong in another (often lower-status) profession. Consider the following sentences:

SEXIST   A doctor must spend many years earning his credentials to practice medicine.

REVISED   Doctors must spend many years earning their credentials to practice medicine.

SEXIST   When the homeowner dusts, vacuums, and launders, she is doing required household maintenance.

REVISED   When homeowners dust, vacuum, and launder, they are doing required household maintenance.

Many doctors are women, and many men do household chores.

Take care to avoid occupational titles and other group descriptions that include the word *man*. Here is a list of some common terms with alternatives that are not gender-biased:

anchorman = anchor

businessman = businessperson

chairman = chair

congressman = representative

craftsman = artist

fireman = fire fighter

foreman = supervisor

freshman = first-year student

insurance man = insurance agent

mailman = mail carrier

mankind = humanity, people

manpower = personnel, workers

newsman = reporter, journalist

policeman = police officer

salesman = sales representative

stewardess/steward = flight
attendant

waitress/waiter = food server

weatherman = weather reporter,
forecaster

workman = worker

You can avoid using gender-specific pronouns to refer to groups that contain both genders by using a plural pronoun, dropping the pronoun, using a "his or her" combination, or alternating gender pronouns within a passage (as *A Writer's Workshop* sometimes does).

The *he or she* method can easily be overworked and sound awkward. When you alternate *he* and *she*, be sure the pronoun references are clear. See Chapter 25 for help with pronoun reference.

OPTIONS TO PREVENT GENDER BIAS WITH PRONOUNS

GENDER BIAS   A student who studies his notes thoroughly should do well on his exam.

REVISED: PLURAL PRONOUN   Students who study their notes thoroughly should do well on the exam. (*their* substituted for *his*)

REVISED: DELETED PRONOUN   A student studying notes thoroughly should do well on the exam.

REVISED: HIS OR HER/SHE OR HE	A student who studies his or her notes thoroughly should do well on the exam.
REVISED: ALTERNATED PRONOUNS	A student who studies his notes thoroughly should do well on the exam. The student will do particularly well if she focuses on the chapter summaries.

ACTIVITY 20.13 | *Revising Sexist Language*

Revise the following sentences (or phrases) by replacing gender-biased language with appropriate alternatives.

EXAMPLE: "To boldly go where no man has gone before . . ."
Revised: *"To boldly go where no one has gone before . . ."*

1. When a baby needs his diaper changed, find his mother in a hurry!

   _____

   _____

2. Dear Sir: I have heard a great deal about your company and the professionalism of your salesmen.

   _____

   _____

3. When the mailman dropped off my package, I thanked her.

   _____

   _____

4. Jackie will be a freshman at JCCC this year.

   _____

   _____

5. If we had more manpower in this office, we could finish the job on time.

   _____

   _____

6. Congressman Andrea Cambiano will now take questions from the newsmen.

   _____

   _____

Using Contractions Carefully

In speech and informal writing, we often use **contractions**—abbreviated words joined with apostrophes—such as *can't* from *cannot* and *haven't* from *have not*. Contractions are largely absent from more formal or academic writing, but there is a good reason for not banishing them altogether from your writer's tool kit. When a construction sounds awkward expressed as two words, you can choose to accept the odd sound, revise the sentence, or use a contraction. Consider the following examples:

A. Would not this sentence seem somewhat stilted if I did not use a contraction?

B. Will not you come with me to the ballgame?

Questions like these sound more natural when they begin with contractions. Compare "Won't you come with me to the ballgame?" with sentence B.

Another good reason for using contractions occasionally is that they can add a welcome note of informality to an otherwise serious paragraph. Like other markers of informal style, such as personal pronouns, dialogue, revealed thought, and common words, contractions can contribute to a more relaxed tone.

As with any stylistic device, you should be cautious about overusing contractions. In particular, avoid these: *could've, would've, should've, they'd, I'd, we'd,* and *when's.*

ACTIVITY 20.14 *Revising Contractions*

Assume that the following sentences appear in college essays trying for a midrange style, neither too distant nor too chummy. Examine the contractions, keep any that seem appropriate, and revise the rest.

1. They'd have made it to the summit if they could've.

   _____

2. When's the last time a president was impeached in this country?

   _____

3. What's the CIA think they could've accomplished through covert means that the Pentagon hasn't been able to achieve?

   _____

4. I can't give you an answer if you haven't a proper question.

   _____

5. Aren't you the one who says it's hardly worth watching network news anymore because it's mostly just sound bites?

   _____

Using Figures of Speech

Figures of speech are expressions that convey their meaning in a nonliteral way or that reinforce their meaning through the arrangement of words. Writers can create comparisons by using metaphor, simile, and personification; play with meaning through overstatement, understatement, and irony; and position words for effect by using emphatic repetition. Figures of speech are common in language, contributing much to its strength, clarity, and color. When we say, "Sam's a couch potato" and "The algebra exam was a nightmare," we are using well-worn figures of speech.

Figures of speech are a valuable resource. They can help you make your writing more concise and connect with your audience.

As style points that draw attention to themselves, figures of speech should be used with discretion: A little spice is welcome, but a lot is not.

Metaphor, Simile, and Personification

Metaphor and simile are perhaps the most useful and widespread figures of speech, often, along with personification, slipping into our expressions unnoticed. A **metaphor** says that one thing is another, whereas a **simile** uses *like* or *as.* For example, a sports reporter might write the following:

METAPHOR   Luis Figo is a $56 million man, soccer's most expensive diamond.

The literal meaning of the metaphor is that Luis Figo is a valuable and well-paid soccer player, but notice how the figure of speech adds interest to the writing. If the reporter had written "as expensive" or "like a diamond," we would have a simile. Here are several other metaphors and similes:

METAPHORS

A. Dunn's knee was done for, a hinge with the pin pulled.

B. Her life was an empty house, a chain on the front door, windows boarded shut, and a sign nailed to the front door saying "Nobody home."

SIMILES

A. His illness crept upon him, barely noticed, draining his life like the fall stealing green from the trees.

B. Jeb shouted downstairs to his son, "That damn noise sounds more like a chainsaw cuttin' galvanized tin than music!"

When creating figurative comparisons, avoid clashing images called **mixed metaphors:**

Seeming to escape the web of her misfortune, at the last possible moment she slammed into the wall of her destiny.

The metaphor is more unified if we use the spiderweb imagery consistently:

Seeming to escape the web of her misfortune, at the last possible moment a strand of her destiny pulled her back down into the spider's lair.

Personification gives human qualities to animals and things, thereby creating a comparison and often establishing a mood. When we say that the sky looks angry or threatening, we are personifying, attributing emotions to the sky. Here are several other examples of personification:

PERSONIFICATION

A. Tired from the weight of years, the old barn leaned hard to one side.

B. The airbus, heavy with fuel and feeling its age, seemed reluctant to leave the runway.

C. The golden arches seemed to smile, saying, "Come on in. The fries are hot."

When you are using figures of speech like metaphors, similes, and personification, watch for clichés and worn expressions. **Clichés** are metaphors and similes that have had the life sucked out of them by overuse—for example, "He stood still as a statue" or "Her heart pounded like a drum."

Worn phrases are similar, but they are not always a comparison—for example, "live life to the fullest" or "a cut-and-dried solution." Because even old figures of speech have some power and are common in casual speech, they will occasionally sneak into your writing. However, since they are secondhand expressions, you should avoid them. Here is a brief list of some common clichés and worn expressions:

CLICHÉS AND WORN EXPRESSIONS

sent chills down my spine	like two peas in a pod	cold as ice
seemed like an eternity	security blanket	butterflies in my stomach
couch potato	iron out the wrinkles	
sparkle (gleam, spark, glint) in her/his eye	window of opportunity	a perfect little angel
	pushing the envelope	glued to
thin as a rail (stick)	get a handle on	a step in the right direction
is a breeze	live life to the fullest	
velcroed to	take things one day (one step) at a time	see the light
make the project fly		a slap on the hand
no strings attached	last but not least	few and far between
between a rock and a hard place	seemed like only yesterday	life flash before her eyes
hated with a passion	go with the flow	winning isn't everything
break a sweat	set in stone	
get the ball rolling	right on the money	up bright and early
moved like lightning	bundle of energy	brushed him/her off
out in left field		
hot as hell		

As you revise paragraphs and essays, find and replace clichés and worn expressions.

[*What comes to mind when you hear "pretty as a picture"? In a sentence, replace this cliché with a specific, vivid description.*]

ACTIVITY 20.15 *Revising Clichés and Worn Expressions*

Revise these sentences to eliminate clichés and worn expressions. You may "translate" the cliché into literal language or try for a fresh metaphor or simile.

EXAMPLE (CLICHÉ): As I waited to take my algebra final, I felt butterflies in my stomach.

Revised (simile): *As I waited to take my algebra final, I felt like a beginning skier about to plunge down her first slope.*

Revised (literal language): *As I waited to take my algebra final, I was nervous.*

1. They should act quickly, for their days are numbered.

2. While driving on the highway, you can lose your life in the blink of an eye.

3. Their relationship was doomed from the start.

4. We need more jobs where money isn't everything.

5. Everyone else was right on target, but Jason didn't have a clue.

_____

6. The last thing I want to do is to end up as another statistic.

_____

ACTIVITY 20.16 | WORKING TOGETHER: *Creating Metaphors and Similes*

Discuss with group members possible metaphors or similes for the following sentences. Imagining and verbally describing a scene as fully as possible can help. For the example, you might visualize a car with a wobbly wheel and then search for images that suggest a spinning object—pinwheel, Ferris wheel, or Frisbee—or the drum of a washing machine. For number 6, create your own metaphor or simile, and explain its meaning.

EXAMPLE: (for number 6)

The blown tire on Mayfield's car wobbled like *a washer with an uneven load.*

Meaning: *The wheels on a racing car move at high speeds, as does the drum inside a washing machine, and both are subject to stress. People can relate to a washer clonking around from an uneven load of clothes and see how the wheel might need the same immediate attention.*

1. My life today is like _____

_____

2. She fell down the stairs like _____

_____

3. The car skidded like _____

_____

4. After pumping iron for 6 years, Mark had become a _____

_____

5. The grease burn felt like _____

_____

6. Your metaphor/simile: _____

_____

How it conveys your meaning: _____

_____

ACTIVITY 20.17 | *Personifying*

Consider the following options for personifying, and then create sentences that include personified imagery. For number 6, explain how the personification of one of the five phrases helps convey your meaning.

EXAMPLE: a boring baseball game

Personification: *After the seventh inning, the game just limped along till the misery was finally over.*

Meaning: *When there is little hitting and baserunning, baseball can slow to a crawl. A person with a limp moves slowly and is often in pain, just the way I feel when I'm stuck in a slow game.*

1. A mountain ridge covered with snow and ready to avalanche

   _____

   _____

2. The sun setting over the ocean as seen from a comfortable perspective (dock, restaurant, cruise ship)

   _____

   _____

3. A 1968 Volkswagen Beetle with the running boards rusted off

   _____

   _____

4. A large building crane carrying a steel beam to a fifth floor

   _____

   _____

5. A litter of 6-week-old beagle puppies playing with a knotted towel

   _____

   _____

6. How one of the above personifications conveys your meaning:

   _____

   _____

Overstatement, Understatement, and Irony

Other figures of speech that can affect your tone are overstatement, understatement, and irony. When you use **overstatement,** you exaggerate for effect: "When they see this speeding ticket, my parents are going to *murder* me." When you use **understatement,** you downplay a situation. If your friend responded, "I hope your parents will be a *little less* drastic," that is understatement—we hope that the parents will be a *lot* less drastic than murder. When you use **irony,** you state the opposite of what you mean. For example, in the hall before your algebra final, you might say to a classmate, "This is going to be fun." Irony can be useful because it reflects on the author's persona, often revealing a sense of perspective and humor, and establishes shared knowledge. In effect, it says to the reader, "I know that you know what I mean." Here are more examples of these figures of speech:

OVERSTATEMENT

A. After her high school win, Terri felt like the best golfer on the planet.

B. DVD players are so cheap now that stores practically give them away.

UNDERSTATEMENT

A. Robert De Niro's character in the film *Backdraft*, after he has been impaled on a wrought iron fence, says, "Hey . . . ah, kid, I think I gotta little problem here."

B. He commented to a friend's uncle who had just bought a Dodge Viper: "That must have set you back a little bit."

IRONY

A. Dilated to 6 centimeters, dripping sweat, and twisting on the hospital bed, Alice gasped between contractions, "Tell me . . . again . . . about the joys of motherhood."

B. While Alice suffered through another round of contractions, her brother-in-law, in the waiting room, suffered his own agony—missing the playoff game between the Lakers and the Bulls.

ACTIVITY 20.18 | *Creating Overstatement, Understatement, and Irony*

Avoid worn phrases and clichés.

Consider how you might revise the following sentences for overstatement, understatement, and irony. As you revise the sentences, expect that it will take some work to create interesting figures of speech. You may notice irony also working in understatement.

EXAMPLE: I don't feel appreciated at work.

Overstatement: *If I died tomorrow and fell on the floor, people would just step around me till they got tired of the nuisance, and then they would toss me in the dumpster out back.*

1. Registering for classes can seem complicated.

   Overstatement: _____

   _____

2. Freddy Krueger, from the *Nightmare on Elm Street* movies, is a spooky character.

   Overstatement: _____

   _____

3. Bill Gates is worth 65 billion dollars.

   Understatement: _____

   _____

4. Drunken driving kills thousands of people annually.

   Understatement: _____

   _____

5. A friend is doing poorly in college: He has not bothered to buy text-books, seldom goes to class, and never studies for exams.

   Irony: _____

   _____

6. Elaine works hard, helps her friends, gives to charity, and is active in her community. She also is overly meticulous. Comment on this habit.

Irony: _____

_____

Emphatic Repetition

Repetition can be a useful way to reinforce meaning and guide readers. Of course, repetition can also be useless, boring readers who wonder why the same word keeps repeating itself endlessly. Which of the following two paragraphs illustrates harmful repetition, and which helpful repetition?

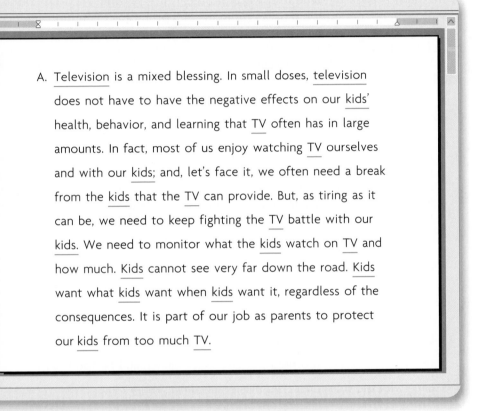

A. Television is a mixed blessing. In small doses, television does not have to have the negative effects on our kids' health, behavior, and learning that TV often has in large amounts. In fact, most of us enjoy watching TV ourselves and with our kids; and, let's face it, we often need a break from the kids that the TV can provide. But, as tiring as it can be, we need to keep fighting the TV battle with our kids. We need to monitor what the kids watch on TV and how much. Kids cannot see very far down the road. Kids want what kids want when kids want it, regardless of the consequences. It is part of our job as parents to protect our kids from too much TV.

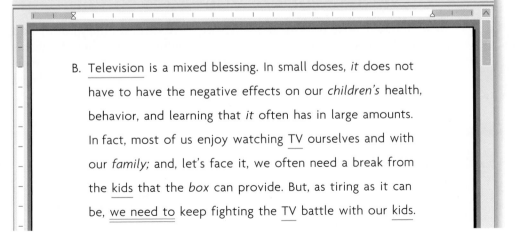

B. Television is a mixed blessing. In small doses, *it* does not have to have the negative effects on our *children's* health, behavior, and learning that *it* often has in large amounts. In fact, most of us enjoy watching TV ourselves and with our *family*; and, let's face it, we often need a break from the kids that the *box* can provide. But, as tiring as it can be, we need to keep fighting the TV battle with our kids.

We need to monitor what *they* watch and how much. *Children* cannot see very far down the road. *They* <u>want</u> what they <u>want</u> when they <u>want</u> it, regardless of the consequences. It is part of our job as parents to protect *them* from themselves.

Paragraph A bogs the reader down and bores through unneeded repetition. On the other hand, paragraph B uses synonyms and pronouns to minimize unneeded repetition, keeping only what is useful for coherence. The author also creates special emphasis with the words "we need to" and "want."

In your own work, try occasionally repeating words that you want to especially emphasize, particularly in conclusions.

ACTIVITY 20.19 | *Revising for Emphatic Repetition*

Read through the following narrative paragraph and revise it (on separate paper) for effective repetition. Replace any word you think is repeated unnecessarily, restructuring a sentence slightly if you think it is needed. Next, underline any *effectively* repeated phrase and explain how the repetition adds to the paragraph's meaning.

Martin dragged into the house at the end of another exhausting workday. Martin had slept little the night before, and Martin had been kept on the job two hours past his regular quitting time. Martin collapsed on the sofa. Staring down at his work boots, Martin thought about unlacing his boots; his feet hurt. But he was too tired to manage it. Martin was too tired to unlace his boots, too tired to think about dinner, and far too tired to cope with the stack of unpaid bills on his dining room table.

ADJUSTING LANGUAGE FOR DIFFERENT AUDIENCES

Conservation in Context

Read today's post on Green Daily, http://www.greendaily.com/, and rewrite it as if you were talking to a friend, telling him or her about this information. Then rewrite the post again in more academic language, as if for a class. Highlight specific words and phrases that you have replaced in each case. ●

ACTIVITY 20.20 | WORKING ONLINE: *Word Choice Review*

Take the Chapter 20 Review Quiz at www.mhhe.com/brannan.

Chapter Summary

1. Style in writing consists largely of word choices and arrangement.

2. Writers choose their words on the basis of their subject, their attitude toward it, and their sense of what the audience wants or needs to know.

3. General and abstract words are necessary for framing larger ideas, particularly in thesis and topic sentences, but specific and concrete terms are essential to develop the more general words.

4. Writing concisely requires cutting words that serve little purpose in a sentence. Sentences, paragraphs, and essays may be concise *and* long.

5. We can improve concision by controlling these elements:
   A. Redundant expressions: *each and every one, true facts*
   B. Empty words and phrases: *very, thing, kind of*
   C. Padded phrases: *due to the fact that = because, at the present time = now*
   D. Excessive qualifiers/emphasizers: *sometimes, maybe/certainly, obviously*
   E. Unneeded detail: postage stamp *rectangular and placed in the corner*
   F. Inflated clauses and phrases: *in an eager way = eagerly*

6. Writers vary their tone on the basis of how they feel about their topic and how they regard their audience.

7. Multisyllable words can be overused. Generally, rely on the more common word: *numerous = many, terminate = end, edifice = house.*

8. Eliminate slang from relatively formal writing, and use colloquial expressions judiciously: *bummed = depressed, psyched up = excited, kid = child.*

9. The connotation of words often affects tone: Connotations of *child* include *innocence, happiness, freedom.*

10. Avoid biased language, including gender bias, in writing: *all men ≠ everyone.*

11. Contractions should be used sparingly in relatively formal writing.

12. Figures of speech can enrich writing, providing concision, color, and emphasis.
    A. Metaphor: *Her life was an empty house.*
    B. Simile: *Her life was like an empty house.*
    C. Personification: *the angry sky*
    D. Overstatement: *My parents will murder me!*
    E. Understatement: *AIDS is a disease that has caused some trouble.*
    F. Irony: *If you want to keep them safe, let children have loaded guns.*
    G. Emphatic repetition: *"I stand here in the name of law; I stand here in the name of justice; and I stand here in the name of human decency."*

13. Avoid clichés and worn expressions: *sent chills up my spine.*

Practicing Sentence Sense

Working with Sentence Parts

21

[*Like the table being assembled in the picture, sentences also consist of many pieces. Before reading further in this chapter, what sentence parts (such as nouns and verbs) do you remember from your earlier education? Write a paragraph telling how much sentence grammar you still recall and discussing how you felt about learning it.*]

KEY TOPICS

- Reviewing the parts of speech
- Identifying the part of speech a word belongs to
- Recognizing the verbs and subjects of simple sentences
- Phrases
- Clauses
- Sentence types

What Are We Trying to Achieve and Why?

Most of *A Writer's Workshop* has focused on helping you discover, organize, develop, and revise ideas. However, once those ideas are in place, you must take the next step by expressing them in sentences that are clear to an audience. By learning the basic parts of a sentence, you will better manage them; and in seeing the relationship among the parts, you will punctuate more effectively as well.

Reviewing the Parts of Speech

All of the words in sentences fall into eight traditional categories based on how they function. These word categories are called the **parts of speech.**

THE EIGHT PARTS OF SPEECH

1. **Verbs** express an action or state of being: *run, is.*

2. **Nouns** name a person, place, thing, concept, or quality: *Tom, Idaho, rock, freedom, pleasure.*

3. **Pronouns** stand in place of a noun: *he, her, they, who, their, it.*

4. **Adjectives** describe nouns and pronouns: *hard* chair, someone *strong.*

5. **Adverbs** describe verbs, adjectives, and adverbs: running *quickly, very* angry, *too* busily.

6. **Prepositions** shape nouns and pronouns into phrases: *on* the table, *near* her.

7. **Conjunctions** connect words, phrases, and clauses: cats *and* dogs, on my desk *or* in that drawer, they left *because* we left.

8. **Interjections** emphasize emotions: *Oh! Ouch!*

We seldom use all of the parts of speech in any one sentence, but we often use many in our most common expressions, as in the following sentence, where they are identified by number:

<pre>
    7   2   1   2   6 3   2   5   1   3   4
Because Timmy threw water on him, Tom immediately chased his younger
    2   6   4   2   7 6   4   2
brother through the house and into the street.
</pre>

Once we see examples from each category and how each works, we will learn where sentences begin and end and how to manage more complex sentences.

Verbs

Verbs, along with nouns, are the core of sentences. The verb expresses an action or state of being, and the nouns (or pronouns) perform or receive the action or experience the state of being. Verbs are of several types:

1. **Action verbs** show something happening—physically, mentally, or emotionally.

   A. Zeus *hurled* a lightning bolt across the sky.

   B. Aristotle *reflected* on the cause.

   C. Zeus's behavior often *angered* his wife, Hera.

2. **Being verbs** (or **linking verbs**) tell about a state of being. The verb *be* in its various forms (*am, are, is, was, were, been, being*) is the most common of

Every English sentence requires a verb.

In English, capitalize proper nouns, including days of the week and months of the year.

these verbs. Others include *look, sound, taste, smell, appear, feel, seem, become, remain, get,* and *grow.*

   A. Sheryl *is* an intelligent woman.

   B. Max *seemed* very nervous.

   C. Hot chocolate with marshmallows *tastes* good in the winter.

3. **Helping verbs** help the main verb of a sentence express meaning. With the main verb, they create a unit called a **verb phrase.** Common helping verbs include *be, have, do, may, might, must, can, could, should,* and *would.*

   A. Martin <u>*should be*</u> making a decision.

   B. Melanie <u>*might have*</u> finished the race.

   C. Margaret <u>*didn't say*</u> anything to anyone.

Notice that the main verb is at the end of the verb phrase. When *be* is followed by another verb, *be* is a helping verb.

   In addition to a base form (*work*), verbs have an infinitive form (*to work*) and can occur in various tenses, which show action as present, past, or future: "John *works* today, *worked* yesterday, and *will work* again tomorrow." (See Chapter 24.)

Nouns

As mentioned previously, nouns, along with verbs, form the core of our sentences, telling who or what is doing or receiving the action of the verb. Nouns can be relatively specific and concrete (*snow*) or relatively general and abstract (*cold*). Here are five categories:

1. **Proper nouns** name specific people (*Maria Gonzalez*), places (*Kansas City*), things (*Statue of Liberty*), and concepts (*Judaism*).

2. **Common nouns** name nonspecific people (*woman*), places (*city*), things (*statue*), concepts (*religion*), and qualities (*width*). Common nouns may be count or noncount nouns.

3. **Count nouns** name objects that can be quantified or enumerated: *rock, dress, car, trouble.* They generally form their plurals by adding *-s* or *-es.*

4. **Noncount nouns** name objects that cannot be counted: *sunlight, music, air.* They have no plural form.

5. **Collective nouns** name a group that is considered a unit and so is grammatically singular: *team, family, gathering, band.* (See Chapter 24.)

Pronouns

Pronouns are words that take the place of nouns. Like nouns, they can perform the action in a sentence ("*She* ran up a horrendous credit card debt") or receive the action ("Anna kicked *it* [the ball] downfield"). Because pronouns have no identity on their own, they must refer to a noun. Readers can easily be confused if a writer does not *always* make the link clear between a pronoun and noun.

TYPES OF PRONOUNS

1. **Personal pronouns:** *I, you, he, she, it, we, they, me, her, him, us, them*

2. **Indefinite pronouns:** *all, any, anybody, anything, both, each, everybody, everyone, everything, few, many, more, most, much, nobody, none, no one, one, several, some, somebody, someone, something*

3. **Relative pronouns:** *who, which, that (whom, whose, what, whatever, whichever, whoever, whomever)*

For more on using general and specific language, see Chapter 5.

Nouns are often introduced by articles: *the, a,* and *an:*

- *The* introduces a noun that is referring to something specific or already known to the reader (*the* flock of sparrows that damaged my rice crop; *the* sun).

- *A* and *an* introduce a noun that is not referring to something specific or known to the reader (*a* flock of sparrows). Use *a* in front of words that begin with a consonant sound (*a* rock) and *an* in front of words that begin with a vowel sound (*an* egg). Keep in mind that it is the sound, not the letter, that matters: *an* F in chemistry, *an* hour, *a* used car.

Distinguish between "he" and "she." In English, pronouns replace nouns, so they are not omitted or repeated. For more on pronouns, see Chapter 25.

For more on adjectives and adverbs, see Chapter 26.

Unlike many other languages, in English, adjectives precede the word they describe. In addition, they do not agree (in number or gender) with they words they modify.

4. **Interrogative pronouns:** *what, who, which, whom, whose*

5. **Demonstrative pronouns:** *this, that, these, those*

6. **Reflexive and intensive pronouns:** *myself, yourself, herself, himself, itself, oneself, ourselves, yourselves, themselves*

7. **Reciprocal pronouns:** *each other, one another*

8. **Possessive pronouns:** *my, mine, your, yours, her, hers, his, its, our, ours, their, theirs*

Adjectives

Adjectives are words that describe nouns or pronouns by answering questions like the following: *Which one? How many? What kind (shape, color, texture)?* Adjectives usually come directly before the word they modify. Many adjectives have three forms, indicating different degrees: *good, better, best; large, larger, largest; loud, louder, loudest.*

A. *The huge* Great Dane drooled on my arm.

B. Jonathan was *the best* child in the room.

Adverbs

Adverbs are words that describe verbs, adjectives, or other adverbs by answering the questions *when, where, why, how,* and *to what degree or extent.* An adverb is a flexible modifier, appearing before or after, and sometimes at a distance from, the word it describes. Consider the following sentences, in which *quickly* modifies the verb *scaled* and *too* modifies *quickly:*

A. Antonio *quickly* scaled the ladder.

B. *Too quickly* for safety, Antonio scaled the ladder.

Many adverbs are created by adding *-ly* to an adjective (*boldly* from *bold, happily* from *happy*), but many do not end in *-ly* (*then, sometimes, very, too*).

Prepositions

Prepositions come before nouns or pronouns, with which they combine in **prepositional phrases**, connecting these words to sentences. Many prepositions indicate location (*near, around, against, beside*), some indicate time (*until, during, for, since*), and some can mean either time or location (*on, in, by, at*). Prepositional phrases function as adjectives (the skateboard *with* the broken wheel) and as adverbs (hiked *up* the mountain path).

Prepositions That Show Location			Prepositions That Show Time	Prepositions That Show Location or Time
above	behind	inside	during	at
against	below	into	for	by
ahead of	beside	near	till	in
along	between	next to	until	on
alongside	beyond	of		
among	down	off		
around	from	onto		
at the side (end)	in front of	opposite		

Location (*cont.*)				
out of	through	up		
outside	to	upon		
over	toward	with		
past	under	without		

Deciding which preposition to use can be tricky because prepositions are often part of **idiomatic expressions**, phrases that may ignore grammar rules and that have a meaning beyond the literal definition of the words used.

Memorize these phrases.

COMMON PREPOSITIONAL PHRASES

abide *by* a decision

abide *in* New York

accuse *of* theft

afraid *of* horror films

agree *with* a wife

agree *to* a proposition

angry *with* a friend

apologize *for* a mistake

arrive *at* home

aware *of* a fact

bored *with* TV

capable *of* reading

charge *for* an oil change

comply *with* an order

concerned *about* (*with*) crime

independent *of* each other

interested *in* politics

proud *of* yourself

responsible *for* a child

rewarded *by* an employer

rewarded *for* work

Conjunctions

Like prepositions, conjunctions connect sentence parts. The seven **coordinating conjunctions** are used to show an equal relationship between words, phrases, or clauses. The acronym FANBOYS can help you remember the coordinating conjunctions.

for	and	nor	but	or	yet	so

CONNECTS WORDS   Jesse *and* Frank James were outlaws.

CONNECTS PHRASES   On the playing field *or* in the classroom, we will do our best.

CONNECTS CLAUSES   Florence works at IHOP, *but* Greg works at Dillard's.

Correlative conjunctions also join words, phrases, and clauses but work in pairs. They include *both/and, either/or, neither/nor,* and *not only/but also.*

A. *Neither* eggs *nor* whole milk will clog arteries if consumed in moderation.

B. *Either* that dog goes, *or* I go.

Conjunctive adverbs link only clauses, not words or phrases. Notice that they can express a relationship of ideas across sentences. Common conjunctive adverbs include *however, therefore, nevertheless, in fact,* and *consequently.*

A. I'm going to the symphony; *however,* Allen is going to the Linkin Park concert.

B. I'm going to the symphony. Allen, *however,* is going to the Linkin Park concert.

Certain prepositions follow adjectives and verbs by convention; when we substitute a different preposition, the phrase becomes nonstandard English. Become fluent with idiomatic phrases by listening carefully to native speakers, reading extensively, and memorizing phrases that are new to you. Practice using prepositions at www.mhhe.com/brannan (Ch. 21).

The three types of conjunctions discussed so far link main clauses; **subordinating conjunctions,** in contrast, connect a subordinate clause to a main clause. A subordinating conjunction, then, signals an unequal relationship between the clauses: The subordinate clause, which it introduces, is less important in the sentence and cannot stand alone but needs the main clause to complete its meaning.

A. *Because* it is 95 degrees out, I am heading for the pool.

B. I am heading for the pool *because* it is 95 degrees out.

Create a chart that incorporates all types of conjunctions. Arrange them according to meaning.

COMMON SUBORDINATING CONJUNCTIONS

after	as though	in order that	so that	whenever
although	because	now that	though	where
as	before	once	till	whereas
as if	even though	rather than	until	wherever
as long as	if	since	when	while

Interjections

Interjections are words used to express emotion. Mild interjections are set off with a comma (*"Well,* I won't be going to the movie"), and more emphatic ones are punctuated with an exclamation point (*"Oh, no!* Sophie forgot the tickets").

Identifying the Part of Speech a Word Belongs To

Identifying the part of speech a word belongs to is often fairly easy, and memorizing some of the "cue" words listed will help you. However, some words belong to more than one part of speech, and we therefore need to look carefully at their use in a particular sentence. For example, we can *light* a fire (verb), turn on a *light* (noun), or feel a *light* breeze (adjective). The best way to identify a word's part of speech is to think about how it *functions*: Does it name, describe, show action or being, connect, or express emotion?

Memorizing a conjunction like *because* will help you remember the larger group of conjunctions.

For more on main and subordinate clauses, see Chapter 22.

ACTIVITY 21.1 *Using Parts of Speech*

Fill in the blanks with the type of word indicated in parentheses at the end of the sentence.

EXAMPLE: My whole family ___*loves*___ to go to the Renaissance Festival. (action verb)

1. Sharks _____ in the deep, cold water of Monterey Bay. (action verb)

2. Iceland relies mainly on geothermal and hydropower for its energy needs instead of _____. (noun)

3. The sound from the furnace would _____ disappear and then begin again. (adverb)

4. Hang gliding is a _____ sport. (adjective)

5. Wild Bill Hickok was shot and killed _____ Deadwood _____ the age of 39. (prepositions)

6. Adolf Hitler was a dictator. _____ was responsible for the deaths of millions. (personal pronoun)

7. Argentina _____ Chile are South American countries that have elected women as presidents. (coordinating conjunction)

8. Benjamin Franklin, _____ was one of the Founding Fathers, lived to be 84. (relative pronoun)

9. _____ football is popular in America, soccer has more followers worldwide. (subordinating conjunction)

10. Just before the performance, Pavarotti _____ unwell. (being verb)

Recognizing the Verbs and Subjects of Simple Sentences

Knowing the parts of speech helps make sentences seem less mysterious. To form sentences, of course, we don't need all the parts of speech. In fact, we can form a one-word sentence—"Stop!" As long as we have both a subject (in this case, *you* is understood as the subject) and a verb, and they represent a complete thought, we have a sentence. In this section, then, we focus on recognizing the basic parts of a **simple sentence** (sentence with one main clause): the subject—often a noun or pronoun—and verb.

Simple sentences in English are usually ordered with the subject (S) coming before the verb (V), which is followed by the object (O), the word receiving the action, if there is one:

```
 S      V      O
Eric  cooked  dinner.
```

Knowing this word order will help you find verbs and subjects and thus help you decide where a simple sentence begins and ends.

Recognizing Verbs

As we have seen, verbs include action words (*work*) and state-of-being words (*be, seem*). One way to find verbs, then, is to ask which word shows action or state of being.

Or you might ask which words change form to show tense: present, past, or future. You can test for tense by including the words *today, yesterday,* and *tomorrow,* as we do here for the sentence "Michael plays with his children":

A. Today, Michael *plays* with his children.

B. Yesterday, Michael *played* with his children.

C. Tomorrow, Michael *will play* with his children.

Because *play* changes form, it has tense and so is a verb.

Identifying verbs becomes more complicated when a simple sentence has several verbs. This can occur for two reasons.

First, we often use **compound verbs,** or two-part verbs, to create variety and concision. These two-part verbs can be hard to spot:

Margaret skipped her lunch *but* later regretted it.

Simple sentences with compound verbs often use the coordinating conjunctions *and* and *but,* so be alert for these conjunctions.

For more on sentence types, see pp. 524–526.

Verbs also include helping words such as *be, do,* and *have,* discussed further in the following section.

To recognize verbs, look for words that change their form to show tense.

No comma is used
with compound verbs.
See Chapter 27.

Keep verb phrases
together unless the
sentence sounds
most natural with
the adverb after a
helping verb. "Brian
has quickly forgotten
every answer on the
exam" sounds less
stilted than "Brian
quickly has forgotten
every answer on the
exam."

For more on phrases,
see pp. 516–521.

Do not repeat a
subject that has been
replaced by a relative
pronoun.

Second, as we have seen, the main verb of a sentence often follows a helping verb like *be, do, have, may, might, must, can, could, should,* or *would.* Together they form verb phrases such as "*might have been* singing" or "*will be* starting." The verbs in these phrases sometimes become divided, often by an adverb, as in "Brian has quickly forgotten every answer on the exam."

Life gets even more complicated when we both split verb phrases and compound the verbs, as in the following sentence:

I will soon be starting back to college and will probably enjoy all my classes.

Keeping these complications in mind will help you identify the subjects, verbs, and sentence boundaries of potentially tricky simple sentences like these.

One final factor can complicate the identification of verbs: Certain other word groups, called **verbals,** are easy to mistake for verbs because they look much like them. Notice that the italicized words in the following sentences are *not* verbs:

A. Jennifer has barely escaped *dieting* herself into a coma.
B. We are often told to *fend* for ourselves.
C. The firefighters scanned the sky again, anxiously *looking* for signs of rain.

We will discuss verbals later in the chapter, but for now just remember that these kinds of words, which often have an *-ing* ending (diet*ing*) or a *to* beginning (*to* fend), are *never* the verbs in a sentence.

Recognizing Subjects

Subjects in sentences are usually nouns or pronouns located in front of a verb and answering the question of who or what is performing the action or experiencing the state.

S   V

Glinda saved Dorothy from a sleeping spell.

Who saved Dorothy? Glinda, so *Glinda* is the subject of the sentence.

As with verbs, there are various complications in identifying subjects. The subject of a simple sentence can be a compound subject, with two parts, as in sentence A, or even more, as in sentence B:

A. *Dorothy* and the *lion* became friends.
B. *Dorothy,* the *lion,* the *scarecrow,* and the *tin man* became friends.

Sometimes subjects have a describing phrase before, after, or within them:

C. *Dorothy,* a young girl from Kansas, and the *lion,* the *scarecrow,* and the *tin man* became friends.

You might also write a sentence with one or more phrases as the subject:

INFINITIVE PHRASE   *To return* to Kansas was Dorothy's dream.

GERUND PHRASE   *Returning* to Kansas was Dorothy's dream.

There are several other situations that can make finding subjects more difficult. First, in command sentences, we often omit the subject:

Pass the salt, please.

In such sentences, the subject is understood to be *you,* the person who is expected to perform the command or request.

Second, in sentences that begin with the words *there* and *here,* the subject follows the verb, and in sentences that ask questions, the subject follows a helping verb:

A. There are four boys in the courtyard.

B. Here lies my best friend.

C. Will you come with me?

In this instance, simply rearrange the sentence mentally, putting the subject back into its usual slot:

A. Four boys are in the courtyard.

B. My best friend lies here.

C. You will come with me.

Finally, it is easy to mistake as subjects the nouns and pronouns within prepositional phrases attached to the subject:

A. The bitter taste [*of lemon peels*] makes him want to spit.

B. One [*of the women*] wants anchovies on her pizza.

In these sentences, the nouns *peels* and *women* cannot be subjects because they are within prepositional phrases. Since subjects *never* appear in prepositional phrases, one way of finding subjects is by mentally crossing out prepositional phrases in the subject part of the sentence.

It can also be hard to spot subjects and verbs in sentences with more than one clause, such as the following complex sentence:

subordinate clause   main clause (= simple sentence)
Although he did not run in it, Alex watched the marathon on TV.

Each clause has a subject and a verb, and later in this chapter, we will look more closely at subjects and verbs in multiple clauses. For more on verbs and subjects, see Chapter 24.

ACTIVITY 21.2 *Locating Verbs and Subjects*

In the following sentences, underline the subject or subjects once and the verb or verbs twice.

EXAMPLE: Over the years, Clint Eastwood has become a fine director.

1. The United States is increasingly conflicted about its immigration policies.

2. There are three good reasons not to take this trip.

3. Protecting the watershed of the river will help to protect the river itself.

4. One of the team's most outstanding players was awarded a scholarship to Michigan State.

5. To pilot commercial jets has always been Teresa's dream.

6. Montana and Wyoming were fighting more than the typical fires of a dry summer and were hoping for a quick end to their troubles.

7. Have you been to see *The Golden Compass* yet?

8. Warren might have quickly started the car but, in his nervousness, dropped the keys.

9. Please open the blinds and raise the window.

10. Residents of Central America and South America sometimes wonder about and resent the habit of many U.S. citizens of referring to themselves as Americans.

Look for the word(s) that express(es) action or state of being, and then ask who or what is performing the action or experiencing the state of being.

In number 9, the subject *you* is understood.

Two-Word (Phrasal) Verbs

One kind of verb that can be confusing is the **two-part** or **phrasal verb,** which consists of a verb followed by a preposition or adverb. For example, when you say, "Leon will *look over* the report," you do not mean that he will try to see across the report to something on the other side; you mean that he will read and think about the report. Phrasal verbs usually express a different meaning than the verb would have by itself.

Most phrasal verbs consisting of a main verb and an adverb can be split or remain together:

SPLIT	Travis will *drop* his sister *off* at school.
NOT SPLIT	Travis will *drop off* his sister at school.

However, when a pronoun is used as the object, it must be placed *between* the two verb parts:

INCORRECT	Travis will *drop off* her at school.
CORRECT	Travis will *drop* her *off* at school.

Some phrasal verbs consisting of a main verb and a preposition are not separable:

NOT SEPARABLE	After that, Travis will *drop in* on his best friend.

We use many phrasal verbs in informal conversation that we would avoid in more formal writing (*drags out* class), often finding a more concise substitute (*prolongs* class).

Phrases

Knowing subjects and verbs will help you distinguish between clauses and phrases, the two word groups that make up sentences.

A **clause** includes a subject and a verb, whereas a **phrase** is missing a subject or a verb, or both. Because phrases can work as nouns, adjectives, or adverbs, knowing these parts of speech will help you manage phrases in sentences and will help you with their punctuation.

Here we will explore six kinds of phrases: prepositional, infinitive, participial, gerund, absolute, and appositive. (For more on phrases, see pp. 464–472.)

Prepositional Phrases

A **prepositional phrase** begins with a preposition (*in, on, of, during*), ends with a noun or pronoun, and works as an adjective or adverb. Notice that prepositional phrases answer the same kinds of questions as do adjectives and adverbs.

ADJECTIVE

TELLS WHICH ONE	The pickup truck *with* the cracked windshield is mine.
TELLS WHO	The woman *in* the blue silk dress is my date.

ADVERB

TELLS WHERE	Houdini escaped many times *from inside* a locked safe.
TELLS WHEN	Arthur talked *during* the whole movie.
TELLS HOW	I struggled out of bed this morning *with* great difficulty.

Prepositional phrases functioning as adverbs are often easy to move, for more sentence variety, clarity, and emphasis. Notice that we could reposition the prepositional phrase in any of the three preceding sentences. For example:

A. *With* great difficulty I struggled out of bed this morning.

B. I struggled out of bed *with great difficulty* this morning.

Infinitive Phrases

An infinitive can be formed by putting the word *to* in front of any base verb—for instance, *to run, to love,* or *to think*. Infinitives, along with gerunds and participles, are called **verbals** because they are verb forms that have a sense of action but do not function as verbs.

Infinitive phrases are formed by adding words, often nouns, after the infinitive: "*to run* a marathon," "*to love* one's country," "*to think* deep thoughts." Infinitives and infinitive phrases work as adjectives, adverbs, or nouns:

ADJECTIVE

DESCRIBES NOUN   Paula has a proposal *to present*.

ADVERB

DESCRIBES VERB   We practiced long hours *to win* the basketball game.

NOUN

IS SUBJECT   *To reach* the top was his driving ambition.

As with prepositional phrases, infinitive phrases that function as adverbs can often be moved within a sentence. For example, we could recast the adverb sentence like this: "*To win* the basketball game, we practiced long hours." Introductory adverbial infinitive phrases require a comma.

Participial Phrases

Participial phrases begin with either a present participle (base verb with *-ing*) or past participle (base verb with *-d/-ed/-n/-t*). Participials can be single-word modifiers of nouns: *struggling* soldiers, *crashing* waves, *wrinkled* jacket, *forgotten* memory. As phrases, too, participials often work as adjectives. As in many of the following examples, they often include prepositional phrases:

Present Participial Phrase

A. *Skimming* close to the ground, the swallow caught a cricket in midhop.

B. Jamie bought 50 more lottery tickets, *praying* for a miracle.

C. The salesclerk *chewing* gum was the one who ignored me for 10 minutes.

Past Participial Phrase

A. *Exhausted* from three final exams in one day, Marilyn fell asleep in her seat.

B. Devin vowed to play his hardest, *thrilled* to finally be on the team.

C. A bluegill *caught* on ultralight tackle can put up quite a battle.

Participial phrases can be *essential* to the meaning of the word they are describing, as they are in the two preceding C sentences, or *nonessential,* as they are in the A and B sentences.

Sentences that begin with two or more prepositional phrases require a comma.

For more on participles, see Chapter 24.

Nonessential phrases, as in sentences A and B, require a comma.

Essential phrases, as in both C sentences, do not use a comma.

For more on punctuating essential and nonessential phrases, see Chapter 27.

Nonessential phrases are set off with commas, and they can often be repositioned. For example, we might move the participial phrase in sentence B:

A. *Thrilled* to finally be on the team, Devin vowed to play his hardest.

B. Devin, *thrilled* to finally be on the team, vowed to play his hardest.

When shifting participial phrases, be careful that they do not appear to describe an unintended word. For example, the participial phrase in this construction might seem to describe the cricket:

The swallow caught a cricket in midhop, *skimming* close to the ground.

Also be wary of dangling and misplaced phrases that clearly modify the wrong word:

Skimming close to the ground, a cricket was caught by a swallow in midhop.

Gerund Phrases

The gerund, another kind of verbal, is formed by adding -*ing* to a base verb and is used as a noun—for example, *backpacking, swimming,* and *laughing*. **Gerund phrases** begin with a gerund and include other words. As shown in the following examples, gerunds and gerund phrases may appear in several places in a sentence:

A. *Backpacking* is a strenuous sport.

B. *Backpacking* in the Bob Marshall Wilderness is an unforgettable experience.

C. Ellen enjoys *laughing* at life's idiotic moments.

Although gerunds and many participials end in -*ing,* the gerund functions as a noun rather than as an adjective. Notice that the gerunds in sentences A and B are subjects and that the gerund in sentence C is an object. To see this difference between gerund and participial phrases, compare the following sentences:

PARTICIPIAL PHRASE   *Backpacking* in the Bob Marshall Wilderness, Nikki learned the meaning of rugged.

GERUND PHRASE   *Backpacking* in the Bob Marshall Wilderness is an unforgettable experience.

The first sentence uses *backpacking* as an adjective that tells about Nikki, the subject of the main part of the sentence; therefore, the phrase is a participial. The second sentence uses *backpacking* as the subject, so the phrase is a gerund. Whereas the participial phrase must be set off by a comma, the gerund phrase cannot be.

Absolute Phrases

The **absolute phrase** resembles a participial phrase in that it uses a present or past participle (-*ing* or -*d*/-*ed*/-*n*/-*t*), but it differs in an important respect: A noun or pronoun always precedes the participle. Absolute phrases describe the rest of the sentence they are attached to, rather than a single word. For this reason, they can be in different places in a sentence, as shown by the following examples:

Absolute Phrase—Present

A. [The wind *blowing* steadily from the south,] we knew that the warm weather would last.

B. Coco said good-bye to her homeland forever, [her eyes *streaming* tears].

No comma should be used with gerunds or gerund phrases.

Because gerunds are nouns, if you can mentally replace the -*ing* phrase with "it" or "this," the phrase is a gerund, not a participial.

Absolute Phrase—Past

C. Adam tried to appear at attention, [his arm _raised_ in a stiff salute].

D. [The thief finally _locked_ in a cell,] everyone felt more at ease.

You can create an absolute phrase by omitting a "to be" verb. For instance, without the _is_, the stand-alone sentence "The wind is blowing steadily from the south" becomes the absolute phrase in sentence A above. Absolute phrases, like nonessential participial phrases, must be set off with a comma.

Absolute phrases require a comma.

Appositive Phrases

An **appositive phrase** is a word group that renames a noun or pronoun. Appositives usually follow the word they are describing, but if describing the subject, they can be useful as sentence openers.

Most appositives are nonessential—giving useful but not vital information. Therefore, as with all nonessential material, we use commas. Here are several examples:

Appositive phrases are a handy way to add ideas or comments without distracting readers too much from the main flow of thought.

A. The dolphin, a _mammal_, lives in family units called pods.

B. A _mammal_, the dolphin lives in family units called pods.

C. The dolphin, a _mammal_ known as a cetacean, lives in family units called pods.

D. The dolphin, a _mammal_ known as a cetacean that is still killed in large numbers by tuna fishers, lives in family units called pods.

In each case, the underlined appositive tells the reader a bit more about dolphins.

ACTIVITY 21.3 _Identifying Phrases_

Over each underlined phrase, write the type of phrase. Don't be confused when you find several phrases within a word group.

infinitive phrase
EXAMPLE: To make it through her study session, Jody drank two pots of coffee.

1. Perched on Jasmine's shoulder, the cockatiel always felt secure.

2. Jumping out of a plane is not Ethan's idea of a relaxing weekend.

3. To find better jobs, many adults long out of school are returning.

4. The new Corvette, redlining at 7,000 rpm, smoked down the interstate.

5. Aging power plants in the United States continue to emit toxic pollutants, increasing asthma and other respiratory illnesses.

6. Robert Downey Jr., an actor with a history of substance abuse, plays recovering alcoholic Tony Stark in _Iron Man_.

7. On a trip from Chicago to Denver, Joanne was stranded in airports for 36 hours.

To identify the phrase, look at the overall structure, at how the words work as a unit. For example, "Slipping on the ice, Ben fell" includes a prepositional phrase, "on the ice," but since the whole word group begins with a participle, the word group is a participial phrase.

8. Online advertising, <u>mostly obnoxious spam and pop-up windows</u>,

continues <u>to flood into our homes</u>.

9. <u>Having clear goals in life</u> helps people to succeed.

10. <u>Stepping quietly into the room</u>, <u>his pipe glowing dimly</u>, Holmes

surveyed the scene <u>of the murder</u>.

ACTIVITY 21.4 WORKING TOGETHER: *Creating Phrases*

With group members, discuss the six phrases and then complete each sentence with the type of phrase(s) indicated in parentheses.

EXAMPLE: Lilly sat (prepositional phrases) *at the end of the pier* and waited.

1. In the morning Anna went (prepositional phrases) _____

_____.

2. _____ (participial phrase), Lauren and Roy had the best

evening of their lives.

3. _____ (absolute phrase), Roger was so hungry that he

nearly fainted.

4. _____ (infinitive phrase), the climbers had to struggle

up the cliff face till nearly dusk.

5. _____ (gerund phrase) would improve people's health.

6. Michael Jackson, _____ (appositive phrase),

bought the rights to almost all of the Beatles' music.

7. _____ (prepositional phrases), the children found six

baby bunnies in a nest.

8. Many hunters support gun control, _____

_____ (participial phrase).

9. _____ (infinitive phrase), Frank finally wrote a check to

the gas company.

10. Whales communicate through body language and song, _____

_____ (absolute phrase).

Notice the use of commas with the phrases in these sentences.

Clauses

Subordinate clauses standing alone are sentence fragments.

In contrast to phrases, clauses have both a subject and a verb. Clauses are of two sorts, main and subordinate. A **main** (or **independent**) **clause** expresses a complete thought, so it can function as a stand-alone (simple) sentence. A **subordinate** (or **dependent**) **clause** lacks a complete thought and so cannot stand alone. Despite having a verb and a subject, a subordinate clause, like a phrase, depends on and must therefore be attached to a main clause to form a sentence.

Notice how these main and subordinate clauses can easily combine:

MAIN CLAUSE	Flea markets are interesting
SUBORDINATE CLAUSE	because they are a walk through history
COMBINED CLAUSES	Flea markets are interesting because they are a walk through history.
MAIN CLAUSE	Many people suffer from arthritis
SUBORDINATE CLAUSE	which can cause excruciating joint pain
COMBINED CLAUSES	Many people suffer from arthritis, which can cause excruciating joint pain.

There are three kinds of subordinate clauses—noun, adjective, and adverb clauses—which work just as their names suggest. We will now focus on each kind of subordinate clause.

Noun Clauses

Noun clauses are subordinate clauses that work the way single nouns and noun phrases do in a sentence and are often used as subjects—for example, as in sentence B:

A. The *candidate* surprised everyone.

B. *What the candidate said* surprised everyone.

Noun clauses are useful because they give more information. In sentence A, we learn that the single-word subject (the candidate) surprised everyone, but we don't know why. However, in sentence B, we find out through the noun clause that it was "what the candidate *said*" that surprised everyone.

Here are some example sentences with noun clauses used in other ways besides as subjects:

To identify a noun clause, try replacing the clause with the pronoun "it."

OBJECT	Jason mentioned *that he would leave for El Paso in the morning.*
OBJECT OF PREPOSITION	Hoang asked for *whatever help his friends would give.*
COMPLEMENT	The administration's feeling is *that no one deserves a salary increase.*

Note: *That* may be dropped from the above noun clauses with no effect on the sentences.

Because noun clauses are an essential part of sentences—unlike many adverb and adjective clauses—they are *not* set off with commas.

COMMON CUE WORDS THAT BEGIN NOUN CLAUSES					
who	that	whatever	what	where	whether
which	whose	whoever	when	why	how

Note: Some of these words can also introduce adjective and adverb clauses.

Adjective Clauses

Adjective clauses (or **relative clauses**) work like single adjectives and adjective phrases, describing nouns and pronouns, as in sentence B:

A. I drive an *old* truck.

B. I drive a truck *that is old.*

Use *who* to refer to people, but use *which* and *that* to refer to things and animals.

The relative pronoun *that* is used only to begin essential clauses, so never use commas to set off adjective clauses that start with *that*. Nonessential adjective clauses are set off with a comma or commas. For more on essential versus nonessential adjective clauses, see Chapters 19 and 22.

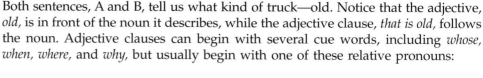

Both sentences, A and B, tell us what kind of truck—old. Notice that the adjective, *old*, is in front of the noun it describes, while the adjective clause, *that is old*, follows the noun. Adjective clauses can begin with several cue words, including *whose, when, where,* and *why*, but usually begin with one of these relative pronouns:

who	**which**	**that**

Note: These words also sometimes introduce noun clauses.

To punctuate adjective clauses correctly, you need to determine whether they are *essential* to the meaning of the sentence. If they are essential, that is, if removing them would alter the main idea, do *not* use a comma or commas:

Essential Adjective Clauses

A. Gina Caldarello is the person *who* is responsible for the accident.

B. The Firestone tires were the ones *that* were recalled.

In sentence A, we don't know why we should be interested in Gina until reading the adjective clause and finding out that she was responsible for an accident. In sentence B, we need the adjective clause to tell us why we should be interested in the Firestone tires. Therefore, the clauses are essential and *not* set off with commas.

Nonessential adjective clauses, however, can be cut from a sentence without significantly changing the meaning, so they are set off with commas:

Nonessential Adjective Clauses

A. Tara Farnsworth, *who* is an exceptional student, is a fine athlete.

B. I stayed out too late, *which* caused me to oversleep my 8:00 class.

Sentence A emphasizes that Tara Farnsworth is a fine athlete but adds a less-important comment about her as a student. *Who* clauses that immediately follow proper nouns are nonessential. Sentence B uses the *which* clause to add a comment about oversleeping. In both sentences, the adjective clauses contain interesting but not essential information.

Adverb Clauses

Adverb clauses function like single adverbs and adverb phrases, describing verbs, adjectives, and other adverbs. They give information about a main clause, telling *when, why, where, how,* and *to what extent,* as in the following sentences:

WHEN	*When* the carolers came to our house, we served hot chocolate.
WHY	*Because* it began to rain, the party headed indoors.
WHERE	*Where* Amanda and her friends go, trouble is sure to follow.
HOW	*As if* he had not eaten for a week, Brad wolfed down his hamburger.
TO WHAT EXTENT	*Until* he could stand it no more, Max listened to the boring lecture.

Adverb clauses, like adverbs, often can be moved in a sentence. For example, we could reverse the subordinate and main clauses in any of the above examples, like this:

We served hot chocolate *when* the carolers came to our house.

When the adverb clause comes before the main clause, it should be set off with a comma. However, when it follows the main clause, a comma is not usually used. (Exceptions: Adverb clauses beginning with *though, although,* and *even*

Adverb clauses that begin sentences require a comma. Adverb clauses that follow main clauses usually do not use commas.

though often use a comma even when following a main clause because they show concession.)

Adverb clauses always begin with a **subordinating conjunction,** such as *when, because, where, as if,* and *until.* (See p. 512 for a more complete list.)

ACTIVITY 21.5 | *Identifying Clauses*

Write the type of clause over each underlined clause. As you analyze each sentence, look at the cue words (*that, who, which, because, what,* etc.) that begin the clauses, and think about how the clauses *function.* Do they work as nouns, as adjectives, or as adverbs? To help tell the difference between adjective and noun clauses, try substituting "it" for the noun clause.

> *adjective clause*
> **EXAMPLE:** The drum set *that* has been reduced in price by 50 percent still costs too much.

1. What the commencement speaker said put everyone in the audience to sleep.

2. When the lead guitarist shows up, the band will go on.

3. What to do with nuclear waste remains a major problem in the movement to build more nuclear power plants.

4. Try raising a chicken if you want a truly messy pet.

5. The police officer who pulled Professor Allen over for speeding was one of his former students.

6. Paul Simon, who began performing in high school, has had a successful musical career for over 40 years.

7. Marla thinks that John Travolta is a fine actor.

8. The elm tree that is leaning over my house concerns me.

9. The Milky Way galaxy, which contains our solar system, looks like a sprinkling of glowing dust in the night sky.

10. After we raced to get to the doctor's office on time, we sat and waited for 45 minutes.

ACTIVITY 21.6 | *Creating Clauses*

Write clauses to complete the following sentences.

> **EXAMPLE:** *"Before I go one step further* (adverb clause), I want to see a map!"

1. _____ (adverb clause), he spends half the game on the bench.

2. The Superfund, created in 1980 to clean up toxic industrial messes, is a government regulation _____ (adjective clause).

3. _____ (noun clause) wins the contest of life.

4. _____ (adverb clause), they are difficult to exterminate.

5. The advertisement that I received in the mail today promised me a "free gift," _____ (adjective clause).

6. I am going to save some money _____ (adverb clause).

7. _____ (noun clause) is a mystery that no one has been able to figure out.

8. Garth Brooks, _____ (adjective clause), has been out of the headlines recently.

9. _____ (adverb clause), you can have your name removed from many junk mail lists.

10. In 2005 the Gulf Coast was struck by Hurricane Katrina, _____ _____ (adjective clause).

Sentence Types

To identify the type of sentence, look at the type and number of its clauses.

Having reviewed the parts of speech, phrases, and clauses, you know most of the basic sentence grammar you need to write interesting and correct sentences. Now you can simply apply this knowledge to work with sentence types.

There are only four sentence types in English, each based on the clauses it contains: simple, compound, complex, and compound–complex.

Simple Sentences

A **simple sentence** contains one main clause with no subordinate clauses. It may be short and truly "simple," as in uncomplicated, or it may have several phrases that lengthen it. Here are some examples:

A. Aaron likes ice cream.

B. Aaron and his younger sister like ice cream.

C. Aaron and his younger sister like ice cream but seldom have the money to buy much of it.

Sentence A has a single subject, *Aaron,* and a single verb, *likes.* But sentence B adds another subject, *sister.* And sentence C also adds another verb, *have,* as well as two phrases, *to buy much* and *of it.* Simple sentences can be short or long and may contain commas, for instance to set off introductory phrases or nonessential phrases. However, they have only one clause, a *main* clause.

Compound Sentences

A **compound sentence** adds one or more main clauses to a simple sentence. This creates a sentence with two or more sets of subjects and verbs (main clauses). The clauses are usually joined by a coordinating conjunction like *and* or *but* and a comma—or by a semicolon if the conjunction is omitted. Short or long, compound sentences do not contain a subordinate clause. Here are two examples:

A. Aaron and his younger sister like ice cream, *so they eat a lot of it.*

B. Aaron and his younger sister like ice cream, so they eat a lot of it, *but they seldom have the money to buy much of it.*

Sentence A has *two* main clauses, two sets of subjects and verbs. If we wanted to create two separate sentences, we could put a period after *ice cream.* Sentence B is a compound sentence with *three* main clauses!

Complex Sentences

Complex sentences are not necessarily any more complicated than simple or compound sentences, but they do contain another kind of clause—the subordinate, or dependent, clause. So a complex sentence has *one main clause* and *one or more subordinate clauses*. As with other sentence types, any clause may include phrases. Here are examples:

A. Aaron and his younger sister like ice cream *because it tastes sweet.*

B. Aaron and his younger sister like ice cream *because it tastes sweet* but seldom have the money to buy much of it.

Sentence A starts with a main clause and attaches a subordinate adverb clause beginning with *because.* Notice that sentence B adds material but still has only *one* main clause. Sentence B uses a two-part subject and a two-part verb in its main clause; the subordinate *because* clause separates the two main verbs (*like* and *have*).

Complex sentences can contain more than one subordinate clause, as in the following example:

Aaron, *who is quickly gaining weight,* likes ice cream because it tastes sweet.

This sentence contains an adjective clause and an adverb clause.

Compound–Complex Sentences

The **compound–complex sentence** combines the two preceding sentence types. It has two or more main clauses and one or more subordinate clauses. As usual, any clause can include phrases. Here are examples:

       main clause   adverb clause   main clause

A. Aaron likes ice cream *because it tastes sweet,* so he eats a lot of it.

       main clause   adjective clause   main clause

B. Aaron likes ice cream *that is full of chocolate chips,* so he eats a lot of it.

    main clause   noun clause   main clause

C. Aaron says *that he likes ice cream,* so he eats a lot of it.

ACTIVITY 21.7 | *Identifying Sentence Types*

Underline each clause, and above it write its type (main clause or noun, adjective, or adverb clause). At the end of the sentence, write the sentence type (simple, compound, complex, or compound–complex).

Compound sentences usually require a comma before a coordinating conjunction. (However, a semicolon can also divide the two main clauses, omitting the coordinating conjunction.)

Stringing too many main clauses together with *and* or *but* makes for monotonous reading.

Note the comma used before the coordinating conjunction *so.*

EXAMPLE:

main clause *adverb clause*
Children love to draw and paint from the earliest ages, and if adults
main clause
continue to encourage them, children will often carry their artistic interests
into adulthood. *Compound–complex*

1. Although swimming is not the best sport for losing weight, it can be a great aerobic workout. _____

2. Carp are said by some to be delicious, but a person must know how to prepare the fish properly. _____

3. Many companies in the United States use underpaid foreign labor to cut costs. _____

4. Many trial lawyers are experts at bending the truth to help their clients. _____

5. Because forests are beautiful, house thousands of species of plants and animals, and clean the earth's atmosphere, they deserve good stewardship. _____

6. I used to think that David was slow moving until I saw him jump up from his chair to shake a centipede off his bare arm. _____

7. Playing an instrument is a good way to learn music and bring joy into a person's life. _____

8. Fireflies, which are also called lightning bugs, produce their glow through a process known as bioluminescence. _____

9. When the weather permits, I love to grill just about anything out on my deck, but my favorite food is hamburgers. _____

10. Jet planes cannot glide well, so if the engines malfunction, the plane is likely to crash. _____

ACTIVITY 21.8 WORKING TOGETHER: *Using Phrases and Clauses to Improve Readability*

Review A Writer's Basic Sentence Grammar on pages 528–529, and then discuss with group members how to improve the clarity and flow of sentences in the following narrative. Keeping all the main ideas, revise the narrative by combining sentences and adding connecting words where needed (prepositions, such as *in, on,* and *near;* conjunctions, such as *because, when, and,* and *but;* and relative pronouns, such as *who, which,* and *that* will be particularly useful). Also try using *-ing* phrases.

EXAMPLE

My older brother Jason should be on a special show called America's Dumbest Criminals. One night in May of 2007, Jason and his best friend, Ken, found a new white Nissan with the keys left in the door in the neighbor's driveway. This was temptation they could not resist. . . .

America's Dumbest Criminal?

My older brother Jason should be on a special show called *America's Dumbest Criminals*. One night in May of 2007, Jason found a new white Nissan. His best friend, Ken, was with him too. The car was in the neighbor's driveway. The car had the keys left in the door. This was temptation they could not resist.

"Hey, look at this," Jason said. "What an idiot to forget your keys."

"Yeah, it's their own fault if we borrow their car," replied Ken.

Both boys jumped in the car. Jason sat on the garage door opener. The door raised.

"Oh, crap!" Jason yelled. They leapt out of the car. Then they ran back home.

They watched the neighbors' house. They didn't see anyone reacting. Jason and Ken thought they were safe to try again. This time they figured they would be smart. They would bring along gloves to mask fingerprints. They climbed back into the car. Once again Jason sat on the garage door opener.

"Dammit, man!" Ken said. They were hiding in some nearby bushes. Still no one was stirring in the house. They tried for the Nissan again. This was the third time. This time they succeeded. So, off they went on their "well-planned" expedition.

They reached the major roads. Ken began to get paranoid. "Man, we just passed a cop. We're gonna get caught!"

"Shut up, dude," ordered Jason. "We're cool. How are they gonna know? The people are still asleep, remember?"

"Uhh . . ." said Ken, "because we're driving around with white gloves on, and it looks a little odd, don't you think?"

"Well then, we'll just take them off," Jason replied.

"Yeah, but when they get the car back, our fingerprints will be all over it."

Jason and Ken idled at a stoplight for a minute. My brother came up with his next brilliant suggestion. They would buy some Armor-All. Then they would wipe off all their fingerprints. Then they would park the car a few blocks from the owner's house. Well, they managed to clean the car half way up. They congratulated themselves on getting away with it. They taped the car key to the hood. Then they walked home.

But Jason had forgotten his gloves. Jason panicked. They went back to the car for them. But someone had called the police. The boys were arrested. Their situation got worse. They had parked across a city line. So they were prosecuted by two cities.

Older brothers and sisters are supposed to set an example. This is one older and "wiser" brother I learned never to follow.

ACTIVITY 21.9 WORKING ONLINE: *Parts of Speech Review*

Take the Chapter 21 Review Quiz at www.mhhe.com/brannan.

Chapter Summary: A Writer's Basic Sentence Grammar

Having learned and practiced recognizing the basic sentence parts in this chapter, you now know more about how to control sentences. Words (parts of speech) build phrases; phrases grow into or are attached to clauses; clauses are sentences or are attached to them. Knowing how words work—to express action or state of being, name, describe, or link—you can now confidently revise your sentences to best express your meaning.

This Chapter Summary offers quick review of key sentence parts:

WORDS (8 KINDS)

verb, noun, pronoun, adjective, adverb, preposition, conjunction, interjection

---

PHRASES (6 KINDS)

prepositional, infinitive, participial, gerund, absolute, appositive

1. **Prepositional:** Phrase beginning with a preposition and ending with a noun or pronoun—used as adjective or adverb

   Example: "Erik ran *down* the hall and *through* the door."

2. **Infinitive:** Phrase beginning with *to* + base verb—used as a noun, adjective, or adverb

   Example: "*To arrive* at class on time, Erik finally set his alarm."

3. **Participial:** Phrase beginning with base verb + *-ing* or *-d/-ed/-n*—used as an adjective

   Example: "*Running* fast, Erik made it to class on time."

4. **Gerund:** Phrase beginning with an *-ing* word—used as a noun

   Example: "*Running* fast always wore Erik out."

Words that begin prepositional phrases include *to, of, on, near, around, beside, at, by, in, about, with, of,* and *for.*

5. **Absolute:** Phrase beginning with a noun followed by base verb + *-ing* or *-d/-ed/-n/-t*—describes whole sentence

Example: "Erik raced toward class, the door *closing* just in front of him."

6. **Appositive:** Phrase that renames a noun or pronoun

Example: "Erik, a chronic *oversleeper,* raced down the hall as the bell rang."

CLAUSES (2 KINDS)

main and subordinate (3 kinds): noun, adjective, adverb

1. **Main:** Clause with a complete thought—stands by itself

Example: "Fran likes double-cheese pizza."

2. **Subordinate:** Clause without a complete thought—used with a main clause

- **Noun:** Clause used as subject, object, or complement

Example: "*That* Fran likes double-cheese pizza is obvious to everyone."

- **Adjective:** Clause that follows and describes a noun or pronoun

Example: "Fran, *who* is a close friend of mine, likes double-cheese pizza."

- **Adverb:** Clause that acts as an adverb, telling when, why, where, how, or to what extent something was done

Example: "*When* she goes to Italian Delight, Fran likes to eat double-cheese pizza."

SENTENCES (4 KINDS)

simple, compound, complex, compound–complex

1. **Simple:** "Karyn likes shoes."
2. **Compound:** "Karyn likes shoes, *so* she owns a lot of them."
3. **Complex:** "Karyn likes shoes *because* they help express her creative style."
4. **Compound–complex:** "Karyn likes shoes *because* they help express her creative style, *so* she owns a lot of them."

Coordination, Subordination, and Parallelism

22

[*Athletes like the cheerleaders in this photo have to coordinate their movements, often mirroring each other's moves and establishing who will lead and who will follow. I a paragraph, discuss one or more situations or groups you have been in where people had to coordinate their actions What value do you see in the ability to coordinate?*]

KEY TOPICS

- Coordination
  - Using coordination
  - Avoiding excessive coordination
- Subordination
  - Adverb clauses
  - Adjective clauses
  - Avoiding excessive subordination

- Parallelism
  - Series
  - Lists and outlines
  - Pairs

The repetition of the *and/and/and* sentence pattern makes the paragraph tedious. If we keep some of the compound sentences but add more subordination, we can clarify meaning and increase the readability like this:

> Comedians are important in a culture <u>because</u> they help people release their frustrations with one another. <u>Even though</u> comics can be mean-spirited, truly injuring people they are lampooning, often comedians express the irritation of millions of people <u>who</u> have been disappointed by some segment of society, for instance, politicians. <u>When</u> Amy Poehler or Jay Leno parodies Hillary Clinton or George W. Bush, there is usually some truth behind the barbs, and recognizing this truth makes us laugh.

Subordination

Coordination helps with clarity and sentence variety, but as you can see from the first paragraph above, coordination alone is not enough to create readable writing. When you add **subordination,** however, you help readers know which of your ideas to pay most attention to.

You can subordinate single words—for example, "<u>Fortunately,</u> Jim made the team"—and you might subordinate phrases, as in the following sentences:

A. <u>With the right front fender missing and the windshield cracked,</u> the old Chevy had seen better days.

B. <u>At the bottom of my purse in the zipper pouch,</u> you will find my lipstick.

C. Alfredo Calderella, <u>a magnificent baritone,</u> is vice president of First National Bank.

Each of the underlined phrases adds useful information to the sentence, but the main thought is in the main clause. For instance, in sentence C, the writer wants to highlight Alfredo's position as a bank vice president; the fact that he is also a baritone is not as important.

Adverb Clauses

We can also subordinate whole clauses that function as nouns, adjectives, and adverbs. For example, the **adverb clause** (beginning with words like *because, if,* and *although*) helps show how ideas relate within sentences. Notice how in the following sentence the writer expects readers to make the cause-and-effect connection:

> Janice hid the Oreos from her husband. He has a sweet tooth and would eat the whole bag.

If we subordinate the second sentence by adding the conjunction *because,* the cause-and-effect relationship becomes clear:

> Janice hid the Oreos from her husband *because* he has a sweet tooth and would eat the whole bag.

Adverb clauses function like single adverbs, answering the questions *why, when, where, how,* and *to what extent or degree.* Why did Janice hide the Oreos? Because her husband has a sweet tooth.

When beginning a sentence with an adverb clause—unless it is very short—set it off with a comma. However, when the adverb clause follows the main clause, you usually do not need a comma. Here are several examples:

A. *Because* he has a sweet tooth and would eat the whole bag, Janice hid the Oreos from her husband.

Note that there is no comma between *husband* and *because.*

For more on adverb
clauses, see
pp. 522–523.

B. *While* temperatures soared past 100 degrees, I lived at the community pool.
C. We are back to fans and misting ourselves with spray bottles of water *until* we fix the beat-up old air conditioner.

Below is a list of subordinating conjunctions that begin adverb clauses.

SUBORDINATING CONJUNCTIONS

after	as though	in order that	so that	whenever
although	because	now that	though	where
as	before	once	till	whereas
as if	even though	rather than	until	wherever
as long as	if	since	when	while

ACTIVITY 22.2 *Subordinating with Adverb Clauses*

Fill in the blanks in the following sentences with clauses that work with the given subordinating conjunction. To be sure you have written a subordinate clause, underline the <u>verb</u> in each subordinate clause twice and the subject once.

EXAMPLE: When _I finish my homework_, I will give you a call.

1. If _____,
   he swears he will hang up his running shoes for good.

2. After _____, we will party till the refrigerator is empty.

3. Although _____,
   this composition class has given me new hope.

4. Once _____, Renee snapped
   an award winning photo of a luna moth.

5. I didn't realize that Gary Larson was truly demented until _____
   _____

6. _____ so that he will be
   marketable when he graduates.

7. _____, some practitioners
   are looking to medicine of the East for solutions.

8. Write three sentences that contain an adverb clause. Remember to use a comma only to set off adverb clauses that *begin* sentences, and be sure to underline the <u>verb</u> in each subordinate clause twice and the subject once.

   A. _____

   B. _____

   C. _____

Adjective Clauses

Almost as useful as adverb clauses for subordinating ideas within sentences are **adjective (or relative) clauses,** which generally begin with the relative pronouns *who, which,* or *that.* While adverb clauses work as adverbs (telling *when, why, where, how,* and *to what degree or extent*), adjective clauses work as adjectives, meaning that they describe nouns and pronouns, answering the questions *which one; how many;* and *what kind, shape, color, texture,* or *condition.*

Adjective clauses may be *essential* or *nonessential* to the meaning of a sentence. In both cases, though, they help condense information, making sentences more economical and fluid. Here are several examples.

For more on essential versus nonessential adjective clauses, see pp. 521–522.

NONESSENTIAL ADJECTIVE CLAUSES

A. The mockingbird has an amazing range of musical voices.

The mockingbird is common to the Midwest.

The mockingbird, *which is common to the Midwest,* has an amazing range of musical voices.

B. Paul Bunyan is said to have created the Grand Canyon by dragging his ax along the ground one day.

Paul Bunyan is a giant out of folklore.

Paul Bunyan, *who is a giant out of folklore,* is said to have created the Grand Canyon by dragging his ax along the ground one day.

Neither of the underlined adjective clauses is essential to the meaning of the main part of the sentence, so they are enclosed with commas.

Nonessential clauses require commas; essential clauses are *not* set off with commas.

ESSENTIAL ADJECTIVE CLAUSES

A. The woman is my sister.

The woman is wearing a bright red scarf.

The woman *who is wearing a bright red scarf* is my sister.

B. The Camaro ended up on its side in a ditch.

The Camaro almost got away from the highway patrol.

The Camaro *that almost got away from the highway patrol* ended up on its side in a ditch.

Both of the underlined adjective clauses are essential to the meaning of the main part of the sentence, so they are *not* enclosed with commas.

In general, use *who* to refer to people, but use *which* and *that* to refer to things and animals.

ACTIVITY 22.3 *Subordinating with Adjective Clauses*

Fill in the blanks in the following sentences with an appropriate clause. Note that commas are used to set off the nonessential clauses but not the essential clauses.

EXAMPLE: My best friend, *who has put himself and his children through school*, will graduate from college in the spring.

1. James Earl Jones, who _____, is still a fine actor.

2. Baseball is still the game that _____.

3. Disposable plastic bags, _____,

   can easily be replaced by reusable cloth bags.

4. SUVs that _____ are driven

   by many people who would never consider taking them off-road.

5. The Trojan Horse, which _____,

   was left outside the walls of Troy and presumed by the Trojans to

   be a gift from the gods.

6. Ireland is a country that _____

   _____.

7. The Three Stooges were slapstick comedians who _____

   _____.

8. Write three sentences that contain adjective clauses. Remember to use
   commas only to set off nonessential adjective clauses.

   A. _____

   B. _____

   C. _____

Avoiding Excessive Subordination

As with coordination, subordination can be too much of a good thing. When a writer puts more ideas into a sentence than readers can sort out, the writing becomes dense. The easy solution to the problem is simply to "unpack" a few of the sentences, splitting them into two or even three parts. Here is an example of overly subordinated writing:

> People who are worried about the high risk of heart attack, which can strike both men and women even in their twenties, have several alternatives that can keep them healthy as long as they are willing to abide by some sensible rules for managing their lives in such a way as to bring their LDL cholesterol to within tolerable limits, which can be done through regular exercise and a low-fat diet, neither of which is beyond anyone's capabilities, although having to give up favorite foods can seem like a terrific sacrifice to many people who have made food a central part of their lives.

Now look at this revision:

> People who are worried about heart attacks have several alternatives for remaining healthy. If they are willing to abide by some sensible rules (regular exercise and a low-fat diet), they can bring their LDL cholesterol to within tolerable limits. It is true, though, that giving up favorite foods can seem like a terrific sacrifice to many people who have made food a central part of their lives.

Notice that, aside from being clearer, the second version is shorter and more concise, without sacrificing any ideas.

Parallelism

When writers use **parallelism,** a form of coordination, they repeat similar grammatical structures for clarity and emphasis. The words may be in a series, list, or pair and are often connected by a coordinating conjunction like *and* or *but*.

Series

Items in a series should be the same grammatical type—nouns following nouns, verbs following verbs, and so forth—although slight variations are fine. In the third sentence, for instance, "watching television" is a phrase, not a single word.

NOUNS	Be sure to pick up milk, eggs, bread, *and* coffee.
VERBS	I will swim, bike, *and* climb my way through my vacation.
GERUNDS	Daryl plans to spend his vacation reading, watching television, *and* sleeping.
PREPOSITIONAL PHRASES	On the playground, in the halls, *and* in the classroom, the children played nonstop.

You should avoid this kind of nonparallel construction:

NONPARALLEL	Daryl plans to spend his vacation reading, watching television, and he wants to sleep in as much as possible.

There are two ways to make this construction parallel:

PARALLEL	Daryl plans to spend his vacation reading, watching television, and sleeping in as much as possible. (three parallel gerunds)
PARALLEL	Daryl plans to spend his vacation reading and watching television, and he wants to sleep in as much as possible. (parallel pair and separate main clause)

Lists and Outlines

Related to items in a series are lists, especially outlines. All outlines should be in parallel form. A sentence outline uses all sentences. A phrase outline uses the same kind of phrases (prepositional, participial, etc.):

FAULTY PARALLELISM	I. Hawaiian people
	    A. The language they speak
	    B. Worshipping gods
	    C. Their culture

CORRECT PARALLELISM	I. Hawaiian people
	    A. Language
	    B. Religion
	    C. Culture

Pairs

You can also use parallelism to balance pairs, usually with a coordinating conjunction, as in the following examples:

A. Bart loved to fish *and* to backpack.

B. As a child, Maryanne learned to whistle like a train *and* to hoot like an owl.

C. Ping-Pong requires fast reflexes *and* long arms.

D. I am going to Seattle by train, *but* Jenny is traveling to the city by plane.

Notice that sentence D is a compound sentence linking two main clauses that mirror one another in grammatical structure: subject, verb, and two prepositional phrases. This type of sentence is called "balanced."

You can also use word groups called **correlative conjunctions** to pair ideas, as in the following sentence:

With my tax refund, I will have *either* the house painted *or* the driveway paved.

Here are several common correlative pairs:

either . . . or   neither . . . nor

both . . . and   not only . . . but also

When creating parallel phrases and clauses, you should be sure to include the words needed to balance both parts of the expression, without leaving any words out. In the following nonparallel examples, the first one has an unneeded infinitive, *to make,* and the second is missing the word *long.*

| NONPARALLEL | Martin wanted both recognition for his hard work and to make money. |
| PARALLEL | Martin wanted both recognition for his hard work and money. |

| NONPARALLEL | Ping-Pong requires fast reflexes and arms. |
| PARALLEL | Ping-Pong requires fast reflexes and long arms. |

When you use parallelism in a series, list, or pair, you can leave out words in front of phrases and clauses, as in the following examples:

A. The puppy chewed on magazines, (on) table legs, and (on) shoes.

B. Helen ordered a chocolate shake, (a) hamburger, and (a) plate of fries.

C. I learned early to trust my parents, (my) close relatives, and (my) best friends.

D. I hope that my education encourages me to look inward, (that it) guides me onward, and (that it) carries me upward.

Note that in sentence A, it would be incorrect to write "on magazines, on table legs, and shoes," dropping the final *on.* If you use the first two *on*'s, you must finish the series using *on.*

HINT

Whether to include the words in parentheses here is an issue of style. Repetition often helps emphasize a point, and some people might find, for example, that sentence D is more forceful with *that it* left in.

ACTIVITY 22.4   *Creating Parallelism*

Complete the following sentences with parallel words, phrases, and clauses.

EXAMPLE: Margaret loves to dance, to ice skate, and _____*to bowl*_____.

1. Singing, writing, and _____ are art forms.

2. Jerome will go either to the mall tonight or _____.

3. In sunny and windy areas, both solar _____ power can provide clean, renewable energy.

4. Brett wanted to spend his days surfing rather than to _____
    _____.

5. Grace is a woman who works hard and who _____
    _____.

6. Neither the football team nor _____ made the play-offs this year.

7. The horse bolted from the stable and then _____.

8. Write three sentences containing parallel forms.

   A. _____

   B. _____

   C. _____

ACTIVITY 22.5 WORKING TOGETHER: *Coordination, Subordination, and Parallelism in Context*

Write a paragraph about an activity you take part in where there is coordination and/or subordination, or where parallelism is a goal. Be specific. To help think of ideas, look at this chapter's opening photograph and note how all three goals apply: The cheerleaders in this photo achieve (1) **parallelism** during a toe-touch jump. When cheerleaders form a pyramid, they use (2) **coordination** to equally balance the base and (3) **subordination** to hoist one cheerleader—the flyer—to the top; the rest of the team works to lift, support, and catch her as the routine progresses. You might write about another team sport or any activity when you have to work with others (a job, a game, a band) to accomplish something. After drafting your paragraph, trade work with a classmate. Next, annotate your partner's paragraph by proofing for parallelism (underlining any incorrect or questionable usage) and by noting wherever he or she uses coordination and/or subordination with "C" and "S."

ACTIVITY 22.6 WORKING ONLINE: *Coordination, Subordination, and Parallelism Review*

Take the Chapter 22 Review Quiz at www.mhhe.com/brannan.

Chapter Summary

1. Coordination in writing gives roughly equal weight to ideas.

2. Coordinating conjunctions are the primary means of coordinating ideas in sentences.

3. Be careful not to overcoordinate sentences in a paragraph.

4. Subordination in writing stresses one idea while deemphasizing another.

5. Single words, phrases, or clauses can be subordinated.

6. Subordinating conjunctions are one important word group that helps with subordination.

7. Be careful not to oversubordinate sentences in a paragraph.

8. Parallelism in writing uses similar structures to achieve clarity and emphasis.

9. Parallel structures may be in the form of series, lists, or pairs.

Run-ons, Comma Splices, and Sentence Fragments

23

[*This fielder flies into the stands crowded with spectators. By crossing a boundary that both other players and the fans usually observe, he causes problems. When sentences push past their boundaries or are improperly divided, they too cause problems as readers try to make sense of them. Write a paragraph discussing what problems might arise from not being able to determine boundaries in one of the following situations: driving, fencing a property, riding a bus or subway.*]

KEY TOPICS

- Run-on sentences and comma splices
  - Fixing run-ons and comma splices with end punctuation
  - Fixing run-ons and comma splices with coordination
  - Fixing run-ons and comma splices with semicolons
- Fixing run-ons and comma splices with subordination
- Sentence fragments
  - Phrase fragments
  - Subordinate clause fragments

What Are We Trying to Achieve and Why?

Chapter 23 focuses on two common sentence problems found in rough drafts: improperly divided and incomplete (fragmented) sentences. When the time comes to edit their work, writers sometimes find that ideas have overlapped and that it is difficult to determine where one main thought ends and another begins.

The key to determining sentence boundaries, and so to controlling **run-ons, comma splices,** and **fragments,** is locating *verbs* and *subjects,* as we practiced in Chapter 21. As you work through this chapter, make a habit of looking for the action (or state-of-being) word(s) in each sentence—the verb—and then asking yourself who or what is performing the action (or experiencing the state of being)—the subject.

Run-on Sentences and Comma Splices

If two main clauses are run together as a single sentence, without any punctuation, the result is a **run-on** or **fused sentence.** If two sentences have been divided with a comma, the result is a **comma splice.**

Both kinds of errors can present problems for readers, as in the following examples:

RUN-ON   Greg says he will take all three of my shifts next week so I can go to the lake if my dad is in a good mood, he might give me the keys to the boat.

COMMA SPLICE Greg says he will take all three of my shifts next week so I can go to the lake, if my dad is in a good mood, he might give me the keys to the boat.

When the first main thought ends with the word *lake,* we need to mark the spot with a strong break so readers know that a new main thought is beginning. A comma alone is not strong enough, but we can use one of the following methods:

- **End punctuation:** period, question mark, or exclamation point
- **Comma with coordinating conjunction** (*and, but, so, or, yet, for, nor*)
- **Semicolon**
- **Subordination:** words, phrases, clauses

Fixing Run-ons and Comma Splices with End Punctuation

The easiest way to fix these two errors is by dividing the sentences with a period or other end punctuation (e.g., question mark or exclamation point).

FIXED   Greg says he will take all three of my shifts next week so I can go to the lake. If my dad is in a good mood, he might give me the keys to the boat.

However, a period is not always the best solution. If the sentences that are run together are short, using a period may create a "choppy" effect, as in the following example:

RUN-ON AND   Paul Moller has been working on an air car for 37 years he is still
COMMA SPLICE   not close to seeing it fly. He hopes to have it operational in his lifetime, most people do not think that he will make it.

REVISED BUT CHOPPY   Paul Moller has been working on an air car for 37 years. He is still not close to seeing it fly. He hopes to have it operational in his lifetime. Most people do not think that he will make it.

For more on problems with sentence variety, see Chapter 19.

For more on coordination, see Chapter 22.

If correcting run-ons or comma splices with end punctuation creates a series of choppy sentences, you should try one of the other methods covered in this chapter.

Fixing Run-ons and Comma Splices with Coordination

If a period is not the best choice, you might find that a comma and a **coordinating conjunction** like *and, but, or, so, yet, for,* or *nor* work better. These useful connecting words help readers understand the relationship between clauses.

For example, *and* lets readers know that the clauses are roughly equivalent and not dependent on each other. *But* and *yet* point out contrast, and *so* shows cause and effect. Revising our choppy example from above, we can eliminate the run-on and comma splice by using coordinating conjunctions:

FIXED   Paul Moller has been working on an air car for 37 years, and he is still not close to seeing it fly. He hopes to have it operational in his lifetime, but most people do not think that he will make it.

Fixing Run-ons and Comma Splices with Semicolons

A semicolon is an alternative to end punctuation or to a comma and a coordinating conjunction for fixing run-ons and comma splices. If the main ideas in the two clauses are closely related, then a semicolon might be a good choice.

RUN-ON	Knitting is not just for old folks many young people enjoy it too.
COMMA SPLICE	Knitting is not just for old folks, many young people enjoy it too.
FIXED	Knitting is not just for old folks; many young people enjoy it too.

A semicolon is probably the best choice for this sentence because the second main clause completes the statement made in the first clause. These two sentences work as a single unit of thought.

You can also separate the clauses with a semicolon and a **conjunctive adverb,** followed by a comma. Here is an example:

Western medicine has much to offer; *however,* Eastern medicine is also a valuable resource.

Sometimes the conjunctive adverb can appear *within* a clause rather than between the two main clauses, in which case it is set off by commas:

Western medicine has much to offer; Eastern medicine, *however,* is also a valuable resource.

Common conjunctive adverbs include *however, therefore, nevertheless, in fact, consequently, meanwhile, furthermore,* and *thus.*

Fixing Run-ons and Comma Splices with Subordination

For more on subordination, see Chapter 22.

A method for correcting run-ons and comma splices that also helps you eliminate unneeded words is **subordination.** When subordinating one main clause to another, you focus readers' attention on the idea contained within the main clause. You can change one of the clauses to a subordinate clause, a phrase, or even a single word.

Notice the following examples:

| RUN-ON | Jamie bought 50 more lottery tickets he was praying for a miracle. |
| COMMA SPLICE | Jamie bought 50 more lottery tickets, he was praying for a miracle. |

FIXED: **ADJECTIVE CLAUSE**	Jamie, *who* was praying for a miracle, bought 50 more lottery tickets.
PARTICIPIAL PHRASE	Jamie, *praying* for a miracle, bought 50 more lottery tickets.
PARTICIPLE	Jamie, *praying*, bought 50 more lottery tickets.

Each of the revised sentences corrects the error—and eliminates unneeded words.

Here are several other examples that show how you can use subordination to fix problem sentences:

RUN-ON	Some Christmas carolers came to our apartment we served them hot chocolate.
COMMA SPLICE	Some Christmas carolers came to our apartment, we served them hot chocolate.
FIXED: **ADVERB CLAUSE**	*When* some Christmas carolers came to our apartment, we served them hot chocolate.
ABSOLUTE PHRASE	Our apartment crowded with shivering Christmas carolers, we served them hot chocolate.

RUN-ON	We practiced long hours we wanted to win the basketball game.
COMMA SPLICE	We practiced long hours, we wanted to win the basketball game.
FIXED: **ADVERB CLAUSE**	*Because* we wanted to win the basketball game, we practiced long hours.
PARTICIPIAL PHRASE	*Wanting* to win the basketball game, we practiced long hours.
INFINITIVE PHRASE	*To win* the basketball game, we practiced long hours.
INFINITIVE	*To win*, we practiced long hours.

RUN-ON	I had an unforgettable experience it was backpacking in the Bob Marshall Wilderness.
COMMA SPLICE	I had an unforgettable experience, it was backpacking in the Bob Marshall Wilderness.
FIXED: **GERUND PHRASE**	*Backpacking* in the Bob Marshall Wilderness was an unforgettable experience.
PREPOSITIONAL PHRASE	*On* my backpacking trip in the Bob Marshall Wilderness, I had an unforgettable experience.

For help with changing independent clauses to subordinate clauses or phrases, review Chapters 19 and 21.

ACTIVITY 23.1 *Recognizing Run-ons and Comma Splices*

Decide which of the following sentences is correct, a run-on, or a comma splice. Underline each <u>verb</u> twice, ask yourself who or what is doing the action or experiencing the state of being, and then underline each <u>subject</u> once. You will find main clauses and a few subordinate clauses. Draw a line where the main clauses meet, and then at the front of each sentence write "RO" for run-on, "CS" for comma splice, or "C" for correct.

EXAMPLE: __RO__ I <u>was having</u> a great time | I <u>didn't want</u> to go home.

1. _____ I think that I must have eaten too much I'm feeling a little sick.

2. _____ The family will be having dinner at Cindy's house, she has prepared a feast.

3. _____ Although some think Jamie is kindhearted, he has a cruel streak.

4. _____ Truck drivers are often away from home, this constant traveling must make them lonely.

5. _____ My daughter learned to swim this summer, I can't keep her out of the pool.

6. _____ Fifty percent of all marriages today end in divorce I am sure that mine will not.

7. _____ The book left me feeling nervous I think that I will sleep with the light on.

8. _____ My uncle used to live in Hawaii, but he moved back to Kansas last year.

9. _____ Some people give good advice others just give lots of it.

10. _____ Harbour Island has beautiful pink sand beaches we will go there again one day.

ACTIVITY 23.2 | Fixing Run-ons and Comma Splices

In the following sentences, underline each <u>verb</u> twice and each <u>subject</u> once. You will find main clauses and a few subordinate clauses. In the blank at the beginning of each sentence, write "RO" for run-on and "CS" for comma splice. Next, correct each of the sentences, using *each* of the four methods we have discussed: end punctuation, coordination, semicolon, and subordination.

EXAMPLE: __CS__ Wal-Mart <u>can sell</u> products at a lower price than small stores, many little retail <u>stores</u> in small towns <u>are going</u> out of business.

Period: *Wal-Mart can sell products at a lower price than small stores.*
Many little retail stores in small towns are going out of business.

Coordinating conjunction: *Wal-Mart can sell products at a lower price*
than small stores, so many little retail stores in small towns are going
out of business.

Semicolon: *Wal-Mart can sell products at a lower price than small*
stores; therefore, many little retail stores in small towns are going out
of business.

Subordination: *Because Wal-Mart can sell products at a lower price*
than small stores, many little retail stores in small towns are going out
of business.

1. _____ Chen loves to draw Virginia prefers to paint.

    Period: _____

    _____

    Coordinating conjunction: _____

    _____

    Semicolon: _____

    _____

    Subordination: _____

    _____

2. _____ A finish carpenter is a master artisan, he or she can bring wood
    to life.

    Period: _____

    _____

    Coordinating conjunction: _____

    _____

    Semicolon: _____

    _____

    Subordination: _____

    _____

3. _____ Bees are an essential part of agriculture, they pollinate thousands
    of species of fruits and vegetables.

    Period: _____

    _____

    Coordinating conjunction: _____

    _____

    Semicolon: _____

    _____

    Subordination: _____

    _____

4. _____ Halley's comet returns to earth every 76 years few people see it
    twice in a lifetime.

    Period: _____

    _____

    Coordinating conjunction: _____

    _____

    Semicolon: _____

    _____

Subordination: _____

_____

5. _____ Hockey is a sport that requires strength, speed, and agility, it
also helps if a player can duck fast.

Period: _____

_____

Coordinating conjunction: _____

_____

Semicolon: _____

_____

Subordination: _____

_____

Sentence Fragments

For a sentence to stand alone, it must have a subject and a verb, and it must express a complete thought. A **sentence fragment** lacks one or more of these requirements. As in the following examples, readers may have difficulty understanding the writer's thought:

PHRASES

A. Trying desperately with all his might.
B. Tired beyond belief but happy.
C. To win the pennant after 85 years.
D. A hard worker and good-hearted person.

CLAUSES

E. When his aching muscles let him try again.
F. Who arrived there late but made it.

None of these examples can stand alone as sentences because they all lack a finished thought. Examples A–D are *phrases*; they lack both subjects and verbs. Examples E and F are *clauses*; they come closer to being free-standing sentences because they do have a subject and a verb, but they lack a main clause to complete their meaning.

Sentence fragments can slip into your writing because they can look and sound like complete sentences within the context of your paragraphs, as in the following example:

FRAGMENTS   Trying desperately with all his might. Walter jerked 200 pounds of free weight above his head. Tired beyond belief but happy. He promised himself to make 220. When his aching muscles let him try again.

FIXED   Trying desperately with all his might, Walter jerked 200 pounds of free weight above his head. Tired beyond belief but happy, he promised himself to make 220 when his aching muscles let him try again.

Some sentence fragments can be fixed by attaching them to the sentence that precedes or follows them, often using a comma as in the corrected version above. When this method does not work, you must replace any missing words, usually subjects or verbs.

The key to finding and correcting fragments is recognizing verbs and subjects so you can identify sentence boundaries. The rest of this chapter will focus on the two most common kinds of fragments—phrases and subordinate clauses.

Phrase Fragments

In Chapter 21, you learned that a phrase has a noun or a verb form but not both a subject and a verb. Phrases must be attached to a main clause to express their full meaning. If they are not attached, they are sentence fragments. There are two ways to fix phrase fragments:

1. Connect them to a main clause.

2. Add words (subjects, verbs, or both) to turn the phrases into main clauses.

PREPOSITIONAL PHRASE FRAGMENT	We finally made it to the stadium. *After* a long, boring delay in traffic.
FIXED: BY ATTACHING	We finally made it to the stadium *after* a long, boring delay in traffic.
BY ADDING WORDS	We finally made it to the stadium. The traffic caused a long, boring delay.
INFINITIVE PHRASE FRAGMENT	*To enter* the water cleanly from a high dive. A diver must keep arms and legs straight, fingers and toes pointed.
FIXED: BY ATTACHING	*To enter* the water cleanly from a high dive, a diver must keep arms and legs straight, fingers and toes pointed.
BY ADDING WORDS	There is a method to entering the water cleanly from a high dive. A diver must keep arms and legs straight, fingers and toes pointed.
PARTICIPIAL PHRASE FRAGMENT (PRESENT TENSE)	*Pushing* hard to get through the sweaty bodies. Shawn struggled to escape from the mosh pit.
FIXED: BY ATTACHING	*Pushing* hard to get through the sweaty bodies, Shawn struggled to escape from the mosh pit.
BY ADDING WORDS	Shawn pushed hard to get through the sweaty bodies. He struggled to escape from the mosh pit.
PARTICIPIAL PHRASE FRAGMENT (PAST TENSE)	*Tired* beyond belief but happy. Walter promised himself to make 220 when his aching muscles let him try again.
FIXED: BY ATTACHING	Tired beyond belief but happy, Walter promised himself to make 220 when his aching muscles let him try again.
BY ADDING WORDS	Walter was tired beyond belief but happy. He promised himself to make 220 when his aching muscles let him try again.
ABSOLUTE PHRASE FRAGMENT	The *earth shaking* violently beneath their feet. Samita and Lane were knocked flat.

FIXED:	
BY ATTACHING	The *earth shaking* violently beneath their feet, Samita and Lane were knocked flat.
BY ADDING WORDS	The earth <u>was</u> shaking violently beneath their feet. Samita and Lane were knocked flat.
APPOSITIVE PHRASE FRAGMENT	A hard *worker* and a good-hearted *person*. Allison was often taken advantage of by her co-workers.
FIXED:	
BY ATTACHING	A hard worker and a good-hearted person, Allison was often taken advantage of by her co-workers.
BY ADDING WORDS	Allison <u>was</u> a hard worker and a good-hearted person. She was often taken advantage of by her co-workers.

ACTIVITY 23.3 | *Recognizing and Fixing Phrase Fragments*

Decide which of the following sentences are fragments, and then correct the error by rewriting the sentence in the space provided. You may attach a phrase to a main clause or add words to the fragment, whichever method seems best to you. If the group of sentences does not contain a fragment, write "Correct."

EXAMPLE: Singing with great power and feeling. Pavarotti received a standing ovation from the audience.

Fixed: *Singing with great power and feeling, Pavarotti received a standing ovation from the audience.*

1. The pancakes were not appetizing. Burned on the bottom and raw on top. They made Elaine want to go out for breakfast.

_____

_____

2. Streaking downfield, shaking off tackles as he went. Allen charged toward the end zone 30 yards away.

_____

_____

3. To save energy nationally. Every homeowner could switch out five traditional electric bulbs for fluorescent bulbs. The equivalent energy exchange of removing 8 million cars from the highway.

_____

_____

4. Ahsan and Fatima spend more time with their children than anyone I know. They have a truly happy family.

_____

_____

5. Although it is expensive, it is a special treat. To eat at the Blue Water Grill.

_____

_____

HINT

When you combine the phrase with a main clause, be sure to punctuate correctly.

6. Two flight attendants were thrown onto the laps of passengers. The plane encountering heavy turbulence.

_____

_____

7. The funniest child in the family. Cicely seemed to have a joke for every occasion.

_____

_____

8. Fishing in his pocket for a handkerchief. Martin finally found one. Buried underneath his car keys, wadded-up dollar bills, and rent statement. He handed the handkerchief to his fiancée, who was feeling depressed. Remembering how opposed her parents were to this marriage.

_____

_____

_____

Subordinate Clause Fragments

While sentence fragments are often phrases, they can also be subordinate clauses. Subordinate clauses, which depend on main clauses to be complete, come in three varieties—noun, adjective, and adverb. Adverb and adjective clauses are the ones that most commonly turn up as fragments. To identify adverb clause fragments, look for sentences that begin with one of these common subordinating conjunctions:

HINT

A **subordinate clause** contains a subject and a verb but not a complete thought (see Chapter 21).

SUBORDINATING CONJUNCTIONS

after	as though	in order that	so that	whenever
although	because	now that	though	where
as	before	once	till	whereas
as if	even though	rather than	until	wherever
as long as	if	since	when	while

If a sentence begins with one of these conjunctions and is not attached to a main clause, it is a fragment. Adverb clause fragments can be fixed either by attaching them to the main clause or by dropping the subordinating conjunction to create another main clause, as in the following example:

ADVERB CLAUSE FRAGMENT	*Because* the Midwest drought and heat wave have lasted for a month. Much of what was once green is now withered.
FIXED: BY ATTACHING	*Because* the Midwest drought and heat wave have lasted for a month, much of what was once green is now withered.
BY DROPPING SUBORDINATOR	The Midwest drought and heat wave have lasted for a month. Much of what was once green is now withered.

Adjective clause fragments can usually be identified by one of these three common relative pronouns: *who, which,* or *that.*

These fragments can be fixed either by attaching them to the main clause or by dropping the relative pronoun and replacing it with a noun or pronoun, as in the following example:

ADJECTIVE CLAUSE FRAGMENT	The first decent bicycle I bought was a Trek. *Which* has given me years of good service.
FIXED: BY ATTACHING	The first decent bicycle I bought was a Trek, *which* has given me years of good service.
BY DROPPING RELATIVE PRONOUN AND ADDING NOUN	The first decent bicycle I bought was a Trek. This bike has given me years of good service.

HINT

When combining the subordinate clause with a main clause, be sure to punctuate correctly.

ACTIVITY 23.4 WORKING TOGETHER: *Recognizing and Fixing Subordinate Clause Fragments*

Rewrite any of the following sentences that contain a fragment, or write "Correct." You may attach the fragment to a main clause or add a subject, whichever method seems best to you. Now compare your answers with a partner's and see where and how your solutions differ. Note which edited version of each you prefer and why.

EXAMPLE: When the Renaissance Festival begins to advertise. I begin to think of all the food I will end up eating. While I am there.

Fixed: *When the Renaissance Festival begins to advertise, I begin to think of all the food I will end up eating while I am there.*

1. If Morgan joins the eco tour in Brazil. She will see some breathtaking rain forest canopy.

   _____

   _____

2. We took the course in emergency CPR for children. Even though our daughter is grown. Because we hope to have grandchildren sometime soon.

   _____

   _____

3. For family pets, many people favor Labradors. Which have a reputation for being friendly and gentle.

   _____

   _____

4. Rather than stay in a dead-end job that you don't like, why not go back to college, retrain, and find a new life?

   _____

   _____

5. When a person recycles aluminum cans. It reduces by 95 percent the amount of energy. That it takes to make these same cans from raw aluminum.

_____

_____

ACTIVITY 23.5 WORKING ONLINE: *Sentence Boundaries Practice*

Practice fixing run-ons, comma splices, and fragments on Gateway; link to exercises at www.mhhe.com/brannan.

ACTIVITY 23.6 WORKING ONLINE: *Sentence Boundaries Review*

Take the Chapter 23 Review Quiz at www.mhhe.com/brannan.

Chapter Summary

1. Writers can identify and correct run-ons, comma splices, and fragments by determining sentence boundaries: locating *verbs* and *subjects* and distinguishing *main clauses* from *subordinate clauses.*

2. A run-on sentence occurs when two or more main clauses run together without punctuation between them. A comma splice occurs when only a comma connects main clauses; by itself a comma is not strong enough to join them.

3. The easiest way to fix a comma splice or a run-on is to separate the two main clauses with end punctuation, such as a period.

4. Comma splices and run-ons can also be fixed by using commas with coordinating conjunctions, by using semicolons, or by using subordination (phrases or clauses).

5. A sentence fragment is missing either a subject or a main verb; it is an incomplete sentence and does not express a complete thought. Fragments may be phrases or subordinate clauses.

6. To make a phrase fragment into a sentence, either connect it to a main clause or add words (subjects, verbs, or both) to turn the phrase itself into a main clause.

7. To make an adverb clause fragment into a sentence, either attach it to the main clause or drop the subordinating conjunction to create another main clause.

8. To make an adjective clause fragment into a sentence, either attach it to the main clause or drop the relative pronoun and replace it with a noun or pronoun.

Verbs

Form and Agreement

24

[*Verbs primarily show action or state of being. Imagine that the cyclist in this photograph is on his way to work. Write a brief paragraph and underline the action verbs to show what could happen to him along the way. Or focus your paragraph on the reasons this man bikes to work, detailing how this choice benefits both the cyclist and the environment; again, underline all the action verbs.*]

KEY TOPICS

- The principal parts of verbs and verb tenses
  - Three primary verb tenses
  - Helping verbs
  - Perfect tenses
  - Progressive tenses
  - Irregular verbs
  - Problem verbs
  - Verb tense sequences and unneeded tense shifts

- Subject/verb agreement
  - Intervening words
  - Compound subjects
  - Indefinite pronouns
  - *Or, either/or, neither/nor*
  - Relative pronouns as subjects
  - Linking verbs
  - Changing the order of subjects and verbs
  - Collective nouns
  - Plural nouns/plural verbs
  - "False" plural nouns

What Are We Trying to Achieve and Why?

As we know from Chapter 21, sentences grow from subjects and verbs, to which all the other describing words, phrases, and clauses are attached. Verbs in particular can cause problems because they take so many different forms and do so much work. In this chapter, we will look at the forms verbs take, paying special attention to **tense**—time change in verbs—and subject/verb **agreement.**

The Principal Parts of Verbs and Verb Tenses

Verbs come in two varieties in English: **regular**—the vast majority—and **irregular.** In both cases, they may appear in one of five different **forms:**

THE FIVE FORMS OF VERBS

	Base Form	Past Tense	Past Participle	Present Participle	-s Ending
Regular	walk	walked	walked	walking	walks
Irregular	sing	sang	sung	singing	sings

The base form is the one you find listed in the dictionary: *walk, talk, eat.* The past tense of regular verbs is created by adding *-d* or *-ed* to the base form, whereas irregular verbs change their past tense in other ways, including vowel changes: *sing/sang, speak/spoke, drink/drank.* We usually form the past participle, like the past tense, by adding *-d* or *-ed* and the present participle by adding *-ing.* In the last form, an *-s* or *-es* is added to create almost all third-person singular present tenses: *he walks, she walks, it walks, somebody walks.*

We combine these five verb forms to create twelve tenses, which we can reduce to the three that we are all familiar with: present, past, and future.

Three Primary Verb Tenses

The **present tense** has several uses, in general showing action happening now: "The mockingbird *sings* in the tree." Here are four other uses:

- To show habitual action: "I *eat* breakfast every morning."
- To express general truths: "Spring *follows* winter."
- To discuss works of art: "*Romeo and Juliet is* not Shakespeare's best play."
- To refer to future events (sometimes): "Bruce Springsteen *begins* his concert soon."

Notice that only one form in the present tense differs from the others, the *-s* ending used with *he, she, it,* and many indefinite pronouns:

I play	we play
you play	you (plural) play
he, she, it, everyone plays	they play

The simple **past tense** tells about actions occurring in the past that do not continue into the present. Regular verbs form the past tense by adding *-d* or *-ed* to the base: "Arnold <u>nailed</u> the horseshoe over his door." The action occurred one time and was not repeated.

I nailed	we nailed
you nailed	you (plural) nailed
he, she, it nailed	they nailed

The primary verb tenses, in terms of form and function, may differ in other languages.

Indefinite pronouns include *each, no one,* etc. (see p. 571).

Irregular verbs change their spellings in the past tense, sometimes radically: *fly/flew, creep/crept, eat/ate.*

The third simple tense is the **future,** which is used to show anticipated action. We usually form this tense by adding the helping verb *will* to the base verb: "Claire *will dance* on Broadway this summer."

I will dance	we will dance
you will dance	you (plural) will dance
he, she, it will dance	they will dance

Helping Verbs

To help verbs express tenses, English uses **auxiliary** or **helping verbs** with a main verb. The most common are forms of the word *be (am, are, is, was, were, been, being), do (does, did, done),* or *have (has, had).* Other typical helping verbs are *may, might, must, can, could, should,* and *would.* When combined with main verbs, helping verbs create phrases like the following:

A. We *were* running behind schedule.

B. Sabato *did* finish the contract yesterday.

C. The thief *had* stripped my Mustang before I got it back.

D. Mark *could have* gotten an internship last semester.

Modals (*may/might, can/could, will/would, shall/should, must*) are helping verbs that express requests, doubt, capability, necessity, and advisability:

REQUEST	*Would (will, could, can)* you pass the salt?
DOUBT	I *might (may)* go to the concert this weekend.
CAPABILITY	I *could (can)* ask Mae to come with me.
NECESSITY	Jade *must* meet her deadline or lose the contract.
ADVISABILITY	You *should* arrive at the airport at least 1 hour before your flight.

Modals help refine the meaning of main verbs and are especially useful in softening requests. For example, while eating dinner, you might say, "Pass the salt," as a command. Or you could reduce the command to a request, using one of the modals: "Would you pass the salt?"

Perfect Tenses

While the simple present, past, and future tenses help express many essential time relationships, they do not cover them all. To discuss an action finished earlier in time than another, we use the **perfect tenses**—present, past, and future. To form a perfect tense, we put *has, have,* or *had* in front of a past participle.

The **present perfect** tells of actions begun in the past and finished at some unknown time or that continue into the present. If we mention a specific time, we use the **simple past** rather than the present perfect.

A. The spring rain *has* brought new life to the earth. (The rain happened at some point in the past.)

B. Alma and Mitch *have* both tried sleeping under a pyramid for their mental health. (They tried it at some past time, but the sentence does not indicate when or that they have stopped.)

C. Alma and Mitch both tried sleeping under a pyramid last night for their mental health. (They tried at a specific time: *last night.*)

See Chapter 21 for information on linking verbs.

The base form of a verb always follows the modal, so be careful not to use the past tense or an infinitive: **Not this**—Francesca *should called* her mother this weekend. **But this**—Francesca *should call* her mother this weekend. (You can practice using modals at www.mhhe.com/brannan under Ch. 24.)

A *past participle* is a base verb usually ending in *-d/-ed* for regular verbs.

The **past perfect** shows one action happening further back in time than another past action:

A. Emily *had* hoped to make the 1:00 flight, but her car <u>stalled</u> on the way to the airport. (Her hoping happened before the car stalled.)

B. As Martin walked into the crowd of friends, he suddenly <u>realized</u> that they *had* <u>carefully planned</u> this surprise party. (He realized after they planned.)

The **future perfect** shows an action that will be completed before another future act:

A. Isaac *will have* <u>finished</u> 200 layups before the game next week. (Isaac will finish the drills in the future but before the more distant event of the game.)

B. Once Dad searches the attic for the oven mitt, he *will have* <u>looked</u> everywhere. (The sentence specifies the time that the search for the mitt will be over.)

It might be helpful to create a timeline of each verb tense and then compare them in terms of function.

ACTIVITY 24.1 | *Distinguishing Simple Past from Present Perfect*

Underline the correct verb form in the following sentences.

> **EXAMPLE:** Mark (won/<u>has won</u>) the Poetry Slam every year since it began.

1. Gerard (wanted/has wanted) a Ford Ranger for as long as he can remember.

2. The crowd (applauded/has applauded) for 5 minutes and is still clapping.

3. For 6 months, Jack's mother (pleaded/has pleaded) with him to cut his hair, and she will keep after him until he does.

4. To save energy, Jenny (raked/has raked) her leaves today instead of using her leaf blower.

5. In competing for the Olympic gold, the skaters (practiced/have practiced) their routine for 2 years, and they are almost ready.

6. In your journal or on separate paper, create three sentences of your own that use the present perfect tense.

HINT

Remember that the *simple past* is used for an action completed in the past, whereas the *present perfect* is used for an action begun in the past that was completed at some unspecified time or that continues into the present.

ACTIVITY 24.2 | WORKING TOGETHER: *Distinguishing Simple Past from Past Perfect*

Underline the correct verb form in the following sentences. After completing number 8, trade sentences with a partner and rewrite his or her sentences in the simple past. Discuss what else you had to change in the sentence and how its meaning has now shifted.

> **EXAMPLE:** Alex's truck (stalled/<u>had stalled</u>) three times before he finally repaired the fuel pump.

1. Vincent swore that he (smoked/had smoked) his last cigarette.

2. The guests (arrived/had arrived) before we were ready for them.

3. The windstorm (did/had done) its worst damage by the time we arrived.

4. Peter's father was angry, wanting to know who (threw/had thrown) the baseball through the living room window.

5. Ashwani (slipped/had slipped) on the ice and fell hard on his back.

6. The building crew (finished/had finished) leveling and smoothing the sidewalk when a dog chased a cat through the wet cement.

7. Krissy sat through another boring time-share presentation because she wanted the iPod Shuffle the sales staff (promised/had promised).

8. Create three sentences of your own that use the past perfect tense:

   A. _____

   B. _____

   C. _____

Progressive Tenses

Whereas the perfect tenses are formed using the past participle (*-ed*), the **progressive tenses** are formed with the present participle (*-ing*) plus a form of the verb *be (is, am, are, was, were, been, being)*. We use the progressive tenses to show ongoing action during the present, past, or future.

The **present progressive** tells of ongoing action in the present. Sentences using this tense imply or sometimes use phrases like *right now* or *at this moment*.

A. I *am* cleaning my kitchen right now. (The cleaning is happening at this moment.)

B. Looking out my window, I see that it *is* raining. (It is raining right now.)

C. It often rains in the spring. (It usually rains at this time.)

Sentence C uses the simple present, which suggests repeated or habitual action.

The **past progressive** tells of ongoing action in the past. Similar to the past perfect, it can indicate one action occurring before another, but it is *ongoing* action that may immediately lead to another past action:

A. I *was* cleaning my kitchen when the phone rang. (He began cleaning the kitchen before the phone rang, and he was still cleaning at the time it rang.)

B. Luis and Maria *were* strolling on the plaza as clouds began to gather. (Luis and Maria were walking before and during the time that the clouds gathered.)

C. Luis and Maria strolled on the plaza, and then clouds began to gather. (Luis and Maria took a stroll but completed it *before* the clouds moved in.)

Sentence C uses the simple past because the action ended at a specified time.

The **future progressive** tells of ongoing action in the future and, like the simple future, uses the helping verb *will:*

A. I *will be* cleaning my kitchen tomorrow afternoon. (The kitchen will be cleaned at a certain time in the future.)

B. Chad *will be* trolling for striped bass all morning. (Chad expects to be in the process of fishing in the future.)

C. Chad *will* troll for striped bass all morning. (Chad will fish in the future.)

Sentence C gives the same idea of future activity using the simple future. Often there is little difference between the future progressive and the simple future.

English Review Note

Do not use the present progressive for **stative verbs,** which indicate that a subject will remain constant and unchanging for a certain time.
EXAMPLE: "Ashwani **understands** *calculus better than I ever will"* is correct, but it is incorrect to write *"Ashwani* **is understanding** *calculus better than I ever will."* Common stative verbs include *be, believe, belong, cost, hate, have, know, like, love, mean, need, own, resemble, think, understand, weigh.* Practice identifying stative verbs at www.mhhe.com/brannan (Ch. 24).

ACTIVITY 24.3 *Distinguishing Simple Present from Present Progressive*

Underline the correct verb form in the following sentences. Remember that the *simple present* suggests habitual action and general truths, whereas the *present progressive* tells us that the action is occurring at that moment.

> EXAMPLE: Dad can't read to you now because he (works/is working) in his office.

1. "Hold down the racket! I (try/am trying) to concentrate."
2. I (go/am going) to school every morning at 8:00 a.m.
3. The wind (blows/is blowing) the chimes, and they are ringing softly.
4. At this very moment, Isabella (walks/is walking) across the stage to receive her associate's degree.
5. The world population (grows/is growing) so rapidly that it will double in 60 years.
6. In your journal or on separate paper, create three sentences of your own that use the present progressive tense.

ACTIVITY 24.4 *Distinguishing Simple Past from Past Progressive*

Underline the correct verb form in the following sentences. Remember that the *simple past* tells that an action has been completed in the past, whereas the *past progressive* tells that the past action is ongoing.

> EXAMPLE: I (worked/was working) in the back of the store when you called.

1. We (went/were going) to the store when Mom was pulled over for speeding.
2. Jessica (typed/was typing) her paper when her computer crashed.
3. The men (smoothed/were smoothing) out the last section of sidewalk as the children (scratched/were scratching) their initials in the first section.
4. We (ate/were eating) at Rio Bravo when we heard the news about Paul's accident.
5. We (ate/were eating) at Rio Bravo last week, and this week we will try Margarita's.
6. In your journal or on separate paper, create three sentences of your own that use the past progressive tense.

Irregular Verbs

Regular verbs in English form their past tense by adding *-d* or *-ed* to the base or dictionary form (*walk/walked*), but **irregular verbs** are not so easy. The past tense and past participle of irregular verbs are usually spelled differently than the base form—sometimes just changing a vowel (*begin/began/begun*), but sometimes changing consonants (*prove/proved/proven*) and sometimes not changing at all (*cut/cut/cut*)!

The most important irregular verb in English is *to be*. Because it is used so often both as a helper (*is* speaking) and on its own as a linking verb (John *is* a strong man), you should learn its seven forms.

SIX FORMS OF *TO BE: AM, ARE, IS, WAS, WERE, BEEN*

	Singular	Plural
Present	I am you are he, she, it is	we are you are they are
Past	I was you were he, she, it was	we were you were they were
Past Participle	I had been you had been he, she, it had been	we had been you had been they had been

Here is a list of the principal parts of some common irregular verbs:

COMMON IRREGULAR VERBS

Present Tense	Past Tense	Past Participle	Present Tense	Past Tense	Past Participle
awake	awoke	awoke/ awakened	drive	drove	driven
become	became	become	eat	ate	eaten
begin	began	begun	fall	fell	fallen
bite	bit	bitten	feel	felt	felt
blow	blew	blown	fight	fought	fought
break	broke	broken	find	found	found
bring	brought	brought	fly	flew	flown
build	built	built	forget	forgot	forgotten
buy	bought	bought	freeze	froze	frozen
catch	caught	caught	get	got	got/ gotten
choose	chose	chosen	give	gave	given
come	came	come	go	went	gone
cost	cost	cost	grow	grew	grown
creep	crept	crept	hang	hung (hanged)	hung (hanged)
cut	cut	cut	hear	heard	heard
dig	dug	dug	hide	hid	hidden
dive	dived/dove	dived	hit	hit	hit
do	did	done	hold	held	held
draw	drew	drawn	keep	kept	kept
drink	drank	drunk			

English Review Note

Two irregular verbs that can work as either helping verbs or action verbs are *to do* (forms: *do, does, did, done*) and *to have* (forms: *have, has, had*).

HINT

The best way to handle these forms is to memorize them and then refer to a dictionary when needed.

Present Tense	Past Tense	Past Participle		Present Tense	Past Tense	Past Participle
kneel	knelt	knelt		say	said	said
know	knew	known		see	saw	seen
lay (put)	laid	laid		set	set	set
lead	led	led		shake	shook	shaken
leave	left	left		show	showed	shown
let	let	let		sing	sang	sung
lie (recline)	lay	lain		sit	sat	sat
light	lit (lighted)	lit (lighted)		sleep	slept	slept
lose	lost	lost		speak	spoke	spoken
pay	paid	paid		steal	stole	stolen
prove	proved	proven		swim	swam	swum
ride	rode	ridden		swing	swung	swung
ring	rang	rung		take	took	taken
rise	rose	risen		tell	told	told
run	ran	run		write	wrote	written

Problem Verbs

Aside from the partial list of irregular verbs above, there are several verbs that are especially tricky: *lie/lay, sit/set,* and *rise/raise.*

COMMON PROBLEM VERBS

Base Form	Past Tense	Past Participle	Present Participle	-s Ending
lie	lay	lain	lying	lies
lay	laid	laid	laying	lays
sit	sat	sat	sitting	sits
set	set	set	setting	sets
rise	rose	risen	rising	rises
raise	raised	raised	raising	raises

English Review Note

Commonly confused verbs:
live/leave
feel/fall
thought/taught

- *Lie* means to rest or recline, as in "I'm tired. I think I <u>will</u> *lie* down now."
- *Lay* means to place something, as in "I <u>will</u> *lay* the book on the table."

- *Sit* means to be seated, as in "I <u>will</u> *sit* in the chair."
- *Set* means to place something, as in "I <u>will</u> *set* the cup on the counter."

- *Rise* means to go up, as in "The balloon is *rising* in the sky."
- *Raise* means to lift, as in "I <u>will</u> *raise* the window to get some air."

Verb Tense Sequences and Unneeded Tense Shifts

Writers often combine verb tenses, speaking in the present, past, and future. As you move from a subordinate clause to a main clause, however, you should be sure that the verb tenses indicate a logical time relationship so you do not confuse the reader. You can show many time relationships by combining tenses, as in the following:

A. Amy <u>spends</u> time with her grandparents because she <u>loves</u> them. (present/present)

B. Amy <u>spent</u> time with her grandparents because she <u>loved</u> them. (past/past)

C. Amy <u>spent</u> time with her grandparents because she <u>loves</u> them. (past/present)

D. Amy <u>spends</u> time with her grandparents because she <u>loves</u> them and they <u>will be</u> gone soon. (present/present/future)

In sentence A, Amy is still spending time with her grandparents, whom she still loves. In sentence B, she used to spend time with them because she used to love them but may not any more. Sentence C says that Amy once spent time with the old folks but may not any more, even though she still loves them. Sentence D explains that Amy spends time with the grandparents because she loves them and because she realizes they may die soon.

However, there are also illogical tense relationships that we want to avoid, such as the following:

Amy <u>spends</u> time with her grandparents because she <u>will love</u> them. (present/future)

It is unlikely that Amy is spending time with her grandparents because she will love them someday.

Another way to confuse readers is to needlessly shift from one tense to another, usually between present and past. Notice how the following passage begins in the present, shifts to the past, and then shifts back to the present.

Here we <u>are</u> at the stadium, looking forward to a great game. Then

Brent <u>told</u> me that he <u>had forgotten</u> the tickets! I <u>was</u> understandably

<u>annoyed</u>. How <u>were</u> we <u>going</u> to get into the sold-out game without tickets?

I <u>try</u> not to scream at my idiot friend, but it <u>is</u> hard not to.

To solve the problem, simply change the tenses so that they are consistent throughout. Either past or present will do, although past is used in narrative passages more often. Here is the revision:

There we <u>were</u> at the stadium, looking forward to a great game. Then

Brent <u>told</u> me that he <u>had forgotten</u> the tickets! I <u>was</u> understandably

<u>annoyed</u>. How <u>were</u> we <u>going</u> to get into the sold-out game without tickets?

I <u>tried</u> not to scream at my idiot friend, but it <u>was</u> hard not to.

Subject/Verb Agreement

In addition to understanding verb tenses, you need to understand how verbs agree with subjects. Singular verbs should be paired with singular subjects and plural verbs with plural subjects. Although it might seem confusing, the -s ending on a present-tense verb usually marks it as singular, whereas the same ending on a subject marks it as plural. We usually observe this distinction without thinking about it when we speak and write, as in the following two examples:

SINGULAR SUBJECT   My cat <u>sleeps</u> in bed with me.

PLURAL SUBJECT   My cats <u>sleep</u> in bed with me.

Learning correct subject-verb agreement can be a challenge. Edit your sentences carefully. Identify each subject and verb and check for correct agreement.

However, as we write more complicated sentences than these, we sometimes have trouble locating our subjects and verbs and then making them agree in number. The rest of this chapter will help you with subject/verb agreement problems.

Intervening Words

<u>One</u> of the most frequent trouble spots in our sentences <u>occurs</u> when a verb is separated from its subject by a number of words—as in this sentence. We often try to connect the verb (in this case, *occurs*) with the closest noun (*sentences*) instead of the actual subject (*one*). Here are several examples with the subjects underlined once and the verbs twice:

A. *The Dark Knight*, one of the decade's many action-packed spectacles, <u>stars</u> Christian Bale.
B. The <u>movie</u> that we enjoyed more than all of the others <u>is</u> *WALL-E*
C. <u>Figures</u> released today from the White House <u>explain</u> the president's proposal.
D. A <u>box</u> with 13 bagels <u>is called</u> a baker's dozen.
E. The defense <u>attorney</u>, along with union members, <u>is protesting</u> the ruling.

Two steps can help you make subjects and verbs agree:

1. Locate the action or state-of-being word.
2. Ask, "Who or what is doing the action or experiencing the state of being?"

For example, in sentence C, what explains? *Figures* explain. Notice that sentence D has a prepositional phrase, "with 13 bagels," between the subject and verb. Subjects are never found within a prepositional phrase.

Also note that sentence E uses the phrase *along with,* one of a small group of phrases that do not affect the number of the subject: *in addition to, as well as, along with, plus, including,* and *together with.*

HINT

Subjects are never found within prepositional phrases. For more on subjects with prepositional phrases, see p. 515.

ACTIVITY 24.5 *Agreement with Separated Subjects and Verbs*

Underline the correct verb in parentheses twice and its subject once.

EXAMPLE: The <u>cars</u> on this lot (<u>cost</u>/costs) much more than I can afford.

1. The undercover officer standing among the teens at the concert (blends/blend) easily with the crowd.
2. Some of the most interesting sculptures in the museum, including one made entirely of soap, (is/are) on the third floor.
3. Music therapy along with other holistic healing methods (is/are) helping many people to overcome stress.
4. The red-tailed hawk in high winds (needs/need) to fly above them or land.
5. The sound of piston rods knocking (makes/make) most car owners a little sick.
6. A stack of red composite shingles (sits/sit) in Harold's pickup truck.
7. One of the cat's paws (has/have) a nasty infection.

Compound Subjects

In a **compound subject** (one with two or more parts), the verb usually becomes plural:

> Firestone and Ford are accusing each other in the latest round of blame fixing over blown tires.

However, some subjects may seem to be two-part but are actually singular:

> My best friend and older brother, Robert, has helped me through tight spots all my life.

Indefinite Pronouns

The singular **indefinite pronouns** in the following list require singular verbs when the pronouns are used as subjects:

SINGULAR INDEFINITE PRONOUNS

anybody	each	everyone	no one	somebody
anyone	either	neither	nothing	someone
anything	everybody	nobody	one	something

A. Nobody wins if everyone is destroyed in the battle.

B. Anyone who thinks she can do better is welcome to try.

C. Everybody listens closely to wolves howling in the distance.

When a singular indefinite pronoun is attached to a subject that has two or more parts, the sentence still requires a singular verb:

> Every man, woman, and child deserves equality under the law.

However, indefinite pronouns like *all, more, most, any, none* and *some* can be singular or plural, depending on the meaning of the sentence:

A. From the whipped cream topping to the bottom crust, all of the key lime pie was delicious.

B. All of the band's instruments were stolen last night.

ACTIVITY 24.6 | *Agreement with Indefinite Pronouns*

Underline the correct <u>verb</u> in parentheses twice and its <u>subject</u> once.

EXAMPLE: Everyone (is/are) here who is going to make it.

1. Some of Julio's best friends (is/are) majoring in business.
2. Nothing (tastes/taste) as good as an ice-cold Coke on a hot summer day.
3. Each of the girls on the team (has/have) a 20-minute warm-up routine.
4. None of the buildings in the path of the hurricane still (stands/stand).
5. Neither of the candidates in the mayoral race (has/have) gone into full mud-slinging mode—yet.
6. Most of Sarah's friends (thinks/think) that she is a hard worker.
7. Everyone watching the surfers (agree/agrees) that this group is the best.

Or, Either/Or, Neither/Nor

When using *or, either/or,* and *neither/nor* to connect compound subjects, we have three possibilities for subject/verb agreement:

- When the subjects are both singular, the verb will be singular.
- When the subjects are both plural, the verb will be plural.
- When subjects are singular and plural, the verb agrees with the *closest* subject.

A. *Either* Tim *or* Diane wins the gold, not both of them.

B. Apples *or* peaches make the perfect pie.

C. *Neither* the minister *nor* the members of his congregation want to abandon school prayer.

Relative Pronouns as Subjects

The relative pronouns *who, which,* and *that* (among others) are the subjects of relative clauses and always refer back to nouns. These pronouns are singular or plural based on the noun they refer to.

A. A person *who* rides motorized scooters will probably say they are fun and safe.

B. People *who* ride motorized scooters say they are fun and safe.

C. An SUV *that* blows a tire is more likely to roll over than a car.

D. SUVs *that* blow tires are more likely to roll over than cars.

Linking Verbs

A linking verb should agree with its subject, not the word(s) that follow(s) the verb and provides information about the subject, known as the **complement.**

A. A deciding factor in many elections today is women.

B. Women are a deciding factor in many elections today.

Even though it is grammatically correct, sentence A sounds a bit awkward. It is best to revise it, as sentence B does.

Changing the Order of Subjects and Verbs

Although the usual order of words in English sentences is subject, verb, object (*Eric threw the ball*), writers sometimes change this order for variety, emphasis, or clarity. When you vary this standard order, especially when you reverse subject and verb, you may sometimes have trouble with subject/verb agreement. Here are four ways writers relocate sentence parts:

For more on inversion, see pp. 472–473.

1. Use inversion to move the subject of a sentence close to or all the way to the end of a sentence, thus emphasizing the final word. Compare sentence A, in standard order, with sentence B, inverted:

   A. A rattlesnake slithered into a hole in the ground.

   B. Into a hole in the ground slithered a rattlesnake.

2. Use there/here sentences to push the subject past the verb:

   A. *There* are three good reasons for exercising regularly.

   B. *There* is a terrible noise coming from the washing machine.

   C. *Here* are the leftovers from last night's dinner.

If passive-voice sentences seem confusing when you are trying to find a subject, ask, "Who or what is having something done to it?"

3. Use questions to reverse the ordinary positions of subject and verb:

   A. <u>Are</u> <u>you</u> <u>coming</u> to the game with me?

   B. Where <u>is</u> the map of Missouri?

4. Use passive voice to downplay or eliminate the active agent of a sentence, the real subject. In sentences in the passive voice, the direct object becomes the subject. Often the active agent is left out altogether. Compare sentence A, in active voice, with B, in passive voice:

   A. <u>Jenny</u> <u>climbed</u> the tree.

   B. The <u>tree</u> <u>was climbed</u> by Jenny.

In sentence A, the subject, *Jenny,* climbs *the tree,* the direct object. In sentence B, the direct object in sentence A becomes the grammatical subject, with a form of *to be* as a helping verb with a past participle.

   When the doer of an action is relatively unimportant or unknown, the passive voice can be an effective choice. But active voice works best when—as in most cases—you want the real doer of the action to receive full attention. However, here are two examples of effective passive-voice sentences, both of which seek to emphasize the words in the subject position:

   A. My friend's <u>home</u> <u>was broken</u> into last night. (A thief did it, but the focus is on the violation of the home.)

   B. Six million <u>Jews</u> <u>were murdered</u> during the Holocaust. (The Nazis did it, but the focus is on the deaths rather than the perpetrators of the crime.)

ACTIVITY 24.7 *Agreement with Reordered Sentences*

Underline the <u>verb</u> in each sentence twice and the <u>subject</u> once.

   EXAMPLE: In the middle of an angry crowd <u>cowered</u> two innocent <u>bystanders</u>.

1. From the back of the old Chevy station wagon clung three young boys, hitching a ride on their sleds.

2. This mess was made by someone.

3. When is Louis going to take the bar exam?

4. By the side of the road was a Ford Explorer with a flat tire.

5. Here are the best facilities for losing weight and toning up.

6. My flight was delayed by the ice storm.

7. There is a hole in the ozone over Antarctica that gets bigger each passing year.

Collective Nouns

In American English, words that stand for groups usually are treated as singular—for example, *army, committee, team, band, class, audience, crowd, gathering, jury, herd, school,* and *flock:*

A. The <u>jury</u> <u>feels</u> that its decision was just.

B. Our <u>committee</u> <u>has beaten</u> this issue to death.

   However, if the members of the group are acting individually, it often sounds more natural to revise the sentence to reflect this—for example, "The <u>members</u> of our group <u>have</u> not <u>reached</u> a decision yet."

Plural Nouns/Plural Verbs

While some nouns are collectively singular, others are always plural—for example, *scissors, pants, clothes,* and *fireworks:*

> The scissors are in the drawer.

"False" Plural Nouns

Some nouns that end in *-s* are not plural—for example, *mathematics, physics, athletics, economics, statistics, measles, mumps, politics, ethics,* and *pediatrics.* Though titles may contain plural nouns—for example, *All Creatures Great and Small*—they take singular verbs. Sums of money, distances, measurements, and time units may also look plural, but when they are being used as a unit, they, too, are grammatically singular:

A. Mathematics is my favorite subject.

B. Thirty minutes is too long to spend listening to Dr. Parrish lecture.

C. Twenty-five thousand dollars sounds like too much to spend on a car.

ACTIVITY 24.8 Agreement with Plural and Collective Nouns

Underline the verb in parentheses twice and the subject once.

> EXAMPLE: Fireworks (is/are) a wonderful sight to many Americans on July Fourth.

1. *Jaws* (is/are) a movie that made many people reluctant to swim in the ocean.

2. The whole gathering (believes/believe) in the imminent destruction of earth.

3. The audience (applauds/applaud) enthusiastically, hoping for one more encore.

4. A whole flock of Canadian geese (is flying/are flying) through the airspace above La Guardia airport.

5. Five hundred dollars (is/are) too much for this guitar.

6. The only pants I have (is/are) in the dryer.

7. Five hundred flat miles across Kansas (is/are) too far to drive to reach Denver.

ACTIVITY 24.9 WORKING TOGETHER: Using Agreement in Context

In a small group, write a paragraph completing the following sentences. Feel free to use humor, and check each other's work.

One of the most popular new bands (is/are)

The lead singer (stands/stand out) because

However, the other members (is/are)

[Name of the band] (plays/play)

Their music and lyrics (sounds like/sound like)

Five minutes of listening to their music (is/are)

ACTIVITY 24.10 | WORKING ONLINE: *Voice Shifts and More Verbs Practice*

Practice verb and voice shifts and subject/verb agreement on Gateway (link at www.mhhe.com/brannan).

ACTIVITY 24.11 | WORKING ONLINE: *Verbs Review*

Take the Chapter 24 Review Quiz at www.mhhe.com/brannan.

Chapter Summary

1. All verbs are either regular or irregular and have five forms: **base, past tense, past participle, present participle,** and **-s ending.**

2. Learning to use verb tenses correctly is an important skill for a writer to develop. There are twelve verb tenses.

3. The **present tense** shows action happening either right now or continuously.

4. The **past tense** shows action that happened in the past but is no longer happening.

5. The **future tense** shows anticipated action.

6. To discuss an action finished earlier in time than another, we use the **perfect tenses,** present, past, and future. To form a perfect tense, we put *has, have,* or *had* in front of a **past participle.** Most past participles use a *-d/-ed* ending.

7. To show ongoing action within tenses—present, past, or future—we use the **progressive tenses.** The progressive is formed by placing a helping verb (*is, am, are, was, were, been, or being*) in front of a **present participle** (which usually ends in *-ing*).

8. The past tense and past participle of **irregular verbs** are formed in a variety of ways. The best approach to learning irregular verb forms is to memorize those that are commonly used.

9. The following verbs may cause confusion: *lie/lay, sit/set,* and *rise/raise.*

10. When moving from a subordinate to a main clause, writers often combine verb tenses; however, the verb tenses should indicate a logical time relationship.

11. Singular verbs should be paired with singular subjects and plural verbs with plural subjects.

12. A verb may be separated from its subject by a number of intervening words.

13. Compound subjects are almost always plural.

14. Some indefinite pronouns are singular, others are plural, and still others can be used in singular or plural constructions, depending on the nouns they refer to. A relative pronoun is singular or plural depending on the noun it refers to.

15. Linking verbs should always agree with their subjects, even when it might sometimes seem that the verb should agree with a complement.

16. The most common way to arrange an English sentence is subject, verb, object, but sentence parts can be reordered for variety, emphasis, or clarity.

17. Most collective nouns are treated as singular and should therefore be used with singular verbs. Some nouns, like *scissors* and *fireworks,* are always plural. Some nouns that end in *-s* (such as *mathematics*) are singular.

Pronouns

Reference, Agreement, and Form

25

[*One woman points at some odd-looking figures, perhaps saying to her companion, "What are they?" Pronouns, like "they," by referring to nouns, help us to name things, like these figures in Barcelona's 2007 Trash People exhibit. Write a brief paragraph describing several works of art on your college campus, underlining every pronoun that you use.*]

KEY TOPICS

- Referring clearly to a specific antecedent
- Agreeing in number with the antecedent
- Choosing proper pronoun case
- Solving common problems with pronoun case
- Avoiding shifts in person

What Are We Trying to Achieve and Why?

Like verbs and nouns, **pronouns** are a common and important part of speech. Pronouns like *he, this, who, myself,* and *everyone* take the place of nouns and help create variety in your writing.

Without pronouns to replace nouns, we might be stuck with paragraphs like this one:

> The leopard crept stealthily through the dry grass, stalking the leopard's prey. As the leopard neared the antelope, the leopard's ears flattened, and the leopard's tail began to twitch in anticipation. Pausing for a moment, seeming to hold the leopard's breath, the leopard sprang from hiding to land on the antelope's back.

Clearly, the repetition of *leopard* becomes monotonous. To solve the problem, we can substitute pronouns, as in the following revision:

> The leopard crept stealthily through the dry grass, stalking her prey. As the leopard neared the antelope, the leopard's ears flattened, and her tail began to twitch in anticipation. Pausing for a moment, seeming to hold her breath, the leopard sprang from hiding to land on the antelope's back.

As useful as pronouns are, they have no identity by themselves. Therefore, they must refer to a noun to achieve meaning. If a friend were to say, "It was a horrible experience," you might respond, "What was horrible?" You cannot know until your friend says, "Root canal." Using a noun tells the reader exactly what the writer means.

Whenever you use pronouns, you must be sure that the reader knows what they refer to and take care to use the correct form of the pronoun. Chapter 25 focuses on pronoun reference, agreement, and form.

Referring Clearly to a Specific Antecedent

A pronoun refers to an **antecedent**—a word that the pronoun substitutes for, most often a noun but occasionally another pronoun or phrase. The antecedent is usually located before the pronoun, either within the same sentence or in a nearby sentence, as in the following: "Jim drinks hot chocolate. He likes it a lot." The words *he* and *it* take the place of *Jim* and *hot chocolate.*

Pronouns that are far removed from their antecedent can cause confusion, as in the following sentences:

UNCLEAR   A. Eileen told Isabella that she would never be happy until she stopped relying on men to define her existence.

            B. After she made this statement, she apologized, not wanting to sound like she was unkind.

In sentence A, who needs to stop relying on men? The confusion increases in sentence B. Who has said what? To clarify the meaning, the writer could recast the sentences this way:

REVISED   A. Eileen told Isabella that Isabella would never be happy until she stopped relying on men to define her existence.

            B. After Eileen made this statement, she apologized, not wanting to sound like she was unkind.

Now the writer's meaning is clear.

Pronouns that can be particularly confusing to readers are *it, they, them, this, that, these, those,* and *which.* These words should usually refer to a specific noun

For more on achieving variety and coherence through the use of pronouns, see p. 455.

For a list of pronouns, see page 573.

Pronouns must clearly refer to specific nouns.

Although some languages do not require subject pronouns, English does.

rather than a general idea, and they should be close to the noun they stand for to avoid unclear meanings, as in the following examples:

UNCLEAR   *They* rudely informed Jenna and Craig at the grocery store that *they* were out of mangoes.

Who informed Jenna and Craig—perhaps a store employee? The employee probably did not tell Jenna and Craig that the two of them were out of mangoes; the store was out.

REVISED   An employee at the grocery store rudely informed Jenna and Craig that the store was out of mangoes.

UNCLEAR   *It* made Jenna and Craig unhappy.

What made them unhappy: the lack of mangoes, the rudeness of the employee, or both?

REVISED   The rudeness of the employee and the lack of mangoes made them unhappy.

UNCLEAR   *This* taught *them* to prepare further in advance for parties, *which* will help *them* prevent *this* in the future.

What taught Jenna and Craig a lesson: the rude behavior, the lack of mangoes, or both? Is *which* referring to the parties—the closest noun—or the idea of preparing in advance? Is *them* referring to the parties—again, the closest noun—or to Craig and Jenna? What is the final *this* referring to?

REVISED   This unhappy shopping experience taught Craig and Jenna to prepare further in advance for parties. The lesson will help the couple to avoid future unpleasant surprises when planning parties.

Pronouns are useful in writing, but they need to be clearly linked with their antecedents.

Often the best fix for ambiguous pronoun reference is to replace the pronoun with a noun, as in the revised examples.

ACTIVITY 25.1 *Clarifying Pronoun Reference*

Revise the following sentences for unclear pronoun reference by replacing the pronouns with nouns and writing the revised sentence in the space provided.

EXAMPLE: When I finally reached the admissions office, they told me my transcripts had been lost.

Revised: *When I finally reached the admissions office, an employee told me my transcripts had been lost.*

1. Nguyen and his wife planned a night walk over the Big Island's lava fields to see the hot lava oozing into the sea, which made them both a bit nervous.

   _____

   _____

2. Many teachers are now aware that they have unconsciously discouraged girls from excelling in science and math. This is why they should now do better.

   _____

   _____

   _____

3. Large asteroids seldom hit the earth, but when they do, they cause terrific destruction, which is a relief to me.

_____

_____

4. Ann was talking to Eva when she saw the accident in the parking lot.

_____

_____

5. After the painters spoke with Jim and Kristi in their dining room, they moved the dining room table and then painted it.

_____

_____

6. Rainbow trout rest behind rocks in streams to conserve their energy and because they channel food toward them.

_____

_____

7. Sheila needed wire cutters or pliers to strip the insulation from the wires, so she asked her husband to hand them to her.

_____

_____

8. Meat and dairy products are high in saturated fats and often have toxic chemicals in them. But they taste good and have many valuable nutrients. For these reasons, though, many people are trying to cut down on their consumption.

_____

_____

_____

_____

Agreeing in Number with the Antecedent

Not only must pronouns be clearly linked to their antecedents, but they also must agree in **number:** Singular nouns take singular pronouns; plural nouns take plural pronouns. Consider the following examples:

A. *The Night of the Living Dead* is a classic horror *film*, but there is much in *it* that is laughable.

B. Many *films* have tried to capture the essence of Mary Shelley's *Frankenstein*, but few of *them* have succeeded.

In sentence A, the singular pronoun *it* refers to the singular *film*. In sentence B, the plural pronoun *them* links with the plural noun *films*.

Difficulties with pronoun/antecedent agreement often occur when the antecedent falls into one of the following categories: **indefinite pronouns, collective nouns,** and **compound antecedents.**

Indefinite Pronouns

Indefinite pronouns as antecedents can be a problem because they do not refer to a specific person or thing. Although most are singular, a few are plural, and several (*all, any, enough, more, most, none, some*) can be either singular or plural, depending on what noun they connect with.

INDEFINITE PRONOUNS

Singular			Plural
anybody	everybody	nothing	both
anyone	everyone	one	few
anything	neither	somebody	many
each	nobody	someone	others
either	no one	something	several

Singular indefinite pronouns take singular verbs even when the indefinite pronoun is connected to a plural noun. Note the following examples. Even though the noun *bands* is plural, the singular pronoun *it* refers back to the singular indefinite pronoun *each*.

INCORRECT   *Each* of the *bands* play until midnight; then *they* move to the next gig.

CORRECT   *Each* of the *bands* plays until midnight; then *it* moves to the next gig.

Even though the noun *players* is plural, the singular pronoun *himself* refers back to *neither*.

INCORRECT   *Neither* of the *players* deserve to be benched for defending *themselves*.

CORRECT   *Neither* of the *players* deserves to be benched for defending *himself*.

Here are several more examples illustrating correct pronoun agreement:

A. *One* of the shoppers was trying to find *her* checkbook.
B. *Anyone* can learn to play a musical instrument if *he* or *she* practices enough.
C. *Most* of the athletes failed *their* drug tests. (The indefinite pronoun *most* is plural because the noun that is connected to it, *athletes,* is plural.)
D. *Most* of the coffee is in *its* container. (Here *most* is singular because the noun that is connected to it, *coffee,* is singular.)

Collective Nouns

Pronouns referring to singular **collective nouns** are also singular:

The *group* feels that *its* membership policy is fair.

However, if the members of the group are acting individually, the noun becomes plural, and so does the pronoun:

The *group* are divided in *their* judgment, *all* members arguing passionately for *their* positions.

Compound Antecedents

We often use as subjects, and as other parts of a sentence, **compound antecedents,** nouns of two or more words joined as a unit by the conjunctions *and, or,* and

Notice that sentence B uses "*he or she*" to overcome gender bias in pronoun usage. (For more on this strategy, turn to Chapter 20.)

In American English, most groups are treated as a single unit, that is, as individuals acting together as one—for example, *army, committee, team, band, class, audience, crowd, gathering, group, herd, school,* and *flock.* See Chapter 24 for more on subject/verb agreement.

nor. When the antecedent is linked by *and,* it is usually plural, requiring a plural pronoun:

A. *Wind* and *sun* suck moisture from the earth, and *they* can destroy a corn crop.

B. *Lauren* and *Bob* will be on *their* favorite float river by this time tomorrow.

When the antecedent is linked by *or* or *nor,* the pronoun should agree with the nearest part:

A. Either Mark or *Luke* will bring *his* Frisbee to the park.

B. Mark or his *brothers* will bring *their* Frisbees to the park.

C. Neither Mark nor his *friends* remembered to bring *their* Frisbees to the park.

When you are using a plural and singular compound antecedent, put the plural word second for smoother-sounding sentences:

AWKWARD   Neither the fans nor the *coach* could control *his* anger at the
            referee's decision.

REVISED   Neither the coach nor the *fans* could control *their* anger at the
            referee's decision.

ACTIVITY 25.2 *Creating Pronoun Agreement*

Underline the antecedent in each of the following sentences, and then write an appropriate pronoun in the blank.

EXAMPLE: We are often told that anybody can be successful in this country if
he or she is willing to work hard.

1. Everyone would like a job that makes _____ happy.

2. A flock of swallows was on _____ way south for the winter.

3. Carl knew that the success of his latest album depended on many
   people and that _____ deserved recognition for _____ help.

4. Each player, giving _____ utmost, makes a team a winner or
   loser.

5. Nobody was able to move _____ vehicle from the crowded
   stadium parking lot.

6. Several of the people at my party called the next day to say that
   _____ had had a great time.

7. A school of tuna found _____ decimated by pursuing dolphins.

8. Every one of the women should know that _____ has an equal
   chance at the job.

9. Either of the boys will clean up the mess _____ made if you bribe
   _____ with candy.

10. Neither the director nor any of the actors thought that _____
    would complete the scene on schedule.

Choosing Proper Pronoun Case

Even after clarifying a pronoun's antecedent and checking for agreement in number, we can still have problems with **case**—the form a pronoun takes to show how it works in a sentence: as subject, object, or possessor.

Subjective Case

Pronouns used as subjects or subject complements are in the **subjective case:**

A. *She* runs 6-minute miles. (pronoun as subject)

B. The person to thank for breakfast is *she.* (pronoun as complement)

Pronouns used as objects follow the verb.

Objective Case

Pronouns used as objects (receiving the action of verbs), objects of prepositional phrases, and subjects of infinitives are in the **objective case:**

A. The whole family happily greeted *her.* (pronoun as direct object)

B. Emily kicked the ball to *him.* (pronoun as indirect object)

C. Alex wanted to share the secret with *you* and *me.* (pronouns as objects of preposition *with*)

D. Patty asked *him* to bring a green salad. (pronoun as subject of infinitive *to bring*)

Its, whose, and *your* are possessive pronouns; *it's, who's,* and *you're* are contractions.

Possessive Case

Pronouns used to show ownership are in the **possessive case:**

A. Is that *your* umbrella?

B. No, that one is not *mine.*

This chart will help you choose the correct pronoun case.

PRONOUN CASE CHART

Singular	Subjective	Objective	Possessive
First person	I	me	my, mine
Second person	you	you	your, yours
Third person	he, she, it, who, whoever	him, her, it, whom, whomever	his, her, hers, its, whose

Plural	Subjective	Objective	Possessive
First person	we	us	our, ours
Second person	you	you	your, yours
Third person	they, who, whoever	them, whom, whomever	their, theirs, whose

Pronouns in the possessive case do not agree with the nouns they modify.

Solving Common Problems with Pronoun Case

Pronoun case often causes problems in three categories: compounds, comparisons, and *who/whom.*

Compounds

Difficulties with compounds occur when two pronouns, two nouns, or a noun and a pronoun are linked by *and* or *or,* as in the following examples:

SUBJECTS   *Jerry* and *I/me* <u>went</u> to the Royals' game last night.

OBJECTS   The game <u>disappointed</u> *him* and *I/me.*

OBJECTS OF PREPOSITION   We left early, <u>which was</u> all right with *him* and *I/me.*

In each of these sentences, writers can be confused about which form of a pronoun to use. If we mentally cross out one of the pair, the remaining word will often guide us to the correct case:

A. ~~Jerry and~~ *I* went to the Royals' game last night. (*"Me* went to the Royals' game last night" does not sound right.)

   Jerry and *I* went to the Royals' game last night.

B. The game disappointed ~~him and~~ *me.* ("The game disappointed *I*" does not sound right.)

   The game disappointed *him* and *me.*

C. So we left early, which was all right with ~~him and~~ *me.* (You would not say "which was all right with *I.*")

   So we left early, which was all right with *him* and *me.*

Comparisons

We often make noun/pronoun and pronoun/pronoun comparisons using the words *than* and *as.* These comparisons can be confusing because they may leave words out of the sentence:

A. Kate sings more beautifully than *I/me.*

B. Dan is as competent as *he/him.*

If we add the missing verbs to sentences A and B, it becomes easier to determine the correct pronoun case. With the verbs in place, we can see that the pronouns are subjects and therefore must be in the subjective case.

C. Kate sings more beautifully than *I* <u>(sing)</u>.

D. Dan is as competent as *he* <u>(is)</u>.

   By adding missing words to the following examples, we can see that the pronouns are direct objects and need to be in the objective case:

A. This study guide will help you more than <u>(it will help)</u> *her/she.*

B. Loud music distracts Jessica as much as <u>(it distracts)</u> *him/he.*

   Sometimes choosing pronoun case will affect the meaning of your sentences:

A. Ian cares for football more than me. (more than he cares for me)

B. Ian cares for football more than I. (more than I care for football)

Who/Whom

The relative pronouns *who/whoever* and *whom/whomever* can also cause case problems. *Who/whoever* are used as subjects and *whom/whomever* have been traditionally used as objects, as in the following sentences:

SUBJECT   *Who* <u>will give</u> Jenny a ride to the game?

OBJECT   I should <u>give</u> your house keys to *whom*?

Being able to locate the verb and subject in your sentence will also help you determine case. If the pronoun is not a subject or a subject complement and does not show possession, it should be in the objective case.

Although the distinction between *who* and *whom* has been fading—*who* is often used in place of *whom*—most academic audiences expect the more formal usage of *whom*. However, if using *whom* seems awkward or overly formal, you can always recast the sentence so that the relative pronoun is unneeded or sometimes just drop it, as in the following example:

FORMAL   The fastest swimmer *whom* Brandon had to face was his archrival from Shawnee Mission South.

LESS FORMAL   The fastest swimmer Brandon had to face was his archrival from Shawnee Mission South.

ACTIVITY 25.3 | WORKING TOGETHER: *Choosing Pronoun Case*

For practice with two-part constructions, comparisons, and *who/whom*, work with a partner to underline the correct pronoun within parentheses in each sentence. Read each sentence aloud to each other to "hear" what sounds right, but also check your instincts against the rules in this book.

EXAMPLE: We finally found a babysitter so that my wife and (me/I) could have a night out.

1. It made George furious to hear (she/her) and Jason laughing together.
2. Anna is the girl (who/whom) Tomas is taking to the spring formal.
3. The sergeant pointed at Carlos and (I/me) and said, "You are volunteering."
4. During the recital, Lewis could see that Amy was more bored than (him/he).
5. Few people have reacted as violently as (they/them).
6. The gold medal belongs as much to the rest of the team as (she/her).
7. My older brother and (me/I) started skateboarding before we began surfing.
8. My boss offered Richard and (she/her) a raise.
9. April is a girl (whom/who) never gives up.
10. (She/Her) and her friend will leave the party by midnight.

Finding verbs and subjects will help you choose the correct pronoun. Also, try crossing out one word of the pair and putting in the implied words.

Avoiding Shifts in Person

As we saw in the Pronoun Case Chart on page 573, pronouns have number (singular or plural) and person (first, second, or third). **Person** is the perspective the author assumes when he or she writes: first person (*I, we*), second person (*you*), or third person (*he, she,* or *they*). Writers should be consistent in both number and person.

The most frequent shift error is from the first-person *I* or third-person *they* to the second-person *you,* as in the following examples:

INCONSISTENT   *I* looked out the window as *I* sat in a huge jet cutting through the clouds. *You* could see tiny green irrigation rings on the ground 25,000 feet below, reminding *me* of the drought still in progress.

FIXED   *I* looked out the window as *I* sat in a huge jet cutting through the clouds. *I* could see tiny green irrigation rings on the ground 25,000 feet below, reminding *me* of the drought still in progress.

INCONSISTENT	To improve *their* lives, American immigrants have often traveled westward. If *you* wanted to farm, ranch, or mine in the 19th century, the West was the place for *you*.
FIXED	To improve *their* lives, American immigrants have often traveled westward. If *they* wanted to farm, ranch, or mine in the 19th century, the West was the place for *them*.

HINT

Use *you* only when there is a good reason to directly address your readers.

Writers often mix persons in their work, but there should always be a good reason for doing so. The *I* of personal experience is sometimes used in introductions and conclusions but then avoided in the body paragraphs of an essay (except in a personal anecdote). You can use *you* occasionally in introductions and conclusions to address your readers directly, and you can use *you* often in process-analysis instructions (as in textbooks like this one). *We, us,* and *our* can help you connect with your audience, especially in persuasive writing. However, watch out for unnecessary shifts in person.

When using the slightly more formal third person, you have several options to avoid an inappropriate second-person *you*. You can use third-person pronouns (*he, she, they*), or nouns that can take their place (*people, students, employees*), or you can leave the pronoun out altogether. Note the following examples:

INAPPROPRIATE PRONOUN SHIFT	Australia was first colonized by English convicts. You would have worked hard in those early settlements.
FIXED: THIRD-PERSON PRONOUN	Australia was first colonized by English convicts. *They* would have worked hard in those early settlements.
NOUN	Australia was first colonized by English convicts. The *colonists* would have worked hard in the early settlements.
PRONOUN DELETED	Working hard in the early settlements, English convicts first colonized Australia.

ACTIVITY 25.4 *Avoiding Shifts in Person*

In the following paragraphs, cross out the inappropriate pronouns, write in the appropriate words in the space above them, and change any verb affected by a pronoun substitution. You may need to make other revisions as well.

1. When I lived on the farm, I had to help with a lot of chores. I had to take care of my animals, help my dad irrigate in the morning and evening, and cook and clean every day. When you live in a city, you end up with fewer responsibilities. All I have to do now is help my father with his landscaping business and help keep our small apartment clean. You don't have all of the extra responsibilities in the city that you have on the farm.

2. People who love downhill skiing regularly risk terrible injury pursuing it. You might think that you are too tough to get hurt, but skiers frequently break bones and, worse, rip their knee joints apart. Hurtling downhill at 40 to 50 miles an hour, you can easily run into a tree or

another person, sending you both to the hospital. Skiers say that a fast run down the mountain is a lot like flying, but you don't have all those trees, boulders, and people to dodge up in the sky.

ACTIVITY 25.5 | WORKING ONLINE: *Using Pronouns in Context*

Watch the preview for the movie *Who Killed the Electric Car?* at http://www.sonyclassics.com/whokilledtheelectriccar/. After viewing the preview, write a paragraph telling a friend why you would or wouldn't be interested in seeing the film, using specific examples from the preview. In your first draft, avoid all pronouns. Then write a revision, substituting pronouns to avoid repetition but being certain not to introduce confusion. ●

ACTIVITY 25.6 | WORKING ONLINE: *Pronoun Review*

Take the Chapter 25 Review Quiz at www.mhhe.com/brannan.

Chapter Summary

1. Pronouns stand in the place of nouns and help create variety in our work.

2. Pronouns can be classified as one or more of the following types: personal, indefinite, relative, interrogative, demonstrative, reflexive and intensive, reciprocal, and possessive.

3. Pronouns must be clearly linked to their antecedents, and they must agree with them in number.

4. Most difficulties with pronoun/antecedent agreement fall into one of these categories: indefinite pronouns, collective nouns, or compound antecedents.

5. Pronouns can be in the subjective, objective, or possessive case.

6. Pronoun case often causes problems in three categories: compounds, comparisons, and *who/whom.*

7. One common pronoun error is shifting (without good reason) from the first-person *I* or second-person *you* to the third-person *they.*

Adjectives and Adverbs

Words That Describe

26

[*Adjectives and adverbs are describing words that add color and interest to our work. Look closely at the image of the elephant and baboon. How can you capture this scene in words? In a paragraph describe this picture for a friend who would not be able to see it. Try to bring it to life. You can name objects specifically (such as "tusks" or "earth") and then add color details. What sensory details might you include (sight, sound, touch, taste, smell)?*]

KEY TOPICS

- Introducing adjectives and related word groups
- Introducing adverbs and related word groups
- Using comparative and superlative forms
- Avoiding overuse of modifiers
- Avoiding dangling and misplaced modifiers

What Are We Trying to Achieve and Why?

One of the ways that we add information to sentences is by using **adjectives** and **adverbs,** words that *describe* or *modify.* Phrases and clauses can also be **modifiers,** functioning as adjectives and adverbs.

Adjectives tell us about *nouns* and *pronouns:* "the *red* pants." **Adverbs** tell us about *verbs, adjectives,* and other *adverbs:* "She sings *melodiously.*" These modifiers are usually located close to the word they tell about, although adverbs in particular may be some distance from the word. The problems most likely to arise with adjectives and adverbs involve choosing the right forms, using them selectively, and attaching them clearly to the words they describe.

Introducing Adjectives and Related Word Groups

Adjectives describe nouns and pronouns, telling of people and things—how many; what kind, color, shape, size, texture, or age; and so on. Here are two examples:

In English, adjectives do not agree in number or gender with the words they modify.

MODIFYING A NOUN   A *tall* sycamore tree stands in my yard. (tells size)

MODIFYING A PRONOUN   I'd like the *new* one. (tells which one)

Phrases and clauses also can function as adjectives, as in the following examples:

PHRASE   A sycamore tree *with an eagle's nest* stands in my yard. (gives further description)

CLAUSE   The sycamore tree *that fell on my house last night* was 110 years old. (tells which one)

Notice from the four sentences above that adjectives come before the noun they modify, whereas adjective phrases and adjective clauses follow the noun. In addition to coming before nouns, adjectives can follow linking verbs (*be, seem, feel,* and so on), as in these examples:

English adjectives usually come before the nouns they modify.

A. Louis feels *sick.*

B. He is *kind.*

Multiple adjectives have a preferred order to follow, according to the category the word fits into:

The Preferred Order for Adjectives

1. **Determiners:** *this, these, that, the, a, an, some, many, my, our, your, all, both, each, several, one, two*

2. **Judgment:** *unusual, interesting, impressive, ugly, beautiful, inspiring, hopeful, smart, funny*

3. **Size:** *large, massive, small, tiny, heavy, light, tall, short*

4. **Shape:** *round, square, rectangular, wide, deep, thin, slim, fat*

5. **Age:** *young, adolescent, teenage, middle-aged, old, ancient*

6. **Color:** *white, black, blue, red, yellow, green*

7. **Adjectives derived from proper nouns:** *American, Buddhist, Kansan, Parisian, Gothic*

8. **Material:** *wood, plastic, cloth, paper, cardboard, metal, stone, clay, glass, ceramic*

Practice using adjectives in the correct order at www. mhhe.com/brannan.

When adjectives add meaning to the ones that precede them, their effect is **cumulative,** and no comma is needed to separate them (*the beautiful tall ancient redwoods*). Adjectives that modify or describe equally are said to be **coordinate** and *do* require a comma between them (*happy, hard-working firefighter*).

Introducing Adverbs and Related Word Groups

Adverbs cannot appear between a verb and its direct object.

Adverbs describe verbs, adjectives, and other adverbs, telling *when, where, why, how,* and *to what degree or extent* something was done. Here are some examples:

MODIFYING A VERB	Matt *quietly* entered the room. (tells how)
MODIFYING AN ADJECTIVE	Matt can be an *exceedingly* quiet man. (tells to what extent)
MODIFYING AN ADVERB	Matt *very* quietly entered the room. (tells to what degree)

As with adjectives, phrases and clauses also can function as adverbs:

PHRASE	*On his tiptoes* Matt entered the room. (tells how)
CLAUSE	*When everyone was sleeping,* Matt entered the room. (tells when)

Many adverbs are formed by adding *-ly* to the end of an adjective.

Adverbs that modify verbs and adverb phrases and clauses often allow us a great deal of freedom with placement. For example, we could recast the sentences above in several ways, including these:

A. Matt entered the room *quietly.* (tells how)

B. Matt entered the room *on his tiptoes.* (tells how)

C. Matt entered the room *when everyone was sleeping.* (tells when)

Knowing how a word *functions* is the best way to determine what part of speech it is.

One way to identify adverbs is to look for the *-ly* ending often attached to adjectives to form adverbs (*bad/badly, happy/happily, sweet/sweetly,* and so on). However, this method is not foolproof because many adverbs do not have the *-ly* ending (*soon, too, very, already, often, quite, then, always, there,* and so on).

Using Comparative and Superlative Forms

Adjectives and adverbs often compare two or more things. Those that compare two things use an *-er* ending or the words *more* and *less,* forms known as **comparatives.** Those that compare three or more things use *-est* or *most* and *least,* forms known as **superlatives.** Here are some examples:

Adjective	Comparative	Superlative
strong	stronger, less strong	strongest, least strong
beautiful	more beautiful, least beautiful	most beautiful, least beautiful
Adverb	**Comparative**	**Superlative**
soon	sooner, less soon	soonest, least soon
easily	more easily, less easily	most easily, least easily

A. Sam is *stronger* than Nick, but Ethan is the *strongest* of all.

B. Sam lifted the weights *more easily* than Nick did, but Ethan lifted them the *most easily* of all.

Often, as in these examples, one-syllable adjectives and adverbs take the *-er/-est* endings and those with two or more syllables appear with *more/most*.

Irregular adjectives and adverbs do not follow the pattern and so must be memorized.

COMMON IRREGULAR ADJECTIVES AND ADVERBS

good, well	better	best
bad, badly	worse	worst
far	farther, further	farthest, furthest

Even apart from their comparative and superlative forms, the words *good* and *well* can cause confusion. Keep in mind that *good* is always an adjective, whereas *well* is often an adverb but sometimes an adjective, as in the following sentences:

A. Claire has a *good* dog.

B. Claire's dog performs *well*.

C. Claire's dog does not feel *well*.

In sentence A, *good* describes the noun *dog*; it is an adjective. In sentence B, *well* describes the verb *perform*, which makes it an adverb. Sentence C has the linking verb *feel*, which connects *well* to *dog*, so *well* in this sentence is an adjective. As an adjective, *well* generally means "healthy, not sick."

The words *bad* and *badly* can also be confusing. Notice the following usages:

A. Puffy was a *bad* cat today.

B. Puffy behaved *badly* today.

C. Puffy felt *bad* today.

Bad is always an adjective, describing nouns (*cat*) and occurring before a noun, as in sentence A, or after a linking verb, as in sentence C. *Badly* is always an adverb, describing verbs—*behaved* in sentence B.

Avoiding Overuse of Modifiers

As helpful as adjectives and adverbs can be in building images and explaining things, we sometimes overuse them. Common culprits include adverbs like *very, really, extremely, awfully,* and *incredibly*. Occasionally these intensifiers are appropriate, but typically three out of four can be cut and the words they describe replaced with more specific words. For example, compare the following sentences:

A. The mercury was *very* high on that *extremely* hot, *awfully* uncomfortable day, making me feel *incredibly* bad.

B. The mercury topped 100 degrees on that blistering day, making me miserable.

Sentence B has more force; it avoids the mushy intensifying adverbs of sentence A.

Another common mistake in early drafts is cramming too many modifiers into one sentence, often simply stacking them in front of a word. Compare the following sentences:

A. A foul-tempered, cruel, 300-pound, gray-haired tyrant mother, whose breath constantly reeked of garlic and coffee, Carleta terrorized me as a child.

B. A foul-tempered, cruel, gray-haired tyrant, my mother terrorized me as a child. Carleta weighed 300 pounds, and her breath constantly reeked of garlic and coffee.

Sentence A stacks too many adjectives in front of the noun *mother*. Sentence B solves the problem by creating two sentences and redistributing the modifiers. Sometimes you will choose to simply cut modifiers; other times you will weave them into other sentences.

ACTIVITY 26.1 *Correcting Problems with Adjectives and Adverbs*

Correct the errors in the following sentences. If the wrong modifier is used, cross it out and write the correct one in the space provided. If too many modifiers are used, just cross out the ones you don't think are needed.

EXAMPLE: Though the room was noisy, he said ~~quiet~~, "My price is now 5,000 dollars." *quietly*

1. When he saw his dad's truck in the driveway, Peter ran home quick. _____

2. We go to Sandstone regular to see outdoor concerts. _____

3. With a 103-degree temperature and upset stomach, Aaron feels badly today. _____

4. Jennifer passed the soccer ball direct to her teammate who scored the winning goal. _____

5. This really extremely very not nice guy kept bothering me at a party that was already awfully, really incredibly boring. _____

6. Trisha Yearwood sang that last song beautiful. _____

7. To make it to state competition, the team will have to play good all season. _____

8. Six feet six, broad-shouldered, potbellied, gray-haired and partly bald, my coach would glare at me with his cold angry, squinting blue eyes and say, "You're either lazy or stupid!" _____

9. Josh swore that if they came for him he would not go quiet to jail. _____

10. Handle the crystal careful, or you will break it. _____

Avoiding Dangling and Misplaced Modifiers

Another problem arises when modifiers are not clearly linked to the word they describe. When a modifier (single word or word group) occurs at the beginning of a sentence, it should describe the noun that follows. If it doesn't describe that noun, it is a **dangling modifier.** Here are several examples:

A. After finishing the meal, my eyelids grew heavy, and I dozed off.

B. Worn to a frazzle, the final exam had sucked out the last of Amy's energy.

C. To make it to the peak, the weather would need to favor the climbers.

D. As a civilian, his family had always come first.

Participial phrases are especially prone to dangling.

As you can see, each sentence begins with a modifier that does not describe the noun that follows it. For example, in sentence A, *after finishing the meal* doesn't describe *eyelids*; it's obviously meant to describe *I*, later in the sentence. You can correct a dangling modifier by inserting a subject into the modifier or placing the noun it is intended to describe directly after it, as in the following examples:

A. After I <u>finished</u> the meal, my eyelids grew heavy, and I dozed off. OR
   After finishing the meal, I felt my eyelids grow heavy, and I dozed off.

B. <u>Amy</u> <u>was</u> worn to a frazzle, the final exam having sucked out the last of her energy. OR
   Worn to a frazzle, Amy felt that the final exam had sucked out the last of her energy.

Misplaced modifiers also appear to modify a word other than the one they are intended to modify, as in the following examples:

A. John called to the beagle in his slippers.

B. Alicia put the calendar on her office wall covered with nature pictures.

C. The machinist drilled a hole in a piece of metal that was a half inch in diameter.

D. We saw a herd of cows from our car grazing in a harvested wheat field.

E. Bill only drank a glass of Pepsi. (meaning he did nothing but drink it)

To correct the misplaced modifier, you need to move it closer to the word it should describe, sometimes adding a word or two:

A. In his slippers *John* called to the beagle.

B. Alicia put the *calendar* covered with nature pictures on her office wall.

C. The machinist drilled a *hole* that was a half inch in diameter in a piece of metal.

D. From our car we saw a *herd* of cows grazing in a harvested wheat field.

E. Bill drank only a *glass* of Pepsi. (meaning just one, and no more)

| **ACTIVITY 26.2** | WORKING TOGETHER: *Correcting Dangling and Misplaced Modifiers* |

Work in pairs to rewrite the following sentences, adding whatever words might be needed to correct the dangling and misplaced modifiers. Before starting to edit, read each sentence aloud and determine where the confusion lies. Which confused meaning do you and your partner find the most humorous?

EXAMPLE: Trying his best to make the team, Isaac's sweat-soaked shirt was proof of his effort.

Revised: *Isaac was trying his best to make the team, and his sweat-soaked shirt was proof of his effort.*

1. Rain soaked the highway that was pouring from the sky.

   _____

   _____

2. Banging two pans together to wake him up, Tim groaned as his mother clanged them together once again.

   _____

   _____

3. To vote in national elections, polling booths should be open until midnight.

_____

_____

4. I felt sorry for the kitten at the pet store meowing in its cage.

_____

_____

5. At 73, Maria watched her grandfather run in the Boston Marathon.

_____

_____

6. Walking through the produce section, the peaches looked delicious.

_____

_____

7. I read about an insect in a magazine that is born, mates, and dies in one day.

_____

_____

8. Vito rode on the subway wearing only shorts and a T-shirt.

_____

_____

9. Miriam learned tae kwon do to defend herself at her community center.

_____

_____

10. Emily went to the Halloween party at Lucy's house dressed like a witch.

_____

_____

ACTIVITY 26.3 WORKING ONLINE: *Describing Your College's Website*

Spend 10–15 minutes exploring your college's website. Now write a paragraph describing your impression of it. How well does it describe your school, and how easy was it to use? What kinds of images does it show? Use at least ten adjectives and five adverbs in your response.

ACTIVITY 26.4 WORKING ONLINE: *Adjective and Adverb Review*

Take the Chapter 26 Review Quiz at www.mhhe.com/brannan.

Chapter Summary

1. Adjectives describe nouns and pronouns, telling *how many*, *which*, or *what kind*.

2. *Adverbs* describe verbs, adjectives, and other adverbs, telling *when*, *where*, *why*, *how*, and *to what degree or extent* something was done.

3. The comparative form of adjectives and adverbs compares two or more things using an *-er* ending or the words *more* and *less*.

4. The superlative form of adjectives and adverbs compares three or more things using *-est* or *most* and *least*.

5. There are several common irregular adjective and adverb forms that are best handled through memorizing: *good*, *well*, *bad*, *little*, *many*, and *far*.

6. Be careful not to stack too many modifiers before a noun.

7. Dangling and misplaced modifiers occur when single words and word groups are not positioned closely enough to the word they mean to describe.

Commas, Other Punctuation Marks, and Mechanics

27

[*As the director of a play or movie organizes the flow of action and helps make sense of the story being presented, so does punctuation organize and control the flow of our ideas on paper. In a paragraph, summarize a movie or play that you have seen recently; however, leave out all punctuation and make all letters lowercase. Trade paragraphs with a classmate to see if you can understand each other's thoughts. Now edit the other student's paragraph, placing punctuation and dividing sentences where you think they should be separated. What value do you see in punctuation?*]

KEY TOPICS

What Are We Trying to Achieve and Why?

After you have labored to gather, organize, and express your ideas, you have one final task as a writer: to make sure that your grammar, spelling, and punctuation are correct and support your hard work. This chapter focuses on punctuation and mechanics, with special attention devoted to commas. Punctuation is essential for sorting our ideas into easily understood units of thought. Notice how changes in punctuation from passage A to passage B dramatically change the meaning.

A. Dear John:

I want a man who knows what love is all about. You are generous, kind, and thoughtful. People who are not like you admit to being useless and inferior. You have ruined me for other men. I yearn for you. I have no feelings whatsoever when we're apart. I can be forever happy. Will you let me be yours?

Susan

B. Dear John:

I want a man who knows what love is. All about you are generous, kind, and thoughtful—people who are not like you. Admit to being useless and inferior. You have ruined me. For other men I yearn. For you I have no feelings whatsoever. When we're apart, I can be forever happy. Will you let me be?

Yours,
Susan

Your work is not likely to shift meaning this abruptly when you misuse a few commas, but you *are* likely to confuse or lose readers if you let punctuation and other mechanical problems pile up. Because commas typically cause the most concern, we will focus on them first.

Commas

Commas are primarily used to separate and enclose words or sentence parts. Because we use them so often, writers have developed a system for placing commas in an orderly way to help sort out ideas. This system of "rules" is not foolproof or even altogether logical, but it works reasonably well, and even professional writers adhere to it most of the time. Comma usage conventions are designed not to frustrate and confuse writers but to serve their needs. There *is* a controlling logic that works in punctuating by convention rather than by ear. Remember that writing is not simply transcribed speech: It is a more complex use of language that requires careful revision and editing. So the pause-and-punctuate method of placing commas will help a writer only about half the time. Fifty percent is not an average that most of us are happy with.

Learning to punctuate accurately depends on knowledge of sentence parts, knowledge you developed in working on Chapter 21. Once you can separate a main clause from a subordinate clause and are familiar with the different kinds of phrases, comma usage will make sense to you, at least most of the time. If you learn the three primary comma categories and the few secondary uses covered in this chapter, you will greatly reduce any problems you have had with comma usage.

The Big Three Comma Categories

Commas have three main uses:

> ## THE BIG THREE COMMA CATEGORIES
>
> 1. To separate a main clause from an introductory word or word groups
> 2. To enclose or separate a nonessential word or word groups that come within or after a main clause
> 3. To separate two main clauses

Memorize the Big Three comma categories.

To put commas in the right place in a sentence, first look for the main clause or main clauses in the sentence. Once you locate a main clause, look for a word or word groups that come *before, within,* or *after* it. Failure to use commas to enclose or separate these words accounts for perhaps half of all comma errors.

The following sentence, which has two main clauses, illustrates punctuating a sentence with commas that serve all three functions:

> Smiling in delight,[1] Miguel,[2] a 2-year-old,[2] stopped to touch a rose,[3] and his father watched closely,[4] trying to keep him away from the thorns.

In this sentence:

1. The first comma sets off an introductory phrase.
2. The next two enclose the nonessential words *a 2-year-old.*
3. The next comma, before the conjunction *and*, separates the two main clauses.
4. The final comma separates the second main clause from the nonessential phrase that follows it.

1-Commas That Separate Introductory Words and Word Groups

We often begin sentences with an introductory word, phrase, or subordinate clause, which should be separated from the main clause with a comma. The following lists show the specific kinds of structures involved:

Words

CONJUNCTIVE ADVERB	*However*, I hope to make it to the bank before it closes. (pp. 511–512)
ADVERB	*Unfortunately*, Jen doesn't have enough money to buy that iPhone. (Chapter 26)
TRANSITIONAL WORD	*Next*, the cat tried to claw the new curtains. (pp. 54–56)
PRESENT PARTICIPLE	*Smiling*, Sal cradled his new catcher's mitt. (pp. 465–466)
PAST PARTICIPLE	*Excited*, Emma ran to meet her mother. (pp. 467–468)
ADVERB	*Yes*, I would love to go to the dance with you.
INTERJECTION	Well, someone must be responsible.

Phrases

PREPOSITIONAL PHRASES	*Near the fence in the backyard*, you will find the lawn mower. (pp. 516–517)
PRESENT PARTICIPIAL PHRASE	*Diving for the football*, Ethan snatched it from the air with one hand. (pp. 517–518)

English Review Note

Be careful not to use the word *although* (a subordinating conjunction) in place of *however.*

HINT

Common conjunctive adverbs include *nevertheless, therefore, in fact,* and *consequently.* Common transitional words include *finally, in addition, first, last, also, for example, of course, in other words, on the other hand,* and *as a result.*

PAST PARTICIPIAL PHRASE	*Thrilled by the sight of presents,* Amaya <u>ran</u> to meet her mother. (pp. 518–519)
PRESENT ABSOLUTE PHRASE	*The car running on fumes,* Latashia <u>coasted</u> into her driveway. (pp. 468–469)
PAST ABSOLUTE PHRASE	*His boat covered with a tarp,* Christopher <u>felt</u> it would survive the hailstorm. (pp. 468–469)
INFINITIVE PHRASE	*To play lead guitar in the band,* Tanya <u>knew</u> that she would need to practice hard. (p. 517)
APPOSITIVE PHRASE	*An athlete with much experience,* Madison <u>could see</u> that the game was headed for disaster. (p. 519)

Clauses

ADVERB CLAUSE	*Because fall had arrived in full force,* Michael <u>was raking</u> his twentieth bag of leaves.

To recognize adverb clauses, keep in mind that they are introduced by sub-ordinating conjunctions, common examples of which include *because, if, since, when, after, until, while, as, although, before,* and *so that.*

Notice in all these examples that the introductory words add meaning to the main clause, in effect introducing the main idea of the sentence. Another way to decide if you need a comma in the front part of your sentence is to find the subject of the main clause and count the words that precede it. If there are five or more words in front of it, you probably need a comma.

Introductory words or word groups can occur before the second main clause in a compound or compound–complex sentence. When you punctuate these sentences, treat the second main clause as if it were the beginning of the sentence, by separating with a comma the word or word group that intro-duces it:

A. I have to work this weekend, and *even though I have a math test on Monday,* I probably won't study much for it.

B. Brianna got a terrible sunburn, but *having spent most of the afternoon under an umbrella,* I was only pink.

Sentence A has an introductory adverb clause after the *and.* Because this adverb clause comes before a main clause, a comma is required after *Monday.* Sentence B is another two-part sentence, this one with a participial phrase after the *but.* Therefore, a comma is needed after *umbrella.*

Writers will often omit a comma if a sentence begins with a short preposi-tional phrase or adverb clause.

A. *In this house* both parents are the bosses.

B. *If we go* we will probably have fun.

However, including the comma in such cases is never incorrect.

See p. 512 for more examples of subordinating conjunctions.

If you have five or more words before a main clause, use a comma to set them off. If you have a two-part sentence, punctuate the second half as if it were the first.

For more on phrases and clauses (including how to tell main from subordinate clauses), see Chapter 21.

ACTIVITY 27.1 *Commas after Introductory Word Groups*

In the following sentences, find the main clause and underline the <u>verb</u> twice and the <u>subject</u> once. Now use a comma to set off introductory word groups. If a sentence is correct, write "C" after it.

EXAMPLE: If we get this job done we can meet everyone at the party.

Corrected: If we get this job done, <u>we</u> <u>can meet</u> everyone at the party.

1. When we get to the top of the hill we can see all of Monterey Bay.

2. Slipping on a slice of tomato Darin fell flat on his back.

3. To have fun at the lake a person needs only sunblock and a towel.

4. In the backseat you will find the new John Mayer CD.

5. Of the cell phones on the warning list the Ericsson T28 World produces the highest level of radiation.

6. His lungs eaten away by cancer the last Marlboro Man dropped from the saddle today.

7. Nevertheless RU 486, the abortion pill, has arrived in the United States.

8. Frightened by a legal system that has finally decided to care deadbeat dads are beginning to pay their child support.

9. Climbing to the fifth floor of her apartment was a daily ordeal for Kendra.

10. On separate paper, write three sentences that use an introductory word group set off with a comma; underline the <u>verb</u> of the main clause twice and the <u>subject</u> once.

2-Commas That Set Off Nonessential Words and Word Groups

The second major reason for using commas is to set off a **nonessential** word and word groups within or at the end of main clauses. *Nonessential* means that the words are not needed to complete the meaning of the sentence. If the word or word groups are cut, the main idea is still clear. Let's compare nonessential and essential word groups:

ESSENTIAL   The Dodge Caravan *that is leaking gasoline* is mine.

NONESSENTIAL   Dodge Caravans, *which are roomy family vehicles*, have hatchback doors.

In the first sentence, we need the *that* clause to identify which Dodge Caravan. In the second sentence, the *which* clause simply adds a comment, so the clause is set off with a comma.

Which clauses frequently signal nonessential material, and when they do, they must be set off with commas. *That* clauses signal essential material and so do not take commas. With *who,* both patterns are common:

ESSENTIAL   A cyclist *who has survived cancer* might work even harder at his sport.

NONESSENTIAL   Lance Armstrong, *who has survived cancer*, may be the world's best cyclist.

In the first sentence, the *who* clause identifies which cyclist might work harder; not all cyclists, but perhaps those who have survived cancer. The second sentence uses a proper noun, *Lance Armstrong*, which identifies the athlete beyond question. Therefore, the *who* clause that follows is nonessential and so uses commas.

We often use nonessential word groups to enrich writing. However, when doing so, we need to signal with commas that the material is of secondary importance. Following, you will see examples of nonessential single words, phrases, and clauses.

Words

CONJUNCTIVE ADVERB	I hope, *however*, to make it to the bank before it closes.
ADVERB	Jen, *unfortunately*, doesn't have enough money to buy that computer.
TRANSITIONAL WORD	The cat, *next*, decided to claw the new curtains.
PRESENT PARTICIPLE	Sal, *smiling*, cradled his new catcher's mitt.
PAST PARTICIPLE	Emma, *excited*, ran to meet her mother.

Phrases

PRESENT PARTICIPIAL PHRASE	Ethan, *diving for the football*, snatched it from the air with one hand.
PAST PARTICIPIAL PHRASE	Amaya, *excited by the sight of presents*, ran to meet her mother.
PRESENT ABSOLUTE PHRASE	Latashia coasted into her driveway, *the car running on fumes.*
PAST ABSOLUTE PHRASE	Christopher, *his boat covered with a tarp*, felt it would survive the hailstorm.
INFINITIVE PHRASE	Tanya knew that, *to play lead guitar in the band*, she would need to practice hard.
APPOSITIVE PHRASE	Madison, *an athlete with much experience*, could see that the game was headed for disaster.

> **HINT**
>
> Notice that the introductory word groups from the previous comma category still require commas when shifted into the main clauses.

We sometimes misuse commas because we confuse essential and nonessential participial phrases within or at the end of sentences. Compare the participial phrases that end the following two sentences:

A. We listened to the cottonwood leaves *rustling in the wind.*

B. We walked up the hill, *taking great pleasure in the sunny day.*

The present participial phrase in sentence A is essential, telling which cottonwood leaves the people listened to. We could rewrite it as an essential adjective clause, "*that were* rustling in the wind." The phrase in sentence B, in contrast, is nonessential, merely adding a comment about the people. Notice that, for this reason, we could easily shift the phrase in sentence B to the beginning of the sentence, whereas the phrase in sentence A must occur next to *leaves*, the word it describes. Therefore, the phrase in sentence B is set off with a comma, but the phrase in sentence A is not.

> **HINT**
>
> If we tried to shift the phrase *rustling in the wind* to the beginning of the sentence, we would have a dangling modifier; see pp. 582–584.

Clauses

ADJECTIVE CLAUSE	Dmitri stayed at the Marriott Hotel, *which is one of the finest in the city.*
ADJECTIVE CLAUSE	Slobodan Milosevic, *who contributed to the deaths of thousands*, is no longer in power in the former Yugoslavia.

In both of these sentences, we know the adjective clauses are nonessential, because they follow proper nouns. Proper nouns themselves identify the person or thing, so what follows must be nonessential commentary.

The same logic applies to an adjective clause that begins with the word *where*. Note that it can be either essential or nonessential, as in the following examples:

A. Gary was not as popular in Topeka as he is in the city *where he now lives.*

B. Gary was not as popular in Topeka as he is in Dallas, *where he moved last fall.*

In sentence A, the *where* clause completes the meaning of the main clause, telling which city he is now popular in. Sentence B uses the proper noun *Dallas,* so the *where* clause becomes nonessential and is set off with a comma.

ACTIVITY 27.2 *Commas with Nonessential Word Groups*

In the following sentences, find the main clause and underline the <u>verb</u> twice and the <u>subject</u> once. Now use commas to set off nonessential word groups within and at the end of the main clauses. If a sentence is correct, write "C" after it.

EXAMPLE: **Kelsey chased after the soccer ball running at full speed.**

Corrected: **Kelsey chased after the soccer ball, running at full speed.**

1. The motorcycle that is blowing oily smoke needs a ring job.
2. *Smithsonian* magazine which has Al Gore on its board of regents is filled with interesting articles.
3. Dustin reacting quickly managed to save the child from falling overboard.
4. Eboni exhausted dragged herself into the shower at 6:30 a.m.
5. The wind which had blown continuously for three days whipped the edge of the flag to ragged tatters.
6. The boxer hoping desperately for an opportunity to attack continued to backpedal around the ring.
7. At midnight a time known as the "witching hour" Halloween parties reach their height.
8. Abby's pediatrician who looked like she had bad news walked slowly toward us.
9. I noticed the purple bruise developing under his left eye.
10. On separate paper, write three of your own sentences that use nonessential word groups; underline the <u>verb</u> of the main clause twice and the <u>subject</u> once.

HINT

Memorizing *and/but* will help you remember to edit for commas in two-part sentences.

3-Commas That Separate Main Clauses

The last major reason for using commas is to separate main clauses within compound and compound–complex sentences—sentences that use a coordinating conjunction (*and, but, or, so, yet, nor, for*) to join two main clauses. Here are some examples:

A. Five-year-old Addie wanted to climb the sweet gum tree in her backyard, *and* her mother wanted to stop her.

B. Jacob wanted to explain to his girlfriend what he was doing at the movies with another woman, *but* he couldn't think of a convincing excuse.

C. You can pay me now, *or* you can pay me later.

D. Michelle hoped to run in the Boston Marathon, *so* she trained all year.

E. New Orleans evacuated in the face of Hurricane Gustav, *yet* nature spared this city still recovering from the ravages of Katrina.

Notice that, with two main clauses, a subject and verb appear on each side of the coordinating conjunction. Remember that coordinating conjunctions are used between words and phrases as well as clauses. If you tried to put a comma before every coordinating conjunction, you would have a mess. Consider the following sentence:

NO COMMA NEEDED   The willow trees <u>were blowing</u> in the wind *and* <u>losing</u> leaves and soon <u>would be</u> bare.

This sentence has only one main clause with a three-part verb, *were blowing, losing,* and *would be.* The words after *and* could not stand alone as a separate sentence. Use a comma before a coordinating conjunction only when the material before and after could be divided into two separate sentences, each ending with a period.

Another common error is using an unneeded comma before the subordinating conjunction *so that* when the *that* has been dropped, as in the following example:

NO COMMA NEEDED   Cinderella's cruel stepmother locked her in a room *so* [that] one of the stepmother's daughters might wed Prince Charming.

This *so* is not a coordinating conjunction; it is a subordinating conjunction that comes before an essential adverb clause.

When the main clauses are only a few words long, some writers omit the comma, as in the following example:

This deal stinks and you do too.

However, a comma between main clauses connected by a coordinating conjunction is never incorrect.

ACTIVITY 27.3 *Commas to Divide Compound Sentences*

In the following sentences, find the main clauses, and in each underline the <u>verb</u> twice and <u>subject</u> once. Now put commas before the coordinating conjunctions wherever needed. If a sentence is correct, write "C" after it.

EXAMPLE: Nina asked her grandfather a question but he did not hear her.

Corrected: Nina <u>asked</u> her grandfather a question, but he <u>did</u> not <u>hear</u> her.

1. The California sea otter and the Chinese panda are endangered species.
2. Sending large robots to distant planets is too expensive but sending miniature ones is not.
3. Suchin tried for years to play piano yet she could not master the bass line.
4. Cell phones in college classrooms can be viewed as a blessing for those who need them or a curse for those who are startled by the ring tones.
5. The principal groaned in the midst of his nightmare and drifted back into dreams of being chased through the halls by students.
6. Athletes should maintain at least a C average or they should be benched until they raise their grades.
7. At first Cecelia favored the younger candidate for town council but then she discovered his real priorities.

Remember that *-ing* words used as nouns (called gerunds) can be sentence subjects.

8. Andy was on his way to Madison Middle School and he fervently hoped that Max, the class bully, would be absent again.

9. Tess wanted to win the lottery so she could quit work at the GM plant.

10. On separate paper, write three of your own compound sentences, underlining the <u>verbs</u> twice and the <u>subjects</u> once.

Secondary Comma Categories

While the Big Three comma categories account for most comma errors, several other structures that call for commas can also cause some confusion.

Items in a Series

When three or more words or word groups are listed in a row, a comma should follow each item except the last in the series:

NOUNS	I'm going to Home Depot to buy some lumber, paving stones, and cement.
VERB PHRASES	We ran for the bus stop, missed the bus, and then chased it all the way to the next stop.
MAIN CLAUSES	Harry did the research, Tenzin organized all the sources, and Rashonda wrote most of the first draft.

Coordinate Adjectives

When two or more **coordinate,** or equal, **adjectives** precede a noun (or pronoun), commas should be used between the adjectives:

It was a *long, hard* hike to get to the top of the mountain.

In this sentence, *long* and *hard* modify *hike* equally. We could also use the word *and* in place of the comma, and we could reverse the two adjectives, saying "a hard, long hike."

This sentence, in contrast, uses **cumulative adjectives:**

Two tired old men sat on a park bench.

The adjectives *two tired old* do not describe the noun *men* equally. Instead, each adjective adds meaning to the others: These are old men who are tired, and there are two of them. Notice that we could neither insert *and* between the words nor reverse them.

Adjectives fall into various categories (adjectives of number, judgment, size, shape, age, color, location, and material). Adjectives from the same category occurring together are coordinate and use commas; adjectives from different categories are cumulative and do not use commas.

Another place *not* to use a comma is directly before or between two-word nouns, as in the following sentence:

Melanie changed the *filthy* <u>furnace filter</u>.

Because *furnace filter* is a single unit, no comma is needed.

Contrasting Expressions

We often contrast ideas using *not*, as in this sentence:

Ashaki, not Tony, deserves the promotion.

The phrase beginning with *not* is nonessential material and so is set off with commas.

Misleading Expressions

If a sentence might be misinterpreted without a comma, either insert a comma or restructure the sentence:

MISLEADING	Cody became angry when his opponent cheated and complained.
COMMA ADDED	Cody became angry when his opponent cheated, and complained.
RESTRUCTURED	When his opponent cheated, Cody became angry and complained.

Numbers, Addresses, Place Names, Dates, and Direct Address

When using numbers, addresses, place names, dates, and direct address, follow the conventions of standard comma placement:

- **Numbers:** 3,985,041
- **Addresses:** "Joanne lives at 4593 Connell Lane, Overland Park, Kansas."
- **Place names:** "Most of my relatives live in Forth Worth, Texas."
- **Dates:** "On October 13, 2006, the dreaded Friday the 13th appeared on the calendar."
- **Direct address:** "Stefanie, would you please close the window?"

ACTIVITY 27.4 *Commas with Secondary Categories*

Put commas where needed in the following sentences. If the sentence is correct, write "C" after it.

EXAMPLE: Everyone I know is going on to college trade school or the service.

Corrected: Everyone I know is going on to college, trade school, or the service.

1. Five young trick-or-treating children came jostling up to the front door.
2. Wallace stood on shaky weak legs that would carry him no farther.
3. Estefana wanted to go to Mardi Gras not the mountains.
4. The wedding will be on May 14 2010 at the Episcopal church at 4966 Birch Mission Kansas.
5. The overworked Canon BubbleJet printer began to run out of ink.
6. Canoeing on Ozark rivers rafting on the Colorado River and kayaking in the ocean are three of Omar's favorite pastimes.
7. "Brianna I hope you are done with your homework," said her mother.
8. At sixteen teenagers are finally able to drive.
9. Alison and her friends decided not to go to the show after all.
10. Anthony has the stereo cranked full blast his sister is channel surfing and little Amy is banging away on the piano—both parents have surrendered, retreating to the porch for a few moments of quiet.

Avoiding Unnecessary Commas

Even if you have practiced the main rules for comma usage, you will sometimes use commas when you shouldn't. Below are four common errors to guard against.

Separating Subject from Verb or Object

Do not put a comma between the subject and the verb or the verb and its object, unless you are using commas to enclose nonessential word groups—for example, "Sunshine, my pet canary, flew away." Notice these incorrectly punctuated sentences:

<table>
<tr><td>INCORRECTLY PUNCTUATED SENTENCES</td><td>A.</td><td>All of Andy's friends, went to see him in the hospital. (subject separated from verb)</td></tr>
<tr><td></td><td>B.</td><td>How the child managed to force his head through the bars, was a mystery to everyone. (subject separated from verb)</td></tr>
<tr><td></td><td>C.</td><td>We finally won, an important away game. (verb separated from object)</td></tr>
<tr><td></td><td>D.</td><td>All day long Myndi hoped, that she had turned the oven off before she left the house. (verb separated from object)</td></tr>
</table>

Separating Compound Constructions

As discussed earlier, commas are used before coordinating conjunctions (*and, but, or, so, yet, for, nor*) only when these link two main clauses (stand-alone sentences). Before using a comma with a coordinating conjunction, make sure a subject and a verb appear on *both* sides of the conjunction.

<table>
<tr><td>INCORRECTLY PUNCTUATED SENTENCES</td><td>A.</td><td>Tara thought that she would see Bruce Springsteen in concert at Sandstone, but found out that he had canceled the tour. (compound verb, no subject after but)</td></tr>
<tr><td></td><td>B.</td><td>T. E. Lawrence survived many hardships and much combat between the years 1916 and 1918, and died in his home country of England from a motorcycle accident. (compound verb, no subject after and)</td></tr>
<tr><td></td><td>C.</td><td>Some long-overdue recognition from his boss, and the promise of an immediate pay raise helped Raymundo decide to stay at his job. (compound subject, one verb)</td></tr>
<tr><td></td><td>D.</td><td>The skiers rocketed down the icy slopes, and then along the narrow trail that connected Fantasy to Suicide Run. (compound prepositional phrases)</td></tr>
</table>

Separating Essential Word Groups

Readers can be confused if you use commas to set off essential information in a sentence.

<table>
<tr><td>INCORRECTLY PUNCTUATED SENTENCES</td><td>A.</td><td>Stephen King's novel, Salem's Lot, has several frightening vampire scenes. (Essential appositive: King has many novels, not just one, so the commas in this sentence are misleading.)</td></tr>
<tr><td></td><td>B.</td><td>The motorcycle, that has no mufflers, wakes everyone in the neighborhood. (Essential adjective clause: The clause that has no mufflers is needed to point out which motorcycle is waking everyone.)</td></tr>
<tr><td></td><td>C.</td><td>The squirrel, missing half a tail, is the one that keeps getting into my bird feeders. (Essential participial phrase: The phrase</td></tr>
</table>

Remember to use *two* commas to enclose nonessential words and word groups within a sentence.

missing half a tail is needed to tell which squirrel is invading the feeders.)

D. The Chili's restaurant, *in the Oak Park Mall Shopping Center,* is the one running the chicken sandwich special. (Essential prepositional phrase: The phrase *in the Oak Park Mall Shopping Center* is needed to tell which Chili's is running the chicken sandwich special.)

Adverb clauses that begin with *although, though,* and *even though* usually do use a comma even when they follow a main clause because these subordinating conjunctions show concession.

Separating Adverb Clauses after Main Clauses

One more common problem is using a comma after a main clause when the clause is followed by a **subordinate adverb clause** (a clause that begins with a word like *because, if, since, when, until, while,* or *as*), as in the following example:

NOT THIS   We went to the hockey game, *because we like the Blades.*

BUT THIS   We went to the hockey game *because we like the Blades.*

OR THIS   *Because we like the Blades,* we went to the hockey game.

ACTIVITY 27.5   *Removing Unnecessary Commas*

In the following sentences, underline the <u>verb</u> of the *main* clause twice and the subject once. Next, cross out incorrect commas, leaving the correct ones.

EXAMPLE: While Roxanne tried on a new dress, her friend wandered around the department store, and finally decided to buy a new purse.

Corrected: While Roxanne tried on a new dress, her friend wandered around the department store and finally decided to buy a new purse.

Reviewing Chapter 21 will help you locate main clauses and subjects and verbs.

1. Wandering listlessly, across the front yard, Helen felt that she had seen her better days pass her by, and wondered, if there was a chance that she still had a future.

2. Everyone, in the class thought, that singular pronouns like *everyone* should be plural.

3. The Saturn, missing its left rear taillight, was being followed closely by a highway patrol car.

4. The Suzuki Grand Vitara, costing less than several of its competitors, has a zippy, six-cylinder engine.

5. Arturo knew, that he was in trouble, when the conductor stopped practice the second time, and pointed at him.

6. Christian Bale performed well in the movie, *The Dark Knight.*

7. The stillness in the air, and the sudden absence of animal activity made Lesha think that a big storm might be on the way.

8. R. J. could see that quitting his job, and moving out of the city would not help him forget his first lost love.

9. The temperatures will remain in the hundreds, if the Jet Stream does not dip back down into the Midwest.

10. The insane engineer blew the whistle for five nonstop minutes as his train rumbled past the crossing at 3:00 a.m., waking residents, some of whom grumbled into their pillows and then dropped back into restless sleep.

Semicolons are one method for correcting comma splices and run-on sentences.

For more on comma splices and run-ons, see Chapter 23.

Other Punctuation Marks and Mechanics

In addition to commas, writers often use semicolons, colons, dashes, and parentheses to group and separate ideas. These are discussed in the following sections, along with punctuation marks that serve other purposes and additional mechanics issues important to your writing.

Semicolons

If periods are full stops in sentences, bringing the reader to a temporary halt, and commas are half stops, mere split-second pauses, semicolons might be thought of as three-quarter stops, marks midway between the other two. We use semicolons in two ways: to separate main clauses without using a coordinating conjunction (such as *and* or *but*) and to separate word groups that are in a series and contain commas.

Separating Main Clauses
Consider these two sentences:

A. Jakob Dylan is following in his father's footsteps; Bob Dylan is proud of his son.

B. Many books have been written about the Beatles; however, *The Beatles Anthology* was written by the surviving Beatles themselves.

In both A and B, while a period could be used to separate the main clauses, the second main clause is so closely related to the first that the semicolon is a good choice. Notice that sentence B uses a conjunctive adverb, *however,* as well as a semicolon between the two main clauses. The semicolon dividing main clauses is one way to fix a comma splice or run-on sentence.

Separating Word Groups in a Series
Look at this sentence:

> When we go to the Renaissance Festival, we end up *devouring* turkey legs,
>
> sausages, and meat pies; *watching* the jousting, acting, and juggling; and
>
> *shopping* for clothing, art work, and musical instruments.

Each of the three main word groups in this sentence—the phrases beginning with *devouring, watching,* and *shopping*—has within it words that are separated by commas. To avoid confusion, we use semicolons, not commas, to separate the main word groups.

Colons

The colon has three primary uses: to introduce a list (as in this sentence), to separate closely related main clauses, and to introduce an appositive (nonessential describing word or phrase) at the end of a sentence. We also use the colon in the salutation of a business letter (Dear Professor Hastings:) and, sometimes, to introduce quotations (John Smith claimed: "There is no gold in the New World.").

When a colon introduces a list, the material before it must be a grammatically complete sentence. Do not use a colon to introduce a list that is needed to make the sentence grammatically complete, as in this example:

INAPPROPRIATE COLON INTRODUCING A LIST	Maria will bring: potato chips, soda, and pasta salad.
CORRECTED	Maria will bring the following items: potato chips, soda, and pasta salad.

Like a semicolon, a colon can be used to separate closely related main clauses:

SEPARATING MAIN
CLAUSES

Lowell finally <u>understood</u> why his girlfriend would not return his calls: <u>she had decided</u> that they were through.

However, a colon should be used only if the second clause restates or completes the meaning of the first. In the example, it completes the meaning, by telling why.

Note: For grammatically complete sentences following a colon, the first letter may be either capitalized or lowercase.

Colons also introduce appositives:

INTRODUCING
APPOSITIVE

Make your purchases on the basis of two criteria: cost and usefulness.

The sentence ends with an appositive, which describes the noun it follows, *criteria*.

Dashes

The dash is a versatile punctuation mark that can help writers in several ways: to set off a series that begins a sentence, to indicate an abrupt break in thought within a sentence, to enclose items in a series, and to emphasize a word or word group at the end of a sentence. **Note:** A dash [—] is longer than a hyphen [-]. If your word processing program does not have a dash, use two hyphens to create it.

Avoid overusing dashes; try to keep to one or two per page.

BEGINNING SERIES

Three novels, one anthology of short stories, and two how-to books—my summer reading list is complete.

BREAK IN
THOUGHT

I will arrive at the party—if Tony shows up to drive me—around midnight.

ITEMS IN SERIES

Last night Carrie packed all her necessities—clothes, shoes, and toiletries—but forgot to include her hair dryer.

FINAL WORD GROUP
EMPHASIZED

Javier had worked hard at Sprint and deserved some recognition—and a salary increase.

Note the possible confusion without the dashes: "Last night Carrie packed all her necessities, clothes, shoes, and toiletries . . . ."

Parentheses

Writers use parentheses primarily to enclose nonessential material. Since commas can often serve this function, writers usually reserve parentheses for more loosely related material:

There were too many players on the team (and coaches, for that matter).

Avoid overusing parentheses; usually more than once or twice a page is too much.

Quotation Marks

Quotation marks are used primarily to enclose the spoken and written words of others—that is, dialogue and quotations from texts. We also use quotation marks to enclose the titles of short creative works (stories, essays, poems, newspaper and magazine articles, songs, and episodes of television shows) and, occasionally, when referring to a word used as a word (the word "dinosaur" means . . .).

DIALOGUE

"I'll get Jamie out of the bath," said Sarah.

QUOTATION FROM
TEXT

In *The Voyage of the Beagle*, Charles Darwin writes, "In five little packets which I sent him, he has ascertained no less than sixty-seven different organic forms!"

Notice that the comma after *bath* and the exclamation point after *forms* are both placed inside the quotation marks.

Apostrophes

Apostrophes have two main functions: to indicate the omission of letters in contractions and to show ownership.

Contractions

Here are some common contractions: *wouldn't* (would not), *won't* (will not), *let's* (let us), *it's* (it is), *you're* (you are), *who's* (who is/has). Be careful not to confuse *it's,* *you're,* and *who's* with the sound-alike words *its,* *your,* and *whose,* which are possessive pronouns.

Possession

To show ownership for singular nouns and some plural nouns, we use the apostrophe and *-s* (*John's book, Stefanie's car keys, the cloud's shadow, the children's pet*). With most plural nouns, the apostrophe follows the *-s:*

Adam and Darin owned the lemonade stand. It was the boys' stand.

The need for an apostrophe may not seem obvious in, for example, *an hour's wait, a dollar's worth of chocolate raisins,* or *a whole season's rain in one week.* To check whether an apostrophe is needed, you can restate the possessive word as an "of" phrase: *the car keys of Stefanie, the wait of an hour,* or *the rain of a whole season.*

Hyphens

Hyphens join word parts or words to make new words:

- **Prefixes:** ex-athlete, anti-Communist, self-respect, pro-democracy
- **Compound words:** son-in-law, go-between, look-alike, twenty-seven
- **Compound adjectives:** well-respected machinist, good-looking quarter horse, hard-fought contest, problem-solving attitude, hard-to-catch outlaw

When the compound adjective follows the noun, no hyphen is used: "The machinist is well respected."

Hyphens can also be used at the end of a line of text to divide a word between syllables.

Capitalization

We capitalize proper nouns—the names of specific, unique individuals or things—and words derived from them. Here are some categories:

- **People, things, trademarks:** Mark, Camry, Coca-Cola
- **Professional titles:** Professor Oden, Doctor Franklin, Senator Edwards
- **Organizations, institutions, sports teams, companies:** the United Way, Centerville High School, New York Mets, Macy's
- **Nationalities, ethnicities, and races:** German, Russian, French, Korean, Syrian, African American, Hispanic, Asian
- **Languages:** Spanish, Mandarin, Swahili, Portuguese, English
- **Religions, followers of religions, deities, holy books:** Catholicism, Buddhism; Protestant, Hindu; Lord, Allah, Adonai; Bible, Koran, Talmud
- **Historical documents, periods, events:** the Constitution, the Renaissance, the Vietnam War
- **Geographic names:** the Ozark Mountains, St. Louis, Pacific Northwest, Middle East, California
- **Days, months, holidays:** Saturday, April, Christmas
- **First word in a direct quote:** Margaret said, "No one agrees with you."
- **Titles:** books, stories, films, magazines, newspapers, poems, songs, and works of art: *The Catcher in the Rye,* "Down at the Dinghy," *Newsweek*

Capitalize all words in titles except prepositions (*on, in, at*), coordinating conjunctions (*and, but, or, so, yet, nor, for*), and articles (*a, an, the*)—unless any of these words begin or end the title or follow a colon in the title (*Sleepwalking: A Comedy*).

Do not capitalize the following: seasons (*spring*), plants (*rose, oak*), animals (*robin, ant*), school subjects (*biology, economics*).

Note that the categories in the preceding list are proper nouns; do not capitalize words that are part of a name when they are used as common nouns. For example, capitalize *doctor* in *Doctor Johnson* but not in *Abby Johnson, who is a doctor*; capitalize *high school* in *Southwest High School* but not in *Tom's high school*.

Numbers

Some writers prefer in most cases to indicate numbers with numerals instead of words. However, a more traditional treatment calls for spelling out numbers of one or two words (*three, fourteen, fifty-six*) and then using numerals for numbers of three words or more (101; 2,098; 5,980,746). Here are several other conventions for number use:

- **Numbers in dates:** "January 3, 2009, at 10:00 p.m." (The endings *-st, -d,* and *-th* are not needed after dates.)
- **Numbers in series:** "The driveway was 140 feet long, 12 feet wide, and 6 inches deep." (Be consistent in using numerals or words.)
- **Numbers that begin sentences:** "One hundred and thirty passengers died in the crash." (Spell out a number or recast the sentence.)
- **Percentages/decimals:** "The solution was 95 percent water." (Use numerals.)
- **Page numbers:** "The authors state on page 34 . . ." (Use numerals.)
- **Identification numbers:** room 14, Interstate 35, channel 41 (Use numerals.)
- **Physical measures:** 6 miles, 12 feet (Use numerals.)
- **Times:** 3 hours, 7:00 a.m. (Use numerals.)

Underlining and Italicizing

Most underlining or, with a word processor, *italicizing* is done to represent titles. For the most part, longer works are italicized or underlined, while shorter works are enclosed in quotation marks.

TITLES THAT SHOULD BE IN ITALICS (OR UNDERLINED)

Books: *The Ox-Bow Incident*

Plays: *Hamlet*

Pamphlets: *Treating Lower Back Pain*

Long musical works: *OK Computer* (whole albums)

Television and radio programs: *Lost*

Long poems: *Beowulf*

Periodicals: *Newsweek*

Published speeches: *Gettysburg Address*

Movies: *The Dark Knight*

Works of art: Michelangelo's *David*

Other common uses for italics include the following:

- **Emphasis:** "Luann said that she would *never* marry a man for money."
- **Names of specific airplanes, trains, ships, and satellites:** the space shuttle *Challenger*
- **Words and letters referred to as such:** "The word *very* is usually expendable."

HINT

Don't be afraid to try italicizing for emphasis, but do so sparingly.

In the following sentences in the *main* clauses, underline the verb twice and the subject once. Then correct the errors in the sentences. Check for semicolons, colons, dashes, quotation marks, apostrophes, capitalization, hyphens, numbers, and underlining/italicizing.

> **EXAMPLE:** The essay Tony wrote called Diminished Capacity was praised by his teacher, who said, This essay should win the schools literary competition.
>
> Corrected: The essay Tony wrote called "Diminished Capacity" was praised by his teacher, who said, "This essay should win the school's literary competition."

1. Harvey said there are many well intentioned people maybe the majority who vote for a president based on a single issue.

2. Here are just a few of the car Manufacturers who have gotten into the mini-SUV line toyota, subaru, suzuki, and nissan.

3. The arrival of the hybrid gasoline/electric cars is a hopeful-sign for the environment these cars might significantly reduce air pollution.

4. Some forget that its the peoples will that is supposed to govern a democracy.

5. Juliet loves cool-Spring days' though she dislikes the rain and says after the earth has slept all winter, I cant wait for the first of Springs Daffodil's.

6. 43 sailboats set out for key west, Florida, but only 39 made it through the *Hurricane.*

7. Thirty year old Alex Carroll has written a best selling book called Beat the Cops: The guide To Fighting Your Traffic Ticket And Winning.

8. No till farming is an established-method for conserving the soil.

9. The AARP organization begins sending out it's membership applications to people when they turn 50.

10. Madonnas CD Ray of Light was overseen by French Producer Mirwais Ahmadzai.

Return to the paragraph that you wrote (and that a classmate punctuated) for the chapter-opening writing activity (p. 586). In pairs, identify and fix any errors in punctuation and mechanics in both of your paragraphs. Explain each of your edits by referencing specific rules from the text.

ACTIVITY 27.8 | WORKING ONLINE: *Editing in the Real World*

The blog *This Is Broken* features photographs of signs with punctuation, grammar, and spelling errors. Go to http://www.goodexperience. com/tib/archives/signs/ and choose five signs that need corrections in grammar or mechanics. Copy down each sign's contents, mistakes and all, on separate paper. Annotating the original wording (crossing out mistakes instead of erasing them), revise each sign so its meaning is both clear and grammatically correct.

ACTIVITY 27.9 | WORKING ONLINE: *Practicing Punctuation and Mechanics*

Practice using commas, semicolons, colons, dashes, parentheses, quotation marks, apostrophes, and various mechanics at www.mhhe. com/brannan. Note areas in which you need additional practice on your Improvement Chart at the back of this book.

ACTIVITY 27.10 | WORKING ONLINE: *Punctuation and Mechanics Review*

Take the Chapter 27 Review Quiz at www.mhhe.com/brannan.

Chapter Summary

1. Punctuation helps readers sort out a writer's ideas.
2. There are three main uses of the comma:
   a. Commas separate a main clause from an introductory word or words.
   b. Commas enclose or separate nonessential words, phrases, or clauses that come within or after a main clause.
   c. Commas separate two main clauses when using a coordinating conjunction.
3. Commas also separate items in a series, separate coordinate adjectives, separate contrasting ideas, and are used in the following conventions: numbers, addresses, place names, dates, titles, direct address, and quotations.
4. Avoid unneeded commas.
5. Use a semicolon to divide main clauses without using a coordinating conjunction and to separate items in a series that are subdivided with commas.
6. Use a colon primarily to begin a formal list, separate closely related main clauses, and mark a formal appositive.
7. Use a dash to set off a series that begins a sentence, to show an abrupt break in thought, to enclose items in a series that contain commas, and to emphasize a word group at the end of a sentence.
8. Use parentheses to add nonessential material to a main clause.
9. Use quotation marks primarily to enclose the spoken or written word.

10. Use the apostrophe to mark contractions and possession.

11. Capitalize proper nouns.

12. Use a hyphen to join words and to show where words are divided into syllables.

13. In general, use numerals for numbers of three or more words, but spell out numbers of one or two words. However, some conventions call for numerals in all instances, such as dates; addresses; percentages, decimals, fractions; scores and statistics; and others.

14. Underline or italicize to emphasize a word or identify the titles of long works, such as books, movies, and television shows.Other common conjunctive adverbs include *therefore, nevertheless, then, in fact,* and *consequently.*

Spelling and Sound-alike Words

28

[*Whoever typed the text projected behind Hillary Clinton failed to edit his or her work—and now a prominently misspelled word, tommorrow, appears behind the senator, detracting from the effectiveness of her speech. Even if you are writing for a much less public purpose, misspelled or misused words can still reflect poorly on your writing.*]

KEY TOPICS

- Improving your spelling
- Learning useful spelling patterns
  - Doubling the final consonant
  - Dropping or keeping the final *e*
  - Changing or not changing the final *y* to *i*
  - Forming plurals: *-s* or *-es*
  - Using *ie* or *ei*
- Distinguishing sound-alike words

What Are We Trying to Achieve and Why?

An explanation or argument that in conversation impresses your listeners with its clarity and logic can, when you write it, be discredited altogether based on nothing more than misspelled words. Although spelling should be a low priority in drafting, when editing, you should try to catch every misspelling because errors in spelling affect readers' perception of you. For example, even the brightest, most qualified job applicant who submits a résumé with miscellaneous misspellings and wrong choices of sound-alike words, such as *there* instead of *their*, will have a hard time getting an interview.

English spelling is quirky at best, and everyone misspells words occasionally. Sounding words out often helps, but not always. A language that produces words like *knight, sign, sugar,* and *ocean* is bound to frustrate its writers. But there are patterns we can depend on to answer many spelling questions. This chapter will help you improve your spelling with some suggestions, some basic rules, lists of commonly misspelled words, and lists of sound-alike words.

Improving Your Spelling

Use the following list to help improve your spelling.

Spelling Suggestions

1. **Decide to work on your spelling.** If you want to improve, you can.

2. **Develop the dictionary habit.** Write with a dictionary close at hand. As you draft, put a question mark by words you are unsure of, and then use your dictionary to find the correct spelling. If you try several letter combinations and still cannot find the correct spelling, mark the word and ask someone for help, perhaps a person in your editing group.

3. **Use an online dictionary** or set your word processing program's option to search using approximate spellings.

4. **Take advantage of the spell-check feature** of your word processing software. Remember, though, that spell check is only a simple-minded device; it can't, for example, catch homonym errors (sound-alike words).

5. **Begin a personal spelling list** of words that you are unsure of or have misspelled in compositions. (See the Improvement Chart at the back of this book.) Pay particular attention to the ordinary words you use regularly and to sound-alike words. Because words like *photovoltaic* and *conundrum* are uncommon, you will probably be alerted to the need to check their spelling. It is the common—and commonly misspelled—words that are more likely to plague you.

6. **In editing, look closely at every word in every sentence.** Sound words out syllable by syllable, keeping in mind that sounding out doesn't always work.

7. **Try to remember pattern words** that are similar to and can help you with other words. If, for example, you are unsure of whether to double the *p* in the word *hopped* but are sure about the double *p* in *stopped, stopped* can help you with *hopped.*

8. **Test yourself on the lists of commonly misspelled words and sound-alike words in this chapter.** Include in your spelling list any word that you misspell along with the correct spelling. It often helps to pronounce the word aloud several times, exaggerating the stresses on the syllables, such as *soph-O-more* or *math-E-mat-ics.*

9. **When you discover you have misspelled a word, make sure of the correct spelling** and then write the word several times, preferably within a sentence.

10. **Study the spelling patterns listed in this chapter.**

Learning Useful Spelling Patterns

Much of spelling hinges on being able to break words into syllables and to recognize vowels and consonants. **Syllables** are simply units of sound—the way a word is divided in the dictionary—for example, *syl-la-ble* or *base-ball*. The vowels and consonants of English are as follows:

- **Vowels:** *a, e, i, o, u*
- **Consonants:** *b, c, d, f, g, h, j, k, l, m, n, p, q, r, s, t, v, w, x, y, z*

The letter *y* can function as either a consonant, as in *yes*, or a vowel, as in *pretty* (where it sounds like *ee*) and *fly* (where it sounds like *i*).

Doubling the Final Consonant

To determine whether to double the final consonant of a word when adding a suffix (an ending like *-ed, -ing, -er,* or *-est*), check to see if three conditions are met:

1. Is the word a single-syllable word (*pot*) or accented on the final syllable (*oc-CUR*)?

2. Are the last three letters of the word consonant–vowel–consonant (*p-o-t, occ-u-r*)?

3. Does the suffix begin with a vowel (*-ed, -ing*)?

If all three of these conditions are met, double the final consonant, as in the following lists:

Double Final Consonant

Single-Syllable Words	Words Accented on the Final Syllable
stun + ing = stunning	oc-CUR + ing = occurring
stop + ed = stopped	sub-MIT + ing = submitting
plan + er = planner	com-MIT + ed = committed
hot + est = hottest	pre-FER + ed = preferred

If any of the three conditions are lacking, do *not* double the final consonant:

en-ter + ing = entering (*enter* is not accented on final syllable)

ask + ed = asked (*ask* does not end in consonant–vowel–consonant)

slow + ly = slowly (*-ly* does not begin with a vowel)

Notice that the following words, while fulfilling conditions 1 and 3, do not fulfill condition 2, as none end in consonant–vowel–consonant:

Do Not Double Final Consonant

Single-Syllable Words	Words Accented on the Final Syllable
crawl + ing = crawling	despair + ing = despairing
stoop + ed = stooped	pretend + ing = pretending
plain + er = plainer	attend + ed = attended
slight + est = slightest	appear + ed = appeared

Dropping or Keeping the Final e

As a general rule, when adding a suffix to a word ending in *e*, you should do the following:

1. **Drop the *e* if the suffix begins with a vowel.** Common suffixes include *-ing, -al, -able, -ence, -ance, -ion, -ous, -ure, -ive,* and *-age.*

   come + ing = coming   congregate + ion = congregation

   survive + al = survival   fame + ous = famous

   excite + able = excitable   seize + ure = seizure

   precede + ence = precedence   create + ive = creative

   guide + ance = guidance   plume + age = plumage

   Exceptions include *noticeable, courageous, manageable, dyeing,* and *mileage.*

2. **Keep the *e* if the suffix begins with a consonant.** Common suffixes include *-ly, -ment, -ness, -less, -ty,* and *-ful.*

   definite + ly = definitely   taste + less = tasteless

   advertise + ment = advertisement entire + ty = entirety

   like + ness = likeness   waste + ful = wasteful

   Exceptions include *acknowledgment, ninth, truly, wholly,* and *argument.*

Changing or Not Changing the Final y to i

When adding a suffix to a word ending in a *y*:

1. **Change the *y* to *i* if it is preceded by a consonant:**

   sky + es = skies   happy + ness = happiness

   rely + ance = reliance   healthy + est = healthiest

   marry + ed = married   merry + ment = merriment

   pity + less = pitiless   mercy + ful = merciful

2. **Do not change the *y* if it is preceded by a vowel:**

   enjoy + able = enjoyable   play + ful = playful

   deploy + ed = deployed   employ + ment = employment

   joy + ous = joyous   coy + est = coyest

   essay + ist = essayist

   Exceptions include *paid, said, laid, daily,* and *gaily.*

When you are adding the suffix *-ing* to a word ending in *y*, always keep the *y*: *crying, studying, enjoying, saying.*

Forming Plurals: -s or -es

Most nouns form their plurals by adding *-s* or *-es* (*birds, batches*):

1. **If the word ends in *ch, sh, ss, x,* or *z,* add *-es*:**

   snitch + es = snitches

   brush + es = brushes

   miss + es = misses

   box + es = boxes

   waltz + es = waltzes

2. **If the word ends in** *y* **preceded by a vowel, add** *-s:*

holiday + s = holidays

Friday + s = Fridays

monkey + s = monkeys

3. **If the word ends in** *y* **preceded by a consonant, change the** *y* **to** *i* **and add** *-es:*

theory + es = theories

sky + es = skies

fly + es = flies

4. **Some words ending in** *o* **add an** *-s,* **while others add an** *-es.* Here are a few common examples, which you might want to memorize:

o + -s	*o + -es*
pianos	tomatoes
memos	potatoes
solos	heroes
radios	mosquitoes

Using ie or ei

In most instances, use *i* before *e*, except after *c*, unless the *ei* sounds like *ay* as in *neighbor* and *weigh*.

ie

believe	piece
niece	yield

ei after c

conceive	receive
deceive	ceiling

ei that sounds like ay

eighth	reign
weight	vein

Exceptions, which use *ei* where we would expect *ie*, include *caffeine, seize, height, leisure, neither, either, weird,* and *foreign.*

LIST OF FREQUENTLY MISSPELLED WORDS

a lot	affect	breathe	choose
accept	all right	business	chose
accommodate	already	calendar	completely
acquaint	argument	cannot	conceive
acquire	beginning	capital	conscience
adolescence	believe	career	conscientious
advice	beside	character	conscious
advise	break	choice	controlled

(cont.)

controlling	guarantee	occurrence	subtle
convenience	height	occurring	success
council	heroes	opportunity	suppose
counsel	hypocrite	parallel	surprise
counselor	immediately	particular	temperature
criticism	independent	passed	than
criticize	interest	past	their
curiosity	interfere	perform	then
curious	interrupt	personnel	there
definitely	it's	piece	therefore
dependent	its	possess	they're
desirability	jewelry	practical	threw
despair	judgment	precede	through
disappoint	knowledge	preferred	to
disastrous	led	prejudice	too
discipline	leisure	principal	transferred
effect	length	principle	truly
eighth	license	privilege	unconscious
environment	likelihood	proceed	unfortunately
equipped	liveliest	professor	until
exaggerate	loneliness	quiet	usually
except	lonely	receive	vacuum
experience	lose	referring	vegetable
fantasies	maintenance	relieve	weight
fascinate	marriage	reminisce	weird
fictitious	mathematics	rhythm	where
field	mischief	roommate	whether
foreign	moral	sense	whole
forty	morale	separate	whose
fourth	necessary	sergeant	without
friendliness	ninety	shining	woman
fulfill	noticeable	similar	written
government	obstacle	since	yield
governor	occasion	sophomore	you're
grammar	occurred	strength	your

Distinguishing Sound-alike Words

A/An/And

A and *an* are indefinite articles; for more on their use, see page 509.

A is an article used before words beginning with a consonant sound:

A rose is a beautiful flower.

An is an article used before words beginning with a vowel sound:

An iris is also a beautiful flower.

And links words:

A rose *and* an iris are both beautiful flowers.

Accept/Except
Accept means "to receive":

Olga *accepted* the silver medal.

Except means "excluding, other than, or but":

Olga *accepted* the silver medal, *except* she still longed for the gold.

Every member of the gymnastics team *except* Marina received a medal.

Advice/Advise
Advice means "an opinion or suggestion":

Brent had some good *advice* to give to his younger brother.

Advise means "to counsel or give a suggestion":

Brent *advised* his younger brother not to take their dad's car again.

Affect/Effect
Affect means "to influence or change":

Graduating from college *affected* Matthew's career plans.

Effect usually means "the result":

The *effect* of Matthew's graduation was to change his career plans.

All Ready/Already
All ready means "prepared":

Are you *all ready* to go to the beach?

Already means "before or by this time":

Everyone was *already* prepared to go to the beach.

Are/Our
Are is a present tense form of *be:*

Wallace and Lupe *are* working on the proposal.

Our means "belonging to us":

Wallace and Lupe *are* working on *our* proposal.

Beside/Besides
Beside means "next to":

Brent sleeps with his cell phone *beside* him.

Besides means "in addition to or except for":

Besides his cell phone Brent also sleeps with his pager.

Brake/Break
Brake means "to stop or a device for stopping":

Most people *brake* when they approach a red light.

Break means "to separate something into pieces or destroy it":

Please don't *break* the vase.

Breath/Breathe

Breath means "the air we inhale":

>   Having climbed five flights of stairs, Austin was out of *breath*.

Breathe means "the act of filling our lungs with air":

>   Having climbed five flights of stairs, Austin needed to *breathe* deeply.

Choose/Chose

Choose means "to select":

>   "Sylvia, which mutual fund will you *choose?*"

Chose is the past tense of *choose*:

>   Sylvia *chose* the environmentally friendly fund.

Clothes/Cloths

Clothes means "something to wear":

>   Allyson is wearing business *clothes* this morning.

Cloths means "pieces of fabric":

>   We will need several damp *cloths* to get the baby's face clean.

Conscience/Conscious

Conscience means "an inner sense of ethical behavior":

>   Natasha's *conscience* troubled her when she took the promotion.

Conscious means "awake or aware":

>   Natasha was *conscious* of her *conscience* troubling her.

Do/Due

Do means "to perform":

>   When she discovered her error, Gabrielle had to *do* the budget again.

Due means "something owing or expected to arrive":

>   Javier was *due* at 3:00 p.m.

Farther/Further

Farther refers to distance:

>   It's *farther* to your house than it is to mine.

Further means "additional":

>   I would like *further* practice before I embarrass myself onstage.

Hear/Here

Hear means "sensing a sound":

>   At the Eagles' concert you are sure to *hear* "Hotel California."

Here refers to a place:

>   Next month the Eagles will play *here* in this city.

Its/It's

Its means "ownership by a thing or animal":

>   The horse hurt *its* hoof.

It's is the contraction of *it is:*

> The horse hurt *its* hoof, but *it's* going to recover soon.

Lead/Led

Lead is a metal and also means "to guide or be in front of":

> *Lead* is heavier than iron.

> Marco has been here before, so he will *lead* the way.

Led is the past tense of *lead:*

> Marco had been here before, so he *led* the way.

Loose/Lose

Loose means "unrestrained":

> I had a pocketful of *loose* change.

Lose means "to misplace":

> If you are not careful with all that *loose* change, you are likely to *lose* it.

Past/Passed

Past means "time before now":

> Michael spends too much time thinking about the *past*.

Passed is the past tense of the verb to *pass,* meaning "to go by":

> Haven't we *passed* this Dillard's sometime in the *past?*

Quiet/Quite

Quiet means "silent":

> At the end of the dock, all was *quiet*.

Quite means "very":

> At the end of the dock, all was *quiet* and *quite* still.

Sit/Set

Sit means "to be seated":

> If you don't mind, I will *sit* on the counter.

Set means "to place something":

> Please don't *sit* on the counter where we are going to *set* the plates.

Suppose/Supposed (to)

Suppose means "to assume or guess":

> I *suppose* Carmaletta will skate today.

Supposed can be the past tense of *suppose* but, combined with *to,* usually means "ought to":

> Carmaletta is *supposed* to skate today.

Their/There/They're

Their means "ownership by more than one":

> Cofia and Travis own that house. It is *their* house.

There refers to a place:

> Cofia and Travis live in that house over *there*.

They're is the contraction of *they are:*

> Cofia and Travis own that house. *They're* living in it.

Then/Than

Then means "afterward or at that time":

> Jocelyn went to the art exhibit and *then* went home.

Than means a comparison is being made:

> Jocelyn likes Impressionist paintings better *than* pop art.

Through/Thru/Threw

Through means "moving from one side to another" or "finished":

> When he was *through* with his errands, David drove *through* the parking lot at McDonald's.

Thru is a commercial shortening of *through,* used in naming places where you do business as you briefly pass by. *Thru* should not be used as a synonym for *through:*

> David drove *through* the drive-*thru* at McDonald's.

Threw is the past tense of *throw:*

> When David drove *through* the drive-*thru,* he *threw* five dollars to the cashier.

To/Too/Two

To means "toward" or marks an infinitive (*to talk*):

> Ashley went *to* the bank *to* get some money.

Too means "also, very, or excessively":

> Ashley arrived at her bank *too* late, and the other banks were closed, *too.*

Two is a number:

> Ashley was *too* late *to* get the *two* hundred dollars she needed.

Use/Used

Use means "to operate or work with something":

> I will *use* the lawnmower.

Used can be the past tense of *use,* but followed by *to, used* means "to be accustomed to":

> I am not *used* to the loud noise the lawn mower makes.

Whose/Who's

Whose shows ownership:

> Jesse found fifty dollars in the street but did not wonder long *whose* it was.

Who's is the contraction of *who has* or of *who is:*

> *Who's* got money for lunch?

> Jesse found fifty dollars, so she is the one *who's* buying lunch.

Were/Where

Were is the past tense of *are:*

> The clowns *were* squirting water all over the ring.

Where refers to a place:

The clowns *were* squirting water only *where* they *were* supposed to.

Your/You're

Your shows ownership:

Is that *your* Jeep?

You're is the contraction of *you are:*

Oh, *you're* driving a rental.

ACTIVITY 28.1 | WORKING TOGETHER: *Editing for Spelling and Sound-alike Errors*

The following essay excerpt has many spelling and sound-alike errors. Applying the rules from this chapter—and using a dictionary—find each error, cross it out, and write the correct spelling above it. Check your work against at least two other classmates', and work together to make sure you've found all the errors and fixed them.

Hudled together in tiny windowless shacks, the first English settlers in the New World struggled to survive the winter. Having little expereince at rough living conditions, planing poorly, and often being led by those unqualified for the job, the colonists in most of the early settlements suffered terribly, many dieing there first year from starvation, illness, injury, and conflicts with Native Americans. Begining with the "lost colony" of Gilbert and Raleigh and progresing thru the Massachusetts Bay Company, early English attempts at colonizeing the New World met with disaster.

Sir Humphrey Gilbert and his half-brother, Sir Walter Raleigh, where the first adventures to try colonizeing America. Obtaining permission from Queen Elizabeth in 1578 to "inhabit and posses" any land in the New World not claimed buy a "Christian ruler," they both tried and failed several times. Gilbert, after two attempts, was drowned in passage, and Raleigh had to abandon two more colonys in 1585. Raleigh's final attempt was in 1587 with the infamous "lost colony," settled by more than a hundred people on Roanoke Island, near the coast of North Carolina. It vanished without a trace within three years.

After Gilbert and Raleigh, colonization efforts stoped untill 1607 when James I allowed two companys, the London and Plymouth, to try again, but niether, at first, met with succes. The London Company financed the first attempt (to be called Jamestown), which from the start ran in to problems. On the four-month voyage across the Atlantic, thirty-nine

Englishmen died. Not knowing any better, the survivors located Jamestown near swampy ground that bred mosquitos and malaria. Instead of prepareing for winter by planting and storeing enough food, the mainly gentlemen settlers searched for gold. As a result many starved too death during the winter, and others died from disease. By 1608 only thirty-eight colonists were alive. Although Jamestown began to prosper after 1630, between 1607 and 1624 80 percent of the colonists—thousand of men, women, and children—died.

ACTIVITY 28.2 WORKING ONLINE: *Going Beyond Spell Check*

 Go to www.accuracyproject.org/odetospellchecker and rewrite the poem "Ode to a Spell Checker," correcting each sound-alike mistake.

ACTIVITY 28.3 WORKING ONLINE: *Spelling Review*

 Take the Chapter 28 Review Quiz at www.mhhe.com/brannan.

Chapter Summary

1. Being able to spell according to accepted conventions is an important writing skill.
2. Because many English spellings are not phonetic, knowing a few spelling patterns and memorizing problematic words will help with spelling conventions.
3. Using a dictionary is an important habit to develop.
4. Editing for spelling is best done slowly—word by word, syllable by syllable.
5. Using pattern words, similar in number of syllables and endings, can help you spell words that you are unsure of.
6. Sound-alike words must be memorized to be used correctly.
7. To become a better speller, start a chart to track your own misspelled words. Study the words often, and test yourself on them until you can spell them correctly.

Learning from Professional Readings

6

B R A N N A N

The student models in the assignment chapters are excellent resources for helping you create paragraphs and essays. However, this unit offers a brief look at how professional writers incorporate the patterns of development in their writing, relying on detailed examples and explanations to produce memorable prose. As you read through these models, consider the elements of good writing we have practiced, and see how many you can spot in the work of these authors. Do not be surprised if a topic or thesis sentence seems "out of place" occasionally. As we have noted previously, not all body paragraphs begin with a topic sentence, and not all introductory paragraphs end with a thesis sentence.

HINT

To review the elements of descriptive writing, turn to Chapter 5.

Description
The Great Tide Pool   JOHN STEINBECK

Description is often used in writing to help make a story more interesting, to convey information, or to help make a point. The following two paragraphs are excerpts from John Steinbeck's novel *Cannery Row*, set in northern California. In this selection, he describes a tide pool at the edge of Monterey Bay. Whether you have seen a tide pool before or been in the ocean, does this description leave you feeling like you have seen a tide pool now?

1   Doc was collecting marine animals in the Great Tide Pool on the tip of the Peninsula. It is a fabulous place: when the tide is in, a wave-churned basin, creamy with foam, whipped by the combers that roll in from the whistling buoy on the reef. But when the tide goes out the little water world becomes quiet and lovely. The sea is very clear and the bottom becomes fantastic with hurrying, fighting, feeding, breeding animals. Crabs rush from frond to frond of the waving algae. Starfish squat over mussels and limpets, attach their million little suckers and then slowly lift with incredible power until the prey is broken from the rock. And then the starfish stomach comes out and envelops its food. Orange and speckled and fluted nudibranchs slide gracefully over the rocks, their skirts waving like the dresses of Spanish dancers. And black eels poke their heads out of crevices and wait for prey. The snapping shrimps with their trigger claws pop loudly. The lovely colored world is glassed over. Hermit crabs like frantic children scamper on the bottom sand. And now one, finding an empty snail shell he likes better than his own, creeps out, exposing his soft body to the enemy for a moment, and then pops into the new shell. A wave breaks over the barrier, and churns the glassy water for a moment and mixes bubbles into the pool, and then it clears and is tranquil and lovely and murderous again. Here a crab tears a leg from his brother. The anemones expand like soft and brilliant flowers, inviting any tired and perplexed animal to lie for a moment in their arms, and when some small crab or little tide-pool Johnnie accepts the green and purple invitation, the petals whip in, the stinging cells shoot tiny narcotic needles into the prey and it grows weak and perhaps sleepy while the searing caustic digestive acids melt its body down.

2   Then the creeping murderer, the octopus, steals out, slowly, softly, moving like a gray mist, pretending now to be a bit of weed, now a rock, now a lump of decaying meat while its evil goat eyes watch coldly. It oozes and flows toward

a feeding crab, and as it comes close its yellow eyes burn and its body turns rosy with the pulsing color of anticipation and rage. Then suddenly it runs lightly on the tips of its arms as ferociously as a charging cat. It leaps savagely on the crab, there is a puff of black fluid, and the struggling mass is obscured in the sepia cloud while the octopus murders the crab. On the exposed rocks out of water, the barnacles bubble behind their closed doors and the limpets dry out. And down to the rocks come the black flies to eat anything they can find. The sharp smell of iodine from the algae, and the lime smell of calcareous bodies and the smell of powerful protean, smell of sperm and ova fill the air. On the exposed rocks the starfish emit semen and eggs from between their rays. The smells of life and richness, of death and digestion, of decay and birth, burden the air. And salt spray blows in from the barrier where the ocean waits for its rising-tide strength to permit it back into the Great Tide Pool again. And on the reef the whistling buoy bellows like a sad and patient bull.

QUESTIONS FOR ANALYSIS

1. What is the dominant impression of these two paragraphs? Does the author state it in a topic sentence, and if so, where?

   _____

   _____

   _____

2. Name five specific words. How do these words contribute to the description?

   _____

   _____

   _____

3. Choose any image that seems clear to you, and tell how the details and explanation make the image appealing.

   _____

   _____

   _____

4. How does the description of action add to the dominant impression?

   _____

   _____

   _____

5. In the second paragraph, Steinbeck personifies (gives human attributes to) an octopus, calling it a "murderer." How does this description of the octopus add interest to the paragraph and help reinforce the dominant impression? (For more on personification, see pp. 498–501.)

   _____

   _____

   _____

6. Whether or not you are familiar with some of the creatures Steinbeck names, how do the metaphors and similes help you visualize them? What can you conclude about the value of comparisons in building description? (For more on metaphors/similes, see pp. 498–500.)

_____

_____

_____

7. John Steinbeck is famous for his descriptions of the Monterey Bay area. Take a tour of Pacific Grove—complete with maps, photographs, and details about Steinbeck's connections to various sites—at http://www.93950.com/steinbeck/. (The tide pool from this selection is the fourth stop.) Describe one of the other sites in a paragraph, imitating Steinbeck's vivid language and attention to detail. You can write from what you see, what you read, and your imagination.

The Truth about Tongass

DOUGLAS H. CHADWICK

In the following article from *National Geographic*, notice how the author uses description to interest readers in his subject, the Tongass National Forest. In particular note the focus of the first two paragraphs. What dominant impression is Chadwick trying to convey?

1   A strange, soft storm of white flakes is floating out of the summer sky, drifting past tall mountainside evergreens onto the nets of golden lichens hung from their boughs, onto the bushes colored by salmonberries and blueberries, onto the bear-tracked shores. This is not an unseasonal snow squall, not a flurry of wind-borne seeds. It's a fall of molted feathers from bald eagles converging on the waterways by the hundreds, bright heads and tails gleaming like beacons all along the dark woodland slopes. A high tide of flesh surges inland from the sea: Every river, every stream, quivers with salmon thrashing upcurrent to spawn like rapids running in reverse. If any more flowing juices and beating hearts crowded in here, the place might start moving around on its own.

2   Big trees, big birds, big fish, big bears, immense peaks wrapped in great glaciers that break off into bays where great whales spout: This is Southeast Alaska, the state's panhandle. It separates northern British Columbia from the open Pacific with a chain of misty, fjord-footed mountains and a jigsaw puzzle of more than a thousand islands. Known as the Alexander Archipelago, the islands help explain how a region less than 500 miles long can have 18,000 miles of shoreline (almost all wild, whereas the longest stretch of undeveloped coast in the contiguous states is 30 miles), more than 10,000 estuaries, and 13,750 river miles that host oceangoing fish. About 5 percent of Southeast Alaska is owned by native tribes or the state. Another 12.5 percent makes up Glacier Bay National Park and Preserve. All the rest—16.8 million acres—is the Tongass National Forest.

3   Three times the size of the next largest U.S. national forest, the Tongass could hardly be further from most citizens' everyday lives. Yet logging on part of this expanse has fueled decades of acrimony, lawsuits, even intervention by Congress. The controversy—and whatever the outcome may be—has turned

the remote Tongass into a central test of how Americans want to manage living resources on public lands.

National forest? National rain forest is more accurate. Make that old- 4 growth temperate rain forest, an exceptionally rich ecosystem that holds more organic matter—more biomass—per acre than any other, including tropical jungles. And that's not counting the equally lush forests of seaweed added to Tongass shores whenever the tide goes out. Temperate rain forest flourished from Alaska to northern California and in nations from Norway to Chile. Much has fallen to the ax and saw. In the lower 48 states, 96 percent of old-growth forest of all types has been cut down. The Tongass now represents not only the greatest remaining reserve of huge trees in the U.S., but also nearly one-third of the old-growth temperate rain forest left in the world.

QUESTIONS FOR ANALYSIS

1. Evaluate the first paragraph as an introduction. Is the hook effective—why? What is the dominant impression? Is it stated outright or implied?

   _____

   _____

   _____

2. In what paragraph does the author state the location of the trees and animals he describes? Why does the author tell the reader the location of his description at this point in the article? Why not wait for several more paragraphs?

   _____

   _____

   _____

3. What seems to be the article's focus, and in what paragraph do you find this out?

   _____

   _____

   _____

4. Why do you suppose the author gives statistics about old-growth temperate rain forests in his fourth paragraph?

   _____

   _____

   _____

5. What does the author hope to achieve by repeating the word *big* in paragraph 2? Is he successful?

   _____

   _____

   _____

6. What does the author mean by the term *fjord-footed mountains* in paragraph 2? (You may need to look up *fjord* in a dictionary.) Do you think most members of his audience would know this term, or should the author have explained it—why?

_____

_____

_____

7. Visit the Tongass Clearinghouse photo gallery of southeastern Alaska at http://www.tongass.com/Photos.html. Using specific details, describe three of these photographs to someone who can't see them. In one or more of your descriptions, try to use figurative language—a simile or metaphor—but be sure to avoid clichés or worn expressions.

To review the elements of narrative writing, turn to Chapter 6.

Narration

The Dare

ROGER HOFFMANN

This personal narrative, by freelance writer Roger Hoffmann, tells how the author as a 12-year-old took a dangerous dare. Though the event occurred many years in the author's past, he is able to recall a number of specific details of the setting, particularly the train, and some significant dialogue. As you read the story (which first appeared in the *New York Times*), ask yourself how Hoffmann holds readers' attention, maintaining suspense until the end.

1   The secret to diving under a moving freight train and rolling out the other side with all your parts attached lies in picking the right spot between the tracks to hit with your back. Ideally, you want soft dirt or pea gravel, clear of glass shards and railroad spikes that could cause you instinctively, and fatally, to sit up. Today, at thirty-eight, I couldn't be threatened or baited enough to attempt that dive. But as a seventh grader struggling to make the cut in a tough Atlanta grammar school, all it took was a dare.

2   I coasted through my first years of school as a fussed-over smart kid, the teacher's pet who finished his work first and then strutted around the room tutoring other students. By the seventh grade, I had more A's than friends. Even my old cronies, Dwayne and O. T., made it clear I'd never be one of the guys in junior high if I didn't dirty up my act. They challenged me to break the rules and I did. The I-dare-you's escalated: shoplifting, sugaring teachers' gas tanks, dropping lighted matches into public mailboxes. Each guerrilla act won me the approval I never got for just being smart.

3   Walking home by the railroad tracks after school, we started playing chicken with oncoming trains. O. T., who was failing that year, always won. One afternoon he charged a boxcar from the side, stopping just short of throwing himself between the wheels. I was stunned. After the train disappeared, we debated whether someone could dive under a moving car, stay put for a 10-count, then scramble out the other side. I thought it could be done and said so. O. T. immediately stepped in front of me and smiled. Not by me, I added quickly, I certainly didn't mean that I could do it. "A smart guy like you," he said, his smile evaporating, "you could figure it out easy." And then, squeezing each word for

effect, "I . . . DARE . . . you." I'd just turned twelve. The monkey clawing my back was Teacher's Pet. And I'd been dared.

As an adult, I've been on both ends of life's implicit business and social 4 I-dare-you's, although adults don't use those words. We provoke with body language, tone of voice, ambiguous phrases. I dare you to: argue with the boss, tell Fred what you think of him, send the wine back. Only rarely are the risks physical. How we respond to dares when we are young may have something to do with which of the truly hazardous male inner dares— attacking mountains, tempting bulls at Pamplona—we embrace or ignore as men.

For two weeks, I scouted trains and tracks. I studied moving boxcars close 5 up, memorizing how they squatted on their axles, never getting used to the squeal or the way the air fell hot from the sides. I created an imaginary, friendly train and ran next to it. I mastered a shallow, head-first dive with a simple half-twist. I'd land on my back, count to ten, imagine wheels and, locking both hands on the rail to my left, heave myself over and out. Even under pure sky, though, I had to fight to keep my eyes open and my shoulders between the rails.

The next Saturday, O. T., Dwayne and three eighth graders met me below 6 the hill that backed up to the lumberyard. The track followed a slow bend there and opened to a straight, slightly uphill climb for a solid third of a mile. My run started two hundred yards after the bend. The train would have its tongue hanging out.

The other boys huddled off to one side, a circle on another planet, and 7 watched quietly as I double-knotted my shoelaces. My hands trembled. O. T. broke the circle and came over to me. He kept his hands hidden in the pockets of his jacket. We looked at each other. BB's of sweat appeared beneath his nose. I stuffed my wallet in one of his pockets, rubbing it against his knuckles on the way in, and slid my house key, wired to a red-and-white fishing bobber, into the other. We backed away from each other, and he turned and ran to join the four already climbing up the hill.

I watched them all the way to the top. They clustered together as if I were 8 taking their picture. Their silhouette resembled a round-shouldered tombstone. They waved down to me, and I dropped them from my mind and sat down on the rail. Immediately, I jumped back. The steel was vibrating.

The train sounded like a cow going short of breath. I pulled my shirttail 9 out and looked down at my spot, then up the incline of track ahead of me. Suddenly the air went hot, and the engine was by me. I hadn't pictured it moving that fast. A man's bare head leaned out and stared at me. I waved to him with my left hand and turned into the train, burying my face in the incredible noise. When I looked up, the head was gone.

I started running alongside the boxcars. Quickly, I found their pace, held 10 it, and then eased off, concentrating on each thick wheel that cut past me. I slowed another notch. Over my shoulder, I picked my car as it came off the bend, locking in the image of the white mountain goat painted on its side. I waited, leaning forward like the anchor in a 440-relay, wishing the baton up the track behind me. Then the big goat fired by me, and I was flying and then tucking my shoulder as I dipped under the train.

11   A heavy blanket of red dust settled over me. I felt bolted to the earth. Sheet-metal bellies thundered and shook above my face. Count to ten, a voice said, watch the axles and look to your left for daylight. But I couldn't count, and I couldn't find left if my life depended on it, which it did. The colors overhead went from brown to red to black to red again. Finally, I ripped my hands free, forced them to the rail, and, in one convulsive jerk, threw myself into the blue light.

12   I lay there face down until there was no more noise, and I could feel the sun against the back of my neck. I sat up. The last ribbon of train was slipping away in the distance. Across the tracks, O. T. was leading a cavalry charge down the hill, five very small, galloping boys, their fists whirling above them. I pulled my knees to my chest. My corduroy pants puckered wet across my thighs. I didn't care.

For more on time transitions, see p. 55. For more on showing versus telling, see pp. 111–112.

QUESTIONS FOR ANALYSIS

1. Summarize the story's primary action in several sentences, and identify the climax. Name several word groups the author uses to keep the action connected from one paragraph to the next.

    _____

    _____

    _____

    _____

    _____

    _____

2. Showing and telling are crucial to effective storytelling. What does Hoffman show us in paragraph 7, and how does this affect the suspense in the story?

    _____

    _____

    _____

    _____

3. What do you think the meaning of this story is for Hoffman, and where in the story does he make this clear?

    _____

    _____

    _____

    _____

4. If you think the introductory paragraph is effective, what makes it work? Look especially at the first sentence. Write out the thesis sentence.

    _____

    _____

    _____

    _____

5. If you think the concluding paragraph is effective, what makes it work? How does the last sentence reflect on the author and the need for approval that drove him to accept the dare?

_____

_____

_____

_____

6. Hoffman uses metaphors and similes in several places. Choose any two and explain how they add to the story. Does he also include any overly used metaphors (clichés) that he might have avoided? (For more on figures of speech, see pp. 498–504.)

_____

_____

_____

_____

7. Specific words, sensory details, and active verbs are critical to effective storytelling. List several of each in paragraph 11 and tell how they add to the story.

_____

_____

_____

_____

8. This article from the University of Nebraska-Lincoln details the increased importance of peers in an adolescent's life: http://www.ianrpubs.unl.edu/sendlt/g1751.pdf. Compare these findings with your own experience. When you reached your early teen years, did friends become more important than family? On separate paper, write your own story called "The Dare," recalling a specific moment when you responded to (or resisted) a challenge by a peer. What happened, and how did it make you feel?

The Jacket

GARY SOTO

Gary Soto—poet, essayist, and novelist—often writes about his childhood in California and the difficulties he and other Mexican Americans have faced as migrant workers in the San Joaquin Valley. The essay that follows is taken from a collection of his shorter works titled *The Effects of Knut Hamsun on a Fresno Boy*. As you read, notice how Soto enriches his narrative with metaphors and similes and how important the jacket is to the story.

My clothes have failed me. I remember the green coat that I wore in fifth 1 and sixth grades when you either danced like a champ or pressed yourself against a greasy wall, bitter as a penny toward the happy couples.

When I needed a new jacket and my mother asked what kind I wanted, I 2 described something like bikers wear: black leather and silver studs with enough belts to hold down a small town. We were in the kitchen, steam on the windows from her cooking. She listened so long while stirring dinner that I thought she understood for sure the kind I wanted. The next day when I got home from school, I discovered draped on my bedpost a jacket the color of day-old guacamole. I threw my books on the bed and approached the jacket slowly, as if it were a stranger whose hand I had to shake. I touched the vinyl sleeve, the collar, and peeked at the mustard-colored lining.

3   From the kitchen mother yelled that my jacket was in the closet. I closed the door to her voice and pulled at the rack of clothes in the closet, hoping the jacket on the bedpost wasn't for me but my mean brother. No luck. I gave up. From my bed, I stared at the jacket. I wanted to cry because it was so ugly and so big that I knew I'd have to wear it a long time. I was a small kid, thin as a young tree, and it would be years before I'd have a new one. I stared at the jacket, like an enemy, thinking bad things before I took off my old jacket whose sleeves climbed halfway to my elbow.

4   I put the big jacket on. I zipped it up and down several times, and rolled the cuffs up so they didn't cover my hands. I put my hands in the pockets and flapped the jacket like a bird's wings. I stood in front of the mirror, full face, then profile, and then looked over my shoulder as if someone had called me. I sat on the bed, stood against the bed, and combed my hair to see what I would look like doing something natural. I looked ugly. I threw it on my brother's bed and looked at it for a long time before I slipped it on and went out to the backyard, smiling a "thank you" to my mom as I passed her in the kitchen. With my hands in my pockets I kicked a ball against the fence, and then climbed it to sit looking into the alley. I hurled orange peels at the mouth of an open garbage can and when the peels were gone I watched the white puffs of my breath thin to nothing.

5   I jumped down, hands in my pockets, and in the backyard on my knees I teased my dog, Brownie, by swooping my arms while making bird calls. He jumped at me and missed. He jumped again and again, until a tooth sunk deep, ripping an L-shaped tear on my left sleeve. I pushed Brownie away to study the tear as I would a cut on my arm. There was no blood, only a few loose pieces of fuzz. Damn dog, I thought, and pushed him away hard when he tried to bite again. I got up from my knees and went to my bedroom to sit with my jacket on my lap, with the lights out.

6   That was the first afternoon with my new jacket. The next day I wore it to sixth grade and got a D on a math quiz. During the morning recess Frankie T., the playground terrorist, pushed me to the ground and told me to stay there until recess was over. My best friend, Steve Negrete, ate an apple while looking at me, and the girls turned away to whisper on the monkey bars. The teachers were no help: they looked my way and talked about how foolish I looked in my new jacket. I saw their heads bob with laughter, their hands half-covering their mouths.

7   Even though it was cold, I took off the jacket during lunch and played kickball in a thin shirt, my arm feeling like braille from the goose bumps. But when I returned to class I slipped the jacket on and shivered until I was warm. I sat on my hands, heating them up, while my teeth chattered like a cup of crooked dice. Finally warm, I slid out of the jacket but a few minutes later put it back on when the fire bell rang. We paraded out into the yard where we,

the sixth graders, walked past all the other grades to stand against the back fence. Everybody saw me. Although they didn't say out loud, "Man, that's ugly," I heard the buzz-buzz of gossip and even laughter that I knew was meant for me.

And so I went, in my guacamole-colored jacket. So embarrassed, so hurt, I couldn't even do my homework. I received Cs on quizzes, and forgot the state capitals and rivers of South America, our friendly neighbor. Even the girls who had been friendly blew away like loose flowers to follow the boys in neat jackets. 8

I wore that thing for three years until the sleeves grew short and my forearms stuck out like the necks of turtles. All during that time no love came to me—no little dark girl in a Sunday dress she wore on Monday. At lunchtime I stayed with the ugly boys who leaned against the chain-link fence and looked around with propellers of grass spinning in our mouths. We saw girls walk by alone, saw couples, hand in hand, their heads like bookends pressing air together. We saw them and spun our propellers so fast our faces were blurs. 9

I blame that jacket for those bad years. I blame my mother for her bad taste and her cheap ways. It was a sad time for the heart. With a friend I spent my sixth-grade year in a tree in the alley, waiting for something good to happen to me in that jacket, which had become the ugly brother who tagged along wherever I went. And it was about that time that I began to grow. My chest puffed up with muscle and, strangely, a few more ribs. Even my hands, those fleshy hammers, showed bravely through the cuffs, the fingers already hardening for the coming fights. But that L-shaped rip on the left sleeve got bigger, bits of stuffing coughed out from its wound after a hard day of play. I finally Scotch-taped it closed, but in rain or cold weather the tape peeled off like a scab and more stuffing fell out until that sleeve shriveled into a palsied arm. That winter the elbows began to crack and whole chunks of green began to fall off. I showed the cracks to my mother, who always seemed to be at the stove with steamed-up glasses, and she said that there were children in Mexico who would love that jacket. I told her that this was America and yelled that Debbie, my sister, didn't have a jacket like mine. I ran outside, ready to cry, and climbed the tree by the alley to think bad thoughts and watch my breath puff white and disappear. 10

But whole pieces still casually flew off my jacket when I played hard, read quietly, or took vicious spelling tests at school. When it became so spotted that my brother began to call me "camouflage," I flung it over the fence into the alley. Later, however, I swiped the jacket off the ground and went inside to drape it across my lap and mope. 11

I was called to dinner: steam silvered my mother's glasses as she said grace; my brother and sister with their heads bowed made ugly faces at their glasses of powdered milk. I gagged too, but eagerly ate big rips of buttered tortilla that held scooped-up beans. Finished, I went outside with my jacket across my arm. It was a cold sky. The faces of clouds were piled up, hurting. I climbed the fence, jumping down with a grunt. I started up the alley and soon slipped into my jacket, that green ugly brother who breathed over my shoulder that day and ever since. 12

1. Summarize the main action in this story and identify the main conflict. What does most of the tension/conflict stem from, and what is the resolution of that conflict?

    _____

    _____

    _____

    _____

2. Why does Soto tell us this story? What is his point? How does the jacket relate to the conflict in the story, and what does it show about the author's life?

    _____

    _____

    _____

    _____

3. Personal narrative often reveals much about a person's life circumstances and character. What do readers learn about Soto's life and character from this story?

    _____

    _____

    _____

    _____

4. Soto uses many metaphors and similes and several instances of personification. Locate one of each of these figures of speech, and tell how they enrich the story.

    _____

    _____

    _____

    _____

5. Although most personal narrative includes direct dialogue, this essay does not. Locate two instances of indirect dialogue, and tell what readers learn about Soto from it. Could direct dialogue have also been used effectively in these places? Why or why not?

    _____

    _____

    _____

    _____

6. Writers sometimes achieve emphasis by using sentence fragments and short sentences. In paragraph 3, locate a sentence fragment and a short sentence, and comment on how they add to the meaning of the scene.

_____

_____

_____

_____

7. How does the introduction arouse readers' curiosity and focus the story?

_____

_____

_____

_____

8. Comment on the conclusion. Does it satisfactorily wrap up the story? How does Soto's final comment about the jacket relate to the significance of the story?

_____

_____

_____

_____

Illustration
The Case for Short Words   RICHARD LEDERER

In the next essay you will see how teacher and author Richard Lederer illustrates his points about language: For those who write, short words have strength and grace and may be the first and best choice. Notice especially how the author makes a case for his claim about short words with paragraphs 1–4, which are composed entirely of one-syllable words.

HINT

To review the elements of illustrating through examples, turn to Chapter 7.

1   When you speak and write, there is no law that says you have to use big words. Short words are as good as long ones, and short, old words—like *sun* and *grass* and *home*—are best of all. A lot of small words, more than you might think, can meet your needs with a strength, grace, and charm that large words do not have.

2   Big words can make the way dark for those who read what you write and hear what you say. Small words cast their clear light on big things—night and day, love and hate, war and peace, and life and death. Big words at times seem strange to the eye and the ear and the mind and the heart. Small words are the ones we seem to have known from the time we were born, like the hearth fire that warms the home.

3   Short words are bright like sparks that glow in the night, prompt like the dawn that greets the day, sharp like the blade of a knife, hot like salt tears that scald the cheek, quick like moths that flit from flame to flame, and terse like the dart and sting of a bee.

4   Here is a sound rule: Use small, old words where you can. If a long word says just what you want to say, do not fear to use it. But know that our tongue is rich in crisp, brisk, swift, short words. Make them the spine and the heart of what you speak and write. Short words are like fast friends. They will not let you down.

5   The title of this chapter and the four paragraphs that you have just read are wrought entirely of words of one syllable. In setting myself this task, I did not feel especially cabined, cribbed, or confined. In fact, the structure helped me to focus on the power of the message I was trying to put across.

6   One study shows that twenty words account for twenty-five percent of all spoken English words, and all twenty are monosyllabic. In order of frequency they are: *I, you, the, a, to, is, it, that, of, and, in, what, he, this, have, do, she, not, on,* and *they.* Other studies indicate that the fifty most common words in written English are each made of a single syllable.

7   For centuries our finest poets and orators have recognized and employed the power of small words to make a straight point between two minds. A great many of our proverbs punch home their points with pithy monosyllables: "Where there's a will, there's a way," "A stitch in time saves nine," "Spare the rod and spoil the child," "A bird in the hand is worth two in the bush."

8   Nobody used the short word more skillfully than William Shakespeare, whose dying King Lear laments:

9   And my poor fool is hang'd! No, no, no life! Why should a dog, a
         horse, a rat have life, And thou no breath at all? . . . Do you see
         this? Look on her, look, her lips. Look there, look there!

10   Shakespeare's contemporaries made the King James Bible a centerpiece of short words—"And God said. Let there be light: and there was light. And God saw the light, that it was good." The descendants of such mighty lines live on in the twentieth century. When asked to explain his policy to Parliament, Winston Churchill responded with these ringing monosyllables: "I will say: it is to wage war, by sea, land, and air, with all our might and with all our strength that God can give us." In his "Death of the Hired Man" Robert Frost observes that "Home is the place where, when you go there,/They have to take you in." And William H. Johnson uses ten two-letter words to explain his secret of success: "If it is to be,/It is up to me."

11   You don't have to be a great author, statesman, or philosopher to tap the energy and eloquence of small words. Each winter I ask my ninth graders at St. Paul's School to write a composition composed entirely of one-syllable words. My students greet my request with obligatory moans and groans, but, when they return to class with their essays, most feel that, with the pressure to produce high-sounding polysyllables relieved, they have created some of their most powerful and luminous prose. Here are submissions from two of my ninth graders:

12   What can you say to a boy who has left home? You can say that he
         has done wrong, but he does not care. He has left home so that
         he will not have to deal with what you say. He wants to go as far
         as he can. He will do what he wants to do.

13   This boy does not want to be forced to go to church, to comb his
         hair, or to be on time. A good time for this boy does not lie in your

reach, for what you have he does not want. He dreams of ripped jeans, shorts with no starch, and old socks.

So now this boy is on a bus to a place he dreams of, a place with no rules. This boy now walks a strange street, his long hair blown back by the wind. He wears no coat or tie, just jeans and an old shirt. He hates your world, and he has left it. —*Charles Shaffer* 14

For a long time we cruised by the coast and at last came to a wide bay past the curve of a hill, at the end of which lay a small town. Our long boat ride at an end, we all stretched and stood up to watch as the boat nosed its way in. 15

The town climbed up the hill that rose from the shore, a space in front of it left bare for the port. Each house was a clean white with sky blue or grey trim; in front of each one was a small yard, edged by a white stone wall strewn with green vines. 16

As the town basked in the heat of noon, not a thing stirred in the streets or by the shore. The sun beat down on the sea, the land, and the back of our necks, so that, in spite of the breeze that made the vines sway, we all wished we could hide from the glare in a cool, white house. But, as there was no one to help dock the boat, we had to stand and wait. 17

At last the head of the crew leaped from the side and strode to a large house on the right. He shoved the door wide, poked his head through the gloom, and roared with a fierce voice. Five or six men came out, and soon the port was loud with the clank of chains and creak of planks as the men caught ropes thrown by the crew, pulled them taut, and tied them to posts. Then they set up a rough plank so we could cross from the deck to the shore. We all made for the large house while the crew watched, glad to be rid of us. —*Celia Wren* 18

You too can tap into the vitality and vigor of compact expression. Take a suggestion from the highway department. At the boundaries of your speech and prose place a sign that reads "Caution: Small Words at Work." 19

QUESTIONS FOR ANALYSIS

1. Is the hook effective—why or why not? Write out the thesis sentence.

   _____

   _____

   _____

2. What similes does the author use in paragraph 3? How do they help make his essay interesting and advance his point?

   _____

   _____

   _____

3. Although the author makes a case for small words, where does he concede that "large" words are also useful?

4. In paragraph 5, the author uses the word *wrought,* a small but infrequently used word. What word of more than one syllable would be a more common replacement? Also, instead of saying *to put across* in the same paragraph, what single word of several syllables could substitute? Which word choices do you think are best for this article—why?

_____

_____

_____

5. Paragraphs 6–14 give many examples to support Lederer's point about small words. Choose any two examples and explain how they clarify the author's points.

_____

_____

_____

6. Do you think that a writer should ever try to limit his or her work entirely, or even mostly, to small words? Why or why not?

_____

_____

_____

7. Go to http://www.freerice.com/ and test your vocabulary (short and long words alike) for 10 minutes; for every answer you get right, the organization donates 20 grains of rice to the UN World Food Program. Does this seem like a helpful way to increase your vocabulary? Why or why not? Answer this question in a short paragraph (on separate paper), using specific examples to back up your point.

A White Woman of Color
JULIA ALVAREZ

In the self-reflective essay, "A White Woman of Color," teacher, poet, and novelist Julia Alvarez uses many detailed examples to explore her past and present, helping readers to see who she was and has become. As you read through this essay, notice how well Alvarez uses patterns of development like comparison and contrast, cause and effect, and narration to develop her ideas.

1   Growing up in the Dominican Republic, I experienced racism within my own family—though I didn't think of it as racism. But there was definitely a hierarchy of beauty, which was the main currency in our family of daughters. It was not until years later, from the vantage point of the United States and an American education, that I realized that this hierarchy of beauty was dictated by our coloring. We were a progression of whitening, as if my mother were slowly bleaching the color out of her children.

The oldest sister had the darkest coloring with very curly hair and "coarse" features. She looked the most like Papa's side of the family and was considered the least pretty. I came next, with "good hair," and skin that back then was a deep olive, for I was a tomboy—another dark mark against me—who would not stay out of the sun. The sister right after me had my skin color, but she was a good girl who stayed indoors, so she was much paler, her hair a golden brown. But the pride and joy of the family was the baby. She made heads turn—strangers approached asking to feel her silken hair. She was white white—an adjective which was repeated in describing her color as if to deepen the shade of white. Her eyes were brown but her hair was an unaccountable towheaded blond. Because of her coloring, my father was teased that there must have been a German milkman in our neighborhood. How could *she* be *his* daughter? It was clear that this youngest child resembled Mami's side of the family.

Mami's family were *really* white, both in terms of race, and also of class. From them came the Spanish surnames, the pale skin, the lank hair. Her brothers and uncles went to schools abroad and had important businesses in the country. They also emulated the manners and habits of North Americans. Growing up, I remember arguments at the supper table about whether it was proper to tie one's napkin around one's neck or not, how much of one's arm one could properly lay on the table, and whether spaghetti could be eaten with the help of a spoon. My mother, of course, insisted on all the protocol of knives and forks and on eating a little portion of everything served; my father, on the other hand, defended our eating whatever we wanted, with our hands if need be, so we could "have fun" with our food. My mother would snap back that we looked like *jibaritas* who should be living out in the country. Of course, that was precisely where my father's family came from.

Not that Papi's family weren't smart and enterprising, all twenty-five brothers and sisters. (The size of the family in and of itself was considered very country by some members of Mami's family.) Many of Papi's brothers had gone to the university and become professionals. But their education was totally island—no fancy degrees from Andover, Cornell, or Yale, no summer camps or school songs in another language. Papi's family still lived in the interior rather than the capital, in old-fashioned houses, which were decorated in ways that my mother's family would have considered, well, tasteless. I remember antimacassars on the backs of rocking chairs, garish paintings of flamboyant trees, ceramic planters with plastic flowers in bloom. Papi's family were *criollos*—creoles, expansive, proud, colorful—rather than cosmopolitans. (Some members had a sixth finger on their right—or was it their left?—hands.) Their money, kept in a wad in their back pockets, still had the smell of the earth on it, whereas my mother's family had money in Chase Manhattan Bank, most of it with George Washington's picture on it, not Juan Pablo Duarte's.

It was clear to us growing up then that lighter was better, but there was no question of discriminating against someone because he or she was dark-skinned. Everyone's family, even an elite one like Mami's, had darker-skinned members. All Dominicans, as the saying goes, have a little black behind the ears. To separate oneself from those who were darker would have been to divide *una familia*—a sacrosanct entity in our culture. Neither was white blood necessarily a sign of moral, intellectual, or political superiority. All one has to do is page through a Dominican history book and look at the number of dark-skinned presidents, dictators, generals, and entrepreneurs to see that power has not resided exclusively or primarily among the whites on the island. The leadership of our country historically has been "colored."

6   But being black was something else. A black Dominican was referred to as a "dark indian" (*indio oscuro*)—unless you wanted to come to blows with him, that is. The real blacks were the Haitians who lived next door and who occupied the Dominican Republic for twenty years, from 1822–1844, a fact that can still so inflame the Dominican populace you'd think it had happened last year. The denial of the Afro-Dominican part of our culture reached its climax during the dictatorship of Trujillo, whose own maternal grandmother was Haitian. To protect Dominican race purity, Trujillo ordered the overnight slaughter of thousands (figures range from 20,000 to 40,000) of Haitians by his military, who committed this atrocity using only machetes and knives in order to make this planned extermination look like a "spontaneous" border skirmish. He also had the Dominican Republic declared a white nation despite the evidence of the mulatto senators who were forced to pass this ridiculous measure.

7   So, black was not so good, kinky hair was not so good, thick lips were not so good. But even if you were *indio oscuro con pelo malo y una bemba de aquá a Baní,* you could still sit in the front of the bus and order at the lunch counter—or the equivalent thereof. There was no segregation of races in the halls of power. But in the aesthetic arena—the ones to which we girls were relegated as females—lighter was better. Lank hair and pale skin and small, fine features were better. All I had to do was stay out of the sun and behave myself, and I could pass as a pretty white girl.

8   Another aspect of my growing up also greatly influenced my thinking on race. Although I was raised in the heart of a large family, my day-to-day caretakers were the maids. Most of these women were dark-skinned, some of Haitian background. One of them, Misiá had been spared the machetes of the 1937 massacre when she was taken in by our family and hidden from the prowling *guardias.* We children spent most of the day with these women. They tended to us, nursed us when we were sick, cradled us when we fell down and scraped an elbow or knee (as a tomboy, there was a lot of this scraping for me), and most important, they told us stories of *los santos* and *el barón del cementerio,* of *el cuco* and *las ciguapas,* beautiful dark-skinned creatures, who escaped capture because their feet were turned backwards, and so they left behind a false set of footprints. These women spread the wings of our imaginations and connected us deeply to the land we came from. They were the ones with the stories that had power over us.

9   We arrived in Nueva York in 1960, before the large waves of Caribbean immigrants created little Habanas, Santo Domingos, and San Juans in the boroughs of the city. Here we encountered a whole new kettle of wax—as my malapropping Mami might have said. People of color were treated as if they were inferior, prone to violence, uneducated, untrustworthy, lazy—all the "bad" adjectives we were learning in our new language. Our dark-skinned aunt, Tía Ana, who had lived in New York for several decades and so was the authority in these matters, recounted stories of discrimination on buses and subways. These Americans were so blind! One drop of black and you were

black. Everyone back home would have known that Tía Ana was not black; she had "good hair" and her skin color was a light *indio.* All week, she worked in a *factoría* in the Bronx, and when she came to visit us on Saturdays to sew our school clothes, she had to take three trains to our nice neighborhood where the darkest face on the street was usually her own.

We were lucky to be white Dominicans. But white as we were, we still 10 encountered prejudice. We found that our accents, our habits and smells added "color" to our complexions. Had we been darker, we certainly could not have bought our mock Tudor house in Jamaica Estates. In fact, the African American family who moved in across the street several years later needed police protection because of threats. Even so, at the local school, we endured the bullying of classmates. "Go back to where you came from!" they yelled at my sisters and me on the playground. When some of them started throwing stones, my mother made up her mind that we were not safe and began applying to boarding schools where privilege transformed prejudice into patronage.

"So where are you from?" our classmates would ask. 11

"Jamaica Estates," I'd say, an edge of belligerence to my voice. It was obvi- 12 ous from my accent, if not my looks, that I was not from there in the way they meant being from somewhere.

"I mean *originally.*" 13

And then it would come out, the color, the accent, the cousins with six 14 fingers, the smell of garlic.

By the time I went off to college, a great explosion of American culture was 15 taking place on campuses across the country. The Civil Rights movement, the Vietnam War and subsequent peace movement, and the women's movement were transforming traditional definitions of American identity. Ethnicity was in: my classmates wore long braids like Native Americans, peasant blouses from Mexico, long diaphanous skirts and dangly earrings from India. Suddenly my foreignness was being celebrated. This reversal felt affirming but also disturbing. As *huipils, serapes,* and embroidered dresses proliferated about me, I had the feeling that my ethnicity had become a commodity. I resented it.

When I began looking for a job after college, I discovered that being a white 16 Latina made me a nonthreatening minority in the eyes of these employers. My color was a question *only* of culture—and if I kept my cultural color to myself, I was "no problem." Each time I was hired for one of my countless visiting appointments to teach creative writing, freshman English, introductory survey courses—never permanent "invitations," mind you—the inevitable questionnaire would accompany my contract, in which I was to check my race: Caucasian, Black, Native American, Asian, Hispanic, Other. How could a Dominican divide herself in this way? Or was I really a Dominican anymore? And what was Hispanic? A census creation—there is no such culture—how could it define who I was at all? Given this set of options, the truest answer might have been to check Other.

Adrift from any Latino community in this country, my culture had become 17 an internal homeland, periodically replenished by trips back "home." But as a professional woman on my own, I felt less and less at home on the island. My values, the loss of my Catholic faith, my wardrobe, my hippy ways, and my feminist ideas separated me from my native culture. I did not subscribe to many of the mores and constraints that seemed to be an intrinsic part of that culture. And since my culture had always been my "color," by rejecting these mores, I had become not only Americanized, but whiter.

18   If I could have been a part of a Latino community in the United States, the struggle might have been if not easier, less private and, therefore, less isolating. These issues of acculturation and ethnicity would have been struggles to share with others like me. But all my North American life I had lived in shifting academic communities—going to boarding schools, then college, and later teaching wherever I could get those yearly appointments—and these communities reflected the dearth of Latinos in the profession. Except for friends in Spanish departments, who tended to have come from their countries of origin to teach rather than being raised in this country as I was, I had very little daily contact with Latinos.

19   I looked for company where I had always found it since coming to this country—in books. At first, the texts that I read and taught were the canonical works that formed the context of the bread-and-butter courses, which as a "visiting instructor," I was hired to teach. These texts were mostly written by white male writers from Britain and the United States, with a few women thrown in, and no Latinos. Thank goodness for the occasional creative writing workshop where I could bring in the multicultural authors I wanted. But since I had been formed in this very academy, I was clueless about where to start. I began to educate myself by reading, and that is when I discovered that there were others out there like me, hybrids who came in a variety of colors and whose ethnicity and race were an evolving process, not a rigid paradigm or a list of boxes, one of which you checked off.

20   This discovery of my ethnicity in books was like a rebirth. I had been going through a pretty bad writer's block: the white page seemed to resist whatever it was I had in me to say. But listening to authors like Maxine Hong Kingston, Toni Morrison, Gwendolyn Brooks, Langston Hughes, Maya Angelou, June Jordan, and to that first wave of Latino writers—Lorna Dee Cervantes, Piri Thomas, Rudolfo Anaya, Edward Rivera, Ernesto Galarza—I began to hear the language "in color," to see that literature could reflect the otherness I was feeling. A story could allow for the competing claims of different parts of ourselves and where we came from.

21   Ironically, it was through my own stories and poems that I finally made contact with Latino communities in this country. As I published more, I was invited to read at community centers and bilingual programs. Latino students, who began attending colleges in larger numbers in the late seventies and eighties, sought me out as a writer and teacher "of color." After the publication of *How the Garcia Girls Lost Their Accents*, I found that I had become a sort of spokesperson for Dominicans in this country, a role I had neither sought nor accepted. Of course, some Dominicans refused to grant me any status as a "real" Dominican because I was white. With the color word was also a suggestion of class. My family had not been among the waves of economic immigrants who left the island in the seventies, a generally darker-skinned, working-class group, who might have been the maids and workers in my mother's family house. We had come in 1960, political refugees, with no money but with "prospects": Papi had a friend who was the doctor at the Waldorf-Astoria and who

helped him get a job; Mami's family had money in the Chase Manhattan Bank that they could loan us. We changed classes in America—from Mami's elite family to middle-class spics—but our background, education, and most especially our pale skin had made mobility easier for us here. We had not undergone the same kind of race struggles as other Dominicans; therefore, we could not be "real Dominicans."

What I came to understand and accept and ultimately fight for with my 22 writing is the reality that ethnicity and race are not fixed constructs or measurable quantities. What constitutes our ethnicity and our race evolves as we seek to define and redefine ourselves in new contexts. My Latinness is not something someone could take away from me, or leave me out of, with a definition. It is in my blood: it comes from that mixture of biology, culture, native language, and experience that make me a different American from one whose family comes from Ireland or Poland or Italy. My Latinness is also a political choice. I am choosing to hold on to my ethnicity and native language even if I can "pass." I am choosing to color my Americanness with my Dominicanness even if it comes in a light shade of skin color.

As we Latinos redefine ourselves in America, making ourselves up and 23 making ourselves over, we have to be careful in taking up the promises of America not to adopt its limiting racial paradigms. Many of us have shed customs and prejudices that oppressed our gender, race, or class on our native islands and in our native countries. We should not replace these with modes of thinking that are divisive and oppressive of our rich diversity. Maybe as a group that embraces many races and differences, we Latinos can provide a positive multicultural, multiracial model to a divided America.

QUESTIONS FOR ANALYSIS

1. Comment on the introductory paragraph. Is the hook effective? Why or why not? Is Alvarez's thesis clearly stated in this paragraph or does it grow from the rest of the essay?

   _____

   _____

   _____

2. In what paragraph(s) does the author most clearly state her main point?

   _____

   _____

   _____

3. Write out the author's topic sentence in paragraph 3. What detailed examples does she give to support this main point?

   _____

   _____

   _____

4. What primary pattern of development does Alvarez use to develop paragraph 4? Name several specific examples that she gives to support the main point of this paragraph.

_____

_____

_____

5. Alvarez states in paragraph 5 that "[n]either was white blood necessarily a sign of moral, intellectual, or political superiority." What example does she give to illustrate this point and, how then does she explain that example?

_____

_____

_____

6. In paragraph 9, the author discusses what her life was like in New York when she first arrived in 1960. Do you think that life has improved for immigrants in recent years, especially those of color—why or why not?

_____

_____

_____

7. What effect is Alvarez trying to achieve by italicizing the words *she* and *his* in the second paragraph? Why can this stylistic device be useful in writing?

_____

_____

_____

Classification

To review the elements of classification, turn to Chapter 8.

The Ways of Meeting Oppression

MARTIN LUTHER KING JR.

In the essay "The Ways of Meeting Oppression," Martin Luther King Jr. classifies the ways people react to oppression and argues that one method is superior. As you read, notice how clearly the author states the methods and develops them through specific examples, several of which are biblical references. Are you convinced after reading this essay that King's method of choice is the best one?

1   Oppressed people deal with their oppression in three characteristic ways. One way is acquiescence: the oppressed resign themselves to their doom. They tacitly adjust themselves to oppression, and thereby become conditioned to it. In every movement toward freedom some of the oppressed prefer to remain oppressed. Almost 2,800 years ago Moses set out to lead the children of Israel from the slavery of Egypt to the freedom of the promised land. He soon discovered that slaves do not always welcome their deliverers. They become accustomed to being slaves. They would rather bear those ills they have, as

Shakespeare pointed out, than flee to others that they know not of. They prefer the "fleshpots of Egypt" to the ordeals of emancipation.

There is such a thing as the freedom of exhaustion. Some people are so 2 worn down by the yoke of oppression that they give up. A few years ago in the slum areas of Atlanta, a Negro guitarist used to sing almost daily: "Been down so long that down don't bother me." This is the type of negative freedom and resignation that often engulfs the life of the oppressed.

But this is not the way out. To accept passively an unjust system is to coop- 3 erate with that system; thereby the oppressed become as evil as the oppressor. Noncooperation with evil is as much a moral obligation as is cooperation with good. The oppressed must never allow the conscience of the oppressor to slumber. Religion reminds every man that he is his brother's keeper. To accept injustice or segregation passively is to say to the oppressor that his actions are morally right. It is a way of allowing his conscience to fall asleep. At this moment the oppressed fails to be his brother's keeper. So acquiescence—while often the easier way—is not the moral way. It is the way of the coward. The Negro cannot win the respect of his oppressor by acquiescing; he merely increases the oppressor's arrogance and contempt. Acquiescence is interpreted as proof of the Negro's inferiority. The Negro cannot win the respect of the white people of the South or the peoples of the world if he is willing to sell the future of his children for his personal and immediate comfort and safety.

A second way that oppressed people sometimes deal with oppression is to 4 resort to physical violence and corroding hatred. Violence often brings about momentary results. Nations have frequently won their independence in battle. But in spite of temporary victories, violence never brings permanent peace. It solves no social problem; it merely creates new and more complicated ones.

Violence as a way of achieving racial justice is both impractical and 5 immoral. It is impractical because it is a descending spiral ending in destruction for all. The old law of an eye for an eye leaves everybody blind. It is immoral because it seeks to humiliate the opponent rather than win his understanding; it seeks to annihilate rather than to convert. Violence is immoral because it thrives on hatred rather than love. It destroys community and makes brotherhood impossible. It leaves society in monologue rather than dialogue. Violence ends by defeating itself. It creates bitterness in the survivors and brutality in the destroyers. A voice echoes through time saying to every potential Peter, "Put up your sword."* History is cluttered with the wreckage of nations that failed to follow this command.

If the American Negro and other victims of oppression succumb to the 6 temptation of using violence in the struggle for freedom, future generations will be the recipients of a desolate night of bitterness, and our chief legacy to them will be an endless reign of meaningless chaos. Violence is not the way.

The third way open to oppressed people in their quest for freedom is 7 the way of nonviolent resistance. Like the synthesis in Hegelian philosophy, the principle of nonviolent resistance seeks to reconcile the truths of two opposites—the acquiescence and violence—while avoiding the extremes and

---

*The apostle Peter had drawn his sword to defend Christ from arrest. The voice was Christ's, who surrendered himself for trial and crucifixion (John 18:11).

immoralities of both. The nonviolent resister agrees with the person who acquiesces that one should not be physically aggressive toward his opponent; but he balances the equation by agreeing with the person of violence that evil must be resisted. He avoids the nonresistance of the former and the violent resistance of the latter. With nonviolent resistance, no individual or group need submit to any wrong.

8   It seems to me that this is the method that must guide the actions of the Negro in the present crisis in race relations. Through nonviolent resistance the Negro will be able to rise to the noble height of opposing the unjust system while loving the perpetrators of the system. The Negro must work passionately and unrelentingly for full stature as a citizen, but he must not use inferior methods to gain it. He must never come to terms with falsehood, malice, hate, or destruction.

9   Nonviolent resistance makes it possible for the Negro to remain in the South and struggle for his rights. The Negro's problem will not be solved by running away. He cannot listen to the glib suggestion of those who would urge him to migrate en masse to other sections of the country. By grasping his great opportunity in the South he can make a lasting contribution to the moral strength of the nation and set a sublime example of courage for generations yet unborn.

10   By nonviolent resistance, the Negro can also enlist all men of good will in his struggle for equality. The problem is not a purely racial one, with Negroes set against whites. In the end, it is not a struggle between people at all, but a tension between justice and injustice. Nonviolent resistance is not aimed against oppressors but against oppression. Under its banner consciences, not racial groups, are enlisted.

QUESTIONS FOR ANALYSIS

1. Classification requires a single organizing principle for focus. What is the SOP (single organizing principle) in this essay? Name two other possible ways to classify oppression.

    _____

    _____

    _____

2. Having a reason for a classification is important. What is King's purpose in writing this essay? What sentence is this most clearly stated in?

    _____

    _____

    _____

3. Classification essays can be organized by space, time, or importance. Name the major categories in this essay and method of arrangement, and then explain why you think King chose this organization.

    _____

    _____

    _____

4. Is the introductory paragraph effective? Why or why not? Where is the thesis located?

_____

_____

_____

5. Essays are usually developed through several patterns, such as cause/effect, comparison/contrast, and definition. Tell which of the patterns of development is used in paragraph 5 and how effectively.

_____

_____

_____

6. Paragraphs 4–6 deal with the issue of violence in responding to oppression. Why does King discuss violence at this length? What groups in his audience might be especially interested in King's message?

_____

_____

_____

7. Is the concluding paragraph effective? Why or why not? What is King's expanded thought?

_____

_____

_____

8. Would you protest for a cause you cared passionately about? If so, what approaches would you consider? Would you join a march or participate in a sit-in? Would you break the law, if peacefully? Would you resort to violence? On separate paper, write a paragraph classifying protests into three categories—ones you would participate in, ones you might participate in, and ones you would not consider. The "Types of Protest" chart at http://www.teachnet-lab.org/unhs/vitulano/types_of_protestexample.htm provides a helpful reference.

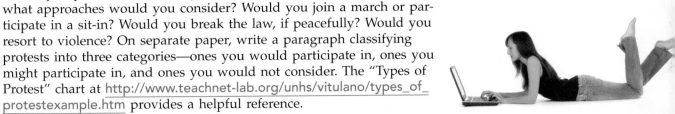

Friends, Good Friends—and Such Good Friends

JUDITH VIORST

Judith Viorst wrote this essay for *Redbook*, a magazine with an audience primarily of women. As you read, ask yourself how well targeted the author's examples and explanations are. Does she choose situations that many women could identify with, perhaps more so than men? Does she choose quotations from people who would be interesting to her readership? Notice the eight categories she groups friendships into. Do you think she misses any important types of friends?

Women are friends, I once would have said, when they totally love and support and trust each other, and bare to each other the secrets of their souls, and run—no questions asked—to help each other, and tell harsh truths to each

other (no, you can't wear that dress unless you lose ten pounds first) when harsh truths must be told.

2   Women are friends, I once would have said, when they share the same affection for Ingmar Bergman,* plus train rides, cats, warm rain, charades, Camus,† and hate with equal ardor Newark and Brussels sprouts and Lawrence Welk‡ and camping.

3   In other words, I once would have said that a friend is a friend all the way, but now I believe that's a narrow point of view. For the friendships I have and the friendships I see are conducted at many levels of intensity, serve many different functions, meet different needs and range from those as all-the-way as the friendship of the soul sisters mentioned above to that of the most nonchalant and casual playmates.

4   Consider these varieties of friendship:

5   1. Convenience friends. These are women with whom, if our paths weren't crossing all the time, we'd have no particular reason to be friends: a next-door neighbor, a woman in our car pool, the mother of one of our children's closest friends or maybe some mommy with whom we serve juice and cookies each week at the Glenwood Co-op Nursery.

6   Convenience friends are convenient indeed. They'll lend us their cups and silverware for a party. They'll drive our kids to soccer when we're sick. They'll take us to pick up our car when we need a lift to the garage. They'll even take our cats when we go on vacation. As we will for them.

7   But we don't, with convenience friends, ever come too close or tell too much; we maintain our public face and emotional distance. "Which means," says Elaine, "that I'll talk about being overweight but not about being depressed. Which means I'll admit being mad but not blind with rage. Which means that I might say that we're pinched this month but never that I'm worried sick over money."

8   But which doesn't mean that there isn't sufficient value to be found in these friendships of mutual aid, in convenience friends.

9   2. Special-interest friends. These friendships aren't intimate, and they needn't involve kids or silverware or cats. Their value lies in some interest jointly shared. And so we may have an office friend or a yoga friend or a tennis friend or a friend from the Women's Democratic Club.

10   "I've got one woman friend," says Joyce, "who likes, as I do, to take psychology courses. Which makes it nice for me—and nice for her. It's fun to go with someone you know and it's fun to discuss what you've learned, driving back from the classes." And for the most part, she says, that's all they discuss.

11   "I'd say that what we're doing is *doing* together, not being together," Suzanne says of her Tuesday-doubles friends. "It's mainly a tennis relationship, but we play together well. And I guess we all need to have a couple of playmates."

12   I agree.

---

*Ingmar Bergman (1918–2007) was a highly praised Swedish film director.

†Albert Camus (1913–1960) was a French novelist.

‡Lawrence Welk (1903–1992) was an American bandleader whose television show ran from 1951 to 1978 on ABC and was then syndicated until 1982.

My playmate is a shopping friend, a woman of marvelous taste, a woman 13
who knows exactly *where* to buy *what,* and furthermore is a woman who always
knows beyond a doubt what one ought to be buying. I don't have the time to
keep up with what's new in eyeshadow, hemlines, and shoes and whether the
smock look is in or finished already. But since (oh, shame!) I care a lot about
eyeshadow, hemlines, and shoes, and since I don't *want* to wear smocks if the
smock look is finished, I'm very glad to have a shopping friend.

3. Historical friends. We all have a friend who knew us when . . . maybe 14
way back in Miss Meltzer's second grade, when our family lived in that three-
room flat in Brooklyn, when our dad was out of work for seven months, when
our brother Allie got in that fight where they had to call the police, when our
sister married the endodontist from Yonkers and when, the morning after we
lost our virginity, she was the first, the only, friend we told.

The years have gone by and we've gone separate ways and we've little 15
in common now, but we're still an intimate part of each other's past. And
so whenever we go to Detroit we always go to visit this friend of our girl-
hood. Who knows how we looked before our teeth were straightened. Who
knows how we talked before our voice got un-Brooklyned. Who knows what
we ate before we learned about artichokes. And who, by her presence, puts
us in touch with an earlier part of ourself, a part of ourself it's important
never to lose.

"What this friend means to me and what I mean to her," says Grace, "is 16
having a sister without sibling rivalry. We know the texture of each other's
lives. She remembers my grandmother's cabbage soup. I remember the way
her uncle played the piano. There's simply no other friend who remembers
those things."

4. Crossroads friends. Like historical friends, our crossroads friends are 17
important for *what was*—for the friendship we shared at a crucial, now past,
time of life. A time, perhaps, when we roomed in college together; or worked
as eager young singles in the Big City together; or went together, as my friend
Elizabeth and I did, through pregnancy, birth, and that scary first year of new
motherhood.

Crossroads friends forge powerful links, links strong enough to endure 18
with not much more contact than once-a-year letters at Christmas. And out of
respect for those crossroad years, for those dramas and dreams we once shared,
we will always be friends.

5. Cross-generational friends. Historical friends and crossroads friends 19
seem to maintain a special kind of intimacy—dormant but always ready to be
revived—and though we may rarely meet, whenever we do connect, it's personal and intense. Another kind of intimacy exists in the friendships that form
across generations in what one woman calls her daughter–mother and her
mother–daughter relationships.

Evelyn's friend is her mother's age—"but I share so much more than I 20
ever could with my mother"—a woman she talks to of music, of books and of
life. "What I get from her is the benefit of her experience. What she gets—and
enjoys—from me is a youthful perspective. It's a pleasure for both of us."

I have in my own life a precious friend, a woman of 65 who has lived very 21
hard, who is wise, who listens well; who has been where I am and can help

me understand it; and who represents not only an ultimate ideal mother to me but also the person I'd like to be when I grow up.

22   In our daughter role we tend to do more than our share of self-revelation; in our mother role we tend to receive what's revealed. It's another kind of pleasure—playing wise mother to a questing younger person. It's another very lovely kind of friendship.

23   6. Part-of-a-couple friends. Some of the women we call our friends we never see alone—we see them as part of a couple at couples' parties. And though we share interests in many things and respect each other's views, we aren't moved to deepen the relationship. Whatever the reason, a lack of time or—and this is more likely—a lack of chemistry, our friendship remains in the context of a group. But the fact that our feeling on seeing each other is always, "I'm *so* glad she's here" and the fact that we spend half the evening talking together says that this too, in its own way, counts as a friendship.

24   (Other part-of-a-couple friends are the friends that came with the marriage, and some of these are friends we could live without. But sometimes, alas, she married our husband's best friend; and sometimes, alas, she *is* our husband's best friend. And so we find ourself dealing with her, somewhat against our will, in a spirit of what I'll call *reluctant* friendship.)

25   7. Men who are friends. I wanted to write just of women friends, but the women I've talked to won't let me—they say I must mention man–woman friendships too. For these friendships can be just as close and as dear as those that we form with women. Listen to Lucy's description of one such friendship:

26   "We've found we have things to talk about that are different from what he talks about with my husband and different from what I talk about with his wife. So sometimes we call on the phone or meet for lunch. There are similar intellectual interests—we always pass on to each other the books that we love—but there's also something tender and caring too."

27   In a couple of crises, Lucy says, "he offered himself for talking and for helping. And when someone died in his family he wanted me there. The sexual, flirty part of our friendship is very small, but *some*—just enough to make it fun and different." She thinks—and I agree—that the sexual part, though small, is always *some*, is always there when a man and a woman are friends.

28   It's only in the past few years that I've made friends with men, in the sense of a friendship that's *mine,* not just part of two couples. And achieving with them the ease and the trust I've found with women friends has value indeed. Under the dryer at home last week, putting on mascara and rouge, I comfortably sat and talked with a fellow named Peter. Peter, I finally decided, could handle the shock of me minus mascara under the dryer. Because we care for each other. Because we're friends.

29   8. There are medium friends, and pretty good friends, and very good friends indeed, and these friendships are defined by their level of intimacy. And what we'll reveal at each of these levels of intimacy is calibrated with care. We might tell a medium friend, for example, that yesterday we had a fight with our husband. And we might tell a pretty good friend that this fight with our husband made us so mad that we slept on the couch. And we might tell a very good friend that the reason we got so mad in that fight that we slept

on the couch had something to do with that girl that works in his office. But it's only to our very best friends that we're willing to tell all, to tell what's going on with that girl in his office.

The best of friends, I still believe, totally love and support and trust each 30 other, and bare to each other the secrets of their souls, and run—no questions asked—to help each other, and tell harsh truths to each other when they must be told.

But we needn't agree about everything (only 12-year-old girl friends agree 31 about *everything*) to tolerate each other's point of view. To accept without judgment. To give and to take without ever keeping score. And to *be* there, as I am for them and as they are for me, to comfort our sorrows, to celebrate our joys.

QUESTIONS FOR ANALYSIS

1. Well-written classification essays establish a single organizing principle (SOP) to group their categories. What SOP does Viorst use?

   _____

   _____

   _____

2. How does the author use contrast to help readers understand her first group, called "convenience friends"? Name three specific examples of convenience friends.

   _____

   _____

   _____

3. Viorst uses quotations from women to help illustrate some of her groupings. Pick two quotations and tell why they are useful. How do they help her connect with her audience?

   _____

   _____

   _____

4. How many paragraphs does the author devote to her introduction? In what sentence do you find her thesis? Does it clearly predict an essay of classification?

   _____

   _____

   _____

5. How many paragraphs does the author devote to her conclusion? How does she frame the essay? What is her expanded thought?

   _____

   _____

   _____

6. What do you suppose is the author's purpose in writing this essay?

    _____

    _____

    _____

7. Viorst uses dashes, parentheses, and italics in several places to create variety and emphasis. Find an instance of each, and tell how they make the essay more readable.

    _____

    _____

    _____

8. Read Dr. Jan Yager's classification of six types of toxic friends at http://love.ivillage.com/fnf/fnffightfriends/0,,nxwf,00.html. What SOP does she use? How are this and Viorst's article applicable to men's friendships? On a separate piece of paper, classify types of friendships between men (or between men and women) using a similar SOP to either Yager's or Viorst's.

To review the elements of cause and effect, turn to Chapter 9.

Cause and Effect

Two by Two, We'll Fill the Planet

BENJAMIN ZUCKERMAN

"Two by Two, We'll Fill the Planet," by Benjamin Zuckerman, first appeared in the *Los Angeles Times* in October 1991. The author raises a question that concerns us all—overpopulation. If we believe his statistics, human overpopulation of the planet is inevitable unless people control how many children they bring into the world. How accurate do you think the author's projections are? Are there any other factors that he has not mentioned that might offset the population explosion? Must couples at some point limit themselves to only two children—the "replacement level"—to save the human race from a miserably overcrowded planet or even extinction?

1   How many angels can dance on the head of a pin? This is a type of question that people asked in the not so distant past when religion reigned supreme, and science and technology played a negligible role in everyday life. Now that the rise of science and technology has enabled enormous increases in the human population, we must face the question: How many people can live on the surface of the Earth?

2   The rate of growth, that is, the percentage increase per year, of the human population is at an all-time high. Many politicians, economists and religious leaders regard rapid population growth as "natural" and extol its virtues. For example, we often read that population growth stimulates the economy and is, therefore, good. This may be true if one's vision is expressed in units of four years and limited to a few decades at most. However, life has existed on Earth for at least 3.5 billion years and human beings for a few million years. So the very rapid population growth of the past 100 or so years is not natural.

If the current rate of growth of world population, about 2% per year, were continued into the year 3400, then each person now alive would have 1 trillion descendants and the total human population would be about 10,000,000,000, 000,000,000,000 (10 sextillion). This is 10% of the total number of stars in the entire observable universe. Well before 3400, the average amount of land per person would have diminished to less than one square inch.

Broken down into shorter intervals, we are talking about a tenfold increase in just over a century. So by about the year 2100, at current rates, there would be 50 billion people on Earth. And 500 billion not long after the year 2200.

What about covering all the deserts and oceans with people? That would only delay the inevitable need for zero population growth by a century at the very most. How about shipping off the extra people (net difference between the number born and the number who die) to outer space? At current growth rates that would mean sending 10,000 people up every hour of every day. And we have trouble launching a few shuttles per year safely.

The issue is not whether an economy that is stimulated by population growth is good, bad, or indifferent. The above calculations show that growth is impossible except in the very short run. The real issue is what kind of world will the people of the present and next few generations leave for the people and other creatures of the next few millennia.

According to UCLA professor and biologist Jared Diamond, the coming century will witness one of the worst extinctions in the history of life on Earth. Roughly one-half of the 30 million species that are estimated to end will become extinct, courtesy entirely of human beings. If yet additional population and economic growth of the sort that some people espouse actually occurs, then the extinction rate will be even worse. A combination of far too many people, greed, and unbridled technological power is destroying the natural world.

Each person plays a role in the population equation. If you and your spouse have two children and four grandchildren, then you are reproducing at replacement levels (zero population growth). But if you have four children and they, in turn, each have four children so that you have 16 grandchildren, then that is roughly equivalent to the 2% per year growth rate that character-izes the world as a whole.

Each of us has his or her own system of values. For me, a planet with relatively few people, each of whom can live with dignity and a high quality of life, is far superior to a world where too many people, awash in pollution, stretch resources to the breaking point, and where billions struggle to survive at mere subsistence levels.

QUESTIONS FOR ANALYSIS

1. If you think the introductory paragraph is effective, what makes it work? Look especially at the hook (first sentence) and the thesis sentence. Write out the thesis sentence.

_____

_____

_____

2. What is the author's purpose, is it stated or implied, and what paragraph reveals it most clearly?

_____

_____

_____

3. Writers sometimes use a transitional paragraph to summarize part of their essay and then move readers into the next discussion point. Which paragraph in Zuckerman's essay functions this way, what is it transitioning from, and what point is it moving the reader to? What effect does any statement in this paragraph have on the thesis?

_____

_____

_____

4. If you think the concluding paragraph is effective, what makes it work? How does the author try to connect with the reader?

_____

_____

_____

5. Is this primarily an essay dealing with causes, effects, or both? What effects are discussed in paragraphs 3 and 4 and in paragraph 7?

_____

_____

_____

6. Cause-and-effect essays often explore problems and solutions. What paragraph is developed this way, and what is the author's point in this paragraph?

_____

_____

_____

7. The author addresses his audience in the third person ("people") and first person ("we") but also speaks to them in the second person ("you"). In what paragraph does Zuckerman speak to his readers as "you," and what effect is he trying to achieve? Is this use of second person effective, or might it alienate his audience? Why or why not?

_____

_____

_____

8. In 2008, Zuckerman contributed this article about sustainability to UCLA's *Today Online:* http://www.today.ucla.edu/voices/080808_population_zuckerman/. On separate paper, summarize his cause-and-effect analysis and then respond to it. Do you agree with his criticism of the Greendex survey? Why or why not?

Black Men and Public Space   BRENT STAPLES

Brent Staples is a journalist who writes about the negative effects—as an African-American male—he has on the people around him. Staples uses a number of well-illustrated examples to show these effects and points out that men of his race are themselves often endangered simply by being black. As you read this essay, try to put yourself in the author's shoes. Have you ever been frightened by someone who appears menacing? Have you ever perceived yourself to be frightening to others? How have these experiences altered your behavior?

My first victim was a woman—white, well dressed, probably in her early 1 twenties. I came upon her late one evening on a deserted street in Hyde Park, a relatively affluent neighborhood in an otherwise mean, impoverished section of Chicago. As I swung onto the avenue behind her, there seemed to be a discreet, uninflammatory distance between us. Not so. She cast back a worried glance. To her, the youngish black man—a broad six feet two inches with a beard and billowing hair, both hands shoved into the pockets of a bulky military jacket—seemed menacingly close. After a few more quick glimpses, she picked up her pace and was soon running in earnest. Within seconds she disappeared into a cross street.

That was more than a decade ago. I was twenty-two years old, a graduate 2 student newly arrived at the University of Chicago. It was in the echo of that terrified woman's footfalls that I first began to know the unwieldy inheritance I'd come into—the ability to alter public space in ugly ways. It was clear that she thought herself the quarry of a mugger, a rapist, or worse. Suffering a bout of insomnia, however, I was stalking sleep, not defenseless wayfarers. As a softy who is scarcely able to take a knife to a raw chicken—let alone hold one to a person's throat—I was surprised, embarrassed, and dismayed all at once. Her flight made me feel like an accomplice in tyranny. It also made it clear that I was indistinguishable from the muggers who occasionally seeped into the area from the surrounding ghetto. That first encounter, and those that followed, signified that a vast, unnerving gulf lay between nighttime pedestrians—particularly women—and me. And I soon gathered that being perceived as dangerous is a hazard in itself. I only needed to turn a corner into a dicey situation, or crowd some frightened, armed person in a foyer somewhere, or make an errant move after being pulled over by a policeman. Where fear and weapons meet—and they often do in urban America—there is always the possibility of death.

In that first year, my first away from my hometown, I was to become thor- 3 oughly familiar with the language of fear. At dark, shadowy intersections, I could cross in front of a car stopped at a traffic light and elicit the *thunk, thunk, thunk, thunk* of the driver—black, white, male, or female—hammering down the door locks. On less traveled streets after dark, I grew accustomed to but never comfortable with people crossing to the other side of the street rather than pass me. Then there were the standard unpleasantries with policemen, doormen, bouncers, cab drivers, and others whose business it is to screen out troublesome individuals *before* there is any nastiness.

I moved to New York nearly two years ago and I have remained an avid 4 night walker. In central Manhattan, the near-constant crowd cover minimizes these one-on-one street encounters. Elsewhere—in SoHo, for example, where sidewalks are narrow and tightly spaced buildings shut out the sky—things can get very taut indeed.

5   After dark, on the warrenlike streets of Brooklyn where I live, I often see women who fear the worst from me. They seem to have set their faces on neutral, and with their purse straps strung across their chests bandolier-style, they forge ahead as though bracing themselves against being tackled. I understand, of course, that the danger they perceive is not a hallucination. Women are particularly vulnerable to street violence, and young black males are drastically overrepresented among the perpetrators of that violence. Yet these truths are no solace against the kind of alienation that comes of being ever the suspect, a fearsome entity with whom pedestrians avoid making eye contact.

6   It is not altogether clear to me how I reached the ripe old age of twenty-two without being conscious of the lethality nighttime pedestrians attributed to me. Perhaps it was because in Chester, Pennsylvania, the small, angry industrial town where I came of age in the 1960s, I was scarcely noticeable against a backdrop of gang warfare, street knifings, and murders. I grew up one of the good boys, had perhaps a half-dozen fistfights. In retrospect, my shyness of combat has clear sources.

7   As a boy, I saw countless tough guys locked away; I have since buried several, too. They were babies, really—a teenage cousin, a brother of twenty-two, a childhood friend in his mid-twenties—all gone down in episodes of bravado played out in the streets. I came to doubt the virtues of intimidation early on. I chose, perhaps unconsciously, to remain a shadow—timid, but a survivor.

8   The fearsomeness mistakenly attributed to me in public places often has a perilous flavor. The most frightening of these confusions occurred in the late 1970s and early 1980s, when I worked as a journalist in Chicago. One day, rushing into the office of a magazine I was writing for with a deadline story in hand, I was mistaken for a burglar. The office manager called security and, with an ad hoc posse, pursued me through the labyrinthine halls, nearly to my editor's door. I had no way of proving who I was. I could only move briskly toward the company of someone who knew me.

9   Another time I was on assignment for a local paper and killing time before an interview. I entered a jewelry store on the city's affluent Near North Side. The proprietor excused herself and returned with an enormous red Doberman pinscher straining at the end of a leash. She stood, the dog extended toward me, silent to my questions, her eyes bulging nearly out of her head. I took a cursory look around, nodded, and bade her good night.

10   Relatively speaking, however, I never fared as badly as another black male journalist. He went to nearby Waukegan, Illinois, a couple of summers ago to work on a story about a murderer who was born there. Mistaking the reporter for the killer, the police officers hauled him from his car at gunpoint and but for his press credentials would probably have tried to book him. Such episodes are not uncommon. Black men trade tales like this all the time.

11   Over the years, I learned to smother the rage I felt at so often being taken for a criminal. Not to do so would surely have led to madness. I now take precautions to make myself less threatening. I move about with care, particularly late in the evening. I give a wide berth to nervous people on subway platforms

during the wee hours, particularly when I have exchanged business clothes for jeans. If I happen to be entering a building behind some people who appear skittish, I may walk by, letting them clear the lobby before I return, so as not to seem to be following them. I have been calm and extremely congenial on those rare occasions when I've been pulled over by the police.

And on late evening constitutionals I employ what has proved to be an 12 excellent tension-reducing measure: I whistle melodies from Beethoven and Vivaldi and the more popular classical composers. Even steely New Yorkers hunching toward nighttime destinations seem to relax, and occasionally they even join in the tune. Virtually everybody seems to sense that a mugger wouldn't be warbling bright, sunny selections from Vivaldi's *Four Seasons*. It is my equivalent of the cowbell that hikers wear when they know they are in bear country.

QUESTIONS FOR ANALYSIS

1. Does this essay deal primarily with causes or effects? Give several examples to support your response.

   _____

   _____

   _____

2. Where in the essay does Staples discuss causes?

   _____

   _____

   _____

3. Where is the thesis located?

   _____

   _____

4. If you think the introductory paragraph is effective, what makes it work? What effect does the hook have on the introduction? Is the introduction effective? Why or why not? Comment on the hook and the sentences that follow. What effect might they have on readers?

   _____

   _____

   _____

5. Is the conclusion effective? Why or why not? How does it connect with paragraph 11? What is the expanded thought? What statement is Staples making with the cowbell simile?

   _____

   _____

   _____

6. What is the author's purpose in adding the information in the second half of paragraph 5, beginning with "I understand"?

_____

_____

_____

7. In what paragraphs does Staples characterize himself in a way that makes it seem ironic that people would mistake him to be a violent person?

_____

_____

_____

8. Read this article about Seattle police officers accused of racial bias: http://seattlepi.nwsource.com/local/suit22.shtml. Clearly, police discrimination is a serious issue. Have you ever felt the police treated you unfairly because of your race? Did they ever treat you unfairly because of your age or your gender? If so, describe the experience. What do you think can be done to combat police discrimination? What role could education and the community play?

Process Analysis
The Fine Art of Complaining
CAROLINE REGO

Caroline Rego, a longtime consumer advocate, wrote this article to show readers how to protest when they receive poor service or shoddy merchandise. The author gives practical suggestions for dealing with personal confrontations and writing effective letters of complaint. Notice as you read that Rego lays out her suggestions in several paragraphs, illustrating them with specific examples and explaining her points carefully. Paragraphs 5 and 6, in particular, benefit from positive and negative examples: "Do this, not that."

1 *You waited forty-five minutes for your dinner, and when it came it was cold—and not what you ordered in the first place. You washed your supposedly machine-washable, preshrunk T-shirt (the one the catalogue claimed was "indestructible"), and now it's the size of a napkin. Your new car broke down a month after you bought it, and the dealer says the warranty doesn't apply.*

2 Life's annoyances descend on all of us—some pattering down like gentle raindrops, others striking with the bruising force of hailstones. We dodge the ones we can, but inevitably, plenty of them make contact. And when they do, we react fairly predictably. Many of us—most of us, probably—grumble to ourselves and take it. We scowl at our unappetizing food but choke it down. We stash the shrunken T-shirt in a drawer, vowing never again to order from a catalogue. We glare fiercely at our checkbooks as we pay for repairs that should have been free.

3 A few of us go to the other extreme. Taking our cue from the crazed newscaster in the 1976 movie *Network*, we go through life mad as hell and unwilling to take it anymore. In offices, we shout at hapless receptionists when we're

kept waiting for appointments. In restaurants, we make scenes that have fellow patrons craning their necks to get a look at us. In stores, we argue with salespeople for not waiting on us. We may notice after a while that our friends seem reluctant to venture into public with us, but hey—we're just standing up for our rights. Being a patsy doesn't get you anywhere in life.

It's true—milquetoasts live unsatisfying lives. However, people who go 4 through the day in an eye-popping, vein-throbbing state of apoplectic rage don't win any prizes either. What persons at both ends of the scale need— what could empower the silent sufferer and civilize the Neanderthal—is a course in the gentle art of *effective* complaining.

Effective complaining is not apologetic and half-hearted. It's not making 5 one awkward attempt at protest—"Uh, excuse me, I don't think I ordered the squid and onions"—and then slinking away in defeat. But neither is it roaring away indiscriminately, attempting to get satisfaction through the sheer volume of our complaint.

Effective complainers are people who act businesslike and important. Act- 6 ing important doesn't mean puffing up your chest and saying, "Do you know who I am?"—an approach that would tempt anyone to take you down a peg or two. It doesn't mean shouting and threatening—techniques that will only antagonize the person whose help you need. It *does* mean making it clear that you know your request is reasonable and that you are confident it will be taken care of. People are generally treated the way they expect to be treated. If you act like someone making a fair request, chances are that request will be granted. Don't beg, don't explain. Just state your name, the problem, and what you expect to have done. Remain polite. But be firm. "My car has been in your garage for three days, and a mechanic hasn't even looked at it yet," you might say. "I want to know when it is going to be worked on." Period. Now it is up to them to give you a satisfactory response. Don't say, "Sorry to bother you about this, but . . ." or "I, uh, was sort of expecting . . . ." You're only asking people to remedy a problem, after all; that is not grounds for apology.

If your problem requires an immediate response, try to make your com- 7 plaint in person; a real, live, in-the-flesh individual has to be dealt with in some way. Complaining over the telephone, by contrast, is much less effective. When you speak to a disembodied voice, when the person at the other end of the line doesn't have to face you, you're more likely to get a runaround.

Most importantly, complain to the right person. One of the greatest frus- 8 trations in complaining is talking to a clerk or receptionist who cannot solve your problem and whose only purpose seems to be to drive you crazy. Getting mad doesn't help; the person you're mad at probably had nothing to do with your actual problem. And you'll have to repeat everything you've said to the clerk once you're passed along to the appropriate person. So make sure from the start that you're talking to someone who can help—a manager or supervisor.

If your problem doesn't require an immediate response, complaining by 9 letter is probably the most effective way to get what you want. A letter of complaint should be brief, businesslike, and to the point. If you have a new vacuum cleaner that doesn't work, don't spend a paragraph describing how your Uncle Joe tried to fix the problem and couldn't. As when complaining in person, be sure you address someone in a position of real authority. Here's an example of an effective letter of complaint.

10 Ms. Anne Lublin
Manager
Mitchell Appliances
80 Front Street
Newton, MA 02159

11 Dear Ms. Lublin:

12 *First section: Explain the problem. Include facts to back up your story.*

13 On August 6, I purchased a new Perma-Kool freezer from your store (a copy of my sales receipt is enclosed). In the two weeks I have owned the freezer, I have had to call your repair department three times in an attempt to get it running properly. The freezer ran normally when it was installed, but since then it has repeatedly turned off, causing the food inside to spoil. My calls to your repair department have not been responded to promptly. After I called the first time, on August 10, I waited two days for the repair person to show up. It took three days to get a repair person here after my second call, on August 15. The freezer stopped yet again on August 20. I called to discuss this recent problem, but no one has responded to my call.

14 *Second section: Tell how you trust the company and are confident that your reader will fix the problem. This is to "soften up" the reader a bit.*

15 I am surprised to receive such unprofessional service and poor quality from Mitchell Appliances since I have been one of your satisfied customers for fifteen years. In the past, I have purchased a television, air conditioner, and washing machine from your company. I know that you value good relations with your customers, and I'm sure you want to see me pleased with my most recent purchase.

16 *Third section: Explain exactly what you want to be done—repair, replacement, refund, etc.*

17 Although your repair department initially thought that the freezer needed only some minor adjustments, the fact that no one has been able to permanently fix the problem convinces me that the freezer has some serious defect. I am understandably unwilling to spend any more time having repairs made. Therefore, I expect you to exchange the freezer for an identical model by the end of this week (August 30). Please call me to arrange for the removal of the defective freezer and the delivery of the new one.

18 Sincerely,

Janice Becker

P.S. (Readers always notice a P.S.) State again when you expect the problem to 19 *be taken care of, and what you will do if it isn't.*

P.S. I am confident that we can resolve this problem by August 30. If the defec- 20 tive freezer is not replaced by then, however, I will report this incident to the Better Business Bureau.

Notice that the P.S. says what you'll do if your problem isn't solved. In 21 other words, you make a threat—a polite threat. Your threat must be reasonable and believable. A threat to burn down the store if your purchase price isn't refunded is neither reasonable nor believable—or if it *were* believed, you could end up in jail. A threat to report the store to a consumer-protection agency, such as the Better Business Bureau, however, is credible.

Don't be too quick to make one of the most common—and commonly 22 empty—threats: "I'll sue!" A full-blown lawsuit is more trouble, and more expensive, than most problems are worth. On the other hand, most areas have a small-claims court where suits involving modest amounts of money are heard. These courts don't use complex legal language or procedures, and you don't need a lawyer to use them. A store or company will often settle with you—if your claim is fair—rather than go to small-claims court.

Whether you complain over the phone, in person, or by letter, be persis- 23 tent. One complaint may not get results. In that case, keep on complaining, and make sure you keep complaining to the same person. Chances are he or she will get worn out and take care of the situation, if only to be rid of you.

Someday, perhaps, the world will be free of the petty annoyances that 24 plague us all from time to time. Until then, however, toasters will break down, stores will refuse to honor rainchecks, and bills will include items that were never purchased. You can depend upon it—there will be grounds for complaint. You might as well learn to be good at it.

QUESTIONS FOR ANALYSIS

1. List the steps Rego lays out for dealing with people in person. Then list the steps (sections) in the letter of complaint.

   _____

   _____

   _____

2. Readers often want to know the why behind a suggestion and need to be warned if something may go wrong. How does the author explain (including defining words) and warn in paragraph 6?

   _____

   _____

   _____

3. What is the author's most important suggestion for successful complaining? Do you agree with the author? Why or why not?

   _____

   _____

   _____

4. How many paragraphs does the author use to introduce her process, and where is the thesis located? How effective is this introduction, and why do you think so?

_____

_____

_____

_____

5. Process-analysis essays can be dry, even boring, reading, so writers often try to enliven their style by creating a friendly tone and varying sentence patterns. List instances in paragraphs 1–9 where you think the author's style is especially engaging. Consider these elements: metaphor and simile; understatement; short sentences; dashes; pronouns like _you, us,_ and _we;_ active verbs; dialogue; and ellipsis points.

_____

_____

_____

6. What suggestions does Rego give in paragraph 23?

_____

_____

_____

7. Read this template for a thank-you letter, a model for what you would send a potential employer after a job interview: http://jobsearch.about.com/od/thankyouletters/a/blthank.htm. Using it as a guide, write a paragraph (on separate paper) explaining to a friend the process of writing one.

Green Roofs Swing Temperatures in Urban Jungles

APRIL HOLLADAY

Process analysis is frequently used to develop parts of longer articles or essays and can give explicit instructions on how to complete a task, as in "The Fine Art of Complaining," the preceding essay, or help people understand a process. In this article, written by April Holladay, we find a process to be understood—how "green roofs" work. Notice as you read the description how much specific information Holladay gives, telling of the construction, function, and value of green roofs. Also note where Holladay uses other patterns of development to develop the process description.

1 **Q: How do green roofs work, and how well do they function? Do they help the environment? (Pete, Washington DC)**

2 **A:** A green roof is a flat roof, usually, that has plants growing in a thin layer of soil, and works much the same as any roof. Its primary job is to shelter the building below from the elements: cold and heat, rain and snow. The plants and soil take the place of conventional roof coverings, such as built-up-roof (BUR), modified-bitumen or metal-standing-seam roofs. The plant/soil layer

protects the roof waterproofing membrane, as do the more conventional coverings.

"Green roofs have the potential to doubling or tripling the life span of the 3 membrane (compared with conventional covering)," says landscape architect Chris Counts of Michael Van Valkenburgh Associates. "The technology is so new [in the United States] the exact lifespan is not actually confirmed yet."

Green roofs, however, cost about twice as much to install, says Seattle's 4 King County government in a 2004 study. The cost of green roofs is about $14 to $25 square foot. The higher cost and longer membrane life, however, appear to offset each other. The King-County study estimates that, over a 40-year life span, the "total costs of ownership for the green roof" is only about 10% higher than for a conventional roof design.

A green roof regains open space lost as we establish cities and pave over 5 countryside. And with an alpine meadow on the roof, city dwellers can still enjoy a bit of nature.

The most common green roof in moderate climates (like Germany, which 6 has used green roofs for over 30 years) is a single non-irrigated 3–4-inch layer of lightweight, compost soil with drought-resistant plants. The Germans find this kind of green roof gives the most benefit for the money; 14% of the new flat roofs in Germany are green roofs.

HOW GREEN ROOFS WORK

The main task for green roofs, like all roofs, is to protect the waterproof mem- 7 brane from the elements to keep the roof from leaking. Well-designed green roofs come in layers to do three jobs:

- **Lower roof temperatures** that, in the summer, can be extremely hot 8 (130° F, 55° C). Lower temperatures and more even temperatures prolong the life of the waterproofing membrane by reducing heat damage and degradation.

- **Drain rainwater** so any standing water doesn't damage the membrane, 9 doesn't rot the plants, erode the soil system or cause the roof structure to sag under water weight.

- **Separate and protect** the membrane from human feet on the rooftop and 10 from plant roots (for example, stray tree seeds that have taken root).

The green-roof layers vary, depending on design, but all include: 11

- Plants and soil—the top layer. Plants lower the waterproofing 12 membrane temperature by absorbing 80% of the sun's radiation and using that energy to synthesize sugars and starches from carbon dioxide and water. The plants and soil also sponge up about 40% of the rain falling on the roof in a major 2-inch rainstorm, which reduces water flowing into storm sewers (more about this later).

- A landscape or filter cloth to keep the soil from washing away. This 13 layer separates the plant system from the rest of the roof. Also, many green roofs have walkways to protect the roof from foot-traffic wear.

- Drainage layers that sometimes include built-in reservoirs. Plastic 14 sheets, fabric or synthetic mats, or granular mineral layers are some of the drainage materials used to collect some of the water and allow the remainder to flow off. The main drainage design feature is, as with all roofs, a slightly sloping roof so gravity can move the water to the drains.

15   • A root barrier (sometimes in the form of root repellant on the membrane) to block roots from penetrating the waterproofing membrane.

16 Below these layers come (not necessarily in this order) the waterproof membrane, insulation and the building structure—which must be especially strong to support the additional weight of the green roof. Sometimes the insulation is placed above the waterproof membrane.

HOW WELL THEY FUNCTION

17 The National Research Council of Canada (NRC) constructed a green-roof testing facility at its Ottawa campus. It consists of a roof area of about 800-square feet that's divided into two parts: one half with a bare waterproofing membrane on top and the other half with a green-roof covering the waterproof membrane. A wildflower meadow grows in six-inches of lightweight soil. The Canadians instrumented both halves of the roof.

18   The University of Central Florida conducted a similar study, except comparing its green roof (6–8 inches of light-weight soil and a variety of native Florida vegetation) with a conventional roof surface. They, likewise divided a larger (3300-square foot) roof into two parts, and instrumented both halves.

19   The two groups found:

20   • Green roofs modify temperature fluctuations of the membranes, thereby reducing thermal stress and possibly extending membrane life.

21   On a typical hot summer day in Ottawa, the outdoor temperature peaked at 95°F. The membrane on the Canadian reference roof reached 158° whereas the membrane on the green roof reached only about 77°F.

22   The Florida group found that "the maximum average day temperature for the conventional roof surface was 130°F while the maximum average day green roof surface temperature was 91°F, lower than the conventional roof." The average was measured over the period from July 4 to Sept. 1, 2005.

23   • Green roofs shade and insulate the roof and evaporate moisture. Thus, they cool the roof, and reduce the demand for air conditioning in the building below.

24   The Canadians found that, in the spring and, particularly, in the summer, the green roof reduced the average daily energy demand by up to 75%, compared with the reference roof.

25   The Floridians estimated that the average energy use to remove the additional heat gain from the conventional roof over the monitored summer period is approximately 700 watt-hours per day.

26   • Green roofs delay runoff and reduce the runoff rate and volume. In a typical 12-hour period during a rainstorm, the Canadian green roof delayed runoff by about 45 minutes, and soaked up about 45% of the rain.

27   As an example of recent design improvements, consider the new green roof going up over the American Society of Landscape Architects (ASLA) building in Washington DC. The roof is a "matrix," says Stephen Noone of the Michael Van Valkenburgh and Associates, the landscape architecture firm that is designing the green roof. An open space that people can stroll and sit on overlays a regular green roof.

More innovations: a metal grating that "floats" about three inches over the 28
greenery and soil, says Counts. The architects hope that plants will grow up
through the grating, and then people, walking on the plants, will give the
plants a "haircut", which regenerates the plants. Also the architects will put
the waterproofing down first, then cover with rigid insulation. The reason,
explains Counts, is so the "various elements, such as deck and the metal grating, will sit or bear on the rigid insulation rather the waterproof membrane as
in the traditional system." This protects the membrane from rubbing caused
by shifting movements in the waves, deck and metal grating as the construction crew builds the elements and as people "occupy the roof." Finally, they
plan to construct greenery-covered "waves" made of foam, and shaped to create a valley-like place to stroll.

THE ENVIRONMENT

Yes, green roofs help city environments. In addition to improving the environ- 29
ment of a single building, as we've discussed, they also improve the environment
of a city. That's the reason the German government gave green roofs a big push.
"Over 77 German municipalities invest in green roofs," says Elevated Landscape
Technologies of Brantfort, Ontario, Canada. As German cities got larger, municipal governments started to tax property owners for releasing storm water from
their properties. "This has been the largest driver in creating the developed
green-roof industry in Europe."

Why? Because green roofs cut runoff from roofs by about 40%, and also 30
delay the flow from roofs about 45 minutes. Both actions help city storm sewers cope with a storm runoff. If rain swamps a sewer's capacity, then storm
sewage overflows in the city.

Other benefits are more speculative. "If widely adopted, rooftop gardens 31
could reduce the urban heat island, which would decrease smog episodes . . ."
says Karen Liu of the NRC. Plants " . . . can also filter out airborne pollutants
washed off in the rain, thus improving the quality of the runoff," she adds. A
study done by Weston Design Consultants for Chicago estimates that the
greening of all of that city's rooftops would cut peak power demand for air
conditioning by 720 megawatts—which is the equivalent of several coal-fired
generating stations or one small nuclear power plant.

QUESTIONS FOR ANALYSIS

1. Where does the author first define what a green roof is and what it does?

_____

_____

_____

2. In which paragraphs does the author use quotations? Why does she give the source's credentials? What is the author's purpose in using quotations from these people? How do their explanations add to the process explanation?

3. What three effects can a green roof have on a building?

4. What are essential elements that make up a green roof? In your own words tell how the plants and soil affect the roof. Has the author clearly explained this step in the process?

5. In which paragraph does the author warn about the weight-bearing capacity of roofs?

6. What section of the article focuses on the positive effects of green roofs? What are some of these benefits?

7. Using *Living Green 365*'s "Ten Actions"—http://www.livinggreen.org/actions.cfm—as a reference, describe (in your own words, on separate paper) the process of "reduce, reuse, then recycle."

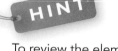

To review the elements of comparison and contrast, turn to Chapter 11.

Comparison and Contrast
Grant and Lee: A Study in Contrasts BRUCE CATTON

In the essay "Grant and Lee: A Study in Contrasts," Bruce Catton compares and contrasts the two leading generals of the North and South during the Civil War. The author's purpose is not to argue for the superiority of one general over the other but rather to give readers some insight into the two men. As you read, think about which of the two you most identify with. Do you think the differences between the two men are still represented as divisions between the North and South in our country?

1   When Ulysses S. Grant and Robert E. Lee met in the parlor of a modest house at Appomattox Court House, Virginia, on April 9, 1865, to work out the terms for the surrender of Lee's Army of Northern Virginia, a great chapter in American life came to a close, and a great new chapter began.

These men were bringing the Civil War to its virtual finish. To be sure, 2
other armies had yet to surrender, and for a few days the fugitive Confederate
government would struggle desperately and vainly, trying to find some way
to go on living now that its chief support was gone. But in effect it was all over
when Grant and Lee signed the papers. And the little room where they wrote
out the terms was the scene of one of the poignant, dramatic contrasts in
American history.

They were two strong men, these oddly different generals, and they rep- 3
resented the strengths of two conflicting currents that, through them, had
come into final collision.

Back of Robert E. Lee was the notion that the old aristocratic concept might 4
somehow survive and be dominant in American life.

Lee was tidewater Virginia, and in his background were family, culture, and 5
tradition . . . the age of chivalry transplanted to a New World which was making
its own legends and its own myths. He embodied a way of life that had come
down through the age of knighthood and the English country squire. America
was a land that was beginning all over again, dedicated to nothing much more
complicated than the rather hazy belief that all men had equal rights and should
have an equal chance in the world. In such a land Lee stood for the feeling that
it was somehow of advantage to human society to have a pronounced inequal-
ity in the social structure. There should be a leisure class, backed by ownership
of land; in turn, society itself should be keyed to the land as the chief source of
wealth and influence. It would bring forth (according to this ideal) a class of
men with a strong sense of obligation to the community; men who lived not to
gain advantage for themselves, but to meet the solemn obligations which had
been laid on them by the very fact that they were privileged. From them the
country would get its leadership; to them it could look for the higher values—of
thought, of conduct, of personal deportment—to give it strength and virtue.

Lee embodied the noblest elements of this aristocratic ideal. Through him, 6
the landed nobility justified itself. For four years, the Southern states had
fought a desperate war to uphold the ideals for which Lee stood. In the end,
it almost seemed as if the Confederacy fought for Lee; as if he himself was the
Confederacy . . . the best thing that the way of life for which the Confederacy
stood could ever have to offer. He had passed into legend before Appomattox.
Thousands of tired, underfed, poorly clothed Confederate soldiers, long since
past the simple enthusiasm of the early days of the struggle, somehow considered Lee the symbol of everything for which they had been willing to die.
But they could not quite put this feeling into words. If the Lost Cause, sancti-
fied by so much heroism and so many deaths, had a living justification, its
justification was General Lee.

Grant, the son of a tanner on the Western frontier, was everything Lee 7
was not. He had come up the hard way and embodied nothing in particular
except the eternal toughness and sinewy fiber of the men who grew up beyond
the mountains. He was one of a body of men who owed reverence and obei-
sance to no one, who were self-reliant to a fault, who cared hardly anything
for the past but who had a sharp eye for the future.

These frontier men were the precise opposite of the tidewater aristocrats. 8
Back of them, in the great surge that had taken people over the Alleghenies

and into the opening Western country, there was a deep, implicit dissatisfaction with a past that had settled into grooves. They stood for democracy, not from any reasoned conclusion about the proper ordering of human society, but simply because they had grown up in the middle of democracy and knew how it worked. Their society might have privileges, but they would be privileges each man had won for himself. Forms and patterns meant nothing. No man was born to anything, except perhaps to a chance to show how far he could rise. Life was competition.

9   Yet along with this feeling had come a deep sense of belonging to a national community. The Westerner who developed a farm, opened a shop, or set up in business as a trader, could hope to prosper only as his own community prospered—and his community ran from the Atlantic to the Pacific and from Canada down to Mexico. If the land was settled, with towns and highways and accessible markets, he could better himself. He saw his fate in terms of the nation's own destiny. As its horizons expanded, so did his. He had, in other words, an acute dollars-and-cents stake in the continued growth and development of his country.

10   And that, perhaps, is where the contrast between Grant and Lee becomes most striking. The Virginia aristocrat, inevitably, saw himself in relation to his own region. He lived in a static society which could endure almost anything except change. Instinctively, his first loyalty would go to the locality in which that society existed. He would fight to the limit of endurance to defend it, because in defending it he was defending everything that gave his own life its deepest meaning.

11   The Westerner, on the other hand, would fight with an equal tenacity for the broader concept of society. He fought so because everything he lived by was tied to growth, expansion, and a constantly widening horizon. What he lived by would survive or fall with the nation itself. He could not possibly stand by unmoved in the face of an attempt to destroy the Union. He would combat it with everything he had, because he could only see it as an effort to cut the ground out from under his feet.

12   So Grant and Lee were in complete contrast, representing two diametrically opposed elements in American life. Grant was the modern man emerging; beyond him, ready to come on the stage, was the great age of steel and machinery, of crowded cities and a restless burgeoning vitality. Lee might have ridden down from the old age of chivalry, lance in hand, silken banner fluttering over his head. Each man was the perfect champion of his cause, drawing both his strengths and his weaknesses from the people he led.

13   Yet it was not all contrast, after all. Different as they were—in background, in personality, in underlying aspiration—these two great soldiers had much in common. Under everything else, they were marvelous fighters. Furthermore, their fighting qualities were really very much alike.

14   Each man had, to begin with, the great virtue of utter tenacity and fidelity. Grant fought his way down the Mississippi Valley in spite of acute personal discouragement and profound military handicaps. Lee hung on in the trenches at Petersburg after hope itself had died. In each man there was an indomitable quality . . . the born fighter's refusal to give up as long as he can still remain on his feet and lift his two fists.

Daring and resourcefulness they had, too; the ability to think faster and 15
move faster than the enemy. These were the qualities which gave Lee the
dazzling campaigns of Second Manassas and Chancellorsville and won Vicks-
burg for Grant.

Lastly, and perhaps greatest of all, there was the ability, at the end, to turn 16
quickly from war to peace once the fighting was over. Out of the way these
two men behaved at Appomattox came the possibility of a peace of reconcili-
ation. It was a possibility not wholly realized, in the years to come, but which
did, in the end, help the two sections to become one nation again . . . after a
war whose bitterness might have seemed to make such a reunion wholly
impossible. No part of either man's life became him more than the part he
played in their brief meeting in the McLean house at Appomattox. Their
behavior there put all succeeding generations of Americans in their debt. Two
great Americans, Grant and Lee—very different, yet under everything very
much alike. Their encounter at Appomattox was one of the great moments of
American history.

QUESTIONS FOR ANALYSIS

1. Essays that compare and contrast organize material by the block or
   point-by-point method and sometimes both. In this essay, which paragraphs are devoted exclusively to Lee and which to Grant? Are these
   paragraphs comparing or contrasting?

   _____

   _____

2. Which paragraphs discuss the similarities of the two generals? Has the
   method of organizing shifted? Are the comparison paragraphs arranged
   by the block method or point-by-point?

   _____

   _____

3. Transitional words are particularly important when moving from one
   paragraph to another in comparison/contrast essays. Identify the transitional words in the first sentences of paragraphs 9–13.

   _____

   _____

4. Identify the topic sentence in paragraph 5, and explain if it is effective
   or not. Which example uses cause and effect for development?

   _____

   _____

5. Contrast the views of Lee and Grant toward their communities as discussed in paragraphs 5 and 9. What is the fundamental difference
   between the two men?

   _____

   _____

6. If you think the concluding paragraph is effective, what makes it work? What final thought does Catton leave us with?

   _____

   _____

7. Using the block method, use the City Comparison at http://www. bestplaces.net/city/ to compare any two locations in the United States. Based on your findings, write (on separate paper) a paragraph comparing or contrasting features like crime, education, climate, and cost of living.

Why Men Don't Last: Self-Destruction as a Way of Life
NATALIE ANGIER

In the following essay, Pulitzer Prize–winning journalist Natalie Angier examines the habits of men and women in the United States, speculating on what drives men to an early death, on average seven years ahead of women. Notice how the author begins her essay with the personal example of her father but then relies heavily on external sources to develop the rest of the essay. As you read this piece, does any of the information surprise you? What traits can you identify in yourself?

1   My father had great habits. Long before ficus trees met weight machines, he was a dogged exerciser. He did pushups and isometrics. He climbed rocks. He went for long, vigorous walks. He ate sparingly and avoided sweets and grease. He took such good care of his teeth that they looked fake.

2   My father had terrible habits. He was chronically angry. He threw things around the house and broke them. He didn't drink often, but when he did, he turned more violent than usual. He didn't go to doctors, even when we begged him to. He let a big, ugly mole on his back grow bigger and bigger, and so he died of malignant melanoma, a curable cancer, at 51.

3   My father was a real man—so good and so bad. He was also Everyman.

4   Men by some measures take better care of themselves than women do and are in better health. They are less likely to be fat, for example; they exercise more, and suffer from fewer chronic diseases like diabetes, osteoporosis and arthritis.

5   By standard measures, men have less than half the rate of depression seen in women. When men do feel depressed, they tend to seek distraction in an activity, which, many psychologists say, can be a more effective technique for dispelling the mood than is a depressed woman's tendency to turn inward and ruminate. In the United States and many other industrialized nations, women are about three times more likely than men to express suicidal thoughts or to attempt to kill themselves.

6   And yet . . . men don't last. They die off in greater numbers than women do at every stage of life, and thus their average life span is seven years shorter. Women may attempt suicide relatively more often, but in the United States, four times more men than women die from the act each year.

7   Men are also far more likely than women to die behind the wheel or to kill others as a result of their driving. From 1977 to 1995, three and a half times

more male drivers than female drivers were involved in fatal car crashes. Death by homicide also favors men; among those under 30, the male-to-female ratio is 8 to 1.

Yes, men can be impressive in their tendency to self-destruct, explosively or 8 gradually. They are at least twice as likely as women to be alcoholics and three times more likely to be drug addicts. They have an eightfold greater chance than women do of ending up in prison. Boys are much more likely than girls to be thrown out of school for a conduct or antisocial personality disorder, or to drop out on their own surly initiative. Men gamble themselves into a devastating economic and emotional pit two to three times more often than women do.

"Between boys' suicide rates, dropout rates and homicide rates, and men's 9 self-destructive behaviors generally, we have a real crisis in America," said William S. Pollack, a psychologist at Harvard Medical School and co-director of the Center for Men at McLean Hospital in Belmont, Mass. "Until recently, the crisis has gone unheralded."

It is one thing to herald a presumed crisis, though, and to cite a ream of 10 gloomy statistics. It is quite another to understand the crisis, or to figure out where it comes from or what to do about it. As those who study the various forms of men's self-destructive behaviors realize, there is not a single, glib, over-arching explanation for the sex-specific patterns they see.

A crude evolutionary hypothesis would have it that men are natural risk- 11 takers, given to showy displays of bravado, aggression and daring all for the sake of attracting a harem of mates. By this premise, most of men's self-destructive, violent tendencies are a manifestation of their need to take big chances for the sake of passing their genes into the river of tomorrow.

Some of the data on men's bad habits fit the risk-taker model. For example, 12 those who study compulsive gambling have observed that men and women tend to display very different methods and preferences for throwing away big sums of money.

"Men get enamored of the action in gambling," said Linda Chamberlain, a 13 psychologist at Regis University in Denver who specializes in treating gambling disorders. "They describe an overwhelming rush of feelings and excitement associated with the process of gambling. They like the feeling of being a player, and taking on a struggle with the house to show that they can overcome the odds and beat the system. They tend to prefer the table games, where they can feel powerful and omnipotent while everybody watches them."

Dr. Chamberlain noted that many male gamblers engage in other risk- 14 taking behaviors, like auto racing or hang gliding. By contrast, she said, "Women tend to use gambling more as a sedative, to numb themselves and escape from daily responsibilities, or feelings of depression or alienation. Women tend to prefer the solitary forms of gambling, the slot machines or video poker, where there isn't as much social scrutiny."

Yet the risk-taking theory does not account for why men outnumber 15 women in the consumption of licit and illicit anodynes. Alcohol, heroin and marijuana can be at least as numbing and sedating as repetitively pulling the arm of a slot machine. And some studies have found that men use drugs and alcohol for the same reasons that women often overeat: as an attempt to self-medicate when they are feeling anxious or in despair.

16   "We can speculate all we want, but we really don't know why men drink more than women," said Enoch Gordis, the head of the National Institute on Alcohol Abuse and Alcoholism. Nor does men's comparatively higher rate of suicide appear linked to the risk-taking profile. To the contrary, Paul Duberstein, an assistant professor of psychiatry and oncology at the University of Rochester School of Medicine, has found that people who complete a suicidal act are often low in a personality trait referred to as "openness to experience," tending to be rigid and inflexible in their behaviors. By comparison, those who express suicidal thoughts tend to score relatively high on the openness-to-experience scale.

17   Given that men commit suicide more often than women, and women talk about it more, his research suggests that, in a sense, women are the greater risk-takers and novelty seekers, while the men are likelier to feel trapped and helpless in the face of changing circumstances.

18   Silvia Cara Canetto, an associate professor of psychology at Colorado State University in Fort Collins, has extensively studied the role of gender in suicidal behaviors. Dr. Canetto has found that cultural narratives may determine why women attempt suicide more often while men kill themselves more often. She proposes that in Western countries, to talk about suicide or to survive a suicidal act is often considered "feminine," hysterical, irrational, and weak. To actually die by one's own hand may be viewed as "masculine," decisive, strong. Even the language conveys the polarized, weak-strong imagery: a "failed" suicide attempt as opposed to a "successful" one.

19   "There is indirect evidence that there is negative stigma toward men who survive suicide," Dr. Canetto said. "Men don't want to 'fail,' even though failing in this case means surviving." If the "suicidal script" that identifies completing the acts as "rational, courageous and masculine" can be "undermined and torn to pieces," she said, we might have a new approach to prevention.

20   Dr. Pollak of the Center for Men also blames many of men's self-destructive ways on the persistent image of the dispassionate, resilient, action-oriented male—the Marlboro Man who never even gasps for breath. For all the talk of the sensitive "new man," he argues, men have yet to catch up with women in expanding their range of acceptable emotions and behaviors. Men in our culture, Dr. Pollack says, are pretty much limited to a menu of three strong feelings: rage, triumph, lust. "Anything else and you risk being seen as a sissy," he said.

21   In a number of books, most recently, "Real Boys: Rescuing Our Sons from the Myths of Boyhood," he proposes that boys "lose their voice, a whole half of their emotional selves," beginning at age 4 or 5. "Their vulnerable, sad feelings and sense of need are suppressed or shamed out of them," he said—by their peers, parents, the great wide televised fist in their face.

22   He added: "If you keep hammering it into a kid that he has to look tough and stop being a crybaby and a mama's boy, the boy will start creating a mask of bravado."

23   That boys and young men continue to feel confused over the proper harmonics of modern masculinity was revealed in a study that Dr. Pollack conducted of 200 eighth-grade boys. Through questionnaires, he determined their scores on two scales, one measuring their "egalitarianism"—the degree to which they think men and women are equal, that men should change a baby's

diapers, that mothers should work and the like—and the other gauging their "traditionalism" as determined by their responses to conventional notions, like the premise that men must "stand on their own two feet" and must "always be willing to have sex if someone asks."

On average, the boys scored high on both scales. "They are split on what 24 it means to be a man," said Dr. Pollack.

The cult of masculinity can beckon like a siren song in baritone. Dr. Frank- 25 lin L. Nelson, a clinical psychologist at the Fairbanks Community Mental Health Center in Alaska, sees many men who get into trouble by adhering to sentimental notions of manhood. "A lot of men come up here hoping to get away from a wimpy world and live like pioneers by old-fashioned masculine principles of individualism, strength and ruggedness," he said. They learn that nothing is simple; even Alaska is part of a wider, interdependent world and they really do need friends, warmth and electricity.

"Right now, it's 35 degrees below zero outside," he said during a January 26 interview. "If you're not prepared, it doesn't take long at that temperature to freeze to death."

QUESTIONS FOR ANALYSIS

1. Evaluate the author's introduction: hook, development, and thesis. Where does the introduction end, and where is the thesis first mentioned? Why do you think beginning an essay with personal examples can be effective?

   _____

   _____

   _____

2. How is this article arranged, by the block or point-by-point method? If the author had chosen the other method, would the presentation be as effective—why or why not?

   _____

   _____

   _____

3. Is this an essay largely of comparison or contrast? List several of the author's points to explain your answer.

   _____

   _____

   _____

4. In which paragraphs does Angier speculate about men's risk-taking tendencies and how they might help explain why men die sooner than women? Choose one or more specific examples she uses and tell how the examples help illustrate her point.

   _____

   _____

   _____

5. In paragraphs 17–19, the author contrasts men's approach to suicide with women's. What is the difference between these approaches, and why do more men than women die from suicide?

_____

_____

_____

6. Metaphorical language links contrasting images to make a point. In the context of paragraphs 21 and 22, explain what Angier means by "the great wide televised fist in their face."

_____

_____

_____

7. The author moves into her conclusion in paragraphs 25 and 26. Why do you suppose she ends with the quotation from the clinical psychologist from Fairbanks, Alaska? How does Alaska figure into the image of "masculinity" for some men who move there? How might freezing to death relate to those who feel they must isolate themselves to be "real men"?

_____

_____

_____

_____

8. According to a 2005 study, men and women share many more similarities than differences. Read this article at http://www.timesonline.co.uk/tol/news/uk/article567852.ece and then write a paragraph (on separate paper) choosing to compare or contrast the sexes using the point-by-point method. Include specific examples from your own experiences.

Definition

They've Gotta Keep It: People Who Save Everything

LYNDA W. WARREN AND
JONNAE C. OSTROM

Lynda W. Warren, a psychologist and psychology professor, and Jonnae C. Ostrom, a clinical social worker, discuss a group of people known as "pack rats," or excessive savers, in this article published in *Psychology Today*. The authors are surprised to learn that compulsive savers are not only older people reacting to the deprivation they felt during the Great Depression; rather, pack rats are often young and can be found in every economic bracket. As is common in definition essays, you will find the term explored through the brief definition strategies listed in Chapter 15—synonyms, negation, comparisons, formal definition—and several of the patterns of development, especially cause and effect.

1   Most of us have more things than we need and use. At times they pile up in corners and closets or accumulate in the recesses of attics, basements or garages. But we sort through our clutter periodically and clean it up, saving

only what we really need and giving away or throwing out the excess. This isn't the case, unfortunately, with people we call "pack rats"—those who collect, save or hoard insatiably, often with only the vague rationale that the items may someday be useful. And because they rarely winnow what they save, it grows and grows.

While some pack rats specialize in what they collect, others seem to save 2 indiscriminately. And what they keep, such as junk mail, supermarket receipts, newspapers, business memos, empty cans, clothes or old Christmas and birthday cards, often seem to be worthless. Even when items have some value, such as lumber scraps, fabric remnants, auto parts, shoes and plastic meat trays, they tend to be kept in huge quantities that no one could use in a lifetime.

Although pack rats collect, they are different from collectors, who save in 3 a systematic way. Collectors usually specialize in one or a few classes of objects, which they organize, display and even catalogue. But pack rats tend to stockpile their possessions haphazardly and seldom use them.

Our interest in pack rats was sparked by a combination of personal expe- 4 rience with some older relatives and recognition of similar saving patterns in some younger clients one of us saw in therapy sessions. Until then, we, like most people, assumed that pack rats were all older people who had lived through the Great Depression of the 1930s—eccentrics who were stockpiling stuff just in case another Depression came along. We were surprised to discover a younger generation of pack rats, born long after the 1930s.

None of these clients identified themselves during therapy as pack rats or 5 indicated that their hoarding tendencies were causing problems in any way. Only after their partners told us how annoyed and angry they were about the pack rats' unwillingness to clean up the growing mess at home did they acknowledge their behavior. Even then, they defended it and had little interest in changing. The real problem, they implied, was their partner's intolerance rather than their own hoarding.

Like most people, we had viewed excessive saving as a rare and harmless 6 eccentricity. But when we discussed our initial observations with others, we gradually came to realize that almost everyone we met either admitted to some strong pack-rat tendencies or seemed to know someone who had them. Perhaps the greatest surprise, however, was how eager people were to discuss their own pack-rat experiences. Although our observations are admittedly based on a small sample, we now believe that such behavior is common and that, particularly when it is extreme, it may create problems for the pack rats or those close to them.

When we turned to the psychological literature, we found surprisingly 7 little about human collecting or hoarding in general and almost nothing about pack-rat behavior. Psychoanalysts view hoarding as one characteristic of the "anal" character type, first described by Freud. Erich Fromm later identified the "hoarding orientation" as one of the four basic ways in which people may adjust unproductively to life.

While some pack rats do have typically anal-retentive characteristics such 8 as miserliness, orderliness and stubbornness, we suspect that they vary as much in personality characteristics as they do in education, socioeconomic status and occupation. But they do share certain ways of thinking and feeling about their possessions that shed some light on the possible causes and consequences of their behavior.

9   Why do some people continue to save when there is no more space for what they have and they own more of something than could ever be used? We have now asked that question of numerous students, friends and colleagues who have admitted their pack-rat inclinations. They readily answer the question with seemingly good reasons, such as possible future need ("I might need this sometime"), sentimental attachment ("Aunt Edith gave this to me"), potential value ("This might be worth something someday") and lack of wear or damage ("This is too good to throw away"). Such reasons are difficult to challenge; they are grounded in some truth and logic and suggest that pack-rat saving reflects good sense, thrift and even foresight. Indeed, many pack rats proudly announce, "I've never thrown anything away!" or "You would not believe what I keep!"

10   But on further questioning, other, less logical reasons become apparent. Trying to get rid of things may upset pack rats emotionally and may even bring on physical distress. As one woman said, "I get a headache or sick to my stomach if I have to throw something away."

11   They find it hard to decide what to keep and what to throw away. Sometimes they fear they will get rid of something that they or someone else might value, now or later. Having made such a "mistake" in the past seems to increase such distress. "I've always regretted throwing away the letters Mother sent me in college. I will never make that mistake again," one client said. Saving the object eliminates the distress and is buttressed by the reassuring thought, "Better to save this than be sorry later."

12   Many pack rats resemble compulsive personalities in their tendency to avoid or postpone decisions, perhaps because of an inordinate fear of making a mistake. Indeed, in the latest edition of the psychiatric diagnostic bible (DSM-III-R), the kind of irrational hoarding seen in pack rats ("inability to discard worn-out or worthless objects even when they have no sentimental value") is described as a characteristic of people with obsessive compulsive personality disorder.

13   Some pack rats seem to have a depressive side, too. Discarding things seems to reawaken old memories and feelings of loss or abandonment, akin to grief or the pain of rejection. "I feel incredibly sad—it's really very painful," one client said of the process. Another client, a mental-health counselor, said, "I don't understand why, but when I have to throw something away, even something like dead flowers, I feel my old abandonment fears and I also feel lonely."

14   Some pack rats report that their parents discarded certain treasured possessions, apparently insensitive to their attachment to the objects. "My Dad went through my room one time and threw out my old shell collection that I had in a closet. It devastated me," said one woman we interviewed. Such early experiences continue to color their feelings as adults, particularly toward possessions they especially cherish.

15   It's not uncommon for pack rats to "personalize" their possessions or identify with them, seeing them as extensions of themselves. One pack rat defiantly said about her things, "This is me—this is my individuality and you are not going to throw it out!"

At times the possessions are viewed akin to beloved people. For example, 16
one woman said, "I can't let my Christmas tree be destroyed! I love my Christmas
ornaments—I adore them!" Another woman echoed her emotional involvement: "My jewelry is such a comfort to me. I just love my rings and chains."
Discarding such personalized possessions could easily trigger fears, sadness
or guilt because it would be psychologically equivalent to a part of oneself
dying or abandoning a loved one.

In saving everything, the pack rat seems to have found the perfect way to 17
avoid indecision and the discomfort of getting rid of things. It works—but only
for a while. The stuff keeps mounting, and so do the problems it produces.

Attempts to clean up and organize may be upsetting because there is too 18
much stuff to manage without spending enormous amounts of time and effort.
One pack rat sighed, "Just thinking about cleaning it up makes me tired before
I begin." And since even heroic efforts at cleaning bring barely visible results,
such unrewarding efforts are unlikely to continue.

At this point, faced with ever-growing goods and ineffective ways of get- 19
ting rid of the excess, pack rats may begin to feel controlled by their possessions. As one put it, "I'm at the point where I feel impotent about getting my
bedroom cleaned."

Even if the clutter doesn't get the pack rats down, it often irks others in 20
the household who do not share the same penchant for saving. Since hoarding
frequently begins in the bedroom, the pack rat's partner is usually the first to
be affected. He or she begins to feel squeezed out by accumulated possessions,
which may seem to take precedence over the couple's relationship.

At first, the partner may simply feel bewildered about the growing mess 21
and uncertain about what to do, since requests to remove the "junk" tend to
be ignored or met with indignation or even anger. One exasperated husband
of a pack-rat client said: "She keeps her stuff in paper bags all over the bedroom. You can now hardly get to the bed. I tried talking to her about it but
nothing seems to work. When she says she has cleaned it out, I can never see
any change. I'm ready to hire a truck to cart it all away."

As the junk piles accumulate, the partner may try to clean up the mess. 22
But that generally infuriates the pack rat and does nothing to break the savings
habit. As the partner begins to feel increasingly impotent, feelings of frustration and irritation escalate and the stockpiled possessions may become an
emotional barrier between the two. This situation is even worse if the pack rat
is also a compulsive shopper whose spending sprees are creating financial
problems and excessive family debt.

Children are also affected by a parent's pack-rat behavior. They may resent 23
having the family's living space taken over by piles of possessions and may
hesitate to ask their friends over because they are embarrassed by the excessive clutter and disarray. One child of a pack rat said, "As long as I can remember, I've always warned people what to expect the first time they come to our
house. I told them it was OK to move something so they would have a place
to sit down." Even the adults may rarely invite nonfamily members to visit
because the house is never presentable.

Children may also be caught in the middle of the escalating tension 24
between their parents over what to do about all the stuff in the house. But

whatever their feelings, it is clear that the children are being raised in an environment in which possessions are especially important and laden with complex emotions.

25   Our clients and other people we have consulted have helped make us aware of the problems pack rats can pose for themselves and those around them. Now we hope that a new study of excessive savers will provide some preliminary answers to a number of deeper questions: What predisposes people to become pack rats, and when does hoarding typically start? Can the behavior be averted or changed? Is excessive saving associated with earlier emotional or economic deprivation? Does such saving cause emotional distress directly or are pack rats only bothered when others disapprove of their behavior? Do pack rats run into problems at work the same way they often do at home?

26   Whatever additional information we come up with, we're already sure of at least one thing: This article will be saved forever by all the pack rats of the world.

QUESTIONS FOR ANALYSIS

1. In which sentence do you first learn the authors' focus for this essay? How do they define the term "pack rat"?

2. Write out the synonym the authors give in paragraph 25 for the term "pack rat."

3. The authors define through negation in paragraph 3. What do they tell us that pack rats are not?

4. Which of the patterns of development (for more on this, see pp. 9–10) do the authors mainly use in paragraphs 9–23?

5. Which one of the paragraphs in this essay begins with a question, and what is the authors' purpose in using it?

6. Drawing from traits and behaviors the authors describe in the article, write out a 10-point profile of a pack rat. What is the essential, defining trait of a pack rat?

7. Are paragraphs 25 and 26 an effective conclusion? Why or why not?

8. Read one blogger's account of excavating a hoarder's home at http://rarenest.blogspot.com/search/label/Hoarding. A short series of entries features before-and-after photographs and descriptions of the house, as well as information about hoarding. What other patterns of development does this writer use to help define *hoarding*?

What Is a Dad?

BOB BRANNAN

The essay "What Is a Dad?" offers several defining elements of fatherhood. Because this is an extended definition, you will find many of the patterns of development represented, as well as points common to brief definitions: synonyms, negation, comparisons, and formal defining. As you read, ask yourself if the designated audience—young married men who have just learned they are about to become fathers—would be interested in the examples and explanations provided.

"Honey, it's going to be a girl!" my wife of ten years said to me as I paused 1 near the top of the living room steps. I looked at the half a dozen pink balloons bouncing on the ceiling and at Beth smiling from above me at the head of the stairs. "Wonderful," I thought, and then immediately, "Oh, no!" Fatherhood was rushing at me like a space shuttle coming in with its payload from outer space, and I wasn't prepared. I dropped my briefcase on the landing, gave her a hug, and lied convincingly: "That's the best news I've heard this year." As we talked over the details of the sonogram, I thought hard about what lay ahead for us and about what I was going to become—a dad. I didn't know then much of what a dad was supposed to be, but I was sure it involved a lot more than just providing food, clothing, and shelter. And that's exactly what the past three years of raising a little girl has taught me: Being a dad is one of the hardest yet most rewarding jobs there is.

I had thought that being a father meant being a child again, just a quick 2 time travel back to the days of bare feet and endless summers, becoming a friend and playmate. Well, I was wrong . . . and right. Fathers can and should play with their children, the more the better. But that's not how I spent the first year with my daughter. No one had prepared me for the seemingly endless routine of feeding, burping, cleaning, rocking, and diaper changing that came with the territory. It wasn't until Lauren was fairly secure on her feet that we were able to play the way I had anticipated. But for the past two years we have been inseparable companions, creating fantasy games, role playing every Disney character that Walt ever helped bring into the world, and both learning to sing lots of drippy songs—God help whoever has to listen.

But becoming a good father requires more than just a willingness and 3 ability to become young again; a man must become fiercely, wholeheartedly protective. Of course we should be alert to the more predictable dangers for our children (put the gate across the stairs, pad all the sharp corners, put the locks on the cabinets, cover all the electrical outlets), but there is another world of potential hurt out there that most of us know next to nothing about. What if your son wakes up at three in the morning coughing uncontrollably? How about the ear infection and runny nose that never seem to go away? What do you do about those angry red welts that appear on, migrate across, disappear from, and then reappear on your little girl's skin? You might think that modern medicine and an enlightened, caring pediatrician could solve the problems. But often this is not so. Fathers and mothers are frequently on their own in this. If we care deeply for our children, we spend a lot of time finding out for ourselves how to help them.

4   However, the parent's life isn't all *that* dismal. Many fathers have supremely healthy children, which leaves the dads with more time for one of the most important roles he will play in his child's life, teacher. Yes, fathers-to-be, whatever you have done for a living up till this point, now you are a teacher. While some might view themselves more as a boss, benevolent monarch, or dictator, the truth is that we will be spending a large part of the next eighteen years (at least) trying to teach our children how to become happy, healthy, complete human beings. All the areas we work with from the initial ABCs and counting to restraining our anger—often at them!—to appreciating a spring daffodil or majestic sunset, all of these lessons, well taught, mark us as the most crucial teachers there can be. If we do our small jobs well, we slowly remake the world.

5   So what is a dad, really? As far as I can tell, he is a man who bravely and foolishly, with only limited vision, steps into a difficult lifelong role that he begins with almost no experience and ends, if he is lucky, having learned a little. Along the way he has profited immeasurably: he has had an attentive, enthusiastic playmate who laughs at his stupidest jokes and thinks his voice impressions are incredibly brilliant; he has become less selfish, if not selfless, learning to put the needs of another ahead of his own; and he has grown by giving daily without counting of his knowledge and wisdom, whatever they may be, as he teaches his son or daughter to the best of his ability. I suppose, in the end, the true measure of a good father is one who loves his children beyond himself—perhaps all others—and who can hope that the adult he has helped shape will for all her life be able to look back at the man and, at least on occasion, say, "I love you, dad."

QUESTIONS FOR ANALYSIS

1. Extended definitions often grow from several patterns of development. Name two from paragraph 2, and explain how they add to the paragraph.

_____

_____

_____

2. If you think the introductory paragraph is effective, what makes it work? Look especially at the hook (first sentence), the author's use of "I," the brief dialogue, revealing thoughts, and the thesis sentence. Write out the thesis sentence.

_____

_____

_____

3. If you think the concluding paragraph is effective, what makes it work? Why does the author use a question as the first sentence? What are the effects of being a father that the author lists?

_____

_____

_____

4. Brief definitions often include negation, comparisons (often as metaphor/simile), and synonyms. List each paragraph in which these occur, and explain how they add to your understanding of "fatherhood."

_____

_____

_____

5. What words in the topic sentence of paragraph 3 relate back to paragraph 2, and are they an effective connector?

_____

_____

6. Choose any paragraph and explain how the examples help develop the author's points.

_____

_____

_____

7. A website called *5 Minutes for Mom* sponsors a Mother's Day contest for photographs that best define "motherhood." You can see one 2008 entry and the story behind it at http://momology.blogspot.com/2008/04/defining-motherhood.html. How would you define "mother" with words and/or images? Find a specific photograph you've either taken or seen, and use it to write a paragraph (on separate paper) defining "mother" or "motherhood."

Persuasion

Abortion, Right and Wrong   RACHEL RICHARDSON SMITH

To review the elements of persuasion, turn to Chapter 16.

In the essay "Abortion, Right and Wrong," Rachel Richardson Smith argues for a broader perspective on the issue of abortion. As you read, think about the author's persona—how she presents herself to the audience—and her position on abortion. For an argument to be successful, does it need to convert a listener, or can it merely ask for greater tolerance and respect?

I cannot bring myself to say I am in favor of abortion. I don't want anyone to have one. I want people to use contraceptives and for those contraceptives to be foolproof. I want people to be responsible for their actions; mature in their decisions. I want children to be loved, wanted, well cared for. 1

I cannot bring myself to say I am against choice. I want women who are young, poor, single or all three to be able to direct the course of their lives. I want women who have had all the children they want or can afford or their bodies 2

can withstand to be able to decide their future. I want women who are in bad marriages or destructive relationships to avoid being trapped by pregnancy.

3   So in these days when thousands rally in opposition to legalized abortion, when facilities providing abortions are bombed, when the president speaks glowingly of the growing momentum behind the anti-abortion movement, I find myself increasingly alienated from the pro-life groups.

4   At the same time, I am overwhelmed with mail from pro-choice groups. They, too, are mobilizing their forces, growing articulate in support of their cause, and they want my support. I am not sure I can give it.

5   I find myself in the awkward position of being both anti-abortion and pro-choice. Neither group seems to be completely right—or wrong. It is not that I think abortion is wrong for me but acceptable for someone else. The question is far more complex than that.

6   Part of my problem is that what I think and how I feel about this issue are two entirely different matters. I know that unwanted children are often neglected, even abandoned. I know that many of those seeking abortions are children themselves. I know that making abortion illegal will not stop all women from having them.

ABSOLUTES

7   I also know from experience the crisis an unplanned pregnancy can cause. Yet I have felt the joy of giving birth, the delight that comes from feeling a baby's skin against my own. I know how hard it is to parent a child and how deeply satisfying it can be. My children sometimes provoke me and cause me endless frustration, but I can still look at them with tenderness and wonder at the miracle of it all. The lessons of my own experience produce conflicting emotions. Theory collides with reality.

8   It concerns me that both groups present themselves in absolutes. They are committed and they want me to commit. They do not recognize the gray area where I seem to be languishing. Each group has the right answer—the only answer.

9   Yet I am uncomfortable in either camp. I have nothing in common with the pro-lifers. I am horrified by their scare tactics, their pictures of well-formed fetuses tossed in a metal pan, their cruel slogans. I cannot condone their flagrant misuse of Scripture and unforgiving spirit. There is a meanness about their position that causes them to pass judgment on the lives of women in a way I could never do.

10   The pro-life groups, with their fundamentalist religious attitudes, have a fear and an abhorrence of sex, especially premarital sex. In their view abortion only compounds the sexual sin. What I find incomprehensible is that even as they are opposed to abortion they are also opposed to alternative solutions. They are squeamish about sex education in the schools. They don't want teens to have contraceptives without parental consent. They offer little aid or sympathy to unwed mothers. They are the vigilant guardians of a narrow morality.

11   I wonder how abortion got to be the greatest of all sins? What about poverty, ignorance, hunger, weaponry?

12   The only thing the anti-abortion groups seem to have right is that abortion is indeed the taking of a human life. I simply cannot escape this one glaring fact. Call it what you will—fertilized egg, embryo, fetus. What we have here is human

life. If it were just a mass of tissue there would be no debate. So I agree that abortion ends a life. But the anti-abortionists are wrong to call it murder.

The sad truth is that homicide is not always against the law. Our society 13 does not categorically recognize the sanctity of human life. There are a number of legal and apparently socially acceptable ways to take human life. "Justifiable" homicide includes the death penalty, war, killing in self-defense. It seems to me that as a society we need to come to grips with our own ambiguity concerning the value of human life. If we are to value and protect unborn life so stringently, why do we not also value and protect life already born?

MISTAKES

Why can't we see abortion for the human tragedy it is? No woman plans 14 for her life to turn out that way. Even the most effective contraceptives are no guarantee against pregnancy. Loneliness, ignorance, immaturity, can lead to decisions (or lack of decisions) that may result in untimely pregnancy. People make mistakes.

What many people seem to misunderstand is that no woman wants to 15 have an abortion. Circumstances demand it; women do it. No woman reacts to abortion with joy. Relief, yes. But also ambivalence, grief, despair, guilt.

The pro-choice groups do not seem to acknowledge that abortion is not a 16 perfect answer. What goes unsaid is that when a woman has an abortion she loses more than an unwanted pregnancy. Often she loses her self-respect. No woman can forget a pregnancy no matter how it ends.

Why can we not view abortion as one of those anguished decisions in 17 which human beings struggle to do the best they can in trying circumstances? Why is abortion viewed so coldly and factually on the one hand and so judgmentally on the other? Why is it not akin to the same painful experience families must sometimes make to allow a loved one to die?

I wonder how we can begin to change the context in which we think about 18 abortion. How can we begin to think about it redemptively? What is it in the trauma of loss of life—be it loved or unloved, born or unborn—from which we can learn? There is much I have yet to resolve. Even as I refuse to pass judgment on other women's lives, I weep for the children who might have been. I suspect I am not alone.

QUESTIONS FOR ANALYSIS

1. A good argument defines its issue early. Where in the first few paragraphs do we learn what the issue is in this essay?

   _____

   _____

2. What is the author's position on the issue, and in which paragraph is it most clearly stated?

   _____

   _____

   _____

3. How would you characterize the author's persona? (For more on persona, see pp. 485–486.) What points in the essay make you feel this way?

_____

_____

_____

4. Strong arguments require clear terminology and refutation of opposing reasons. In which paragraph does the author define a key term? How does the definition help refute a pro-life reason?

_____

_____

_____

5. In which paragraph does the author deal with the issue of the fetus as human? Does her position support pro-life or pro-choice?

_____

_____

6. All arguments grow from assertions supported by detailed examples and explanations. Identify the topic sentence in paragraph 9, and then list the examples the author offers to support her assertion.

_____

_____

7. What three reasons does the author list in paragraph 6 that support the pro-choice position?

_____

_____

8. To preserve their credibility by limiting overstatement, writers qualify frequently in argument (using words like _seems, might, often,_ and _frequently_). Name three instances of qualifying in paragraphs 5–7. (For more on qualifying in argument, see pp. 465–484.)

_____

_____

9. Spend some time on www.prolife.com and www.prochoice.com. Can you articulate the central point each site makes? What is the purpose of each site? What arguments does it offer, and what support does it provide? In a paragraph (on separate paper), explain why you would refer a woman to one site over the other, to both, or to neither.

What Is Biodiversity and Why Should We Care about It?

DONELLA MEADOWS

"What Is Biodiversity and Why Should We Care About It?" comes from the book _The Global Citizen_, written by Donella Meadows in 1991. The author argues that people do not care enough for their planet, that if we continue to destroy plant and animal habitats we will ultimately destroy ourselves. As

you read this article, imagine yourself as part of Meadows's target audience— people who are interested in the environment but not well informed on matters like "biodiversity." Does the author hold your interest and speak persuasively to you, or do you feel alienated at any point, as if the author is reprimanding you?

1　Most of us have grasped the idea that there's a hole in the sky over the South Pole that could give us skin cancer. We are beginning to understand that a global warming could inundate Miami Beach and make New York even more unbearable in the summer. There is another environmental problem, however, that doesn't have a catchy name like "ozone hole" or "greenhouse effect," and that hasn't yet entered the public consciousness. It's the loss of biodiversity.

2　Bio-*what?*

3　Biodiversity sounds like it has to do with pandas and tigers and tropical rain forests. It does, but it's bigger than those, bigger than a single species or even a single ecosystem. It's the whole, all of life, the microscopic creepy-crawlies as well as the elephants and condors. It's all the habitats, beautiful or not, that support life—the tundra, prairie, and swamp as well as the tropical forest.

4　Why care about tundras and swamps? There's one good reason—self-interest. Preserving biodiversity is not something to do out of kindness of our hearts, to express our fondness for fuzzy creatures on Sunday mornings when we happen to feel virtuous. It's something to do to maintain the many forms of life we eat and use, and to maintain ourselves.

5　How would you like the job of pollinating all trillion or so apple blossoms in the state of New York some sunny afternoon in May? It's conceivable, maybe, that you could invent a machine to do it, but inconceivable that the machine could work as efficiently, elegantly, and cheaply as honeybees, much less make honey.

6　Suppose you were assigned to turn every bit of dead organic matter—from fallen leaves to urban garbage to road kills—into nutrients that feed new life. Even if you knew how, what would it cost? Uncountable numbers of bacteria, molds, mites, and worms do it for free. If they ever stopped, all life would stop. We would not last long if green plants stopped turning our exhaled carbon dioxide back into oxygen. The plants would not last long if a few beneficent kinds of soil bacteria stopped turning nitrogen from the air into fertilizer.

7　Human reckoning cannot put a value on the services performed for us by the millions of species of life on earth. In addition to pollination and recycling, these services include flood control, drought prevention, pest control, temperature regulation, and maintenance of the world's most valuable library, the genes of all living organisms, a library we are just learning to read.

8　Another thing we are just learning is that both the genetic library and the ecosystem's services depend on the integrity of the entire biological world. All species fit together in an intricate, interdependent, self-sustaining whole. Rips in the biological fabric tend to run. Gaps cause things to fall in unexpected ways.

9　For example, attempts to replant acacia trees in the Sahel at the edge of the Sahara desert have failed because the degraded soil has lost a bacterium called rhizobium, without which acacia trees can't grow. Songbirds that eat summer insects in North America are declining because of deforestation in their Central American wintering grounds. European forests are more vulnerable to acid rain than American forests because they are human-managed, single-species plantations rather than natural mixtures of many species forming an interknit, resilient system.

10   Biodiversity cannot be maintained by protecting a few charismatic megafauna in a zoo, not by preserving a few greenbelts of even large national parks. Biodiversity can maintain itself, however, without human attention or expense, without zookeepers, park rangers, foresters, or refrigerated gene banks. All it needs is to be left alone.

11   It is not being left alone, of course, which is why biological impoverishment has become a problem of global dimensions. There is hardly a place left on earth, where people do not log, pave, spray, drain, flood, graze, fish, plow, burn, drill, spill, or dump.

12   Ecologists estimate that human beings usurp, directly or indirectly, about 40 percent of each year's total biological production (and our population is on its way to another doubling in forty years). There is no biome, with the possible exception of the deep ocean, that we are not degrading. In poor countries biodiversity is being nickeled and dimed to death; in rich countries it is being billion-dollared to death.

13   To provide their priceless service to us, the honeybees ask only that we stop saturating the landscape with poisons, stop paving the meadows and verges where bee food grows, and leave them enough honey to get through the winter.

14   To maintain our planet and our lives, the other species have similar requests, all of which, summed up, are: Control yourselves. Control your numbers. Control your greed. See yourselves as what you are, part of an interdependent biological community, the most intelligent part, though you don't often act that way. Act that way. Do so either out of a moral respect for something wonderful that you did not create and do not understand or out of a practical interest in your own survival.

QUESTIONS FOR ANALYSIS

1. Evaluate the introduction. Does the first sentence arouse readers' curiosity? Do the middle sentences speak to the audience's interests and knowledge? Does the paragraph indicate what the article will be about? What pronouns help connect the writer to the audience?

_____

_____

_____

_____

2. Effective arguments quickly clarify their issue. One way to do this is by defining terms. In which paragraph does Meadows begin to define her key term, and what specific examples does she use to illustrate her definition? Has the author made a mistake by not also defining the term *ecosystem*? Why or why not?

_____

_____

_____

_____

3. Persuasive writing gives people reasons to accept a writer's position. What is the author's primary reason to support her position, where does she first state it, and how clearly does she explain it? What objection or misconception in this paragraph does she anticipate and counter?

_____

_____

_____

_____

4. Without support, reasons are unconvincing. What paragraphs does Meadows devote to supporting her primary reason? What main examples does she offer for support in paragraphs 5 and 6? Does the author's use of *you* in these paragraphs seem appropriate? Why would she combine *you* with a question as the first sentence in paragraph 5?

_____

_____

_____

_____

5. Because writers regularly combine the patterns of development in supporting their ideas, you will find several in this article, including cause and effect. Locate two instances of cause and effect, and explain how effectively they are used to help make the author's point.

_____

_____

_____

_____

6. All arguments deal with counterreasons and objections to the author's position. What is the counterreason offered in paragraph 10, and how well does Meadows refute it?

_____

_____

_____

_____

7. Connecting paragraphs in essays is important to ease readers from one idea into the next. What connecting methods does Meadows use to link paragraphs 1–4?

_____

_____

_____

_____

8. How effective is the concluding paragraph? What points does the author remind us of; what is the expanded thought? What device does Meadows use to keep from having to criticize her audience, even though she does use the pronoun *you*?

9. Go to http://www.biodiversityhotspots.org/ and choose one "hotspot" to read about. After reading the information, write an information paragraph summarizing what you have read in your own words. Then rephrase this material in a new paragraph that argues a point persuasively.

Nobel Acceptance Speech (excerpt) AL GORE

Persuasive writing seeks to move people to think or act a certain way. In Al Gore's Nobel acceptance speech, you will see that the author's purpose is quite clear: to move his listeners to take action on global warming. As you read through this article, remember that it is a speech, meant to be delivered at a measured pace with pauses built in for effect and short paragraphs, some only one sentence. Does the author appeal to his immediate and more distant worldwide audience through evidence to support claims; examples that create an emotional response; and a persona that seems sincere, caring, knowledgeable, and reasonable?

1   [T]oday, we dumped another 70 million tons of global-warming pollution into the thin shell of atmosphere surrounding our planet, as if it were an open sewer. And tomorrow, we will dump a slightly larger amount, with the cumulative concentrations now trapping more and more heat from the sun.

2   As a result, the earth has a fever. And the fever is rising. The experts have told us it is not a passing affliction that will heal by itself. We asked for a second opinion. And a third. And a fourth. And the consistent conclusion, restated with increasing alarm, is that something basic is wrong.

3   We are what is wrong, and we must make it right.

4   Last September 21, as the Northern Hemisphere tilted away from the sun, scientists reported with unprecedented distress that the North Polar ice cap is "falling off a cliff." One study estimated that it could be completely gone during summer in less than 22 years. Another new study, to be presented by U.S. Navy researchers later this week, warns it could happen in as little as 7 years.

5   Seven years from now.

6   In the last few months, it has been harder and harder to misinterpret the signs that our world is spinning out of kilter. Major cities in North and South America, Asia and Australia are nearly out of water due to massive droughts and melting glaciers. Desperate farmers are losing their livelihoods. Peoples in the frozen Arctic and on low-lying Pacific islands are planning evacuations of places they have long called home. Unprecedented wildfires have forced a half million people from their homes in one country and caused a national emergency that almost brought down the government in another. Climate refugees have migrated into areas already inhabited by people with different cultures, religions, and traditions, increasing the potential for conflict. Stronger storms in the Pacific and Atlantic have threatened whole cities. Millions have been displaced by massive flooding in South Asia, Mexico, and 18 countries

in Africa. As temperature extremes have increased, tens of thousands have lost their lives. We are recklessly burning and clearing our forests and driving more and more species into extinction. The very web of life on which we depend is being ripped and frayed.

We never intended to cause all this destruction, just as Alfred Nobel never 7 intended that dynamite be used for waging war. He had hoped his invention would promote human progress. We shared that same worthy goal when we began burning massive quantities of coal, then oil and methane.

Even in Nobel's time, there were a few warnings of the likely conse- 8 quences. One of the very first winners of the Prize in chemistry worried that, "We are evaporating our coal mines into the air." After performing 10,000 equations by hand, Svante Arrhenius calculated that the earth's average temperature would increase by many degrees if we doubled the amount of CO_2 in the atmosphere.

But unlike most other forms of pollution, CO_2 is invisible, tasteless, and 9 odorless—which has helped keep the truth about what it is doing to our climate out of sight and out of mind. Moreover, the catastrophe now threatening us is unprecedented—and we often confuse the unprecedented with the improbable.

Indeed, without realizing it, we have begun to wage war on the earth itself. 10 Now, we and the earth's climate are locked in a relationship familiar to war planners: "Mutually assured destruction."

More than two decades ago, scientists calculated that nuclear war could 11 throw so much debris and smoke into the air that it would block life-giving sunlight from our atmosphere, causing a "nuclear winter." Their eloquent warnings here in Oslo helped galvanize the world's resolve to halt the nuclear arms race.

Now science is warning us that if we do not quickly reduce the global 12 warming pollution that is trapping so much of the heat our planet normally radiates back out of the atmosphere, we are in danger of creating a permanent "carbon summer."

As the American poet Robert Frost wrote, "Some say the world will end 13 in fire; some say in ice." Either, he notes, "would suffice."

But neither need be our fate. It is time to make peace with the planet. 14

We must quickly mobilize our civilization with the urgency and resolve 15 that has previously been seen only when nations mobilized for war. These prior struggles for survival were won when leaders found words at the 11th hour that released a mighty surge of courage, hope and readiness to sacrifice for a protracted and mortal challenge.

These were not comforting and misleading assurances that the threat was 16 not real or imminent; that it would affect others but not ourselves; that ordinary life might be lived even in the presence of extraordinary threat; that Providence could be trusted to do for us what we would not do for ourselves.

No, these were calls to come to the defense of the common future. They 17 were calls upon the courage, generosity and strength of entire peoples, citizens of every class and condition who were ready to stand against the threat once asked to do so. Our enemies in those times calculated that free people would not rise to the challenge; they were, of course, catastrophically wrong.

Now comes the threat of climate crisis—a threat that is real, rising, immi- 18 nent, and universal. Once again, it is the 11th hour. The penalties for ignoring this challenge are immense and growing, and at some near point would be unsustainable and unrecoverable. For now we still have the power to choose our fate, and the remaining question is only this: Have we the will to act vigorously and in time, or will we remain imprisoned by a dangerous illusion?

19   We must abandon the conceit that individual, isolated, private actions are the answer. They can and do help. But they will not take us far enough without collective action. At the same time, we must ensure that in mobilizing globally, we do not invite the establishment of ideological conformity and a new lock-step "ism."

20   That means adopting principles, values, laws, and treaties that release creativity and initiative at every level of society in multifold responses originating concurrently and spontaneously.

21   This new consciousness requires expanding the possibilities inherent in all humanity. The innovators who will devise a new way to harness the sun's energy for pennies or invent an engine that's carbon negative may live in Lagos or Mumbai or Montevideo. We must ensure that entrepreneurs and inventors everywhere on the globe have the chance to change the world.

22   When we unite for a moral purpose that is manifestly good and true, the spiritual energy unleashed can transform us. The generation that defeated fascism throughout the world in the 1940s found, in rising to meet their awesome challenge, that they had gained the moral authority and long-term vision to launch the Marshall Plan, the United Nations, and a new level of global cooperation and foresight that unified Europe and facilitated the emergence of democracy and prosperity in Germany, Japan, Italy and much of the world. One of their visionary leaders said, "It is time we steered by the stars and not by the lights of every passing ship."

23   In the Kanji characters used in both Chinese and Japanese, "crisis" is written with two symbols, the first meaning "danger," the second "opportunity." By facing and removing the danger of the climate crisis, we have the opportunity to gain the moral authority and vision to vastly increase our own capacity to solve other crises that have been too long ignored.

24   We must understand the connections between the climate crisis and the afflictions of poverty, hunger, HIV-AIDS and other pandemics. As these problems are linked, so too must be their solutions. We must begin by making the common rescue of the global environment the central organizing principle of the world community.

25   The pace of our response must be accelerated to match the accelerating pace of the crisis itself.

26   The great Norwegian playwright, Henrik Ibsen, wrote, "One of these days, the younger generation will come knocking at my door."

27   The future is knocking at our door right now. Make no mistake, the next generation will ask us one of two questions. Either they will ask: "What were you thinking; why didn't you act?"

28   Or they will ask instead: "How did you find the moral courage to rise and successfully resolve a crisis that so many said was impossible to solve?"

29   We have everything we need to get started, save perhaps political will, but political will is a renewable resource.

30   So let us renew it, and say together: "We have a purpose. We are many. For this purpose we will rise and we will act."

QUESTIONS FOR ANALYSIS

1. Does the first line of the speech arouse your curiosity? Why?

   _____

   _____

2. How does Gore personify (to give human attributes to an inanimate object or animal) in paragraph 2? How does this image help or hurt his argument?

   _____

   _____

3. Choose any three metaphors or similes from the speech and explain why you think they are effective or not.

   _____

   _____

4. Where does Gore first clearly state his thesis? Is his assertion too strong? Why or why not?

   _____

   _____

5. What examples does Gore give in paragraph 6 to support his thesis? How do these examples help his argument?

   _____

   _____

6. Why does the author refer to Alfred Nobel in paragraph 7? What is Gore hoping to accomplish with his audience by using the pronoun *we* in this paragraph?

   _____

   _____

   _____

7. At http://www.climatecrisis.net/takeaction/whatyoucando/ you can learn specific ways to help reduce your impact on the environment. Choose two suggestions that you feel would be easy to follow and one that you find inconvenient or unappealing. Write an argument to yourself about making all three of these changes, countering your objections. Or write an argument defending your decision not to change your ways. Either way, support your point with reliable, concrete evidence.

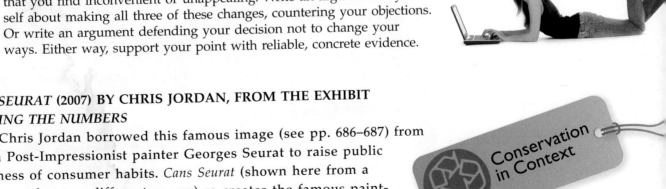

CANS SEURAT (2007) BY CHRIS JORDAN, FROM THE EXHIBIT *RUNNING THE NUMBERS*

Artist Chris Jordan borrowed this famous image (see pp. 686–687) from French Post-Impressionist painter Georges Seurat to raise public awareness of consumer habits. *Cans Seurat* (shown here from a distance and at two different zooms) re-creates the famous painting entirely with aluminum cans—106,000 of them, the number that Americans open every 30 seconds. ●

Conservation in Context

[partial zoom]

[detail at actual size]

A WRITING ASSIGNMENT

Go to www.chrisjordan.com, and after viewing Jordan's other work, write a paragraph responding to how much U.S. citizens consume daily. Using one or more of the nine patterns of development—description, narration, process, comparison/contrast, cause/effect, classification, definition, persuasion, illustration—use your response to Jordan's works of art as a jumping-off point for discussing the role recycling does, could, or should play in our society. ●

Conservation in Context

Credits

Text Credits

pp. 11–12, "Tree house." *Wikipedia, The Free Encyclopedia*. 3 Sep 2008, 16:23 UTC. 27 Oct 2008 <http://en.wikipedia.org/w/index.php?title=Tree_house&oldid=236053135>. All text is available under the terms of the GNU Free Documentation License. Wikipedia© is a registered trademark of the Wikimedia Foundation, Inc., a U.S. registered 501(c)(3) tax-deductible nonprofit charity.

p. 618, John Steinbeck, "The Great Tide Pool" from *Cannery Row* by John Steinbeck. Copyright 1945 by John Steinbeck, renewed © 1973 by Elaine Steinbeck, John Steinbeck IV, and Thom Steinbeck. Used by permission of Viking Penguin, a division of Penguin Group (USA) Inc., and by permission of Penguin Group (UK) Ltd.

p. 620, Douglas H. Chadwick, "The Truth about Tongass" from *National Geographic*, July 2007, pp. 108-9. Copyright © 2007. Reprinted by permission of National Geographic Society.

p. 622, Roger Hoffmann, "The Dare," first published in *The New York Times*, "About Men," March 23, 1986. Copyright 1986 Roger Hoffmann.

p. 625, Gary Soto, "The Jacket" from *The Effects of Knut Hamsun on a Fresno Boy: Recollections and Short Essays* by Gary Soto. Copyright © 1983, 2001. Reprinted by permission of Persea Books, Inc. (New York).

p. 629, Richard Lederer, "The Case for Short Words" from *The Miracle of Language* by Richard Lederer (New York: Pocket Books, 1991). Copyright 1990 Richard Lederer. Used by permission of the author.

p. 632, Julia Alvarez, "A White Woman of Color"; first published in *The Hungry Mind Review*, 1998; reprinted in *Half and Half: Writers Growing Up Biracial and Bicultural*, ed. Claudine C. O'Hearn, Pantheon Books. Reprinted by permission of Susan Bergholz Literary Services, New York, NY, and Lamy, NM. All rights reserved.

p. 638, Martin Luther King Jr., "The Ways of Meeting Oppression." Reprinted by arrangement with The Heirs to the Estate of Martin Luther King Jr., c/o Writers House as agent for the proprietor, New York, NY. Copyright 1963 Dr. Martin Luther King Jr., copyright renewed 1991 Coretta Scott King.

p. 641, Judith Viorst, "Friends, Good Friends—and Such Good Friends." Copyright 1977 by Judith Viorst. Originally appeared in *Redbook*. Reprinted by permission of Lescher & Lescher, Ltd.

p. 646, Benjamin Zuckerman, "Two by Two, We'll Fill the Planet." First appeared in the *Los Angeles Times*, October 1991. Copyright 1991 by Benjamin Zuckerman. Used by permission of the author.

p. 649, Brent Staples, "Black Men and Public Space." First appeared in *Harper's*, December 1986. Copyright 1986 by Brent Staples. Brent Staples writes editorials for *The New York Times* and is author of the memoir *Parallel Time*.

p. 652, Caroline Rego, "The Fine Art of Complaining." Reprinted by permission of Townsend Press.

p. 656, April Holladay, "Green Roofs Swing Temperatures in Urban Jungles" from *USA Today* (April 24, 2006). Reprinted with permission.

p. 660, Bruce Catton, "Grant and Lee: A Study in Contrasts." Copyright 1958 by U.S. Capitol Historical Society. Used by permission.

Photo Credits

Index

IMPROVEMENT CHART

Name: _____

This chart will help you track and correct errors in your major writing assignments. Chapter numbers (in parentheses) follow each error. List words that you consistently misspell or sound-alike words that cause problems in the last two columns.

	1	2	3	4	5	6	7	8	Spelling	Soundalike
1. Subject/verb agreement (24)										
2. Verb tense shift (24)										
3. Verb form (24)										
4. Pronoun agreement (25)										
5. Pronoun shift (25)										
6. Pronoun case (25)										
7. Pronoun reference (25)										
8. Parallelism (22)										
9. Misplaced and dangling modifier (26)										
10. Adverb form (26)										
11. Run-on sentence (23)										
12. Comma splice (23)										
13. Sentence fragment (23)										
14. Unneeded comma (27)										
15. Comma to introduce (27)										
16. Comma to enclose/end (27)										
17. Comma to divide (27)										
18. Comma with a series (27)										
19. Comma with coordinate adjective (27)										
20. Comma for contrast (27)										
21. Comma with numbers, dates, addresses, place names, direct address (27)										
22. Semicolon (27)										
23. Quotation marks (27)										
24. Apostrophe (27)										
25. Capitalization (27)										
26. Hyphen (27)										
27. Spelling (28)										
28. Soundalike (28)										
29. Wrong word (20)										
30. Missing word (1)										

Abbreviations and Symbols for Revising and Editing Your Writing

(Page numbers are indicated in parentheses.)

ad	Problem with adjective or adverb *(578–585)*
agr	Problem with subject/verb agreement *(560–566)* or pronoun agreement *(570–572)*
apos	Apostrophe error *(599–600)*
cap	Capitalization error *(600–601)*
case	Pronoun case problem *(573–575)*
coh	Coherence problem *(53–59)*
:	Colon needed *(598–599)*
,	Comma needed *(587–595)*
no ,	Comma not needed *(596–597)*
cs	Comma splice *(541–546)*
dm	Dangling modifier *(582–584)*
dev	Development needed—add details *(42–49)*
frag	Sentence fragment *(546–551)*
hyph	Hyphen problem *(600)*
ital	Italics needed *(601)*
lc	Lowercase letter needed
mm	Misplaced modifier *(582–584)*
¶	Paragraph indent needed
no ¶	No paragraph indent needed
par	Parallelism problem
quot	Problem with quotation marks *(599)*
ref	Pronoun reference problem *(568–570)*
ro	Run-on sentence *(541–546)*
;	Semicolon problem
shift	Pronoun shift *(575–577)* or verb tense shift *(559–560)*
sp	Spelling error *(605–616)*
trans	Transition needed *(54–57)*
und	Underlining needed *(601)*
verb	Verb form or tense problem *(553–560)*
wordy	Too many words *(481–489)*
ww	Wrong word *(481–504, 610–615)*
?	Unclear
ℒ	Delete this letter or word
^	Add a letter or word